THE OXFORD ENGLISH
LITERARY HISTORY

Volume 5: 1645–1714

THE OXFORD ENGLISH LITERARY HISTORY

General Editors: Jonathan Bate and Colin Burrow

*already published

This series was conceived and commissioned by Kim Walwyn (1956–2002), to whose memory it is dedicated.

THE OXFORD ENGLISH
LITERARY HISTORY
Volume 5: 1645–1714

The Later Seventeenth Century

MARGARET J. M. EZELL

OXFORD
UNIVERSITY PRESS

OXFORD
UNIVERSITY PRESS

Great Clarendon Street, Oxford, OX2 6DP,
United Kingdom

Oxford University Press is a department of the University of Oxford.
It furthers the University's objective of excellence in research, scholarship,
and education by publishing worldwide. Oxford is a registered trade mark of
Oxford University Press in the UK and in certain other countries

Published in the United States of America by Oxford University Press
198 Madison Avenue, New York, NY 10016, United States of America

British Library Cataloguing in Publication Data
Data available

Library of Congress Control Number: 2017931330

ISBN 978–0–19–818311–2

Printed and bound by
CPI Group (UK) Ltd, Croydon, CR0 4YY

Acknowledgements

The Reader will yet find something New and Entertaining, and I hope, not unuseful in this Essay; at least accept of my Good-Will which is all I ask, besides his Pardon (or Act of Oblivion indeed rather) of Typographical Errata, and my own Imperfections.

> John Evelyn, *Numismata. A Discourse of Medals, Antient and Modern. Together with some Accounts of Heads and Effigies of Illustrious, and Famous Persons, in Sculps, and Taille-Doucel* (1697)

A project such as this that has taken so many years to arrive at completion has necessarily incurred many debts. First would be to my series editor Jonathan Bate, who thought I would be a good match with the project many years ago, and more recently to Colin Burrow for his keen editorial eye at the end. My thanks go to the editors at Oxford University Press, Sophie Goldsworthy who patiently believed, and Jacqueline Norton and Eleanor Collins, who persisted until the end.

I could not have completed this volume without the general support of my senior academic administrators at Texas A&M University, who saw the value of pursuing this long project, in particular my Deans of the College of Liberal Arts, the late Woodrow Jones and Charles Johnson, and my long-serving and patient department head, J. Lawrence Mitchell. While they were in office, I was also able to secure support from the American Council of Learned Societies and the John Simon Guggenheim Foundation for necessary travel and research time at crucial points in its development. The generous donors of the John Paul Abbott Professorship and the John H. and Sara H. Lindsey Chair in Liberal Arts were my silent sponsors for the last ten years, and this volume would not exist without them.

Innumerable librarians and archivists have made doing the research for this volume such a pleasure. To the staff, especially in special collections, I am very grateful: the Bodleian Library, the British Library, Cambridge University Library, Edinburgh University Library, the Folger Shakespeare Library, Glasgow University Library, the Guildhall Library, London, Huntington Library, the Brotherton Library at Leeds University, Dr William's Library, London, the National Library of Ireland, the National Library of Scotland, the National Library of Wales, the Newberry Library, the University Library at Nottingham, the Northamptonshire County Record Office, and the Princeton University Library.

Throughout the process, my writing has been helped by my current and former colleagues at Texas A&M giving their input on the project and individual sections, including Courtney Beggs, Jaemin Choi, Jeffrey Cox, Laura Estill, Robert Griffin, Lawrence Griffing, Laura Mandell, Mary Ann O'Farrell, Meghan Parker, James Rosenheim, and Jennifer Wollock. I am enormously grateful as well to colleagues elsewhere for their discussions and encouragement, as well as assistance in reading portions of the manuscript, which helped me to clarify the conceptualization of the volume, to save me from many embarrassing errors, and to point out better paths to explore: Deborah Brown, Vera Camden, Elizabeth Clarke, Elizabeth H. Hageman, Robert D. Hume, J. Paul Hunter, Jurgen Mainzer, James Raven, Cynthia Wall, and James Winn. While they did their best, the errors still present are mine alone.

Throughout its long gestation period, the work of producing the physical text itself was immeasurably helped by the enthusiastic assistance of my students at Texas A&M University, who not only served as trial readers but also materially aided in proofing and checking details. In particular, Evelyn Teng did the heavy work towards the end of the process with the bibliographical sections and overall continuity, while Emily Teng, Benjamin Alexander, Amanda Black, Julia Nicole Taylor, Sarah Jones, Carla Schuster, Rebecca Morris, Jaeeun Yi, Seunghee Lee, and Soha Chung checked quotations and asked important questions as they read. Meah and Shadow Mainzer likewise made their marks on this work. One of my most important debts is to Joanna North, my indefatigable and patient editor in the process of formatting and preparing the volume for the wider world, without whom I would have simply given up. The final version benefited enormously from the attentions of my excellent editorial production team at OUP.

In conclusion, with much love, I dedicate this work to the Griffing family.

General Editors' Preface

The Oxford English Literary History is the twenty-first-century successor to the Oxford History of English Literature, which appeared in fifteen volumes between 1945 and 1997. As in the previous series, each volume offers an individual scholar's vision of a discrete period of literary history. Each has a distinctive emphasis and structure, determined by its author's considered view of the principal contours of the period. But all the volumes are written in the belief that literary history is a discipline necessary for the revelation of the power of imaginative writing to serve as a means of human understanding, past, present, and future.

Our primary aim is to explore the diverse purposes of literary activity and the varied mental worlds of writers and readers in the past. Particular attention is given to the institutions in which literary acts take place (educated communities, publishing networks, and so forth), the forms in which literary works are presented (traditions, genres, structural conventions), and the relationship between literature and broader historical continuities and transformations. Literary history is distinct from political history, but a historical understanding of literature cannot be divorced from cultural and intellectual revolutions or the effects of social change and the upheaval of war.

We do not seek to offer a comprehensive survey of the works of all 'major', let alone 'minor', writers of the last thousand years and more. All literary histories are inevitably incomplete—as was seen from the rediscovery in the late twentieth century of many long-forgotten women writers of earlier eras. Every literary history has to select; in so doing, it reconfigures the 'canon'. We cast our nets very widely and make claims for many works not previously regarded as canonical, but we are fully conscious of our partiality. Detailed case studies are preferred to summary listings.

A further aim is to undertake a critical investigation of the very notion of a national literary heritage. The word 'literature' is often taken to refer to poems, plays, and novels, but historically a much wider range of writing may properly be considered as 'literary' or as belonging within the realm of what used to be called 'letters'. The boundaries of the literary in general and of *English* literary history in particular have changed through the centuries. Each volume maps those boundaries in the terms of its own period.

For the sake of consistency and feasibility, however, two broad definitions of 'English Literary History' have been applied. First, save in the polyglot cultures of the Anglo-Saxon and Anglo-Norman eras, we have confined ourselves to the English language—a body of important work written in Latin between the fourteenth and the seventeenth centuries has been excluded. And, secondly, we have concentrated on works that come from, or bear upon, England. Most of the writing of other English-speaking countries, notably the United States of America, is excluded. We are not offering a world history of writing in the English language. Those Americans who lived and worked in England, however, fall within the scope of the series.

So too with Scottish, Irish, Welsh writers, and those from countries that were once part of the British Empire: where their work was produced or significantly disseminated in England, they may be included. Indeed, such figures are of special importance in many volumes, exactly because their non-English origins often placed them in an ambivalent relationship with England. Throughout the series, particular attention is paid to encounters between English and other traditions. But we have also recognized that Scottish, Welsh, Irish, African, Asian, Australasian, and Caribbean literatures all have their own histories, which we have not sought to colonize.

It would be possible to argue endlessly about periodization. The arrangement of the Oxford English Literary History is both traditional and innovative. For instance, the period around the beginning of the nineteenth century has long been thought of as the 'Romantic' one; however we may wish to modify the nomenclature, people will go on reading and studying the Lake Poets and the 'second-generation Romantics' in relation to each other, so it would have been factitious to introduce a volume division at, say, 1810. On the other hand, it is still too soon for there to be broad agreement on the literary–historical shape of the twentieth century: to propose a single break at, say, 1945 would be to fall in with the false assumption that literature moves in tandem with events. Each volume argues the case for its own period as a period, but at the same time beginning and ending dates are treated flexibly, and in many cases—especially with respect to the twentieth century—there is deliberate and considerable overlap between the temporal boundaries of adjacent volumes.

The voices of the last millennium are so various and vital that English literary history is always in the process of being rewritten. We seek both to chart and to contribute to that rewriting, for the benefit not just of students and scholars but of all serious readers.

Jonathan Bate
Colin Burrow

Contents

List of Figures

Abbreviations

Acts and Ordinances	*Acts and Ordinances of the Interregnum, 1642–1660*, ed. C. H. Firth and R. S. Rait, 3 vols (His Majesty's Stationery Office, 1911) <http://www.british-history.ac.uk/no-series/acts-ordinances-interregnum>
Aubrey, *Brief Lives*	John Aubrey, *Brief Lives with An Apparatus for the Lives of our English Mathematical Writers*, ed. Kate Bennett, 2 vols (Oxford University Press, 2015)
bap.	baptized
Baxter, *RB*	*Reliquaiae Baxterianae: Or, Mr Richard Baxter's Narrative of the Most Memorable Passages of His Life and Times*, ed. Matthew Sylvester (1696)
Beinecke	Beinecke Rare Book and Manuscript Library, Yale University, New Haven
BHO	British History Online
BL	British Library, London
Bodl.	Bodleian Library, Oxford
Burnet, *History*	*Bishop Burnet's History of his own Time*, ed. M. J. Routh, 6 vols (Oxford University Press, 1823)
CCISP	*Calendar of the Clarendon State Papers*, ed. O. Ogle et al., 5 vols (Clarendon Press, 1869–1970)
CISP	*State Papers Collected by Edward, Earl of Clarendon*, ed. R. Scrope and T. Monkhouse, 3 vols (Oxford, 1767–86)
CJ	*Journal of the House of Commons, 1547–1696*, 12 vols (Printed by Order of the House of Commons, 1802)
Clarendon, *History*	Edward Hyde, Earl of Clarendon, *The History of the Rebellion and Civil Wars in England*, 6 vols (Clarendon Press, 1888; repr. 1958; repr. 1992).
CSPD	*Calendar of State Papers, Domestic Series, 1640–1680*, ed. M. A. E. Green, 13 vols (Longman, 1875–86)
CSPT	*A Collection of the State Papers of John Thurloe, Esqu.*, ed. Thomas Birch, 7 vols (London, 1742)
CSPV	*Calendar of State Papers and Manuscripts, Relating to English Affairs, Existing in the Archives and Collections of Venice, and in Other Libraries of*

	Northern Italy, ed. Rawdon Brown (Longman, 1864–1947)
CUL	Cambridge University Library
CV	*The Oxford English Literary History* Volume 5: 1645–1714: *The Later Seventeenth Century* (Companion Volume)
Dunton, *Life and Errors*	*The Life and Errors of John Dunton, Citizen of London* (1705)
ELH	*English Literary History*
EMS	*English Manuscript Studies*
Evelyn, *Diary*	*The Diary of John Evelyn*, ed. E. S. De Beer, 6 vols (Oxford University Press, 1955; repr. 2000)
FSL	Folger Shakespeare Library, Washington
HMC	Historical Manuscripts Commission
London Stage	*The London Stage, 1660–1800; a Calendar of plays, entertainments & afterpieces, together with casts, box-receipts and contemporary comment. Compiled from the playbills, newspapers and theatrical diaries of the period, Part 1: 1660–1700*, ed. William Van Lennep, introduction by Emmett L. Avery and Arthur H. Scouten (Southern Illinois University Press, 1968); online <http://hdl.handle.net/2027/mdp.39015020696632>
Luttrell, *State Affairs*	Narcissus Luttrell, *A Brief Historical Relation of State Affairs from September 1678 to April 1714*, 6 vols (Oxford University Press, 1857; repr. Cambridge University Press, 2011)
MV	*The Oxford English Literary History* Volume 5: 1645–1714: *The Later Seventeenth Century* (Main Volume)
n.d.	no date
NLI	National Library of Ireland
NLS	National Library of Scotland
NLW	National Library of Wales
North, *Examen*	Roger North, *Examen, or An Equiry ... Together with Some Memoirs Occasionally Inserted* (1740)
ODNB	*Oxford Dictionary of National Biography* online
Pepys, *Diary*	*The Diary of Samuel Pepys*, ed. R. Latham and W. Matthews, 11 vols (University of California Press, 1970–83; repr. 1995; repr. 2000)
Plomer, *Dictionary, 1641*	Henry Robert Plomer. *A Dictionary of the Booksellers and Printers Who were at Work in England ... 1641–1667* (Bibliographical Society, 1907)

Plomer, *Dictionary, 1668*	Henry Robert Plomer, *Dictionary of the Printers and Booksellers . . . 1668 to 1725* (Oxford University Press, 1922)
PMLA	*Publications of the Modern Language Association*
POAS	*Poems on Affairs of State: Augustan Satirical Verse, 1660–1714*, ed. George de F. Lord, 7 vols (Yale University Press, 1963)
Reresby, *Memoirs*	*Memoirs of Sir John Reresby: The Complete Text and a Selection from his Letters*, ed. Andrew Browning, Mary K. Geiter, and W. A. Speck (Offices of the Royal Historical Society, 1991)
RES	*Review of English Studies*
RETD	*A Register of English Theatrical Documents, 1660–1737*, ed. Judith Milhous and Robert D. Hume, 2 vols (Southern Illinois Press, 1991)
SEL	*Studies in English Literature, 1500–1900*
SRO	Somerset County Record Office
UG	University of Glasgow Library, Glasgow
Wood, *Ath. Oxon.*	A. Wood, *Athenae Oxonienses*, 2 vols (1691–2); 2nd edn. (1721); new edn., ed. P. Bliss, 4 vols (1813–20); repr. Georg Olms, 1967, 1969)

A Note on the Texts

For ease of reading, this project has been divided into two volumes, the Main and a Companion (*MV* and *CV*).[1] This in no way implies that the materials in the Companion Volume are in some sense of less interest than those in the Main Volume, but is to provide multiple ways in which a reader can explore the history of a complex period's literary culture. To gain a general, chronological overview of the years covered, 1645–1714, one can read the Preface to the Main Volume along with the first long section in each chapter; these initial longer sections, designated by date, offer a thick description of a single year or two and are concerned with what was being written, read, performed, and heard during that slice of time. To follow a particular topic in more depth, the Main and Companion volumes offer, within each chapter, sections that are more narrowly focused. If one is interested in a certain genre—for example, drama—one can read together the appropriate sections from the Companion Volume and Main Volume to have a comprehensive topic-focused account within the larger framework.

To convey better a sense of the English reading experiences available in the late seventeenth and early eighteenth centuries, the primary sources quoted in this book are taken from digitalized copies found on the Early English Books Online (EEBO) and the Eighteenth-Century Collection Online (ECCO) databases, as well as from unique annotated volumes in special collections and archived manuscript holdings. As modern readers will quickly discern, seventeenth- and early eighteenth-century printed texts were not the stable, uniform product we now expect of mass-produced texts; instead, variations in punctuation, capitalization, pagination, and spelling could occur even within a single print run, as well as in different editions set at different times. Also adding to possible confusion, the date on the printed title page may not be the year in which readers could actually obtain a text: title pages sometimes indicate one year while advertisements suggest that they might have been in the hands of readers in the late winter months of the previous year. The goal here was not to attempt to impose a modern uniformity of presentation on these materials, or to filter them through a modern editorial lens, but instead within the bounds of coherence to highlight the unique aspects and often very personal nature of texts produced during this time period in a variety of media.

Although the Gregorian calendar was not adopted in England until 1751—when George II decreed that, in order to conform to it, 2 September

---

[1] The Companion Volume is available as an ebook and on Oxford Scholarship Online.

1752 should be followed by 14 September 1752—I have chosen for clarity's sake to give the years in this volume in 'New Style', that is, the year begins on 1 January rather than 25 March, while preserving the 'Old Style' for the day and month. Following the conventions established by *The London Stage, 1660–1800* (1960–8), performances are indicated by theatre year—for example, the 1672–3 season, which, after the theatres were reopened in 1660, ran from September through August.

In terms of currency, during this period English money consisted of silver coinage, including the pound (£) worth 20 shillings (*s.*), with a shilling equalling 12 pence (*d.*). The term 'guinea' is a reference to a gold coin issued after 1663, intended to be worth the same as a £ but whose value could vary with the price of gold until stabilized by royal proclamation in 1717, which limited the exchange of a golden guinea to no more than 21 silver shillings. A 'half crown' is 2*s.* 6*d.* All coins created during this period showed a profile of the reigning monarch's head. Calculating the value of money from earlier historical periods has vexed generations of historians; as a recent study has declared, the hope of creating a modern equivalent, what £1 would buy in 1700 and today, using a single multiplier is fraught with difficulties.[2]

While every effort has been made to ensure accuracy and conformity concerning publication and performance details, future readers will no doubt find things to correct and, I hope, texts and authors to inspire them to further investigations and discoveries.

---

[2] See Milhous and Hume, *The Publication of Plays*, ch. 3.

A Preface to the Reader: Describing 'Literary Life' in the Mid- and Late Seventeenth Century

This volume covers a mere seventy years, 1645–1714, but during that block of time there were several civil wars, repeated rebellions, and the so-called Glorious Revolution, all posing severe challenges to the existing forms of government and notions of authority, whether political or domestic. At least at the beginning of this period, it would have been almost impossible to separate a writer's political and literary lives. Literary life in the 1645–1714 period was affected in direct, material ways by the English Civil Wars and subsequent rebellions and revolutions, with their violent, disorienting political and theological shifts, changing economic opportunities, and renegotiations of roles of authority and submission. Simultaneous with this reshaping of English self-perceptions was the English expansion into strange overseas worlds: this bringing of the new worlds back into England over the course of these decades increased the variety of materials available for consumers to enjoy, in terms of both new fashions and goods and new ways of situating England's place in the world, as well as new words. Finally, during this seventy-year period, even the technologies of circulating writing and the legal structures associated with authorship changed, with the first law concerning what we understand as copyright being enacted in 1709.

Under close inspection, all periods in history are more complex than they might first appear and involve intricate, subtle shifts in culture to repel or embrace particular local events, but, for this period, its complexities—its volatility and multiplicity of identities—are the first aspects one sees. Laws both civil and cultural changed repeatedly with regard to what was and was not legal to read, write, perform, own, wear, hear, and say. In terms of faith, this period experienced constant turmoil, with the official institutions and forms of religious expression changing almost every twenty years. It was a period during which new forms of literature came into being and were consumed by readers and audiences in new media and new theatrical spaces. This period staged the first public trial and execution of a divine right monarch, featured prophets from all social classes publishing advice to rulers, offered audiences their first view of professional women actresses performing in roles created by professional women writers, saw the publication of the first newspaper, the *London Gazette*, provided dictionaries for new readers seeking to understand 'hard words', offered 'novels' that could be carried in one's pocket, and saw translated into English many of the classical writers such as Horace, Virgil,

Homer, Juvenal, Ovid, and Plutarch, whose works previously had been the entertainment and inspiration of only those with an elite or university education.

The use of the phrase 'literary life' to describe the scope of the contents of this book is also more complicated than one might think. There are no commanding literary movements or genre labels for this period such as Romanticism or Modernism, which have been used to characterize other blocks of literary time. Traditionally, studies have been organized around its perceived great figures: the Age of Milton, the Age of Dryden, the Age of Pope. Most nineteenth- and twentieth-century literary histories slide over the war years and the Interregnum as a period during which literary and artistic culture was under attack and in hiding, the famous 'Cavalier winter', described by the critic Earl Miner. In these models, at the Restoration, literary life supposedly emerged from hibernation more or less intact; the period that followed is characterized in such histories as dominated by libertine excesses and demand for novelty and entertainment (although this model makes little room for many of the great works of religious and devotional writing appearing in these decades, including Milton's *Paradise Lost* and John Bunyan's *The Pilgrim's Progress*). These types of literary histories suggest that by the turn of the century we find a well-established, professional literary culture able to satisfy the desires of a new type of reading public and a backlash again the excesses of Charles's courtiers. Ian Watt's theory of 'the rise of the novel' as a genre is set using this model, with the rise of the new urban middle class rejecting the excesses of the Restoration elite in search of a bourgeois morality. Thus, in contrast with the goals of this study, many previous ones organized around great figures and the rise of genres treat this span of years as a series of ruptures or clean breaks with past practices, with the war and Interregnum years seen as a cultural vacuum or dead zone compared to the Stuart eras that preceded and succeeded it.

In the same way that 'literary' is found to be a slippery term during this period, however, determining who were the readers and writers during this turbulent period in British history is an evolving field of study. 'Literate' is only rarely included in dictionaries of the time, defined when it does appear as 'learned'. In general, in the twentieth and early twenty-first centuries 'literary' has been used to describe the activities of a small, elite group with access to education, whether through academies and universities or privately in the home, and with the financial security to have access to books and manuscripts, the leisure to enjoy owning and reading them, and the desire to participate in creating new texts for other readers.

This is a far cry from both the seventeenth-century understanding of the word and from more recent historians' use of the term to describe the ability of a person to read and/or write at the most basic, functional level. Social historians studying the period have used various methods to determine rates of historical literacy, from the simple ability to sign one's name on documents, to expanded definitions that include shades of literacy, but they, in general, are based on a set of assumptions about reading and writing, print texts and manuscripts. Until quite recently, the assumption was that the literacy rate was quite low and that the rate for women of all classes was lower than that of men. As we shall see, in the last few decades of the twentieth century and the first ones of the twenty-first these figures have been greatly revised upwards for both sexes, which has implications for what constitutes the literary history of the period.

Although the assumptions about literacy as they relate to class and gender have served us well to think about readers, particularly those in urban settings in the mid-eighteenth century and onwards, it is problematic how well they represent the reading and authorship experiences of men and women in the countryside and small villages at the later part of the seventeenth century and the start of the eighteenth. This is especially true during the 1645–1714 period because of the instability in the cultural and legal institutions controlling socially acceptable behaviours and the rapid expansion of the press during the Civil War and Interregnum. Printers and booksellers faced changing circumstances under which to produce texts, when the laws governing printing and distribution of potentially politically sensitive materials were poorly enforced or in flux, and during which the market for printed leisure reading was being formed. During this period, too, we see further strategies for marketing literature as a consumer product for a variety of levels of reader being created.

Such changes in reading practices and the general literary environment were noted, not always with approval, by contemporary writers. The anonymous author of *The Justice of Peace His Calling: A Moral Essay* (1684) in describing the qualities necessary for being a Justice observed:

The Age we live in is full of Learning, and the great Plenty of Books that come every day into the World, have fallen so thick in all places, that they have not escaped the Soft Hands of Ladies, nor the Hard fists of Mechanicks, and Trades-men...and therefore if a Justice of the Peace be not indifferently well qualified in this Point, he will sometimes discover it, and that will (if it have no worse effect) betray him to the Contempt of those, who ought to honour and respect him for his Place.[1]

One cannot always assume during this period that gentry gentlemen were well read or that common maidservants and labouring men were illiterate, especially in godly households overseen by pious masters and mistresses who wished their servants to read the Bible. While there are certainly classes and types of reading materials that required money for a library and extensive formal education in the classics to own and enjoy, this is also the period in which there was an unprecedented amount of translation of classical writers into English: while folio volumes required an allowance to purchase and space to keep them, daily papers, broadsides, and copies of popular songs could be had for a penny, and popular octavo and duodecimo volumes could be easily carried in one's pocket. By the end of this period, canny booksellers would

---

[1] *The Justice of Peace His Calling*, 23.

offer editions with expensive leather bindings to those who wished them, but would also sell the same texts in less expensive paper versions.

What sorts of texts were being read by these soft-handed ladies and hard-fisted working men? To see more closely how the fabric of the period's literary texts was woven from competing discourses, the chapters in this volume will attempt first to describe simply what was available to be read, viewed, and written about, using a series of discrete one- to two-year periods. Based on these descriptions of the texts and performances available during selected years— 1645, 1659–60, 1674–5, 1685–6, 1700—the issues that are raised by the texts, their authors, performers, audiences, and readers will then be looked at more closely in separate topical essays in the shorter sections that follow. This organization is not intended to provide exhaustive, encyclopaedic coverage, even if such a thing were possible; by reading the first longer descriptive sections in each chapter, one has the chance to see both the continuities and changes play out over the period, while the shorter topical sections sharpen the focus on particular issues found at different moments.

Thus, what this volume seeks to do—thanks in part to the newly available electronic databases of early modern texts—is to investigate and to describe more comprehensively the wide range of literary materials that were being written, read, and performed over this seventy-year span rather than to concentrate on particular individuals, texts, or genres. It is intended as a starting point for thinking about both change and continuity in literary practices broadly conceived, not a map of an individual author or type of writing. It will offer a contextual description of the ways in which literary culture responded to changing times, the different modes of literary production and performance, and the ways in which shared discourses and rhetorics circulated through many different types of texts, both literary and historical. It will be looking at what continued as well as what changed, and how the literary discourses of earlier generations still had resonance and vitality during volatile times.

While the terms 'literary' and 'literature' have specific connotations for readers after the mid-eighteenth century, for the period in question, 1645–1714, 'literature' was defined in dictionaries such as Thomas Blount's *Glossographia: or a Dictionary, Interpreting all such Hard Words* (1656) as 'learning, cunning, grammer [*sic*], knowledge of letters'. Other key terms we associate with the discussion of literary texts also have different meanings—for example, John Bullokar's definition of 'Library' in his *An English Expositour, or Compleat Dictionary: Teaching the interpretation of the Hardest Words, and Most Useful Terms of Art used in our Language* (1674) as being a 'study or Shop full of Books', while the words 'author' and 'text' are absent from definition or discussion. Blount's definition of 'poesy' mingles what we would distinguish as being different, separate genres, poetry and drama:

Poesie = a Poets work, Poetry; There are six sorts of Poesie; the Heroick Poem Narrative is called an Epique Poem; the Heroick Poem Dramatique is Tragedy; the Scommatick

Narrative, is Satyr; Dramatick is Comedy; The Pastoral Narrative is called simply pastoral (anciently Bucolique) and the same Dramatique, Pastoral Comedy. The figure therefore of an Epique Poem, and of a Tragedy ought to be the same; for they differ more, but that they are pronounced by one or many person.[2]

While modern readers share a vocabulary concerning literary matters with readers and writers in the late seventeenth century, it is clear from the usage and definitions of the literary terms that do appear in such books that earlier readers' assumptions about being an author and about what constitutes a literary event are often quite different from later generations' expectations. One of the purposes of this study is thus to highlight such differences, and to attempt to situate mid- and late-seventeenth-century literary texts back into the social matrix whence they arose.

Authors, of course, are readers, too. In the period 1645–1715, their world was filled with texts, written, verbal, and visual, informing them how a king speaks to his people, how a man seduces the object of his desire, how a prophetess converses with God, and a mother with her children. Not all of these texts are what have traditionally been defined as literary ones, but, even in the proclamations issued by monarchs, the newsbook accounts of wonderful sights, criminals' repentant confessions, and texts teaching everything from grammar to horsemanship, we find the vocabulary of lived experience that writers and readers during this period had in common, which permeates their lyrics, their dramas, and their fictions.

Not only are the terms associated with literary life often at odds with the ways modern criticism makes use of them, but also our understanding of the ways in which texts were created, transmitted, performed, and preserved during a period that at its end saw the first steps in creating formal copyright law. Literary life during this period was conducted not just through leather- or cloth-bound printed books, but also through a variety of related media, which circulated among readers, listeners, and writers in complex networks of exchange. Expensive new folio editions of old Elizabethan dramas, ephemeral broadsides and mercuries recording contemporary news, and affordable pocket-sized books instructing one on 'modish' style appeared simultaneously; street entertainers, aristocratic theatricals, dictionaries of hard words and of thieves' cant, civic pageants, domestic letters containing friends' attempts at lyric and family news, clandestine manuscript lampoons targeting public figures, charismatic religious leaders in the pulpit or in the gaol, multi-volume romances translated from French and Italian, and less expensive short octavo novels all competed for readers' interest and response.

From this variety of sources, those writers traditionally seen as the period's 'major' literary figures such as Katherine Philips, John Milton, John Bunyan, John Dryden, Aphra Behn, Joseph Addison and Richard Steele, Daniel Defoe,

[2] Blount, *Glossographia.*

Anne Finch, Alexander Pope, and Jonathan Swift absorbed the multiple voices of their cultures and were active participants in continuing its vitality. This volume hopes to place such figures back in the textual conversations of their contemporaries, whether it be the provocative pamphleteer William Prynne, whose prolific career spanned the reigns of Charles I, Cromwell, and Charles II, the royalist poet Hester Pulter responding to the events of the war and Interregnum from her country house and recording them in her manuscript volume, Abiezer Coppe's divinely inspired prophetic messages to Cromwell's government, or Aphra Behn's and Susanna Centlivre's successful commercial comedies, the ongoing debates over the virtues of coffee and tea in shaping the character of its drinkers, and Ned Ward's literary tours of London's underworld.

Literary life in this period, when the printing press was coming into new prominence, but not yet the inevitably preferred mode of transmitting those texts we think of as 'literary', is likewise a complicated thing to reconstruct. Printed texts provided only a part of the vocabulary of literature and news of the world. Handwritten texts, whether one's own hand or that of a professional scribe or a secretary, provided another conduit for information as well as modes of discourse. Manuscripts were circulated among friends as well as being produced and sold commercially. Most professional, commercial writers participated in circulating handwritten manuscripts in addition to printing their works for profit, but many social or coterie writers' texts were never published. Handwritten compositions were diffused through extended epistolary networks linking country and city, connecting England and the Continent and the Americas; handwritten materials were transformed through copying, involving multiple authors participating in creating and circulating them. They were also sometimes 'pirated' and printed, sometimes to the dismay of their original creators and readers, but sometimes to their benefit, as a means that introduced poets such as Anne Bradstreet to a wider paying readership.

Finally, in addition to the printed and handwritten word, this was a period of performance, even though during part of it the theatres were officially closed, from the pulpit and stage to the cockpit and street corner. The texts themselves, whether printed or handwritten, sometimes in their contents suggest that they were intended to be read aloud. Reading itself was very often during this period a social activity. Oral culture and written are inextricably linked during this period, not only among the illiterate and semi-literate population with their passion for ballads, broadsides, and chapbooks, but also in ways readers in general shared their reading material, from epistles to friends, the performance of popular lyrics, and reading aloud of devotional works for the benefit of the household, to *The Spectator*'s ambition to be read and discussed in coffee shops and over tea tables.

Thus, in addition to the printed titles as found in rare book rooms and digitalized in Early English Books Online (EEBO) and Eighteenth-Century Collection Online (ECCO), this volume also seeks to involve the literary life of mid- and late-seventeenth-century men and women participating in a dynamic exchange of texts in manuscript forms, as well as in the performance of dramas, sermons, speeches, spectacles, prophecies, and ballads that made up the sound of literary life before it was captured on the printed pages. All of these types of materials taken together form the basis for what readers and authors in the middle and later part of the seventeenth century would have had at their disposal as the common modes of expression—what 'worked' in rhetorics of authority and submission, of physical description and investigatory exploration, of public statements and private devotions.

A child born in the early 1640s when Charles I was on the throne would, theoretically, have entered a tightly structured world organized around the theory of the divine right of kings and the authority of the established English Church hierarchy and its ministers, one where social position and domestic roles were represented as being innate and natural. The year was marked with traditional festivals and rituals that celebrated the seasons and important life events. In his or her early teenage years in the 1650s, after Charles had been defeated and executed and the government was controlled by Parliament and Oliver Cromwell, that child would have experienced a completely different scheme of power and rhetoric of politics, where kings were expected to answer to Parliament, governance could be construed to be a social contract between different levels of power, and the supposedly powerless could, through the medium of cheap print and petitions, find a national audience.

Daily life and the forms of entertainment enjoyed by every class came under legislation, from the closing of the London theatres in 1642, the repeated ordinances attempting to regulate printing, and the 1647 ordinance abolishing the celebration of Christmas, Easter, and other holidays as pagan, to the 1657 ordinance regulating what could and could not be done on Sundays. This ordinance declared:

All persons keeping, using or being present upon the Day aforesaid at any Fairs, Markets, Wakes, Revels, Wrestlings, Shootings, Leaping, Bowling, Ringing of Bells for pleasure, or upon any other occasion, (saving for calling people together for the publique Worship) Feasts, Church-Ale, May Poles, Gaming, Bear-Baiting, Bull-Baiting, or any other Sports and Pastimes; All persons unnecessarily walking in the Church or Church-Yards, or elsewhere in the time of Publique Worship; And all persons vainly and prophanely walking on the day aforesaid; And all persons Travelling, carrying Burthens, or doing any worldly labour or work of their ordinary Calling on the Day aforesaid, shall be deemed guilty of prophaning the Lords-Day. (*Acts and Ordinances*, June 1657)

Furthermore, 'all persons Contriving, Printing or Publishing any Papers, Books or Pamphlets for allowance of Sports and Pastimes upon the Lords-Day, or against the Morality thereof, shall forfeit the Sum of Five pounds, or be committed to the House of Correction'.

In matters of faith, the Church of England with the King as its head and its institutional hierarchies of power, unified with a common book of prayer, was shaken by radical Protestants. Some sectarians during this decade went so far as to hold that all believers are equal before God, requiring not church or minister, but only a believing heart to achieve salvation. With all equal before the Lord, even labourers and women could preach, prophesy, and publish their experiences based on the validity of their personal experiences rather than doctrine or ordination. Many believed that the second coming of Christ and the rule of the saints on earth was imminent and worked diligently to prepare a godly England to receive the Lord. Ordinances passed in the 1650s ensured that 'scandalous, ignorant and insufficient Ministers and Schoolmasters' could be removed by local commissions for failing to propagate the Gospel in an approved manner (August 1654).

When that child was a mature adult in 1660, after fifteen years of war and Puritan rule, within a short period after the death of Oliver Cromwell, the army invited the exiled King Charles II and his courtiers and all that they symbolically represented to return and re-establish the institutions and culture of monarchy as well as the Anglican Church. This invitation, however, did not result in simple return to the conditions under Charles I—for example, while the theatres quickly reopened under royal patent and patronage, they were not the same buildings, stages, sets, nor always the same actors and writers who had been there before.

In politics, the relationship between the king, the government, and the governed would be marked forever by a new set of expectations and strategies of political negotiation. For the child, who was now an adult in the 1660s and 1670s while Charles II reigned, national politics was frequently marked by conspiracies and stratagems, avidly reported in broadsides, newsletters, and newsbooks. The creation of rival political parties with competing rhetorics and propaganda created pamphlet wars and a taste for contemporary satire. The Restoration court itself was a form of entertainment: as recorded in contemporary memoirs and diaries, it provided a lavish spectacle with its sometimes shocking performances of libertine lifestyle played out before a society increasingly aware of and interested in celebrity figures including writers, actors, and the King's many mistresses. The crowd watched and read about the real-life drama of who would be Charles's successor, a drama that would culminate shortly after his death with unsuccessful rebellion and execution of his natural son, the glamorous if ultimately sad figure of the Duke of Monmouth, and the temporary securing of the throne for Charles's brother, James.

Ironically, the 1660 Restoration of monarchy and the Anglican Church in fact led in the 1680s to a practising Catholic king on the throne, James II. His reign was brief, and his subsequent flight to France indicated how unwilling were the countries of his kingdom—England, Scotland, and Ireland—to defend his principles. This so-called Glorious Revolution was accomplished with little bloodshed and led once again to a group of English exiles living in France and to James's supporters who stayed behind, such as the poet laureate John Dryden, either redirecting their literary energies or, like Anne Finch, retiring from the public scene. It also led to the re-establishment of a Protestant line through a series of English-born queens, James's daughters Mary and Anne, with their foreign-born husbands. In 1707, Queen Anne would legislate that 'the two Kingdoms of Scotland and England, shall...be united into one Kingdom by the Name of Great Britain' and with that phrase, a new national identity would begin to be created.[3]

A child born in the 1640s who lived into the first decade of the eighteenth century, as did the diarist Lady Cowper (1644–1720), the playwright William Wycherley (1641–1716), and the actor Edward Kynaston (1643–1712), would have experienced revolutions in government and religious practice, new modes of circulating information to an expanding readership, challenges to the perception of roles within the family, and challenges to how the world was seen and understood, from the ways in which gender roles and sexuality were defined and represented, to a growing sense of the myriad ways in which individuals played their part in shaping public culture in general. Given these dramatic changes in public life, it can be easy to forget that, as with all cultures, on the one hand, there was the official, institutional representation of a 'good' or godly society and the appropriate behaviour of its members as represented in its laws and ordinances and prescriptive literature, but, on the other, there were also the ways in which individuals actually conducted their lives. The theatres were officially closed after 1642, for example, but performances continued; while Charles II and his libertine courtiers pursued the royal maids of honour dishonourably, at least some of them, including Margaret Blagge and Anne Killigrew, were noted for their piety, devotional writings, and poetry. There was virulent anti-Catholic sentiment throughout the period, but two of its most successful commercial writers, John Dryden and Alexander Pope, were unashamedly practising Catholics. It must have been frequently a bewildering, astonishing, and alarming period in which to live and yet, as witnessed by the many diaries, memoirs, and private life writings that men and women during that time left behind, it was a period rich in literary culture and exploration, one that continued to enjoy many of the literary forms of earlier generations while also transforming them and inventing new genres that endure today.

---

[3] *First Article of Act of Union.*

Ending the War, Creating a Commonwealth, and Surviving the Interregnum, 1645–1658

I. 1645

This book was engendred in a cloud, born a Captive, and bred up in the dark shades of melancholy...

> James Howell, dedication to the second edition of
> *Epistolae Ho-Elianae* (1647), sig. A3ʳ

Oh Englishmen! Where is your freedoms? and what is become of your Liberties and Privileges that you have been fighting for all this while ...?

> John Lilburne, *Englands Birth-right Justified* (1645), 11

For those living in England, Scotland, Ireland, and Wales, 1645 was a year marked in public by spectacles of death and triumph and swirling rumours of bloody battles and secret plots, in private by individuals facing terrifying possibilities, monotonous continuity, and fearful hopes. The conflicting emotions and loyalties generated by civil war are woven into the very fabric of the texts that English people were reading, writing, and hearing during this period, whether newsbook accounts of battlefield atrocities, scholarly debates over religious issues, or lyric poetry speaking with the voice of an earlier generation. It is not an insignificant point that the two authors whose books sold the most copies during the seventeenth century, Francis Quarles (1592–1644) and George Wither (1588–1667), both now at the end of their literary careers, were actively engaged on opposing sides of this conflict. Pens that had created religious emblem poems and pastorals were now engaged in generating polemic pieces to raise the spirits of their Royalist and Parliamentary readers.

The majority of writers we today classify as literary figures were heavily involved in the events of the war and the resulting political and religious debates. The military conflicts of the English Civil War begun in 1642 were by 1645 turning against the King and his followers, and, while Parliament was

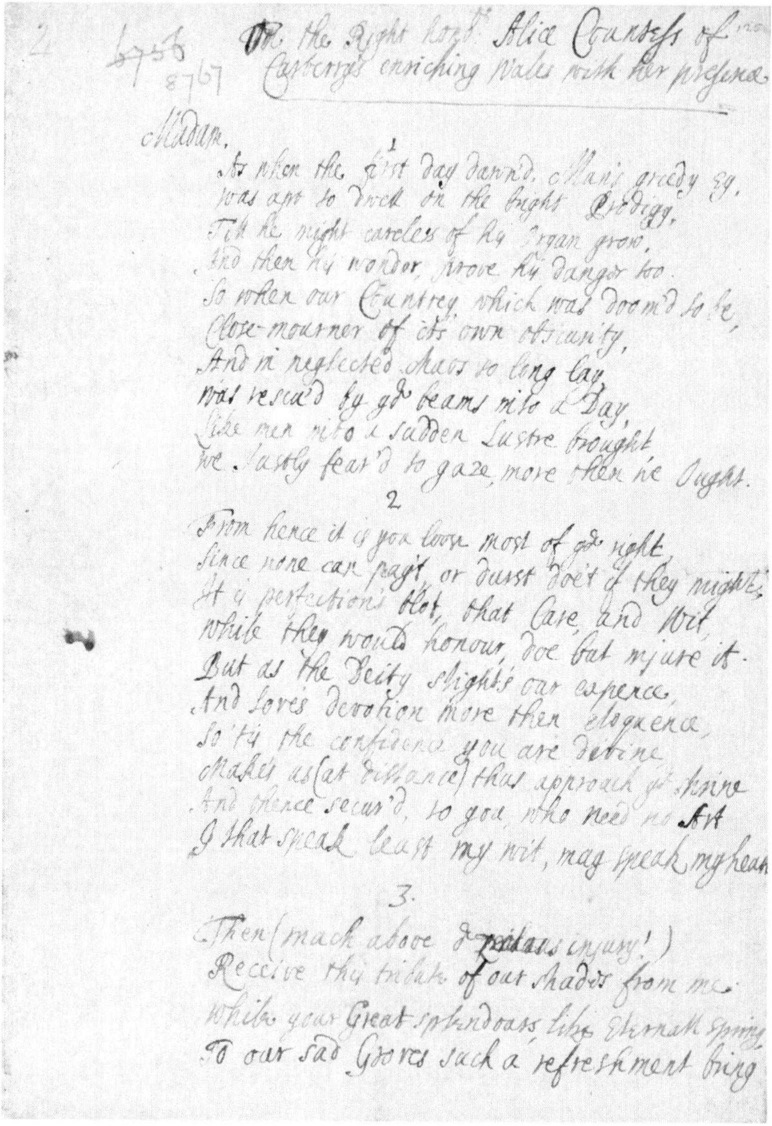

Figure 1. Katherine Philips, autograph 'On the Right Honrble Alice Countess of Carberry' (*c*.1652). MS EL 8767, Egerton family papers, The Huntington Library, San Marino, California

claiming victory over the Royalists, among its own ranks dissent and division proliferated. The two poets whose volumes of verse appearing late in 1645/ January 1646 are hailed by subsequent generations as the significant literary landmarks for this period were otherwise occupied: Edmund Waller (1606–87) was in exile in France with the Queen, after having been arrested for participating in a plot to take over Parliament for the King in 1643, and John Milton (1608–74) was in London writing polemical prose tracts for the Parliamentarians. Other famous literary figures were likewise employed: Richard Lovelace (1617–57) and Henry Vaughan (1621–95) were both serving as soldiers for the King, while John Bunyan (bap. 1628–88) was serving as a foot soldier for Parliament. During this period, one cannot neatly separate a writer's civil life from his or her literary output, whether the poetry from the politics, or the satirist from the newsbook writer. We find in the collections of verse published in 1645, for example, that, while some volumes consisted of traditional, formal compilations of the poet's work from their earlier life, others were spontaneous responses to the immediate events of the day.

The year 1645 opened, according to our calendar terms, with the beheading of Archbishop of Canterbury, William Laud, on 10 January, an event grimly foreshadowing future ones. As the King's chaplain, Laud had rigorously promoted strict religious uniformity and had encouraged the Bishops' War against the Scottish Presbyterians in 1633; Laud had been tried and found not guilty by the House of Lords, but was subsequently convicted and executed through a bill of attainder by the heavily Presbyterian Commons. Laud's final sermon before his execution was immediately put into print; on 24 January, it was quickly attacked by his old foe, Henry Burton (bap. 1578–1647/8), in a pamphlet entitled *The Grand Impostor Unmasked*, which warned readers that, 'when the Fox preacheth, let the Geese beware'.[1] In this example, we can see how both sides of the conflict used the press, and, by looking at what each associated with the act of putting one's words into print rather than speech or script, we can find traces of the habits of reading and writing that also involve literary matters as well as political.

Burton, a clergyman who, along with William Prynne (1600–69) and John Bastwick (1595?–1654), had earned the title of 'The Protestant Martyrs' in 1637 after they were sentenced to having their ears cut off for publishing attacks on Laud, is at pains to assure his readers about his motives for printing his text. First, he explains he was 'earnestly importuned by two reverent godly Ministers' to unmask the fraud of Laud's text, and, second, it is important to Burton that someone do so in print. Laud's sermon was not 'preached' as the text represents it, Burton claims, but instead read from a prepared text, 'for without his book he could neither preach, nor pray', Burton asserts. Furthermore, Laud's text is filled with 'legerdemain', whereby Laud casts the blame on his executioners rather than acknowledging his faults. Burton states that his prime

---

[1] Burton, *The grand imposter unmasked*, 'Preface to the Reader'.

concern arises from the printing of such dangerous materials, so corrupting to the uninformed reader: 'that such a poysonfull peece as this should be so licentiously published in Print, before some Antidote were prepared, either to correct its Malignancy, or to corroborate the simple hearted people, apt to drink in such a sugared potion, from the mouth of such a bold dying man, though a Traitor'. To counteract this 'licentious' printing, this spread of 'poisonous lies', Burton put his own thoughts on paper to be printed. For Burton, Laud's writing out of his supposedly spontaneous dying thoughts smacks of the artificiality of a 'show' of learning that marked a 'feigned' holiness, a text that relies on carefully contrived rhetoric to control its listeners and hearers rather than sincere emotions; the appearance of the text in print, in Burton's opinion, gives the contents a spurious authority for those 'simple hearted' readers who were not present to witness the actual events. For this 'simple' reader Laud's printed text is 'poysonfull', requiring a second printed text, Burton's, to act as an 'Antidote' ('Preface to the Reader').

In this example, to print a text was to make a claim about not only the nature of its contents but also its author's right to speak, and the authority of his or her words. In 1645, the textual battlefield was the pamphlet form, where the goal was to shape public opinion and win the readers' hearts and loyalties. By far the largest number of texts printed during this year were these short, ephemeral pamphlets, whose writers were capable of responding quickly not only to events of the day, but also to other writers.[2] While their subject matter may seem arcane and obscure to a modern reader, at the heart of the controversies was the control over the reader's perception of the nature of authority, whether divine or civil, and an attempt to direct the individual's response to those in power.

On the physical battlefield, 1645 saw repeated victories for Parliament and Lord Fairfax's New Model Army, a new-styled professional fighting force formed in April 1645, all of which were reported in the numerous diurnal or newsbooks of the day. Many of those whose poetry has been anthologized by later generations of critics as being characteristic of this period were in 1645 either in prison or serving in the military. In 1645, the royalist gentleman soldier Richard Lovelace was released from Gatehouse Prison, where he had been incarcerated since 1642 for presenting the Kentish Petition to Parliament in favour of the King and where, while imprisoned, he had written the song that concludes, 'Stone walls do not a prison make, | Nor iron bars a cage', passionately declaring his loyalties.[3] Lovelace rejoined the King's forces in 1645, but the military tide had turned against the Royalist armies during the years of his imprisonment. Lovelace's friend the enigmatic Andrew Marvell (1621–78), who would contribute a commendatory verse to Lovelace's 1648 collection of

[2] See Smith, *Literature and Revolution*; Achinstein, *Milton and the Revolutionary Reader*; Raymond, *Pamphlets and Pamphleteering*, ch. 6.

[3] Richard Lovelace, *Lucasta, epodes, odes, sonnets, songs* (1649), 98, 'To Althea, from Prison'.

poems *Lucasta*, had left England, and, according to Milton, passed his time travelling in Holland, France, Italy, and Spain, acquiring languages as he went. On Marvell's return to London in 1647, the future assistant to the then blind Milton in the Latin secretaryship would go on in the early 1650s to write poems praising Oliver Cromwell.

Three years after Charles I had raised his standard at Nottingham, Charles and Prince Rupert were defeated by the Parliamentary generals Fairfax and Cromwell at Naseby on 14 June 1645.[4] Although James Graham, the Marquis of Montrose, who had had notable early victories in Scotland, continued the attempt to advance in the west in Bristol, he lost in Wales at the battle of Philiphaugh. The poet Henry Vaughan (1621–95) left his job as the secretary to Judge Marmaduke Lloyd of Brecon and joined the King's forces in Wales in 1645 in time to participate in another defeat by Parliament at the battle of Rowton Heath in September; in the following year, his book *Poems, with the Tenth Satire of Juvenal Englished* would be published. On 20 July, the situation of the Royalist forces was sufficiently alarming that King Charles I wrote to the Prince of Wales to warn him to be ready to flee the country; the Prince had already moved west from Oxford for safety, taking with him in his entourage Edward Hyde (1609–74), the future Lord Clarendon, and Sir Richard Fanshawe (1608–66), a poet, translator, and diplomat. The beleaguered father wrote to his 15-year-old son warning him 'to prepare for the worse... whensoever you find yourself in apparent danger of falling into the rebels' hands, that you convey yourself into France, and there to be under your mother's care'.[5]

While the Royalist forces struggled on in many parts of the country, such as in the city of Chester, which continued to resist the siege by Parliamentary troops, the plight of the individual Royalist supporters in the countryside was often perilous and became the stuff of loyalist memories. David Jenkins, a judge of Great Sessions for Carmarthen, Cardigan, and Pembrokeshire, was captured at the battle of Hereford in 1645; while sitting as a judge, he had indicted several Parliamentarians for high treason, and, after his capture, John Aubrey (1626–97) records: 'Parliament intended to have hanged him, and he expected no lesse, but resolved to be hangd with the Bible under one arme and Magna charta under the other' (Aubrey, *Brief Lives*, 2. 1522). Parliament, apparently recognizing the power of such a symbolic spectacle and fearing to make him a Royalist martyr, instead kept Jenkins imprisoned for the next fifteen years.

While the men in the family were engaged in the military campaigns and languishing in prisons, the women of both warring sides likewise experienced battle conditions, caught up in sieges and raids, and no doubt uneasy isolation. In Nottinghamshire, the sisters Jane Cavendish (1620/1–69) and Elizabeth Egerton (1626–63) weathered the series of sieges at Welbeck Abbey that began

---

[4] See Worden, *The English Civil Wars, 1640–1660*, and Braddick, *God's Fury*.
[5] Gregg, *King Charles I*, 398.

in 1644: first, it was captured by the Parliamentary forces, then in the summer of 1645 it was briefly returned to Royalist troops, only again to be surrendered after four more months back to Parliament in November 1645. The writings of these women during these years offer an example of the ways in which the practices of social authorship and the literary genres of peaceful times were shaped by the conditions of war. The two women had grown up in a network of powerful political families as well as those noted for the patronage of writers. They were the daughters of the former commanding general of the north, William Cavendish (bap. 1593–1676), at that time the Earl of Newcastle, the future Duke of Newcastle; Elizabeth was married in 1641 to John Egerton, Lord Brackley, the future Earl of Bridgewater, who as a young boy had appeared in Thomas Carew's masque *Coelum Britanicum* and Milton's *A Masque Presented at Ludlow Castle*.

While their father, husband, and brothers were away fighting, the sisters endured siege. During these years, the two sisters were also compiling a manuscript miscellany, *The Concealed Fansyes. Poems, Songs, a Pastorall, and a Play*. Encouraged from an early age by their father to write, during 1644 and 1645 the women had collected in two fair copies, apparently done by their father's secretary John Rolleston, their occasional poems to friends and relatives as well as poems praying for the safety of their soldier father.[6] They had grown up in a household where, before the war, dramatists were welcomed and masques and entertainments were frequently performed; their father not only commissioned works by Ben Jonson, James Shirley, and Sir William Davenant, but also had his own plays, *The Country Captaine* and *The Varietie*, performed at Blackfriars in the early 1640s.

The collaborative comedy written by his daughters, *Concealed Fansyes*, concerns two young motherless sisters, who, while their father is away, attempt to 'educate' their suitors, Courtly and Presumption, about the benefits of 'an equall marriage'. The other long piece in the Bodleian Library volume is also collaborative, a pastoral, a genre associated with the courtly entertainments of Queen Henrietta Maria, which had so provoked the wrath of William Prynne in *Histriomastix*. This piece tellingly opens with an anti-masque of witches, who celebrate their powers to create civil strife, 'to make Brother hate brother'. The volume's contents are like snapshots of the literary education of these well-born Englishwomen, reflecting not only their literary tastes for friendship poems and pastoral comedy, but also their commitment to shared values and beliefs among the besieged Royalists; in their poems to their relatives and friends, they reaffirm the bonds of love and loyalty that are threatened by civil war.

Not far away, Lucy Hutchinson (1620–81) found herself indignantly recording in her diary the strife between factions competing for power on the Parliamentary side. The future translator of Lucretius' *De Rerum Natura* had accompanied her husband, John Hutchinson, when he had been appointed

---

[6] See Bodl., MS Rawl. poet. 16, and Yale University, Beinecke Library, Osborn MS b. 233.

governor of Nottingham Castle and had nursed wounded soldiers, including those of the opposing side. In the memoir of his life she wrote in the 1670s for their children, she describes how, after a battle in 1643, one of the Parliamentary officers, a Captain Palmer, criticized her saying 'his soul abhorred to see this favour to the enemies of God'.[7] Referring to herself in the third person, Lucy Hutchinson records that 'she had done nothing but what she thought was her duty, in humanity to them, as fellow-creatures, not as enemies' (p. 183). She also recalls the effect of the publication of the King's private correspondence, captured at Naseby, 'which letters being carried to London were printed, and manifested his falsehood'. 'Contrary to his professions', she notes, the King 'had endeavoured to bring in Danes and Lorrainers and Irish rebels to subdue the good people here, and had given himself up to be governed by the queen in all affairs both of state and religion' (p. 282).

The view of the King as being the catspaw of the Queen was reinforced with the publication in 1645 by special order of Parliament of *The Kings Cabinet Opened: or, Certain Packets of Secret Letters & Papers*, creating widespread interest and dismay. 'It was a great sin', the pamphlet opens, 'against the mercies of God, to conceale those evidences of truth, which hee so graciously (and almost miraculously) by surprizall of these Papers, hath put into our hands'.[8] Readers may see for themselves 'in his privat Letters what affection the King beares to his people, what language and titles he bestowes upon his great Councell' (sig. A3ʳ). Although later historians have proved that the letters were selectively edited, the 1645 publishers went to great lengths to assure the readers of the letters' authenticity, including having the originals on display in London and including at the end of each printed letter a statement 'a true Copy examined by' a Member of Parliament.[9] The preface concludes with a flourish that the publication of these personal letters, 'by Gods good providence the traverse Curtain is drawn, and the King writing to *Ormond*, and the Queen, what they must not disclose, is presented upon the stage'.[10]

The majority of the letters in the volume are addressed by Charles to his 'Deare Heart', Henrietta Maria, on the Continent attempting to raise money for his army. In her letters to Charles written from Paris in the early months of 1645, Henrietta Maria bluntly warns her husband against going to London to meet with Parliament: 'I cannot conceive where the wit was of those who gave you this counsel', she declares, 'unlesse it be to hazard your person to save theirs'. 'For the honour of God', she pleads, 'trust not your selfe in the hands of these people'. 'If you ever goe to London before Parliament be ended, or without a good Army', she concludes, 'you are lost'.[11] In 'annotations' at the end of the pamphlet, the editors bluntly state 'It is plaine, here, first, that the Kings Counsels are wholly managed by the Queen; though she be of the weaker sexe,

---

borne an Alien, bred up in a contrary religion' (p. 43). Perhaps as damning, 'the Queen appears to have been as harsh, and imperious towards the King, *pap[er]* 34 as she is implacable to our Religion, Nation, and Government' (p. 44).

On the other side of the conflict, the heroism of the women in the town of Lyme Regis, which successfully repelled Royalist troops led by Prince Maurice, was the subject for heartfelt if laboured verse in *Joanereidos: Or Feminine Valour* by James Strong published in 1645. The long title of this fourteen-page poem of praise explains that, while the town was being besieged, the women of Lyme 'defying the meciless Enemy at the face abroad, as by fighting against them in Garrison Towns; sometimes carrying stones, anon tumbling of stones over the Works on the Enemy, when they have been scaling them, some carrying powder, other charging of Pieces to ease the Souldiers…to maintain that Christian quarrel for the long Parliament'.[12] Strong marvels at 'Womens vertues in the West | Like Grapes ne'r drop till they were prest', and that the siege merely provided the opportunity for these 'western' women to demonstrate their courage.

> There see the field
> Maintain'd by Women tho men Yield:
>
> .   .   .   .   .
>
> Who could see the sword not daunting
> A Woman's heart, but stand still vaunting? (sig. E1ʳ)

Strong parallels the strength of the Parliamentary women during the siege with heroic women in the Bible, concluding that

> Nor fancy, frenzy, or blind passion,
> Or ought but pious resolution
> Moves them with constant courage thus to hold. (sig. E3ʳ)

Of course, in a civil war, it is not only castles and cities that are targets of raiding soldiers. Nor did one have to be a theatrical romance heroine to become involved in dramatic events encroaching on one's domestic space. During the war, we find women such as Dame Anne Filmer (d. 1671), who continued to manage the family's agricultural estate at East Sutton Park in Kent near Maidstone, despite nine raids by Parliamentary forces that took food, animals, and bedding. Her husband, Sir Robert Filmer (1588?–1653), was imprisoned at Leeds Castle from 1644 through 1645. Although in failing health, Filmer, like Lovelace, turned to writing to occupy his time and thoughts. Not a poet by temperament, Filmer, best known for the posthumous publication of his support of the theory of divine right monarchy, *Patriarcha*, nevertheless appears to have composed several short essays bearing obliquely on the crisis of his times, including a treatise on the virtues of a good wife, who demonstrated 'courage' as her most necessary quality.

---

[12] Strong, *Joanereidos*, title page.

Like many other Royalists who escaped being imprisoned, after his forces had been defeated in 1644 Newcastle had fled the country to France along with his sons. In February 1645, a Parliamentary newsbook *Mercurius Britanicus* announced sarcastically after the defeat at the battle of Marston Moor that Newcastle, who 'in time of peace tired the stage in Black-Fryers with his Comedies', had in time of war participated in a type of national drama, where as commander of the army he 'strode the stage in the North with the first Tragedies, travers'd his ground between York and Hull…help't Rupert to a sound beating, and Exit'.[13]

Exiled in France in 1645 from such former congenial literary pursuits, Newcastle met and married a young lady-in-waiting in Henrietta Maria's court, Margaret Lucas (1623?–1673), the future poet, playwright, and essayist, and the future Duchess of Newcastle. Other prominent literary figures and intellectuals living in exile in 1645 included Edmund Waller, Thomas Hobbes (1588–1679), Abraham Cowley (1618–67), Sir Kenelm Digby (1603–65), John Earle (1598x 1601–1665), Endymion Porter (1587–1649), and Richard Crashaw (1612/13–48), all of whom had either followed in Henrietta Maria's path when she fled in 1643 or arrived over the course of the next two years. Some, like Cowley, had been ejected by Parliament from their university fellowships, while others such as Crashaw had been removed by Parliament from their livings. By 1645, as the military phase of the war was signalling victory for Parliament, the number of English living abroad as exiles increased—the end of this phase of the Civil War was drawing near, and, in 1646, Charles I would surrender to the Scots.

When considering the questions of what was being read, written, and heard in 1645, it is necessary, too, to consider exterior forces that might affect the circulation or performance of texts. Between 1642 and 1645, Parliament issued numerous ordinances and acts that consolidated its control over the composition of the government, the army, and the Church. It also passed legislation that directly affected English readers and audiences, attempting to control what could be published, what could be viewed in a public setting, and what could be read in church. In 1643, Parliament had renewed the Licensing Act in an attempt to control radical pamphleteers of all persuasions, a move that provoked Milton's famous argument for freedom of the press, *Areopagitica*, but that remained in effect until 1660. On 4 January 1645, Parliament banned the use of the Book of Common Prayer; its forms and language were deemed too 'popish' and too representative of what was seen as the absolute power of the bishops embodied by Laud himself. In 1644, William Chillingworth had invoked a theatrical metaphor to describe what many viewed as the political imposition of an artificial hierarchy on the true Church: 'When I shall see therefore all the Fables in the Metamorphosis acted and prove stories…then will I beginne to beleeve that Presbyteriall government, having continued in the Church during the Apostles times should presently after, against the Apostles

---

[13] Hotson, *Commonwealth and Restoration Stage*, 20.

doctrine and will of Christ, be whirld about like a scene in a masque, and transformed into Episcopacy.'[14] In addition to the power of the bishops, many Puritans believed the reliance on the set texts found in the Book of Common Prayer interfered with the individual's seeking God, replacing personal prayers with formulaic texts to be learned, but not experienced, texts whose authority derived from the power of the bishops rather than the individual worshipper's spiritual strivings.

Parliament also attempted, without complete success, to control the presentation of texts on stage. The London theatres had been closed by the order of Parliament in 1642 to control public assembly. The Houses of Commons and Lords published a resolution on 2 September 1642 announcing that, 'whereas publike Sports doe not well agree with publike Calamities, nor publike Stage-playes with the Seasons of Humiliation', in order to 'appease and avert the Wrath of God', while 'these sad Causes and set times of Humiliation doe continue, publike Stage-playes shall cease, and been forborne'. The Globe Theatre had been pulled down in 1644. In July 1645, the Commons ordered the demolition of Charles's Masque House, which stood in Whitehall and which had been used to stage the productions of Inigo Jones (1573–1652), the brilliant architect and theatrical designer for Charles I's court; its timber was to be sold and the proceeds used to pay off the King's former servants.[15] Other London theatres remained intact, but were used for different purposes. The Fortune was used for fencing matches, and the newsbook *Mercurius Veridicus*, 19–26 April 1645, reports that, during the midst of the matches, constables interrupted the play to press men into the army.[16]

The last Master of the Revels, Sir Henry Herbert (bap. 1594–1673), the younger brother of Edward Lord Herbert of Cherbury and the older sibling of the poet George Herbert, was thus out of a job. He joined King Charles's followers in Oxford, the new centre for Royalist life and literature, but the next year he took the National Covenant and paid the fine for being a Royalist supporter. Many of the actors from the King's Company at the Globe and Blackfriars had enlisted in the King's army in 1642; according to the hostile Parliamentary newsbooks, while in residence in Oxford, these actor/soldiers occasionally performed for the King's followers. Some of these actors would flee to France in 1646 to entertain the exiled English and eke out a penurious existence, while others, after the defeat at Naseby, followed the lead of the Master of the Revels, and in September 1645 laid down their arms and returned to London, and threw themselves upon 'the mercy of the Parliament . . . offer[ing] to take the Covenant, & (if they may be accepted) are Willing to put themselves into their service'.[17]

[14] Chillingworth, *Apostolicall Institution*, 6.
[15] Hotson, *Commonwealth and Restoration Stage*, 13.
[16] Hotson, *Commonwealth and Restoration Stage*, 19.
[17] *Perfect Occurrences*, sig. R[r–v], 19–26 September 1645.

In 1645, there is also the question of where one could have one's texts printed and where one could purchase them. Charles had moved the royal press to Oxford, where, in 1645, it continued to produce numerous news-sheets such as *Mercurious Aulicus* and Royalist pamphlets by John Taylor, John Birkenhead [Berkenhead] (the licenser of the Royalist press), Sir George Wharton, and others, to bolster the spirits of Charles's followers during the days of military defeat. While publishing remained mostly the business of London printers, Oxford and other scattered provincial presses continued to provide outlets not only for Royalist sympathizers and pamphleteers, but also for writers producing the traditional literary forms, although many of the leading literary lights from before the war years, such as Sir John Suckling who had died in France in 1642, and many of its future ones, such as Edmund Waller and Abraham Cowley, had already fled to the Continent.

Many writers at this time, of course, did not write with a view to publishing, especially during the years involving active fighting. If Royalist sympathizers were struggling to preserve their homes and livelihoods and their manuscript verse celebrates the bonds of loyalty and friendship in adversity, Parliamentary supporters found themselves engaged in creating new roles for themselves and their families. It is also clear that, in 1645, many were discovering on their own side a lack of agreement over fundamental religious and social issues. These conflicts and controversy often mark the type and tone of the entries found in the diaries and meditations written during these times as well as the literary genres, seen in the Cavendish sisters' volume. Mary Carey (*c.*1609–*c.*1680) created a manuscript volume that combined prose meditations and verse, many lamenting the untimely deaths of her children; during this period, she travelled with her second husband, George Payler, the paymaster for Parliamentary forces, as they moved from garrison to garrison. In order not to be separated from her husband, she made her home in a variety of places, recording her unsettled life in her book, noting that, while it was being composed, 'I have liv'd in Barwick; London; Kent; Hunsden; Edenbroughe; Thistleworth; Hackney; Tottrige; Grenwicke; Bednellgrene; Claphame; York; [Nun] Mountaine; James's; Newington; [and] Coven-garden'. Conscious of her good fortune compared to others, she observes that 'in all thes warres, I was safe in Garrison, & was not straitned; nor plundred; nor separated from my deare Relations'.[18] Wherever she went, her pen and papers went with her, the act of reading and writing a part of the daily fabric of her life, even in times of turmoil.

What could one read in 1645? Social authors such as the Cavendish sisters continued to circulate texts among friends and family in manuscript form; letters and epistles clearly functioned as a key means for the transmission of literary texts as well as information. Manuscript volumes from this period were often shared household books, where, for example, Mary Carey and her

[18] Bodl., MS Rawl. D. 1308, fo. 195.

husband George Payler alternated in creating its contents. For readers relying on booksellers, on the other hand, they would find less than a dozen titles of what we typically define as fine 'literature' that were published during this year from the London and provincial presses combined. Of the less than 1,000 titles recorded as printed in 1645, only a very few were volumes of collected verse, although many broadsides and pamphlets used verse in making their political statements. Although small in number, the contents of these volumes of poetry are of no little importance in understanding the literary environment of the war years and the dominant models of literary authorship as well as providing several of the key texts used to define the literary tastes of that and the immediately following generations.

In addition to poetasters such as Matthew Stevenson (d. 1684), who printed *Occasions Off-spring Or Poems Upon Severall Occasions* in 1645, we also find John Milton's *Poems* (dated 1645, but appearing in January 1646), and Edmund Waller's *Poems e&*, which were both published in London by Humphrey Moseley. Like Stevenson's collection (which among other pleasant topics celebrates the virtues of Yorkshire ale and the numerous innkeepers with whom the poet imbibed), the contents of both Waller's and Milton's volumes were largely composed in the years before the fighting and contain notable lyrics and occasional verse. On the other hand, Waller's and Milton's collections also bear the mark of being produced during a time of civil strife, and their presentation in print signals their writers' political participation. Moseley, who in 1645 also produced *Epistolae Ho Elianae: Familiar Letters Domestic and Forren* by the Royalist supporter James Howell (1594?–1666), became the foremost publisher of literary texts for the next twenty years, and, as we shall see, produced volumes whose uniform format suggests the development of a national literary canon.

In 1645, London printer Richard Cotes also produced three other volumes of collected poetry, although much of his production focused on social and occasional verse. Like Moseley, his list featured poets who were engaged on opposing political sides. George Wither (1588–1667), the 'Rustick Poet' who in earlier days had published the pastoral *Fidelia* (1615), the *Psalms of David* (1631), and a collection of *Emblems* (1635), had become a captain in the Parliamentary army, raising the first cavalry troop for Parliament in Hampshire. Ironically, after attempting unsuccessfully to fortify Farnham Castle in Surrey in 1642, he was captured by Royalist forces, and, according to a story retold by John Aubrey, was spared from execution only when another poet, Sir John Denham, the author of *Cooper's Hill* (1642), interceded for his life: Denham supposedly begged the King not to hang Wither, for 'whilest G.W. lived he should not be the worst poet in England' (Aubrey, *Brief Lives*, I. 351–2).

While Denham may have disliked Wither's verses, Wither was one of the favourite writers of Oliver Cromwell. Like so many literary soldiers on both sides, Wither continued to compose, publishing *Campo-Musae, Or The Field-Musings of Captain George Wither* in 1643; in 1645, Wither had anonymously printed his satirical account of a parliament of newsbook authors, *The Great Assises holden in Parnassus by Apollo and his assesours*. The long title indicates his primary targets as the writers of newsbooks on both sides, but, in the process of Wither's condemnation, one also receives interesting portraits of the preceding generation of writers, many known personally to Wither, including Ben Jonson and Thomas Carew, as a means of contrasting the writers of earlier times with those of the war years.

This unease with the politics and practices of both sides of the war is also clearly manifest in Wither's long poem written after the battle of Naseby, *Vox Pacifica: A Voice Tending to the Pacification of God's wrath* (1645). In this four-canto poem, Wither declares that

> Though none they please, my *Musings* must be told.
> Mistake not tho, as it should be thought
> That by *Enthusiasme*, now, I write;
> Or, that the matter which to me is brought,
> But GODS immediate dictates, I indite.[19]

Positioning himself as a poetic vessel to transmit the 'VOICE' of prophecy, Wither opens by recounting the original transgressions of Charles I:

> The Cup and Fornication of the WHORE, |
> Do seeme to have bewicht his royall brest

and

> The *Soverainge*, from the *Subject* is estranged;
> And *Kingship* into *Tyranny*, is changed
> .   .   .   .   .
> none, but *Slaves*, are now true Subjects thought. (canto I, p. 27)

Equally, Wither warns his reader, the Parliament 'ev'ry day your sorrowes more increase'. The discord between King and Parliament has become the standard for the common man of the nation, and the soldiers of both armies,

> … equally oppresse both Friends, and Foe;
> They plunder, scoffe, insult, game, drink and whore,
> And ev'rie day corrupt each other so. (canto I, p. 30)

'These foure years of *Discord*, have so changed, | The gentleness, already, of this Nation' and Wither fears that not only the political relationships but even fundamental social ones have become monstrous:

> Men and women are so far estranged,
> From civill, to a barb'rous inclination:
> .   .   .   .   .
> …they whom you have arm'd for your defence,
> Will shortly ruine you, unless preventions.

---

[19] Wither, *Vox Pacifica*, canto I, p. 3.

Pleading for moderation and a united desire for peace through reformation, Wither continues to extend his opening emblem of the diseased state thrown into a mad distemper, one that can be cured only by God:

> Yea, bid both *King*, and *Parliament*, make hast,
> In penitence, united to appeare:
> Lest, into those Confusions, they be cast,
> Which will affright them both; and, make them feare,
> And know, there is, on earth, a *greater-thing*,
> Then, an unrighteous *Parliament*, or *King*. (canto IV, p. 199)

In addition to publishing Wither's *Great Assisses* in 1645, Cotes also produced two volumes of verse, which in both their contents and their format evoke the literary cultures of earlier, more peaceful times. The anonymous third edition of *Witt's Recreations* is a compilation of epigrams, epitaphs, and figure poems. This volume continued the tradition of social verse popular before the war; in its light-hearted poetic puzzles, it offers a contrast to the events experienced by many of its readers. In its collection of epitaphs, it reminded readers of the virtues of departed worthies, perhaps offering a contrast or a model for contemporary leaders.

The final title in Cotes's list of poetry was the 3rd Lord North's *A Forest of Varieties*, a volume of his collected poetry, letters, and occasional writings. Dudley, Lord North (bap. 1582–1666) added to some copies of the work a handwritten subtitle, 'or rather A Wildernesse', suggesting the author's appreciation of the ungroomed appearance of its contents, which transfers to the printed page the dynamics of a social, coterie writer in its exchanges of verses and compliments.[20] Mingling prose and verse and covering many years of labour, the meditations and reflections are those made by an author for whom writing was a passion rather than a profession, and a life-long practice rather than a single act of publication.

In 1645, North like many was uneasily positioned between political loyalties, declaring in the opening of *Forest* that 'the direfull extremities and convulsions which my unhappy Country, and my self in it have suffered these last yeers make good with the saying of *Ingenes Curae Stupent*: Partiality found much, ingenuity little freedom'.[21] North continues, employing the theatrical metaphor we have seen associated with the war, that 'the first surprize was such as caryed me to an affection of dissolution rather then to endure the spectatorship of the growing miseries & approaching tragedies; nay, spectatorship was not allowed' (sig. A2ʳ).

A former courtier in the service of James I, North dedicated his volume to Elizabeth of Bohemia, the sister of Charles I and the mother of the Princes Rupert and Maurice who were engaged fighting for the royalists. The handsome large volume, with its fine type and presentation, solidly embodies the

---

[20] FSL, call no. N1283.   [21] North, *A Forest of Varieties*, sig. A2ʳ.

variety of the writings and interests of an educated gentleman, deeply involved in the literary culture of his times, with little or no concern about securing a widespread readership but rather with the preservation of a literary life and its friendships. 'My Writings are somwhat like a Mart', he observes in a later revised version retitled *A Forest Promiscuous of Various Seasons Productions* (1659), 'much choice, not all allowable' (title page). Many of the epistles he includes reconstruct the literary currents flowing among his friends: 'Madam, the Verses which I read to your Ladyship the other day, at your casement', opens one, 'were occasioned by some disorder of the preceding week' (p. 211). In other epistles, he reflects on the nature of poetry of his younger days in James I's court, descrying its tendency to be 'like fine colored ayery bubbles or Quelque-choses, much ostentation and littel food; conceits, similies, and allegories are good, so the matter bee carried along in them, and not interrupted by them' (p. 2). For his own work, North hopes his readers will appreciate that 'in definance of Critiques, my births are naturall, easie, and hasty, sometimes foure peeces to my breakfast in the beginning of a morning…I love not Verses of the ragged staffe, but wish them fluent and gentle' (p. 213). He also wished the contents to reflect his life as a poet, lover, courtier, and gentleman, one whose writings bound him together in friendship with like-minded men and women readers.

These 1645 volumes of verse offer a starting point for considering the range of literary activity, its venues and production, and the general state of literary culture during a time of armed civil war. The specific contents of Milton's and Waller's volumes will be discussed in more detail later in this section as well as the ways in which they help to represent different models of being an author and different concepts of audience.

While other singular titles appeared in 1645, such as *Trissotetras*, a guide for understanding trigonometry for the 'benefit of those that are mathematically affected', by the future translator of *Rabelais*, Sir Thomas Urquhart of Cromarty (1611–60), the majority of the other items published during this year were ordinances, proclamations, and instructions issued by both the King and Parliament. It is instructive to look at the names and titles of the individual writers who had several titles printed during this year as an indicator of the nature of print during the war years. The two most prolific publishers during 1645 with seven titles each were William Prynne (1600–69) and John Lilburne (1615?–57). Prynne, whose persecution by Archbishop Laud had made him a virtual martyr for the Protestant cause, was a lawyer who published some 200 pamphlets and books in his lifetime, including *Histriomastix* (1633), an attack upon the decadence of the stage; in the 1640s he was actively engaged in promoting the principle of Parliamentary supremacy, including his assemblage of supporting legal texts sponsored by Parliament, *The Sovereigne Power of Parliaments* (1643).

In Prynne's 1645 publications, his titles indicate that he was continuing his part in the pamphlet wars, the rapid exchanges by opposing polemicists.

Prynne's 1645 titles include *A Vindication of Four Serious Questions* and *Truth Triumphing over Falshood*, the last written in response to attacks on *Foure Serious Questions of Grand Importance* and *A Fresh Discovery of some Prodigious News*, which had appeared in 1644. Prynne's numerous opponents, who were frequently prolific writers for print themselves, charged him with using so much paper that he had increased its price: in a typical blast, Henry Robinson declared in *The Falsehood of Mr William Pryn's Truth Triumphing* (1645) that 'I could much rather have bemon'd in private that perverse and implacable spirit of yours, had not you of late so inconsiderately bespatter'd so many Pamphlets, which have infected the very aire, far worse than any most malignant contagion'.[22] Pamphlets such as Prynne's and Robinson's typically appear to have been printed in batches of 1,000,[23] so Prynne could look back on his work in 1645 and perhaps have seen some 7,000 items with his name printed on them in circulation.

No less prolific in pamphlet production was his one-time associate and later political enemy John Lilburne. In 1645, Lilburne printed several responses to others' pamphlets, such as his *An Answer to Nine Arguments*, but perhaps most importantly, he produced while imprisoned by the Long Parliament one of his most famous tracts, *England's Birth-right Justified against all arbitrary usurpation, whether Regall or Parliamentary, or under what Vizor soever* printed in October 1645. Lilburne, who also had left the Parliamentary army in that year, voiced the feelings of the radical supporters of Parliament, who had become disenchanted with its reforms and some of whom would eventually come together to be known as the Levellers. The pamphlet's long title declares that the text will lay forth: *divers Queries, Observations and Grievances of the People, declaring this Parliaments present Proceedings to be directly contrary to those fundamentall Principles, whereby their Actions at first were justfiyable against the King, in their present Illegall dealing with those that have been their best Freinds, Advancers and Preservers: And in other things of high concernment to the Freedom of all the Free-born People of England.*

One of Lilburne's charges is Parliament's continued use of the practice of granting 'monopolies' for commodities, even after they had been banned, and, in particular, 'that insufferable, unjust and tyrannical Monopoly of Printing'.[24] In contrast to Milton's *Areopagitica* (1644), which had been presented in the form of a classical oration to Parliament concerning its licensing ordinance, Lilburne's pamphlet plays upon the emotions of its common readers with a list of charges and complaints, culminating with the cry for all 'free-born' Englishmen to guard against the encroachment of the individual's liberties by any institution, royal or Parliamentarian, the two being in reality closer in their beliefs and absolutist practices than they are different:

---

[22] Robinson, *Falsehood*, sig. A2r.   [23] Smith, *Literature and Revolution*, 30.
[24] Lilburne, *England's Birth-right*, 10.

a great company of the very same Malignant fellows that Canterbury [Laud] and his Malignant party engaged their Arbitrary Designes, against both the Peoples and Parliments just Priviledges...are invested with Arbitrary unlimmitted Power, even by a generall Ordinance of Parliament, to print, divulge and dispense whatsoever Books, Pamphlets and Libells they please, though they be full of Lyes, and tend to the poysoning of the Kingdom with unjust and Tyrannicall Principles. (p. 10)

Itself a masterpiece of radical political prose, Lilburne's tract asserts against the existing powers of Parliamentary censorship that the possessors of such privilege 'most violently...suppress every thing which hath any true Declaration of the just Rights and Liberties of the free-borne People of this Nation, and to brand and traduce all such Writers and Writings with the odious termes of Sedition, Conspiracie and Treason' (p. 10).

Such ordinances, obviously, did not silence Lilburne, who also printed seven titles in 1645. And, while Lilburne and others may have wished they did, the ordinance did not control the appearance and spread of royalist writings, either, most of which came out in Oxford. The ageing John Taylor (1578–1653), who would live through the reigns of Elizabeth, James I, Charles I, and into that of Cromwell, was one of the most active of the Royalist writers in 1645. Called 'the water-poet' because of his earlier employment as a London waterman, Taylor had published his first book, *The Sculler*, in 1612—in 1645, he produced with the press at Oxford numerous political satires and rebuttals including *Oxford besieged*, *The Causes of the Diseases and Distempers of this Kingdom*, *Rebells Anathematized, and Anatomized*, *The Generall Complaint of the most oppressed, distressed Commons*, *Aqua-Musae: or, Cacafogo, Cacadaemon, Captain George Wither wrung in the Withers*, and *A Most Learned and Eloquent Speech, spoken (or delivered in the Honourable House of Commons at Westminster...[by] Miles Corbet* (but written by John Taylor). Perhaps he would have rivalled Prynne and Lilburne in his output, but, as he lamented in 1644 in *Crop-Eare Curried, or, Tom Nash his Ghost, Declaring the pruining of Prinnes two last Parracidicall Pamphlets*, his attack on Prynne had to wait because the Oxford printers were so busy.

One of the projects occupying the Oxford printers in 1645 was the production of diurnals or newsbooks, also called 'mercuries', to promote the Royalist cause. The newsbook came into its own as a form in the 1640s and was extensively used by all parties throughout the 1640s and 1650s. The typical newsbook would have been about eight pages of text and published weekly, containing accounts of important events delivered typically as reports from eyewitnesses, sometimes containing verse. In 1645, Sir John Birkenhead, also the licenser for the royal press, was producing *Mercurius Aulicus*; Marchamont Nedham was the answering voice for Parliament with *Mercurius Britanicus*, each accusing the other of lying, distorting, and maligning the truth. *Mercurius Britanicus* goes so far as to accuse *Aulicus* of conducting a spectacular cover-up in the 20–27 January issue: 'as sure as can be King Charls is dead, and yet we never heard of it; I wonder we have not his Funerall Sermon in Print [in *Aulicus*], and the young Prince sent up to London'.[25]

Another writer whose texts occupied the Oxford printers was the poet and essayist Francis Quarles (1592–1644), whose *Emblems* first appeared in 1635 and was frequently reprinted. In the year after his death, his pamphlets 'The Loyall Convert', 'The New Distemper', and 'The Whipper Whipt', were gathered together and published as *The Profest Royalist: His Quarrell with the Times* by Leonard Lichfield in Oxford in 1645. Dedicated to King Charles by Quarles, the first treatise explores the puzzle of how England,

> that hath for many Ages continued the happiest Nation on the habitable earth . . . a thriving and well-contented People, in so much that shee became the Earths Paradise, and the Worlds Wonder, is now the Nursery of all Sects; her Peace is violated; her Plenty wasting; her Government distempered, her People discontented, and unnaturally imbroyld in her own Blood, not knowing the way, nor affecting the meanes to Peace, Insomuch that she is now become the By-word of the Earth, and the scorne of Nations.[26]

In the three tracts, Quarles explores not only the charges against Charles brought by Parliament, but also the ways in which Parliamentary writers have presented the issues to readers.

Quarles, like many of the royalist pamphleteers, had believed that the source of the trouble originated in 'Nationall Transgressions' and 'from the abuse of the Peace wee now want'. Reading the accusations from both parties, Quarles declares that he found his sympathies 'tost and turned as a Weather-cocke' between the two sides; to establish the truth, Quarles turns to the Bible for enlightenment. Both the King and Parliament contributed to the initial breach he now believes, but the resistance to the King's authority, whether it is good or bad, is a violation of God's appointment of Charles as the sovereign ruler of the nation. For Quarles, the present existing strife stems from this transgression of the principle of divine right monarchy. Quarles firmly rejects those who claim that Charles derives his authority from the people, that 'his Crowne was set up upon his Head by his Subjects, upon such and such conditions' (p. 5), asserting instead that, whether the King and his minister are good or evil, they are in their position through God's proclamation of royal authority, not a human ceremony of coronation. In his 'Post-script to the Reader', Quarles contrasts his exposition of the troubles with that of his opponents: 'Now thou hast heard the Harmony of Scriptures, without Corruption, and the language of Reason, without Sophistry.' He urges his readers to view with suspicion any interpretation of Scripture which is figural and instead to stay with a literal reading, to 'faithfully examine, and ponder the plaine Texts which thou hast read, and yeelding due obedience to them, stop thine eares against all sinister expositions, and remember, that historicall Scripture will admit no allegoricall

---

[25] *Mercurius Britanicus*, 20–27 January 1645.   [26] Quarles, *Profest Royalist*, 1.

interpretations' (p. 17), a request that may seem paradoxical coming from the author of the popular collection of *Emblems* twenty years before.

While Charles had an able army of writers devoted to explaining the principles of divine right monarchy, Parliament also had its eloquent spokesmen, very often, like Wither, writers who themselves were actively engaged in the military campaigns. An example from 1645 is *The Idolaters Ruine and Englands Triumph; Or The Meditations of a Maimed Souldier*; its author, William Whitfield, in contrast to Quarles, dedicates his treatise to 'All Noble, Valiant, and Faithfull Souldiers, which Fight under the Banner of the Lord Jesus',[27] declaring that he himself has suffered for the cause, having been under a surgeon's care for seventeen weeks. Since he cannot now fight on the battlefield, 'I have presumed to write this booke, for the incouragement of such Souldiers which have their limbes, to be faithfull and valiant, in, and for the Cause of God, for the pulling downe the Kingdome and Throne of Antichrist'. Comparing himself to Priscilla and Aquila in the Bible, women who 'though not much learned' nevertheless were used by God to instruct Apollos, Whitfield offers in his 'Apologie' the declaration that what he writes, he never heard a minister preach upon, 'neither did I read any mans workes in the time of my writing of it, save onely the Bible' (sig. A3ʳ). Instead of dry scholarly erudition or the formulaic statements from the institutes of religion, therefore, the source of and the authority for his writings rest in his own reading of the Scriptures and his own personal experiences as a soldier.

In addition to the prolific pamphleteers on both sides offering their interpretations and meditations upon the Scriptures, London and Oxford printers were kept busy in 1645 producing copies of sermons, many of them directly addressing the issues of the war. We see in these publications some of the different types of audiences being reached from the pulpit and their correspondence with a reading population. There were sermons addressed specifically to women auditors and readers, and some commenting on 'old England's' sad state from 'new England's' perspective; there were sermons demonstrating that God was on the side of the Parliamentary forces, and also those that declared God favoured the King. There were two new catechisms to remind soldiers that their profession could, and should, be a godly one, and there were still more catechisms for the King's soldiers, obviously different from those for the Parliament's.

In 1645, Samuel Torshell printed the sermon he preached at Whitehall on Princess Elizabeth's birthday in 1644, *The Womans Glorie. A Treatise, asserting the due Honour of that Sexe, and Directing wherein that Honour consists*. In this small, elegant, pocket-sized book, listeners and readers are exhorted to remember that, as God's creations, 'Women [are] capable of the highest improvements', including not only extraordinary piety, but also advanced secular learning.[28] While the book is dedicated to the Princess as the exemplar of all

---

[27] Whitfield, *The Idolaters Ruine*, sig. A2ʳ.   [28] Torshell, *The Womans Glorie*, 2.

virtues, Torshell offers to his English women readers as an example of the truly learned, literate woman Anna Maria von Schurman of Utrecht, who had attended the university there, albeit behind a screen in order not to distract the male students, wrote in several languages, and was in correspondence with Descartes and other leading European intellectuals. Van Schurman would herself publish two treatises arguing women's innate intellectual abilities. Torshell, while advocating women's education, nevertheless earnestly desires that his women readers would burn all their 'lewd' books and pamphlets, including seemingly harmless literary ones: 'Away with your Tragedies, and Comedies, and Masques, and Pastorals, & whatsoever other names they have, that soften the spirit, and take away the savour of heavenly matters', he urged. 'Away with your Spenser, your Ariosto, your deare Arcadia too, if these doe steale away your hearts and time from your Scripture-study and Meditation' (pp. 124–5). The danger for women readers, Torshell declares, is that, by consuming poetry, romances, and dramas, they are left vulnerable to their imaginations; 'the Imagination is a great thorough-fare', he warns his courtly readers, and it is a woman's duty to 'keep out bad [books], at least let them not lodge with you, but on go as Vagrants' (p. 221).

Perhaps in sympathy with such views on reading fictions, Elizabeth Richardson, Baroness Cramond (1576/77–1651), created more appropriate reading materials for her four daughters and two daughters-in-law. Composed in 1625 when she was the newly widowed Elizabeth Ashburnham, the text, which the Baroness permitted to be published in 1645 under the title *A Ladies Legacie to her Daughters*, contains three short sections of prayers and meditations. In her opening epistle to her daughters, she announces that 'I had no purpose at all when I writ these books, for the use of my selfe, and my children, to make them publicke: but have beene lately over perswaded by some that much desired to have them'.[29] She hopes that readers 'whose exquisite judgements may finde many blameworthy faults' will not fault the subject matter, which is 'but devotions or prayers, which surely concernes and belong to women, as well as to the best learned men' (p. 3). The content of the volumes provides short prayers for every day of the week, meditations on special days, and prayers for times of affliction, sickness, and when faced with temptation.

In contrast to these 1645 texts, the danger John Brinsley saw for his women readers did not come from reading Spenser's *Faerie Queene* or Sidney's *Arcadia*, but from listening to and reading seditious political pamphlets. Brinsley, a minister at Great Yarmouth, was addressing a much humbler audience than those celebrating the Princess's birthday at Whitehall; in 1645 he had printed his sermon *A Looking Glasse for Good Women*, directing it to 'all the well affected, but ill advised of the weaker Sex, who are either turned, or turning from the way of the Church of Christ in Old England, to the refined Error of separation'.[30] Concerned over the number of women in his flock who were leaving the

[29] Richardson, *Ladies Legacie*, 3.   [30] Brinsley, *A Looking Glasse*, sig. A2ᵛ.

traditional church, Brinsley was moved to print his sermon so that 'what you could not vouchsafe to heare with the eare, you may yet have the opportunity to see with the eye' (sig. A2ᵛ). Framing his sermon in the narrative of the Fall, Brinsley reminds his female audience that as women, they, like Eve, are more prone to be deceived, for 'as the Mother was deceived, so are her Daughters'. The modern serpents, he warns, are 'Romanish Jesuits' and 'some English Anabaptists[,] dangerous seducers', but they are equally pernicious and, like the serpent in Eden, adept at manipulating their listener's sense of contentment, 'they first fall into dislike with their present state and condition: Notwithstanding, that they are well, yet they are not so well, so well as they could be, and as they apprehend some others to be' (p. 8).

Sowing the seeds of discontent, these separatist preachers and writers encourage women to step outside their traditional roles in the church. Brinsley is particularly distressed by 'Publick Administration' by women: he offers for an example 'that notorious Mistris [Anne] Hutchinson of New-England, who under a colourable pretext of repeating of Sermons, held a weekly Exercise, whereby in a little time she had impoysoned a considerable part of that Plantation with most dangerous and detestable, desperate and damnable Errors and Heresies'. 'Henceforth', Brinsley concludes, 'no more Women Preachers' (p. 35).

Nearer to home than the colonies, Brinsley could have found numerous examples of women preaching, prophesizing, and publishing. During the 1640s and 1650s, it has been estimated by some historians that women were the majority members in the radical sects. Although the extent of participation differed from group to group, one of the characteristics of the sectarians always attacked by their enemies was the public behaviour of their women members, which ranged from preaching, printing of polemics, prophecies, and visionary warnings found among Brownist, Fifth Monarchist, and Independent groups, to the accusations of free love and communitarianism levelled at those called Adamites and Familists. Brinsley could have found examples of publishing women preachers much nearer home, such as Katherine Chidley (fl. 1616–53), who, in 1645, printed two of her treatises, or Lady Eleanor Douglas Davies (1590–1652), who printed no less than six pieces in that year. The two women, from very different social backgrounds and circumstances, shared a belief in the necessity of publishing one's writings and participating actively in London politics.

Chidley, the wife of a London tailor and mother of seven children, took on the conservative Presbyterian forces as represented in the person and writings of Thomas Edwards, author of *Gangraena: Or a Catalogue and Discovery of Many of the Errours, Heresies, Blasphemies and Pernicious Practices of the Sectaries of This Time* (1645). Chidley, a Brownist who along with her son Samuel became associated with the Leveller movement, advocated among other positions that ministers should earn their own living through manual labour rather than through church offices, and she herself led her own Independent congregation; in 1653, she and a group of women presented Parliament with a petition to free John Lilburne that had been signed by 6,000 women.[31] In her two texts printed in 1645, *A New Yeares-Gift, or a Brief Exhortation to Mr Thomas Edwards* and the broadside 'Good Counsell, to the Petitioners for Presbyterian Government', she exhorts the existing powers to remember the plight of the poor and not to betray the reforms they had initially proposed. In *A New Yeares-Gift*, Chidley addressed 'the Godly Reader', explaining that she writes to refute Edwards's 'slanderous accusations' against the Separatists as the sources of discord, when, indeed, 'the Hyrarchy' and 'the Bishops-Priests' have for sixteen years persecuted those 'who feare God and walke in his way, [I mean the way of Separation]'.[32] 'People rightly informed will not have their necks captivated, under Jewish yoakes of tithes paying, to maintaine a papish ordained Clergie', Chidley declares, for God 'requiredth his people to maintaine no Ministry but their owne, even such as labour with them in the Word and doctrine' (A2r). Chidley's emphasis on the established church as being a mercenary profession spreading false reports through its writers to mislead the simple reader is a common thread throughout her writings.

Unlike Katherine Chidley, Lady Eleanor Audeley Davies Douglas was personally familiar with ways of political power in her day. She was the daughter of George Audeley, Earl of Castlehaven, and the wife of the attorney general for Ireland, and, unlike Chidley's petitions to a humbler audience, she typically chose to address readers in positions of power, whether King or Parliament. She began prophesizing events in the 1620s, correctly predicting the death of the Duke of Buckingham in 1628; she also predicted the death of Archbishop Laud and Charles I, and she had been imprisoned for her outspoken commentary before the war itself began. Lady Eleanor represented herself in her writings as a prophetic descendant of Daniel, one who had come to warn her nation of peril rather than to write propaganda for a particular party. In her accounts of the events of the 1640s, she does not hesitate to label Parliament as 'the nursing mother of dragons' but also attacks the Church of England as an 'indulgent witch, the mother of harlots'.[33] In 1645, she printed her prophecy that, in her lifetime, England would witness the Second Coming of Christ, a hope apparently shared by many of her readers.

Lady Eleanor was not alone in her predictions of disaster for the English nation at the millennium. Perhaps not surprisingly against a backdrop of sensational prophecy, in addition to the erudite prophecy of Lady Eleanor based on her biblical scholarship, more popular and sensational accounts of miracles, apparitions, witches, and monsters invading the lives of average Englishmen and women were reported in the pamphlets printed in 1645. *A Strange and Wonderful Example of God's Judgements* retells the story of a London tailor, James Braithwaight, a man of 'very loose life and conversation, given to many

[31] Mack, *Visionary Women*, 123.　　[32] Chidley, *A New Yeares-Gift*, sig. A2r.
[33] Mack, *Visionary Women*, 118.

ill vices',[34] much given to swearing and making oaths; after his death, however, his drunken oath, that dogs could eat his flesh and bones if he was a liar, mysteriously comes true, his body being repeatedly uncovered and apparently eaten by unseen hounds, no matter how often or how deep it was reburied. The significance of this story for the times, the pamphlet writer points out, is that one should take heed of 'rash vows, false oaths or imprecations' since 'oftentimes men were punished in the same way that they themselves offended' (p. 1).

Another group of pamphlets appearing in 1645 also used supposedly factual narratives as a means of interpreting God's anger with England in general and his capacity to send warnings and punishments. Both sides of the political conflict claimed significance for their position in these accounts, both ask the reader to interpret supposedly factual narratives analytically and allegorically, to make the connections between the secular and the divine, the material and the spiritual conditions of their lives. *The Most Strange and Wonderful Apparitions of Blood and Signs and Wonders from Heaven with a True Relations of a Monster Born in Ratcliffe Highway* recounts the stories of monstrous or unnatural births that happened to godly women or to an animal, rather than being a result of human sin: in the first, a perfect child is born connected to a 'monstrous' partial Siamese twin, which as the author interprets, might signal the birth of a new perfect England from the corpse of a deformed monarchy. In the second, a pious woman gives birth to an hermaphrodite lacking limbs, and a London goldsmith's cat gives birth to a kitten with eight feet, two tails, no head, and the hands of a child. This author concludes that the unnatural conflict between Charles and Parliament is mirrored in these unnatural births and that God has sent them as a warning to those attempting to overturn natural order.

In popular pamphlets in general, women characters frequently figure either as the innocent vehicles of God's messages through their monstrous offspring and their perception of apparitions or as the destructive agents of evil forces contributing to England's disorder. In addition to favourable verses about Amazonian women warriors such as Strong's *Joanereidos* mentioned before, 1645 saw the printing of several accounts of witchcraft trials, a genre that would continue to flourish in the 1640s: the sensational pamphlets highlighted the crimes and unnatural desires of such village women, offering the reader the drama of a trial with the fascination of perverse desires being acted upon by one's neighbour. The printed confessions in *A True and Exact Relation of the Several...Late Witches...at Chelmesford* (1645) recount for the reader's horrified pleasure specific lurid details of how Elizabeth Clark, Anne Leech, Anne Cooper, and Margaret Landishe enjoyed their intimate relationship with the devil and his minions, as did the confessions in *The Examination, Confession, Trial and Execution of Joan Williford, Joan Cariden and Jane Holt* (1645). Each narrative offers in addition to the events of the trial a search for an

---

[34] *A Strange and Wonderful Example*, 2.

explanation of the human impulses that permit the devil access to everyday, common women.

Englishmen and women living in the American colonies in 1645 viewed this chaotic scene in dismay and published their fears. Anne Bradstreet (1612/13–72) in 1642–3 had composed her verse 'Dialogue between Old-England and New' addressed to the 'brave Nobles' defending Charles I and the monarchy; in her long poem 'Four Ages' composed between 1643 and 1646 and published in 1650 as part of *The Tenth Muse*, she continued to interweave her dismay over England's war and Charles's execution into her history of the biblical ages of mankind. Ministers in the New World wrote to their friends and former schoolmates still in England to express their horror over the religious chaos. We see, for example, in Thomas Shepard's letter 'New Englands lamentation for old Englands present errors', sent from Cambridge, Massachusetts, to his friend in Suffolk, printed in 1645, the recurring use of metaphors of disease and infection to describe the English national condition. Shepard blamed an increase of 'Anabaptists, rigid separatists, antimoniams and familists' for the crisis.[35]

As we have seen, in the texts of 1645, Shepard was not alone in characterizing the Civil War as a type of disease. The sectarians were commonly metaphorized as having been overcome by pestilence, their ideas and errors spreading like the plague to cause madness, disorder, and death. John Taylor extended the metaphor to its full length in his 1645 pamphlet *The Causes of the diseases and distempers of this kingdom; found by feeling her pulse, viewing her urine, and casting her water*. The long title concludes, 'The remedies are left to the skill and direction of more able and learned physitians'. Both sides claimed the metaphor of illness and of cure; both sides viewed the war as a national epidemic whose agents of infection were the seditious pamphlets and tracts of the opposite party.

In 1645, the issue that drew some of the most inflamed pamphlet responses was not overtly a political one, but the topic of infant baptism. This controversy split the Parliamentarian supporters between the Presbyterians and the so-called Anabaptists, a general label for several groups that rejected the practice of baptizing infants. Through their rejections of this central ritual of the established church, the Anabaptists were perceived as challenging not only the convention of the sacrament, but also the implied relationship between the individual, the officers of the church, and God. Numerous treatises, sermons, and reprints of early tracts on the defence of paedobaptism appeared in the year 1645, written by moderate members of both the Parliamentarian side as well as the Royalist, who were eager to characterize all their Parliamentary opponents as Anabaptists. The pamphlets from this period demonstrate a lively, ongoing literary shouting match of a group of opinionated writers responding quickly to other specific texts, to sermons, and to their opponents' imagined personalities. Writers such as Praisegod Barbon [Barebone] (*c.*1598–1679/80) published

---

[35] Shepard, *New Englands Lamentation*, 2.

A defence of the lawfulness of Baptizism, while, on the other side, Henry Deen (1606/07–60?) attempted in *AntiChrist Unmasked* (1645) both to refute Daniel Featley's (1582–1645) text written while he was imprisoned, *Katabaptistai Kataptustoi: The dippers dipt, or The Anabaptists duck'd and plung'd over head and earers* (1645), and also to attack Stephen Marshall's sermon on infant baptism preached at Westminster Abbey and printed that year. In the previous year, Christopher Blackwood had likewise been moved to attack Marshall in his text *The storming of AntiChrist*, which also included an attack on Thomas Blake (1596/97–1657) and his 1644 text *The birth-priviledge together with the rights of infants to baptisme*, which in turn provoked Blake's 1645 attack on Blackwood, *Infants baptisme, freed from antichristianism*. The controversy over infant baptism in 1645, at its heart a fight between conflicting views of fallen man's relationship to God and the powers of the earthly church, exemplified the pattern of intertwined pamphlet publication during the rest of the decade.

Compared to the invective and passion generated over the issue of infant baptism, John Milton's two tracts on divorce published in 1645 seem models of restraint and scholarship, but they were no less radical in their implications. In 1642, Milton had married Mary Powell, who had returned to her family shortly after their marriage. In 1643, Milton had published *The Doctrine and Discipline of Divorce*, which was singled out for attack in 1645 in *Gangraena* by Thomas Edwards, the same Edwards against whom Katherine Chidley wrote. Here, Edwards accuses Milton of arguing that 'man in regard of the freedome and eminency of his creation, is a law to himself in this matter, being head of the other sex, which was made for him, neither need he hear any judge therein above himself'. In Edwards's representation of Milton's text, its readers are misled into dangerous licence in the name of liberty, and he cites as a particularly frightening example the 'lace-woman' preacher Mrs Attaway, who, supposedly based on her reading of Milton, considered putting aside her 'unsanctified husband, that did not walk in the way of Sion, nor speak the language of Canaan'.[36] Milton's *Tetrachordon* and *Colasterion*, which both appeared in 1645, are in part a response to attacks made by Edwards and others.

Addressed to Parliament, *Tetrachordon: expositions upon the foure chief places in scripture, which treat of mariage, or nullities in mariage* is a continuation of Milton's exploration of what constitutes a true marriage based on a close examination of Scriptures. Milton argues, given the Bible's representation of the union of Adam and Eve, that divorce should be permitted not only for adultery but also for mental and spiritual incompatibility, pressing strongly against a definition of marriage that defines the needs of the body—the prime function of matrimony being defined as procreation—as being the central feature of the union between the sexes.

What courts of concupiscence are these, wherein fleshly appetite is heard before right reason, lust before love or devotion? They may be pious Christians together, they may be loving

---

[36] Edwards, *Gargraena*, pt 1, p. 34.

and friendly, they may be helpful to each other in the family, but they cannot couple; that shall divorce them, though either party would not. They can neither serve God together, nor one be at peace with the other, nor be good in the family one to other; but live as they were dead, or live as they were deadly enemies in a cage together: it is all one, they can couple, they shall not divorce till death, no though this sentence be their death.[37]

What else can one call such law, demands Milton, other than tyranny? 'The law is to tender the liberty and the human dignity of them that live under the law', Milton concludes, combining the rhetoric of radical politics with his close reading of Scriptures, 'whether it be the man's right above the woman or the woman's just appeal against wrong and servitude' (p. 32). In *Colasterion: A Reply to a Nameless Answer Against the Doctrine and Discipline of Divorce*, Milton defends his divorce tracts from the 'jolly slander' that has characterized his arguments as 'Divorce at Pleasure'.[38] Prynne, for one, had called on Parliament to suppress 'atheisticall opinions' including 'divorce at pleasure' in his 1644 pamphlet *Twelve Considerable Serious Questions*.[39] Turning to the language of polemic, Milton concludes on reading his opponent's attack that 'his very first page notoriously bewrays him an illiterate and arrogant presumer in that which he understands not'.[40] For Milton, the anonymous author is betrayed by his own words and his literary style: his Greek and Hebrew being such that 'the boys at school might reckon with him at his grammar' and his 'low and homespun expression of his mother English' make Milton conclude that the author must be 'not other than some mechanic…a contentious and overweening pretender' to learning and claims to authorship (p. 3).

In January of the year after these final two divorce tracts were published, Milton's *Poems of Mr John Milton, both English and Latin, compos'd at several times* also appeared, although the volume apparently did not initially circulate widely. It contains Milton's collected poetic work composed over a fifteen-year span, moving from his early paraphrases of Psalms 114 and 136 done as a teenager and 'On the Morning of Christ's Nativity' composed in 1629, through 'L'Allegro' and 'Il Penseroso' and 'Lycidas', which had appeared in 1638 in a volume dedicated to the memory of Edward King. The volume also includes Milton's experiments with Italian sonnets and epitaphs, a 1630 poem on Shakespeare, and two poems on the death of the Cambridge University Carrier, 'old Hobson'. The centrepiece in the volume is *A Masque Presented at Ludlow Castle* [*Comus*], which was extensively enlarged and revised by Milton from its performance in 1634 featuring three of the children of the Earl of Bridgewater: in August 1645, ironically, Ludlow Castle became a refuge for the King as he made his way north to Scotland after defeat at Naseby. The final half of the volume is devoted to Milton's Latin verses.

Humphrey Moseley (c.1603–61) published both Milton's and Edmund Waller's volumes of verse, each having a similar style of presentation that would

---

[37] Milton, *Tetrachordon*, 11.   [38] Milton, *Colasterion*, 1.
[39] Prynne, *Twelve Considerable Serious Questions*, 7.   [40] Milton, *Colasterion*, 2.

be repeated in the subsequent years' editions of Lovelace, Suckling, and others. The title page of Milton's poems informs the purchaser that these pieces were 'Compos'd at several times' and that this volume was 'Printed by his true Copies', by the London printer Ruth Raworth. In addition, one is informed that the songs had been set by Henry Lawes, 'Gentleman of the Kings Chappel and one of his Majesties Private Musick', which serves in a sense to recontextualize the verse in its original courtly setting as opposed to Milton's recent reputation as a radical pamphleteer. The portrait opposite it (the so-called Marshall Portrait) reinforces this impression, showing Milton with long, loose, curling hair, dressed plainly but still with some richness, looking very much like a portrait of a cavalier, surrounded by the figures of 'Melpomene', 'Erato', 'Clio', and 'Urania' fixing him at the centre of classical literature. The title page includes an epigram from Virgil's *Eclogue* 7: 27–8, which expresses the desire that the poet be protected from evil tongues exciting the envy of the gods at his talents. Moseley's own preface to the volume does lay large claims for the poet's merit while simultaneously suggesting that it was Moseley's efforts rather than Milton's initiative that secured their publication, since 'the Authors more peculiar excellency in these studies, was too well known to conceal his Papers, or to keep me from attempting to sollicit them from him'.[41]

Moseley begins by commenting on the state of literature at the time and his overall design in bringing out volumes such as Milton's and Waller's. Given that 'the slightest Pamphlet is now adayes more vendible then the Works of learnedst men', Moseley asserts that it is only 'the love I have to our own Language that hath made me diligent to collect, and set forth such Peeces both in Prose and Vers, as may renew the wonted honour and esteeme of our English tongue' (sig. a3ʳ). In establishing the Parliamentarian pamphleteer within the fold of fine literature, Moseley directly ties Milton's volume to Waller's, which he had published earlier in the year and which had met with great success; he concludes by suggesting that Milton is the Spenser of their times.

Indeed, most of the contents of Milton's volume are not overtly political or radical in their tone or subject. 'L'Allegro' and 'Il Penseroso' explore the opposing psychological states of mirth and melancholy in a classical rather than Parliamentary fashion, suggesting that pleasure can be derived both from

> Jest and youthful jollity
> Quips and cranks, and wanton wiles

and

> Or sweetest *Shakespear* fancies childe,
> Warble his native wood-notes wilde,
> And ever against eating Cares,
> Lap me in soft *Lydian* airs,
> Married to immortal verse' ('L'Allegro', *Poems*, 36)

[41] Milton, *Poems*, sig. a3ʳ, 'Preface'.

and also from the pleasure of melancholy,

> To walk the studious Cloysters pale,
> And love the high embowed Roof
> With antick Pillars' massy proof,
> And storied Windows richly bright,
> Casting a dim religious light

and to become lost in 'gorgeous Tragedy' ('Il Penseroso', *Poems*, 43, 60). The volume contains the masterful English sonnet 'How soon hath time the subtle thief of youth', where Milton reflects on the passing of his twenty-third year, and five elegant Italian sonnets celebrating the pleasures of charming ladies and of being in love.

'Lycidas', however, does bear references to its historical moment apart from the immediate occasion of its composition, the untimely death by drowning in the Irish Sea of Milton's Cambridge acquaintance Edward King, on 10 August 1637. Shortly after King's death, William Prynne and Henry Burton were transported in late August and September across the Irish Sea under Laud's orders, with Burton sent to Guernsey and Prynne to Jersey to keep them a safe distance from the sympathetic London crowds. Milton's Trinity College manuscript dates the composition of 'Lycidas' as being November 1637 before it was printed at Cambridge in *Justa Edouardo King* (1638). At the time of his composing 'Lycidas', some seven years before Prynne's attack on his divorce tracts, Milton was already committed to the position against Laud. In the 1645 volume, printed after Laud's death, Milton apparently added the head note that 'In this monody the author bewails a learned friend, unfortunately drowned in his passage from Chester on the Irish Seas, 1637 and by occasion foretells the ruin of our corrupted clergy in their height' (*Poems*, 57). Critics have pointed to the similarities between Milton's account of the pastoral flock in disarray and attacks on Laud's care for his flock:

> The hungry Sheep look up, and are not fed,
> But swoll'n with wind, and the rank mist they draw,
> Rot inwardly, and foul contagion spread:
> Besides what the grim Woolf with privy paw
> Daily devours apace, and nothing sed. (*Poems*, 62)

By the addition of the head note in 1645, Milton makes clear that both his political allegiances and those events in the poet's private world are in some senses inseparable from the events in the larger public one.

The longest piece in the volume is the masque *A Masque Presented at Ludlow Castle*, the story of the capture and attempted seduction of virtuous young Lady by Comus, a malignant spirit born of Circe and Bacchus but residing in an English forest. Comus, whose techniques of temptation foreshadow Satan's verbal legerdemain in *Paradise Lost*, is a creature of darkness and sensual revelry, who transforms heedless travellers into monsters with human forms but animal heads, who then lose themselves in bestial pleasures. Unlike

Milton's later tempted lady, Eve, this Lady preserves herself through her incorruptible chastity and disdain for Comus's 'glosening speech', although she does require the assistance of her two brothers, an attendant good spirit (performed by the musician Henry Lawes), and the native river nymph Sabrina to rescue her from her physical enslavement.

The printed text differs extensively from the Trinity College manuscript with its corrections and from the first printed edition in 1637.[42] *A Masque Presented at Ludlow Castle*, too, has had scholars who argue that its performance by the young children of the Earl of Bridgewater in 1634 would have had reverberations in the courtly and literary world because of the peculiar events of that family's private history, which had become public scandal. In 1631, Mervin Touchet, Lord Audley, 2nd Earl of Castlehaven, was tried and executed by the House of Lords for sodomy and rape; during the trial, it became clear that the Earl had, in addition to enjoying an illegal relationship with his groom, also instructed his servants to rape his wife, Lady Anne Stanley, the sister to the Countess of Bridgewater, and his young stepdaughter Elizabeth. The charges against him were brought by his son James, for whom he had arranged a marriage with the 12-year-old girl. Although blameless in the events, the two women were publicly stigmatized by the sensational public trial.

The choice by Milton to feature a pure young heroine whose adamantine virtue protects her from the sexual manipulation of the evil Comus, and to write that role for the 15-year-old niece and cousin of the women abused seems particularly poignant in this family context. 'Virtue may be assailed, but never hurt', asserts her Elder Brother:

> Surpriz'd by unjust force, but not enthrall'd,
> Yea even that which mischief meant most harm
> Shall in the happy trial prove most glory.
> But evil on itself shall back recoyl,
> And mix no more with goodness, when at last
> Gather'd like scum, and settle'd to itself
> It shall be in eternal restless change
> Self-fed, and self-consumed. (*Poems*, 101)

By the time of its appearance in the 1645 volume, much of this family history of the performers would have been erased from the reader's memory, and Milton did not provide any sort of head note, as he did with 'Lycidas', concerning the larger social issues to which the literary event was tied. Given the nature of the other texts in circulation in 1645, however, the Lady's defiant rebuff of Comus's temptations—

> Fool do not boast,
> Thou canst not touch the freedom of my minde
> With all thy charms although this corporal rinde
> Thou hast immanacl'd, while Heav'n sees good. (*Poems*, 104)

[42] Cambridge University, Trinity College, 'The Milton MS', Trinity College MS R.3.4.

—when read in the context of the radical rhetoric of the imprisoned pamphlet-eers such as Lilburne and the Protestant martyrs attacked earlier by Laud might well have taken on an added realm of significance to a reader of this volume.

Preceding the appearance of Milton's volume, Moseley had also brought forth *Poems, &c.* by Edmund Waller and *Epistolae Ho-Elianae Familiar Letters Domestic and Forren* by James Howell (1594?–1666). Waller's *Poems*, like Milton's, are a collection of verses composed over a lengthy period of years, opening with a poem addressed to Charles I on the death of the Duke of Buckingham in 1628, followed by one on Charles's escape from danger on the road at St Andero in 1625. Likewise, Howell's letters, which open with a dedi-cation to King Charles, have as their contents 'a Relation of those Passages of State that happen'd a good part of King James His Reign, and of his Maties now Regnant: As also of such Outlandish Occurrences that had reference to this Kingdom'.[43] On the title pages of both volumes, Moseley clearly identifies the political positions of the authors, noting in Waller's case that 'Mr Ed. Waller of Beckonsfield, Esquire' was 'lately a Member of the Honourable House of Commons' and that Howell was 'one of the Clerks of his Maties most Honorable Privy Counsell'.

Such an identification of Waller as a former Member of Parliament might well have carried strong resonance for purchasers of this volume. In 1643, Waller followed the Queen into exile in France, having been part of a failed attempt to seize Parliament for the King, for which he had been imprisoned in the Tower and fined; Aubrey records that he sold his estate in Bedfordshire, 'which was procured in 24 hours time or els he had been hanged: With which money he Bribed the whole House, which was the first time a house of Commons was ever bribed' (Aubrey, *Brief Lives*, 1. 374–5). Edward Hyde, Lord Clarendon, writing in later years, was even more severe, accusing Waller of 'an insinuation and servile flattery to the height the vainest and most imperious nature could be contented with; that it preserved and won his life from those who were most resolved to take it, and in an occasion in which he ought to have been ambitious to have lost it';[44] in his *History of the Rebellion*, Clarendon presents Waller as having been initially viewed as 'the boldest champion the crown had in both houses', but when Parliament caused Waller and his brother-in-law Mr Tomkins to be arrested, 'Mr Waller was so confounded with fear and apprehension, that he confessed whatever he had said, heard, thought, or seen; all that he knew of himself, and all that he suspected of others; without concealing any person of what degree or quality soever' (Clarendon, *History*, 3. 44–5). Tomkins and another conspirator, Chaloner, were hanged, and Waller sentenced to exile.

As with Milton's volume, the title page also informs us that the lyrics had been set to music by Henry Lawes, furthering contextualizing Waller within

---

[43] Howell, *Epistolae*, sig. a1ʳ.   [44] Clarendon, *Life*, 1. 54–5.

the courtly literary culture. In addition to the occasional poems addressed to specific members of the royal family, the volume contains some of Waller's best-known lyrics, including 'Go, Lovely Rose', a classic exposition of the carpe diem theme continued in other verses, such as that addressed 'To the Mutable Fair' and 'To Phillis':

> Phillis, why should we delay
> Pleasures shorter then the day?
> Could wee (which we never can)
> Stretch our lives beyond their span?
> Beauty like a shaddow flies
> and our youth before us dies,
> Or would youth and beauty stay,
> Love had wings and will away.[45]

There is also a set of poems directed to Lady Dorothy Sidney (Sacharissa) and to her family home Penshurst, the object of Ben Jonson's famous country-house poem. Although Waller told Aubrey he had not known Jonson (who died in 1637), many of his occasional poems bear a strong resemblance to his in style and tone: in his 'Upon Ben Johnson', Waller salutes him as 'Mirrour of Poets, Mirror of our Age' and writes in praise of his comedies, where

> Who ever in those Glasses looke, may finde
> The spots return'd, or graces of the mind;
> And by the helpe of so divine an Art,
> At leisure view and dresse his nobler Art.[46]

The content and genre of Howell's volume, too, might well have had particular associations for the purchaser in 1645. The publication of supposedly private 'letters' was a particularly charged one during this period: after the defeat of the King at Naseby in June, the private correspondence between Charles and his family was intercepted and as we have seen published under the title *The King's Cabinet Opened*. Although some disputed the publication as another attempt by Parliament to blacken the King's reputation, the letters were reprinted several times during 1645 and frequently cited in pamphlets. Howell's collection of letters on topics 'Historical. Political. Philosophical' opens with a verse epistle to the reader by Howell, which concludes that 'Letters as Ligaments the world do tie, | Else all commerce and love 'twixt men would die'.[47] In 1645, Howell was imprisoned in the Fleet, where he would remain until 1651; his loyalty to his King and his dedication to serving the royal family is never shaded in this collection of unabashedly Royalist musing. His opening address is to the King, declaring that, 'as the Law stiles You, [you are] the Center of our happiness, as well as the fountain of honor' and concluding that 'letters can treasure up, and transmit matters of State to posterity, with as

---

[45] Waller, *Poems*, 131. [46] Waller, *Poems*, 153, 154.
[47] Howell, *Epistolae*, 'To the Reader'.

much Faith, and be as authentic Registers, and safe repositories of Truth, as any Story whatsoever' ('The Epistle Dedicatory').

The author's circumstances in 1645 raise questions not only about the contents of the letters, but also how they would be transmitted and received. In an early letter written to his university friend Richard Altham while Howell was abroad, Howell observes that, 'tho you be now a good way out of my reach, yet you are not out of my remembrance; you are still within the horizon of my love'. In writing the letter, Howell conjures up before him the absent friend and, since 'the horizon of love is large and spacious, it is as boundless as that of the imagination; and where the imagination rangeth, the memory is still busy to usher in, and present the desired object it fixes upon' (p. 15). While held prisoner in the Fleet, Howell had already produced one text, *Instructions for Foreign Travel*, a guidebook for Englishmen travelling abroad; it has been widely debated whether during this time he may or may not have fabricated some of the letters or at least altered his originals, since, as he states, his papers were seized when he was imprisoned.

While many such as Howell kept writing steadily through 1645, some publishing their work, others collecting it in manuscript, there were of course other individuals who would later figure prominently in the world of books and literary life who during this time turned away from the pen in order to serve their causes in the armies. Richard Baxter (1615–91), the Puritan divine who in 1650 would publish *The Saints Everlasting Rest*, left his ministry in Kidderminster and became a chaplain in the Parliamentary army, attempting through his preaching to control the spread of what he viewed as dangerous sects such as the Seekers, the Ranters, and the Familists. John Bunyan (bap. 1628–88) was serving as a foot soldier in a garrison in Newport Pagnell, having been mustered into the army in November of 1644. Still others were forced into new professions as the times dictated: Eyllaerdt Swanston, formerly a London actor, upon the closing of the theatres had 'profest himself a Presbyterian, [and] took up the Trade of a Jeweller'.[48] During 1645, the next generation of literary writers were also being shaped through their travels and their studies. Around this date, the young John Dryden (1631–1700), the future author of 'Heroic Stanzas' on Cromwell's death, entered Westminster School as a King's Scholar.

Writing in 1645, Howell, like so many writers on both sides of the conflict, found that imprisonment called for all his powers of love, memory, and imagination to sustain him. As he noted in the 1647 second edition, like many of the texts created during this time, 'this book was engendered in a cloud, born a captive, and bred up in the dark shades of melancholy'.[49] And, as with so many literary texts printed in the year 1645, whether the subject matter was travels in Naples or the politics of foreign courts or the conquest of the heart, the politics of that year are rarely far from the writers' allusions and the listeners' and readers' apprehensions.

---

[48] Wright, *Historia histrionica*, 8.   [49] Howell, *Epistolae*, A3ʳ.

II. Laws Regulating Publication, Speech, and Performance, 1645–1658

When the so-called Long Parliament suspended the King's prerogative powers in 1641 and thus abolished the Star Chamber and the High Commission, among the many significant effects for authors and publishers was to open an occasion to question the legality of the royal patents issued to particular printers for the monopoly of printing lucrative texts, such as the Bible, law books, and grammars. This in part led to an increase of so-called pirated texts, as unlicensed printers seized the opportunity presented to expand their own list of publications. There was also a rapid and unprecedented increase in the number of cheap pamphlet publications offering multiple points of view on the war and those in power. In 1640, there were only some 848 titles published, 676 of them in London; in 1641 there were 2,034 in total, of which 1,789 were from London. By 1645, with the enforcement of the 1643 Act for the Regulation of Printing, numbers were lower, but still much higher than under Charles I, staying around 1,174.[50] The Stationers' Company had rapidly lost control. Parliament had set up in 1641 a Committee of Printing to investigate complaints concerning illegal publications, but it lacked effective authority to enforce it.

In 1643, Parliament had passed the Act for the Regulation of Printing, which prompted John Milton's famous polemic against censorship, *Areopagitica* (1644), itself published without a licence at an unidentified press. This Act required that all printed materials, books, pamphlets, and broadsides had to be entered in the Register at Stationers' Hall and licensed by an approved licenser. In the late 1640s, Parliament appointed various committees to enforce the regulations—for example, the Committee on Sequestrations, which was given the task of suppressing the sale of royalist pamphlets being printed in Oxford. The Committee of Both Kingdoms controlled the publication of materials concerning Scottish and foreign matters, and several special committees were appointed to deal with specifically pernicious texts or types of publications. In 1647 a special committee was formed to investigate unlicensed newsbooks (see *MV* 1.III). On 20 September 1647, it was recommended that enforcement of licensing and the suppression of illegal printed materials be taken out of the separate committees and given over to the Committee of the Militia of London.

This Act detailed specific penalties for illegal publication and distribution. Authors were to be fined 40 shillings or imprisoned for forty days; printers were likewise to be either fined 20 shillings or jailed for twenty days, but they would also lose all printing materials and presses. Booksellers were liable for only a 10-shilling fine or ten days' imprisonment, and the vendors on the streets, the hawkers and peddlers, forfeited all their goods and were to be whipped as

---

[50] See Barnard, McKenzie, and Bell (eds), *The Cambridge History of the Book in Britain*, 4. *1557–1695*, app. I, table I; for a discussion of the impact of the sudden increase in printed reading materials, see Achinstein, *Milton and the Revolutionary Reader*, ch. 1.

'Common Rogue' (*Acts and Ordinances*, 1. 1021).[51] The specificity of the language of the bill for the regulation of printing reveals the web of connections existing among speakers, writers, printers, and sellers of texts: 'the Penalties in this Ordinance', the Act announces, extend to 'any person or persons that shall Make, Write, Print, Publish, Sell or Utter, or cause to be Made, Written, Published, Sold or Uttered, any Book, Pamphlet, Treatise, Ballad, Libel, Sheet or Sheets of News that shall contain any Seditious, Treasonable or Blasphemous matter' (*Acts and Ordinances*, 1. 1023). The expression of seditious ideas was treason whether it appeared in verse or prose, handwriting or print, was sung in the street, preached in a pulpit, or sold for a penny.

While the penalties for illegal publication were made clear in this Act, it is less clear how successful they were in deterring publication or how effectively they could be enforced. The numbers of publications issued during this period, however, suggest the very limited control the government actually had over printed materials: in 1641 there were only four publications classified as newspapers or newsbooks, in 1643 there were 402, in 1645 there were 722, and in 1648 there were an estimated 612.[52]

Numerous unlicensed pamphlets in the years following 1645 directly attacked Parliament for its attempts to censor publications as being part of its perceived threat to remove the King only to replace him with an equally arbitrary governing body. The group known as the Levellers were particularly vocal in their attacks on press censorship as a hallmark of arbitrary and illegal government. The printer Richard Overton (fl. 1640–1663), who operated a secret press in Coleman Street whose imprimatur was 'the Martin Mar-Priest Press' (1645–6), was an early critic of Parliament's attempts to control speech and printing.[53] In 1645, he issued *The Arraignement of Mr Persecution*, whose title page declared that it was 'Printed by *Martin Claw Clergie*, Printer to the *Reverend Assembly of Divines*, and are to be sould at his shop in *Toleration Street*, at the *Signe* of the *Subjects Liberty*, right opposite to *Persecuting Court*, 1645'. It notes ironically that 'This is Licensed, and printed according to Holy Order, but not Entered into the Stationers Monopole'. Primarily an attack on the Presbyterian Parliament, the pamphlet is an allegorical arraignment of 'Mr Persecution' by 'Mr Gods-vengeance', arguing for freedom of conscience, which is inextricably tied to freedom of expression.

John Lilburne (1615?–57), the soldier and polemical writer who had been sentenced by the Star Chamber in 1638 to be whipped and pilloried for illegal publications, found himself in 1645 being jailed by Parliament for unlicensed publications critical of the government. The title of the second edition of one of Lilburne's polemics suggests the range of his grievances: *Englands Birth-right Justified against all arbitrary usurpation, whether Regall or Parliamentary, or under what Vizor soever....by a well-wisher to the just cause for which*

[51] See Seibert, *Freedom of the Press*, ch. 9.   [52] Siebert, *Freedom of the Press*, 203, n. 1.
[53] See Plomer, 'Secret Printing'.

Lieutenant Col. John Lilburne is unjustly imprisoned in New-gate. In this tract, he particularly attacks government-controlled monopolies, listing as his third example of this practice 'the insufferable, unjust and tyrannical Monopoly of Printing'.[54] Needless to say, it was published without a licence, probably from a secret press in Goodman's Fields.[55]

Lilburne's imprisonment and his sufferings, well publicized through numerous unlicensed pamphlets, led to a series of Leveller petitions to the House of Commons in 1647 outlining a series of fundamental changes to government, one of which was the freedom of the press to publish without licensing, culminating in the petition of 18 January 1649. In this petition, it is argued that all ordinances governing printing should be revoked by Parliament, which, in effect, came to power with the help of unlicensed publications against the King. Government, it asserts, if it is just and good, will need and wish 'to hear all voices and judgments, which they can never do, but by giving freedom to the Press'. To institute government licensing, 'or to put the least restrain upon the Press, seems altogether inconsistent with the good of the Common-wealth, and expressly opposite and dangerous to the liberties of the people'.[56] The apparently alarmed Parliament's response to this call for complete freedom of expression in print was to pass an ordinance that expanded the definition of treason to include seditious publication, a change that would lead in the tumultuous years following to numerous trials and executions of printers and their agents (see *MV* 1.II; *MV* 2.II; *MV* 3.II, *MV* 4.II; *MV* 5.II).

Newsbooks were, of course, particularly worrisome to the government (see *MV* 1.III). On the same day as the Ordinance for Regulating printing was passed in September 1647, Gilbert Mabbott (bap. 1622–c.1670) was given the thankless task by Sir Thomas Fairfax, the commander in chief of the Parliamentary army, of licensing weekly pamphlets. Mabbott was himself a newsletter writer, of both published versions such as *The Perfect Diurnall* and scribal ones commissioned by individuals to send accounts of domestic and foreign happenings. He was unsuccessful in controlling the illegal opposition newsbooks, some of which, in fact, used his imprimatur without his permission, and he resigned or was relieved of his post in May 1649.

By 1645, Parliament had officially closed the public theatres and places of popular public entertainments such as bear-baiting as not suitable pastimes during war but also because they might serve as potentially dangerous meeting spaces for discontented citizens. However, as with the licensing of printed materials, it is clearly questionable how effective they were in stopping all theatrical performances (see *CV* 1.IV). There were repeated admonishments to the Justices of the Peace and the sheriffs to enforce the 1642 Act: Justices should 'be very diligent and strict in improving their Authority, for the suppressing and

---

[54] Lilburne, *Englands Birth-right*, 10.

[55] Plomer, 'Secret Printing', 387–8. 'Martin Mar-Priest' is an allusion to the name used in the anonymous illegal pamphlet controversy in 1588 and 1589, Martin Marprelate.

[56] Steele, *Tudor and Stuart Proclamations*, 1, no. 282.

preventing any Stage Plays, Dancings of the Ropes, Bearbaitings, or Bullbaitings' urges one issued 11 August 1647. After Charles's execution, the need to control London public spaces became even more acute, and, in March 1649, the acting spaces at Salisbury Court, the Phoenix, and the Fortune were dismantled (see CV 1.IV), thus following the second Globe's destruction in 1644. Even the physical demolition of the Fortune and other acting spaces did not completely suppress performances, however. As we will see, there is a consistent gap between the law's delineation of what could and could not be done and what Londoners and those in the countryside wished to and were able to see, read, and hear.

The official government culture of the Interregnum passed numerous Acts and Ordinances setting forth fines and penalties restricting entertainments in general, but Londoners and those living outside the city apparently nevertheless managed to buy forbidden pamphlets, ballads, and pictures throughout this period. The government may have banned 'merry books', but the 1650s saw a popular expansion of the genre known as 'academies' containing jests, songs, and amusing dialogues (see CV 1.V). There was a £5 fine for writing about recreational activities on Sundays, a position repeated in Acts passed in 1650 and 1657, which suggests Sunday sports likewise persisted as a problem despite the law.

Some speech acts themselves were targeted by Parliament in the late 1640s and 1650s, but, again, the repeated injunctions that they should be better enforced makes one wonder how successful they were in shaping actual behaviours. Prior to the passage of the Act regulating printing, on 4 February 1647, Parliament passed the Ordinance concerning 'the growth and spreading of Errors, Heresies, and Blasphemies', requiring a national day of public humiliation to bring the country to its senses, highlighting the danger of spoken heresy and blasphemy to listeners through infection 'of their plagues' (*Acts and Ordinances*, 1. 913). The prophetic Welshman Arise Evans (see MV 1.IV), who had been placed in Bedlam in the 1630s for representing himself as 'God's Secretary', was brought up on blasphemy charges at Old Bailey and put in Bridewell. Parliament passed another Act on 2 May 1648 condemning those that, 'by Preaching, Teaching, Printing, or Writing, Maintain and publish that there is no God, or that God is not present in all places'. This lengthy Act sets out specific beliefs and acts deemed blasphemous, including that penalties shall be enforced on 'every person or persons that shall publish or maintain … as all men shall be saved, or that man by Nature hath free will to turn to God, or that God may be worshipped in or by Pictures or Images' (*Acts and Ordinances*, 1. 1133).

The Blasphemy Act of 1650 was directed at the Ranters, and chargeable offences included asserting that one was God, that God dwelled within one, or denying that 'whoredom, adultery, drunkenness or the like open wickedness' was in fact sinful. The prophet preacher and writer Abiezer Coppe (1619–72) was granted a vision from God instructing him to go to London to preach and to write. *A Fiery Flying Roll* (1650) is Coppe's stylistic rejection of the institutional language of faith and its conventions (see *MV* 1.IV). He declared that 'my most Excellent Majesty (in me) hath strangely and variously transformed this forme. And behold, by mine owne Almightinesse (In me)'.[57] In his transformed state, he has an apocalyptic vision of England's future; Coppe condemns the wealthy and the clergy for having forsaken the poor of the land, describing how he would accost the wealthy in the street as they passed in their carriages. In the second part of the *Fiery Flying Roll*, he again asserts he speaks directly from God, and warns censors 'in the Name and Power of the eternall God, I charge thee to burn it not, tear it not, for if thou dost, I will tear thee to pieces'. In February 1650, Parliament declared that Coppe's books had so many 'horrid blasphemies' they were ordered seized and burned. When he was brought to court after the passage of the new Blasphemy Act, he refused to remove his hat, answered questions by talking to himself, and tossed fruit and nuts into the room; the examining committee sent him back to Newgate, where he remained until his recantation in 1651.

Puritanism, almost from its beginning, was founded in the belief that Christian magistrates 'had a religious duty to punish heresy, idolatry, and apostacy...to halt the spread of false religion'.[58] Radical sectarian groups such as the Muggletonians, the Seekers, and the Ranters preached and worshipped in ways directly in conflict with the official laws governing speech and public behaviour during the Interregnum. In 1645, Laurence Clarkson and Hanserd Knollys were arrested and examined by the county committee at Bury St Edmunds for irregular practices, including allegations that Clarkson had performed adult baptism on six naked women. Clarkson and Knollys were confined for six months. Upon release, Clarkson travelled to London, where he continued preaching and published his second treatise, *Truth Released from Prison* (1646). Its long title makes clear its stance in relationship to official, institutional culture: '*Or, A true discovery, who are the troublers of true Israel; the disturbers of Englands peace. With a brief Narration; in which is impartially debated of, who are the true Embassadors of that great Jehovah, the Prince of Peace. By Lawrence Clarkson, a labourer in that great Mysterie of godlinesse.*' It was printed by Jane Coe, but not licensed by anyone. Its argument is essentially anticlerical and calls for liberty of conscience.

In addition to the Ranters, the Baptists, and the Seekers, who had been in existence prior to the Civil War years, the Quakers, who came into existence in the 1650s, faced intense persecution for their ways of speaking and worshipping. At the same time, there are increasing numbers of voices urging religious toleration. In 1655, the then Baptist and eventual Quaker Samuel Fisher (bap. 1604–65) declared in *Christianismus redivivus* (originally published as

---

[57] Coppe, *A Fiery Flying Roll*, 1.
[58] Coffey, 'Puritanism and Liberty Revisited', 962–3.
See Bauman, '*Let Your Words be Few*'.

Baby-Baptism Meer Babism) that 'heathens, Jewes, Turks, or Pagans' have the right to 'lawfully be licensed to live in civil States, or in any Common-wealth under the Sun' and that magistrates should 'leave all men to worship God according to their several wayes'.[59] Samuel Richardson (fl. 1637–8), a member of one of the seven Baptist congregations in London, urged on the title page of *The necessity of toleration in matters of religion* (1647) that 'in matters of Religion, men ought not to be compelled, but have liberty and freedome'.[60] He argues that 'it is the best for the publick peace to give every one content, for if there be set up an Order in Religion for a Law, and thereby please one sort of people, another sort will be displeased' (p. 5).

More conservative Puritan leaders and the legislators in Parliament naturally found such sentiments remarkable. Thomas Edwards, in *Gangraena*, declared 'who ever thought seven years ago he should have lived to have heard or seen such things preached and printed in England; all men then would have cryed out of such persons, Away with them, Away with them'.[61] As mystifying to Edwards as these calls for toleration was the highly visible presence of women preaching both in London and travelling about the countryside (see *MV* 1.IV). Katherine Chidley's *A New-Yeares-Gift...to Mr Thomas Edward* (1645), Priscilla Cotton and Mary Cole's *To the Priests* (1655), Anne Audland's *The Saints Testimony* (1655), and Francis Gawler's *A Record of Some Persecutions* (1659), along with Margaret Fell's *Women's Speaking Justified* (1666), and Richard Farnworth's *A Woman Forbidden to Speak* (1654), recount some of the exploits of these highly visible women preachers and the responses they drew forth from bystanders who heard them preach, ministers who read their writings, and the juries who tried them.

Of these women, Anna Trapnel (fl. 1642–60) was one of the more spectacular prophetic speakers who gathered large audiences to hear her speak and attracted the attention of magistrates. The daughter of a shipwright, Trapnel after the death of her godly mother in 1645 pursued her faith through various radical congregations in London. She became associated with the Fifth Monarchists, a millenarian group who believed through the prophecies in the Old Testament that the four great monarchies of the secular world had ruled their allotted span and that the next ruler would be Christ himself returning to rule the godly. She had received prophetic visions concerning battles and Cromwell's closing of Parliament in 1653. During the charismatic Vavasor Powell's trial for treason in Whitehall, she fell into a rhapsodic trance for eleven days, her utterings taken down by the spectators who crowded around her bedside and published as *The cry of a stone, or, A relation of something spoken in Whitehall* (1654). Her prophecies, all of which emerged in verse, dangerously alluded to God's future punishment of Cromwell for misusing his powers as well as denouncements of institutional religion and the universities (see

<hr>

[59] Fisher, *Christianismus redivivus*, 534, 537.   [60] Richardson, *The necessity of toleration*, 4.
[61] Edwards, *Gangraena*, pt 1, p. 121.

MV 1.IV). Such inflammatory remarks, although claimed by Anna Trapnel to be simply God's words uttered through her weak female voice, nevertheless attracted the attention of Cromwell's government, and, when she travelled to Cornwall to visit two imprisoned Fifth Monarchist ministers, Christopher Feake and John Simpson, she was taken by the authorities and brought before the assize on charges of witchcraft, whoredom, seditious intent, and vagrancy. She recorded her successful defence of herself in *Anna Trapnel's 'Report and plea, or, A narrative of her journey from London into Cornwall'* (1654).

As a group, the Quakers felt the legal restrictions most brutally, both men and women (see *MV* 1.IV). Perhaps one of the most celebrated and notorious of the Quaker trials was that of James Nayler (1618–60). Along with Martha Simmons, the sister of the radical publisher Giles Calvert (see *MV* 2.II), in 1656 Nayler and several associates dramatically performed a prophetic 'sign'. Nayler, accompanied by several others, rode into Bristol; this by itself was no crime, but the group attracted scandalized attention when the women dismounted from their horses and, with Martha Simmonds, 'the wife of *Thomas Simmods* of *London*, Bookbinder' leading Nayler's horse on one side and '*Hannah Stranger*... Wife of *John Stranger* of *London* Combmaker', on the other, they sang '*Holy, holy, holy, Lord God of Sabboth*' all the while they 'bestrewed the way with their garments'.[62] To those watching, this was a plainly blasphemous imitation of Christ's entry into Jerusalem.[63] They were all arrested under the 1650 blasphemy law, and authorities seemed to find supporting evidence against Nayler in particular in the letters to him by his associates, which stated baldly 'thy name is no more to be called *James* but *Jesus*'. Historians have interpreted Nayler's actions as a symbolic dramatization intending to signal the living presence of Christ in all believers in the present time, rather than being a conscious claim to divinity for himself. The authorities, however, had Nayler brought from Bristol to be questioned before Parliament. A committee of fifty-five members conducted what was in effect a ten-day trial, which was recorded by one of them, Thomas Burton, in his diary.[64]

Even though Nayler again repeatedly denied believing that he himself was Christ, he was found guilty of 'horrid blasphemy' by Parliament. He also denied any subversive political intent: 'I am one that daily prays that magistracy may be established in this nation', he asserted firmly. 'I do not, nor dare affront authority.'[65] Before sentencing him, the committee asked Nayler if he had any final remarks, to which he replied that 'it pleased the Lord to set me up as a sign of the coming of the righteous one; and what hath been done in my passing through the Towns, I was commanded by the power of the Lord to suffer such things to be done to the outward as a sign'.[66]

[62] Deacon, *The Grand Impostor Examined*, 2–3.
[63] Deacon, one of Nayler's severest critics, published a graphic account in *The Grand Impostor Examined*, while a more sympathetic account can be found in Rich and Tomlinson, *A true narrative*.
[64] Burton, *Diary*, vol. 1.   [65] Burton, *Diary*, 1. 48.
[66] Rich and Tomlinson, *A true narrative*, 28.

The penalties decided on by Parliament far exceeded the suggested six-month imprisonment of the 1650 Act: Nayler was whipped through the streets, leaving no skin upon his back, exposed in the pillory, his tongue bored through with a hot iron, and the letter B for blasphemy branded on his forehead; he was returned to Bristol to be publicly shamed and then brought back to be confined indefinitely in Bridewell, where he remained until 1659. The dramatic effects of both his original prophetic performance and the punishment continued to play out allegorically among his followers: Martha Simmonds, Dorcas Erbury, and Hannah Stranger knelt around him when he stood whipped and bloody in the pillory, in the eyes of many enacting a tableau of a crucifixion scene, the logical ending for the faithful of his trial and persecution. His punishment and imprisonment likewise did not silence Nayler, who continued to produce short treatises that were smuggled out and printed. In the 1657 sympathetic account compiled by Robert Rich and William Tomlinson, *A true narrative of the examination, tryall and sufferings of James Nayler*, they demand indignantly of the reader in a side gloss to 'take good notice of his answers from first to last, and see if in any of them you can finde blasphemy, or any thing that is contrary to the Scriptures, and the Saints practice' (p. 28).

The life and writings of Anne Audland (1627–1705), later Anne Camm, also illustrate what Quaker writers, preachers, and those who witnessed their public performances experienced during the Interregnum. While she travelled widely both with her husband John Audland and by herself spreading the Quaker word in the 1650s, she was often imprisoned. In Auckland, Durham, she was briefly jailed for preaching in the public market square, and her response was to continue preaching out of her jail cell window. More serious was her encounter with authorities in Banbury, where the mayor found the necessary two witnesses to swear that she had uttered blasphemy. In her *A True Declaration of the suffering of the innocent ... Wherein is discovered the zeale of the magistrates and people of Banbury ... By Anne Audland, whom the world scornfully calls Quaker* (1655), published by Giles Calvert, she narrates her defence of herself. Her trial was attended by many supporters, some of whom joined the Quakers, and the judge noted her 'innocent fearlessness of her deportment' in the dock. She was found not guilty of blasphemy by the local jury but guilty of 'misdemeanor'; unfortunately, her refusal to 'swear' to future 'good behavior' landed her back in jail for the next seven to eight months.[67] She was joined there by Jane Vaugh, another women preacher.

The period of the war years and the Interregnum, on the one hand, saw a complete breakdown of the previous forms of royal control over what was printed, performed, and preached, and, on the other, a transfer of authority from the King to Parliament. Many of the functions of the old Star Chamber, the Archbishop of Canterbury, and the Master of the Revels would be taken on by parliamentary committee and published in numerous Acts and Ordinances.

---

[67] See Budge, *Annals of Early Friends*, 33–4.

From the trials and the newsbook accounts, it is clear that some authors, performers, and preachers were effectively silenced by these means, but it is also clear that the civil authorities could not completely control the variety of new voices, from middle-class women and mechanic preachers, from disposed royalists, and from opposition within their own government. During the 1650s, too, as we shall see, there was a growing appetite and market for secular reading materials, entertaining fictions, and vernacular advice books of all sorts, as well as the successful regeneration of the theatre through William Davenant's 'operas'.

III. Humphrey Moseley and London Literary Publishing: Making the Book, Image, and Word

Humphrey Moseley (*c.*1603–61) published some 300 titles between the years 1645 and 1660 from his shop at the sign of the Prince's Arms in St Paul's Churchyard, where he had done business since 1638. The majority of these titles were literary texts that covered a wide variety of genres. In his 1646 edition of John Milton's poems, Moseley explained in a letter to the reader what motivated him to publish the works he did: 'it is not any private respect of gain, Gentle Reader, for the slightest Pamphlet is now adayes more vendible then the Works of learnedest men', he opens, 'but it is the love I have to our own Language that hath made me diligent to collect, and set forth such Peeces both in Prose and Vers, as may renew the wonted honour and esteem of our English tongue'.[68] In his numerous prefaces to his readers, Moseley lays out both his scale of literary merit and his anticipated readers' desires; in his descriptions of the ways in which various volumes came to be printed, he offers an unmatched window into the intersections of courtly performance, social manuscript circulation, and the world of a London commercial printer. Likewise, in his publication practices, he serves as an introduction in the making of books, images, and words during the Commonwealth period.

In addition to publishing living contemporary poets, including Milton, Edmund Waller, William Davenant, Abraham Cowley, John Cleveland, Sir John Denham, William Cavendish Duke of Newcastle, James Shirley, Henry King, Richard Fanshawe, and Henry Vaughan, Moseley was also responsible for publishing works by earlier generations of writers, often for the first time. Readers in the 1650s thus could purchase Sir Walter Ralegh's *Essays*, the *Works* of Ben Jonson, John Donne's sermons, *Paradoxes*, and his defence of suicide *Biathanatos*, Beaumont and Fletcher's complete plays, individual plays by Thomas Middleton, such as his tragicomedy *No Wit Like a Woman's*, the collected poetry and plays of William Cartwright, Lancelot Andrewes's

---

[68] Milton, *Poems*, sig. a3^{r-v}.

sermons, Thomas Carew's courtier poems, and Richard Crashaw's spiritual verses.

This decade also found him publishing important English translations of Juvenal, Seneca, Anacreon, Theocritus, and the odes of the so-called Polish 'Horace', Casimire (Maciej Kazimierz Sarbiewski, 1595–1640) whose writings, artfully blending Christian and classical images and themes, would directly influence Henry Vaughan, Abraham Cowley, and Isaac Watts, among others (see CV 1.V). Through Moseley's publications, English readers could enjoy translations of popular European romances, fictions, and important poems, including Corneille's *The Cid* (1650), Gaultier de Costes's *Cassandra*, and the eight volumes of *Cleopatra* (1652–58) translated by Lord George Digby, Madeleine de Scudéry's *Ibrahim*, done by Henry Cogan (1652), and Richard Fanshawe's translation of the Portuguese epic poem of exploration by Luis de Camões, *The Lusiad* (1655) (see MV 1.V). English readers could follow the adventures of romance heroes and heroines even as their multiple volumes were being penned abroad: in Moseley's note to the reader prefacing the second volume of Madeleine de Scudéry's multi-volume romance *Artamenes* in 1654, he observes that, 'when lately I began to publish the First in English [1653], the Author had not finish'd his [*sic*] own Originall French'. Moseley intends to follow the French pattern of publishing successive volumes, 'though I make but Five Volumes of his [*sic*] Ten', which will result in great savings for the English reader in terms of cost, since 'in France they pay above Four times the value of what you have them here', he points out shrewdly. Finally, he apologizes for the printer's errors ('I could have conceal'd this, but I chose to deal openly, especially in a Work that deserve so well'), and warns his reader to purchase the individual volumes as they appear as he will not publish a second complete version of the text.[69]

Although the contents of the volumes of English verse and plays typically highlight the popularity of conventional genres of the early and mid-century such as lyrics, odes, and pastoral dialogues, both Moseley and his authors often used their prefaces to readers or dedicatory prefaces and poems to surround and infuse these pre-war writings with their political allegiances. These allegiances, especially during the period before the execution of Charles I in 1649, could be complicated. The one-time seeming successor to Ben Jonson as poet laureate, Thomas May (c.1596–1650), who in happier times had some recognition as a dramatist and more as the translator of Lucan's *Pharsalia*, was still able to address a staunch Royalist as 'my honoured Friend Mr Ja. Shirley, Upon the Printing of this Elegant Poems',[70] even though, by the 1640s, May's allegiances had changed from the court to Parliament. May commented on the ways in which politics and literature could not be separated during this period.

[69] Scudéry, *Artamenes*, 'The Stationer to the Reader'.   [70] Shirley, *Poems*, sig. A5ʳ.

> Although thou want the Theaters applause,
> Which now is fitly silenc'd by the Lawes,
> Since these sad times that Civil swords did rage,
> And make three Kingdoms the lamented stage
> Of real Tragedies, it was not fit
> We quite should lose such monuments of wit
> As flowd from thy terse pen. (sig. A5ʳ)

May continues that, during these difficult times,

> the Presse alone
> Can vindicate from dark oblivion
> Thy Poems, Friend; those that with skill can read,
> Shall be thy Judges now, and shall instead
> Of ignorant spectators, grace thy name,
> Though with a narrower, yet a truer Fame. (sig. A5ʳ)

Interestingly, May seems to be suggesting that the transition from performance and courtly social authorship practices into the realm of the printed page makes Shirley's writings available now to 'those that with skill can read' and will more truly prove the enduring qualities of Shirley's work than the ephemeral applause of merely 'ignorant spectators' (sig. A5ʳ) (see *MV* 1.VI).

Political sentiments also infused the paratexts in Moseley's edition of William Cartwright's *Comedies, tragi-comedies, with other poems* (1651). Moseley dedicated the volume not to an individual, but to 'the most renowned and happy Happy Mother of all Learning and Ingenuitie, the (Late most Flourishing) University of Oxford', signing himself 'her most devoted honourer and admirer'.[71] One of the commemorative verses signed by 'K.P.' (Katherine Philips), 'To the Memory of the most Ingenious and Vertuous Gentleman Mr. Wil: Cartwright my much valued Friend', opens with a plea for Cartwright not to abandon his friends: 'such horrid Ignorance benights our Times, | That *Wit* and *Honour* are become our Crimes'. One 'Jo. Leigh, Esquire', addresses Moseley directly in his commendatory verse, declaring that, having now lost his estate in the war and 'Return'd with much adoe to my own Clime', he now has leisure 'to admire those Noble Souls' possessing wit 'Whose high Achievements Thou hast brought to light, | Setting forth Wits who best knew how to write'. He follows that with a list of poets Moseley published in the 1640s highlighting Suckling, Carew, Waller, Beaumont, and Fletcher, Denham, Fanshawe, Davenant, and Newcastle, but notably absent from his catalogue of Moseley's authors is Milton.

In his own letter to the reader, Moseley is at pains to stress that Cartwright viewed his poems as '*Recreation*' rather than his '*works*', and that, without the diligence of Moseley and his friends, 'so strangely scatter'd were these excellent Peeces that till now they never met all together'. Moseley also points to the problem of '*Plagiaries* (whereof this Great Town hath no small number, even

---

[71] Cartwright, *Comedies*, 'Dedication'.

now when 'tis empty)', one of whom after the death of the writer 'had the Forhead to affirm, that himself made Verses this last Summer, which our Author wrote (and whereof we had Coppies) Ten years since'. Moseley also explains the choice of the frontispiece—Cartwright dressed in a scholar's robes, as opposed to 'with *Chaplets* and *Laurel*, *Cloak'd* and *Embroyder'd*'—and the decision to print it in a small octavo format as 'we see it is such weather that the ingenious have least money; else the Lines are as long as in *Folio*, and would equall those of trebble its price'.[72]

This sense of a literary and cultural community banding together in the face of the national 'tragedy' is continued in Moseley's 1646 publication of Shirley's *The Triumph of Beautie, As it was personated by some young Gentlemen, for whom it was intended, at a private Recreation*. His posthumous publication of Suckling's writings, *Fragmenta aurea* (1646, 1648, 1658) and *Last remains* (1659)—Suckling had died abroad in 1641 having fled after failing to bring the army in line to support Charles I—keeps alive the voices of the courtiers with whom Suckling lived and conversed as well as his own in his occasional pieces addressed to his friends and to the King. In 'To the Reader' for *Fragmenta aurea* (1646), Moseley with passion declares that, 'in this Age of Paper prostitutions, a man may buy the reputation of some Authors into the price of their Volume', but Suckling, 'the Name that leadeth into this Elysium, is sacred to *Art* and *Honour*, and no man that is not excellent in both, is qualified a *Competent Judge*' (A3ʳ). Poetic abilities and political allegiances seem naturally bound together in Moseley's volume.

In addition to his political sympathies and critical perspective on the writers he published, Moseley was also a shrewd marketer of literary options. As critics have commented, he was also responsible for publishing most of the highly popular and influential translations of French, Spanish, and Italian romance fiction; Moseley made two large entries of plays with the Stationer's Register, one in 1646 of forty-three plays and another in 1653. Many of his publications were in compact octavo format, convenient for carrying around, and many featured an author portrait commissioned by Moseley. This uniformity in his literary publications has led some critics to view him as the originator of the practice of serial publication, or of issuing uniform volumes that might be collected in relation to one another.

Moseley was also clearly sensitive as to who the prospective purchaser of his books might be and what in particular they desired in terms of format and presentation. In his remarks to the readers of the folio edition of Beaumont and Fletcher's collected *Comedies and Tragedies* (1647), Moseley is aware that the size might be a concern both in terms of the volume's price but also in practical terms: he explains the decision to omit plays that had been previously printed separately on the grounds that they would have 'rendred the Booke so Voluminous that *Ladies* and *Gentlewomen* would have found it scarce

---

[72] Cartwright, *Comedies*, 'To the Reader'.

manageable, who in Workes of this nature must first be remembered'.[73] Also a consideration was that 'those former Pieces had been so long printed and re-printed, that many Gentlemen were already furnished; and I would have none say, they pay twice for the same Booke'. In addition, he points out that if a person desired to purchase a copy of an individual play text during 'these *Publike Troubles*', they would likely procure a mangled version and 'the meanest piece' in the collection would 'cost them more then foure times the price you pay for the whole *Volume*'.

As with many of his books, Moseley was keen to include the authors' portraits in this collection of their plays. 'I was very ambitious to have got Mr *Beaumonts* picture; but could not possibly, though I spared no enquire in those *Noble Families*, whence he was descended, as also among those Gentlemen that were his acquaintance when he was of the *Inner Temple*', Moseley laments; nevertheless, 'the best Pictures and those most like him you'l finde in this *Volume*'. Concerning Fletcher's portrait, Moseley notes that it was 'cut by severall Originall Pieces, which his friends lent me', although 'his unimitable Soule did shine through his countenance in such *Ayre* and *Spirit*, that the Painters confessed it, was not easie to expresse him'. 'As much as could be', he concludes, 'you have here, and the *Graver* hath done his part' (sig. A4^v).

During his lifetime, Moseley was widely respected as a knowledgeable critic of literary works in both English and continental languages and as the publisher of fine quality books. His prefaces and remarks to the reader in his volumes stress his care in gathering together manuscript sources, whether from the author and his circle of friends or by purchasing plays from the theatres, including the Cockpit, Red Bull, and Whitefriars (see *MV* 1.VI). As he declares in his letter from 'the Stationer to the Reader' in the Beaumont and Fletcher volume, 'I had the Originalls from such as received them from the *Authours* themselves; by Those, and none other, I publish this Edition' (sig. A4^v). Moseley was even willing to risk the author's wrath in collecting such authenticated manuscripts in the service of preserving English literary standards: in the instance of his edition of Abraham Cowley's verse *The Mistress* (1647), Moseley declares that it is based on 'A Correct Copy of these verses...(as I am told) written by the Authour himselfe' and had been rushed into print by Moseley apparently without Cowley's direct involvement.[74] Moseley justifies this decision on the grounds of protecting literary merit and also of national good, 'cheifely because I heare that the same is like to be don from a more imperfect' copy, and he concludes that he hopes Cowley will forgive 'this my boldnesse, which proceedes onely from my Love of Him, who will gaine reputation, and of my Countrey, which will receive delight from it' (sig. A2).

Moseley and his printing shop thus served multiple functions in the late 1640s and the 1650s, preserving and promoting those he felt best embodied

---

[73] Beaumont and Fletcher, *Comedies and Tragedies*, sig. A4^r.
[74] Cowley, *The Mistress*, sig. A2^r.

English as a literary language, printing correct editions based on the author's own manuscript copies, bringing out translations of important classical texts as well as popular contemporary European romances, and giving both praise and a continued presence to Royalist writers during officially unsympathetic times. Although the decade of the 1650s at first might not seem a propitious one for a publisher of Royalist sympathizing literary works, Moseley nevertheless took on five apprentices between 1647 and 1658. The catalogues that he printed in the 1650s show a steady increase in the titles he offered readers, starting in 1650 with an eight-page separate catalogue with 75 texts listed, which increased in 1651 to 93, and by 1654, the catalogue had doubled its pages and recorded 180 titles for sale.[75]

Moseley died in 1661 after a period of ill-health, bringing to a close a remarkable decade of literary production. In his will, dated 1660, he named his wife, Anne, and his only surviving child, a daughter also named Anne, joint executrices, and he requested to be buried with his three children in the 'South Isle of the Parish Churche of St Gregories, just behind the pulpit'. In a request reminiscent of his marketing of books that satisfied the needs and desires of both authors and readers, he desired his wife and daughter handle the funeral ceremonies in a 'meet' and 'convenient' way, but one that will cause 'as little Trouble as may bee'.[76] After his death, following the practice found in many of the close-knit publishing families, his wife and daughter continued to publish titles at the Prince's Arms under their own names in the early 1660s.[77]

Looking more generally at the book trade, we find in Moseley's publications many features that would become common among books produced in the later decades of the century. Although war years and a following regime supposedly characterized for its rejection of ornamentation and iconography would not appear to favour the development of book arts such as illustrations, elaborate title pages, and author portraits, nevertheless, publishers such as Moseley who were active through the end of the 1640s and 1650s produced increasing numbers of such items for their readers. England kept pace with the Continent in its increasing demand for engravings of authors and ornamented title pages from the 1640s onwards, to the point where some engravers such as Thomas Cross worked almost entirely for booksellers and printers.[78]

Most of the texts published in the 1620s–40s by authors now considered to be the period's leading literary figures, including Shakespeare, Ben Jonson, John Donne, Sir Walter Ralegh, and George Herbert, included an author's portrait only in posthumous editions of their works. In the 1630s through the 1650s, however, one begins to find more texts including portraits of the living author as a feature of the paratexts ushering the reader into the work.[79]

[75] Reed, *Humphrey Moseley*, 117.　　[76] Reed, *Humphrey Moseley*, 140.

[77] See Bell, 'A Dictionary of Women', and Raven, *The Business of Books*.

[78] See Hind, *Engraving in England*, vol. III, pt 3, p. 1: *The Reign of Charles I*.

[79] See Howe, 'The Authority of Presence', and Ezell, 'Seventeenth-Century Female Author Portraits'.

Likewise, even cheap pamphlet literature, which had such a dramatic increase in numbers during the 1640s and 1650s, used portraits of famous people, graphic illustrations, and sensational images to lure the reader into their stories and songs and to reinforce visually the content of the texts.

Cheaper publications including newsbooks and pamphlets relied on wood-cuts for their simple line pictures (see CV 1.III). During this period, portraits obviously were charged with political significance for the reader. Henrietta Maria's image appears in a woodcut oval portrait in two 1640s publications done by Robert White, who along with his partner Thomas Brudenell was printing the Bible in 1647 as well as publishing news-sheets; the first portrait was in a 1647 pamphlet entitled *The Queen of England's prophecie concerning Prince Charles. And her letter, advice, and proposals, to His Highnesse, touching the three crowns of England, Scotland, and Ireland* and the second in 1649, *The Queens Majesties letter to the Parliament of England, concerning her dread soveraign Lord the King, and her proposals and desires, touching his royall person.* Likewise simple images of Charles I, Prince Rupert, and other Royalist leaders reminded readers of the monarchy in broadsides and news-books and added a symbol of authorization and authority to the printed words.

Much like modern news media print of today, pro-Parliament publishers also offered readers images of the key leaders of the army in appropriate garb and postures. A 1646 broadside, a large format print intended for public dis-play, offers readers and semi- or illiterate viewers a catalogue of both the names and images of important figures. *A perfect list of all the victories obtained (through the blessing of God) by the Parliaments forces under the command of his excellency, Robert Earl of Essex and Ewe…to this present moneth of August, 1646* features four large oval woodcuts of the Parliamentary army's key leaders Essex, Lesley, Fairfax, and the Earl of Manchester, with six smaller ones of individual commanders, including a young Oliver Cromwell as 'Generall of the Horse'.

Even the Leveller John Lilburne had his portrait included in the 1641 pamphlet account of his imprisonment and questioning, *The Christian mans trial.* This same portrait was also used as the frontispiece in Richard Overton's *A remon-strance of many thousand citizens, and other free-born people of England, to their own House of Commons. Occasioned through the illegall and barbarous imprisonment of that famous and worthy sufferer for his countries freedoms, Lievtenant Col. John Lilburne,* but this time with the addition of a prison grate superimposed over Lilburne's face. The portrait of Lilburne behind bars appears again in the 1649 *The legal fundamental liberties of the people of England, revived, asserted and vindicated.* No publisher is listed for this last text, only the information that it was printed 'in the grand yeer of hypocriticall and abominable dissimulation', 1649, after the execution of the King.

In addition to portraits of famous or infamous persons, broadside ballads, broadsheets, and pamphlets typically featured a woodblock illustration show-ing the nature of the song or narrative (see also MV 4.III). One can find the same images of the wooing couple or the penitent sinner being endlessly recycled for different ballads. Some, however, related to the specific topical events described in the text. For example, in a 1650 publication denouncing the practices of radical sectarians, the space left on the title page after a lengthy title— *The Ranters declaration, with their new oath and protestation; their strange votes, and a new way to get money…their new way of ranting, never before heard of; their dancing of the hay naked, at the white Lyon in Peticoat-lane… their Christmas carol, and blaspheming song; their two pretended-abominable keyes to enter heaven, and the worshiping of his little-majesty, the late Bishop of Canterbury…Licensed according to order, and published by M. Stubs, a late fellow-Ranter*—shows four scenes of events described inside. These include naked male and female dancers ('Hey for Christmas'), a man standing on a barrel preaching 'We have over come the devil' to a motley crowd including a headless man, a drinking scene where the toast is 'No way to the old way', and a kissing couple being told 'Increase multiply'. Other pamphlets used graphic title-page illustrations simply to shock the reader. The 1647 pamphlet *Bloody newes from Dover. Being a true relation of the great and bloudy murder, committed by Mary Champion (an Anabaptist) who cut off her childs head, being 7. weekes old, and held it to her husband to baptize* has a severely dressed woman with 'Anabaptist' over her head, a knife at her feet, and holding out an infant's head gushing blood to her husband, who has the label 'Presbyterian' over his head and who holds up both hands in horror at his wife's unnatural act.

Such sensational 'news' with its violent title-page images served both sides of the conflict in depicting the atrocities attributed to each. *A great and bloudy fight at Scarborough-castle in Yorkshire, between the Kings forces under the command of Col. Bointon, and the Parliaments forces under the command of Col. Bethel* (1648) printed by 'G.W'. to be sold at the Old Bailey featured on its title page a picture of two plumed knights on horseback firing pistols at each other, which also served as the illustration for the 1648 *Bloody newes from the Scottish Army, concerning the late bloody Fight upon* Munday *last, six Miles on this side Carlisle, between the 2. Armies of England and Scotland* printed in London '*for general satisfaction, of the* English *and* Scottish'. Other pamphlets show soldiers with infants impaled on spikes as their weeping mothers are slaughtered. Words are hardly necessary.

Even during times of war, popular songs about traditional themes of love, adventure, and the escapades of heroes such as Robin Hood and his men were still in demand and published. Broadside ballads (see *MV* 4.III) typically featured a generic woodcut, in addition to long descriptive titles, such as the 1655 'Loves victory obtained, or, A pleasant sportful joyful meeting, between a young man and his sweeting':

> At first they met, and then they kist, and afterwards did what they list:
> 'Twas all within a Garden green, where pretty sport was to be seen,
> Then listen to my Song a while, i'm sure here's that will make you smile.

This ditty, to be sung to the tune of 'True blew: Or, Ha ha ha', like most of the ballads is printed in black letter and features a woodcut of a fashionable couple from a generation earlier, the lady wielding a protective fan and the gentleman wearing boots and spurs. The woodblocks for these types of publications could be mixed and matched to suit general themes and reused for decades. Ballad publishers such as Francis Grove in Snow-Hill, who had been producing broadsides since the 1620s, continued to flourish in the latter part of the 1640s and 1650s.

For more expensive publications there were more expensive forms of illustration. For more detailed illustrations, title pages, and author portraits, a different form of print technology, engraving, was used to produce a finer line and greater complexity in the image. Because such fine line engravings required a copperplate press to produce them rather than the letterpress used to create the book's text, book printers and publishers collaborated with engravers and print sellers to create their books. Peter Stent operated one of the most successful print shops in London between 1642 and 1665; in 1653 he published a broadside listing his prints for sale at his shop at the sign of the White Horse on Gilt-Spur Street with 160 items. Stent himself was not an engraver, but purchased plates from other printers and commissioned them from artists, with the most commonly employed being Wenceslaus Hollar, Peter Williamson, John Dunstall, and Hollar's English student Richard Gaywood, whom it is estimated produced some 350 plates for illustrating over two dozen books.[80] In his shop, Stent sold portraits, maps, charts, landscape views, engraved volumes illustrating architecture, natural history and anatomy, and copybooks (see CV 1.II).

The expensive volumes of engravings such as John Ogilby's (1600–76) translations of Aesop's *Fables* (1651) and of Virgil, published first as an unillustrated octavo volume in 1649 and subsequently in folio in 1654 and in 1658, required funding by subscription to help support the cost of the illustrations. Done as a 'royal folio' or oversized text, *The Works of Publius Virgilius Maro. Translated, adorn'd with Sculpture, and illustrated with Annotations* published in 1654 included an engraved frontispiece by Pierre Lombart, a portrait of Ogilby by William Faithorne based on a portrait by Peter Lely, Hollar's two-page-wide map of Aeneas' journey, and 101 full-page illustrations by Hollar, Faithorne, Lombard, and William Carter based on paintings done by the German artist Clein (Cleyn) (1582–1658). Patrons' coats of arms and specific dedications take up full pages; the first six plates were dedicated to the royalist commander William Seymour, marquess of Herford, and his son Henry, Lord Beauchamp, and other family members. Although it had features of classical texts published on the Continent from the sixteenth century, Anthony à Wood described the volume as 'the fairest Edition that till then the English Press ever produced', but also noted that, because of its size and cost, it would be 'reserved for libraries and the Nobility'.[81]

---

[80] See Globe, *Peter Stent*, 31–4.   [81] à Wood, *Athenae Oxonienses*, 2. 263.

Readers in the 1640s and 1650s were already familiar with the elaborate emblematic title pages in folio volumes that gained popularity in the 1630s, such as George Wither's 1635 *Collection of Emblemes*, which featured not only an emblematic title page but also the poet's response to seeing his picture published and a rebuke to the engraver for not having understood the text's meaning. Likewise, readers in the 1640s and 1650s would have been able to see Robert Burton's *Anatomy of Melancholy*, first published in 1621 and enjoying numerous reprints and expansions by its author. Its sixth edition appeared in the posthumous edition of 1651, which was reprinted with the title page and explanatory poem in 1652, 1660, and 1676. The title page done by Christian Le Bon in the 1632 edition features a series of vignettes illustrating the text framing the title itself, with Burton's portrait in an oval frame at the bottom; it is faced by Burton's verses explaining 'The Argument of the Frontispiece'. Burton apparently liked this title page and its author portrait so much that he had his image aged as the editions succeeded one another.[82]

Volumes made in the 1640s and 1650s, especially folio ones, continued this rich and detailed style of frontispiece and title-page engraving, often including a small oval portrait of the author or translator as part of its overall emblematic scheme. William Faithorne (*c.*1620–91), who would become one of the most popular engravers in England in the 1660s, especially for his portraits, and be appointed engraver in copper to the King, had been imprisoned in 1645 after being captured at the fall of Basing House. His portrait of the Parliamentary general Thomas Fairfax apparently helped his sentence to be changed to banishment; Faithorne subsequently went to Paris, where he learned the new techniques of Robert Nanteuil and refined his skills. Upon his return to London he set up his own print shop and was a leading importer of French prints. During the 1650s he provided illustrations and frontispieces for the posthumous editions of Lovelace's *Elegies* (1659) and *Lucasta* (1659) as well as providing the portrait for John Bulwer's *Anthropometamorphosis, or, The Artificiall Changeling* (1650), renamed in its third edition illustrations *A view of the people of the whole world* in 1654, whose title page announced that 'For the Readers greater delight Figures are annexed to most of the Relations'.

The frontispiece and illustrations of the races and peoples of the world in this volume were done by another prolific if less refined engraver, Thomas Cross (fl. 1644–1682). His more elaborate frontispiece engravings were for David Papillion's *A Practical Abstract of the Arts of Fortification and Assailing* (1645), and for Henry Holcroft's 1653 translation of *The History of the Warres of the Emperor Justinian*, which featured triumphant Roman soldiers framing the centre title as somewhat classical angels crown a bust of Justinian at the top and defeated Persians and Goths grovelling underneath. Unlike Faithorne, Cross appeared to work almost exclusively for the book trade throughout the 1650s.

---

[82] See Corbett and Lightbown, *The Comely Frontispiece*, ch. 17.

One of the most famous of the emblematic title pages from this period was done for Thomas Hobbes's *Leviathan*, written while Hobbes was in exile in Paris and published in London in 1651 (see CV 1.I). Featuring a large panel across the top of the title page showing a hilly landscape with little towns and cities and church spires, the title page is dominated by the upper-half of a man's body with outstretched arms; one hand wields a sword, the other a crozier staff, showing his rule over both the secular state and the ecclesiastical. Wearing a crown upon its head, the body is made up of the tiny bodies of his subjects. Hobbes describes the figure in the 'Introduction' as 'an Artificiall Man; though of greater stature and strength than the Naturall, for whose protection and defence it was intended...created that great LEVIATHAN called a COMMONWEALTH, or STATE', thus giving the reader an iconographical image of the nature of the covenant entered into by individuals to form a power to protect them from both foreign invasion and domestic crime and violence.[83] *Leviathan*'s frontispiece has been identified as the work of a highly regarded French engraver Abraham Bosse (1602–76) and historians of book engravings suggest that Hobbes was directly involved in its composition; indeed some assert that the face of the Leviathan is Hobbes's own.[84]

Other frontispieces offer readers an image of the author facing the title page to amplify its contents. The minute details of the entirely imaginary domestic scene which serves as the frontispiece for Margaret Cavendish, Duchess of Newcastle's 1656 edition of *Natures pictures drawn by fancies pencil* serve to establish the nature of the entertainment being offered by the contents of the book. The facing frontispiece shows Cavendish and her husband in a social setting with a crowd around a table in front of a cheerful fire, servants busy in the background; the verse below the picture explains, 'Thus in this Semy-Circle, wher they Sitt, | Telling of Tales of Pleasure & of witt. | Heer you may read without a Sinn or Crime, | And how more innocently pass your tyme'. Engraved by Peter Clout after an Abraham van Diepenbeeck painting, the picture is contemporary in furnishings and dress, except that the Duke and Duchess are pictured wearing laurel wreaths. Not all copies of this text contain a frontispiece and critics have speculated that either the Duchess sent too few copies for the number of books printed in London from Antwerp, where she and her husband remained in exile, or that she had frontispieces included only in selected volumes, perhaps designed for presentation copies.[85]

Cavendish had three different frontispiece portraits done by van Diepenbeeck, a fashionable painter and pupil of Rubens who, when he had been in England in 1641, had created a series of paintings of her husband, his family, and his horses. In one she sits in the contemplative pose of the author, seated at a table

---

[83] Hobbes, *Leviathan*, 1–2, 'Introduction'.
[84] See Corbett and Lightbown, *The Comely Frontispiece*, ch. 20.
[85] See Fitzmaurice, 'Front Matter and the Physical Make-up'.

with writing implements on it while angels bearing laurel wreaths hover overhead, and the other, most frequently reproduced and one she used with several of her publications, has her in semi-classical attire standing on a pedestal in a niche, flanked by admiring figures of Athena and Apollo. The latter appeared in her 1653 *Poems, and fancies written by the Right Honourable, the Lady Margaret Newcastle* (see Figure 2), but, as critics have observed about her other frontispieces, it, too, is not always present in all copies.

In its design, this frontispiece recalls the use of classical architectural frames one sees in many earlier and contemporary emblematic title pages and frontispieces. These range from the 1616 folio of Ben Jonson's *Works* to Michael Drayton's editions of *Poly-olbion, or a chorographical Description of Great Britain* (1612–22), to the arched entrance way framed by heroic classical figures in John Bulwer's *Philocophus: Or, the deafe and dumbe mans friend*, which is topped by the six-breasted figure of 'Nature' holding the hands of admiring young Roman males. Done by William Marshall, the complicated picture introducing *Philocophus* is explained in the accompanying poem 'A Reflection of the sence and minde of the Frontispiece': '*Nature*' is joining in a 'masque' to dance with the other senses so that those who are born deaf and mute may learn to 'hear' with their eyes and then speak with their tongues.

Cavendish was obviously not alone in publishing her portrait invested with classical motifs of fame during the 1650s. Robert Herrick's portrait facing the title page of his 1648 collected verse *Hesperides* shows the author in profile, a stout contemporary Englishman transformed into a classical bust wearing a toga, whose prominent nose appears to be a tribute to portraits of Ovid; whimsical pastoral figures both Christian and classical appear at play on Parnassus behind him, and angels bear laurel wreaths overhead and scatter flowers, while the Latin verse on the pedestal testifies to his poetic skills. Also done by William Marshall, this frontispiece offers a visual montage of the contents of the volume Herrick explains in its opening poem 'The Argument of his Book'.

This layering of classical and contemporary is found in the posthumous portraits that were published for poets including Sir John Suckling, Richard Lovelace, and John Cleveland, whose passing is typically signalled by the presence of a laurel wreath crowning them. Likewise, in the author portraits of living writers published in the 1650s by Moseley, including James Howell, Thomas Stanley, and even lesser-known lights including Nicholas Murford who wrote *Fragmenta Poetica* (1650), the author's face introduces his writings and typically positions the text within the author's contemporary social circumstances, scholar, gentleman, philosopher, Royalist, or Parliamentarian.

Some publishers, as we have seen with Moseley, made a point of publishing the author's portrait wherever they could obtain a copy or convince the author to have one made. The verses by the young barrister poet Alexander Brome

(1620–66) under Thomas Cross's engraving of Richard Brome (no relation) for the posthumous edition of his *Five New Playes* (1653) declare a typical sentiment and explanation for the presence of the author's image: 'Reader, lo heere thou wilt two faces finde, | One of the body, t'other of the minde.' The image of the author keeps him 'alive' in the reader's mind, while inside the book he states 'That who reads it, must thinke hee nere shall dy'. The most notorious, however, of Moseley's author portraits probably was the unflattering portrait which serves as the frontispiece to John Milton's *Poems* (1645) (see *MV* 1.I). Looking rather like Moseley's other royalist authors, Milton's portrait does no favours to its sitter. In fact, Milton had engraved in Greek under the portrait 'On the Engraver of his Likeness' a denunciation of the picture and the artist, which declares that Milton's friends would find it impossible to recognize him in this botched version by a poor artist.

A decade later Milton explained that he had agreed to the portrait because of pressure from Moseley. 'At the suggestion and solicitation of a bookseller, I suffered myself to be crudely engraved by an unskillful engraver because there was no other in the city at that time', he asserted bluntly. The artist in question, however, was none other than Moseley's most popular one, William Marshall, who a few years later in 1649 created the period's most famous author portrait frontispiece, the martyred Charles I in *Eikon Basilike*.[86] The figure of Charles I kneeling in prayer amidst a landscape of emblems symbolizing his laying-down of his earthly crown for a heavenly one, served as a powerful visual text for the Royalists in England and abroad (see *CV* 1.I), and such was its impact that the accompanying explanation of the meaning of the frontispiece was copied and preserved in books of prayers and meditations, such as that kept by a relative of Oliver Cromwell, Anna Cromwell Williams.[87]

While copperplate line engraving and woodblocks were the most common ways in which books, pamphlets, broadsides, and other printed materials were decorated and illustrated during the war years and Interregnum, a new technique was being developed that at the end of the century would replace line engraving. Called mezzotint, it would permit plates to be made more quickly and inexpensively than line engraving; the Royalist general Prince Rupert in exile in Frankfurt is credited with helping to create the tools that would make this possible.[88] Upon his return to London at the Restoration, he demonstrated the technique to an admiring John Evelyn, and thus the style of engraving that would dominate images created for the publishing trade by the end of the century was officially introduced to English viewers. The sons of important mid-century engravers such as Robert White's son George and William Faithorne the younger would discard their fathers' line-engraving techniques and embrace the new technology.

---

[86] See Skerpan-Wheeler, 'Authorship and Authority'.   [87] BL MS Harleian 2311.
[88] See Griffiths, *Prints and Printmaking*, 85–8.

IV. Hearing, Speaking, Writing: Religious Discourse from the Pulpit, among the Congregations, and from the Prophets

> What could a man require more from a Nation so pliant and so prone to seek after knowledge. What wants there to such a towardly and pregnant soile, but wise and faithfull labourers, to make a knowing people, a Nation of Prophets, of Sages, and of Worthies.... Where there is much desire to learn, there of necessity will be much arguing, much writing, many opinions; for opinion in good men is but knowledge in the making.
>
> John Milton, *Areopagitica; a speech of Mr John Milton for the liberty of unlicens'd printing, to the Parlament of England* (1644), 30

The spoken and written word at the end of the 1640s and throughout the 1650s was saturated with the language of seeking God, hearing God, and speaking to God. It was a rich and complex time for the development of new modes of religious discourse, created and performed by a new group of individuals outside the established institutional orthodoxy of the Church. While Church of England clerics continued to struggle to hold their flocks together, new Protestant congregations were being formed and new voices were heard and read. It was a decade during which highly influential preachers also used the press to argue points of religion; it was a period during which farmers, artisans, shoemakers, university-educated scholars, and women of all classes heard the voice of God within and spoke as prophets on the streets and in the press.

In general, preachers were moving away from the highly erudite style of sermons as given by those who in earlier times had regularly preached at court, such as Lancelot Andrewes, John Donne, and William Laud. Richard Baxter, then a chaplain for the Parliamentary army, referred to that style as one that 'did but play with holy things' with its extended metaphors and academic allusions far above the grasp of most of the congregation.[89] Many of the more orthodox ministers of the Church of England would be ejected from their livings during this period, such as the poet Robert Herrick, who was forced to leave his congregation in Dean Prior in Devonshire by the county commissioners in 1646 and reside in London, not to return until 1660, aged 69. A select few, such as John Earle, accompanied members of the royal family into exile and served as family chaplains in Paris and Antwerp. Historians have estimated that over 2,000 clerics were turned out of their parishes by Parliamentary commissions, along with their curates, chaplains, and assistants.[90]

---

[89] Baxter, *Mr Baxters rules & directions.*
[90] See Green, 'The Persecution of "Scandalous" and "Malignant" Parish'.

Charges levied against the clerics and submitted to the Parliamentary Committee for Scandalous Ministers, created in late 1640, included inappropriate behaviour, primarily drunkenness, preaching false or erroneous doctrine, and 'malignancy'. Other crimes included refusing to obey Parliamentary orders to dismantle altar rails and to desist from bowing at the name of Jesus, encouraging sports on Sundays, refusing to use the Directory rather than the Book of Common Prayer, and continuing to observe Christmas as a holiday. The charges recorded also highlight the parishioners' concerns that were less doctrinal in nature, and more to do with being an effective minister, including failing to preach on a regular schedule, being dull or abstruse, or giving sermons that were merely monotonously read aloud from books.

In 1645, Thomas Fuller (1607/8–61), royal chaplain to the newborn Princess Henrietta, published his first work, *Good Thoughts in Bad Times* (1645), printed in Exeter where he was living, but quickly reissued in London. Dedicated to Lady Dalkeith, the child's governess, the text offers Fuller's personal meditations, observations on Scripture and historical application of them, concluding with what he called 'mixt contemplations'. In his fourth meditation, Fuller asks for divine guidance for what must have been a common heartache: '*Lord*. Since these wofull Warres began, one, formerly mine Intimate Acquaintaince, is now turned a Stranger, yea, an Enemy', he laments. 'Teach me how to behave my self towards him': 'must the new Foe', he asks, 'quite justle out the old Friend?'[91] In his mixed meditations, Fuller ranges from the gently humorous personal reflection—'HA, is the Interjection of Laughter. *Ah*, is an Interjection of Sorrow. The difference betwixt them very small, as consisting onely in the Transposition of what is no Substantiall Letter... How quickly in the Age of a Minute, in the very turning of a Breath, is our Mirth chang'd into Mourning' (pp. 223–4)—to reflections on the nation as they relate to individuals. 'This Nation is scourged with a wasting Warre. Our Sinnes were ripe; God could no longer be Just, if we were Prosperous', he observes.

Blessed be his Name, that I have suffered my Share in the Calamities of my Countrey. Had I poised my self so politickly betwixt both Parties, that I had suffered from neither, yet could I have took no Contentment in my safe escaping. For why should I, equally ingaged with others in Sinning, be exempted above them from the punishment. (pp. 226–7)

'It is therefore some comfort', he concludes, 'that I draw in the same Yoak with my Neighbours, & with them joyntly bear the Burthen which our Sins joyntly brought upon us' (p. 227).

Fuller, educated at Cambridge, had moved steadily from appointment to appointment in the Church; his writing career would continue even after the execution of Charles and the deconstruction of the court, with his scholarly histories of the Church and its key figures, *Pisgah-Sight of Palestine* (1650), describing the landscape and history of the Holy Land, and *The Church*

---

[91] Fuller, *Good Thoughts*, 8–9.

History of Britain (1655). Before the war, he had written a well-received history published at Cambridge in 1639, *The Historie of the Holy War*, followed in 1642 by a popular collection of exemplary characters and historical biographies, *The Holy State*; as he became increasingly engaged in London, he began a gentle debate with John Milton in the 1640s over the nature of Church reformation. Throughout the war, he never ceased preaching for peace and reconciliation between the King and Parliament and moderation and tolerance in reform of the Church.

Shortly before returning to London from Exeter, he was invited by the city corporation to preach the lecture endowed by Laurence Bodley, the brother of the founder of the Bodleian Library in Oxford; the sermon was subsequently published in Exeter and then London under the title *Feare of Losing the Old Light* (1646). In it, Fuller reflects upon the duty of the minister to reach his audience: 'Preachers must vary their voices interchangeably using frownes, smiles, swords, salves, cordials, corrasives as occasion is offered. If all the Body of our Sermons', he notes, 'be Praising, where is reproving? if all be Reproving, where is Comforting?'[92] Using Revelations 2:5 as his text ('*and will remove thy Candlestick out of his place, except thou repent*'), Fuller addresses the very real fear that, in the war, England has gone too far away from 'the old light': he admonishes his listeners that England 'by her sinnes, which have caused this war', is positioned like Ephesus in Scripture, leaving the terrifying question, will God remove his light from the country? Answering the anticipated objection that preaching now 'daily encreaseth . . . The Gospel formerly going afoote, now rides on horsebacke', Fuller warns 'all is not light that shines' and 'many Incendiaries, which without either authority of calling, or ability of learning invade the Ministeriall function' merely create confusion with their 'tedious and impertinent discourse' (p. 19).

Jeremy Taylor (bap. 1613–67), the future Church of Ireland bishop of Down and Connor, expounded on his calling as a minister of the Church of England frequently in both the pulpit and in print. He had often preached before the displaced court of Charles I when it was in Oxford, leading to the loss of his living in Uppingham in 1644; early in 1645, he had been taken prisoner after the defeat of Cardigan Castle in Wales, on which occasion he was described by a Parliamentary newsbook as being a 'most spruce neat formalist, a very gingerbread Idoll, [and] an Arminian in print'.[93] Once released, he remained in Wales, teaching at a school in Newton Hall in the parish of Llanfihangel Aberbythch, Carmarthenshire, where he assisted the sons of gentlemen to prepare for Oxford, and he soon became the chaplain to Richard Vaughan, 2nd Earl of Carbery at his Elizabethan house, 'Golden Grove'.

---

[92] Fuller, *Feare of Losing the Old Light*, 2–3.

[93] See John Spurr, 'Taylor, Jeremy (*bap.* 1613–1667) Church of Ireland bishop and Down and Connor and religious writer', *ODNB*. Arminianism in contrast to Calvinism rejects predestination as absolute, and holds that Christ's Atonement is in intention universal.

There he prepared some of his most popular and enduring publications, *The Great Exemplar* (1649), *Holy Living* (1650), and *Holy Dying* (1651), as well as entering into the literary network of Katherine Philips (see *MV* 1.VI) and maintaining an active correspondence with Bishop Brian Duppa, who helped to circulate his writings through his correspondence with Sir Justinian Isham.[94] While in Wales, he also was imprisoned and threatened with reimprisonment repeatedly for his unabashed advocacy of the Church of England. In particular, *A Collection of Offices, or Forms of Prayer* (1657) drew attention to his strongly orthodox views; it was published while he was resident in London, where he also baptized John Evelyn's child in 1657 and preached in the private homes of Anglican worshippers.

Taylor's *Holy Living* (1656) was continuously in print during the rest of the century. As its long running title explains, it is not only reflections on the ways in which one's entire life should be spent in devotion to God but also it offers prayers and devotional exercises to aid in the resistance of daily temptations: *Holy living in which are described the means and instruments of obtaining every virtue, and the remedies against every vice, and considerations serving to the resisting all temptations.*

It is necessary that every Man should consider, that since God hath given him an excellent nature, wisdom and choice an understanding soul, and an immortal spirit, having made him Lord over the Beasts, and but a little lower then the Angels; he hath also appointed for him a work and a service great enough to imploy those abilities, and hath also designed him to a state of life after this to which he can only arrive by that service and obedience.[95]

As its title suggests, Taylor offers a systematic programme designed to guide his Anglican reader through the events of daily life in a spiritual frame. His first 'general instrument' is 'Care of our time', reminding the reader that Christ demands that we must 'account for every idle word'; not, he assures us, that 'every word which is not designd to edification, or is lesse prudent, shall be reckoned for a sin, but that the time which we spend in our idle talking and unprofitable discoursings, that time which might and ought to have been imployed to spiritual and useful purposes, that is to be accounted for' (p. 5). The spiritual can be sought and found within even the most mundane and trivial duties. The use of formulaic prayers and devotional guides can assist those striving to live a holy life in the world when they encounter difficulties or are in distress: for example, Taylor offers 'Ejaculations and short meditations to be used in the Night when we wake' (p. 57) to bring comfort and order to combat the terror of night thoughts.

On the opposite side of the argument concerning the beneficial use of formulaic prayer, the charismatic minister and controversialist Richard Baxter (1615–91), while serving as a minister at Bridgnorth, Shropshire, in the 1630s,

---

[94] *Correspondence of Duppa and Isham.*   [95] Taylor, *Holy living*, 5.

had arrived at the conclusion that the Book of Common Prayer had 'much *disorder* and *defectiveness* in it' (*RB*, pt 1, p. 14). Baxter was unusual in that he had been ordained without having had a university education, but throughout his life was an omnivorous reader. As with Taylor, Baxter would continue to be engaged in religious controversies with leading theologians throughout his long life (see *CV* 2.V). Baxter served as chaplain in the Parliamentary army in the early 1640s, having finally chosen sides when he refused to pray publicly in 1639 against the threatened invasion of the Scots. In his younger years, he noted in his diary that he believed that the Book of Common Prayer had many failings; it was acceptable to use it, but he was troubled by the Church's lax administration of the sacraments, the '*promiscuous giving of the Lord's Supper to all Drunkards, Swearers, Fornicators, Scorners at Godliness &c*' (*RB*, pt 1, p. 3). A noted preacher, Baxter would also go on to publish nearly 100 titles over his long life, in addition to scrupulous recording of the events of his life in a volume that would be published after his death (see *CV* 1.VI).

In his ministry in Kidderminster, which he occupied from 1647 through the 1650s, his skills as a preacher drew in the local inhabitants, so that he noted in his diary that 'on the Lord's Day ... you might hear an hundred Families singing Psalms and repeating Sermons, as you passed through the Streets', with some 600 individuals who received communion in his church (*RB*, pt 1, pp. 84–5). His was a moderate Puritanism, which rejected the more radical notions he had encountered in the Army of the Anabaptists and the Ranters, but also the more rigid system of Presbyterianism: while he himself prayed extempore, without a book, he did not object if others used written prayers and he felt that some human inventions were aids to devotion rather than distractions; he wrote hymns and encouraged hymn-singing among the congregation; he would baptize infants, although he saw Christmas as a fraudulent human invention.

His own book of devotion published in 1650, *The Saints Everlasting Rest*, promises on its title page that the reader will learn the way to attain 'their enjoyment of GOD' and 'how to live in the continual delightful forecasts of it'. This massive 800-plus-page volume, which includes George Herbert's poem 'Home' from *The Temple* in the concluding section of part III, urges the reader to seek 'Heavenly Conversation', and that 'one hour thus spent will more effectually revive thee, then many in bare external duties; and a day in these contemplations will afford thee truer content, then all the glory and riches of the Earth'. 'When thou hast neither wealth, nor health, nor the pleasure of this world, yet wilt thou have comfort', Baxter concluded. 'Comfort without the presence, or help of any Friend, without a Minister, without a Book, when all means are denied thee, or taken from thee, yet maist thou have vigorous, real comfort' (*RB*, pt 3, p. 839).

Although Baxter was a well-known controversialist, he was not seen as an 'incendiary' preacher such as alarmed both Fuller and Baxter himself.[96] Fuller

---

[96] Cooper, *Fear and Polemic*.

may have been referencing the preaching and writing of John Saltmarsh (d. 1647), with whom he maintained a steady exchange of pamphlet disagreements in the early 1640s concerning the need for radical reform within the Church of England. Saltmarsh had also been educated at Cambridge, gaining his MA in 1636; during that period he published his first work, a collection of Latin and English verse, *Poemata Sacra* (1636), demonstrating his familiarity with extended metaphysical style conceits. That polite erudition faded as his religious doubts escalated after his ordination as a deacon; he resigned his position as rector in Yorkshire in 1643 rather than accept tithes. When appointed rector of Brasted in Kent in 1645, he refused its salary, living instead on what parishioners freely offered. Saltmarsh moved from there to become the chaplain to the Parliamentary General Sir Thomas Fairfax and thus gained his largest audience, the army.

While with Fairfax and the army, Saltmarsh became widely known for his advocacy of the concept of 'free grace'.[97] Saltmarsh explains the term on the title page of his 1645 pamphlet *The Fountaine of free grace* proving that 'the Foundation of Faith to consist only in Gods Free Love in giving Christ to dye for the sins of all'.[98] He expanded on this in another 1645 publication which was frequently reprinted through the 1650s, *Free-grace: or, the flowings of Christ's blood freely to sinners*. His own personal crisis of faith, he explained, was the foundation for his new understanding of 'the Gospel in its glory, liberty, freenesse, and simplicity for Salvation'.[99] Those terms, liberty and simplicity, would mark his explanations of salvation for all believers.

In 1646, he published a response to John Ley's [Leigh] (1584–1662) pamphlet *Light for Smoke*, one of a lengthy series of exchanges between them, in which Ley accused Saltmarsh of being an Anabaptist, or of rejecting religious participation in civil government and its forms in any way. Saltmarsh's title page for *An end of one controversie* declares that he, the author, is '*not revolted (as Master LEY saith) from a Pastoral Calling; but departed from the Antichristian Ministery by Bishops, and now a Preacher of the Gospel*'. It was printed by Ruth Raworth (who also printed Moseley's edition of John Milton's *Poems* in 1646), to be sold at the shop of the radical publisher Giles Calvert (bap. 1612–63) and his wife, Elizabeth, at the sign of the Black-Spread-Eagle.

Saltmarsh opens by denying any interest in engaging in a pamphlet war with Ley, 'It is indeed the way of the *Popish Schools* to fill the world with *Volumes* and *Tomes*, and rather to astonish then convince'.[100] In the same way that the Catholic writers sought to overwhelm the reader, '*There is no end in making many Books*', he quotes Ecclesiastes 12:12, 'How hath *Truth* been carried out of sight from the *Reader* in the Labyrinth of *Replies* and *Rejoynders*'. Nor is Saltmarsh interested in continuing an academic debate about the state of the

---

[97] Hill, *The World Turned Upside Down*, ch. 9.

[98] Saltmarsh, *The Fountaine of free grace*, title page.

[99] Saltmarsh, *Free-grace*, title page.   [100] Saltmarsh, *An end of one controversie*, 3.

Church of England. 'Nor am I lesse a *Disputant* in *Divinity*, because against *forms* of *Art* and *Logick* (as you say)', he counters (p. 6). 'If you will chalenge me in any point of *Philosophie*, I shall not refuse you *there* in *Logick* or *Forms of Art*', he warns; however: 'They are forms onely for the wisdom of men, not the wisdom of God.' Unlike Ley, 'Nor dare I take my discoveries of Christ from Reason, nor seek the glory of *him* in *forms* so much *belowe him*, and fashion the *Creator* like to the *Creature*, who is *God blessed for ever*'. 'I allow *Learning* its place anywhere in the kingdoms of the world', Saltmarsh concludes, 'but not in the *Kingdom of God*' (p. 6).

Saltmarsh's rejection of his conventional theological training in favour of personal revelation is clearly manifest in his *Sparkles of glory, or Some beams of the morning-star* (1647). Addressed not to fellow clergymen or learned opponents, the 300-plus-page volume takes Hosea 3 ('His coming is prepared as the morning') as the starting point for his rebuke of Parliament for the persecution of true believers, especially the fining and imprisonment of those 'That such as shall *speak* upon the *Scriptures*, or open them, *Publikely*, or in *Private*, and are not *ordained* by the laying on of the *hands* of that present established *ministery* of a *kingdome*'.[101] God, he charges 'dwelleth not in *Temples* made *with hands*...what is *man* that he should conceive that *God* is only in a *place*, or *Temple*, or *form* of *Worship*, or *Systeme* of *Doctrine* of his *forme* or *making*...but they that *worship*, must *worship* in *spirit* and *truth*' (sig. A3ᵛ). In his epistle to 'all true Christians', he reassures them that he is not 'against the *Law*, nor repentance, nor *duties*, nor *ordinances*, as some would say', but 'I am only against any form, as it becomes an engine of *persecution* to all *Christians* differing from it'. In his book, he tells his readers that his brief, direct style is intentional, for 'I finde less of *man* in writing the *substance* and *truth* of things, so far as revealed in us, then in tedious *discourses* and *Paraphrases*, which are many times rather the works of *reason*, and *wit*, and *art*, then of the *Spirit* of God; and I have writ not in that *common method* of men, because I received it not accordingly' ('Epistle to the Reader').

Saltmarsh's rejection of conventional religious forms, practices, and language in favour of a plain, simple, and direct expression arising from his personal experience in grappling with issues of faith was a common thread in the writings and preaching of the multiple new groups of sectarians that emerged during the war and the Interregnum. John Bunyan (bap. 1628–88) began serving in the New Model Army at the age of 16; while in the army he would have been exposed to a variety of preachers, but his personal conversion did not occur until after his marriage in 1649.[102] Becoming convinced of his sinful nature, Bunyan records in his spiritual autobiography *Grace Abounding to the Chief of Sinners* (see CV 2.V) how in the 1650s he pursued outward religious conformity, ultimately joining a separatist Baptist church in Bedford, where he

---

[101] Saltmarsh, *Sparkles of Glory*, sig. A2ᵛ, 'To the High and Honourable Court of *Parliament*'.
[102] See Greaves, *Glimpses of Glory*.

began his career as a preacher. He found himself still in spiritual turmoil, but he had no doubts but that Quakers were preaching false doctrine. His first book, *Some Gospel-Truths Opened* (1656), expresses his fears that members of the Bedford congregation might easily be dazzled by these new ideas. A letter to the reader by John Burton that prefaces Bunyan's refutation of the Quakers, warns the reader:

be not offended because Christ holds forth the glorious treasure of the gospel to thee in a poor earthen vessell, by one, who hath neither the greatness nor the wisdome of this world to commend him to thee . . . this man is not chosen out of an earthly, but out of the heavenly University . . . And though this man hath not the learning or wisdome of man, yet, through grace, he hath received the teaching of God, and the learning of the spirit of Christ, which is the thing that makes a man both a Christian and a Minister of the Gospell.[103]

Consciousness of the divisions between those who have stature and power in the secular world and those like Bunyan, who received his education from the university of heaven and faced prosecution for unlicensed preaching, infused his writings and preaching in the late 1650s. In his third book, *A Few Sighes from Hell* (1658), Bunyan recounts the resistance he encountered as a minister, leading to an indictment before the assizes for preaching. In his explication of the parable in Luke of the rich man and the beggar, Bunyan reminds his reader that 'if a man would judge of men according to outward appearance, he shall oft-times take his mark amiss'.[104] 'Methinks to see how the great ones of the world will go strutting up and down the streets sometimes, it makes me wonder', Bunyan observes. 'Surely, they look upon themselves to be the onely happy men' (p. 7); 'How many pounds do some men spend in a year on their dogs', he continues, 'when in the mean while the poor Saints of God may starve for hunger' (p. 15). 'O you that are the tempted, persecuted, afflicted, sighing, praying Saints of the Lord', Bunyan comforts, 'though your adversaries look upon you now with a disdainful, surly, rugged, proud and haughty countenance, yet the time shall come, when they shall spie you in *Abrahams* bosome' (p. 54).

Both the social origins of these groups of believers and the unorthodoxy of their modes of expression were highlighted in hostile accounts of the proliferation of non-traditional forms of worship. One such critic was Ephraim Pagett [Pagit] (1574–1646), who had precociously translated a sermon on the book of Ruth from Latin into English at the age of 11 and after his education at Oxford became the rector of St Edmund the King, Lombard Street in London. In the 1630s he had gained fame for his attacks on the Catholic Church and his calls for unity among Protestants across Europe. Resolutely grounded within the doctrines of the Church of England, he preached against English heresy and published his sermon *The Mysticall Wolfe* (1645), which was reissued with a more straightforward title *The Tryall of Trueth*. This sermon became the

---

[103] Burton, 'To the Reader', in Bunyan, *Some Gospel-Truths.*
[104] Bunyan, *A Few Sighes*, 5.

foundation for *Heresiography, or, A Description of the Heretickes and Sectaries of these Latter Times* (1645), which enjoyed six further ever-expanding editions through 1661.

In the second edition issued in 1645, he names forty-three different sects, ranging from the familiar 'Papist', 'Independents', and 'Arminians', to the obscure 'Bewkeldians', 'Grindletonians', and 'Familists of the mountains'. All of these, he warns in his dedication to the Lord Mayor of London, 'preach, print, and practise their hereticall opinions openly'.[105] Not only are their pamphlets shocking to Pagett: 'since the suspension of our Church-government, every one that listeth turneth Preacher, as Shoo-makers, Coblers, Button-makers, Hostlers and such like, take upon them to expound the holy Scriptures, intrude into our Pulpits, and vent strange doctrine, tending to faction, sedition, and blasphemie' ('The Epistle Dedicatory').

Likewise, Thomas Edwards's (*c*.1599–1648) *Gangraena* (see MV 1.II), which appeared a year later, targeted what he saw as 16 defined sects and 176 'errors' of belief, excluding Catholics. Another Cambridge-educated cleric, Edwards lacked the early literary and professional successes of Fuller or Saltmarsh. While in London in the early 1640s, Edwards published polemical pamphlets decrying the 'independant government of particular congregations' as stated in the title of a 1641 work;[106] by 1647, however, he had found his cause, as summarized in the title of his 1647 publication, *The casting down of the last and strongest hold of Satan. Or, A treatise against toleration and pretended liberty of conscience.*

His rigid insistence on a Presbyterian model for the congregation and church government was rewarded by his being granted a weekly lecture at Christ Church, Newgate, during which he violently denounced sectarian believers, to the point that it was reported that fights would break out and hecklers attempted to shout him down. One contemporary observer, Katherine Chidley, a leading figure in London's separatist churches, described the atmosphere at Edwards's sermons as being more like a cockpit than a church.[107] Composed of 3 parts and over 200 pages long, *Gangraena* was described by Chidley in her treatise *A new-yeares gift or a Brief Exhortation to Mr Thomas Edwards* (1645) as being lacking in logic and force, an incoherent '*rangling—insinuating—contradictory,—revengefull story*'. In the preface to part I of *Gangraena*, Edwards himself situates the book and its aggressive tone as being part of an extensive paper war and attacks on him from the pulpit: 'the many reproachfull scornfull speeches, and railings both in publike Sermons and printed Pamphlets', made him resolved to 'appear again in publike against the errours of the times'.[108]

---

[105] Paget, *Heresiography*, 'The Epistle Dedicatory'.

[106] Edwards, *Reasons against the independent government of particular congregations*, title page.

[107] See P. R. S. Baker, 'Edwards, Thomas (*c*.1599–1648)', *ODNB*, and Hughes, *Gangraena and the Struggle*, 30, 52–3.

[108] Edwards, *Gangraena*, pt 1, sigs A4ᵛ, B1ʳ.

In his appendices, Edwards includes depositions of charges brought against specific individuals as part of his evidence of the dangerous nature of the sectarians. John Boggis was arraigned on the evidence of an informer for 'horrid and unheard of Blasphemy' in January 1645 in Great Yarmouth: upon being asked to say grace by his host's wife over dinner where the informant was a servant, Boggis supposedly responded '*to whom hee should give thanks, whether to the Butcher or to the Bull, or to the Cow*, (there being then a Shoulder of rosted Veale upon the Table)' (pt 2, pp. 161–2). He compounded the blasphemy by demanding provocatively: '*Where is your God, in Heaven, or in Earth, aloft or below, or doth hee sit in the clouds, or where doth hee sit with his—*'. Concerning the Bible, '*Boggis* wished, *he had not knowne so much of the Bible*, which hee said, *was but only paper*' (pt 2, p. 162).

In addition to displaying crude vulgarity in a pious domestic setting, Edwards's sectarians also promoted social disorder and the dismantling of hierarchies within families. In part I, Edwards tantalized his readers with the assertion that sectarian meetings were characterized by 'horrible disorders, confusions, [and] strange practices not only against the light of Scripture but nature; as in womens preaching, in stealing away women naked in the presence and sight of men, etc.' (pt 1, p. 143). Targeted as one of the 'principall Ringleaders of corrupt opinions and Errours', the 'preaching woman' Mrs Attaway is charged with having seduced William Jenny to leave his wife. According to Edwards's informants who had gone to hear her preach, she had demanded to know what they thought of Milton's writings on divorce (see *MV* 1.I), 'for she had an unsanctified husband, that did not walk in the way of *Sion*, nor speak the language of *Canaan*; and how accordingly she hath practised in it running away with another womans husband' (pt 2, pp. 9–10).

Mrs Attaway, regardless of whether she divorced her husband or not, was hardly alone among English women who felt that the perilous nature of the times called for them to preach publicly and to prophesy warnings. It has been estimated that there were some 300 women who during the war years and the Interregnum were 'visionaries', women who delivered prophecy both in person and in print.[109] Historians have described this particular span of years as being particularly receptive to prophecy in general, by both men and women, delivered in the streets, in meetings, and through print. Discussing the nature of cheap print during the revolution, historians have commented that 'England was awash in prophecies'.[110] Titles such as *A Warning Piece for the World, Or, A Watch-Word to England. Being many Strange and Wonderful Visions & Apparitions, that appeared To one Mr William Morgan a Farmer Neer the City of Hereford, and to one John Rogers, His Shepherd July 15, 1655. The*

---

[109] See Mack, *Visionary Women*, 1–11 and apps 1 and 2, and Thomas, 'Women and the Civil War Sects'.

[110] Friedman, *The Battle of the Frogs*, 62. See also Smith, *Literature and Revolution*; Hinds, *God's Englishwomen*; and McDowell, 'A Ranter Reconsidered', and *The English Radical Imagination*.

truth whereof is confirmed by divers Letters, etc. suggest that even farmers and shepherds were speaking and writing about their visions.

At the opposite end of the social spectrum, Lady Eleanor Audeley Douglas Davies defied both husband and monarch to spread her warnings. Sharing the vocabulary of the 'strange and wonderful', her pamphlet published in 1649 records a long-existing desire by her to communicate her visions, 'Which She Prophesied sixteen years agoe, and had them printed in Holland, and there presented the said Prophesies to the Prince Elector', explains the long title of her *Strange and Wonderfull Prophesies by The Lady Eleanor Audeley* and this publication of them contains 'Notes upon the said Prophesies, how farre they are fulfilled, and what part remains yet unfulfilled, concerning the late King; and Kingly Government, and the Armies and people of ENGLAND'.

Many of these printed prophecies were a record of earlier public performances. The Fifth Monarchist Anna Trapnel (fl. 1642–60) fell into an ecstatic trance during the trial of Vavasor Powell, a charismatic preacher charged with treason, and for eleven days lay motionless while singing prophetic verses about God's anger with Oliver Cromwell for dissolving Parliament and declaring himself Lord Protector. Bystanders took turns recording her verses and they were subsequently printed as *The Cry of a Stone, or, a relation of something spoken in Whitehall* (1654). Her prayers and songs promised both the coming of Christ and the destruction of those in power: 'Oh King Jesus thou art longed for, | Oh take thy power and raign', opens one song that concludes:

> Write how that Protectors shall go,
> And into graves there lye:
> Let pens make known what is said, that,
> They shall expire and die.[111]

Fifth Monarchists were among the more radical and visible of the sects, as they believed England should be purified in preparation for the imminent return of Christ to rule the earth and were highly critical of Cromwell's rule. Trapnel's public performances alarmed the government sufficiently that, when she travelled to Cornwall later in 1654, she was arrested and brought before the magistrates to answer charges of blasphemy and witchcraft (see CV I.VI).[112]

Other prophets seem less well defined in their motives and beliefs and drifted from sect to sect. Arise Evans, a tailor from Wales, published numerous accounts of his call by God to seek out and confront those in power. Invoking the right to petition, Evans visited both Charles I and Cromwell attempting to convey God's wishes concerning the state of England. He explained in a 1655 pamphlet *The Voice of the Iron Rod, to his Highness the Lord Protector* that he had written a petition urging Cromwell to recall Charles II, but, Cromwell having given orders to bar him from access, Evans was forced to print it rather than present it in person.[113]

---

[111] Trapnel, *The Cry of a Stone*, 19–20.   [112] See Magro, 'Spiritual Autobiography'.
[113] Ezell, 'Performance Texts'.

The Oxford educated Abiezer Coppe (1619–72?), who was described as a 'Ranter', also practised direct confrontation in addition to publishing his warnings. He recorded in *A Fiery Flying Roll* (1650) how he himself 'have been made such a signe, and a wonder before many of thine Inhabitants faces…beholding me, fall down flat at the feet of creeples, beggers, lazars, kissing their feet, and resigning up my money to them'.[114] When encountering those of a more genteel class, however, Coppe with a 'mighty loud voyce' denounced them with gnashing teeth and he declared that he accosted the carriages of '100. of men and women of the greater ranke, and many notorious, debois, swearing, roystering roaring Cavalliers…and other wilde sparks of the Gentry: And have proclaimed the notable day of the Lord to them' (p. 15).

Not all sectarians took to the pulpit or engaged in scandalous public behaviour, although espousing radical beliefs. Although not mentioned by Pagett or Edwards, women such as Elizabeth Avery, also considered to be a Fifth Monarchist like Trapnel, addressed similar concerns as Saltmarsh, Bunyan, and Baxter concerning the shallowness of formal institutions of religion in dealing with matters of the spirit. In 1647 she had published by Giles Calvert her *Scripture Prophecies Opened*. Writing in the form of letters to friends, Avery opens by telling her reader that, while the letters were initially intended only for private friends, 'I finde the immediate acting of the Spirit in giving in, and so accordingly in carrying me forth to communicate it to others'.[115] Because she is simply the method of transmission of God's will, 'I dare not conceal it in oblivion, but I must hold it forth to the view of the whole world, not fearing any thing in way of opposition from the creature' (sig. A3ʳ). In publishing these letters, she clearly understands how her actions will be viewed by worldly readers, but 'I fear not the prison, having such enlargements in God: I fear not reproach; for I can wear it as my Crown', Avery announces resolutely, 'though I may be counted mad to the world, I shall speak the words of sobernesse: and if I am mad, as the Apostle saith, it is to God; and if I am in my right mind, it is for the benefit of others' (sig. A3ʳ).

She also warns her readers that what they will encounter will not resemble conventional language of religion. 'I am resolved not to contend for it with carnal weapons, as by Argument', she declares, 'but rather I shall witnesse the truth of it with my Blood'. Casting aside any reliance on learned commentaries or other religious texts, she places the authority and the agency of the text outside of herself: 'if God shall call me to it', she concludes, 'I have nothing to do, but to hold it forth, and so I must leave it to God, who I know will witnesse to his own Truth, and reveal it unto all his in his good time' (sig. A3ᵛ).

Avery believed that her readers 'live in this age, wherein the Prophecies are to be accomplished in a spiritual sense' (p. 2). Eschewing marginal annotations and any reference to human authorities, Avery interweaves her condemnation

---

[114] Coppe, *A Fiery Flying Roll*, 13.
[115] Avery, *Scripture Prophecies Opened*, sig. A3ʳ, 'To the Reader'.

of the Church of England and the coming relief of the beleaguered 'Saints' currently suffering under its regime with partial references to a wide range of Scripture for her readers to pursue and thus read and see for themselves. The connection between Elizabeth Avery and her readers is thus a collaborative and personal one. Acknowledging her seeming unsuitability for the role she is playing both because of her sex and her frail health, 'I am weakest in my self; and more enable to act by the Spirit, when I am most straightned in the flesh', she declares. '*I possesse all things* in my God, in whom I live, and he in me', she assures her concerned readers; 'my joy and consolation is not in my self, in that I live in God, in mine own particular; but my joy is the joy of you all; for sure my soul is bound up with yours in the same bundle'. Avery concludes, 'as the Apostle says: I am alive, if you stand fast in these terrible times, wherein the *powers of heaven* are *shaken*, and not onely the powers of heaven shaken in the Saints, but heaven it self is *passing away with a great noise, and the element melts with fervent heat*' (p. 17).

Although Avery does not directly attack Church of England ministers for their education and their institutionalized discourse, others did not hesitate to do so. Among the sects variously identified as Ranters, Seekers, and Quakers, refuting the arguments of local ministers and magistrates very frequently took the form of attacks on institutionalized and commercialized religion. The 'Seeker' Richard Coppin (*c*.1645–59) represents one of many interesting and provocative figures, who, even though it appears he was university-educated himself, turned aggressively to denounce those former colleagues: in his pamphlet *Truths Testimony* (1655), he asserts that he needs no licence to preach, 'not from *Oxford* and *Cambridge*, or the Schools of the Antichrist'. One of his associates, Abiezer Coppe in *Some Sweet Sips of Some Spiritual Wine* (1649), likewise described ordained ministers and academics as 'muddy men, profound men are Muddy, Diviners, mad, and muddy'. Like many other of the radical writers, Coppe cites Galatians 1:12 as his authority to preach: 'For I neither received it of men, neither was I taught it by men, but by the revelation of Jesus Christ.' Indeed, as critics have noticed, Coppe uses his university training to ridicule his opponents through textual parody, interweaving phrases of Greek, Latin, and Hebrew in his arguments denouncing faith by book, knowing that his texts 'to the Pharisee [are] blasphemy, who hath [*ad unquam*] at's fingers ends'.[116]

Coppe's rejection of formulaic religious rhetoric and forms extends to the printed page of his writings. In the same fashion that he performed his prophecies to the passers-by in the streets, the pages of his pamphlet *A Fiery Flying Roll* (1650) make a dramatic visual departure from the formatting of more traditional spiritual writings. While he preserves the convention of the preface or address to the reader, the customary formulas for identifying both the audience and the author are both linguistically and philosophically at odds with conventional forms of address:

---

[116] See McDowell, 'A Ranter Reconsidered', 188–91.

The Preface
My Deare One.
All or None.
Every one under the Sunne.
Mine own.
My most Excellent Majesty (in me) hath strangely and variously
transformed this forme.
And behold, by mine owne Almightinesse (In me) I have been
changed in a moment, in the twinkling of an eye, at the
sound of the Trump.

As he warns his reader in *Some Sweet Sips of Some Spiritual Wine*, 'Here is
Scripture language throughout these lines: yet Book, Chapter, and Verse sel-
dome quoted. The *Father* would have it so; And I partly know his designe in it;
And heare him secretly whispering in me the reason thereof: Which I must (yet)
burie in silence, till—'.[117]

The Quakers, who were gathered together in the early 1650s by George Fox
(1624–91), were the largest and the most prolific publishers of the sects, with
some 40,000 members by 1660, and publishing more than 2,500 titles by 1700,
many produced by presses run by Quakers, including polemical pamphlets,
prophecies, and life writings (see CV 1.VI).[118] Fox, who had experienced an
intense spiritual crisis as a young man, spent much of his time in the early 1640s
travelling as an itinerant shoemaker, engaging in religious disputes with ministers of all inclinations. Then, 'the Lord opened unto me', Fox wrote in 1646,
that 'being bred at Oxford or Cambridge was not enough to fit and qualify men
to be ministers of Christ; and I stranged at it because it was the common belief
of the people'.[119] He recorded in his journal how in 1647 he heard a voice which
told him that 'there is one, even Christ Jesus, that can speak to thy condition',[120]
and thus he realized that, in seeking external authorities to answer his spiritual
questions, he was ignoring the 'Inner Light' or the presence of God within,
which was all that was necessary for salvation. Once the Inner Light had been
recognized, Quakers both male and female believed that, if called upon by God,
it was their duty to evangelize and spread the word, not only in England, but in
America and the New World as missionaries. The response of their listeners
could be violent: when Elizabeth Fletcher and Elizabeth Leavens attempted to
speak with Oxford students, the infuriated scholars 'violently pushed Elizabeth
Fletcher against a grave-stone, and then threw her into the grave...they threw
them into a miry ditch through which they dragged Elizabeth Fletcher', resulting a short time later in Fletcher's death.[121]

---

[117] Cope, *Some Sweet Sips*, 3.
[118] See Ezell, *Writing Women's Literary History*, ch. 5; Peters, *Print Culture*, chs 1–3.
[119] Quoted in Barber, *The Quakers*, 98; see also Ingle, *First among Friends*.
[120] Fox, *Journal*, 8.
[121] Sewel, *The History*, 1. 126. See also Gill, *Women in the Seventeenth-Century Quaker Community*, ch. 3.

The language and behaviours of the early Quakers presented an immediate provocation to authority, and many of them were fined, imprisoned, and even exiled. It also caused considerable conflict among the movement itself. James Naylor (1618–60) and his followers, including Martha Simmonds (bap. 1624–65), the sister of the printer Giles Calvert, Hannah Stranger, and Dorcas Erbury created a scandal when in 1656 in Bristol they re-enacted Christ's entry into Jerusalem (see *CV* 1.VI). While Naylor rode on horseback, the women walked at his side singing 'Holy, holy, holy, Lord God of Israel'. John Deacon's *The Grand Impostor Examined, Or, The Life, Tryal and Examination of James Nayler: The Seduced and Seducing Quaker* (1657) gave a full and horrified account of Naylor's blasphemy. Part of the evidence produced against him at his trial was found in letters where Hannah Stranger addresses Naylor as the 'prince of peace' and her husband John salutes him as 'thou onely begotten Son of God'.[122] Under questioning, Naylor freely admitted to what seem to be miracles:

Q. How long hast thou lived without any corporal sustenance, having perfect health?
A. Some fifteen or sixteen days, sustained without any other food except the Word of God.
Q. Was Dorcas Erbury dead two days in Exeter? and didst thou raise her?
A. I can do nothing of my self: the Scripture beareth witness to the power in me which is everlasting; it is the same power we read of in the Scripture. The Lord hath made me a signe of his coming: and that honour that belongeth to Christ Jesus, in whom I am revealed, may be given to him, as when on earth at Jerusalem, according to the measure. (p. 18)

Naylor was sentenced to horrific punishment, including 300 lashes and to be branded with a B for blasphemy. While he was in the pillory, Simmonds, Stranger, and Erbury knelt at his feet, suggesting to observers the women at Christ's crucifixion.

The early Quakers were equally embattled with other radical sects including the Baptists and the Ranters; John Bunyan as a fledgling Baptist minister would publish his first writing, *Some Gospel-Truths Opened* (1656), attacking both the Quakers and the Ranters. The Quakers' way of speaking, dressing, and praying was distinctive and set them apart in the community at large. Because they recognized no earthly hierarchy, they refused to show the appropriate social behaviours indicating respect for social rank: the men did not remove their hats in the presence of social superiors or authorities, nor did Quakers bow before magistrates, nor use honorific titles such as 'Sir and Madam', 'Your Honour', or even 'Your Majesty'. In using 'thee' and 'thou', in their speech and writing, they were using the form of the pronoun 'you', which was by that time commonly used when addressing familiar acquaintances or social inferiors, thus levelling ranks. They did not use pagan names for days of the week and months, preferring instead 'first day' and 'second day', and they refused to take

---

[122] Deacon, *The Grand Impostor Examined*, 9, 10.

any oaths.[123] Often their confrontations with those they believed to be 'false professors' or mercenary clerics resulted in extremely dramatic denunciations. Sarah Blackborow, writing in 1659 to 'hireling' ministers, warned: 'You Priests who preach for money, and prepare for war if you have it not, the blood of the innocent ones who have dyed in stinking holes and dungeons, (thrown in there by you because they could not deny Gods Witness in them, to pay you your money) that blood cryeth loud, *Vengeance*, *Vengeance*'.[124]

The presence of women preaching and actively proselytizing was considered by Fox to be one of Quakerism's defining characteristics.[125] Fox noted tartly that '*Moses* and *Aaron*, and *the* seventy Elders, did not say to those Assemblies of the Women, we can do our Work our selves, and you are more fitter to be at home to wash the Dishes'.[126] Elizabeth Hooton (d. 1672) is credited as being the first of the Quaker women to preach; as recorded in Fox's journal in 1649 her 'mouth was opened to preach ye Gospell'.[127] Imprisoned in Derby in 1651 for confronting a minister, she repeated the offence in 1652, criticizing a minister in front of his congregation, and was imprisoned in York Castle; she was imprisoned in Carlisle in 1653 along with Fox and other leading Quakers including James Nayler and William Dewsbury for preaching without a licence and again in 1654 in Lincolnshire, where she was incarcerated for five months. She would continue her ministry after the Restoration and travel to New England, where she met with an equally hostile reception.

Margaret Fell (1614–1702), who would marry Fox in 1669, wrote directly to Cromwell to stop the persecutions of the Quakers, warning him that 'thou art feasting and feeding with Riotous Persons, with Musick, and sporting with them; which Practices are abominable to God; as also thy upholding such an abominable Priesthood; who instead of allowing the Liberty of Conscience promised, do Persecute and Sue Men to Treble Damages for obeying Truth, and seize on their Goods, and Imprison their Persons'.[128] Priscilla Cotton and Mary Cole were Quakers from Plymouth in Devon who were imprisoned when proselytizing in Exeter; in their letter directed to *The priests and people of England we discharge our consciences and give them warning* (1655) they wrote: 'thou tellest the people, Women must not speak in a Church…the Scriptures do say, that all the Church prophesie one by one [I Cor. 14:31]';[129] when the ministers came to examine the women, 'two of your Priests came to speak with us, and when they could not bear sound reproof and wholesome Doctrine, that did concern them, they railed on us with filthy speeches…and so ran from us'. The epistle concludes, 'leaving you to the light in all your

---

[123] See Bauman, '*Let Your Words Be Few*', ch. 4.

[124] Blackberrow, *Herein is Held Forth the Gift and Good-Will of God*, 8. See Corns, *Uncloistered Virtue*, 13–16, for a discussion of the strategies of oppositional voice in radical writings.

[125] See Gill, *Women in the Seventeenth-Century Quaker Community*, ch. 1.

[126] Fox, *A collection of many select and Christian epistles*, pt 1, p. 369, Epistle no. 320.

[127] Fox, *Journal*, 2. 325.

[128] See Bonnelyn Young Kunze, 'Fell, Margaret (1614–1702)', *ODNB*.

[129] Cotton and Cole, *The Priests and People of England*, 3.

consciences to judge of what we have writ, we remain Prisoners in *Exeter* gaol for the word of God' (p. 8).

In the decade of the 1650s, God's word was spoken, written, and heard in ways that shocked and amazed many, but it also clearly invigorated the language of faith and forever unyoked Protestant preaching from the university-trained minister in the pulpit. Lay readers of the Bible were also prolific devotional writers, seeking to understand their place in God's will and in the troubled secular world through meditations, prayers, and autobiographical works. As many have described it, this was also a time of public prophecy, and both men and women from all walks of life from the aristocrat Lady Eleanor Davies Douglas to housewives from Exeter were empowered through their faith to speak and publish that word.

V. Fiction and Adventure Narratives: Romantic Foreigners and Native Romances

During the waning years of the war followed by the trial and execution of Charles I, little of what we would consider to be entertaining fiction writing was being printed for obvious reasons. During the late 1640s, presses were engaged in producing government documents, sensational newsbook reports of contemporary events (see CV 1.III), and increasing numbers of religious and political polemical pamphlets. That said, even in the late 1640s there was a market for fiction, and, during the Commonwealth in the 1650s, certain publishers and booksellers were actively promoting fiction, both translations of European titles and original English works, on their lists.

One of the new titles during this period was by Robert Baron (bap. 1630–58), a 17-year-old student from Cambridge at Gray's Inn, who produced in 1647 and 1648 a pastoral romance brought out in parts, *Erotopaignion, or, The Cyprian Academy*. It is a substantial volume, illustrated with his portrait by William Marshall and an engraved title page. The author portrait by Marshall is not the only aspect this romance tale shares with John Milton's *Poems* (1645). As later critics noted with disapproval, Baron incorporates passages from contemporary popular poets including Milton, Waller, Suckling, and Lovelace as well as Shakespeare and Webster in constructing his multilayered fiction.[130] Romances produced during the 1650s have been declared by critics to be a literary genre particularly identified with and used by Royalist sympathizers, and certainly Baron's precocious effort seems tied to his political sympathies.[131]

Dedicated to James Howell, still imprisoned in the Fleet for his passionate and outspoken royalist views (see MV 1.I), Baron's romance blends prose and verse, and includes two masques to tell his tale: 'It was in that time of the Year

---

[130] See Forker, 'Robert Baron's Use'.
[131] See Potter, *Secret Rites*, ch. 3, and Patterson, *Censorship and Interpretation*, ch. 4.

wherein party-colour'd *Flora* had diapred the Earth with her cheifest Treasurie, and *Silvanus* the Rustick ruler of the woods had deckt the spreading trees, with his choicest Livery', he begins, 'when the Illustrious and Heroick *Flaminius* (the delight of his Age, and the glory of his Nation) cast his love-infected eyes upon the faire *Clorinda*, a Lady who fill'd all mouthes with prayses of the amiable Physiognomy of her Face'.[132] Eleven of Baron's friends from Oxford, Cambridge, and Gray's Inn offer congratulatory poems at the start, highlighting both his youth and his fluid style, which one poet compares to that found in Sir Philip Sidney's romance *Arcadia*. Some later critics have found political commentary embedded in the narrative; for example, in part three, the henchman of the villain Lycidus, 'Lemuroc', which some read as an anagram for Cromwell, stirs the mob against the hero, a rabble-roster who 'congregated, and seduced the rout, and scumd the mud and froth of the people' (pt 3, p. 53).[133]

A prolific writer, in 1649 Baron published another pastoral fiction, *An Apologie for Paris. For rejecting of Juno and Pallas, and presenting of Ate's golden ball to Venus*, followed in 1650 with a book of verse, *Pocula Castalia*, and in 1655, the drama *Mirza* dedicated to 'his Majestie'. *An Apologie for Paris* is dedicated to 'Lady E:R.', and the preface explains that it was the result of an evening's entertainment at her brother 'Sir Johns' home where the company took sides concerning whether Paris was correct in his judgement or not. Baron's defence of Paris and his choice of Venus was apparently so popular that the lady 'bad me file them upon the Register of time, lest they should evaporate into aire, and be lost, and enjoined me to give you an exact Copy of them, promising to overvalue them so far, as to let them find roome in your Cabinet'.[134] In Baron's account, the language of love is extravagant and seductive, as Venus persuades Paris to give her the prize by promising that 'she that hath been the rack of thousand soules, the flame of thousands hearts; (who would willingly have offered up themselves in their owne fires sacrifices to her) she shall not cost thee one sigh, or teare of despaire, but shall freely come to meet thy embraces, and shall every day increase thy affection by new merits'. 'Tell me for Loves sake, is it not more lovely to lie intwined in her foulding armes, like a Lilly imprisoned in a Jaile of snow, or Ivory in a band of Alablaster, than to sit muffled in furres like a bedrid Miser?' Venus demands (p. 31). Paris capitulates.

Another fiction based on an appreciation of earlier English pastoral romance appeared in 1651, Anna Weamys's (fl. 1650–1) *A Continuation of Sir Philip Sydney's Arcadia: Wherein is handled The Loves of Amphialus and Helena Queen of Corinth, Prince Plangus and Erona ... Written by a young Gentlewoman, Mris A.W.*, which would enjoy a second edition in 1690.[135] Like Baron, Weamys was connected to Howell and to other Royalist sympathizers: in

---

[132] Baron, *Erotopaignion*, pt 1, pp. 1–2.

[133] See Maul, 'Robert Baron's *Cyprian Academy*', which also contains a good overview of Baron's use of others' verse.   [134] Baron, *An Apologie for Paris*, 'Preface'.

[135] See Cullen, 'Introduction' to the modern edition of this work (Weamys, *A Continuation of Sir Philip Sidney's Acadia* (1994)) for further biographical information and a discussion of the identities of the authors of the commendatory verses.

Howell's *Epistolae Ho-eliannae* (1650), there is a letter to one Dr Weames, thanking him for sending Weames's daughter's 'continuance of Sir Philip Sidney's Arcadia' and in the printed version of her text one of the five commendatory poems is by Howell, 'To Mistress A.W. Upon her ADDITIONALS to Sir PHILIP SYDNEY'S ARCADIA'. In their poems, all the commentators marvel at the way in which

> His gallant generous spirit, a reprieve
> From's sleeping dust hath punchas't, Deaths malice
> Defying with a timely Metempsychosis.
> He breathes through female Organs, yet retains
> His masculine vigour in Heroick strains. (F.W., 'On the Continuation
> of Sir Philip Sydney's ARCADIA')

Likewise, all are approving of a woman taking on this task: 'Lay by your Needles, Ladies, take the Pen, | The onely difference 'twixt you and men' (F. Vaughan, 'On the Continuation'). Dedicated to the daughters of the staunchly Royalist man of letters Henry Pierrepont, marquess of Dorchester (1606–80), the Ladies Anne and Grace Pierrepont, this text is an imaginative completion of Sidney's original that manages to avoid the florid flourishes of Baron's romance in favour of a brisk narration of the plot lines within a traditional romance structure. The book was published by William Bentley and Thomas Heath, who in 1652 would publish Madame de Scudéry's romance *Ibrahim*, which, as critics have noted, is another romance by a woman writer primarily for women readers. These publishers also worked with Humphrey Moseley, which further strengthens Weamys's possible links to Royalist writers and readers (see *MV* 1.III).

   Other fictions modelled on continental romances during this period include the Royalist newsbook-writer Samuel Sheppard's (*c*.1624–55?) *Loves of Amandus and Sephronia* (1650), Walter Charleton's frequently reprinted *The Ephesian and Cimmerian matrons* (1651) (see also *MV* 3.V), Roger Boyle, Earl of Orrery's (1621–79) never-finished six-volume *Parthenissa* (1651–5), and the anonymous *Cloria and Narcissus*, 'written by an honorable Person' (1653, 1654), the last of which enjoyed several reprints through the early 1660s. Charleton, a physician who would later become one of the first fellows of the Royal Society and produce important treatises on physiology and natural history (see *MV* 2.V), attacks in his early fictions one of the key elements of romance fiction, the notion of Platonic love; this fictional representation of it preceded his translation and defence of Epicurean philosophy by several years.[136]

   Sheppard began his writing career in support of Parliamentary reforms but changed his views after the King's imprisonment; by 1647 he had written the satirical play *The Committee-Man Curried* [groomed] depicting Parliament as self-serving and hypocritical. Between 1647 and 1649 Sheppard was writing for several of the Royalist newsbooks, including *Mercurius Aulicus*, the *Royall*

---

[136] See Mish, *English Prose Fiction*, 27, for this dating of the fictions.

Diurnall, and *Mercurius Pragmaticus*. In 1649, he was arrested for a second time and he remained in prison, where he composed a defence of Charles I, *The Faerie King*, and probably his romance. Sheppard gives no information about the composition of his fiction, the piece having neither a dedication nor a preface. Interestingly, its contents are much more engaged with the conventions of romance than with the events happening outside his prison cell. The summary of the first chapter suggests its concerns remain within the traditions of the romance, the villainous pursuit of a noble maiden: 'Embassadours (from divers parts of Europe) arrive at Verona, the occasion thereof. *Rhoxenor* courts *Sophronia*. Her Reply. He resolves her Ruine.'[137] Boyle's *Parthenissa*, which appeared in various parts starting in 1651 involving several different printers, including Humphrey Moseley in 1655 for volume four, is dedicated to Lady Northumberland and Lady Sunderland. As with Sheppard, it is amazing that Boyle found the time to write; unlike Baron, Weamys, and Sheppard, Boyle, an Irish Protestant, was fighting in Ireland in the late 1640s with the Parliamentary forces. Unlike his brothers who went into exile after the execution of Charles, in 1650 Boyle was part of the siege of Limerick mounted by Cromwell's forces, and, in 1651, Cromwell made him lieutenant-general of the ordnance. In 1654, he was elected to the First Protectorate Parliament, so *Parthenissa* is less a candidate for a Royalist reading than the others published during this period.

Boyle's romance, published in a folio format, is much in the style of the French romances, using many of their standard plot complications.[138] The hero Artabanes is banished for fighting a duel with a rival for the hand of Parthenissa, who is besieged by unwelcome attentions from King Arsaces once he is gone. As critics have noted, there are also strong similarities to Shakespeare's *Romeo and Juliet*, as the heroine supposedly drinks poison to rid herself of her persecutor. Unlike Juliet, however, she and the reader believe she is drinking real poison. The reader of the romance is informed of her death on page 595; unfortunately, Boyle had not revived her by page 727, which is where the unfinished story ends, but one is reassured, as is the hero by the Oracle of Venus at Hierapolis that 'From *Parthenissa's* Ashes I will raise | A Phoenix, in whose Flames thou shalt be blest'. Since there are two other characters in the romance who come back to life over the course of the long romance, one can comfortably imagine a happy ending was planned.

The anonymous *Cloria and Narcissus* (1653) is likewise styled as a 'continuation' of *Princess Cloria*, while at the same time its title describes it as 'a delightfull and new ROMANCE, Imbellished with divers Politicall Notions, and singular Remarks of Moderne Transactions'. *Cloria* returns the 1650s romance as a genre to its Royalist associations. It is not until 1661 that all five of the parts of this romance are united under the title *The Princess Cloria, or, The royal Romance*. In the epistle to the reader of that edition, the still anonymous author comments 'some of it being printed formerly in the worst of times; that

---

[137] Sheppard, *Loves of Amandus and Sephronia*, 1.   [138] See Miller, 'A Source Note'.

is to say, under the Tyrannical Government of *Cromwel*; when but to name or mention any of the Kings concernments, was held the greatest crime'.[139] 'Do not look for an exact History, in every particular circumstance', he or she warns, 'though perchance upon due consideration you will finde, a certain methodical coherency between the main Story, and the numerous Transactions that passed, both at home and abroad' (sig. A1ʳ).

Finally, although not itself a sustained narrative, *Natures Pictures drawn by fancies pencil to the life* (1656) by Margaret Cavendish, Duchess of Newcastle (1623?–73) is an assortment of love stories, some in prose, some in verse, along with the fragment of her autobiography, 'A True Relation', which was omitted in the second edition in 1671. Written while in exile with her newly married husband, the royalist general and man of letters William Cavendish, future Duke of Newcastle, Cavendish's preface to her reader declares that 'I hope this work of mine will…beget chast Thoughts, nourish the love of Vertue'.[140] There is little question for a reader that this collection of stories, supposedly told by a group of men and women sitting around a fireside for entertainment, is highly critical of the Commonwealth regime. A former maid of honour in the court of Henrietta Maria who had accompanied her in exile to Paris, Cavendish set her stories in a pre-Civil War society. Critics have suggested that the narrative pattern might be based on Boccaccio's *Decameron* or perhaps Plato's *The Symposium*, where men and women take turns speaking. The stories range from fictionalized versions of herself, as some critics have suggested about one entitled 'The She-Anchoret', to revisions of romance motifs, as, for example, in the tale 'An Assaulted and Pursued *Chastity*'.[141] In the first, a daughter heeds her dying father's desire that she not marry but instead to 'Live chaste and holy, serve the Gods above', but she is pursued by a lustful married king and ultimately ends up killing herself to avoid plunging her country into war. In the second, the heroine is a young noblewoman who is shipwrecked, a favourite romance plot convention, and is threatened with being sold as a slave to the lascivious Prince of 'the Kingdom of Sensuality'. Both young women preserve their virtue by using their wits to outmanœuvre the schemes of the threatening males, the She-Anchoret holding a learned salon in her cell where intellectuals come to debate philosophy.

For those who could not read languages other than English, the 1650s offered a steady increase in the publication of European romances in translation. In 1647, a posthumous edition of the five-part French romance by Marin Le Roy, sieur de Gomberville, *The history of Polexander* translated by William Browne (1590/91–1645?), was published. The romance is dedicated to Philip Herbert, Earl of Pembroke and Montgomery, in whose family Browne had lived in the

---

[139] *The Princess Cloria*, sig. A1ʳ.
[140] Cavendish, *Natures Pictures*, 'To the Reader'. See Rees, *Margaret Cavendish*, for a discussion of the works written by her while on the Continent.
[141] See Sarasohn, *The Natural Philosophy*, 78–85, for a discussion of the ways in which the fictions prefigure Cavendish's later writings in natural philosophy.

1620s and 1630s. That same year, the Royalist Thomas Stanley (1625–78), who would publish Charles I's *Eikon Basilike* transformed into verse a decade later (see CV 1.I), translated a Spanish romance by Don Juan Perez de Montalvan, *Aurora, & the prince*, which was bound together with his translation of an Italian poem by Girolamo Pretti, *Oronta the Cyprian Virgin*, published by Humphrey Moseley. This appeared the same year that Stanley's *Poems and Translations* was also printed by him (see CV 1.V).

Spanish romances were frequently translated during the 1650s, notably several picaresque or 'rogue' romances. Carlos Garcia's *Lavernae, or the Spanish Gypsy* was translated by William Melvin in 1650. Robert Codrington translated *The troublesome and hard adventures in love*, incorrectly attributed on the title page to Cervantes in 1652, the sixth edition of *Lazarillo de Tormes*, which appeared in 1653, and an abridgment of Mateo Alemán's *The rogue, or The second part of the life of Guzman de Alfarache* (1655).[142] Unlike the pastoral based on Sidney or the courtly French romances, these fictions chronicled the lives and adventures of lower-class men and women as they tricked, swindled, and seduced their way through contemporary Europe. At the opposite end of the social spectrum Codrington also translated Marguerite de Navarre's *Heptameron, Or the History of the Fortunate Lovers* in 1654.

Competing for readers' attention were the translations of Italian romances also appearing in the 1650s. *The honour of chivalry; or The famous and delectable history of Don Bellianis of Greece* was originally put into English in 1598 and was reissued in 1650. 'J.B. Gent' translated Luca Assarino's *La Stratonica; or the Unfortunate Queen* published by Moseley in 1651, and Francesco Carmeni's *Nissena, an excellent new romance* was put into English by 'an Honourable anti-Socordist' and published by Moseley in 1652. Also in 1652 appeared *Choice Novels and Amorous Tales*, described as 'written By the most Refined Wits of Italy and made English by "T.N." for Moseley. Sir Aston Cokayne (1608–1684), who in 1651 had been in Marshalsea prison for his royalist views, had his translation of *Dianae: an excellent new Romance* published by Moseley in 1654. In his prefatory letter to the author, Cokayne dates it as being done in Venice in 1635.[143]

Many of the title pages of these romances from the 1650s announce the genteel or aristocratic origins of the original author, the translator, or both. This is particularly visible in the translations of the French romances that came to dominate the market in the mid-1650s. Moseley again was the publisher of many of them. Translations of French romances from the period brought English readers popular and influential titles by Madeleine de Scudéry, Gautier de Costes La Calprenède, and Honoré d'Urfé. Translating the many parts of La Calprenède's massive *Hymen's praeludia: or, Love's master piece*, comprising *Cassandra* and *Cleopatra*, occupied the talents of Robert Loveday, John

---

[142] See Bjornson, 'The Picaresque Novel', for a useful overview.
[143] See Scott, 'Elizabethan Translations', 478.

Davies, James Webb, 'F.L.', and John Coles. The first complete translation of Urfé's influential *Astrea* appeared in 1657 and united Moseley, Thomas Dring, and Henry Herringman in producing it. Because of the length of these romances, they frequently appeared over a span of several years and involved multiple translators and printers: Scudéry's *Artamenes or The Grand Cyrus*, which is often cited as being among the longest novels in publication, with over two million words in ten volumes, first appeared in 1653 and was still being translated in 1655 and involved both Thomas Dring and Moseley to support its production. The first part of Scudéry's *Clelia, an excellent new romance* (1655) was also translated by Davies and again published jointly by Moseley and Dring only a year after it first appeared in French; new parts of the ten volumes in this romance fiction would appear on a regular basis thereafter. Using exotic oriental or classical settings, Scudéry's translated fictions provided English readers with many of the stock conventions in terms of plot, characters, setting, and even the publication format that came to be associated with 'French Romances' as a group.

Fiction-writing during the final years of the war and during the Commonwealth shows a surprising resiliency. Original romances in English, whether in the continental style or the pastoral, are very frequently associated with the Royalist sympathies of the author. Translators such as the bookseller Francis Kirkman, who would have a major influence on the publication of dramas during this period (see CV 1.IV), and anonymous members of the Inns of Court and other 'Gentlemen' brought a new world of elegant entertainment, in massive folio volumes whose stories were issued in parts over several years, to an appreciative English audience often identified as being women readers. Translations from the Italian and Spanish highlighted another aspect of entertainment, with tales of adventure and exploits of 'vulgar' heroes and heroines surviving by their wits in a real-world setting. The somewhat limited output of original fiction during the decade of the Commonwealth nevertheless provided many of the models for future readers and writers who would in the following decades become avid readers of what were called 'novels'.[144]

VI. Sociable Texts: Manuscript Circulation, Writers, and Readers in Britain and Abroad

The end of the 1640s and the decade of the 1650s, although politically dangerous and socially disruptive, was a period in which sociability continued to play an important part in shaping literary culture, with manuscript texts of poems, plays, and essays circulated widely through various networks of exchange, both within England, Scotland, Wales, and Ireland and extending abroad.

---

[144] For women readers in particular, see Eckerle, *Romancing the Self*.

Often these social networks had been formed prior to the war, at university or the Inns of Court, or at the court itself; some were based on family and geographical location; and some expressed political as well as poetical allegiances. Although there is a marked decline from the 1620s and 1630s in terms of the amount of manuscript material in circulation during the war years and the Commonwealth,[145] often one can track literary friendships—who was reading what by whom before publication—through the increasing number of volumes of verse by individual authors that were published in the 1650s, in their prefatory materials in praise of the poet, their dedications, and their intertextual voices (see CV 1.V).

One multi-purpose and highly organized network for manuscript circulation was Samuel Hartlib's (*c.*1600–62) notion of 'Correspondency', proposed in 1646. Since the 1630s, Hartlib—who had come to England from the Baltic, studied at Cambridge, and founded a school in London—had acted as an agent for the exchange of multiple types of information from the Continent conveyed by letter, and his house served as a meeting place for intellectuals. His manuscript newsletter service had enabled Protestant ministers and refugees scattered across Europe to remain connected and circulated news of science and technological inventions as well as matters ecclesiastical and political.[146] During the war years, Hartlib had remained in London at his house in Duke's Street serving Parliament, although in an unofficial fashion, as an intelligencer. Milton had dedicated his treatise *On Education* (1644) to Hartlib, and Hartlib's vision of a community based on freely circulating correspondence underlies Milton's *Areopagitica* (1644). In 1650, Hartlib moved to Charing Cross, near Angel Court, and continued with his task of furthering the open exchange of news and information of a variety of types between England and the Continent. The intended purpose of his proposed 'Addresse of *Communications*' was to record 'Matters of Religion, of Learning and Ingenuities' while acting as 'Center and Meeting-place of Advices, of Proposalls, of Treaties and of all Manner of Intellectual Rarities'.[147]

Although the treatise was well received and Hartlib received a pension from Parliament for it, the scheme was never officially instituted by the government. Instead, Hartlib himself hired a team of scriveners to copy portions of correspondence concerning a host of topics including science, medicine, Ireland, the American colonies, natural history, and a variety of related topics that he received through his international network of 'ingenue', to be recirculated in England and abroad.

Less formal networks of friends, family, and acquaintances were also using correspondence to share poems, essays, and meditations. Catholic recusant families in particular had well-established networks of textual transmission

---

[145] See Beal, *Index of English Literary Manuscripts*, 2, pt 2.
[146] See Webster, 'Introduction'; Trolander, *Literary Sociability*, chs 5, 6.
[147] Hartlib, *Considerations Tending*, 46, 48.

from the Elizabethan period onwards.[148] Constance Aston Fowler (1621?–64) compiled a manuscript volume containing the poems of herself and her family and their wide circle of acquaintances begun in the 1630s and continued into the 1660s. The same manuscript was also used by a different person to preserve the love poems of William Habington (1605–54).[149] As scholars have noted, the content of the volume as a whole[150] demonstrates not only Constance Fowler's familiarity with the conventions of miscellany compilation but also the existence of an extended network of acquaintances outside her immediate family and the family home at Tixall in Staffordshire from whom she asked for materials to include in it.

These contributors included members of other Catholic families in England as well as connections to the court of Queen Henrietta Maria and to members of convents and schools on the Continent. Her older brother Herbert Aston (bap. 1614–88/9) had accompanied his father to the English embassy in Madrid in the latter part of the 1630s and became friends with Sir Richard Fanshawe; in addition to sending his own verses to his sister for her volume, Aston also created his own poetic miscellany, which went through several iterations with the help of his wife, Katherine, before she died in 1658. Aston, who fought for the King during the war, sent in the late 1650s two of his daughters to be educated at the Augustinian priory at Louvain in France headed by their aunt, Mary Thimelby (1618/19–90), who maintained a steady correspondence with her extended family network in England.[151]

In addition to Fowler's entries in her volume, the different scribal hand that entered Habington's verses has also been found in another 1650s Warwickshire verse miscellany (Bodl. OD MS Eng. poet. b5).[152] Both volumes feature poems ascribed to the early Catholic martyr Robert Southwell; this miscellany also includes banned Christmas carols and other devotional poems intended to promote Catholic community and worship, leading recent scholarship to speculate that the shared hand may have belonged to a travelling Jesuit missionary.[153]

Many English Catholics who resided abroad as part of devotional communities created multiple manuscript texts as part of their devotional practices that were shared among members and sent back to England to support lay Catholics there. Elizabeth Cary, Viscountess Falkland and her daughters Anne, Elizabeth, Lucy, and Mary, all created substantial spiritual writings that associated with the English Benedictine monastery at Cambrai in France; Lucy, with

---

[148] See Walsham, *Catholic Reformation*, ch. 8; Kilroy, *Edmund Campion*, ch. 3. See also Shell, 'Divine Muses, Catholic Poets and Pilgrims'.

[149] Hackett, 'Women and Catholic Manuscript Networks'.

[150] Huntington Library MS HM904.

[151] See Connelly, *The Women of the Catholic Resistance*.

[152] Brown, 'Recusant Community', 5.

[153] Hackett, 'Women and Catholic Manuscript Networks', 1110–11; Brown, 'Recusant Community', 309.

additions from Mary and their brother Patrick, wrote the biography of their mother, *Lady Falkland: Her Life.*[154]

Likewise, Barbara Constable (1617–84) was born in Yorkshire and entered the English Benedictine monastery in Cambrai in 1638, in the company of Lucy and Mary Cary and three other young English girls.[155] Like the Cary women, after taking her vows, Constable devoted the rest of her long life to spiritual writing, leaving behind a large corpus of bound manuscript volumes. She dedicated these volumes to individuals ranging from her confessors to missionaries and other nuns; she gave each the appearance of a printed books with title pages, prefaces, and dedications, and the texts were read among her family in Yorkshire and members of the Benedictine community. Reading, she declared, was a guard against an overactive secular imagination, as 'many haue so little to doe both in religion & out of religion', she observed, that 'if they doe not replenish their minds with such good things as are in spirituall bookes they must needs be full of vaine & idle images since the imagination is continually inuenting'.[156] Often her texts were compilations of her own wide reading and study designed to be accessible and useful to her readers, whether members of her order or Catholic laypeople in need of good words during dark and dangerous times.

Other extended networks also used the creation and exchange of manuscripts as a way of sustaining and reinforcing loyalties and friendships over many years before and after the war. Certainly, the shocking events of the trial of Charles I and his execution in 1649 (see CV 1.I) created networks of sympathetic readers and writers. Edward Benlowes (1602–76), having been educated briefly at St John's College, Cambridge, followed by a period in one of the Inns of Court in London in the 1620s, concluding with the grand tour, had been managing his family's estates in Essex, living at Brent Hall, since 1630. Before the war, Benlowes served as a patron to numerous writers, including Phineas Fletcher (1582–1650), who dedicated his lavish edition of *Purple Island* (1633) to him, and the emblem writer Francis Quarles, to whom he appears to have given two Jesuit emblem books that would inspire and infuse Quarles's *Emblemes* (1635). Benlowes's patronage extended beyond financial matters, as he purchased and had installed at Brent Hall his own rolling press for the printing of copperplates and hired a printer who resided at Brent Hall to provide elegant frontispieces and illustrations for his own and his friends' works, including Fletcher's volume. In fact, the frontispiece of *Emblemes* features a globe, which has as its identifying markers the names of the three villages in which Benlowes, Fletcher, and Quarles lived, Finchingfield, Roxwell, and Hilgary, thus mapping out this literary friendship.[157]

During the war, Benlowes had participated on the Royalist side, commanding a troop of cavalry during the siege of Colchester, which caused him to be

[154] See Wolfe, 'Scribal Hands'.
[155] See Heather Wolfe, 'Constable, Barbara (1617–1684)', *ODNB*.
[156] 'Excellency of mental prayer', Ampleforth MS, SS84, fos 7–8.
[157] See Karl Josef Höltgen, 'Quarles, Francis (1592–1644)', *ODNB*.

heavily fined by Parliament and placed him under financial duress and very much limited his previous generous patronage of poets and translators. Nevertheless, during the late 1640s and early 1650s, Benlowes was the dedicatee for several published volumes, including John Quarles's (Francis's son) *Gods Love and Mans Unworthiness* (1651), as well as a volume by a young gentleman residing in Benlowes's neighbourhood, Thomas Wincoll, *Plantagenets Tragicall Story* (1649), a long poem on 'the unnaturall Voyage of *Richard the Third*, through the Red Sea of his *Nephews* innocent bloud, to his usurped Crowne'.[158] During the late 1640s and 1650s, Benlowes had diverse publications dedicated to him by friends and struggling authors whose work he had supported, including the philosophical essayist and clergyman Alexander Ross's (1591–1654) *Medicus Medicatus: Or The Physicians Religion Cured* (1645), the translator and one-time member of St John's College, John Davies of Kidwelly's (1625–93) *Apocalypsis* (1655), and the curate of Waltham Abbey in western Essex Thomas Fuller's (1607/8–61) *The History of the University of Cambridge since the Conquest* (6th edn, 1655) appended to Fuller's *The Church History of Britain*.

At the same time as he was receiving printed volumes dedicated to him, Benlowes was circulating parts of his long religious poem *Theophila*, believed to have been in progress as early as 1646 although not published until 1652 (see CV 1.V). As critics have observed, the poem seems strongly related to the poet Joseph Beaumont's (1616–99) *Pysche, or, Love's Mysteries* (1648). Beaumont, along with his friend the poet Richard Crashaw, had been ejected from Peterhouse College, Cambridge, in 1644; at his death he left behind 177 poems in manuscript texts composed between 1644 and 1652. In *Pysche*, which he began after returning to live at his father's home in Hadleigh, Suffolk, he, like Benlowes, explores the suffering of a pure soul in a dangerous world that searches for perfect unity with the divine; there is some speculation that, as the two writers lived in relatively close proximity, the two may have influenced and been influenced by each other's texts.[159] Likewise, some critics have pointed to the close textual similarities found in the first canto of *Theophila* and John Cleveland's (bap. 1613–58) 'Fuscara, Or the Bee Errant'; Cleveland, who became known for his biting satires against the Scots and Cromwell, in earlier days had contributed an elegy on the death of Edward King in the collection that included Milton's 'Lycidas'. The former fellow of St John's did not print 'Fuscara' until 1651, suggesting that, like many of Cleveland's poems, it was in circulation in manuscript several years before its publication.

It is believed that Benlowes had been working on the poem *Theophila* since 1646, when he makes a reference to it in a now lost letter to a young clergyman and poet Clement Paman. Paman, who like Benlowes had been at Cambridge and who stayed with relatives living in Benlowes's village of Finchingfield,

---

[158] See Jenkins, *Benlowes*, 182–4.
[159] See P. G. Stanwood, 'Benlowes, Edward (1602–1676)', *ODNB*.

responded that *Theophilia* was like the 'South Indies', a 'Kingdome of jewells undiscovered' that Time and Fame would 'break ope ye volume & reade ym out aloud unto ye world'.[160] Others were clearly reading as he composed it as well, and Alexander Ross responded by translating a canto into Latin before it was published. As the title page announces, parts of the thirteen-canto poem had been set to music by the former court composer John Jenkins (1591x6?–1678), believed to be residing with the Derham and L'Estrange families at Hunstanton in Norfolk in the late 1640s before moving to the North family residing in Kirtling, Cambridgeshire. Jeremy Collier of St John's, Cambridge, offered an enthusiastic prefatory poem, as did Walter Montagu, William Davenant, and several others. Thomas Pestell, of whom nothing is presently known, seems to confirm the early circulation of the verse, pointing to the unsuitability of war times for such divine poetic creation:

> Wonder arrests our Thought; That you alone
> In such *Combustions*, wherein *Thousands* grone,
> (And when some Sparkles of the *publick Flame*
> Seiz'd on your *private State*, and *scorcht* the same)
> Could warble Thus.

> ('For the Author, Truly Heroick, by Bloud, Virtue, Learning')

Another literary network that remained active throughout the end of the war years and through the Commonwealth and was far more well known to both writers of the time and also later literary critics than that of Benlowes was the one in which Katherine Philips (1632–64), the 'matchless Orinda', participated (see Figure 1). Although she was living at a considerable distance from London in the Welsh town of Cardigan, she nevertheless maintained contact with her female friends from her schooldays there, including the antiquarian John Aubrey's sister Mary (1631–? 'Rosania') and Anne Owen (1633–92 'Lucasia'), to whom Philips addressed a poem, 'To the Excellent Mrs Anne Owen upon Her Receiving the Name of Lucasia and Adoption into our Society, 29 December, 1651'.

Philips's early poetry had been admired by the Welsh poet and 'silurist' Henry Vaughan (1621–95) in *Olor Iscanus* (1651) (see CV 1.V). In his poem 'To the most Excellently accomplish'd, Mrs *K. Philips*' he wrote:

> Say wittie fair one, from what Sphere
> Flow these rich numbers you shed here?
> For sure such Incantations come
> From thence, which strike your Readers dumbe,
>
> .   .   .   .
>
> The Poem smooth, and in each line
> Soft as your selfe, yet Masculine.[161]

---

[160] Quoted in Jenkins, *Benlowes*, 156–7; see also 164.
[161] Vaughan, *Olor Iscanus*, 28.

In the late 1640s and 1650s, Philips was clearly actively circulating her poetry, eventually to establish a 'society of friendship', including not only her female schoolfriends, but also other poets whose work she admired, not necessarily living in Wales.[162] These included Sir Edward Dering (1625–84), during this time residing in Kent, Sir John Birkenhead (1617–79), the author of the royalist newsbook *Mercurius Aulicus* (see CV 1.III), and Francis Finch (*c.*1602–77), who dedicated his treatise *Friendship* (1654) to Anne Owen and Philips, and received in return a poem from Philips, 'To the Noble *Palemon*, on his incomparable discourse of Friendship'. She sent a long poem to one Lady Fletcher, apparently a friend of Mary Aubrey, 'Orinda. To Parthenia: A Shaddow of Rosania', which has survived in five other manuscripts from the period. Philips's unpublished poems from this period survive in an autograph volume[163] and in many other compilations of Royalist verse, including a massive folio volume done in the mid-1650s by a single hand bringing together some 220 songs and poems (University of London MS Ogden 42), suggesting the extent to which a poet could have a public readership that went beyond one's geographical location through the medium of manuscript circulation (see Figure 1).[164]

Philips's verses written during the 1650s range from overtly political pieces ('on the Double murther of K. *Charles I*') to songs, occasional verses on her husband's travels, and verses on important events of her life, including the marriage of friends and the loss of children (see MV 2.VI). As with many of the verses of the Royalist poets, Philips urges the preservation of friendship's bonds in the face of vexing and dangerous times: 'Come, my *Ardelia*, to this Bower', she invites in 'A retir'd Friendship': 'Where kindly mingling Souls awhile | Let's innocently spend an hour, | And at all serious follies smile.'

> Here is no quarrelling for Crowns,
> Nor fear of changes in our Fate;
> No trembling at the great ones frowns
> Nor any slavery of State.

Philips concludes by declaring 'In such a scorching Age as this', those who fail to seek the solace of like-minded friends 'Deserve their Happiness to miss'. With a nod towards Donne's 'Valediction forbidding Mourning', she ends with the reassurance that, although the times are out of joint, their relationship creates their own world:

> But we (of one anothers mind
> Assur'd) the boisterous World disdain;
> With quiet Souls and unconfin'd
> Enjoy what Princes wish in vain.[165]

---

[162] See Hageman and Sununu, ' "More copies of it abroad than I could have imagin'd" '; Wright, *Producing Women's Poetry, 1600–1730*, ch. 3.

[163] NLW MS 775B.   [164] See Beal, *In Praise of Scribes*, ch. 5.

[165] See Barash, *English Women's Poetry, 1649–1714*, ch. 2, and Scott-Bauman, *Forms of Engagement*, chs 3, 4.

Dering described the literary community as being a 'generous designe' by Philips to 'unite all those of her acquaintance, which she found worthy, or desired to make so' into a social correspondence group tied by friendship. They famously addressed each other under various *noms de plumes* derived from contemporary works such as Cartwright's pre-war court drama *The Royal Slave*, with Dering being 'Silvander', Cotterell 'Poliarchus', Philips's husband James 'Antenor', Sir John Birkenhead 'Cratander', and later Sir Charles Cotterell 'Poliarchus'. Cotterell, residing mostly in London, appears to have made her acquaintance when he was a suitor to her friend Anne Owen in 1661, and it would be to him that Philips would appeal when a pirated edition of her poems was printed in 1664 to have it recalled.

Another important public figure and one who travelled between Wales and London, Jeremy Taylor (bap. 1613–67) also dedicated his thoughts on friendship to her in 1657, *Discourse on the Nature, Offices, and Measures of Friendship with rules of conducting it written in answer to a letter from the most ingenious and virtuous M.K.P.* Taylor, who had accompanied Charles I as a chaplain and been captured in 1645 near Cardigan Castle in Wales, upon his release had become chaplain to the 2nd Earl of Carbery, Richard Vaughan, at his home Golden Grove, where he published some of his most famous works, including *Holy Living* (1650) and *Holy Dying* (1651); Taylor was repeatedly confined for his outspoken views, publishing *A Collection of Offices or Forms of Prayer* (1657) in direct conflict with Parliament's prohibition against using the Book of Common Prayer (see *MV* 1.IV).

In his address to Philips, Taylor suggests that they were well acquainted: 'But to consult with a friend in the matters of friendship is like consulting with a spiritual person in Religion; they who understand the secrets of Religion, or the interior beauties of friendship are the fittest to give answers in all inquiries concerning the respective subjects', he begins, 'a friends fairest interest is the best measure of the conducting friendships: and therefore you who are so eminent in friendships could also have given the best answer to your own'.[166]

Philips and others in her 'society of friends' were not completely averse to publishing their occasional poetry, but the majority of it appears to have circulated in manuscript. Philips, for example, published under her initials 'To the Memory of the most Ingenious and Vertuous Gentleman Mr Wil: Cartwright, my much valued Friend' in the posthumous edition of his works published in 1651 by Moseley (see *MV* 1.III), a volume that also included poems by Dering, Finch, Birkenhead, Thomas and Henry Vaughan, and the musician Henry Lawes (bap. 1596–1662). Lawes, the royal musician who had devised the music for Milton's *Masque Presented at Ludlow Castle 1634* (*Comus*) before the war, lived in London in the 1650s, where he taught music and gave concerts (see *CV* 1.I) believed to have been attended by Dering, Finch, and Birkenhead as well as Margaret Cavendish, Duchess of Newcastle, and published his anthologies of

---

[166] Taylor, *Discourse on…Friendship*, 2–3.

songs *Ayres and Dialogues* (1653, 1655, 1658). Philips, Dering, Birkenhead, and Finch published several pieces in the second volume, including her tribute to Lawes 'On his Excellent Compositions in Musick', which she signed with her full name and her coterie poem, 'Friendships Mysteries, To my Dearest Lucasia'.

In London, the Inns of Court served as one focus for displaced young men interested in poetry, the classics, and reflecting on the nature of the times in the late 1640s and 1650s. Thomas Stanley (see CV 1.V) moved into the Middle Temple in 1646 next door to his Catholic kinsman Edward Sherburne (bap. 1616–1702), whose estates had been confiscated by Parliament and who had come to live with his cousin William Povey. While living in the Middle Temple, Sherburne would publish two translations from Seneca, including *Medea* (1648) and *Answer to Lucilius...why good men suffer misfortunes seeing there is a divine providence* (1648) dedicated to Charles I. Stanley and Sherburne occupied their time studying and translating together, which resulted in the 1647 publication of Stanley's translation of two romances, one in Spanish and one in Italian, as well as his *Poems and Translations* (see MV 1.V); Stanley describes it as entering 'into a near Communication of Friendship and Studies'.[167] The year 1651 saw the publication of Sherburne's *Poems and Translations* dedicated to Stanley as well as Stanley's revised edition of his 1647 *Poems* with additional translations of the Greek poet Anacreon, the first English translation of Pico della Mirandola's *A Platonick Discourse upon Love*, as well as neo-Latin love lyrics by Dutch, Italian, and French poets.[168]

Stanley appears to have served as a stabilizing force for poets who had lost their livings and/or estates. These included Stanley's uncle William Hammond (1614–?), whose poems Stanley would publish posthumously, Robert Herrick (bap. 1591–1674), Henrietta Maria's court dramatist James Shirley (bap. 1596–1666), and Richard Brome (c.1590–1652), William Fairfax, who had been Stanley's tutor, and for a brief period probably Andrew Marvell. Stanley, in a later unpublished poem 'A Register of Friends', also lists his cousin Richard Lovelace and John Hall as members of his circle during this period.[169] Upon the execution of Charles I, Stanley left London and the Inns of Court and resided at Rushden Manor in Hertfordshire, where he lived with his new wife and soon-to-be large family, along with Edward Sherburne. His wife, Dorothy, signed her name on a bound volume manuscript copy of his *Poems and Translations* (printed 1647), whose calligraphed title page is dated 1646 and has an emblem of two hands tearing apart a heart. This volume records, as does the printed version, the enthusiastic commendatory poems of his circle of readers, including William Hammond, James Shirley, William Fairfax, and John Hall; the original fair copy volume subsequently served as a working

---

[167] Stanley, *Poems and Translations*, 363.

[168] *Poems by Thomas Stanley*; see McDowell, *Poetry and Allegiance*, 14–18, and Revard, 'Thomas Stanley and "A Register of Friends"'.

[169] See Osborn, 'Thomas Stanley's "Lost" Register; Crump, 'Thomas Stanley's Manuscript'.

space for Stanley to revise his 'A Paraphrase upon Psalme 148' and other poems in the 1650s.[170]

John Hall's (bap. 1627–56) involvement in several very different literary and scholarly networks suggests the ways in which politics and literature sometimes clashed, but often was suspended in the recognition of talent. Hall had been a prodigy during his time at St John's College, Cambridge, publishing *Horæ vacivæ or, Essays* in 1646 with commendatory verses by Stanley, Shirley, and Hammond among others. This led to his becoming the patron of John Davies of Kidwelly (who also enjoyed Benlowes's friendship) and beginning a correspondence with Hartlib. Through Hartlib, it is believed, Hall became acquainted with Milton and Robert Boyle.

In 1647, Hall would move from Cambridge to Gray's Inn, publish his *Poems*, and produce a translation requested by Hartlib of Johann Christian Andreae's utopian work *A Modell of a Christian Society*. In 1648, still working from Gray's Inn, Hall began the Parliamentarian-oriented newsbook *Mercurius Britanicus*, which did not prevent him from writing commendatory verses for Lovelace's *Lucasta* (1649) and others to James Shirley and Richard Brome, and even collaborating on *Mercurius Politicus* with Marchamont Nedham, who had by then switched allegiances to the royal cause (see CV i.III). In 1649 Hall was employed by the Council of State 'for answering pamphlets against the commonwealth' (*CSPD, 1649–50*, 139) and in 1650 he would accompany Cromwell on his campaign in Scotland, publishing in 1651 his political analysis *The Grounds and Reasons of Monarchy*. Nevertheless, Hall had such admiration for Benlowes's *Theophila* that he supposedly translated a whole canto of it into Latin in a single day. Lovelace, in turn, would offer his commendatory verses on Hall's posthumously published translation of *Hierocles Upon the Golden Verses* (1657): 'Alas! Our *Faiths* made different *Essayes,* | Our *Minds* and *Merits* brake two sev'rall ways.'

Of course, it was not only Royalists scattered abroad and in the countryside who were occupying their poetical talents in writings and translations not intended for general public reading. Andrew Marvell, an admirer of Lovelace the man and the poet, was after the execution of Charles I moving more clearly into Cromwell's sphere. Critics have long believed that 'The Nymph complaining for the death of her *Faun*' was completed shortly after the execution in 1649, a veiled lament for the loss of the martyred king. His next publicly known poem, however, left few doubts about his future allegiance. 'An *Horation* Ode upon *Cromwel's* Return from *Ireland*' announces Marvell's admiration at least for the man, if not all the elements of the Parliamentary side (as his subsequent satire on Thomas May, the publisher of *The King's Cabinet Opened* and chronicler of Parliamentary history, robustly demonstrates). Although the poem laments the execution of Charles—

> That thence the *Royal Actor* born
> The tragic *Scaffold* might adorn:
> While round the armed Bands
> Did clap their bloody hands

—Cromwell emerges as a divinely appointed force of nature, albeit a dangerous one:

> 'Tis Madness to resist or blame
> The force of angry Heavens flame:
> And, if we would speak true,
> Much to the Man is due.

Shortly after writing this in the summer of 1650, Marvell left London to travel to Yorkshire and the estate of the former commander of the New Model Army, Lord Fairfax, to serve as a tutor to his 12-year-old daughter Mary. At Nun Appleton, Marvell published two short dedicatory pieces in local physician Robert Wittie's translation of *Popular Errours, Or the Errours of the People in Physick*, one in English and one in Latin, addressing the extent to which a poet must infuse a translation with his or her own spirit in a free translation or adhere strictly the words. More important to the young writer was Marvell's growing acquaintance with Fairfax as a patron and as a poet.

Critics have speculated that Marvell's 'Upon Appleton House', one of his longest poems, was composed in the summer of 1651.[171] Like other poems on great country houses, such as Ben Jonson's 'To Penshurst' in celebration of the Sidney family, 'Upon Appleton House' alludes to classical models in which the virtues of the family are manifest in the history of the physical space they have inhabited for generations and the natural and bountiful beauty of its lands. Marvell, in his description of the gardens and grounds of Nun Appleton, additionally uses biblical allusions that will recur in his poem 'The Garden', a green world before the fall of man. Critics differ on the extent to which this poem was also intended as a didactic guide for the young Mary Fairfax, preparing her for her future as a great heiress by reminding her of her family's illustrious past. Certainly, the sections devoted to her towards the end of the poem insist that her purity and goodness actively infuses the natural world around her, while the particular place itself has helped to form her:

> 'Tis *She* that to these Gardens gave
> That wondrous Beauty which they have;
> She straightness on the Woods bestows;
> To *Her* the Meadow sweetness owes;
> Nothing could make the River be
> So Chrystal-pure but only *She*;
> *She* yet more Pure, Sweet, Straight, and Fair,
> Then Gardens, Woods, Meads, Rivers are.[172]

---

[171] See Smith, *Andrew Marvell*, 88–99.
[172] Marvell, *Poems*, canto lxxxxvii, p. 239.

Also, while resident at Nun Appleton and creating his poetic vision of an Eden-like natural setting, Marvell apparently was composing a series of more troubling pastorals. Unlike the poet speaker in 'Upon Appleton House' who happily merges himself in the natural world, 'The Mower to the Glo-Worms', '*Damon the Mower*', and 'The Mower's Song' create a pastoral landscape where the mower's harmony with his rural surroundings is repeatedly interrupted by his tormenting thoughts of Juliana and of death.

Following his employment with Fairfax, Marvell again briefly disappears from view and it is unclear the extent to which the poems he wrote while at Nun Appleton were read by others, as we have fewer manuscript versions of his poems than of many of his contemporaries, and many of his poems would not be published until 1681, three years after his death. Critics have typically assigned 'To his Coy Mistress' to this period, the *carpe diem* lyric opening 'Had we but World enough, and Time, | This Coyness Lady were no crime', but, again, it is unclear who would have been reading it at the time. It would be in 1653 that John Milton, whom some critics feel had read Marvell's 'Horatian Ode', suggested to Parliament that Marvell be employed as his assistant, a request that was at that point denied. Having initially failed to secure employment in Cromwell's government, Marvell again took up the post of tutor, moving to another rural setting, Eton College, to oversee the education of William Dutton, Cromwell's ward. Staying in the household of the staunchly Puritan John Oxenbridge, Marvell was once again in congenial company, and critics believe he probably wrote 'Bermudas' as a poem praising Oxenbridge and his wife, who had gone into exile there in 1635 and 1641. There, too, he made the acquaintance of the elderly scholar John Hales (1584–1656), who had been expelled from Eton and was living in the Richings Lodge in the household of Lady Salter, and whose treatise on schisms Marvell would eventually quote admiringly in *The Rehearsal Transpros'd* (1672), as representing the 'Majesty and Beauty which sits upon the Forehead of masculine Truth and generous Honesty'.[173]

Another staunch republican but no admirer of Cromwell in his later years, Lucy Hutchinson was in the 1650s at Owthorpe in Nottinghamshire, and she most likely began her translation of Lucretius's *De Rerum Natura* during this period. In her subsequent dedication of a fair presentation copy of the manuscript to Arthur Annesley, 1st Earl of Anglesey (1614–86), done in 1675, Hutchinson describes the work self-deprecatingly as an exercise she pursued in her children's schoolroom: while the children recited their lessons, 'I numbred the sillables of my translation by the threds of the canvas I wrought in, & sett them downe with a pen & inke that stood by me'.[174] Twenty years later, she looks back on this seemingly harmless task and shudders over the dangers to her soul for this time spent with the pagan philosophers: 'having by rich grace scaped the shipwreck of my soule among those vaine Philosphers, who by

---

[173] Marvell, *The Rehearsal Transpros'd*, 102.
[174] Hutchinson, *Works*, vol. 1, *Translation of Lucretius*, pt 1, p. 7.

wisedome knew not God', she writes to Anglesey, 'I could not but in charity
sett up this seamarke, to warne incautious travelers, and leave a testimony, that
those walkes of witt which poore vaineglorious schollars call the Muses groves,
are enchanted thickets'. 'While they tipple att their celebrated Helicon', she concludes, 'they loose their lives, and fill themselves with poison' (p. 8). Nevertheless,
she was clearly unwilling to destroy her translation, preferring instead to
entrust it to the judgement and safe-keeping of Anglesey.

Her poem is done in couplets and adheres closely to Lucretius' Latin rather
than attempting a freer translation. Hutchinson also adds short 'arguments'
explaining the contents of each of the books for the assistance of the reader.
For book one, she introduces the key concepts to be explored:

> That unseen Bodies and Vacuitie
> The two first principles of all things be,
> That Time is nothing but the accident
> Of mortal bodies while their race is spent. (p. 29)

The subsequent books explain topics ranging from the Epicurean notions of
atomism, the nature of sensation and thought, to the causes of earthquakes
and thunder. Central to Lucretius' poem is that the natural world and the universe at large are governed by *fortuna* and not the whims of the Roman gods, a
point of view that would become increasingly of interest to members of the
Royal Society when it formed during the Restoration, but also increasingly
abhorrent to the ever more Calvinist Hutchinson.

John Evelyn (1620–1706) had published his translation of the first book of
Lucretius in 1656, complete with an author portrait frontispiece that Hutchinson
mocks, 'a masculine Witt hath thought it worth print his head in a lawrell
crowne for the version of one of these books' (p. 4). The rest of his translation
of Lucretius done during the late 1640s and early 1650s, however, remained in
manuscript, supposedly because of his displeasure over the poor quality of the
first volume's publication. Although a prolific publisher during his lifetime,
Evelyn during the 1650s was busily engaged in a variety of reading and writing
projects at Sayes Court in Deptford, especially during this period, his developing interest in botany and horticulture. The resulting compendium, *Elysium
Britannicum*,[175] was first mentioned to his friend Sir Thomas Browne in 1655
and subsequently referenced in Evelyn's translation of a French gardening text
he published in 1659, *The French Gardiner*. This vast manuscript would be
added to for decades and would involve him in a widespread correspondence
network of professional gardeners and botanical enthusiasts and it also would
serve as the source for several of his works after the Restoration, such as *Sylva*
(1664) on trees and *Terra: a philosophical discourse* (1676).

This final example of Evelyn's active writing and reading pursuits in the
1650s highlights the social, reciprocal nature of reading and writing embodied

---

[175] BL Add. MS 78342–4.

in handwritten texts in the late 1640s and 1650s. It also draws attention to the extent to which printed publications and literary reputations would emerge and be consolidated in the 1660s and 1670s. Whether Royalist or Parliamentarian, male or female, writers in the 1650s very often had their initial readers in the handwritten social networks that could spread texts throughout the country-side and extending abroad to the Continent as well as to the New World, as well as being sheltered in numerous private households composed of intellectually inclined readers.

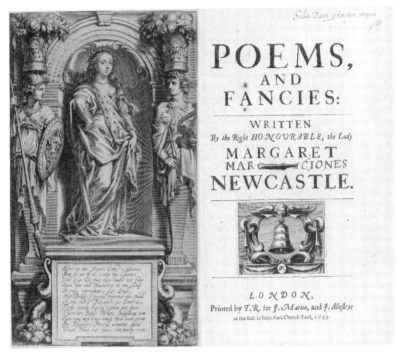

Figure 2. Margaret Cavendish, Duchess of Newcastle, *Poems and Fancies* (1653). RB 120141. The Huntington Library, San Marino, California

2

The Return of the King, Restoration, and Innovation, 1659–1673

I. 1659–1660

Without a doubt no man with more wickedness ever attempted anything, or brought to pass what he desired more wickedly, more in the face and contempt of religion and moral honesty; yet wickedness as great as his could never have accomplished those trophies without the assistance of a great spirit, an admirable circumspection and sagacity, and a most magnanimous resolution.

> Edward Hyde, Earl of Clarendon, on the death of Oliver
> Cromwell, *The History of the Rebellion*, 6. 91

The Word of the Lord came unto me, saying, Write, and again I say, Write with speed, to the Heads and Rulers of this Nation; Oh! earth, earth, earth, hear the Word of the Lord, and be awakened unto righteousness, for the hour of his Judgements are come one the earth...

> Dorothy White, *Upon the 22 day of the 8ᵗʰ Month* (1659)

Sir, the Countrey, as well as the Town, abound with vanities; now the reins of Liberty and Licentiousness are let loose: May-poles, and Playes, and *Juglers*, and all things else now pass current; sin now appears with a brazen face: That wicked spirit amongst men, self, with boasting and gloriation.

> Letter quoted by Henry Jessey, *The Lords loud call to England:*
> *being a true relation of some late, various, and wonderful*
> *judgments, or handy-works of God* (1660)

Late in 1658, politics again became the national drama for English readers and writers. On 3 September, Oliver Cromwell died, and his son Richard succeeded him as Lord Protector of the Commonwealth. For obvious reasons, the transition of power from the Lord Protector to his son and the subsequent political

Figure 3. Elkanah Settle, *The Empress of Morocco* (1673), interior of Duke's Theatre. RB 32739. The Huntington Library, San Marino, California

chaos as rival parties attempted to define the form of the government and the nature of its authority permeated much of the literary material produced during 1659 and 1660, and the political and religious rhetoric of the time was passionate in its urgency to persuade readers. For some, the return of the King was a welcome event, a providential restoration of order and stability for many men and women, but, for others, it was a disheartening return to the worldly vanities and aristocratic culture that had played their parts in Charles I's loss of his crown.

In 1659, once again the outpouring of cheap pamphlets, broadsides, and petitions that had characterized the early war years bombarded readers with arguments, icons, and prophecies. It is noteworthy that even artisan and labouring-class Englishmen and women could now turn to print to voice their concerns using petitions and broadside announcements; in 1659, nearly 100 petitions were printed for distribution, such as the one from *The humble petition of divers inhabitants of the county of Hertford, who have faithfully adhered to the Good Old Cause. Presented to the Parliament, by Dr Barber, with many free-holders, and other inhabitants of the said county, May 13. 1659.* Apprentices, the officers and the soldiers in the army, ministers, seafarers, tavern-keepers and sellers of wine, freemen of the city, and groups of women joined together to amplify their voices, to plead their causes, and to publish their fears about the future to those in power, making use of the traditionally sanctioned right to petition.

The rhetoric they employ is striking. 'Free' is the key word that reverberates in these formulaic publications, and it is this status that validates the writers' voices and their right to be heard and read. So common had such large-scale petitions become by this point, one could obtain pre-printed appeals: the opening salutation had an appropriate blank space to inscribe the particular location, and there was space at the end for signatures, resulting in publications such as *The just petition of the free-borne commoners of the county of* [blank] *whose names are hereunto subscribed, earnestly desiring, the prosperity of the gospell, the removall of bad, the setlement of just lawes, the freedome of this nation, and the peace and tranquilety of all men.*

As part of this national debate, key political and military figures became woven into contemporary fictions. After his death, Cromwell became an iconic figure, at once both heroic and diabolic, and, by the end of 1660, even Cromwell's wife had become a target for satire in John Tatham's comedy *The Rump, or, The Mirrour of the late Times*. Prior to that, however, Cromwell's body had served as a focus for national grief, reviving the pageantry of mourning reserved for monarchs. Thomas Burton recorded in his diary a detailed account of Cromwell's elaborately staged public funeral, for which Burton believed some £60,000 had been reserved. Because of the nature of his illness and the time of year, Cromwell's physical body had decayed rapidly, 'although thus bound up and laid in the coffin, [the body] swelled and bursted, from whence came such filth, that raised such a deadly and noisome stink, that it was found prudent to bury him immediately, which was done in as private a manner as possible'.[1]

Cromwell's public funeral took place several days later, and, as had been done for kings before him, an effigy of him was used for the lying in state. Burton records that 'the effigies of his Highness was, with great state and magnificence, exposed openly, multitudes daily crowding to see this glorious, but mournful sight'. John Evelyn recorded in his diary that Cromwell's effigy was costumed in 'royal robes, & Crown'd with a Crown, scepter & *Mund*, [globe] like a King' and carried from Somerset-house 'in a velvet bed of state drawn by six horses houss'd with the same', and he admits, the staged spectacle was a 'superb Funerall'. For Royalist sympathizers such as Evelyn, however, 'it was the joyfullest funeral that ever I saw, for there was none that Cried, but dogs, which the souldiers hooted away with a barbarous noise; drinking & taking *Tobacco* in the streetes as they went' (Evelyn, *Diary*, 3. 224, 1 November 1658).

After Cromwell's recumbent effigy had been viewed by the crowds, on 23 November, it was raised upright and a crown placed on its head. Then, in a formal procession, the effigy of Cromwell was taken through the streets to Westminster Abbey: Burton's diary entry, which is based on an account preserved in manuscript from the Revd John Prescott, describes how 'this great funeral was performed with very great majesty, in this manner following'.

---

[1] Burton, *Diary*, 2. 516.

All things being in readiness, the waxen effigies of the Protector, with a crown on his head, a sword by his side, a globe and sceptre in his hands, was taken down from his standings, and laid in an open chariot, covered all over with black velvet. The streets, from Somerset-House to Westminster-Abbey, were guarded by soldiers, placed without a railing, and clad in new red coats, with black buttons, with their ensigns wrapped in cypress. These made a lane, to keep off spectators from crowding the procession.[2]

One cannot help but observe the extent to which the Puritan Lord Protector in his death was transformed into the King he had refused to be during his life, or rather how the waxen image of him was carefully costumed and its actions choreographed in an elaborate staging of the passing of a kingly man, in a manner intelligible to all viewers, from the elite mourners who guarded this wax figure to the people who had crowded in to see it lying in state, or who lined the procession route.

  This use of royal iconography would be sneeringly offered up as evidence against him by his detractors writing in the early 1660s: James Heath's (1629?–64) *Flagellum: Or The Life and Death, Birth and Burial of O. Cromwell The late Usurper: Faithfully Described* (1663), which went through three editions by 1665, repeatedly emphasized that Cromwell's body had exploded because of his innate filthiness of character and that the effigy used in the funeral was a 'shew' with manipulated 'scenes'. As early as 1659, Cromwell was the hero and the villain of political dialogues and ballads, but the ghost of Charles I also begins to appear again in pamphlets and broadsides, offering counsel and advice. By 1660 and the return of the monarch, even Parliament as a body became a type of entertaining spectacle: the name itself of the group, the 'Rump Parliament', so-called because they were the surviving remnants of the republican Parliament elected in the autumn of 1640, the group who had tried and convicted Charles I, provided effortless occasions for crude humour in broadside ballads and lampoons. Satirists poured forth pieces with titles such as *Rump rampant, Arsy Versy: Or the Second Martydom of the Rump*, the broadside playlet *The life and death of Mris Rump. And the fatal end of her base-born brat of destruction, with her own first hatching and bringing forth from the Devils arse a peake, it being the only place, from whence this illegiti-mate bastard or monster had its nativity*, and Alexander Brome's ballad *Bumm-foder or, waste-paper proper to wipe the nation's Rump with, or your own*.

  Aiming for more ambitious literary merit, writers of heroic and panegyric verses found themselves within a relatively short space of time in the position of publicly lamenting the loss of Cromwell and shortly thereafter rejoicing in the restoration of Charles II. The verses on Cromwell 'Heroique Stanzas' by the future Poet Laureate, John Dryden (1631–1700), were published after Cromwell's elaborately staged state funeral; Dryden attempted to place Cromwell's virtues in the tradition of Roman panegyrics, praising the private citizen of innate merit and valour who rose to meet his country's needs. 'His

Grandeur he deriv'd from Heav'n alone, | For he was Great e'er Fortune made him so', avers Dryden, 'And Wars like mists that rise against the Sun, | Made him but greater seem not greater grow.'[3] Dryden's measured panegyric seeks to strike a balance between the excess found in laments accorded previous royal leaders, and the man who had refused Parliament's request to become king: clearly the passing of this great figure must be paid appropriate tribute, 'Yet 'tis our duty and our interest too | Such monuments as we can build to raise' (p. 4) by associating him not with departed sovereigns but rather with heroic states-men. Dryden concludes:

> His ashes in a peaceful Urn shall rest,
> His Name a great example stands to show
> How strangely high endeavours may be blest,
> Where *Piety* and *Valour* joyntly go. (p. 12)

Other poets, such as Andrew Marvell (1621–78), by then serving along with John Milton as the Latin secretary for the Council of State run by Cromwell's master of intelligence gathering, John Thurloe, found the occasion of Cromwell's passing a more emotionally charged event. Marvell had celebrated Cromwell's victories in Ireland in 1650 by casting Cromwell as a peaceful man drawn from his quiet country garden to serve as the fierce hunting falcon for Parliament (see *MV* 1.VI). In his 1658 poem 'A Poem upon the Death of his Late Highness the Lord Protector', he described to the departed spirit of Cromwell how his people

> Since thou art gone, with heavy doom,
> Wander like ghosts about thy loved tomb;
> And lost in tears, have neither sight nor mind
> To guide us upward through this region blind.
>
> .   .   .   .   .
>
> Since thou art gone, who best that way couldst teach,
> Only our sighs, perhaps, may thither reach.

Marvell, like John Milton, Dryden, Samuel Hartlib, and Thomas Sprat, was given money by the government to purchase cloth for mourning clothes to walk in Cromwell's funeral procession. Marvell's poem was originally intended to be published with a group of other panegyrics by Dryden and Sprat in January of 1659, but it was Waller's that was used instead. John Milton, who had previously written several poems about the living Cromwell, offered nothing on his passing.

Edmund Waller (1606–87), who had written a 'Panegyric to my Lord Protector' in 1655 that coincided with Waller's appointment as a Commissioner of Trade, interpreted the natural world's response to Cromwell's passing in a one-page broadside later published with Dryden's and Sprat's poems, *Upon the late storme, and of the death of His Highnesse ensuing the same.*

---

[3] Dryden, *Poem on the Death of His late Highness*, 5.

> We must resign; Heav'n His great Soul do's claime
> In storms as loud as His *Immortal Fame:*
> His dying *groans*, his last *Breath*, shakes our Isles;
> And Trees uncut fall for His *Funeral Pile.*

Waller also highlights the connections between Cromwell's career and those of classical rulers rather than recent:

> Nor hath he left us Prisoners to our Isle;
> Under the Tropick is our language spoke,
> And part of Flanders hath receiv'd our yoke.
> From Civil Broils he did us disingage,
> Found nobler objects for our Martial rage,
> And with wise Conduct to his Country show'd
> Their Ancient way of conquering abroad:
> Ungrateful then, if we no Tears allow
> To him that gave us Peace, and Empire too.

In 1659, however, the anonymously published *The Panegyrike and the Storme Two Poetike Libells by Ed. Waller Vassall to the Usurper, Answered by More Faithful Subjects to His Sacred King Charles ye Second* (1659), issued by the exiled Royalist clergyman Richard Watson (1611/12–85), made clear from its title page that strongly different views of Cromwell and his passing existed simultaneously in other poetic spirits. In 'To the Pusillanimous Author of The Panegyrike', the writer points out that Waller would have been answered sooner had not

> … your late Dictator of the Presse,
> Whose spreading Power, like an Erratike Plague,
> Though bred at London, met me at the Hague[4]

and a side note informs the reader that the printer there 'confessed he was to print nothing against the New English state' and had rejected the following satires. This piece also targets John Milton, noting that, had 'that poetike *Areopagite*' obtained the liberty of an unlicensed press, not only Waller, but also Milton's own prose pieces such as *Pro Populo Anglicano Defensio* (1651), would have been answered long ago.

Ironically, another public figure who was both celebrated and reviled during life as an icon of what was wrong with the world as well as being a favourite in the popular imagination died with much less fanfare in 1659. Mary Frith (1584x–1659), aka Moll Cutpurse, the inspiration for Thomas Middleton and Thomas Dekker's comedy *The Roaring Girl* (1611), passed away and was buried in St Bride's, Fleet Street. A petty thief, a fence for stolen goods, and criminal intelligencer who had played a cameo role as herself in performances of *The Roaring Girl* at the Fortune Theatre, her cross-dressing, sword-wearing,

---

[4] Watson, *The Panegyrike and the Storme*, 'To the Pusillanimous Author'.

tobacco-smoking antics had provided materials for pamphleteer and playwrights into the 1650s; she figured in Samuel Shepherd's humorous almanac *Merlinus Anonymous…for the year 1653* and *Endlesse queries: or An end to queries laid down in 36 merry mad queries for the peoples information* (1659), which suggested that 'having formerly done so good service at the *Bear, Garden*, and many other things for the good of the Nation', she might now appoint an heir to return all the purses she had stolen.[5] Three years after her death her reputation was turned to another purpose: *The life and death of Mrs Mary Frith* (1662) appeared, complete with a portrait of her in men's clothes, smoking a pipe, with her pet monkey and parrot gazing at her in admiration. According to this account of her life, Frith had been a staunch Royalist during the war years who had become a highwayman to persecute Parliamentarians, notably supposedly robbing and wounding the general Sir Thomas Fairfax on Hounslow Heath.

Initially, the transition from one Protectorate to the next was peaceful. *The Commonwealth Mercury* (Thursday, 2 September–Thursday, 9 September 1658) describes Richard's procession through the streets of London and how, at the last stop of the procession at Cornhill, 'the largest Demonstrations of Love and Loyalty were lively set forth in the Tongues and Countenances of the Citizens of that renowned City…manifested by their reiterated Shouts and Acclamations upon this great Occasion'.[6] The three armies of England, however, were still standing and awaiting both payment and action, General Charles Fleetwood's in England itself, Oliver's son Henry Cromwell's in Ireland, and General George Monck's in Scotland.

The Parliament likewise quickly manifested uneasy divisions. The confirmed republican Sir Arthur Hesilrige [Haselrig] (1601–61), who figures prominently in many of the broadside satires, organized a filibuster against the approval of Richard Cromwell, while supporting the army's charges against the Parliament. In April 1659, the generals Fleetwood and Disbrowe [Desborough] had convinced Richard to dissolve Parliament, but John Evelyn recorded in his diary on 25 April 1659 'a wonderfull & suddaine change in the face of the publique: The new *Protector Richard* slighted, severall pretenders, & parties for the Government, all *Anarchy* and confusion; Lord have mercy on us' (Evelyn, *Diary*, 3. 228). By July 1659, Richard and his brother Henry had been forced to step down from their positions, and the Rump Parliament had been recalled. Following Richard Cromwell's departure, the government of England went through the summer 'of great fear', and the government shifted its shape no fewer than seven times in twelve months: in October, as the soldiers were demanding payment and their officers and generals a new government, Lambert dissolved the Rump Parliament and created 'a Committee of Safety'.

Outside London, the future anecdotal biographer of his generation, John Aubrey (1626–97), was in the midst of selling off his inherited estates in order

[5] Shepherd, *Merlinus Anonymous*, 6.
[6] *The Commonwealth Mercury*, 7.

to settle debts and lawsuits. Aubrey was also in the midst of beginning yet another ambitious antiquarian project that was never quite completed. His natural history of Wiltshire, one of the earliest archaeological texts produced about English artefacts, had been begun in 1656 in part as a response to reading Inigo Jones's observations on Stonehenge, but in 1659 it was still in preparation, although being circulated in manuscript among his friends. In 1659, he began a second study of his native Wiltshire, 'An Essay towards the Description of the North Division of Wiltshire', as part of a projected county history of England, modelled after Dugdale's *Illustration of Warwickshire*, with William Yoke, T. Gore, Jeffrey Daniel, and Sir John Ernley. In this account, also never finished, Aubrey included for his reader's pleasure not only facsimiles of seals and deeds with accounts of noble buildings and great families, but also 'curious' knowledge and reflections on the juxtaposition of past and present histories. In recounting the origins of some important local families, Aubrey describes how, in the days of Henry VIII, the King had fallen from his horse into mud, '*with which, being fatt and heavie, he had been suffocated to death had he not been timely relieved by his footman Mody, for which service, after the dissolution of the Abbies, he gave him the manour of Garesdon*'. His reason for including this historical tale appears to have been to contrast it with practices during the Commonwealth, or, as he later referred to it, '*Oliver's Triumphant Usurpation*', when such gallant acts did not result in the creation of noble families.[7]

Reflecting later on how the Commonwealth had changed even the physical landscape of England, Aubrey lamented not completing the 1659 survey, 'since the Time aforesaid, many Things are irrecoverably lost. In former Days the Churches an great Houses hereabouts did so abound with Monuments and Things remarkable that it would have deterr'd an Antiquary from undertaking it'. The Civil War, as Aubrey notes, changed more than just the buildings and the families who occupied them, but even affected the telling of natural lore and local legends, the fabric of antiquarian histories. '*At Fausby (near Daintre) in Northamptonshire*', he noted,

a Raven did build her Nest on the Leads between the Tower and the Steeple. The oldest Peoples Grandfathers here, did never remember, but that this Raven yearly made her Nest here; and in the late Civil warre, the Soldiers killed her. I am sorry for the Tragical end of this old Church-Bird, that lived in so many changes of Government and Relegion.[8]

In the autumn of 1659, the young Aubrey moved from Wiltshire to London and took part in the Rota, a political club formed by James Harrington (1611–77). There the still dangerous topic of republicanism was debated, even though Aubrey at this time believed 'the Doctrine was very taking, and more because, as to human foresight, there was no possibility of the King's returne' (Aubrey, *Brief Lives*, 2. 153).

---

[7] Quoted in *Aubrey's Brief Lives*, ed. Dick, pp. xlv–xlvi.
[8] Quoted in *Aubrey's Brief Lives*, ed. Dick, pp. xlv–xlvi.

The death of Cromwell and the unsteady reign of his son, however, did create a climate of tentative hope and activity among the defeated followers of Charles I who still remained in England. In April of 1659, Ann Fanshawe (1625–80) was in the process of gathering her family together to leave England and join her husband, the poet and translator Richard Fanshawe (1608–66). The Fanshawes had spent seven years of the Interregnum under close surveillance by Parliament for their Royalist activities; Richard had occupied his time translating Luis de Camões's *The Lusiads* and revising his translation of Gaurini's *Il Pastor Fido* (see *MV* 1.VI; *CV* 1.I). After the death of Cromwell, Richard Fanshawe had been permitted to leave England for France along with Sir Robert Howard (1626–98), himself newly released from imprisonment in Windsor Castle for his Royalist sympathies, as the companion to the Earl of Pembroke's 18-year-old son. Ann Fanshawe, however, was denied a pass for herself, three of their children, and two servants, as being 'Malignants'. She dramatically recounts in the memoirs she wrote for her son that, to escape and join her husband, she disguised herself as a young merchant's wife 'Anne Harrison' and, having received her pass, used her pen to change 'the great H of Harrison two *ff*, and the rr's an *n*, and i an *s*, and the s, an *h* ... so completely, that none could find out the change'.[9] At Dover, 'the searchers came and, knowing me, demanded my pass, which they were to keep for their discharge. When they had read it they sayd, "Madam, you may goe when you please". "But", says one, "I little thought they would give pass to so great a Malignant, especially in such troublesome time as this"' (p. 139).

By 1659, Parliament was hearing heated criticism not only from Royalist supporters, but also from radical sectarian groups, in particular the Quakers, for the ways in which the godly government operated (see *MV* 1.IV). George Fox (1624–91), the founder of the Society of Friends, or, as their opponents called them, the Quakers, published some twenty short pamphlets and one-page broadsides in 1659 directed at Parliament, the army, and the civil authorities. In Fox's address to Parliament, *Fifty-nine Particulars laid down for the Regulating things, and the taking away of Oppressing Laws, and Oppressors, and to ease the Oppressed* (1659), tithes are the first item on the list: 'Let no man be prisoned for Tithes, which have been set up by the Apostates (the Papists) since the days of the Apostles'.[10] In response to the trials that had imprisoned many of the Quakers for their refusal to pay tithes, to swear oaths, and to observe the social customs of hierarchy, he pragmatically urged that the language of the law and of courts should be reformed: 'Let all laws in *England* be brought into a known tongue, that every Countryman may plead his own cause, without Attorney or Counsellour, or for mony' (p. 4). More idealistically his sixteenth suggestion was that 'let none that is high, proud, or lofty, envious or scornful bear Office, for he will turn the sword backward, and do the Divels

---

[9] Halkett, *Memoirs*, 138.
[10] Fox, *Fifty-nine Particulars*, 3.

work, which is to bring the World into a Wildernesse, and quench the spirit of God' (p. 5). Item 28 returns to the issue of a salaried clergy or ministers in contrast to those called to the vocation by God and speaking the Word directly from the Inner Light: 'Let all this money, and stipends, and Tithes, and hour glasses for preaching by the hour be taken away from men, who make a trade of the Scripture, but let every one speak freely as they have received' (p. 8) and again in item 44, 'let not preaching be made a trade, nor the Word of God made Merchandize' (p. 12).

In terms of the general public good, items 45 through 56 concern public places of amusement and their effect on the citizens of a godly nation. 'Let none keep Ale-houses or Taverns, but who fear God', Fox suggests, 'let all the Stage-playes, May-Games, Shoffel-boards, Dice, Cards, Nine-holes, Foot-balls and Hand-balls, and Fidlings, and all these vain Musicks, which stirs up the light vain minds of people…be taken away that stirs up the light mind, and maketh provision for the flesh, or else they will lye upon you'. In the same spirit, 'let all these jangling of Bells cease, which do feed peoples pleasures and vain minds. Let all those Ballad-singers, and Ballad-makers, and Jest book-makers which stirs up vain and light minds, be taken away' (p. 12). Finally, Fox reminds his Parliamentary readers of their duty to the less fortunate: speaking with certain knowledge of the conditions many Quakers endured while incarcerated, 'let all Goals [gaols] be in wholesom places, that the Prisoners may not lye in their own dung, and Piss, and straw like Chaffe'. Invoking the creed of the Quakers that all are equal in the sight of God: 'Let neither Beggars nor Blind people, nor Fatherless, nor Widows, nor Cripples go a Begging up and down the streets…let all this wearing of gold Lace, and costly attire, more like Anticks then sober men, let this be ended, and cloath the naked, and feed the hungry with the superfluidity'. 'Justice and Righteousness exalteth a Nation', he concludes, 'but sin is a shame both to Rulers and people' (p. 13).

Other prominent and prolific Quaker writers, such as the young Edward Burrough (1633–63), who had been a child during the war years, and Richard Hubberthorne (bap. 1628–62), who had served in Cromwell's army and were both soon to die in prison in the early years of the Restoration, issued broadsides and pamphlets, attacking both the army and Parliament for abandoning '*the Good Old Cause*'. Texts by Quakers were all sent to Fox for his approval before printing, resulting in a uniform message but with distinctively different voices and styles. Burrough's broadside *To the Whole English Army* (1659) offered 'wholesome *Animadversions* in this day of Distractions', but opened with the pointed demand 'Where is the *Good Old Cause* now?' That cause, he reminded his readers, stood for 'liberty, both in Spiritualls and Temporalls', and 'the *just Freedom* of all People'. Because the army has not sustained the cause, 'so many of the people of the Lord, and of the free people of this Nation have been, and are at this day grievous sufferers under the Oppressions and Cruelties of men, and under unjust men, and unjust Lawes'. Francis Howgill (1618?–69) used his fiery rhetoric to refute published attacks on the Quakers for their views and actions and drew dramatic attention to the persecution of the Quakers in both England and New England. Signing himself 'a Lover of Mercy and Truth, and an Enemy to Envy and Cruelty', Howgill attacked *The Popish inquisition New Erected in New-England, whereby Their Church is manifested to be a Daughter of the Mysterie Babylon, which did drink the blood of the Saints* (1659). Richard Crane, who published in 1660 a pamphlet with Thomas Simmons, the Quaker publisher closely tied to the more radical elements of the London group (see *MV* 1.II, 1.IV), decried the return of 'Christian ministers' who accepted money for their services. For Crane, the restoration of the Church of England was the restoration of the Whore of Babylon and the start of the apocalypse, as seen in the long title of his *A Short But a Strict Account Taken of Babylons Merchants, Who are now Forcing the Sale of their Old, Rusty, Cankered Ware, upon the People of these Nations.* The return of the Anglican hierarchy for Crane and those who believed similarly was the return of human-centred religious ritual and costumed theatrical spectacle, 'your *Altars...* your *Organs,* your *Singing-Men* and *Boyes,* with *Surplices, Tippets, Scarffs, Long Garments, and Girdles,* with your invented *prayer* called *Common*',[11] a silencing of the voice divine within each believer.

Quaker women were also highly visible in both their publications and their public actions during this critical time of transition. Through petitions, prophetic writings, and public displays, Quaker women invoked the 'Inner Light', which guided their words and gave them the authority to speak and to publish warnings, appeals, and testimonies to those in power. Like Sarah Blackborow (n.d.) and Judith Eedes (n.d.), the prolific Dorothy White (d. 1686?), who published in 1659 her *A Warning to all the Inhabitants of the Earth where this shall come; but especially to those that are called Magistrates and Rulers, and so pretend to bear a Sword of Justice,* reached an intense pitch as the secular powers in charge waivered. Clearly, White states, God's day of judgement was at hand: 'the Lord God is coming to shake you like a leaf, & to break down your invented imagined Laws, made by your evil hearts, hearts full of corruption and deceit, with guile in your mouths'.[12] White states that she takes no pleasure in this task but that 'I do see a storm of vexation coming on you, shewed unto me by the Lord God, and I am constrained by him to make it known to you' (p. 7). Her signature highlights her role as simply the vehicle to transmit the warning, 'a warning and a message, as received by the Spirit of the living God, as it was given to me to be delivered to you, for you to read in the fear of God, and in meekness to receive it as the Counsel of God. Given forth by *Dorothy White*' (p. 8).

Other Quaker women wrote not as prophets but as citizens to put pressure on Parliament to fulfil their promises. In May 1659, Mary Forster (*c.*1619–86) presented a petition against tithes signed by nearly 7,000 women, *These Several Papers was Sent to Parliament*: speaking for the 'Hand-maids and Daughters of

---

[11] Crane, *A Short But a Strict Account*, 19.
[12] White, *A Warning to all the Inhabitants of the Earth*, 1.

the Lord', she notes that 'it may seem strange to some that women should appear in so publick a manner, in a matter of so great concernment as this of *Tithes*' but she avers 'Behold our God is appearing for us...*choosing the fool- ish things of the World to confound the wise, weak things to confound the Mighty*'.[13] It was printed for Mary Westwood and sold at Giles and Elizabeth Calvert's the Black-Spread-Eagle, whose presses along with those of Thomas Simmons printed many of the most radical texts of their times by Quakers and unrepentant republicans.

The first signer of the petition was Margaret Fell (1614–1702), the so-called mother of Quakerism and future wife of George Fox. She herself in 1659 pub- lished a short treatise on the dangers of following ministers who were appointed by law rather than led by God, *A Paper concerning such as are made Ministers by the will of man*. She cites the example of Paul and Galatians 1:11–12: 'But I certify you, brethren, that the gospel which was preached of me is not after man. For I neither received it of man, neither was I taught it, but by the revela- tion of Jesus Christ' and she asks her readers/hearers to consider 'whether *Paul's* Ministry was not according to what you now persecute, who went into the Synagogues to reason with them, after the same manner as wee doe now, who received not his Ministry from Man'.[14] 'Though he was brought up at the feet of *Gamshell*', Fell points out, 'he counted that which he learned there, as dung and drosse, in comparison of the excellency of Jesus Christ; and now with the Same light, your form of prayer, and form off preaching, without the power, it is as drosse and dung to me, and to all that live in the life, who know Christ to be the high Priest over the houshold of God' (p. 1).

The passionate and apocalyptic 'alarms', pamphlets, petitions, and broad- sides issued by the Quakers, of course, brought equally hyperbolic hostile responses from those who felt that the Quakers were an ignorant and deluded rabble of labourers and artisans, or power-seeking hypocrites, or both. The authors of the satiric *A Phanatique league and covenant, Solemnly enter'd into the Assectors of the good old cause*, ironically represent themselves as being 'we Ignoble men, Barbers, Coblers, Colliers, Draymen, Grocers, Hucksters... Pedlers, Sowgauters, Tinkers, Taylors, and Mechanicks of all sorts, being of the Fanatick party within the Kingdomes (formerly so called) England, Scotland and Ireland, living under, and submitting to only the Government of one Prince, Belzebub Emperor of the Infernal Regions'.[15] Signed at the bottom of the mock petition are the supposed conspirators, including the unlikely combination of the regicides Hugh Peter and John Harrison, along with the republican Arthur Hesilrige, in collaboration with Praisegod Barbon, the con- troversial Quaker James Nayler (see *MV* 1.IV; *CV* 1.VI), and the newsbook- writer Marchamont Nedham (see *CV* 1.III) as extremists who exploit the times for their extreme views.

---

[13] Forster, *These Several Papers was Sent to Parliament.*
[14] Fell, *A Paper*, 1.   [15] *A Phanatique league and covenant.*

This parody of a petition has five points, the first being that 'we shall from the very root of our corrupt hearts and consciences, endeavour by all means possible, in our several capacities, to obstruct and abolish all Decency, Order, and Form whatsoever, in the Government of Church or State'. The petition declares that 'we shall with a most perverse obstinacy, to the hazard of our lives and fortunes, assert our own interests and right of conquest, we had usurpt over the three Nations, against all pretended Priviledges of Parliament, Liberties of the People, and any general good whatsoever'. They furthermore agree to band together,

whether under the Notion of Quakers, Anabaptists, Fifth Monarchists, Ranters, &c. And notwithstanding we differ in judgement from our selves, as well as from all Orthodox Christians, yet we will make it appear to the world, and to the Author of that model of a Commonwealth, call'd the *Rota*, that we are a Wheel, whose Spokes, though divided in circumference, yet concenter in this, *viz*, A total extirpation and subversion of all Government, both Ecclesiastical and Civil.

It was clear from the pamphlets and broadsides issued by angry or frightened observers and the seeming general lack of confidence in Parliament that even the very concept of the Commonwealth was in jeopardy. The 'Rota' sneeringly referred to in the satire was the same one mentioned by Aubrey as having ideas 'very taking'; the Rota Club, meeting nightly at the Turk's Head Coffee House, centred around James Harrington and his radical concept of a Commonwealth based on the yearly rotation of magistrates and voting by ballot, which he had described in *The Commonwealth of Oceana* (1656). In early 1660 he published *The Rota: Or a Model of a Free-State, or equall Commonwealth...debated by a free and open Society of ingenious Gentlemen.* Harrington's chief concern was to urge Parliament to resist the creation of any hereditary oligarchy such as the House of Lords or permanent structures of power, whether in the government, the army, or the Church. On Monck's entering the city, the Rota Club ceased to meet, and Harrington stopped his publications.

John Milton, who was not a member of the Rota, apparently followed its debates through his pupil, friend, and future biographer Cyriack Skinner (1627–1700). In 1659, Milton wrote two pieces urging Parliament to do away with the unpopular tithe system and to take appropriate steps for securing itself as the lasting form of government. In February of 1659, Milton published *A treatise of civil power in ecclesiastical causes, shewing that it is not lawfull for any power on earth to compell in matters of religion*, addressed to the Parliament seated by Richard Cromwell's government, which he addresses as the 'supream Councel' without mentioning Richard. In an argument closely reminiscent of the positions he laid out in *Aeropagitica* in 1644 concerning the necessity of free choice, Milton announces that his topic will be 'Christian libertie', and that he feels 'an inward perswasion of Christian dutie' to address this topic at this particular time.[16] 'Two things there be which have bin ever

---

[16] Milton, *A treatise of civil power*, 1.

found working much mischief to the church of God, and the advancement of truth', he opens, 'force on the one side restraining, and hire on the other side corrupting the teachers thereof' (p. 1).

Given that the only foundation of Protestantism is the Holy Scripture itself, and none can know the inner workings of the Scriptures on any except themselves, Milton argues that for a civil magistrate or authority to presume to judge another's religious beliefs is worse than any possible '*heresie*' or schism among Protestant believers. 'If then we count it so ignorant and irreligious in the papist to think himself dischargd in Gods account, beleeving only as the church beleevs, how much greater condemnation will it be to the protestant his condemner, to think himself justified, beleeving only as the state beleevs?' (p. 7). In answering the fear that appropriate religious observances might not be kept by licentious people unless they are constrained by law to perform them, Milton again returns to the theme of the uselessness of external forms and ceremonies—what spiritual value is there, he argues, in constraining people to attend particular services or perform specific duties if they do so only when under force and not from desire and a believing spirit? Foreshadowing the heart of the argument in *Paradise Lost* concerning free will, he concludes:

On these four scriptural reasons as on a firm square this truth, the right of Christian and evangelic liberty, will stand immoveable against all those pretended consequences of license and confusion, which for the most part men most licentious and confus'd themselves, or such as whose severitie would be wiser then divine wisdom, are ever aptest to object against the waies of God as if God without them when he gave us this libertie, knew not of the worst which these men in their arrogance pretend will follow: yet knowing all their worst, he gave us this liberty as by him judgd best. (pp. 78–9)

Milton published the second part of this project in August 1659, again addressed to Parliament, but by this time it was the Rump Parliament, which had established a Commonwealth after Richard had abdicated the title. *Considerations touching the likeliest means to remove hirelings out of the church, wherein is also discoursed of tithes, church-fees, church revenues, and whether any maintenance of ministers can be settled by law* (1659) focuses less on the damage to the individual who is forced by law to maintain and support ministers and churches that are not embraced by his conscience than on the corruption of the teachers of the flock, the 'hirelings' who have turned the ministry into a professional trade rather than a spiritual calling. On 27 June, a petition had been presented to Parliament with 1,500 signatures urging Parliament not to enforce tithes—Parliament's response on the same day was a resolution continuing them. Recalling his scorn in 'Lycidas' for the 'shepherds' who neglect their flocks to feed themselves at the trough, Milton depicts the 'Simonious decimating clergie' who perform ceremonies such as burial and baptism for a fee and who demand a salary wage as being first embodied in Judas and then transmitted to England through the practices of the Catholic Church.

As with Margaret Fell's invocation of Paul, Milton, too, derides the 'fond error, though too much beleevd among us, to think that the universitie makes a minister of the gospel; what it may conduce to other arts and sciences, I dispute not now: but that which makes fit a minister, the scripture can best informe us to be only from above'.[17] 'In the first evangelic times (and it were happy for Christendom if it were so again)', Milton observes, 'ministers of the gospel were by nothing els distinguishd from other Christians but by thir spiritual knowledge and sanctitie of life' (p. 148). Once, however,

they affected to be calld a clergie, and became as it were a peculiar tribe of levites, a partie, a distinct order in the Commonwealth, bred up for divines in babling schooles and fed at the publick cost, good for nothing els but what was good for nothing, they soone grew idle: that idlenes with fulnes of bread begat pride and perpetual contention with thir feeders the despis'd laitie, through all ages ever since; to the perverting of religion, and the disturbance of all Christendom. (p. 149)

Now in England, Milton avers:

our ministers think scorn to use a trade, and count it the reproach of this age, that tradesmen preach the gospel. It were to be wishd they were all tradesmen; they would not then so many of them, for want of another trade, make a trade of thir preaching: and yet they clamor that tradesmen preach; and yet they preach, while they themselves are the worst tradesmen of all. (p. 99)

Concerning the need for churches, special buildings, or specific places designated and kept only for worship, Milton notes with some irony that, 'notwithstanding the gaudy superstition of som devoted still ignorantly to temples, we may be well assur'd that he who disdaind not to be laid in a manger, disdains not to be preachd in a barn' (p. 93).

Views such as these, argued with the rhetorical powers of a highly skilled polemicist, were hardly to the liking of many of the Presbyterian and Independent voices in the Rump Parliament. Charles II's sympathizers could not help but be encouraged by the very public dissent that raged inside and out of Parliament and within the army. As recounted later in his *L'Estrange, His Apology, with a short view of some late remarkable transactions leading up to the happy settlement of these nations* (1660), Roger L'Estrange (1616–1704) and other Royalists helped to stir up the London apprentices to guard the city against the army and then encouraged the unpaid soldiers to unite with them. There were so many broadsides, petitions, and pamphlets being distributed in the London streets by mercury women and hawkers on the eve of Monck's entering the city that Parliament commanded the Lord Mayor to enforce the 1649 Act that 'no hawkers and dispersers of scandalous books and papers shall be permitted'.[18] As during the height of the war years, authorities were

---

[17] Milton, *Considerations touching the likeliest means*, 133.
[18] Quoted in Kitchin, *Sir Roger L'Estrange*, 54.

completely unable to control these publications, which were avidly collected by readers (see *MV* 1.II; *CV* 1.III).

The secret Royalist society the Sealed Knot revived, and other Royalist sympathizers also began organizing, for action as well as rhetoric, to try to bring the King back in. As with the members of Parliament and the army, there was dissent among the different groups following the King. This can perhaps be seen in part as based on the tensions between the older generation of cavaliers, who had seen their estates ruined and who had lived in penury on the Continent for many years, and the younger generation, ready for action and gallantry and perhaps revenge. In England, Royalist sympathizers began to organize a large-scale uprising across the country. In June 1659, the physician poet William Chamberlayne (*c.*1619–89) published his heroic verse epic *Pharonnida*, and in July he was directly involved in a plot to raise troops in his native Dorsetshire to support the return of the King; although the plot was betrayed to the government by informers, Sir George Booth did manage to raise an army of 6,000 and occupied Cheshire before being captured. *Pharonnida*, described by the poet and critic Robert Southey, who is representative of the nineteenth-century view of the text, as 'one of the most interesting stories ever told in verse',[19] is on one level a conventional Heliodoran romance following the trials and separations of two Greek lovers. Argalia (the long-lost prince of Aetolia) and Pharonnida, the princess of Morea, fall in love at first sight only to have Pharonnida repeatedly abducted by the malignant Almanzor, leader of the discontented rabble of the kingdom and later a bandit chief. Through five books of five cantos each, the lovers overcome being captured by Turks, mock trials where they are sentenced to death, being buried alive with a corpse, and other romance perils. It concludes with the reinstatement of Argalia to his rightful kingdom, and, through his marriage to Pharonnida, the uniting of the three crowns of Sicily (representing England, Scotland, and Ireland) under one rule.

However, in addition to Chamberlayne's attention to the conventions of heroic romance, according to the publication notice printed in the newsbook *Mercurius Politicus*, the text is 'An Heroic Poem relating to the past and present time'.[20] As Chamberlayne relates, he had begun the work before the outbreak of the Civil War and had taken the manuscript with him when he joined the King's army and fought at Newbury; interwoven in book II, cantos ii and iii, with the exploits of the princely hero Argalia are Chamberlayne's descriptions of the gathering of Charles's forces and the disordered countryside through which they marched and fought. At the end of book II, canto v, the poet speaks of his own adventures:

> I must
> Let my Pen rest awhile, and see the rust
> Scour'd from my own Sword,[21]

---

[19] Quoted in Parsons, 'A Forgotten Poet', 304.   [20] *Mercurius Politicus*, 9–16 June 1659.
[21] Chamberlayne, *Pharonnida*, bk II, canto v, p. 171.

the poet informs his readers,

> for a fatal day
> Draws on those gloomy hours, whose short steps may
> In *Britains* blushing Chronicle write more
> Of sanguine Guilt then a whole Age before, (bk II, canto v, p. 171)

which is glossed in the margin as referring to the second battle of Newbury. However, he promises that

> if in
> This rising storm of blood which doth begin
> To drop already, I'me not washt into
> The Grave, my next safe Quarter shall renew
> Acquaintance with *Pharonnida*, till then,
> I leave the Muses to converse with men. (bk II, canto v, p. 171)

With its passages directly relating to the Civil War, the casting of the villain as a feigned champion of 'an overtaxed and oppressed people' who uses them to further his own ambitions, and the prophecy that three kingdoms should be united under one ruler, the romance published by the young bookseller Robert Clavell on the eve of the return of Charles II was a perfect fusion of literary heroics and royalist fervour.

In November 1659, Evelyn published his *An Apology for the Royal Party: Written in a Letter to a Person of the Late Councel of State.* It was 'my bold *Apologie* for the *King*', he recorded in his diary, 'in this time of danger, when it was capital to speake or write in favour of him' (Evelyn, *Diary*, 3. 235). Styling himself on the title page as 'a lover of Peace and of his Country', Evelyn characterizes the Interregnum years as marked by 'ignorant and furious zeal', and that 'this pretence of a universal perfection Religion and the Secular' had been achieved with 'this *Hydra* of Impostures with a mask of Piety and Reformation', leaving England in such a state of confusion and poverty that foreigners 'stand amazed at our *Buffoonery* and madnesse'.[22]

Opening with a lively attack on the current regime, the nameless writer exclaims, 'what a condition you have already reduced this once flourishing Kingdome, since all has been your own' (p. 4). As to their claims to be Puritan reformers, 'there were ever heard of so many *Schismes*, and *Heresies*, of *Jews* and *Socinians*, *Quakers*, *Fifth-Monarchy-men*, *Arians*, *Anabaptists*, *Independents*, and a thousand severall sorts of Blasphemies and professed Atheists, all of them spawned under your government; and then tell me what a Reformation of Religion you have effected!' Speaking of himself as 'being neither a *Courtier*, *Souldier* or *Church-man*, but a plain Country Gentleman, engag'd on neither side' (p. 12), Evelyn concludes by defending the exiled Charles from charges that 'he has lived amongst Papists, is viciously inclin'd,

---

[22] Evelyn, *An Apology*, 2, 8, 12.

and has wicked men about him', retorting 'for his Vertues and Morality, I invoke the most refined family in this Nation, to produce me a Relation of more piety and moderation' (p. 10). Indeed, Evelyn challenges the Council of State to 'shew me a Fraternity more spotless in their honour, and freer from the exorbitances of youth, then these three Brothers [Charles, James, and Henry], so conspicuous to all the world for their Temperance, Magnanimity, Constancy, and Understanding' (p. 10). Two printings were done of the pamphlet, which indicated to him that 'so universaly it tooke' (Evelyn, *Diary*, 3. 235). In December, Evelyn's diary records his continued work for the return of the King, although still in fear of reprisals: on meeting with the Lieutenant of the Tower, Colonel Morley, to discuss the ways in which the King might come back, he records that it was 'to the greate hazard of my life; but the Colonel had ben my Schole-fellow & I knew would not betray me' (Evelyn, *Diary*, 3. 237–8).

In Scotland, General Monck began a march to London on 1 January 1660 to support a growing demand for a free Parliament. To Royalists on the Continent, this seemed like a breach in the opposition against them. Because of the diffi-culty in obtaining news for those in exile, there were many doubts as to what it might signify. 'Monck is so dark a man', wrote John Mordaunt (1626–75) to the widowed Queen Henrietta Maria in Paris, 'no perspective can looke through him... it will be like the last scean of some excellent play, which the most judicious cannot positively say how it will end'.[23] London taxpayers revolted and refused to support the old Rump Parliament or the Committee of Safety, and, by the time Monck arrived in London in February 1660, confusion reigned on multiple fronts. A broadside published in 1659 attributed to Sir John Denham (1614/15–69) captured the feelings of Royalist supporters at Monck's arrival and the possibilities it raised. 'If *England's* bleeding Story may transmit | One Renown'd Name to Time, Yours must be it', the piece opens, asserting that through his negotiations rather than force of arms 'THOU SAV'ST THREE SHATTER'D KINGDOMS gasping Life'.[24]

In effect, there were almost too many possibilities present in the air and in the pamphlets of the day for competing types of authority and rule. In his diary begun in January of 1660, the Londoner Samuel Pepys (1633–1703) records he heard an 'exceeding good argument' at the coffee house on James Harrington's theories of government. Pepys noted in his newly started diary on 2 March 1660 that 'great is the talk of a single person, and that it would now be Charles, George [Monck], or Richard again' (Pepys, *Diary*, 1. 74). The nature of the talk in town was quickly changing, however, and Pepys noted a few days later that 'everybody now drinks the King's health without any fear, whereas before it was very private that a man dare do it' (Pepys, *Diary*, 1. 79).

Certainly the plays that were printed in London in 1659 (although still not permitted legally to be staged publicly), in their titles, advertisements, and

---

[23] Quoted in Smith, *The Cavaliers in Exile*, 166.
[24] Denham, *A panegyrick on His Excellency the Lord General George Monck*, 1.

nostalgic recollections of previous performances, suggest that the time was ripe for a consideration of the pleasures and entertainments of previous times. The preface to a translation of Aristophanes' *Plutus* by 'H.H.B'. defends its publication by declaring that 'some dare affirm that Comedies may teach | More in one hour that some in ten can preach'. Lodowick Carlell's [Carlile] (1601/2–75) *The Deserving Favorite* included as part of the advertising allure on its title page that 'it was presented before the KING and QUEENES Majesties at *White-hall*, and very often at the Private house in *Black-Friers*, with great Applause'. The piece is dedicated to Thomas Cary, the son of the Earl of Monmouth, and Mr William Murrey, of whom it is pointed out that they are 'both of the Bed-chamber to his MAJESTY' Carlell underscores the royal connections of the play, pointing out its origins as 'not design'd to travel so farre as the common Stage', and the publisher, Humphrey Moseley, also establishes the author's courtier rather than commercial concerns for his 'fair Courtly Piece', which was 'drawn to th'*Presse*, not for a golden fleece' but supposedly barely with the author's knowledge.

Other titles in bookshops reintroduced readers to the name and image of both Charles I and Charles II. Lambert van den Bos (Lambert Wood) published a sizeable biography entitled *The Life and Raigne of King Charles, from his birth to his death. Faithfully and impartially performed by Lambert Wood Gent* (1659). Short pamphlets such as *Bradshaw's Ghost: being a dialogue between said ghost and an apparition of the late King Charles* (1659) imagined the regicide and the deposed monarch discussing the contemporary situation with a decidedly Royalist slant. Broadsides were printed and posted such as the *Declaration of the Peaceable Royallists* (1659) urging moderation and a return to times of peace and prosperity. Even reprints of former editions of popular poets emphasized their connections with the departed sovereign: William Drummond's poems were reissued in 1659 with the assertion that this gentleman's works were a favourite of Charles I, as well as of all readers of wit and taste.

The year 1659 also saw the posthumous publication of the three volumes of verse by writers closely associated with the late King and with the Royalist cause: Richard Lovelace's *Lucasta*, which was initially published in 1649, was reissued as *Lucasta. Posthume Poems*, Sir John Suckling's *Last Remains*, and E. Williamson's edition of *John Cleveland Revived*. Dated 1659 and entered into the Stationers' Register on 14 November, Lovelace's remaining poems were published in 1660, joined with a collection of elegies by his brother Dudley and by his friends Sir Charles Cotton and James Howell. Although his elegists point directly to his involvement with the war, the poems in this volume do not deal directly with the events of being imprisoned or of leaving one's loved ones to fight. Instead, they recall the gentle pastoral eroticism of the younger man in short pieces such as 'Love made in the first Age':

> No Serpent kiss poyson'd the Tast,
> Each touch was naturally Chast,

> And their mere Sense a Miracle.
> Naked as their own innocence,
> And unimbroyder'd from Offence
> They went, above, poor Riches, gay.[25]

Also included are several whimsical animal fables, featuring 'The Falcon', 'The Snayl', and 'The Ant'. In the last, unlike in the later poem to his friend Cotton, 'The Grasshopper', which laments the fate of the feckless creature who failed to prepare for the harsh winter, Lovelace urges the industrious ant to

> Cease large example of wise thrift a while,
> (For thy example is become our Law)
> And teach thy frowns a seasonable smile. (p. 13)

For the readers in 1659 and 1660, the publication of Lovelace's and other cavalier poets' posthumous verses might serve to revive the memory of a past literary culture, re-creating in the volumes former times and manners, and provide an alternative expression from the works produced in the late 1640s and 1650s, absorbed in war and politics.

Cavalier gentlemen were not the only ones for whom the fate of the late King's exiled son and the form of government were topics worth passionately debating. In that same year, Arise Evans (*c.*1607–*c.*1660), the Welsh tailor, prophet, and political commentator, published *A Rule from Heaven* (1659). Although in his earlier 1650s treatises such as *A Voice from Heaven to the Common-Wealth of England* (1652) and *The Bloudy Vision of John Farley* (1653) he had represented himself as a supporter of monarchy and had urged a negotiated peace between Cromwell and Charles II (see *MV* 1.IV), in 1659, he urged his readers to consider the possibility of a totally new system of government, one based on the ability to read. Formerly, 'the Scripture was ingrossed ... in the great mens hands, so that they might do as they pleased with the people that knew little or nothing of Scripture'.[26] Evans believed, because of what he perceived as the spread of literacy and the increase in readers during the 1650s, 'knowledge is increased among the People, and shall increase: So that they will not be ruled by the Kings set up after the manner of the Gentiles any more' (p. 45). Evans then suggests choosing a king out of this new class of readers: the king should be poor but literate, over 50 years of age, who was not worth £5 nor was £5 in debt, but who had at some point been forced to accept alms. This individual, chosen by lot, would become 'king', although the Protector and the Parliament should remain; a king chosen by such means from 'the low and poore', Evans believed, would protect the interests of all his subjects and come closest to the goal of Jesus Christ coming to reign on earth.

The new readers emerging out of the 1650s perhaps did not share Evans's view of their potential to become future kings. Pamphlets offered increasingly

---

[25] Lovelace, *Lucasta. Posthume Poems of Richard Lovelace* (1659), 27
[26] Evans, *A Rule from Heaven*, 50.

bold and open speculations about the possibility of the return of Charles II to reclaim his father's throne. By 1659, opinions that had been uttered privately among friends or had been circulated in manuscript copies begin to appear in print. In February 1660, Evelyn continued publishing his defence of Charles II as the only solution for England's dilemma. To counter this, an anonymous pamphlet edited by Edward Bowles (1613–62), *Newes from Brussels*, purporting to be a letter from a member of Charles's retinue to a Royalist sympathizer in England, suggested that Charles was bent on revenge and retribution if permitted to return to England: 'can't fancy, that our Master can forget he had a Father...A Roundhead is a Roundhead; black and white Devils are alike to us'.[27] Evelyn's response was that the letter was clearly 'forged and fictitious stuff', and the lies penned with 'lascivious, black and sooty quill' would not convince any true Englishman of stains upon the character or motives of 'a Prince as He, together with his Illustrious, Heroick, and high-born Bretheren (all of them...the renown and glory of our Nation)'.

John Milton had one further major publication before the return of the King. Written in the early days of 1660 as Monck approached London, the first edition of *The Readie & Easie Way to Establish a Free Commonwealth* appeared in February and was strongly attacked in March; an expanded edition was issued in April, shortly before the Restoration on 1 May. 'After our liberty and religion thus prosperously fought for, gaind, and many years possessd', Milton argued,

now that nothing remains, but in all reason and the certain hopes of a speedie and immediat settlement forever in a firm and free Commonwealth, for this extolld and magnifi'd nation...to fall back or rather to creep back so poorly as it seems the multitude would to thir once abjur'd and detested thraldom of Kingship...not only argues a strange, degenerated contagion suddenly spread among us, fitted and prepar'd for a new slaverie, but will render us a scorn and derision to all our neighbours.[28]

Disagreeing with Harrington's model of a rotating group of elected officials, Milton proposes a perpetual parliament, 'so thir business is or may be, and oft times urgent; the opportunitie of affairs gaind or lost in a moment'. Milton is uncertain about the use of a partial rotation of members: 'I could wish that this wheel or partial wheel in State, if it be possible, might be avoided; as having too much affinitie with the wheel of fortune' (p. 49).

Having shown how easy and efficient it would be at that time to establish a perpetual parliament, Milton returns to the larger philosophical issues that he foregrounded in his other 1659 pieces: 'the whole freedome of man consists either in spiritual or civil libertie' (p. 89), he begins his concluding sections. 'This liberty of conscience, which above all other things ought to be to all men dearest and most precious, no government more inclinable not to favour only, but to protect, then a free Commonwealth; as being most magnanimous, most

<hr />

[27] Bowles, *Newes from Brussels*, 98.   [28] Milton, *The Readie & Easie Way*, 19.

fearless and confident of its own fair proceedings' (pp. 88–9). Lashing out directly at Charles and his exiled courtiers, Milton expostulates: 'what liberty of conscience can we then expect of others far worse principl'd from the cradle, traind up and governd by *Popish* and *Spanish* counsels, and on such depending hitherto for subsistence?' (p. 90).

Pamphlet attacks both on Milton and on his ideas followed quickly. In the satiric *The Censure of the Rota*, perhaps by Samuel Butler, both Milton and Harrington are under attack, as well as the idea of a Commonwealth in general. Speakers within it urge Milton to cease writing, 'since you have always done it to little or no purpose', even though the labour has 'scribled your eyes out'.[29] Roger L'Estrange published anonymously his *Be Merry and be Wise, Or, a Seasonable Word to the Nation* specifically targeting Milton's pamphlets. L'Estrange, who would be appointed the official licenser of the press in 1664 (see *MV* 2.II), also went directly after Milton and his body of political writings in NO *Blinde Guides, In* ANSWER *To a seditious Pamphlet of* J. MILTON'S, (1660). 'Mr Milton', it opens, 'Although in your Life, and Doctrine, you have Resolved one great Question; by evidencing that Devils may indue Humane shapes; and proving your self, even to your own Wife, an Incubus', the question remains whether Milton is indeed a disciple of the devil himself.[30] Certainly, L'Estrange asserts, there is ample evidence of the association in Milton's writings. 'Was it not You, that scribled a Justification of the Murther of the King,...and made it good too, Thus? That murther was an Action meritorious', L'Estrange charges, and 'not content to see that Sacred Head divided from the Body; your piercing Malice enters into the private Agonies of his struggling Soul; with a Blasphemous Insolence, invading the Prerogative of God himself: (Omniscience)' (p. 1).

Milton clearly was an easy target for satirists. The anonymous *The Character of the Rump* only slightly more moderately calls Milton '[the Rump's] Goosquill Champion', describing him as

an old Heretick both in Religion and Manners, that by his will would shake off his Governours as he does his Wives, four in a Fourt night...I believe that when he is condemned to travel to Tyburn in a Cart, he will petition for the favor to be the first man that ever was driven thither in a *Wheel-barrow*.[31]

Milton was well aware that publishing his opinions bearing his widely recognized signature initials was increasingly dangerous; Milton concluded his April edition of *The Readie & Easie Way to Establish a Free Commonwealth* stating, 'with all hazard I have ventur'd what I thought my duty to speak in season, and to forewarne my countrey in time'.[32] Matching the Quaker prophetess Dorothy White's invocation of Jeremiah, Milton closes with the declaration that, if he

---

[29] Harrington, *The Censure of the Rota upon Mr Miltons Book*, 11–12.

[30] L'Estrange, *no Blinde Guides*, 1.

[31] *The Character of the Rump*, 2–3. [32] Milton, *The Readie & Easie Way*, 2nd edn, 353.

had no hearers but the stones and trees, '"*O earth, earth, earth!*" to tell the very soil it self, what her perverse inhabitants are deaf to', he must do it: even if the monarch is returned, '(which Thou suffer not, who didst create mankinde free; nor Thou next, who didst redeem us from being servants of men!)', he must utter this warning, even if they are 'to be the last words of our expiring libertie' (p. 353).

The same month as *The Readie & Easie Way* was issued in its second edition, Charles II wrote in April 1660 to the House of Commons and issued his Declaration of Breda. With the royal rhetoric of a monarch speaking for all his people, Charles assured the House that 'We look upon you as wise and dispassionate Men and good Patriots, who will raise up those Banks and Fences which have been cast down'; he presents himself as one who had 'made that right Christian Use of our Affliction, and that the Observations and Experience We have had in other Countries hath been such, as that We, and We hope all Our Subjects, shall be the better for what We have seen and suffered'.[33] The Declaration of Breda was likewise a triumph of rhetorical tactics, offering a free and full pardon to all who applied within forty days, with the exceptions to be decided by Parliament. No properties would be confiscated in retribution. Monck's army and its officers would be paid their arrears in salary. Charles promised in contrast to the existing 'Uncharitableness of the Times', a 'Liberty to tender Consciences' in matters of religion.[34] Charles's letter and the Declaration were printed and also read aloud on 1 May, a traditional day of festivities, which (along with Christmas) Parliament had previously attempted to suppress: Parliament passed an official resolution inviting Charles to return to the throne without a single condition being stated.

Celebrations began both in England and in Europe before Charles's physical return (see CV 2.I). Poets found more than ample material for their pens and eager readers. Broadsides blossomed announcing 'ENGLANDS JOY For the Coming in of our Gratious Soveraign King CHARLES the II', predicting that

> The Parliament will rise no more in armes
> To fight against their lawfull King,
> Nor be deluded by their factious charms.[35]

Published by Henry Brome (d. 1681), who had printed L'Estrange's pamphlets during the crisis months, *Englands Joy* announces happily that social order and domestic hierarchy will also return with the monarch:

> The Coblers shall not edifie their Tubbs,
> Nor in Divinity set stitches,
> Wee'l not b'instructed by Mechanick scrubs,
> Women shan't preach with men for breeches.

---

[33] Charles II, *King Charles II. his declaration to all his loving subjects*.
[34] *A Common-Councell holden the first day of May 1660*, 11–12.
[35] *England's Joy* (1660).

Katherine Philips (1632–64), writing in Wales, marvelled at the large number of people who travelled to Holland to welcome the exiled monarch and escort him home, and urged Charles's speedy return lest 'As we unmonarch'd were for want of thee | So till thou comest we shall unpeopled be'.[36] Ann Fanshawe and her family were among the crowds who joined the court in The Hague and sailed back to England. Her husband had been rewarded for his services and was now Sir Richard Fanshawe. 'Who can sufficiently express the joy and gallantry of that voyage', she wrote to her son, 'to see so many great ships, the best in the world; to hear the trumpets and all other musick, to see near an hundred brace ships saile before the wind with their wast clothes and streamers...but above all, the glorious Majesties of the King and his 2 brothers was so beyond man's expectation and expression'.[37] Also in this crowd were Roger Palmer and his recent bride, Barbara, the future principal royal mistress of Charles II, who would be rewarded with the title of Duchess of Castlemaine and become the object of Samuel Pepys's and many others' fascinated attention and dismay (see *MV* 2.IV).

In England, the Speaker of the House observed that 'Our Bells and our Bonfires have already began the Proclamation of his Majesty's Goodness and of our Joys'.[38] In The Hague, some 50,000 people came to watch Charles's departure on an English ship formerly named the *Naseby* (the site of the Parliamentary force's defeat of his father), now newly christened the *Royal Charles*. Pepys recorded on 23 May how Charles and his brother the Duke of York amused themselves after dining by altering the names of the other ships accompanying the royal party, transforming the limbs of power of the Protector into those of the King, making the *Richard* (Cromwell) into the *James* (Duke of York) and transforming the *Speaker* (of the House of Commons) into *Mary* (Princess of Orange).

From the very beginning of the process of the restoration of the monarchy, this 'publication' of royal authority in a myriad of media, with its careful attention to both the language and the symbols of power would infuse the perception of these momentous events by Charles's subjects (see *CV* 2.I).

> Go, wondrous Prince, adorn that Throne
> Which Birth and Merit make your own.
> And in your Mercy brighter shine
> Then in the Glories of your Line; Find Love at home and abroad Fear
> And Veneration everywhere,[39]

wrote Katherine Philips in her poem '*Arion* to a Dolphin, On his Majesty's in this passage into *England*'. The hastily printed broadside *Caledons Gratulatory Rapture* reminds readers of the phoenix arising from the ashes:

---

[36] Philips, *Poems by the most deservedly admired Mrs Katherine Philips*, 2, 'On the numerous Access of the English to wait upon the King in *Flanders*'.

[37] Halkett, *Memoirs*, 140–1.   [38] Fraser, *Royal Charles*, 174.

[39] Philips, *Poems by the most deservedly admired Mrs Katherine Philips*, 3.

> With what transcending glory doth he rise,
> To clear the shads of our long dark'ned skies;
> The Thron's repaired, Majesty restor'd,
> The Regal Race return'd, admir'd, ador'd!

On 29 May 1660, his thirtieth birthday, Charles II took the part of the leading actor in a magnificently staged, triumphant return to London. Riding bareheaded and flanked by his two brothers, all wearing doublets of silver, Charles met the Lord Mayor at Deptford, rode through Southwark, and then crossed London Bridge. His entrance was a clear signal that he did not come as broken exile: he was attended by some 300 gentlemen also in silver and their equal number garbed in velvet, all accompanied by servants and footmen wearing splendid liveries. His troops were likewise wearing uniforms with silver cloth and silver lace. Some 20,000 people stood to cheer as he rode through the city; John Evelyn recorded in his diary that 'I stood in the strand & beheld it, & blessed God' (Evelyn, *Diary*, 3. 246). So great was the crowd that Charles did not reach Whitehall until that evening. The only competition to this royal spectacle would be Charles's coronation in 1661, which likewise invoked as many as possible images of historical authority and legitimacy (see CV 2.I).

Gilbert Burnet (1643–1715), writing in hindsight in 1683 in a manuscript he called 'Original Memoirs' or the 'Secret History' of his times, observed that, with the return of the King, 'a spirit of extravagant joy overspread the nation, which was soon attended with all manner of profaneness and immorality' (Burnet, *History*, 1.157). On 29 August 1660, the Act of Indemnity and Oblivion was passed granting amnesty to all, except for fifty individuals, including the thirteen regicides or signers of Charles I's death warrant, and Sir Henry Vane, who had vigorously opposed the Restoration. In December, Pepys recorded uneasily that

the Parliament voted that the bodies of Oliver, Ireton, Bradshaw, and [Pride] should be taken up out of their graves in the abbey, and drawn to the gallows, and there hanged and buried under it. Which (methinks) doth trouble me that a man of so great courage as he was, should have that dishonour, though otherwise he might deserve it enough. (Pepys, *Diary*, 1. 309)

Persons of lesser fame and stature would also experience official censorship of their reading, writing, and public speech with the return of the monarch and the Church of England, in spite of the assertions promising mildness and toleration. Although the Declaration of Breda had offered 'gentleness' concerning different religious practices, in truth most of the existing laws regarding group assemblies actively conflicted with the practices followed by religious groups such as the Baptists and the Quakers. Many of the key texts for such groups, like those by defeated Royalists a generation earlier, would be written in prison over the next three decades.

To many writers on religious matters, the Restoration meant a return to active persecution for activities that had flourished in the 1650s. John Bunyan

(1628–88), who would later write *Pilgrim's Progress* while in prison for preaching illegally, was first arrested in November 1660 under the old Elizabethan conventicle law against illegal assembly. In a manuscript epistle to his followers in Bedford, he recounts his arrest and examination. The justice, Mr Francis Wingate, hearing that Bunyan would be conducting a meeting in Harlington, caused the house to be kept under watch, 'as if we that was to meet together in that place did intend to do some fearful business, to the destruction of the country'.[40] Although he had been warned in advance, Bunyan decided to hold the meeting regardless, for, 'if I should fly, it might be a discouragement to the whole body that might follow after' (p. 109).

Bunyan recorded the subsequent examination by the Clerk of the Peace in the form of a polite dialogue, where an increasingly exasperated authority figure was pleasantly met by Bunyan's resolute faith in his calling. The Clerk began by explaining that 'it is desired, you would submit yourself to the laws of the land, or else at the next sessions it will go worse with you, even to be sent away out of the nation', to which Bunyan mildly replied, 'I did desire to demean myself in the world, both as becometh a man and a Christian'. But, to the Clerk's request that he not hold public assemblies but instead 'do as much good as you can, in a neighborly way, without having such meetings?', Bunyan voiced the response which would cause so many of his fellow lay preachers to spend much of the 1660s in prison: 'every man that hath received a gift from God, he may dispense it, that others may be comforted; and when he that done, he may hear, and learn, and be comforted himself of others' (p. 126). For Bunyan and other sectarians, not to preach, not to share their religious experiences and convictions, was a crime against the Gospel and far more serious than transgressing any man-made statute. As a result, the 1660s would be rich in the writings of men and women determined to share their gift of the light in spiritual autobiographies, exemplary lives, tales of imprisonment and trials, as well as books of prophecy and of poetry.

In contrast, Charles II rewarded many of those who had followed him into exile and who had served the Royalist cause in England during the Interregnum. As we have seen, literary and political lives continued to be deeply intertwined, not only in terms of poets celebrating the return of Charles but also as members of the new government and City of London. It is easy to forget that the writers we variously regard primarily as poets and dramatists were viewed otherwise by their contemporaries. They were producing during this time not only texts and reports, but also roads and buildings to mark the restoration of the old order. Sir John Denham, author of *Cooper's Hill* (1642), was appointed in 1660 to replace Inigo Jones as His Majesty's Surveyor of Works; he would divide his time in the 1660s between preparing his *Poems and Translations* for press in 1668 and improving the pavements in London. Sir Robert Howard (1626–98), whose volume *Poems* was published in 1660, was also that year

---

[40] Bunyan, *A Relation of My Imprisonment*, 109.

commissioned as colonel of an infantry regiment in Hampshire; in 1661, the year before he was appointed as a commissioner for reforming the streets and buildings of London, he would with Thomas Killigrew (1612–83) receive permission to build the new Theatre Royal in Bridges Street.

The young John Wilmot, 2nd Earl of Rochester (1647–80), was at Oxford, but he would reap the benefits of his father's loyalty when Charles II summoned him to court. Others actively used the occasion of Charles's return to create poems in celebration. Rachel Jevon (bap. 1627–?) produced two poems, one in Latin and one in English, *Exultationis Carmen*, whose title page announces was 'presented with her own Hand' and which some critics believe was the first step in petitioning for a position in the court.[41] She describes herself as 'the Unworthiest of His MAJESTIES HAND-MAIDS', but nevertheless establishes clearly her command of Latin as well as the panegyric form. His subjects, she declares, have 'hearts subdu'd by Love, not by the Sword', and even the sea plays its part, 'proud to bring | Three widdow'd Kingdoms their espoused King!'

Surely few could have been more pleased by the re-establishment of the royal court than the theatre managers, actors, and playwrights. In the late summer of 1660, two patents for theatres would be granted by Charles. The first warrant to form an acting company issued in July would go to Thomas Killigrew. Ten days later, William Davenant, resurrecting a warrant granted in 1630 by Charles I to build a theatre, resubmitted it, asking in addition that he and Killigrew be granted a monopoly. By August, both men were assembling their companies out of the existing illegal groups who had been performing unauthorized entertainments: the 'old Actors' who performed at the frequently raided Red Bull, a younger company headed by John Rhodes at the Cockpit in Drury Lane, and William Beeston's group at Salisbury Court (see CV 1.IV). Pepys records in his diary that, on 8 October 1660, a troupe he called 'His Majesty's Comedians' performed Shakespeare's *Othello* at the old Cockpit theatre; the performance, which Pepys pronounced 'well done', included the talents of Davenant's future leading male actor, Thomas Betterton. After strenuous efforts on the part of Killigrew and Davenant to suppress the independent acting groups and force them to join their monopoly, on 5 November 1660 two companies headed by Killigrew and Davenant were officially formed, with the King offering patronage to Killigrew's troupe and his brother James, Duke of York, the patronage of Davenant's.

Having secured their actors, the managers found their next problem became performance space and plays. Both initially used former indoor tennis courts: Killigrew's was in Lincoln's Inn Fields and Davenant's at Salisbury Court in Whitefriars. Killigrew successfully argued that his company was a continuation of the pre-war company the King's Men and thus initially had retained the right to perform all existing plays, including those by Davenant himself. Davenant countered, and in December 1660 the Lord Chamberlain restored to

---

[41] See Hobby, *Virtue of Necessity*, 18–19, 210.

him his own works, as well as a considerable number of Shakespeare's plays, including *The Tempest, Romeo and Juliet, King Lear, Macbeth, Hamlet, Twelfth Night,* and *Henry VIII.* As part of his grant, however, Davenant was required to 'reform' or modernize all the plays except his own, resulting in the seemingly odd enthusiasm for altering Shakespeare's plays during the Restoration.[42]

While the first public performance by the new theatre companies was not until 1661, that is not to say that there were no theatrical performances in London and elsewhere. General Monck had been feted by the London guild of Vintners with *Bacchus Festival, or, a New Medley A* Musical Representation *at the Entertainment of his excellency the Lord General Monck At Vinters-Hall, April 12. 1660,* published as a broadside after its performance. It starred Bacchus, the god of wine, accompanied by a Frenchman, a Spaniard, a German, and a Greek, all praising the virtues of their national wines. This pageant piece was by Thomas Jordan (*c.*1614–85), one-time boy actor in the King's Revels Company in the 1630s, and in the 1640s a playwright and prolific poet who collected Royalist verses, which he subsequently published in 1685 as *A Choice collection of 180 Loyal Songs.* Although the entertainment is a celebration of Monck's entrance into the city, it also expresses the political desires of many of the merchants in the audience: 'Since thou brave *George* hast us redeem'd from sleepie slavery', it opens,

> you have our Laws,
> our Faith, our Cause
> Restor'd to happiness.
> There yet remains behind one truly grateful thing,
> which is that you
> give *Cesar* h's due,
> And help us to our King.[43]

Also initially privately performed, John Tatham's (fl. 1632–64) satiric comedy *The Rump, Or, the Mirrour of the late Times* (1660) highlights the ways in which by 1660, even before the actual return of Charles II, London audiences were willing to enjoy the spectacle of ambitious politicians and their wives being reduced to their original 'tradesmen' origins. The Puritan characters are represented as being relentlessly secular and driven simply by the desire for power and social position. Tatham, who since 1657 had been employed annually providing spectacular 'pageants' to be performed for the Lord Mayor of London celebrating the commercial successes of the city, turned his pen to topical characters and offered viewers a chance to laugh at the figures who had once seemed poised to take over leadership of the nation. It was performed in February or March 1660 while General Monck was in control of the city and before the return of the King; its title page declares that it was 'Acted Many

---

[42] See Hume, *The Development of English Drama*, 20, and Freehafer, 'The Formation of the London Patent Companies'.   [43] Jordan, *Bacchus Festival* (1660).

Times with Great Applause at the Private House in *Dorset*-Court', which scholars have identified as being the old Salisbury Court theatre, then restored to use by the actor William Beeston.[44] The play was restaged in June after Charles's return; in July of the same year, the City of London staged Tatham's celebration of monarchy with the pageant *Londons Glory Represented by Time, Truth, and Fame.*

The Rump opens with several soldiers celebrating their successful seizure of control of the City of London and how they will advance themselves as a result. The chief villains, Bertlam and Lockwhite (Major General John Lambert and the lawyer and politician Bulstrode Whitelocke), are likewise scheming to become the new Lord Protector, having successfully ousted Richard Cromwell. Their earlier oaths of allegiance to Oliver Cromwell do not disturb these plans, Lockwhite cynically observing:

What though I took the Oath of Allegiance as Oliver, your Lordship and others did, (without the which I could not have sat there?) yet it Conducing not to Our Advantage, It was an ill Oath, better broke then kept, and so are all Oaths in the stricter sense.... Oaths, what are they, but Bubbles, that break with their own Emptiness.[45]

'My Lord', he concludes, 'take it from me, He that will live in this world, must be endowed with these three rare Qualities; Dissimulation, Equivocation, and Mental reservation' (I. iii, pp. 8–9).

As the men scheme for political power, the women in the play manœuvre for the trappings of social status. Lady Bertlam, confident her husband will be named Lord Protector, instructs her maid to stop calling her 'Madam' and say instead 'your Highness', and makes it a point to scorn the supposedly common-born widow Madam Cromwell, who has fallen on hard times. Scolding like a Jacobean shrew, Mrs Cromwell loudly makes her own points about the world's ingratitude: 'Highness in the Divels Name, it is not come to that sure yet, is it? hah! Thy Husband may be hang'd first like a Crafty knave as he is', replies the older woman, 'Did my Husband make him a Lord for this? to Ruine our Family?' (II. i, p. 18). There are jokes about the ways in which Lady Bertlam assisted in her husband's advancement during the previous reign (Lambert's wife Frances was a noted favourite of Oliver Cromwell's) and how, at the end of the play, 'Gamer' Cromwell (Elizabeth Cromwell had been styled 'the Lady Protectoress' during her husband's reign and 'her Highness dowager' after his death) and the other scheming politicians are reduced to being street peddlers, selling pens and ink, kitchen stuffs, lemons, limes, and shoe repairs after the noble general (Monck) arrives.

Upon Charles II's return, there is also evidence that he was entertained by private pageants and musical entertainments similar to the ones performed for Monck. William Cavendish, Duke of Newcastle (bap. 1593–1676), had returned

---

[44] See Freehafer, 'The Formation of the London Patent Companies'.
[45] Tatham, *The Rump*, I. iii, pp. 8–9.

from exile in Antwerp with the King (see CV 1.I). A manuscript exists of his 'The King's Entertainment',[46] a 'show' intended to be performed in Newcastle's private home, probably at Dorset House, for the King's pleasure, similar to one Newcastle had staged in his home in Antwerp in 1658 where the King's triumphant return to the throne had been predicted.[47] The entertainment would have required a small number of musicians, singers, and dancers as well as actors to speak the parts, but little staging.

Its plot is simple—on hearing that the King will grace his house once more, the 'Poet' suffers an extreme form of writer's block, 'a deepe dispaire, a cold palsey, seasing his Tongue to dumbness, his parelitick hands so weake as not to hold a pen'.[48] The doctor is summoned and suggests various applications of former writers, first classical, then contemporary, to ease the disease: 'What say you to a cordial of Horace, lapt up in a fine Odes?', he enquires of the anxious waiting gentleman. 'They will not worke not, in these days Doctor', he replies sadly. To the suggestion that a dose of Ovid might help, the objection is that 'from then he will be metamorphosing himself into Trees, Beasts, and Birds, and they will make him much'. Shakespeare is suggested and rejected, and 'Ben: Jonson plaster-wise in this Neck and pills of him a little gilded over' likewise fails to take (p. 389). In the following scene, a Welshman comes to address the King directly in a comic Welsh dialect, congratulating the King for overcoming 'the uglie Treasons and rebellions in the Orlde [world], These filthy Rebells they did thrive, and grow fatt, looke you, of Treasons and Rebellions'. The third scene features a 'rogue' fiddler and the fourth 'excellent dancers, apparil'd in strange formes and as strange postures in their Dances, wth as strange Tunes', followed by a 'running banquet', after which the King may himself dance 'again with the Ladys and when his Majesty is weary & would repose', the stage directions state, 'comes in the sick Poet again in his Chaire with the Gentleman & the Doctor' to conclude the event (p. 390).

The cure is found, once they remember that 'the Braine, Doctor, is like a cleane sheet of paper, and it can be but full, and when it is full of all these Authors, he hath rather memory then Witt . . . and being so full of other Mens witts, hee hath no roome for his owne'. A 'Moore' enters along with a musician in 'Indian Cotes', singing plaintively for the poet's recovery. The music succeeds, but, as the restored Poet announces,

> The influence thus by your Sight
> Hath wraught this miracle to Night
> It is the Kinge who heales by Touch
> And now by sight has done as much.

The Moor closes the entertainment with the song, 'What Joyes can wee expect, nothing | Like to the presence of our King' (p. 395).

---

[46] MS PwV23 Portland Papers, University of Nottingham.
[47] See Hulse, ' "The King's Entertainment" '.
[48] Hulse, ' "The King's Entertainment" ', 387.

This taste for heroic, beleaguered aristocrats overcoming villains and adversity appears to have been equally entertaining for average English readers, continuing the increasing popularity of fiction writing that had expanded in the 1650s (see *MV* 1.V). Both before and after the spectacular return of Charles and his courtiers, English readers were buying translations of French and Italian romances with their accounts of nobles and princes facing dangerous situations and their chivalric behaviour during times of hardship. In 1659, as Parliamentary debates raged and a real army marched on London, English writers were also experimenting with the genre, including using the expensive folio as well as other formats. Gaultier de La Calprenede's enormous Cleopatra series *Hymen's Praeludia: Or, Loves Master-piece* was published by Humphrey Moseley (see *MV* 1.III) in eight separate quarto volumes during 1659–60; the fourth part of Madame de Scudéry's *Clelia*, which started appearing in 1653, became available in 1660, and Vaumoriere's *The Grand Scipio* in a handsome folio was dedicated by G.H. to the Right Honourable Lady Mary Cary. Girolamo Brusoni's *Arnaldo, or the Injur'd Lover* was also available in translation. All such works offered English readers insights into the romantic lives of high-born aristocrats in foreign places, with an enormous cast of characters and multiple storylines to follow from volume to volume.

In emulation of these foreign models in 1660 in Edinburgh, the future King's Advocate in Scotland Sir George Mackenzie (1636/8–91) published his youthful attempt at the genre, *Aretina; or, The Serious Romance*. Like Chamberlayne's *Pharonnida*, it is a romance heavily marked by political allegory and the events of the Civil War. Having spent the final years of the Interregnum studying law in France and the Netherlands, and apparently creating his political romance, he returned to Scotland in 1658 and petitioned in 1659 to become a member of the Faculty of Advocates in Edinburgh. *Aretina*, which consists of four parts, distinguishes itself on its title page with its claim to be a 'serious' romance and that it was 'written originally in English', rather than being a translation.

Dedicated to 'All the LADIES of this NATION', the work is compared by Mackenzie to a premature infant, unlikely to survive without assistance. 'Yet if it be admitted to suck the breasts of your favour, it may possibly prove strong enough (shielded by your affection) to graple with malice, and all other opposition', he suggests,[49] and, by seeking the patronage of all women rather than a single male patron, he acknowledges that 'we may conclude that there is something in you, which nothing in man (who seigneurises over all other creatures, and who can pretend to nothing stronger then courage and reason) can ever equal' (p. 4). In the preface, 'An Apologie for ROMANCES', he begins by noting that 'IT hath been rather the fate, then merit of Romances in all ages, to be asperst with these vices, whereof they were not only innocent, but to whose ante-doting vertues they might justly pretend' (p. 5). Rejecting the claims that romances promote real lust, that reading them wastes time, and that their

---

[49] Mackenzie, *Aretina*, 3.

contents are 'lies' because fiction, Mackenzie declares 'who should blush to trace in these paths, which the famous *Sidney, Scuderie, Barkly*, and *Broghill* hath beaten for them, besides the thousands of Ancients' (p. 6). In fact, 'where Romances are written by excellent wits, and perused by intelligent Readers... the judgement may pick more sound information from them, then from History, for the one teacheth us onely what was done, and the other what should be done' (pp. 6–7). Because romances are entertaining, 'lazy Ladies and luxurious Gallants, are allured to spend in their Chambers some hours, which else, the one would consecrate to the Bed, and the other to the Bordell[o]'. Especially during this time, 'wherein the appétit of mens judgements is become so queasie, that it can relish nothing that is not either vinegared with Satyres, or sugared with Eloquence', romances are the ideal means to bring about the improvement of both sexes of readers (pp. 9–10).

The plot of *Aretina* ('the virtuous') includes the obligatory elements of romance fictions, including pirates, hermits in caves, ladies in distress, long-lost princes, various battle scenes, and monsters to be overcome. It is set in a mythical Egypt, but the court is that of Charles I; book III is mainly concerned with the English Civil War. As Mackenzie noted in his preface, readers should be prepared to read allegorically: 'albeit they seem but fables, yet who would unkernel them, would finde budled up in them reall truthes; and as naturalists observe, these kernels are best where the shells are hardest; and these mettals are noblest, which are mudded over with most earth' ('Preface'). Equally intriguing is his reversal of the conventions of the genre: the male characters, as critics have observed, are driven by their passions, but the heroines are coolly sensible and governed by reason.[50]

Rulers lose power in this story when they have evil counsellors, but also because they show too much mercy to their enemies. These male rulers are overwhelmed by their own passions such as melancholy, which makes them incapable of acting, whether to rescue those they witness in distress or to con-trol their kingdom. Monanthropus, formerly the Chancellor of Egypt, has been forced from office: 'melancholy having lodged it self in the generous breast...did, by the chain of its Charms, so fetter the feet of Reason, that nothing pleased him now but that whereby he might please his passion' (p. 1). Corrupt priests, Malchus, and his self-selected successor, a foreigner named Sophander, take over the chancellor's role, and Malchus 'did by the hand of his pleasure sway the Sceptor of Soveraignity, his fancy being the sole and supream Judge' (p. 32). Two young knights errant—princes in disguise—encounter Monanthropus, and part of book III is devoted to their discussions of the downfall of a neighbouring kingdom Lacedemonian (England)—namely, 'the nimious [extravagant] clemency of the Prince', who wants to reign by 'the scep-ter of love', but who proves to be 'swayed by the hand of a popular affection, which was as volatile as themselves; and by it he was rather their slave, than

---

[50] See Beesemyer, 'Sir George Mackenzie's *Aretina*'.

their Prince' (pp. 245–6). Anaxagius, the King, is betrayed by his own servants and, in fear for his life, is forced to flee the city in a scene that clearly recalls Charles I's flight from London to Oxford in 1642. As critics have noted (even as they are despairing over the unreadability of *Aretina*), it is unique in its attention to the role of the Scots aristocracy in Charles I's court and their part in the politics leading into the Civil War, with the figures of Montrose, Argyll, and the Hamiltons becoming the leaders of various 'tribes' in the nation of 'Athens', tribes whose loyalties always were to their chieftains rather than the King.

Other works of fiction published that year also make direct references to the transition from Commonwealth back to monarchy and its effect on the people and their entertainments. *Don Juan Lamberto: Or, a Comical History of the Late Times by Montelion, Knight of the Oracle* (1660) is often attributed to the miniature painter and poet Thomas Flatman (1635–88) (see *MV* 3.I). It is a satire parodying romance conventions (see *CV* 2.IV) and was used to mock the generals after Cromwell's death restoring Charles to the throne. With its text printed in old-fashioned black letter and its chapter titles in italics, the text leaves the reader in little doubt who the heroes, villains, and clowns are. Opening with 'How *Cromwell* Soldan [sultan] of *Brittaine* dy'd, and what befell his Son the *Meek Knight*' (ch. I), the tale moves briskly to Richard Cromwell's departure from the Protectorate as prompted by the army: 'How the Knight of the *Golden Tulip*, and the Knight of *the mysterious Allegories* came to the Castle of Sir *Fleetwood* the contemptible Knight, where they met with the grim Gyant *Desborough*, and how they went all three and pulled the *Meek Knight* who was then chiefe Soldan out of his Palace by night' (ch. IX).

The Eton fellow and associate of Andrew Marvell in the 1650s (see *MV* 1.VI), Nathaniel Ingelo (1620/1–83), conceived of a higher moral purpose for romance fiction. In his four-part romance *Bentivolio and Urania* (which appeared in two parts, the first in 1660 and the second instalment in 1664), his lengthy 'Preface to the Reader' explains Ingelo's decision to defend the '*Writing and Reading of Romances*'.[51] He admits that there are romances whose '*chief Design* is to put fleshly Lust into long stories, and sometimes not without very unhandsome mixtures, tending onely to the service of brutish Concupiscence, the nourishment of dishonorable affections, and by exciting the Readers muddy fancies, to indispose them for their attendance upon God by their better part'. His goal, in contrast, is to use fiction as Sidney had suggested to delight and to teach, 'the design to please is then as well accomplish'd; but not terminating in the surface of Recreation, it is improv'd into a higher advantage of those nobler faculties which God hath given us' (sig. C1[r]). Although court wits such as Rochester would use the notion of the edifying platonic romance as a source for satire, Ingelo's text was generally popular enough to require four editions by 1682.

---

[51] Ingelo, *Bentivolio and Urania*, 'Preface to the Reader'.

Not all writers, however, were interested in the didactic potential of the romance as a genre. At the opposite end of the moral spectrum, *The Practical Part of Love. Extracted out of the Extravagant and Lascivious Life of a Fair but Subtle Female* (1660), has no redeeming moral position other than, as the preface warns the reader, to demonstrate that 'Pleasure, Recreation, and varietie of Delight, is the Center of most men's desires and wishes. But above all, that of Love, and *Venery,* have the greatest power'.[52] In a foreshadowing of the popular female rogue fictions by Richard Head in the 1670s (see *MV* 3.V), love has little to do with the stories of Lucia and her daughter Hellena. Although gestures are made towards the need for repentance and the bitterness of a sinful life and 'because Example is both pleasing to our Memory, and profitable to our Judgement; This following History shall confirm' (pp. 1–2), the women mostly get the better of the besotted males. Set in contemporary England, beginning in a small country town and then transporting its heroine to London and the Inns of Court, the story has both the beautiful mother of 'mean birth' in the country and her beautiful bastard daughter in the city easily persuaded to share their charms with a variety of males. It is hard to see much repentance as Hellena, the daughter, after leading a sinful life, marries an elderly man and terrorizes him into giving her an annuity; when he dies of a broken heart, Hellena is left 'a most triumphant rich now regnant Whore' (p. 84) at the end of the tale.

By 1660, some readers and writers alike appear to have been getting a little weary of the massive, multi-part French romances so dominant in the fiction market in the 1650s. Only seven romance titles appeared in 1659 and 1660, and, of these, several were parodies of the genre. Samuel Holland had printed at his own expense *Romancio-Mastix: Or a Romance on Romances* in 1660. Hoping, as his long title declared, to lay bare the 'deformities' of the genre so that readers would pursue 'more honourable and profitable Studies', Holland nevertheless displays an impressive familiarity with the popular conventions in his parody. His hero is Don Zara del Fogo, whose sword, that 'Thunder-crack of terrour *Slay-a-Cow,* the very same that he lately won on *Monta-Mole-hill* from the great Gyant *Phrenedecrenobroso,* the son of Pediculo', is described in loving detail.[53] When he encounters a fair maiden disporting herself in a grove, Glyo 'knew not what Responsion to yield' to his compliments 'not to be parallel'd in any Grubstreet Romance' and flees back to her marble Mansion. His adventures conclude when he and his servant are carried off on the back of a winged hog.

The author of *Don Samuel Crispe* turns his attention to the picaresque style of Spanish amorous romances. Purporting to be an autobiography, *Don Samuel Crispe: Or, The Pleasant History of the Knight of Fond Love* (1660) is dedicated to women readers: 'All the Madams, Ladies and Gentlewomen in *England, Scotland* and *Ireland*, and the Dominions thereunto belonging.' 'That I might no longer hide my light under a Bushel', opens the dedication, 'I have here made bold to present you with the choicest Flowers of my *Amorous*

---

[52] *The Practical Part of Love,* sig. A3ʳ, 'Prologue'.   [53] Holland, *Romancio-Mastix,* 3

Frolicks; and to set these my Adventures as so many *Centinels* to guard Melancholy from your thoughts'.[54] In the course of the story of his adventures, he lays out 'Rules for the Order of Fond Love':

1. That they should never speak sence to any Lady they went to visit.
2. That they should give their Ladies often Treatments, and not minde what theye spend upon them.
3. That they go every day to the *Exchange*, to see the exact Modes of Whisks, and Trimmings of Gloves, and give their Ladies information accordingly.
4. That their Handkerchiefs be always perfume'd with Orange-flower-water.
5. That they love every Lady they see; and that they have not so bad an opinion of the said Ladies, as to believe they do not love them again. (ch. 2)

Such comic fictions expand upon the vignettes of 'modish' talk and exchange of compliments found in the 1650s academies of wit and eloquence (see CV 1.II). Soon, however, the court of Charles II itself would provide a living spectacle of amorous frolics and fashionable living, and the commercial world of the Exchange would help create the costumes, accessories, and language that came to define the mode in the 1660s and early 1670s (see MV 2.IV).

For many people in England, the years 1659 and 1660, culminating in the return of the King, were seen as the long-awaited conclusion to an aberrant period of chaos and misrule. The Restoration was a providential act, with Charles, experiencing the trials of exile but being preserved by God, returning to restore his father's royal legacy. For others, such as Milton and supporters of the Commonwealth, it was a tragic conclusion to a shining vision. For many, it must also have been a time of intense anxiety: Ralph Josselin, who had been a chaplain for the Parliamentary army and was residing in Essex during the year of the Restoration, recorded in his diary in January 1660: 'Our poor England [is] unsetled, and her physitians hitherto leading her into deepe waters. Cromwells family cast down with scorne to the ground, none of them in command or imployment; the nation looking more to Charles Stuart, out of love to themselves, not him.' Josselin's conclusion seems to summarize the feelings of confusion over the events of the Interregnum and also perhaps of the possibilities for the 1660s and early 1670s with the return of the King: 'wee have had sad confusions in England, the issue god only knoweth'.[55]

II. Laws Regulating Publication, Speech, and Performance, 1660–1673

In the year of Charles's return, there were still considerable numbers of news pamphlets and political materials of all sorts from satiric ballads to

---

[54] *Don Samuel Crispe*, sig. A1ʳ.   [55] Josselin, *Diary*, 457–8.

impassioned treatises in circulation in opposition to the Restoration, both of
the Church of England and of the monarchy itself. Presbyterians, Quakers,
Scottish Covenanters, and a variety of other sects were preaching and worshipping in ways not conformable with the tenets of the Church of England. Many
of those who had supported the abolition of the House of Lords and the execution of the King were still alive and active in politics. Many had good cause to
fear the return of Charles: in October 1660, the first of the trials of the thirty-
nine regicides took place, and ten of the prisoners were executed. Around the
countryside, books perceived as being in support of the old Commonwealth
regime, the execution of Charles I, or being in opposition to the return of monarchy or of Charles II's legitimacy were gathered up and burned in Exeter,
Chester, and Sherborne.[56] In its own gesture to undo the past, Parliament in its
first session after the Restoration ordered a public burning of the *Solemn
League and Covenant*, the agreement made by the Scottish Presbyterians to
support Parliament against Charles I. This act, however, was quickly answered
by a pamphlet reprinting the original text entitled *The Phoenix, or the Solemn
League and Covenant*.

   While there was no move to resurrect the Star Chamber, the official institution of censorship under Charles I, royal proclamation was again used to control inflammatory publications. On 13 August 1660, a proclamation was issued
calling in and suppressing *Eikonoklastes* (1649; see CV 1.I), John Milton's
scathing rebuttal of the Royalist account of Charles I's final days and *Defensio
pro Populo Anglicano* (1651), 'in both which are contained sundry Treasonable
Passages against Us and Our Government, and most Impious endeavours to
justify the horrid and unmatchable Murder of Our late Dear Father, of Glorious
Memory'.[57] In this proclamation, John Goodwin's *The Obstructors of Justice*,
'written in defence of the traitorous Sentence against his said late Majesty', is
also identified as pernicious. The proclamation orders all copies of the books to
be seized by the magistrates and the vice-chancellors of the universities and
delivered to the sheriff of the county so that they might be burned by the common hangman. Both Milton and Coleman were forced to go into hiding.

   So unsteady were the times that every effort was made to reduce public alarm
over the transition back to monarchy. A proclamation was soon issued requiring
all almanacs predicting future events and books of prognostications to be
licensed before publication, naming Sir George Wharton (1617–81), the almanac
writer and astrologer, as the licenser. Another of the early acts to regulate
publication by the government, in November 1660, was to appoint Sir John
Birkenhead (1617–79), the Royalist newsbook-writer and editor of *Mercurius
Publicus*, as the official licenser for the press (see MV 1.II; CV 1.III).[58] Birkenhead
was the friend of many of the prominent literary figures of his day, including

---

[56] See Bell, 'Elizabeth Calvert', 14.
[57] Charles II, *A proclamation for calling in and suppressing of two books written by John Milton*.
[58] See Steele, *Tudor and Stuart Proclamations* (1910), and Siebert, *Freedom of the Press*, ch. 12.

Edmund Waller, Jeremy Taylor, John Evelyn, John Dryden, Henry Vaughan, and Katherine Philips, in whose circle Birkenhead's sobriquet was 'Cratander'. Wharton and Birkenhead would continue in these roles until the passage in 1662 of *An Act for preventing the frequent Abuses in printing seditious treasonable and unlicensed Bookes and Pamphlets and for regulating of Printing and Printing Presses*, commonly referred to as the Licensing Act (14 Car. II. c. 33). It was clearly based on the model of the Star Chamber decree of 1637, and it was originally to run for two years.

As with the earlier decrees, printing was limited to the master printers who were members of the Stationers' Company and the printers for Oxford and Cambridge University and for the Archbishop of York. Each printer could operate only two presses. The Act also demanded a reduction in the numbers of printers, from fifty-nine master printers in operation at the time of the Act to a mere twenty, with no new masters to be approved until that time. Any new printers, once the reduced number had been achieved, would have to be approved by the Bishop of London and the Archbishop of Canterbury. Master printers were also required to put in surety of £300 to ensure that they would not do any unlawful printing. By 1668, only twenty-eight printers remained, a drastic reduction, which the official licenser appointed by this Act, Sir Roger L'Estrange (1616–1704), attributed to the heavy death toll for the 1665 plague year. In Scotland, which had no Stationers' Company, control of the press remained in the hands of the crown and the Privy Council, which issued monopolies on specific titles. After 1660 'printing burghs' such as Aberdeen maintained the right to publish their almanacs, diurnals, and news-sheets under the protection of local magistrates.[59]

The number of booksellers was likewise limited under the Act to members of the Stationers' Company or those who were licensed by the Lord Bishop of the diocese in which they resided. It specifically barred shopkeepers and 'Habersdasher of Small Wares, Ironmongers, Chandlers' from selling books. Interestingly, unlike previous regulations, it did not specifically target the activities of hawkers, typically women servants and printers' wives such as Elizabeth Calvert, Ann Brewster, Joan Dover, and Hannah Allen, who carried manuscripts to the printer and binders, took printed books and pamphlets to fairs and markets to sell, and in general carried on the printing trade when their husbands were imprisoned.[60] Printers were required to present a copy of every book to each of the university libraries and one to the royal library. There were restrictions on what books could be imported and by whom: nothing could be brought in that was 'heretical, seditious, schismatical or offensive' to the Church of England or to any member of the government, or any private person, although there is no record of any criminal charges being brought on behalf of a private individual during this period.

---

[59] See Mann, ' "Some Property is Theft" ', 35.
[60] See Kitchin, *Sir Roger L'Estrange*, and Bell, 'Offensive Behavior'.

To determine if material was offensive in any of these categories, two copies of the manuscript in English had to be presented to the official Surveyor of the Press for licensing before being printed. This Act specifically forbade any changes to be made in the printed edition after the manuscript was licensed, and the office of the licenser held back one of the manuscript texts to ensure this was so. Upon approval of the manuscript, the licenser would testify that it contained nothing 'contrary to Christian Faith or the Doctrine or Discipline of the Church of England or against the State or Government of this Realme or contrary to good life or good manners', which would then be printed at the start of the book with the name of the licenser. Also required to be on every item printed in his shop was the printer's name; he was furthermore supposed to know the name of the author and to supply it if required by the authorities. Everything printed, whether an epistle or a preface, had to be entered in the Stationers' Register before it was published.

The official licensers divided overseeing these publications among several agents. The licensers for books of history and affairs of state were the principal secretaries of state or their designated appointees. Apart from law and her-aldry, all other books including divinity, art, science, and philosophy came under the purview of the Archbishop of Canterbury and the Bishop of London. University printers required the licence of their chancellor or vice chancellor. Usually the licensers for divinity and philosophy were appointed from the chaplains of the Bishop of London. It is traditionally believed that when Milton's *Paradise Lost* was presented there was some concern expressed over lines in book one, lines 594–9, concerning monarchs who fear change with eclipses, to the point that a licence was given only with hesitation.[61]

Between 1662 and 1679, almost all the licensing of histories and books on affairs of state was done by Roger L'Estrange personally. L'Estrange had resumed his career as a political journalist after the death of Oliver Cromwell. He collected his pro-monarchy texts together in *L'Estrange his Apology: with a Short View of some Late and Remarkable Transactions* (June 1660), and con-tinued after the Restoration vigorously to support the position of the Royalist party and to attack the Presbyterians in power in pamphlets such as *Interest Mistaken, or, The Holy Cheat* (1661). During this period before the Licensing Act, he also operated as an informant concerning illegal political publications. This record of open defiance to the opponents of Charles's interests placed him in a good situation to be named the government's official censor in 1662. Historians of the press, however, are divided over how successful L'Estrange was in controlling pamphlet publication in particular, and apparently nearly half of the publications printed at Oxford did not have a licence.[62] L'Estrange was noted for his zeal in pursuing individuals whom he felt were particularly transgressive—he was the character 'Mr Filth' in John Bunyan's *The Holy War*

---

[61] See Milton, *Paradise Lost: Book III and IV*, p. xlv.
[62] See Siebert, *Freedom of the Press*, ch. 12, esp. pp. 242–3, 249–60.

and 'Towzer' or bloodhound in various Whig writings—but, as his time in office continued, charges that he was open to bribes of various sorts became more and more common (see *MV* 3.II). In 1664, Richard Atkyns, in *The Original and Growth of Printing* (1664), estimated that there were 'at least 600 Booksellers that keep Shops in and about *London*...Two or Three thousand free of the Company of *Stationers*; the Licensed Books of the Kingdome cannot imploy one third part of them',[63] so that it is clear than many were able to avoid his grasp.

There were four principal ways for the government and its agents to enforce the Act. First was by proclamations by the King or his Council, urging the Act to be upheld more rigorously or ordering the suppression of a specific text. Charles II issued eight of these during his reign. The second was through the principal secretary of state enforcing the Act; during this period Lord Arlington and Joseph Williamson had this duty, which also included overseeing newspapers, issuing warrants for arrest or release, and holding examinations and prosecutions, through agents called 'messengers of the press'. To discover unlicensed printed materials and illegal presses, the third means of enforcement was to empower the messengers of the press and the office of the Surveyor and his agents to enter and search any residence, except for that of a peer of the realm, for evidence of illegal printing. Finally, the fourth agency for enforcement was the Stationers' Company itself, but it was by far the least diligent and effective: 'not a little of the responsibility for the failure to enforce the regulation of the Printing Acts in the later part of the seventeenth century can be laid at the door of the Stationers Company'.[64] The increasing resentment among its members over the printing patents, the strong Puritan and Presbyterian presence among the printers themselves, and a general discontent with government restrictions of their trade made the Stationers' Company less than willing partners in suppressing texts and limiting publishing opportunities.

Nor, as we have seen, were all convinced of the need or the effectiveness of the Licensing Act. The soldier and author Richard Atkyns (1615–77), in an elaborately produced book dedicated to Charles II, *The Original and Growth of Printing* (1664), emphasizes in its longer title that 'PRINTING apperताineth to the *Prerogative Royal*; and is a Flower of the *Crown* of *England*'. Identifying himself as one who had known and suffered for Charles I, Atkyns was concerned for personal reasons to re-establish his family's royal patent for the lucrative business of publishing law books, which had been granted to his wife's family in 1618 but was lost during the war. In this obviously self-serving history of printing in England, Atkyns asserts that '*Printing* belongs to Your Majesty, in Your publique and private Capacity, as Supream Magistrate, and as Proprietor'.[65] It is essential, Atkyns argues, that the control of the printed word

---

[63] Atkyns, *The Original and Growth of Printing*, 16.
[64] Siebert, *Freedom of the Press*, 259.
[65] Atkyns, *The Original and Growth of Printing*, sig. B1ᵛ.

must be the King's, as 'it ties, and unties the very Hearts of the People, as please the Author: If the *Tongue*, that is but a little Member, can set the Course of Nature on Fire', he argues, 'how much more the *Quill*, which is of a flying Nature in it self, and so Spiritual, that it is in all Places at the same time; and so Powerful, when it is cunningly handled, that it is the Peoples Deity' ('TO THE KINGS MOST Excellent Majesty', sig. B1ᵛ).

L'Estrange himself was not satisfied with the Act as a means of controlling publication of dangerous materials. In *Considerations and Proposals in order to the regulation of the press* (1663), he declares '*not One Person has been Fin'd, and but one Prosecuted...since the Late Act*, notwithstanding so much Treason and Sedition Printed and disperst since That time'.[66] L'Estrange singles out specific publications for their seditious content, and many of them were printed by a group of printers he refers to as 'the *Confederate Stationers*', Brewster, Chapman, Dover, Creake, and Giles and Elizabeth Calvert. 'The breaking of That Knot would do the work alone. For the *Closer* Carriage of their business they have here in the Town, Their Private *Ware-Houses*, and *Receivers*' (p. 6). Giles and Elizabeth Calvert operated their shop at the Black-Spread-Eagle and were among the most prolific publishers of radical materials, from the 1650s onwards. Thomas Brewster was a former apprentice with them. Livewell Chapman and Francis Smith were booksellers, who were usually supplied with their materials by Simon Dover and Thomas Creake. In 1660, Chapman and Smith published Henry Jessey's *The Lord's Loud call to England*, a text that interpreted various signs and portents as manifestations of God's displeasure with the King and the government. This was the start of a series of pamphlets appearing in 1661, *Mirabilis annus, or the year of prodigies and wonders, Mirabilis annus secundus or the second year of prodigies* (1662), and its second part issued later that same year, *Mirabilis annus secundus: or, the second part of the second years prodigies*. These texts heaped example upon example of 'strange SIGNS and APPARITIONS', 'many remarkable *Accidents*, and signal *Judgments* which have befel divers Persons who have Apostatized from the Truth'. They were published, their titles declare, 'as a Warning to all, speedily to Repent, and to meet the Lord in the way of his Judgments', and to the government they were clearly an attack upon it.[67]

They were also associated with the publication of *The Phoenix* mentioned earlier, and, through an investigation of that text's origins and distribution, the close cooperation of this group of printers and booksellers became clearer to the authorities. They were repeatedly brought in for examination and frequently committed to prison for making and selling seditious materials. After her husband was imprisoned and released, Elizabeth Calvert, who printed *Mirabilis annus*, was herself imprisoned for three months, being finally released in December 1661; her husband, in the intervening time, fled London.

---

[66] L'Estrange, *Considerations and Proposals*, 25.   [67] *Mirabilis annus*, title page.

After his return a year later, Giles Calvert was again imprisoned, along with their maidservant Elizabeth Evans, 'for dispersing seditious books and pamphlets' along with Constance Batty, who in her petition asking for release pleaded on the grounds that, as she could not read the books she sold, she had intended no harm.[68] Thomas Brewster, avoiding questioning in London, was apprehended in Bristol with 'two boxes of books, many of which the Bishop of Bristol finds to be unlicensed and seditious'.[69]

In 1663, acting on informants, L'Estrange raided the home of the printer John Twyn (bap. 1619–64), who was taken in the process of printing *A Treatise of the Execution of Justice*, a text that supposedly urged a revolt against the King. Twyn said he had the manuscript from the Calverts' maidservant Elizabeth Evans, which resulted in a wave of warrants for the arrests of the Calverts, their servants, their apprentices, and their known distributors. John Twyn the printer was tried for treason in February 1664, and trials for seditious libel for the others directly involved in the text's physical production and distribution, the printer Simon Dover, the bookbinder Nathan Brookes, and Thomas Brewster, happened a few days later. Twyn offered as his defence that he had not read the book but was merely printing it for the Calverts, while L'Estrange brought witnesses to swear that Twyn had declared the contents to be '*mettlesome stuffe*' and that he had refused to name the author other than '*the man was a hot fiery man that wrote it*'.[70] Twyn was convicted of high treason: four days after his trial he was hanged, drawn, and quartered. The others were convicted, fined, and sentenced to stand in the pillory. The actual author was never discovered. Dover and Brewster died in prison that year, preceded by Giles Calvert. By 1664, the 'Confederate Knot' had been effectively broken, although it should be noted that the clandestine publishing activities of the printers' wives appear to have continued well into the 1680s.

Another case of illegal publication has a happier ending for the author and his agents. Ralph Wallis (d. 1669), also known as 'the Cobbler of Gloucester', was arrested by L'Estrange in September 1664 for writings that Wallis described as 'drollery' and satire. Although under close observation by authorities in Gloucester and Bristol, Wallis happily published several more works, the verse satire *Rome for Good News* (1665), followed by *More News from Rome, or Magna Charta, Discoursed of between a Poor Man & his Wife* (1666), which chronicles shameful behaviours of Anglican clergymen and describes L'Estrange as a cowardly 'blood-hound' tracking him, a poor naked man. '*Crack-fart*', as he also styles L'Estrange, is clearly a member of the '*Antichristian Armory*'. Wallis's work, with the final title *Room for the cobler of Gloucester and his wife with several cartloads of abominable irregular, pitiful stinking priests* (1668), contains scandalous and scatological anecdotes about living clergymen, describing the rituals of the Anglican Church as '*parings of the Devil's*

---

[68] See Bell, 'Elizabeth Calvert', 21–2.   [69] Quoted in Bell, 'Elizabeth Calvert', 22.
[70] *An exact narrative of the tryal and condemnation of John Twyn*, 13.

Bum-Hole', and was described by L'Estrange as 'the damnedest thing has come out yet'.[71] All Wallis's post-Restoration works, even the most scurrilous, contain loving epistles dedicating them to his 'Dear and Loving Wife' Elizabeth, who supported him and their children throughout the time he was being pursued by L'Estrange.

One of the most difficult and troubling areas for the licensers and the authorities in general in the early years after Charles II's return concerned matters of religious practice. Under the Protectorate, a multitude of independent religious movements had come into being, and Charles's goal was to unify the country under a single religious code once again. In addition to the Licensing Act, a series of four laws sometimes referred to as the Clarendon Code and named for the Lord Chancellor, Edward Hyde, Earl of Clarendon were passed between 1661 and 1665, which had significant impact in shaping public discourse in matters political, religious, and secular.[72]

The first was the Corporation Act in 1661, which required all municipal officials to take Anglican communion and reject the Solemn League and Covenant (1643), the agreement made between the English Parliament and the Scottish Covenanters in which the Scottish party agreed to support Parliament in return for the reformed religion of Scotland becoming the established orthodoxy in England and Ireland. The effect of the Corporation Act was to prevent nonconformists, such as the Presbyterians, from serving in public office. The second law was the Act of Uniformity passed in 1662. This made the Book of Common Prayer the only permitted text in public worship; in response, nearly 2,000 clergymen who refused to adopt the book were forced to resign their ministries. The third Act also targeted those outside the Anglican Church: the Conventicle Act passed in 1664 prohibited meetings of more than five people not all members of the same household for unofficial worship, which had a heavy impact on dissenting groups such as John Bunyan's Baptist congregations and the Quakers. Between July 1664 and December 1665, there were 909 convictions in London of conventiclers, and there were trials in 23 other counties.[73] The final Act in this series likewise attempted to control unauthorized preaching by nonconforming ministers: the Five Mile Act (1665) prohibited nonconforming ministers from residing within 5 miles of the parish from which they had been ejected by the Act of Uniformity, unless they would swear an oath never to resist the King or make any attempt to alter the government of either the Church or the state.

Richard Baxter (1615–91), the Puritan minister who had been chaplain to Parliamentary troops (see *MV* 1.I, 1.IV) but who had steadily opposed Cromwell's rule, noted the irony of his situation under the Clarendon Code. During the Interregnum, Baxter had the 'Liberty and Advantage to preach his Gospel with Success, which I cannot have under a King to whom I have sworn and

---

[71] See Keeble, *The Literary Culture*, 106–8.   [72] See Keeble, *The Literary Culture*, chs 1, 3.
[73] See Hutton, *The Restoration*, and Harris, *Restoration*.

performed true Subjection and Obedience'.[74] In part empowered by this Act and previous personal antipathy, Roger L'Estrange and his agents made Baxter a particular target, L'Estrange having already written two pamphlets in 1661 attacking Baxter's championing of the Presbyterian position in *The Relapsed Apostate* and *State-Divinity.*

Indeed, L'Estrange's animosity towards Presbyterianism and nonconformist writers was so pronounced and widely known that the independent polemicist Edward Bagshaw (1629/30–71) published a rebuttal to him in anticipation of L'Estrange's attack, *An Answer to All that L'Estrange Intends to Write* (1662). Although an ordained minister and briefly the chaplain to the 1st Earl of Anglesey, Bagshaw was forbidden to preach in Ireland by the Archbishop of Dublin in 1662 and was charged with holding illegal conventicles in his rooms. He was sent to the Tower in London for 'treasonable practices' in 1663, during which time L'Estrange in his new role of Surveyor of the Press during a search of Bagshaw's room discovered a manuscript of a fellow prisoner considered so inflammatory by the King that Bagshaw remained incarcerated until his death in 1671.

The Baptist John Bunyan, who was not an ordained minister in the eyes of the church (see *MV* 1.IV), was arrested for public preaching in 1661. He refused the offer of release if he would refrain from preaching, and from jail published his sermon *I will Pray with the Spirit* (1662). In this text, he succinctly sets forth the grounds on which the separatists and independents objected to the mandated use of the Book of Common Prayer, declaring that true prayer is from the inner working of the Spirit and that formalized prayers such as the Book of Common Prayer are merely human, perhaps demonic, inventions. It was also during this period of incarceration that he turned to writing verse

> I am (indeed) in Prison (now)
> In Body, but my Mind
> Is free to study Christ, and how
> Unto me he is kind.[75]

Under this law, Bunyan would remain in Bedford jail, where he wrote his autobiography *Grace Abounding to the Chief of Sinners* as well as *Pilgrim's Progress*, until the Declaration of Indulgence in 1672 (see *CV* 2.III, 2.IV; *MV* 3.V).

In a similar fashion, Vavasor Powell (1617–70), the charismatic Welsh preacher and polemical writer whose verses on the execution of Charles I had so inflamed Katherine Philips (see *MV* 1.V; *CV* 1.I), was in custody by April 1660 as being a danger to the Restoration, even given his forceful opposition to Cromwell, which had led to his earlier treason trial (see *MV* 1.II). Once released, he refused to take the Oaths of Supremacy and Allegiance, published an attack on the Book of Common Prayer, and as a result was put into Fleet Street Prison, where he wrote *The Bird in the Cage Chirping* (1662). This text

---

[74] Baxter, *Reliquiae Baxterianae*, 1. 98–100.   [75] Bunyan, *Prison-Meditations*, 2.

casts the Restoration as being the result of the godly becoming too complaisant during the Interregnum: 'we have been stomach-ful, sick, and surfeited, with the sweet and fat things of Gods house'.[76] Once released, he immediately returned to preaching travelling in Wales, and was once again imprisoned in Cardiff. He ended his days back in London in the Fleet Prison in 1669, where, in spite of the conditions, he managed to continue to preach occasionally until his death in 1670.

Quakers were also severely persecuted under these laws. In spite of their declaration presented to Charles in 1660, *A Declaration from the Harmless and Innocent People of God, Called Quakers*, thought by some to be one of their earliest statements of pacifism ('All bloody Principles & Practices we (as to our own particular) do utterly deny, with all outward wars & strife, and fightings with outward Weapons, for any end, or under any pretence whatsoever, And this is our Testimony to the whole world'[77]), the refusal by Quakers to take oaths of any sort, to pay Church of England tithes, and to stop meeting in public groups for worship ensured the imprisonment and even the death of many. It has been estimated by historians that some 400 Quakers died in prison and 1,000 others were released permanently injured; Quaker writings from this period, like so many religious texts, are marked with the shadow of the prison.[78]

With the return of the court, the office of Master of the Revels, which had been suspended during the Interregnum, suddenly found itself revived if not restored. Sir Henry Herbert (bap. 1594–1673) was sworn in again as Master of the Revels in June 1660. However, when Charles granted two licences to Thomas Killigrew and William Davenant to build new theatres and create acting companies, he also gave them the power to license their own plays. The patents stated that they must not 'cause to be acted or represented any Play, Enterlude, or opera, Containing any Matter of Prophanation, Scurrility or Obscenity', and that they should also 'peruse all playes that haue been formerly written, and to expunge all Prophanesse and Scurrility from the same, before they be represented or Acted'.[79] Herbert filed suit to re-establish his powers over London licensing, but after two years he was able to retain only limited licensing and censorship powers over printed plays and those produced in London.

Although Herbert was supposed to control the licensing of all forms of entertainment outside London, such as strolling players, rope dancers, and puppet shows, he likewise appears to have had little success in restraining the newly restored world of the theatre. Throughout 1663, Herbert issued warrants for the arrest of entertainers such as Paul Reames 'for setting up Modells

[76] Powell, *The Bird in the Cage Chirping*, 8.
[77] *A Declaration from the Harmless and Innocent People of God*, 2.
[78] See Moore, *The Light in their Consciences*, 163.
[79] Quoted in Adams (ed.), *The Dramatic Records of Sir Henry Herbert*, 87–8.

and dumb Shewes without leave first obteyned of the Master of the Revels'.[80] Often town mayors were less than pleased to have these strolling, itinerant players in their towns; a letter from the King to the city of Norwich commiserated with their complaints that 'by the frequency of Lotteries Puppet playes and other shows resorting thether... the meaner sort of people are diverted from the their labors & manufactures & tempted to a vaine expense of their time & money', and thus Charles granted the mayor the right to restrict the number of performers and the number of days they stayed, regardless of any licence they might have from the Master of the Revels.[81] Herbert's instructions to his agents attending the upcoming fairs in London and Bristol were to check that all performers have current licences issued by him, except 'if you find any persons there, wch are Inhabitants of Wales, or other remote places, who seldom or never come to London, and without very great prejudice cannot attend the office'. Herbert notes: 'you are to permitt them for the faire time onely, provided they keep good rule, and pay a present acknowledgement to the office'.[82]

Eventually Herbert came to agreements with Killigrew and Davenant and returned to his job of examining manuscripts of plays to be performed, but, even with the advent of actresses on the stage and the potential for profanity and scurrility of a tantalizing new variety, few performances were censored between 1660 and 1674. Five texts are presently known that show Herbert's efforts as licenser. In John Wilson's *The Cheats* (performed in 1663 by the King's Company), oaths such as 'faith', 'pox', and 'troth' were crossed out along with vulgar words such as 'fart' and insults about the Welsh. A character named Scruple, a hypocritical nonconforming minister, also had his speech in Act Three removed in which he urged his congregation to remain faithful to the Solemn League and Covenant. When Wilson had the play printed in 1663, it was censored by L'Estrange, who saw no harm in Scruple's speeches, and they were left in.

Herbert also licensed Edward Howard's *The Change of Crowns*, but the comedian John Lacy (c.1615–81), a leading performer in the King's Company at the Theatre Royal, apparently added his own improvisations and managed to offend thoroughly the King and Queen who were in the audience during his performance on 15 April 1667. Howard's play was viewed as satirizing the court: Samuel Pepys, who saw it the day after, when the most offensive lines appear to have been removed, recorded in his diary that, even with the alterations, Lacy's part was a country gentleman Asinello who 'do abuse the Court with all the imaginable wit and plainness about selling of places, and doing everything for money' (Pepys, *Diary*, 8. 167–8, 15 April 1667). In 1672, Herbert licensed the revival of William Cartwright's (1611–43) comedy *The Ordinary*, with the annotation '[the Reformations observed] nay [*sic*] bee acted,

---

[80] Bawcutt (ed.), *Control and Censorship*, 268.
[81] Quoted in Bawcutt (ed.), *Control and Censorship*, 269.
[82] Quoted in Bawcutt (ed.), *Control and Censorship*, 270.

not other wise'.[83] Herbert once again was busy crossing out oaths and vulgar words. There is also a note on the manuscript of Elizabeth Polewheele's (1651?–91?) tragedy *The Faithful Virgins*, affirming that it can be performed by the Duke's Company 'only leaving out what was Cross'd by Hernry Herbertt M.R',[84] and evidence suggests it was performed in the early 1670s. The passage in this play that particularly alarmed Herbert was a warning given to the lovely Isabella that the lecherous Duke of Tuscany, whom she is about to marry, will not be true to her, perhaps coming uncomfortably close to Charles's court:

> he must have mistresses and often change
> And when a does, you must not think it strange
> such shall the soule of Tuscany Comand
> Whilst a Scornd' Wife Must as a Cypher stand.[85]

Some plays never made it past rehearsal to the Master of the Revels for approval. In 1669, Sir Robert Howard (1626–98) along with George Villiers, Duke of Buckingham (1628–87), concocted a comedy 'The Country Gentleman'. The King had just dissolved the recalcitrant Parliament in 1668, the concern being that it, along with his own Privy Council, was becoming too factionalized between country (landed nobility, agricultural interests) and city (mercantile, trade interests, supportive of war to secure these interests) parties. Howard, who favoured the country opposition party, wrote a comedy featuring Sir Richard Plainbred, a wealthy and articulate gentleman from the country whose two daughters have recently become heiresses through the death of their uncle; the family travels to the city to settle the estate and encounters 'city' manners, starting with their landlady Miss Finical Fart, who loves all things French. The girls meet a series of suitors representing various political factions—Sir Cautious Trouble-all and Sir Gravity Empty are businessmen who attempt to influence politics, Vapor and Slander are two town fops devoted to court fashions, and Worthy and Lovetruth, two young men from the country who epitomize masculine virtue.

The problem with this seemingly innocuous confection was the scene in Act Three written by Villiers, which directly mocks William Coventry, the Commissioner of the Treasury, as Sir Cautious. When Coventry heard about the play, he challenged Villiers to an illegal duel and ended up off the Privy Council and imprisoned in the Tower. The scandal was recorded by Pepys in his diary, circulated in newsletters, and reported to the French King by his ambassador.[86] While Charles was clearly willing to dispense with the services of Coventry in favour of those of Villiers, he was not willing to have a play so clearly representing a living member of his Privy Council staged. According to Pepys, Coventry himself made it known to the members of the King's Company

---

[83] Quoted in Bawcutt (ed.), *Control and Censorship*, 294.
[84] Quoted in Bawcutt (ed.), *Control and Censorship*, 297.
[85] Quoted in Bawcutt (ed.), *Control and Censorship*, 105.
[86] Patterson, 'The Country Gentleman', 492.

that he would 'slit the nose of anyone who impersonated him on stage', and his friends supposedly happily agreed to cudgel any actors attempting to perform it. Not surprisingly, Howard never presented the play's manuscript to the Master of the Revels, and it was neither performed nor published, its rehearsals merely serving as a source of fresh gossip as the scandal played out, and its text surviving in a single manuscript.[87]

On Herbert's death in 1673, the office of Master of the Revels was briefly assigned to the ageing Thomas Killigrew. Killigrew, whom Pepys describes in 1668 as 'King's fool or jester...and may with privilege revile or jeere any body...without offence' (Pepys, *Diary*, 9. 66–7), was perhaps not as dedicated to his task as Master of the Revels. He did make use of the right to license 'pedlars and petty chapmen' and lotteries. In 1677, his son Charles brought a Chancery suit against him to secure his promised shares in the acting company and the post of Master of the Revels. Two days after the suit had been settled, Charles Killigrew was appointed to that office, which he held until his death in 1724/5, and would in the later part of the century play an active role in the movement to reform the stage (see *MV* 3.II; *MV* 4.II).

III. Renovating the Stage: Companies, Actresses, Repertoire, Theatre Innovations, and the Touring Companies

Within three months of his own triumphantly staged return to London, Charles II in July 1660 signed royal patents permitting Thomas Killigrew (1612–83) and Sir William Davenant (1606–18) to 'erect two playhouses' and to form two companies of players in London, 'suppressing all other playhouses' (*CSPD, 1660–61*, 124). When it was finalized in August 1660, this document would give the two men what amounted to a monopoly over theatrical entertainments in London: they paid the actors, set the price of tickets, and licensed the plays submitted for their approval. Killigrew formed the King's Company, and Davenant, acting under the patronage of James, Duke of York, created the Duke's Company. As the court worked to restore its presence in London and the country at large (see *CV* 2.I), so did theatrical entertainments supported by it re-establish themselves in London and other English towns, returning to popular venues such as Norwich and Oxford. The revival of the theatre in towns outside London was led by the now little known, but still remarkable, rival to Killigrew and Davenant, George Jolly (bap. 1613–c.1683), while, in Dublin, John Ogilby, who had designed the processional arches for Charles's return to London and had been appointed Master of the Revels in Ireland, opened a new royal theatre in Smock Alley in 1662.

---

[87] Auchter, *Dictionary of Literary and Dramatic Censorship*, 68.

Precise information about the specific performances that were happening in London immediately before Charles's return and the very early days of the patent theatres is fragmentary. In addition to the legal documents relating to the theatres and the actors involved with them, some of the key sources for historians of performance have been John Downes's *Roscius Anglicanus* (1708) and the diary entries of the enthusiastic playgoer Samuel Pepys. Downes's 'Historical Review of the Stage' is a particularly valuable source, as Downes himself appeared briefly as an actor in Davenant's opera *The Siege of Rhodes* in 1661, when it was used to open the Duke's Company new theatre at Lincoln's Inn Fields (according to Pepys he mangled his lines so badly he was hissed from the stage). Subsequently, Downes became the company's bookkeeper and prompter until 1706.[88] Written in part from memory and also in part from his records and those of the King's Company acquired from their bookkeeper, Charles Booth, Downes's history focuses on the casting of the plays and the productions' commercial successes and failures rather than any aspect of literary quality or dramatic technique, and its chronology has frequently been found to be unreliable. It is still, however, a remarkable behind-the-scenes look at how Restoration theatre worked: as he states in his note to the reader, Downes was for over forty years 'writing out all the Parts in each Play; and Attending every Morning the Actors Rehearsals, and their Performances in Afternoons'.

From such sources, it is clear that the restoration of the London stage in 1660 and the shaping of the next two decades of plays and performances were deeply connected to the world of the court and Charles's courtiers, from their preferences in types of drama to the material presentation on stage. In 1661, when Davenant revived his 1634 tragicomedy *Love and Honour*, the leading man, Thomas Betterton, was wearing the King's own coronation robes as he played the part of Prince Alvaro; the Duke of York also obligingly lent his robes to Henry Harris, who played a prince.[89] Killigrew, who had spent the previous few years in exile with Charles's court and served as his groom of the bedchamber, was described by Samuel Pepys as being highly esteemed by Charles and perhaps not surprisingly received his patent first on 9 July, which was quickly followed by Davenant's petition.[90] Davenant, who had lived in exile in Paris for a number of years before returning to England (see CV 1.I), had received from Charles I in 1639 a warrant to build a new playhouse on Fleet Street, but he had never been able to build it. In his revision of the document in 1660, he highlighted the need to be able to charge appropriate amounts for tickets in order to restore the physically damaged London theatres, but also to innovate the stage, with 'scenes, musick and new decorations as have not bin formerly used'.[91]

---

[88] See Downes, *Roscius Anglicanus*, pp. v–xxi.   [89] Downes, *Roscius Anglicanus*, 52.
[90] For Killigrew's role and standing in the exile court of Charles II, see Philip Major, 'Introduction: "A Man of Much Plot"', in Major (ed.), *Thomas Killigrew*.
[91] Edmond, *Rare Sir William Davenant*, 143–4.

Killigrew for his part moved quickly to obtain control over the existing body of play texts, including Davenant's own pre-war ones, as well as those by Ben Jonson and Shakespeare. His grounds were that his King's Company was the successor to the previously existing King's Men, the company to which Shakespeare had belonged. Killigrew, after forming his company, began performances at the site of the old Red Bull theatre in early November 1660, but moved within days to Gibbon's Tennis Court on Vere Street. Davenant quickly followed suit, and his company opened performances in mid-November at the old private theatre, Salisbury Court, where they would stay until their new theatre in Lincoln's Inn Fields was built in June 1661, specifically designed to incorporate the proposed innovations in scenery and staging.

Although their patents were granted by the King, Killigrew and Davenant still faced competition from other theatrical agents. Their monopolies had not gone unchallenged, and much of the opposition to them came from three veterans of the stage before the war and during the Commonwealth: Michael Mohun [Moone] (*c.*1616–84), William Beeston (1610/11?–82), and John Rhodes. Rhodes, about whom the least is known, had obtained the lease of the Cockpit Theatre in Drury Lane by 1649; previously, in 1644, he lived in the small house next to the theatre as its keeper. From the arrest records of his actors, he also supported a small company of players even as General Monck's army was entering London to force the Restoration of Charles.[92] Even after the Restoration, Rhodes is sighted largely in legal documents: on 28 July 1660 he was fined £4 6s. for illegal performances at the Cockpit during the spring. He made ends meet by also working as a bookseller during the Interregnum and Restoration, but his life was clearly invested in the theatre.

Mohun, on the other hand, was a well-known, established figure in both the world of the theatre before the war and also the travails of the exiles on the Continent. He had served in the Royalist army as a captain and ultimately a major, and had been wounded and imprisoned at the siege of Dublin in 1649. When he was freed, he travelled to the Continent to join the other Royalist exiles; in 1658, he was in Antwerp, performing the prologue and epilogue to the Earl of Newcastle's entertainment for Charles II (see CV 1.I). Early in 1660, he was back in London, and, by the time of Charles II's return, he had formed a group of actors who first put on plays at the old Red Bull and then moved to the Cockpit.

Beeston, likewise, had a long lineage in the London theatres. A manager rather than an actor, he had worked with his father, Christopher Beeston, in running the very successful Cockpit Theatre in the 1630s, inheriting it in 1638 and being appointed in 1639 to be the 'Governour & Instructer of the Kings and Queens young Company of Actors'. Beeston, whose list of plays under his control included many of the most popular and successful playwrights working after Shakespeare, including Beaumont, Fletcher, Shirley, Ford, and Middleton, had been briefly imprisoned before the war in May 1640 for staging

---

[92] See Hotson, *Commonwealth and Restoration Stage*, 90, 99–100, 197–8.

an unlicensed play, which the Master of the Revels declared inappropriately made allusion to Charles I's unsuccessful northern campaign against the Scots. This affront had caused the ownership of the Cockpit to be transferred to Davenant, who held it for only a year before being imprisoned himself, but for his Royalist sympathies rather than offensive dramas. While Mohun had fled to the Continent, Beeston had stayed in London, attempting to train a new company of boy actors and to purchase the lease of Salisbury Court theatre from the family of the Earl of Dorset, who owned the land. He managed to do this in 1652, after it had been severely damaged by soldiers in 1649 and was slated to be turned into a brewery: a contemporary noted of the first event that 'the playhouse in Salisbury Court, in Fleet Street, was pulled down by a company of soldiers set on by the sectaries of these sad times', and, regarding the second, Frances, Countess of Dorset, declared that she would prefer that 'the house and ground [be] made into a fishpond than that a brewhouse should be so near her dwelling'.[93] When Charles II returned, Beeston started a new company to perform at Salisbury Court.

The London actors and theatre managers already performing when the royal patents were issued were joined in their resistance to the monopoly by the Master of the Revels, Sir Henry Herbert (bap. 1594–1673). From 1623 until the war years, Herbert had functioned as the arbiter of what would be performed in London and who would tour the provinces, as well as what texts would be licensed for performance and print (see *MV* 2.II). During the Interregnum, having made his peace with Parliament, Herbert had lived with little notice in London and on his estate; on the return of Charles II, he was sworn in again in May 1660 as a gentleman of the Privy Chamber and, in June, as Master of the Revels. Killigrew and Davenant, however, had been expressly given in their patents the right to license plays, and Herbert launched an unsuccessful two-year-long legal battle to recover the lucrative licensing of texts and performances. Although his name appears throughout the period as an official censor (see *MV* 2.II), his impact on the stage both in London and outside it was considerably lessened.

As they outmanoeuvred their opponents, it was essential for both Killigrew and Davenant, the latter of whom had successfully staged his 'operas' during the last years of Cromwell's reign (see *CV* 1.IV), to secure the rights to perform the existing repertoire of dramas. It was also necessary to find or build suitable spaces in which to perform them, to assemble companies of actors who could present them, and then to convince a London audience, many of whom, like Samuel Pepys, having been born during the war years or the Interregnum, had probably never seen a stage play, to lay out their money for this new entertainment. George Jolly was an additional complication and actively competed for this audience; he, too, had fled for the Continent in the 1640s and had led a troupe of players that performed in Germany and Sweden during the 1650s,

---

[93] Quoted in Hotson, *Commonwealth and Restoration Stage*, 101, 104–5.

the 'Englische commödianten'. He returned to London late in 1660, and by December had also been granted a royal licence to create an acting company. While Jolly was successful for two years in staging performances of old plays, including Marlowe's *Doctor Faustus* at the Cockpit and Salisbury Court, Killigrew and Davenant eventually bought him out in 1662 for £4 a week paid for the rest of his life and a licence to form a touring company for the provinces, although this agreement would collapse before the end of the decade.

Initially, the repertoire of the King's and Duke's companies, like Jolly's, necessarily rested on tried and true plays from before the war. As already stated, Killigrew's opening gambit was to claim for the King's Company all the surviving pre-war plays, which involved over half of Shakespeare's and almost all of Jonson, Beaumont, and Fletcher. Davenant countered by offering the Lord Chamberlain a 'proposition of reformeing some of the most ancient Playes that were played at the Blackfriers and makeinge them, fit, for the Company of Actors'.[94] He was successful in this ploy, and, significantly, the requirement that most of the older plays that he presented had to be 'adapted' would strongly influence the public's perceptions of Shakespeare from the Restoration through the eighteenth century.

Davenant was not slow to stage his adapted versions of the Shakespeare plays he controlled. He had been allotted *Hamlet*, which became a steady money-spinner for the Duke's Company without significant alterations, but in 1662 Davenant staged the first of his Shakespearean adaptations, *The Law Against Lovers*: it combined *Measure for Measure* with the wooing plot of Beatrice and Benedick from *Much Ado About Nothing* and ended with three happy marriages. This was followed by his transformation of *Macbeth* into an opera in 1663–4, and, in 1667, his most commercially successful adaptation, *The Tempest, or The Enchanted Island*. His first version of *The Tempest* was written with John Dryden and incorporated the music and special scenery effects available to him at the new theatre at Lincoln's Inn Fields and was a significant financial success. In general, however, Shakespeare's comedies were much less popular with Restoration audiences than his tragedies: Samuel Pepys's response to a 1662 performance of *A Midsummer Night's Dream* was that it was the 'most insipid ridiculous play that ever I saw in my life' (Pepys, *Diary*, 3. 208). Thus, although a staple in the repertoire of both companies and a consistent draw for an audience, Shakespeare's appeal was not universal: John Evelyn noted of Davenant's 1661 production of *Hamlet* that 'the old playe began to disgust this refined age; since his Majestie being so long abroad' (Evelyn, *Diary*, 3. 304), foreshadowing the demand for new plays by new writers who better reflected the taste for continental-style theatres and staging.

As popular, if not more so, than Shakespeare in the opening years of the 1660s were the plays by Beaumont and Fletcher.[95] This may have been due in

---

[94] Quoted in Nicoll, *History of Restoration Drama*, 314.
[95] See Sprague, *Beaumont and Fletcher*.

part to Humphrey Moseley's handsome folio publication of their works in 1647 (see *MV* 1.III), which would have ensured that those who had not seen the plays performed before the war would be familiar with their merits from reading them. Historians of the drama have calculated that between 1660 and 1671, of the 105 older plays presented, Beaumont and Fletcher's made up 28 of them.[96] Even before the Restoration, their plays were popular sources for the farces and drolleries that were staged at the Red Bull in an attempt to circumvent the prohibition against staging full-length plays (see *CV* 1.IV).

On the other hand, Shakespeare's *Othello* was among the first productions mounted by Killigrew in 1660, and, notably, it was the occasion for the first English professional female actress to appear on a London commercial stage. Killigrew and Davenant competed fiercely for the talents from the existing pool of experienced actors still in London or returning from the Continent with the Royalists. Michael Mohun was a seasoned veteran of the stage, and Charles Hart (bap. 1625–83), who had been apprenticed to the King's Men and performed women's roles in the early 1640s, had also served in the Royalist army after the war broke out, before joining the travelling English players on the Continent. Mohun and Hart were the backbone of the King's Company for over twenty years, with Hart becoming a shareholder in the company and both eventually becoming part of the theatre's management. Walter Clun (d. 1664) was another key figure in the newly restored theatre: according to the account in James Wright's *Historia Histrionica* (1699), Clun, like Hart, had been apprenticed at Blackfriars and performed on the Continent for the exiled Royalists, and with Hart had been arrested for attempting to form a new London company in 1649. He, too, was one of the thirteen original shareholders in Killigrew's new King's Company, and the versatile performer shone as Iago in *Othello* and Falstaff in *The Merrie Wiues of Windsor*, and starred in the title role of Fletcher's comedy *The Humorous Lieutenant*, which Killigrew used to open the new Theatre Royal in Drury Lane. Pepys records going to see it and being disappointed that the King had insisted that Clun be replaced by his favourite comic actor, John Lacy (*c.*1615–81). Clun's name is less well known in Restoration theatre history probably because of his untimely death: Pepys records in his diary for 4 August 1664 that, after going to see *The Rival Ladies* by Dryden at the King's Theatre: 'Here we hear that Clun, one of their best actors, was, the last night, going out of towne (after he had acted *The Alchymist*, wherein was one of his best parts that he acts) to his country-house, set upon and murdered...the house will have a great miss of him' (Pepys, *Diary*, 5. 232).

Lacy, who had been born in Yorkshire and apprenticed in 1631 to John Ogilby at his dance school in Gray's Inn Lane, also had a long career in the theatre before and after the war years. As a young apprentice actor, he supposedly provided a list of northern dialect terms for some of Ben Jonson's comedies. Like Hart and Mohun, Lacy also served in the King's army, acting as a lieutenant

---

[96] See Clarke, 'Shakespeare in the Restoration', 2, and Maguire, *Regicide and Restoration*, 56.

and quartermaster. In Killigrew's Restoration company, Lacy excelled at the revivals of Jonson's plays, in particular as the pompous Sir Politic Would-Be in *Volpone* and in playing comic foreigner roles, such as the Irish footman in Sir Robert Howard's *The Committee* (1663) and Monsieur Galliard in *The Varietie* by William Cavendish, Duke of Newcastle.

If the King's Company had the cream of the pre-war actors, the Rhodes company performing at the Cockpit in Drury Lane between March and November 1660 had several young actors who would come to dominate the stage during their long lifetimes and whose acting inspired dramatists to create numerous roles specifically for them. In addition to the young James Nokes (*c*.1642–96), whose career with Davenant's company lasted over thirty years and set the standard for comic acting on the restored stage, Rhodes's company also had Thomas Betterton (bap. 1635–1710) and Edward Kynaston (bap. 1643–1712?), who between them shaped the ideal of both male and female performance on stage for a generation. Both began and pursued celebrated careers as actors, but both were also actively involved in their later years in managing theatres and companies of actors (see *MV* 4.IV; *CV* 5.II).[97]

Betterton, whose father was employed as a cook in the household of Charles I, grew up in London, but little is known about his early years and education; it appears that, like Kynaston, he was apprenticed to a bookseller, some sources suggesting John Rhodes.[98] In any event, Downes records that his earliest stage appearances were in Rhodes's company at the Cockpit in Drury Lane in 1659, noting that even at the age of 24 'his Voice [was] then as Audibly strong, full and Articulate, as in the Prime of his Acting'.[99] His performances in Rhodes's company were mostly in plays by Beaumont and Fletcher, and he was 'highly Applauded for his Acting in all these Plays'. In October 1660, Killigrew, while forming the King's Company, lists Betterton as one of his actors, but, in November 1660, Betterton along with nine other actors independently signed a sharing agreement with Davenant and became part of the Duke's Company, where he quickly rose to the status of leading man.

Kynaston was born in Shropshire, supposedly 'well-descended'. When he was 11, he was bound apprentice to John Rhodes for nine years, and in early 1660, he, like Betterton, made his appearance on stage at the Cockpit. Unlike Betterton, however, the 17-year-old played mostly women's roles in the successful dramas from the 1630s, including the female title role in Sir John Suckling's court drama *Aglaura* and Arthiope in Davenant's *The Unfortunate Lovers*. Downes observed 'he being then very Young made a Compleat Female Stage Beauty'. He was particularly effective in portraying feminine distress and suffering, those 'parts greatly moving Compassion and Pity', Downes asserts. 'It has since been Disputable among the Judicious', Downes concludes, 'whether any Woman that succeeded him so Sensibly touch'd the Audience as he'.[100]

---

[97] See Milhous, *Thomas Betterton*, ch. 1.   [98] Roberts, *Thomas Betterton*, ch. 3.
[99] Downes, *Roscius Anglicanus*, 45.   [100] Downes, *Roscius Anglicanus*, 46.

Pepys certainly agreed. On seeing Kynaston perform in the role of the Duke's Sister in Fletcher's tragedy *The Loyal Subject* on 18 August 1660, Pepys recorded in his diary that Kynaston was 'the loveliest lady that ever I saw in my life', with the caveat, 'only her voice not very good' (Pepys, *Diary*, 1. 224). Pepys had never seen a woman on stage, and would not until a performance he records on 3 January 1661, when his response seems somewhat muted compared to his reaction to Kynaston: 'I eat our dinner of a roasted leg of pork which Will did give us, and after that to the Theatre, where was acted [Fletcher and Massinger's comedy] *Beggarsbush*—it being very well done; and here the first time that ever I saw Women come upon the stage' (Pepys, *Diary*, 2. 5).

Although women had been acting professionally in Italy, Spain, and France for many generations, and, indeed, George Jolly's travelling company in Germany had employed several, English commercial theatres such as the Red Bull and Blackfriars typically had employed women only for behind-the-scenes work such as seamstresses and dressers, and in the front of the theatre as hawkers and orange women. There was an English tradition, however, of female performance, on the popular level as entertainers in the bear gardens, in provincial civic and religious pageants, and female balladeers, and at the highest elite level in court masques and private house entertainments.[101] The term 'actress' itself has recently been discovered to have first been used about women's performances in the elite private entertainments at court, in particular in reference to Henrietta Maria and her ladies performing in a court pastoral in 1626.[102] The ladies of Henrietta Maria's court would have been taught to be able to perform credibly, to dance, sing, and act for their select private audiences. Unlike the continental system, where theatres, especially in Italy and France, were organized as family-run enterprises, English actors were trained through an apprenticeship system, with boys being apprenticed typically between the ages of 10 and 13, initially being trained in women's roles before graduating into adult male roles, or drawn from the children's companies associated with the choir schools.[103]

The exiled Royalists would have had ample opportunity to enjoy the talents of female actors in their travels. Both Davenant and Killigrew were certainly familiar with the practice, and it appears that they both envisioned actresses as being part of the ways in which the London stage would become closer to the continental models. Davenant himself had employed female performers to sing in his operas in the 1650s, notably a 'Mrs Coleman' who sang the role of Ianthe in his *The Siege of Rhodes* done at Rutland House in 1656 (see CV 1.IV). The first mention of actresses to appear on the Restoration stage comes from a protest lodged by Michael Mohun and several other of the older actors, charging that Killigrew was refusing to permit them to act until 'wee had by

---

[101] See McManus, 'Women and English Renaissance Drama'.
[102] See Tomlinson, ' "She that Plays the King" ', 189.
[103] See Fisk, 'The Restoration Actress'.

covenant obleiged our selues to Act with Woemen a new Theatre and Habitts according to our Scaenes'.[104] Something similar appears to have been transacted with Davenant's company: the November 1660 'Articles of Agreement' drawn up between Davenant and the actors who had been performing at Salisbury Court stipulated that they would 'remove and Joyne with the said Henry Harris and with other men and women prouided by the sd Sir Wm Davenant'. Furthermore, the articles specifically provide for the maintenance of 'all ye Women that are to performe or represent Womens parts in the aforesaid Tragedies Comedies Playes or representations'.

It was not until the revised royal patents issued in 1662 that actresses were specifically mentioned by Charles II: focusing on the controls in place to permit actresses to be seen on stage, this patent states 'we do likewise permit and give leave that all the women's parts to be acted in either of the said two companies from this time to come may be performed by women'. The patent adds a warning and a justification for women's presence on stage: women actresses are permitted 'so long as these recreations, which by reason of the abuses aforesaid were scandalous and offensive, may be such reformation be esteemed not only harmless delights', the document concludes, 'but useful and instructive representations of human life, by such of our good subject as shall resort to see the same'.[105] The justification, officially, for women taking the stage in public performances is thus framed in terms of reforming previously scandalous theatrical behaviours.

Thomas Jordan, who had scripted Charles II's coronation procession (see CV 2.I), announced in his prologue for a production of *Othello* on 8 December 1660 what is generally believed to mark the first appearance of these actresses on the London commercial stage. Indeed, Jordan trumpets the novelty of the evening's entertainment, declaring 'the first Woman that came to Act on the Stage in the Tragedy, call'd The Moor of Venice', announcing that 'The Woman plays today; mistake me not, | No Man in Gown, or Page in Petty-Coat'. 'In this reforming age', he continues, 'We have intents to civilize the Stage': no longer will audiences have to endure the sight of 40-year-old men pretending to be 15-year-old females. It is not known who this actress was, although claims have been made for Anne Marshall and Margaret Hughes by various sources.

Downes records the names of the first women Killigrew and Davenant employed, and it is notable how several had very long careers. Katherine Corey worked in the King's Company for over twenty years, progressing from sprightly comic roles in Jonson's *The Alchemist* to Octavia in Dryden's *All for Love* and ending her career with a string of secondary parts for elderly widows and wives. Mary Saunderson married her leading man Thomas Betterton and was famous for twenty-five years for her performance in Shakespearean roles. Anne

---

[104] See Bawcutt (ed.), *Control and Censorship*, 235–8.
[105] Quoted in Fitzgerald, *A New History of the English Stage*, 1. 77.

Gibbs, one of the original eight women who signed with Davenant, married the dramatist, critic, and future poet laureate Thomas Shadwell; during her career, she had four children, acted in several of her husband's plays, and was still acting in Christopher Rich's company in 1699. She also oversaw the posthumous publication of Shadwell's *The Volunteers* and dedicated it to the Queen. Others are recorded for only a season or two, but the long continuation of this group of original women players would strongly influence the ways in which parts for women were written in the new dramas created for them.

The women who formed the first generation of professional actresses in London came from a variety of backgrounds.[106] Anne Shadwell's father was a public notary in Norwich, while Mary 'Moll' Davis (*c.*1651–1708) was said to be the illegitimate child of Thomas Howard, the future 4th Earl of Berkshire. Nell [Eleanor] Gwyn's (1651?–87) early life has proved hard to document, although her mother was reputed (at least in contemporary lampoons) to have run a brothel and sold oranges in the theatres; Pepys records that Gwyn herself stated that she was 'brought up in a bawdy-house to fill strong waters to the guests' (Pepys, *Diary*, 8. 503), before she started selling oranges in Killigrew's King's Theatre in 1663. The father of Anne and Rebecca Marshall, in contrast, was the chaplain to Lord Gerard of Gerard's Bromley, Staffordshire: while Anne was known for her prowess in comedy, Rebecca's forte was the passionate and tempestuous female in tragedies. Writers such as Dryden frequently paired her with Elizabeth Bowtell [Boutel] (1648/9–1714/15), who played parts for sweet, innocent young women. Bowtell, born Elizabeth Davenport, and her sister Frances, were both contracted to the King's Company in the early 1660s. The most famous and celebrated of the Restoration actresses, Elizabeth Barry (1656x58–1713) was the daughter of a barrister, Colonel Robert Barry, and was raised along with several other young girls including young Mary Davis in the household of Davenant and his wife, and given a 'genteel' education.

Restoration actresses as a group have traditionally been characterized as occupying an uneasy social position between servant and artist, performer and prostitute.[107] Certainly, the frissons created by actual women on stage in revealing costumes and breeches parts was part of the highly sexualized nature of the theatre that would cause reformers at the end of the century once again to condemn the stage for promoting immorality. More recent historians of the theatres, however, draw attention to the number of women active in the theatre who enjoyed both long successful onstage careers and marriages, often to other actors, and participated in the management of the theatres. The highly publicized romantic affairs of several leading actresses, however, including Nell Gwyn and Mary Davis, mistresses of Charles II, Elizabeth Barry, the Earl of Rochester's mistress, Margaret 'Peg' Hughes, the mistress of Prince Rupert,

---

[106] See Highfill, Burnim, and Langhans, *A Biographical Dictionary*.

[107] See, e.g., the studies by Howe, *The First English Actresses*; Payne, 'The Restoration Actress'; Bush-Bailey, *Treading the Bawds*.

and Hester Davenport, the Earl of Oxford's Roxalana, all contribute to the image of the Restoration actress as being a woman for sale, looking for a powerful and well-to-do keeper. Pepys's records of the freedoms taken by male visitors behind the scenes, including himself, suggest that many men who had no claims to wealth or title also viewed actresses as available for private liaisons.[108]

The theatre was clearly a locus for gossip in general, as actors and actresses gained what today would be described as celebrity status, and the audiences contained members of royalty. Pepys records a conversation with the actress Elizabeth Knipp on 11 January 1668 in which she brought him up to date: 'Knipp come and sat by us, and her talk pleased me a little, she telling me how Mis Davis is for certain going away from the Duke's house, the King being in love with her; and a house is taken for her, and furnishing; and she hath a ring given her already worth 600*l*' (Pepys, *Diary*, 9. 19). Not only was Charles setting up house for Moll Davis, but Knipp assures Pepys 'that the King did send several times for Nelly [Nell Gwyn], and she was with him, but what he did she knows not; this was a good while ago'. He concludes his conversation with her with the information that 'she says that the King first spoiled Mrs Weaver, which is very mean, methinks, in a prince, and I am sorry for it, and can hope for no good to the State from having a Prince so devoted to his pleasure'.

For the audiences, knowing the gossip about the private lives of many of the leading actors and actresses made watching them as characters on stage even more entertaining. Pepys notes in his diary for 7 May 1668 that, when he called backstage to visit Elizabeth Knipp, 'the play being done, I did see Becke Marshall come dressed, off of the stage, and looks mighty fine, and pretty, and noble—and also Nell, in her boy's clothes, mighty pretty'. 'But, Lord', he added, 'their confidence, and how many men do hover about them as soon as they come off the stage, and how confident they [are] in their talk'. In spite of his apparent dismay over the bold behaviour of Marshall and Gwyn, Pepys himself took advantage of the backstage atmosphere: 'Here I did kiss the pretty woman newly come, called Pegg, that was Sir Ch Sidly's mistress—a mighty pretty woman, and seems, but is not, modest' (Pepys, *Diary*, 9. 189).

Nell Gwyn quickly became a public figure after her debut in 1664. When she and Charles Hart were teamed as a pair of witty lovers in the 1665 production of James Howard's *All Mistaken, or, the Mad Couple*, part of the enjoyment of the audience was the knowledge that the clever, romantic couple on stage were also lovers off it.[109] The new comedies began to feature this style of witty young romantic pairs, called by earlier generations of critics 'the gay couple'. They feature clever, intrepid young heroines matched with equally attractive and witty, sophisticated 'man of the town' male protagonists, typically with rakish propensities, whom the virtuous women lead into reform. The teenaged

[108] See Payne, 'Theatrical Spectatorship in Pepys's Diary'.
[109] See Holland, *The Ornament of Action*, ch. 3; Roach, *It*, 63–8.

Nell Gwyn's talents as a comedian and her quick wit in ad libbing lines to play to the gallants in the pit won her quick recognition among theatregoers and many suitors outside of Hart.

Some historians believe Nell Gwyn was an early conquest of the Earl of Rochester, but she without doubt subsequently caught the attention of Charles Sackville, the future Lord Dorset, beginning a relationship with him in 1667 and eventually with the King himself, which soon became part of the persona she assumed every time she stepped upon the stage or was seen in public off it. On 3 April 1665, Pepys records in his diary going to see Lord Orrery's play *Mustapha* at the Duke's Theatre and finding the audience more interesting than the play:

> to a play at the Duke's . . . which being not good, made Betterton's part and Ianthe's but ordinary too, so that we were not contented with it at all. . . . All the pleasure of the play was, the King and my Lady Castlemayne were there—and pretty witty Nell, at the King's house, and the younger Marshall [Anne] sat next us; which pleased me mightily. (Pepys, *Diary*, 6. 73)

Gwyn's performance in Dryden's *Secret-Love, or, The Maiden-Queen* on 2 March 1667 apparently pleased not only Pepys and his wife but also the King and his brother with her portrayal of the 'wild mistress':

> After dinner, with my wife, to the King's house to see *The Mayden Queene*, a new play of Dryden's, mightily commended for the regularity of it, and the strain and wit; and, the truth is, there is a comical part done by Nell, which is Florimell, that I never can hope ever to see the like done again, by man or woman. The King and Duke of York were at the play; but so great performance of a comical part was never, I believe, in the world before as Nell do this, both as a mad girle, then most and best of all when she comes in like a young gallant; and hath the notions and carriage of a spark the most that ever I saw any man have. It makes me, I confess, admire her. (Pepys, *Diary*, 8. 91)

A later contemporary of Nell Gwyn who would equally attract the public eye for her private relationships as much as her performances on stage was Elizabeth Barry (1656x8–1713). The daughter of a royalist soldier, Colonel Robert Barry, Elizabeth was taken into the Davenant household by Lady Davenant along with several other young girls and trained to be an actress. The initial three occasions she appeared on stage in the early 1670s were not successful; according to Betterton's account, when the 'Persons of Wit and Quality' seated in the pit declared she had no future, John Wilmot, the Earl of Rochester, accepted a bet that he could make her 'the finest Player on the Stage'.[110] In 1676, she played in Etherege's *The Man of Mode*, taking the role of the fiery cast-off mistress, Mrs Loveit, and her career as the most celebrated actress of her generation had begun (see *CV* 3.I; *MV* 4.IV).

Public celebrity was not restricted only to the women. Betterton and Hart were also very much part of public discourse. Elizabeth Pepys, Samuel's wife,

---

[110] See Betterton, *The History of the English Stage*, 15–16.

was so enamoured of the leading man of the Duke's Company that she named her dog 'Betterton'. In his entry for 4 November 1661, Pepys describes their pleasure at seeing *The Bondman*, a tragicomedy by Massinger with Betterton as the lead, 'but for Baterton he is called by us both the best actor in the world' (Pepys, *Diary*, 2. 207). He also records a conversation with his barber Tom Benier, 'who being acquainted with all the players' tells him that Betterton is a 'very sober, serious man, and studious and humble, following of his studies, and is rich already with what he gets and saves' and, contrary to rumour, is not yet married to 'Ianthe' (whom Betterton did indeed marry in 1662) (Pepys, *Diary*, 3. 233, 22 October 1662).

Hart, the leading man of the King's Company, in addition to his affair with Nell Gwyn, also gained brief notoriety for his relationship with the King's most powerful mistress, Barbara Palmer, Lady Castlemaine, starting in 1668, when Castlemaine was no longer Charles's primary interest. Pepys, as always following the gossip of the theatre and the court, recorded that, on taking Elizabeth Knipp out to dinner on7 April 1668, she 'tells me mighty news, that my Lady Castlemayne is mightily in love with Hart of their house: and he is much with her in private, and she goes to him, and do give him many presents' (Pepys, *Diary*, 9. 156). Hart's public reputation, however, was primarily as a remarkably effective and enduring stage player. Downes describes how, 'if he Acted in any one [of his best-loved roles] but once in a Fortnight, the House was fill'd as at a New Play'. For Downes, Hart was the consummate professional actor: 'in all the Comedies and Tragedies, he was concern'd he Perform'd with that Exactness and Perfection, that not any of his Successors have Equall'd him'.[111] By the early 1670s, Hart and Mohun had also taken over most of the management of the company from the ageing Thomas Killigrew.

The London theatrical season ran from September through June, and actors performed six days a week during that period, Monday through Saturday. The theatres were also periodically closed on the Fridays of Lent and the week before Easter. The longest closure was caused by the Great Plague, followed by the Great Fire in London, which kept the actors offstage between 5 June 1665 and 29 November 1666. Performances typically began at three or three-thirty in the afternoon, with rehearsals starting in the morning at ten. The evenings were devoted to practising new songs or dances, fixing scenery and staging issues, and, several times a month, a special evening performance at Whitehall might be commanded. As many as three different plays might be performed by a company in a single week, and seasons where fifty different plays were presented were recorded. This placed a high demand on actors and actresses to master their multiple roles and to be able to ad lib quickly and appropriately in places where memory failed.

It was worth the effort, however, to an actor or actress to perfect a crowd-pleasing part. Once an actor or actress had succeeded in a part, he or she

---

[111] Downes, *Roscius Anglicanus*, 41.

typically became identified with it by the public, who demanded that their favourite performers be matched with their favourite roles. Downes notes that Charles Hart so excelled in playing the parts of kings and emperors that he could 'teach any King on Earth how to comport himself'.[112] Joseph Haines, John Lacy, and Cave Underhill (1634–1713) could be counted on for their portrayal of fops, fools, country bumpkins, and characters with names such as 'Old Moody' in Dryden's *Sir Martin Marr-all*. Nell Gwyn's attempts at serious drama were greeted with dismay by her many admirers: Pepys notes on 22 August 1667 that he 'saw "The Indian Emperour;" where I find Nell come again, which I am glad of; but was most infinitely displeased with her being put to act the Emperour's daughter; which is a great and serious part, which she do most basely' (Pepys, *Diary*, 8. 395). The critic John Dennis (1658–1734), writing in 1711 about the drama of the Restoration period, noted that 'many of the Writers for the Stage in my time, have not only adapted their Characters to their Actors, but those actors have as it were sate [posed] for them'.[113]

The new status of the prologue and epilogue, being delivered by a costumed actor or actress in a direct address to the audience, also helped to add to the feeling of a personal relationship between those on stage and in the audience. Occasionally, actors' freedoms with a role, especially when they were deliberately (or accidentally) referential to current events and people, could have a violently negative response. Pepys records in his diary on 1 February 1669 that, after a performance of William Cavendish's comedy *The Heiress*, Kynaston was set upon by hired thugs: 'Kinaston, that did act a part therein, in abuse to Sir Charles Sidley, being last night exceedingly dry-beaten with sticks, by two or three that assaulted him—so as he is mightily bruised and forced to keep his bed' (Pepys, *Diary*, 9. 435).

In addition to the personalities and capabilities of the leading actors and actresses in the two companies, the new theatres constructed by each were an important feature of the types of plays created during the Restoration period. Davenant's company was the first to move into new quarters, and in 1661 the Duke's Company occupied the newly enlarged theatre on the site of the former Lisle's Tennis Court in Lincoln's Inn Fields. Davenant had expanded the original 75-foot-long and 30-foot-wide structure in order to accommodate the type of spectacular staging he had first envisioned with his operas in the late 1650s; what distinguished it from pre-war theatres and converted tennis court theatres was its ability to display changeable scenery and its use of a proscenium arch or 'picture frame' stage, in addition to preserving an 'apron' stage that extended towards the audience.

The novelty of changeable scenery painted on screens, which ran on grooves in the stage floor and could be altered between and during acts to create new playing spaces, was a success with London audiences. To open on 28 June 1661,

---

[112] Downes, *Roscius Anglicanus*, 18.   [113] Dennis, *Reflections*, 1. 418.

Davenant shrewdly chose to restage one of his earlier operas, *The Siege of Rhodes*, which played for a remarkable twelve straight days to full houses. Tradition has it that this was the first time Charles II had visited a public theatre.[114] The popularity of the novel staging had demonstrable effect: when Pepys attended a play by Killigrew's rival troupe at the Vere Street theatre on 4 July, he noted that 'I went to the Theatre and there I saw *Claracilla* (the first time I ever saw it), well acted. But strange to see this house, that use to be so thronged, now empty since the Opera begun; and so will continue for a while, I believe' (Pepys, *Diary*, 2. 223). An Italian visitor in 1669, Prince Cosimo III of Tuscany, likewise admired the technical artistry of the acting space in Lincoln's Inn Fields, as well as the general comfort of the theatre, observing in his diary that 'the scenery is entirely changeable, with various transformations and lovely perspectives. Before the play begins, to render the waiting less annoying and inconvenient, there are very graceful instrumental pieces to be heard, with the result that many go early just to enjoy this part of the entertainment.'[115]

In response to this challenge from Davenant's new-style theatre and its multiple entertainments, Killigrew's newly built Theatre Royal in Bridges Street, Drury Lane, opened on 7 May 1663. It had 3 tiers of seats and was only about 112 feet long and 59 feet wide (a modern tennis court is typically 78 feet long and 27 feet wide by comparison), but it could hold 700 spectators. This was a considerable increase over the King's Company's original home in the converted Gibbons's Tennis Court on Vere Street, which had the capacity for a mere 400 in its limited seating space and no accommodation for scenery. The new Theatre Royal on Drury Lane would house the King's Company until 1672, when it was destroyed by fire; its replacement, possibly based on a design by Wren, was built in 1674 and would host the King's Company until 1682, when the two companies were united into one (see CV 1.1).

Pepys, as usual, was keen to see the new style of scenery and frequently comments on it in his diary. Writing about the 13 June 1663 production of *The Faithfull Shepherdesse*, he noted that he did not care for either the acting or the play itself, 'a most simple thing, and yet much thronged after, and often shown, but it is only for the scenes' sake, which is very fine indeed and worth seeing' (Pepys, *Diary*, 4. 182). Likewise, in his account of a performance of Corneille's *Heraclius* on 8 March 1664, he declared: 'at the beginning, at the drawing up of the Curtaine, there was the finest Scene of the Emperor and his people about him, standing in their fixed and different postures in their Roman habitts, above all that ever I yet saw at any of the Theatres' (Pepys, *Diary*, 5. 79).

In 1671, after the death of Davenant and led by Betterton and the remaining Davenant family, the Duke's Company moved to a new and even more technologically sophisticated theatre, Dorset Garden on the Thames, located near the old Salisbury Court. It cost a staggering £9,000 to build, and theatre historians

---

[114] Milhous, *Thomas Betterton*, 19.   [115] Quoted in Langhans, 'The Post-1660 Theatres', 16.

have attributed its design both to Christopher Wren and also to Robert Hooke. Nearly twice the size of the Duke's Company Lincoln's Inn Field theatre, it was some 140 feet long and 57 feet wide, with its benches in the central pit, two tiers of box seats, and an upper gallery able to seat up to 850 people. Featuring a proscenium arch carved by the master artist Grinling Gibbons, the stage included two raked acting areas, a forestage area extending in front of the arch, and a scenic stage estimated at being around 50 feet in depth and 30 feet high. The forestage and a box seating area above the proscenium arch could hold up to ten musicians for incidental music in the plays, while the pit area had space for a complete orchestra.

The need for the great height of the stage as well as its depth was to accommodate the special scenery and stage machines that would characterize performances at this theatre. Davenant had already experimented with using painted scenes that could slide in grooves on the stage to create different settings in his Lincoln's Inn Field theatre. In the new Dorset Garden theatre, in addition to changeable scenery, the stage had several trap doors in the acting floors and also 'machines' propelled by 'engines' that could fly objects such as clouds and actors and actresses in various chariots and the like for spectacular entrances and exits. Many of these were based on French theatre effects, and Betterton had taken the time to travel to Paris in 1671 specifically to learn more about their staging of *tragédie en machines*.

Most of the plays produced at Dorset Garden after its opening were heroic dramas or operas, which made full use of the physical possibilities of the stage, but were also extremely expensive to stage and required larger than normal casts of actors, musicians, and dancers. The first of these done in Dorset Gardens was Davenant's *Macbeth* (1672–3), followed by Elkanah Settle's *Empress of Morocco* (c.1673), for which a lavish print edition of the play's text was accompanied by engravings of the spectacular scenes, and the revised opera version of Davenant's and Dryden's *Tempest* (1673–4) created by Shadwell. The illustrations for Settle's publication of *Empress of Morocco* (1673) gives a good sense of the ways in which the sliding panels could create, among other scenes, a naval battle, a dungeon, and a 'Moorish' court setting, complete with a very large artificial palm tree (see Figure 3).

Ticket prices for the 1670s Dorset Garden spectacular plays were always more expensive than a regular play. The companies generally charged a similar scale for their seats, with boxes being the most expensive at 4s., while the pit was 2s. 6d., and the galleries the cheapest at 1s. 6d. and 1s.[116] Prices apparently doubled for *The Tempest* (1673). While the older outdoor theatres such as the Globe and the Red Bull had room for some 3,000 patrons, who might pay as little as a penny for entry, the Restoration theatres were closer in both size and price to the 'private' theatres before the war, and, likewise, the composition of their audiences was more restricted.

---

[116] See Avery and Scouten, *The London Stage*, pp. lxx–lxxiii.

As critics have observed, the original dramas staged in the early part of the 1660s not surprisingly attempted to match the tastes of the court. If nothing else, the long exile had given Charles and his companions an appreciation for French drama, and Charles's courtiers themselves provided some of the early new translations (see *MV* 2.IV). There were two productions of *La Mort de Pompée* (one in Dublin by Katherine Philips in 1663 and the other London in 1664 done by the courtiers Edmund Waller, Sir Charles Sedley, Edward Filmer, Sidney Godolphin, and Lord Buckhurst) staged along with Sir Thomas Clarges's *Héraclius* (1664). Sir Robert Howard combined his career as an MP and serving on the King's committee for the recovery of concealed lands with designing stages for the Theatre Royal and writing plays, including political comedies such as *The Committee* (1662), in which true cavalier love overcomes Puritan Parliamentarians, and tragedies such as *The Great Favourite, Or, the Duke of Lerma* (1668), which targeted the then disgraced and exiled Earl of Clarendon. The rake Sir Charles Sedley created another comedy set in the Commonwealth period where young witty cavaliers best crotchety Puritans in *The Mulberry-Garden* (see *MV* 2.IV). Charles's former tutor and ally in exile Sir William Cavendish (see *CV* 1.I) saw the London restaging of his comedies including *The Country Captaine* (first printed in 1649), *The Humorous Lovers* (1667), and *Sir Martin Marr-all, Or, The Feign'd Innocence* (1666). The last was based on his translation of Molière's *L'Etourdi*, but, as Pepys declared in his 16 August 1667 entry, 'every body says, [it was] corrected by Dryden', and indeed it is almost always attributed to Dryden. This reworking would become one of Dryden's most successful comedies: Pepys declared: 'It is the most entire piece of mirth, a complete farce from one end to the other . . . I never laughed so in all my life' (Pepys, *Diary*, 8. 387).

Other plays by titled authors during this early period included those by Katherine Philips's Irish patron Roger Boyle, Earl of Orrery (1621–79). Orrery, who notably served under Cromwell in the conquest of Ireland and as part of the inner cabinet of his council during the 1650s, offered the London public a series of rhyming heroic dramas in the 1660s, all of which concern usurpation and the restoration of legitimate hierarchy. The first, *The Generall*, was produced in London in 1664; it appears to be a direct reference to the events of the Restoration, as a heroic general Clorimum (based on Monck) moved by conscience turns against a usurper he had served and brings back the rightful king. Orrery's heroes display a self-sacrificing regard for public good over private passion, and his plays return almost obsessively to themes of regicide and usurpation.[117] *The Generall* was followed by *The History of Henry the Fifth* (1664), in which that king recovers his kingdom; these plays had the unusual good fortune to be so popular that Orrery enjoyed having two plays being staged by the rival companies in a single year. *The Tragedy of Mustapha, The Son of Solyman the Magnificient* (1665), set in Hungary as it is besieged by the

---

[117] See Maguire, *Regicide and Restoration*, ch. 6; Willie, *Staging the Revolution*, ch. 4.

Turks, has the evil and ambitious Vizier Rustan persuading the Sultan to execute his virtuous son Mustapha, a character marked by his resemblance to Charles I in the hagiographical descriptions bestowed on him by the other characters. *The Black Prince* followed in 1667, written, according to Orrery, at Charles's command. In it, Orrery uses the historical character of Edward, the Black Prince, and his capture of the French king John II at the battle of Poitiers; Kynaston played the lead, with Mohun and Hart in supporting roles. In its prologue, Orrery directly compares Charles II with Charlemagne, declaring 'Our Charles, not theirs, deserves the name of Great', and the play makes clear that English swords and kings shall always triumph over French ones.

John Dryden ably continued and expanded the fashion for heroic drama in rhyme with his two offerings set in exotic locales, *The Indian Queen* (1664) and *The Indian Emperour, or, the Conquest of Mexico by the Spaniards* (1665). The first was written in collaboration with his brother-in-law Sir Robert Howard and, like Orrery's dramas, deals with the usurpation of a throne, this time by an unlawful queen. Zempoalla and her general have usurped the Mexican throne from an unknown legitimate heir and then successfully seized power from Peru's old king Ynca. In the midst of this triumph, she falls in love with the honourable Peruvian general Montezuma, who had become best friends with her son Acacis, whom he previously had captured; both young men love Ynca's virtuous daughter, Orazia. After many complications, legitimate rule is restored as Zempoalla and Acacis kill themselves, Orazia is offered to Montezuma by her grateful father, and Montezuma is ultimately discovered to be the rightful heir of the Mexican throne.

In the sequel, *The Indian Emperour*, Dryden drew on Davenant's popular Commonwealth opera *The Cruelty of the Spaniards in Peru* (see CV 1.IV) to highlight the conquest of the Aztecs by Cortez. This spectacular production, to which Aphra Behn allegedly lent her feathered cloak brought from Surinam, as she assured her readers in her fiction *Oronooko* (see CV 4.II), was a huge success, perhaps because Dryden offered audiences on opening night a programme outlining the ways in which the two plays were connected. Michael Mohun took the lead as the tragic Indian emperor, with Charles Hart as the conquering Cortez. A famous miscasting had Nell Gwyn in her first serious role as the virtuous daughter of the doomed emperor, Cydaria: as Pepys noted, London audiences were pleased that she had returned to the stage, but not in this type of role.

The need for new plays in the late 1660s to showcase the abilities of the new companies and their new theatres meant that playwrights needed to devise materials rapidly, often, as we have seen, turning to older plays or to adaptations of French ones. Thomas Shadwell and Edward Ravenscroft in the late 1660s and early 1670s excelled in making use of Molière's comedies. Shadwell's popular *The Miser* (1672) and Ravenscroft's *The Citizen Turn'd Gentleman* (1671), drawing extensively on *L'Avare* and *Le Bourgeois Gentilhomme*, were adapted to English society to poke fun at the encroaching new money men such as Sir Giles Overreach but also to suggest the decline of gentility among the former class of gentle folk.

In addition to the iconic roles of the witty lovers found in the comedies of the 1660s and 1670s and the rhymed heroic dramas, another recent genre, tragicomedy, likewise highlighted the particular acting talents of the newly formed companies. As the name suggests, this hybrid required actors and actresses who could carry comedic subplots as well as those capable of declaiming noble and pathetic sentiments. In Dryden's *Marriage à la Mode*, written for the King's Company and first performed around 1671, the comic subplot is concerned with the antics of a pair of libertine rakes Palamede and Rhodophil—one married and bored, the other facing an arranged marriage—who unsuccessfully attempt to arrange a series of affairs with mysterious ladies, who in fact turn out to be their wives and fiancées. It opens with Doralice, Palamede's wife, singing a quintessential libertine lyric:

> Why should a foolish Marriage Vow
> Which long ago was made,
> Oblige us to each other now
> When passion is decay'd?[118]

Hart and Mohun played the hapless rakes with Rebecca Marshall and Elizabeth Bowtell as the witty Doralice and the frivolous Melantha. Their intrigues are counterbalanced by the heroic plot of Leonides and Palmyra, who, having been raised as simple country shepherd and shepherdess, are discovered to be a long-lost prince and princess; this couple must then sort through various confusions of identity and survive dire threats from the usurper Polydamas to regain their rightful places in the kingdom and claim their love. Kynaston took the part of Leonidas, who even in his shepherd's garb speaks majestically, declaring boldly to the wondering court, 'I can fear nothing but the Gods' (I. i, p. 13). As with all the heroic dramas of the 1660s and early 1670s, the ability to govern one's passions and willingness to sacrifice personal happiness to the demands of duty suggest noble origins, even of seemingly defeated or humble characters; they eventually will be revealed to be the true rulers and restored to their appropriate place.

Dryden's numerous successes with this new style of tragicomedy as well as his rhymed heroic dramas, which featured long speeches of noble passion and sentiments, clearly established him as a popular playwright for general audiences, but it also made him the target of the court wits (see *MV* 2.IV). George Villiers, Duke of Buckingham, created his parody of Dryden and the heroic in *The Rehearsal* (1671). Working with several other collaborators, including it has been suggested the author of *Hudibras* Samuel Butler (see *MV* 2.VI) and Thomas Sprat (1635–1713) of the Royal Society (see *MV* 2.V), Buckingham not only attacks the absurdity of bombastic heroic speeches and contrived situations

---

[118] Dryden, *Marriage à la Mode*, I. i, p. 1.

found in contemporary rhyming dramas, but also specifically targets Dryden and his plays. The lead character, Mr Bayes (the name suggests the position of the poet laureateship, which Dryden assumed after Davenant in 1668), is in the process of putting on a new play and invites two young men from the country, Johnson and Smith, to watch the rehearsal. The young men are justifiably confused, as the prologue and epilogue featuring characters named Thunder and Lightning are interchangeable and the plot seems to be going in several different directions. Throughout the play, Bayes comically attempts to convince the actors whom he is rehearsing, who are also baffled, to perform nonsense as though it was sense, including having four soldiers appear on stage to kill each other for no reason, then rise and do a lengthy dance.

The real epilogue to *The Rehearsal* confirms that there actually was no plot, merely scenes and speeches from Dryden's own plays, especially *The Conquest of Granada*, haphazardly stitched together using stock situations, such as lost princes being raised by fishermen:

> The Play is at an end, but where's the Plot?
> That circumstance our Poet *Bayes* forgot,
> And we can boast, though 'tis a plotting Age,
> No place is freer from it than the Stage.[119]

It concludes, summarizing the perceived inadequacies of the previous decade's dramas:

> Wherefore, for ours, and for the Kingdoms peace,
> May this prodigious way of writing cease.

Instead, the actor urges:

> Let's have, at least, once in our lives, a time
> When we may hear some Reason, not all Rhyme:
> We have these ten years felt its Influence;
> Pray let this prove a year of Prose and Sence. ('Epilogue')

Undaunted, Dryden published in 1672 his two-part play with a fulsome dedication to the Duke of York in praise of 'Heroique Poetry' supposedly modelled on the Duke's own valorous behaviour as a military leader. 'I have alwaies observ'd in your Royal Highness', Dryden announces, 'an extream concernment for the honour of your Country 'tis a passion common to you with a Brother, the most excellent of Kings: and in your two persons, are eminent the Characters which *Homer* has given us of Heroique virtue'. It is his duty as a poet, Dryden asserts, to devise a means to 'transmit you to Posterity', and to this end he creates the hero Almanzor, who demonstrates, in his words and acts, 'a frank and noble openness of Nature; an easiness to forgive his conquer'd enemies; and to protect them in distress; and above all, an inviolable faith in

---

[119] Villiers, *The Rehearsal*, 'Epilogue'.

this affection. This, Sir, I have briefly shaddow'd to your Royal Highness, that you may not be asham'd of that Heroe whose protection you undertake.'[120] To attack the heroic, Dryden is asserting, is to attack the royal family itself.

Clearly, the theatres were an important venue for the King and his courtiers to see and be seen. Because of the afternoon staging, with the audience enjoying the same lighting as the performers, watching the audience sometimes proved a distraction from watching the play itself. Pepys was torn between irritation and fascination observing members of the audience at a performance of *The Maids Tragedy*:

vexed all the while with two talking ladies and Sir Ch. Sidley; yet pleased to hear their discourse.... one of the ladies would, and did sit with her mask on, all the play; and, being exceeding witty as ever I heard woman, did talk most pleasantly with him; but was, I believe, a virtuous woman, and of quality. He would fain know who she was, but she would not tell. (Pepys, *Diary*, 8. 71–2, 18 February 1667).

The exchange apparently overwhelmed the action on stage, for 'he was mighty witty; and she also making sport with him very inoffensively, that a more pleasant rencontre I never heard. But by that means lost the pleasure of the play wholly' (Pepys, *Diary*, 8. 71–2, 18 February 1667). A foreign visitor in 1667, Samuel Chappuzeau, was also taken by the distracting presence of ladies in the audience: the London theatres 'are attended by well-to-do people and above all by beautiful women'.[121] The theatres, as they became less of a novelty, also began to attract more moderately well-to-do citizens and even apprentices, which did not entirely please Pepys, who noted in his 1 January 1663 entry that 'The house was full of Citizens, and so the less pleasant' (Pepys, *Diary*, 4. 2).

As their repertoire developed and deepened with the addition of new writers such as Aphra Behn in the 1670s, the two patent companies were frequently invited to stage performances for the King at Whitehall. The old Cockpit Theatre there had been damaged during the Interregnum, but it apparently served its purpose until a new theatre, designed more on continental models, was opened in April 1665. Located in what had formerly been the 'Great Hall', this space was remodelled under the direction of John Webb to serve as a permanent court theatre, with scenery and a new stage. Pepys initially was unimpressed: in 1666 on 29 October, he records that 'to White Hall, and into the new playhouse there, the first time I ever was there, and the first play I have seen since before the great plague' (Pepys, *Diary*, 7. 347). Pepys seems more entertained by watching who attended the performance, noting: 'By and by the King and Queene, Duke and Duchesse, and all the great ladies of the Court; which, indeed, was a fine sight.' The play, however, Etherege's comedy *Love in a Tub*, he dismissed as 'a silly play, and though done by the Duke's people, yet having neither Baterton nor his wife—and the whole thing done ill, and being ill also,

[120] Dryden, *The Conquest of Granada*, 'To His Royal Highness the Duke'.
[121] Quoted in Langhans, 'The Post-1660 Theatres', 16.

I had no manner of pleasure in the play'. 'Besides', he concluded, 'the House, though very fine, yet bad for the voice, for hearing. The sight of the ladies, indeed, was exceeding noble; and above all, my Lady Castlemayne' (Pepys, *Diary*, 7. 347).

In addition to the commercial theatres and the court, the Inns of Court also continued their tradition of hiring one of the two companies to provide entertainment on their festival days, All Hallows (1 November) and Candlemas (2 February). The company was typically paid £20 for one of these performances, which would occur, like the Whitehall ones, in the late afternoon or evening after their daily performance in the commercial venues. The plays selected by the Inns of Court to entertain their guests, including justices and leading London citizens, were often from the companies' pre-war repertoire, but a request would occasionally be made for a new, successful play to be performed.

There were several other theatrical enterprises that sprang up after the Restoration that brought the stage to those living outside London. Katherine Philips's adaptation of Corneille's *Tragedy of Pompey*, as already mentioned, was staged in 1663 in Dublin at the newly created Theatre Royal in Smock Alley. Managed by Joseph Ashbury from 1662 until his death in 1720, the Theatre Royal's original company was founded by John Ogilby, who had turned London's streets into a vast theatre for Charles II's triumphant return to the city, published as *The Entertainment of his Most Excellent Majestie Charles II* (1661; see CV 2.1). The peripatetic Ogilby was in Dublin for only a short time, between 1662 and 1666, but during that period he opened his second theatre there, which would be the site of a Theatre Royal until the present day. His first attempt, the Werburgh Street Theatre or the New Theatre, had opened between 1634 and 1637, but had been closed and wrecked during the 1641 rebellion.

Philips, who had finished her rhymed couplet translation of *Pompey* while staying in Dublin, had the enthusiastic support of Robert Boyle, Earl of Orrery, for its staging at the new Smock Alley theatre. Orrery had already had his own heroic drama, *The Generall*, staged there, probably in October 1663 under the title *Altemera*.[122] The women of Orrery's family—his sister-in-law the Countess of Cork and her daughters Lady Elizabeth, Lady Anne, and Lady Frances Boyle—along with the Duke of Ormond's daughter, Lady Mary Butler, had become Philips's friends and patrons during this period in Dublin. Philips wrote to another friend in London, Sir Charles Cotterell, that she had gone to see the ever-popular revived Beaumont and Fletcher comedy *Wit without Money* at the new Dublin playhouse, 'which in my Opinion is much finer than D'Avenant's; but the Scenes are not yet made'.[123] Writing again to Cotterell, Philips in a letter dated 31 January 1663 declared that, when the additional songs she had created for *Pompey* had been set to music, Orrery insisted that it

---

[122] See Mambretti, 'Orinda on the Restoration Stage', 235–6, 242–3.
[123] Philips, *Letters from Orinda to Poliarchus*, 88–9.

be publicly staged, 'which notwithstanding all my Intreaties to the contrary, he is going on with, and has advanc'd a hundred Pounds towards the Expence of buying Roman and Egyptian Habits' (p. 119). The music was provided by trained musicians from the Cathedral, and Ogilby himself choreographed the *entre acte* dances. Its premiere—the first play to have had its debut performance at Dublin's new theatre—apparently had all the tensions encountered when mounting a new play by a new playwright, including a quarrel among the actors 'whether Caesar or Ptolemy shall have the best Hobbyhorse' (pp. 158, 164–5).

Some of the actors performing in Dublin had previously been members of the two London companies. John Richards left the Duke's Company to join Ogilby's in the summer of 1662, which so angered Davenant that he had a warrant drawn up demanding his return. In addition to staging performances in Dublin, the Smock Alley players were also periodically given licences to tour and performed in Oxford and other locations. In this they had competition, both from the patent companies in London, who spent part of their time when the London theatres were closed by the plague in 1665–6 touring the provinces, and also from the touring company of George Jolly. In 1663, at last ousted from London by Killigrew and Davenant, Jolly was granted permission to play in any city except London and Westminster. Norwich became more or less his primary venue, and his players used the space provided by the King's Arms Inn. Following the practice they had used during the brief time they had performed in London after the Restoration, Jolly's company used older plays, including John Ford's Jacobean tragedy *'Tis Pity She's a Whore* and Philip Massinger's satiric *A New Way to Pay Old Debts*.

The theatre after the restoration of Charles II was both restored and innovated. The changes made to the physical playing spaces, the introduction of actresses, and the establishment of two rival companies vying for audiences significantly shaped the types of dramas that were adapted from earlier plays and that were written for the new stages. Many of the theatrical spaces outside London were likewise recovered for the touring companies, and new venues such as Smock Alley in Dublin provided opportunities for new playwrights and texts. Unlike the audiences that initially greeted the first productions in London in 1660 and 1661 in which some in the audience had never seen a staged play, the performances at new London theatres and companies guaranteed that the next urban generation would grow up with notions of theatricality, performance, and celebrity as being an essential part of literary culture.

IV. Enacting Libertinism: Court Performance and Literary Culture

> The King sups at least four or [five] times every week with my Lady
> Castlemaine; and most often stays till the morning with her, and goes

home through the garden all alone privately, and that so as the very centrys [sentries] take notice of it and speak of it. She tells me, that about a month ago she [Lady Castlemaine] quickened at my Lord Gerard's at dinner, and cried out that she was undone; and all the lords and men were fain to quit the room, and women called to help her. In fine, I find that there is nothing almost but bawdry at Court from top to bottom.

Pepys, *Diary*, 4. 1, 1 January 1663

The behaviour of the King after his return in 1660 soon scandalized many who had hoped ardently for his restoration to the throne. Charles openly consorted with his mistresses and illegitimate children and lavished them with property, titles, and wealth; his complete disregard of religious and social codes controlling sexual behaviour was mirrored in the actions of many of his male courtiers and their female counterparts. As recent critics have observed, the hedonistic atmosphere of the court that has come in later generations to represent the whole of the Restoration period was self-consciously transgressive and libertine in nature, although certainly not all members of the court participated in it.[124] For some, however, their public behaviours gained for them an early form of celebrity: their sexual and usually drunken exploits were recorded in diaries, circulated in letters, re-created on stage, discussed in coffee houses, and denounced in sermons. Although they were christened by Andrew Marvell as 'the Merry Gang', sometimes their choices or even their whims led to violence and death, for which the King almost inevitably would issue a pardon. In 1666, for example, George Villiers, Duke of Buckingham (1628–87) and one of Charles's closest companions and advisers, embarked on a public affair with Anna-Maria Brudenell, the married Countess of Shrewsbury; in 1668, Villiers killed the Duke of Shrewsbury in a duel for which Charles pardoned him. As Samuel Pepys recorded: 'This will make the world think that the King hath good councillors about him, when the Duke of Buckingham, the greatest man about him, is a fellow of no more sobriety then to fight about a whore' (Pepys, *Diary*, 9. 27, 17 January 1668).

Historians and critics have observed of Charles's courtiers such as Sir Charles Sedley (bap. 1639–1701), Charles Sackville, Lord Buckhurst (1643–1706), and John Wilmot, Earl of Rochester (1647–10) that such public, transgressive performances were an essential element of creating and sustaining their positions in Charles's court at the beginning of the Restoration. They both asserted an aristocratic privilege to behave in public as they pleased and displayed a performance designed to attract the attention of and amuse the King. Charles II reinstituted the practice of politics of access and government through favourites (see CV 2.1).[125] This created a competitive atmosphere, as the courtiers

---

[124] See Turner, *Libertines and Radicals.*   [125] Love, *English Clandestine Satire*, 30–1.

jostled for proximity and attention, and at the apex of this power positioning was the King's favourite mistress of the moment.

With the exception of Buckingham, who was a contemporary of the King, most of the key libertine figures in Charles's court were young men, too young to have fought in the war; the place of Thomas Killigrew at court, who had accompanied the royal family throughout their exile, was soon taken by his much wilder son, Harry Killigrew.[126] As we shall see, however, many of these same courtiers by the mid-1670s had lost favour, in part because their scandalous behaviour had gone beyond sanction and, like Buckingham, Sedley, and Rochester, they began to mock the politics of the court and its personages in their widely circulated satires and lampoons. Buckingham eventually would go from being one of the chief wits of the court to joining those in Parliament who would comprise the opposing Whig party.

The women they consorted with in the decade of the 1660s and early 1670s were publicly labelled whores, but nevertheless some, such as the actress Nell Gwyn and Barbara Palmer, Countess of Castlemaine, secured wealth and titles for their numerous illegitimate offspring. In addition, they became regular characters in contemporary political satires in the form of libels (poems directed at specific individuals, which were made illegal in both print and handwritten copy in the Licensing Act of 1662) and lampoons (originally a drinking song that became a satiric ballad form), whose number would sharply increase in the 1670s and 1680s.[127] Such satiric snapshots of vices of the court were typically anonymous. For example, 'On the Ladies of the Court', judged to be written around 1663 from the names included in it, catalogues the sexual misconduct of the maids of honour, those women surrounding the new Queen and the Duchess of York. One is Winifred Well, a minor mistress of Charles about whom rumour had it that she had actually 'dropped child' (i.e. given birth) during a ball at court, as recorded by Pepys on 8 February 1663 (Pepys, *Diary*, 4. 37). Of her the lampoon declares:

> Well's broken vessels leak,
> Though fools their freedom have to speak,
> They take no honor from them:
> Whilst thou art there
> They are sure bear
> All that is laid upon them.[128]

Outside of the maids of honour, the theatre provided several of Charles's amorous interests, as it did for his brother the Duke of York and his courtiers, including Mary 'Moll' Davis, who would remain associated with the court for many years and appear in court theatricals (see *MV* 3.I).[129]

---

[126] See Smith, ' "A Gentleman of Great Esteem" ', 160, 168–70.
[127] See Wilson, *Court Satires*, introduction; Linker, *Dangerous Women*, introduction.
[128] Quoted in Wilson, *Court Satires*, 4.   [129] See Howe, *The First English Actresses*.

The King's public display of his many mistresses, even while attending church, set the tone for his court. The most powerful of them, Castlemaine, continued until the end of the King's life to exert influence, long after both the King and she had moved on to other lovers. She was a frequent target of lampoons and satires: the anonymous ballad 'Good people, draw near', composed prior to Clarendon's exile in 1667, declares that 'the world's ruled by cheating and swiving', and that in this world Castlemaine ruled through her avaricious sexual appetites: 'That prerogative quean; | If I had such a bitch I would spay her.'

Castlemaine, however, was an adroit, if not always subtle, manipulator of her own public image and representation, commissioning grand portraits of herself and her offspring almost yearly. These lush and vibrant portraits, many by Sir Peter Lely, challenge the viewer directly in their representation of the royal mistress. In 1663, for example, she had Lely portray her and her eldest son by Charles in the robes and traditional postures of Madonna and child.[130] In the decade of the 1660s, Lely also painted her as a pastoral shepherdess and, in 1667, as her power was waning, as St Catherine; this choice seemingly deliberately invoked Jacob Huysmans's portrait of the young Queen Catherine of Braganza in this same role of saintly martyr and thus forced a direct comparison between queen and mistress. Pepys, who collected prints of her image made by William Faithorne based on Lely's paintings, famously recorded in an early response to her on the occasion when she left her husband to reside openly as the King's mistress that, 'strange it is, how for her beauty I am willing to construe all this to the best and to pity her wherein it is to her hurt, though I know well enough she is a whore' (Pepys, *Diary*, 2. 139, 16 July 1662).

Like the male courtiers, the women associated with the courtiers were highly self-conscious in acting their libertine parts for the King's entertainment, even when it might appear to go against their best interest. Castlemaine scandalized more than Pepys with her unsuccessful seduction of unwilling maid of honour Frances Stuart for the King in a mock wedding: 'Another story was how my Lady Castlemaine, a few days since, had Mrs Stuart to an entertainment, and at night began a frolique that they two must be married', Pepys records avidly, 'and married they were, with ring and all other ceremonies of church service, and ribbands and a sack-posset in bed, and flinging the stocking. But in the close, it is said that my Lady Castlemayne, who was the bridegroom, rose, and the King came and took her place with pretty Mrs Stuart.' 'This is said to be very true', Pepys concludes (Pepys, *Diary*, 4. 37–8, 8 February 1663), and true or not, this episode has entered many subsequent accounts of Charles and his court.

Castlemaine and the other ladies of the court also appeared in court entertainments, sometimes with jarringly ironic results. A translation of Corneille's play *Horace*, begun by Katherine Philips before her death and finished by John Denham, was produced at court in February 1668 with the young Duchess of

---

[130] See MacLeod and Alexander, *Painted Ladies*, 116–35, for a discussion of Castlemaine's involvement with Lely in constructing her portraits.

Monmouth and Castlemaine in leading tragic parts. The play, which highlights the suffering of noble heroes and heroines who sacrifice all personal happiness for the good of the country, showcased instead the royal mistress wearing the crown jewels, a costume estimated to value £200,000, an irony surely not lost on the courtiers in the select audience.[131]

Along with John Evelyn, Samuel Pepys is a key source for recording what Londoners considered newsworthy in the 1660s (see CV 2.III). As seen, his diary records, with a mixture of astonishment, indignation, and perhaps also an occasional touch of admiration, the deeds of those closest to Charles II, which frequently displayed an extravagant disregard for the institutions that had hitherto structured Pepys's society, the Church, the family, and even at times the court itself. On 1 July 1663, only a few months after Castlemaine's supposed mock marriage with Frances Stuart, Pepys's diary contains an account of Sir Charles Sedley dining with Buckhurst and Sir Thomas Ogle at the appropriately named Cock Inn. Sedley, during dinner,

coming in open day into the Balcone and showed his nakedness . . . and abusing of scripture and as it were from thence preaching a mountebanke sermon from that pulpit . . . a thousand people standing underneath to see and hear him. And that being done, he took a glass of wine and washed his prick in it and then drank it off, and then took another and drank the King's health. (Pepys, *Diary*, 4. 209)

Sedley was heavily fined for this behaviour, and the presiding judge declared that it was because of such actions that 'God's anger and judgment hang over us'. It is clear from this example that simply being inebriated or pushing the limits of socially condoned sexual acts was in itself not enough to define the rake: it is the dramatic, public staging of these challenges to conventional morality, even if one's audience is only an angry, titillated crowd outside a tavern. In such plays, poems, and public appearances, the libertines were the heroes of a sexual theatre, one that mixed politics, art, and Eros, and the chief among the court wits was, of course, Charles II himself.

In contrast, only a few months later, Sedley and Buckhurst, along with Edmund Waller, Sidney Godolphin, and Sir Edward Filmer, collaborated in translating Corneille's high-minded tragedy *La Mort de Pompée*, responding to the King's interest in French dramas, which was presented by the Duke's Company at Lincoln's Inn Fields. Sedley's own comedy *The Mulberry-Garden* (1668), notably, was set in Commonwealth England and involved the romantic adventures of two sets of daughters, one the offspring of Sir Samuel Forecast, a rigid Puritan, and the other the children of Sir John Everyoung, an easy-going cavalier; in the final act, marriages are arranged and conventions restored. This will not be the case in Sedley's later comedy, *Bellamira, or The Mistress* (1687), whose heroine is a satiric portrait of Lady Castlemaine: upon her merchant father losing his money, Bellamira uses her lush sexuality to keep a string of male

---

[131] See Hughes, *English Drama*, 37–8.

lovers interested and secure the financial backing of the easy-going 'Keepwell', and so unrepentant was the libertine heroine that it provoked charges of obscenity (see *MV* 4.IV).

As seen in the example of Sedley, it is notable that many of the most prominent of the libertine courtiers, sometimes referred to as the 'Court Wits' in studies of the period—such as John Wilmot, the Earl of Rochester; Sedley; Charles Sackville, Lord Buckhurst (later styled Lord Dorset); Sir George Etherege (1636–91/2); George Villiers, Duke of Buckingham; John Sheffield, Earl of Mulgrave (1647–1721); and William Wycherley (bap. 1641–1716)—were also men of letters, poets, and dramatists, and they helped to create a literature of libertinism as well as living it.[132] Several of these writers were closely involved in the initial production of their plays, with Buckingham and Etherege overseeing the ways in which actual contemporary notables were represented as characters in their plays, such as John Dryden in *The Rehearsal* and Rochester in *Man of Mode*.

Rochester, one of the most publicly visible of the libertine wits, might declare in his verse his desire to 'Leave this gaudy gilded stage', but he also performed his part in creating a libertine ethos for the court through his actions and his lyrics and satires, which circulated widely (see *MV* 2.VI; *MV* 3.I).

> I'll tell of *Whores* Attacqu'd their Lords at home,
> *Bawds Quarters* beaten up, and *Fortress* won,
> *Windows* demolisht, *Watches* overcome,
> And handsome ills, by my contrivance done.

> Nor shall our *Love-fits Cloris* be forgot,
> When each the well-look'd *Link-boy,* strove t'enjoy,
> And the best Kiss was the deciding *Lot,*
> Whether the *Boy* us'd you, or I the *Boy.*[133]

Rochester also chronicled the enthusiasm with which some Londoners responded to the general air of sexual libertinism set by the court. In 'A Ramble in St James Park', written in the early 1670s when he was in his early twenties, he describes how nightly in the park

> Unto this All-sin-sheltering *Grove,*
> *Whores* of the *Bulk,* and the *Alcove.*
> *Great* Ladies Chamber-Maids, Drudges;
> The *Rag-picker*; and *Heiresse* trudges. (pp. 76–7)

They are met there by

> Car-men, Divines, *great* Lords, *and* Taylors,
> Prentices, Pimps, Poets, *and* Gaolers;
> *Foot-Men,* fine *Fops,* do here arrive, (p. 77)

---

[132] See Webster, *Performing Libertinism*, ch. 1.
[133] Wilmot, *Works*, ed. Love, 'The Diabled Debauchee', 44–5.

and it concludes: 'And here promiscuously do swive.' Social order and hierarchy vanish in the 'Strange woods' of St James's, 'consecrate to *Prick* and *Cunt*'. Rochester would do the same with poetic conventions in his occasional verses as he did with social ones in his satires: 'As Cloris full of harmless thoughts, | Beneath a *Willow* lay', a thoroughly conventional pastoral lyric with a blushing innocent shepherdess and charming shepherd, is rendered in a second version as 'Fair *Cloris* in a *Pig-Stye* lay, | Her tender *Herd*, lay by her' (p. 39), and she enjoys erotic fantasies while dozing with her pigs.

The poem 'Régime de Vivre', believed to have been composed around 1673, and sometimes attributed to Rochester and sometimes to Charles Sackville, Lord Buckhurst, describes the imagined typical day of a libertine:

> I Rise at Eleven, I Dine about Two,
> I get drunk before Seven, and the next thing I do;
> I send for my *Whore*.[134]

On his passing out after vomiting in her lap, the '*Bitch,* growing bold, to my Pocket does creep' and sneaks away, leaving the speaker to awake

> hot-headed, and drunk
> What a coyle do I make for the loss of my *Punk*?
> I storm, and I roar, and I fall in a rage
> And missing my *Whore*, I bugger my *Page*.[135]

Recent social historians often find evidence in the flamboyant sexuality of the court in both life and literature of contemporary attitudes towards sexuality and, in particular, what defines masculinity, a conceptualization that would be shifting by 1700. Paradoxically, in the early 1660s the love of boys was apparently defined not as homosexual or aberrant sexual behaviour, even though sodomy was illegal and punishable by death, but instead as an extreme form of libertinism that was associated with a radical scepticism or 'free thinking' concerning the institutions of religion and social custom, and at times of the government as well.[136] Certainly in the verse of Rochester and his fellow libertine poets, sex with attractive servants, male or female, is viewed as opportunistic, and as being an expression of the poet's unlimited sexual appetite and prowess rather than a more modern conceptualization of homosexuality.[137]

The bisexual rake as a figure on stage is more common in the later 1670s, but Aphra Behn's second play, *The Amorous Prince, Or, The Curious Husband* (1671), is, for example, constructed around a libertine disdain for wedded bliss and the willingness to have sex wherever one's fancy hit. Behn complicates the customary breeches role of the female character as the seduced innocent Cloris disguises herself as a page and thus excites the interest of Lorenzo, a favourite

---

[134] See Vieth, *Attribution of Restoration Poetry*, 86–7, 168–72, and 411–12, for a discussion of the issues in attribution for this poem.
[135] Wilmot, *Works*, ed. Love, 74.   [136] See Trumbach, 'The Birth of the Queen'.
[137] See Rousseau, 'The Pursuit of Homosexuality'; Goldberg, *Sodometries*, ch. 1.

of the amorous prince in the title. The opening scene of the play has Prince Frederick in the process of getting dressed in the bedroom of Cloris, still in her night clothes, after a night of obviously illicit sex; the Prince quickly and easily moves on to another conquest, causing Cloris to disguise herself as a page, Philabert, in order to stay near him. Lorenzo's response to the new page is immediate:

> —Hah, I vow to gad a lovely Youth;   [*Lor.* gazes on *Phill.*]
> But what makes he here with *Frederick?*
> This stripling may chance to mar my market of women now—
> 'Tis a fine lad, how plump and white he is; [Aside.]
> Would I could meet him somewhere i'th' dark,
> I'd have a fling at him, and try whether I
> Were right *Florentine*.[138]

Behn's own lover in the 1670s was John Hoyle, a lawyer known for his radical republican views as well as his libertine lifestyle; he was indicted but not convicted in 1687 for sodomy and died in 1692 in a tavern fight occasioned by his 'railing against the government'.[139]

Sedley and friends also figure in another of Pepys's entries as he describes 'among other news, the late frolick and debauchery of Sir Charles Sidly and Buckhurst, running up and down all the night with their arses bare, through the streets; and at last fighting, and being beat by the watch and clapped up all night'. What Pepys found noteworthy in this event was that 'the King takes their parts; and my Lord Chief Justice Keeling hath laid the constable by the heels to answer it next Sessions—which is a horrid shame' (Pepys, *Diary*, 9. 335–6, 23 October 1668). Pepys records that a few days later he passed these stories along to his patron as an illustration of 'the ill posture of things at this time'. The popular pornographic literature of the day likewise mirrors some real-life exploits (see CV 2.IV); titles such as *The Wandering Whore*, a series of pamphlets that began appearing between 1660 and 1663, likewise feature drunken young men assailing whores, damaging property, and assaulting those supposed to keep the law, all without much penalty.[140]

In the comedies of the 1660s and early 1670s, however, the rake character on stage is typically reformed and presumably domesticated by marriage to a virtuous and witty young lady at the end of the play.[141] Most of these, such as Wellbred in *The English Monsieur* (1663) and Philidor in *All Mistaken* (1665) by James Howard and *Secret-Love, or, The Maiden-Queen* (1667) by Dryden, are attractive young men who are wits and well-bred as their names suggest; they fall in love with equally respectable and clever young women and presumably

---

[138] Behn, *The Amorous Prince*, IV. Iii, p. 59.
[139] Quoted in Trumbach, 'The Birth of the Queen', 164.
[140] See Turner, 'The Wandering Whore's Return: The Carnivalization of Sexuality in the Early Restoration', in *Libertines and Radicals*, ch. 4.
[141] See Chernaik, *Sexual Freedom*.

leave behind with marriage their wilder ways (see *MV* 2.III). Other rake figures, however, are more problematic. Rodophil in Dryden's comedy *Marriage-à-la-Mode* (1673) is not tamed by marriage, but instead finds being wed boring and cloying; his friend Palamede, who attempts to seduce his wife, Doralice, resigns himself to marry for money, as his father desires. By the mid-1670s, rakes such as Horner in Wycherley's *The Country-Wife* (1675) and Dorimant in Etherege's *The Man of Mode* (1676) are left unmarried at the end, and any conversion to social respectability is left pointedly unresolved (see *CV* 3.I).

It would be inevitable, given the circulation of their exploits through gossip and the publication in manuscript copies of satires and lampoons, that individual courtiers in Charles's court were loosely identified with characters portrayed on stage. Even the libertine lives of the performers figured in the audience's appreciation of the plays. In 1667, Charles Hart and Nell Gwyn appeared in Dryden's *Secret-Love, or, The Maiden-Queen* in which she played Florimel to Hart's Celadon. The audience, including Pepys, the King, and the Duke of York, no doubt enjoyed an extra element of the performance in the knowledge that the clever, ambitious young girl who woos and finally wins the rakish hero was his lover in real life, and, indeed, would soon become the King's (see *MV* 2.III; *CV* 3.I).

Another literary genre based on a recognizable individual was the personal lampoon or libel.[142] As critics have observed, there is a long tradition of this type of writing, with Royalist satires of the figures in the Interregnum government circulating widely both in script and orally; several volumes of such epigrams and satires had been published, such as *Sportive Wit* and *Choyce Drollery*, both in 1656, and both had been ordered destroyed by the government. In the Restoration, the humiliations of the second Dutch War (1665–7), with the Dutch fleet's raid on the Medway and the destruction of part of the English fleet, again featured figures at court and their politics as the targets for such satires. In addition to poems satirizing these specific events, there was always a steady stream of poetic invective in circulation, designed to topple favourites and advance individuals' own interests at court. Rochester, Buckingham, and Lord Buckhurst (also eventually styled the Earl of Dorset) initially occupied positions of personal access at court, being gentlemen of the bedchamber, and, in the mid-1660s, came to form a faction against the ageing Clarendon, who was famously under attack in the 'Advices to a Painter' satires (see *CV* 2.II).

By the early 1670s, however, Charles himself became increasingly a target for his own court wits, with the famous story of Rochester 'accidently' handing Charles the wrong lampoon and having to escape from court as a result.

> I'th'isle of Britain, long since famous grown
> For breeding the best cunts in Christendom,

---

[142] See Love, *English Clandestine Satire*, ch. 2.

> There reigns, and oh! Long may he reign and thrive,
> The easiest King and best-bred man alive.
>
> .   .   .   .   .
>
> Nor are his high desires above his strength:
> His scepter and his prick are of a length;
> And she may sway the one who plays with th'other,
> And make him little wiser than his brother.
> Poor prince! Thy prick, like thy buffoons at Court,
> Will govern thee because it makes thee sport.[143]

The satire memorably continues 'Restless he rolls about from whore to whore, |
A merry monarch, scandalous and poor', and concludes with a roster of
Charles's mistresses and their skills in manipulating the ageing monarch.

Libertinism, as it was played out in the early years of the Restoration and
as it permeated politics over the course of Charles II's reign, was a hedonistic
lifestyle, a political posture, a body of literature, and a performance art. While
it became increasingly associated with philosophical scepticism about human
institutions and human nature in the 1670s and 1680s, in its earliest manifestations among Charles and his courtiers, male and female, it functioned as a
clear and simple rejection of the ethos of the Interregnum and an assertion of
both aristocratic privilege as well as personal promotion.

V. Creating Science: The Royal Society and the New Literatures of Science

> There is one thing more, about which the *Society* has been most
> sollicitous; and that is, the manner of their *Discourse*: which, unless
> they had been very watchful to keep in due temper, the whole spirit
> and vigour of their *Design*, had been soon eaten out, by the luxury
> and redundance of *speech*.... I can hardly forbear recanting what
> I said before; and concluding, that *eloquence* ought to be banish'd
> out of all *civil Societies*, as a thing fatal to Peace and good Manners.
>
> Thomas Sprat, *History of the Royal Society* (1667)

> ...at her Majesties displeasure concerning their Telescopes, [they]
> kneel'd down, and in the humblest manner petitioned that they might
> not be broken; for, said they, we take more delight in Artificial delu-
> sions, then in natural truths.
>
> Margaret Cavendish, *The Description of a New World,*
> *called the Blazing-World* (1668)

---

[143] Wilmot, *Works*, ed. Love, 85–6, 'A Satyr on Charles II'.

Although science and the literary arts have come to occupy separate cultures in the recent past, this was not yet so during the seventeenth century, when rhetoric, poetry, and music were considered to be important parts of the studies of the new academic societies. Historians are divided over the exact origins of what would become the extraordinarily influential gathering of intellectuals and writers in the late seventeenth century who formed the Royal Society of London, but it is clear that the ways in which English science was conceptualized and the ways in which scientific findings would be disseminated throughout the country and abroad was significantly shaped by this new society.

On 15 July 1662, Charles II granted a Royal Charter bringing into being the Royal Society of London, but it had had several precursors during the late 1640s and 1650s. There were groups meeting in Oxford throughout the war years and during the Commonwealth and also in London, notably at Gresham College. Some contemporaries suggested that the English society was modelled after the Montmor Academy in France, based on reports of it sent by visiting English scientists, including Henry Oldenburg (c.1619–77), who would become the first secretary of the Royal Society. Robert Hooke (1635–1703) in the late 1690s, however, flatly denied this foreign influence on English science and scientific organization: '[Cassini] makes, then, Mr Oldenburg to have been the instrument, who inspired the English with a desire to imitate the French, in having Philosophical Clubs, or Meetings; and that this was the occasion of founding the Royal Society, and making the French the first', Hooke notes. In truth, he asserts, ''tis well known who were the principal men that began and promoted that design, both in this city and in Oxford; and that a long while before Mr Oldenburg came into England'.[144] In a tone and gesture that came to characterize not only the hot-tempered Hooke, the Society's only paid professional member, but also the frequently competitive style of seventeenth-century scientific writing, Hooke concludes with a snap: 'And not only these Philosophic Meetings were before Mr Oldenburg came from Paris; but the Society itself was begun before he came hither; and those who then knew Mr Oldenburg, understood well enough how little he himself knew of philosophic matter.'

Of the 'well-known' groups mentioned by Hooke, one of the most prominent was based at Gresham College in London, a gathering that was seemingly founded on a sociable, shared pursuit of new methods for understanding the physical and spiritual universes. On 28 November 1660, they met in the Gresham College rooms of Lawrence Rooke, following a lecture by the architect Christopher Wren. Rooke, a staunch supporter of the Parliament during the Commonwealth period and who had held the chair of Astronomy at Gresham between 1652 and 1657 until it was assumed by Wren, was presently the chair of Geometry for the College; other members of the College included the future Sir William Petty, economist, being the chair of Music, William Croone, chair of Rhetoric, and Jonathan Goddard, holding the chair of Physic. This London

<hr>

[144] Quoted in Syfret, 'Origins', 81.

circle, encompassing what we would term the natural and pure sciences as well as rhetoric and music, had been meeting twice weekly until the disruptions of 1659 and the conflicts between Richard Cromwell, Parliament, and the army; after Charles II's return, they began to meet again.

In the minutes of this meeting, it was proposed that a new college be formed for 'the promoting of physico-mathematical experimental learning'.[145] Its initial conveners were thus both Royalist supporters and Parliament men, with members from all three kingdoms, England, Ireland, and Scotland. What they shared was a common interest in the 'new' science proposed by Sir Francis Bacon based on observation of natural phenomenon and experimentation. The members came from a variety of professions and backgrounds: William Ball was a royalist astronomer who was also a lawyer; Robert Boyle (1627–91), who had been in active contact with the Hartlib circle in the 1650s (see *MV* 1.VI), was a supporter of Parliament and the son of Richard Boyle, the 1st Earl of Cork in Ireland, and wrote on religious matters and performed experiments in several different subjects. Also from Ireland at this first meeting was William Brouncker (1620–84), a peer of Ireland and a Royalist mathematician who would go on to be named the first President of the Royal Society when it received its charter in 1662. Alexander Bruce (*c*.1629–80), the future 2nd Earl of Kincardine, was an inventor from Scotland, and Sir Robert Moray (1608/9?–73) was another Scot who had gone into exile abroad during the 1650s. William Petty (1623–87) and Lawrence Rooke (1619/20–62) were both mathematicians and both supporters of Parliament; they were balanced by Royalists Sir Paul Neile (bap. 1613–82x6) and Christopher Wren (1632–1723). Jonathan Goddard (bap. 1617–75), a physician, and John Wilkins (1614–72), a natural philosopher, both supporters of Parliament, rounded out this initial group, along with the wealthy Londoner Abraham Hill (bap. 1635–1722). A friend of John Evelyn, Hill was the son of a prominent merchant; on the death of his father, he took rooms in Gresham College, pursuing his passions for languages and collecting, and he would subsequently go on to serve as the treasurer of the Royal Society for many years.

These twelve, as historians have traced, continued throughout their lives to be the driving influences shaping the work of the Society.[146] They drew up the initial list of persons to be invited to join, including many well-known English writers and virtuosi such as Sir Kenelm Digby and John Evelyn, along with the antiquarian astrologer Elias Ashmole (1617–92), who had in 1652 published *Theatrum chemicum Britannicum*, a collection of alchemical poems in English. Evelyn recorded in his diary for 13 January 1661 how he had been nominated for membership by the King himself and how, 'by Suffrage of the rest of the Members', he was made a 'Fellow of the *Philosophical Society*, now meeting at *Gressham* Coll.... it being the first meeting since the returne of his *Majestie* in

---

[145] Birch, *The History of the Royal Society of London*, 1. 3.
[146] See Hunter, *The Royal Society and its Fellows*.

Lond: but begun some years before at *Oxford*' (Evelyn, *Diary*, 3. 266). Evelyn went to the college several times a month during this early period: on 20 February 1661, he records, 'To Lond: about buisinesse: & to our *Meeting*, trying several Exp: about refining Metalls', and later, on 25 April, 'I went to the *Society* where were divers Experiments in Mr *Boyls Pneumatique* Engine' (Evelyn, *Diary*, 3. 271). These experiments had mixed results, however: 'we put in a *Snake* but could not kill it, by exhausting the aire, onely made it extreamly sick, but the chick died of Convulsions out right, in a short space' (Evelyn, *Diary*, 3. 284–5).

Thomas Birch, an early historian of the Society, records that, although the original intent was to hold the membership to fifty-five, it rapidly expanded. By the end of 1661, the Society could boast nearly 100 paying members, ranging from physicians such as the philosophical romance writer Walter Charleton (1620–1707) (see *MV* 1.V; *CV* 2.IV) to William Cavendish, 3rd Earl of Devonshire; it included university academicians such as the astronomer Seth Ward (1617–89) and the well-known linguist and mathematician John Wallis (1616–1703), as well as the professional inventor Robert Hooke. Evelyn chronicled Charles II's continuing interest in the Society, noting on 14 May 1661 that 'His *Majestie* was pleased to discourse with me concerning severall particulars relating to our *Society*, & the *Planet Saturne* &c: as he sat at Supper in the withdrawing roome to his Bed-Chamber' (Evelyn, *Diary*, 3. 288). In 1665, Charles II was made a member, and eventually the roster swelled to boast other luminaries of the court and men of power and influence, including the Duke of York, Clarendon, General Monk, Buckingham, Shaftesbury, and the Archbishops of Canterbury and York.

Even those with more modest court connections were drawn to join the Society. Samuel Pepys recorded in his diary for 15 February 1665 his initiation into it: 'to Gresham College—where I had been by Mr Povy the last week proposed to be admitted a member; and was this day admitted, by signing a book and being taken by the hand by the President, my Lord Brunkard, and some words of admittance said to me'. He continues: 'it is a most acceptable thing to hear their discourse, and see their experiments; which were this day upon the nature of fire, and how it goes out in a place where the ayre is not free, and sooner out where the ayre is exhausted; which they showed by an engine on purpose'. Perhaps as enjoyable, he describes how, 'after this being done, they to the Crowne Taverne, behind the 'Change, and there my Lord and most of the company to a club supper. . . . Here excellent discourses till 10 at night, and then home' (Pepys, *Diary*, 6. 36–7).

Among the very early members of the Society was the poet Abraham Cowley (1618–67), who had spent his time in exile in the 1650s managing the secret correspondence between the late King and Henrietta Maria (see *CV* 1.I, 1.V) and who on his return to England in 1660 devoted himself to botany and writing. Joining him as fellows as the Society matured were other public literary figures, including Edmund Waller, Sir John Denham, and John Dryden. Of these literary men, Cowley seems to have been the most devoted to the scientific issues. In 1661, just prior to the founding of the Society by Charter, he published *A Proposition for the Advancement of Experimental Philosophy*, and in 1667, at John Evelyn's urging, he contributed the dedicatory poem to Thomas Sprat's *History of the Royal Society* (1667), which would lay out poetically the distinctions between the old science and the new.

Cowley laments in the preface to his short essay that, while the universities have done well in training young scholars in 'humane' philosophy, by which he means that which depends 'solely upon Memory and Wit, that is, Reading and Invention', other types of philosophical enquiry have fared less well. 'The other two Parts' of learning, he avers, 'the Inquisition into the Nature of Gods Creatures, and the Application of them to Humane Uses (especially the latter) seem to be very slenderly provided for, or rather almost totally neglected, except onely some small assistances to Physick, and the Mathematicks'.[147] To overcome this deficiency in English universities, Cowley proposes the establishment of a physical college with fellows to oversee a school of some 200 promising students. In proposing this, he states he knows that many feel that all the knowledge that can come within human grasp has already been gathered by 'the Ancients', Aristotle in particular, and 'that it were a folly to travel about for that which others had before brought home to us'. However, he argues: 'As we understand the manners of men by conversation among them, and not by reading Romances, the same is our case in the true Apprehension & Judgement of Things. And no man can hope to make himself as rich by stealing out of others Truncks, as he might by opening and digging of new Mines' (sig. A4ʳ).

Cowley is primarily interested in discoveries that benefit society in its broadest sense. He notes towards the conclusion of the preface that 'for above a thousand years together nothing almost of Ornament or Advantage was added to the Uses of Humane Society, except only Guns and Printing', which he considers to be a lamentable rate of progress. With the advent of the new science, however, 'whereas since the Industry of Men has ventured to go abroad, out of Books and out of Themselves, and to work among Gods Creatures, instead of Playing among their Own, every age has abounded with excellent Inventions, and every year perhaps might do so' (p. 11). This emphasis on the application of knowledge gained through experiment in the living world is a constant thread in the writings of the Society during its first decade.

Although Bacon himself does not appear to have used the term 'experimental philosophy' as such, it became a key phrase in the scientific publications in the early 1660s. Robert Boyle had used the term 'experimental philosophy' in his 1660 essay *Spring of the Air*, and several other titles were published using it in the early years. Boyle again used it in 1663 in his *Usefulness of Experimental Natural Philosophy*, the same year Henry Power (*c*.1626–68) published his

---

[147] Cowley, *A Proposition*, sig. A3ʳ.

Experimental Philosophy.[148] As the title page of Power's book declares, it contains his experiments '*Miscroscopical*', '*Mercurial*', and '*Magnetical*' and 'some *Deductions*, and Probable *Hypotheses*, raised from them, in Avouchment and Illustration of the now famous *Atomical Hypothesis*'.[149] Power as a young man had been advised by a family friend, the physician and essayist Sir Thomas Browne (see *MV* 1.VI), to study medicine; while at Cambridge in the 1650s he had joined the philosophical circle of the physician Francis Glisson (1599?–1677), another early fellow of the Society who also had in the 1640s and 1650s organized meetings among London physicians to discuss medical experiments and present papers.

Setting up his practice and his household outside London in Halifax, Power, along with his neighbour and fellow enthusiast Richard Towneley, procured the latest instruments from London to pursue their passion for natural history and natural philosophy. News of their work reached the Society, and, in 1663, Power was elected a fellow and visited London, presenting his microscopical findings there. While in London, he also arranged for them to be published by the Society's printers, John Martyn and James Allestry, resulting arguably in the first English book on the use of the microscope.

Power is passionate about the importance of these new 'dioptrical Glasses', the previous lack of which 'incomparable Artifice made them not onely erre in their fond Coelestial Hypothesis, and Crystalline wheel-work of the Heavens above us, but also in their nearer Observations of the minute Bodies and smallest sort of Creatures about us'. In describing the appearance of the first of his microscopic investigations of the physiognomy of a flea, Power exclaims with delight, '(alas!) those sons of Sense', early thinkers in classical times, 'were not able to see how curiously the minutest things of the world are wrought, and with what eminent signatures of Divine Providence they were inrich'd and embellish'd, without our Dioptrical assistance' (pp. 1–2). As he had declared in his preface, 'were *Aristotle* now alive, he might write a new History of Animals'. Continuing his observation of the flea, he points out that 'one would wonder at the great strength lodged in so small a Receptacle' who 'will frisk and curvet so nimbly' with its shell, even when the observer sticks a 'large brass pin through his tayl and he will readily drag it away'. Power concludes admiringly: 'I have seen a chain of gold (at *Tredescants* famous reconditory of Novelties) of three hundred links, though not above an inch long, both fastened to, and drawn away by a Flea' (p. 3). As we shall see, early on in its history members of the Society moved away from this mode of enthusiastic description, seeking a more technical language to convey with more accuracy their observations.

While Power may have produced the first English book in praise of the microscope, Robert Hooke's *Micrographia, or, Some physiological descriptions*

[148] See the University of Otago's web-based project 'Early Modern Experimental Philosophy' <https://blogs.otago.ac.nz/emxphi/tag/cowley/> (accessed 13 April 2017).
[149] Power, *Experimental Philosophy*, title page.

of minute bodies made by magnifying glasses (1665) stands as the landmark in the history of science publications.[150] Containing beautifully engraved illustrations, it is dedicated to Charles II. Hooke's letter to the King establishes Charles as both the man of science and the bringer of peace: 'Amidst the many *felicities* that have accompani'd *your Majesties* happy *Restauration* and *Government*, it is none of the least considerable, that *Philosophy* and *Experimental Learning* have *prosper'd* under your *Royal Patronage*', Hooke opens.[151] Because of this halcyon period of quiet and retirement brought about by Charles's return, the members of the Royal Society are 'now busie about *Nobler* matters: The *Improvement* of *Manufactures* and *Agriculture*, the *Increase* of *Commerce*, the *Advantage* of *Navigation*: In all which they are *assisted* by *your Majesties Incouragement* and *Example*'. Hooke modestly disclaims such 'noble' ends, concluding that 'I here presume to bring in that which is more *proportionable* to the *smalness* of my Abilities, and to offer some of the *least* of all *visible things*, to that *Mighty King*, that has *establisht an Empire* over the best of all *Invisible things* of this World, the *Minds* of Men' (sig. A^v).

In his general preface, Hooke lays out the rationale behind this new style of observation. 'It is the great prerogative of Mankind above other Creatures, that we are not only able to *behold* the works of Nature, or barely to *sustein* our lives by them, but we have also the power of *considering, comparing, altering, assisting*, and *improving* them to various uses', he asserts. Given this privileged position, human perception is nevertheless 'capable of being so far advanced by the helps of Art, and Experience, as to make some Men excel others in their Observations, and Deductions, almost as much as they do Beasts'.

By the addition of such *artificial Instruments* and *methods*, there may be, in some manner, a reparation made for the mischiefs, and imperfection, mankind has drawn upon it self, by negligence, and intemperance, and a wilful and superstitious deserting the Prescripts and Rules of Nature, whereby every man, both from a deriv'd corruption, innate and born with him, and from his breeding and converse with men, is very subject to slip into all sorts of errors.

For Hooke and others, the capacity of natural human perception is sharply limited in comparison with the vastness of Nature itself. Hooke continues, 'some parts of it are *too large* to be comprehended, and some *too little* to be perceived. And from thence it must follow', he concludes, 'that not having a full sensation of the Object, we must be very lame and imperfect in our conceptions about it, and in all the propositions which we build upon it'. Furthermore, Hooke warns, 'These being the dangers in the process of humane Reason, the remedies of them all can only proceed from the *real*, the *mechanical*, the *experimental* Philosophy'. Physical experimentation 'has this advantage over the Philosophy of *discourse* and *disputation*, that whereas that chiefly aims at the subtlety of its Deductions and Conclusions ... so this intends the right ordering of them all, and the making

---

[150] Bennett et al., *London's Leonardo*.   [151] Hooke, *Micrographia*, 'To the King', sig. A^v.

them serviceable to each other'. 'The truth is', concludes Hooke, that 'the Science of Nature has been already too long made only a work of the *Brain* and the *Fancy*: It is now high time that it should return to the plainness and soundness of *Observations* on *material* and *obvious* things' ('Preface').

Obviously not all parties engaged in scientific investigations welcomed this new style of science, one so entranced by instruments and the material world. Established scholars at Oxford and Cambridge felt challenged by the overt dismissal of their understanding of how natural history should be conducted and written. Cowley, in effect, had thrown down the gauntlet in his dedicatory poem that opened Sprat's history of the Society published in 1667. In his nine-canto poem 'To the *Royal Society*', Cowley opens with an attack on 'the Guardians and the Tutors', who have confined masculine personified 'Philosophy' for their own ends:

> (Some negligent, and some ambitious men)
> Would ne're consent to set him Free,
> Or his own Natural Powers to let him see,
> Lest that should put an end to their Autoritie.[152]

To keep Philosophy under control,

> They amus'd him with the sports of wanton Wit,
> With the Desserts of Poetry they fed him,
> Instead of solid meats t' encreas his force. (sig. B1ʳ)

Instead of studying Nature, they offered 'painted Scenes, and Pageants of the Brain' until Bacon,

> a mighty Man arose,
> Whom a wise King and Nature chose
> Lord Chancellour of both their Laws,
> And boldly undertook the injur'd Pupils caus. (sig. B1ᵛ)

Cowley credits Bacon with redirecting the scientific gaze to the 'real' through the use of the 'mechanic'.

> From Words, which are but Pictures of the Thought,
> (Though we our Thoughts from them perversly drew)
> To Things, the Minds right Object, he it brought. (sig. B2ʳ)

No longer would memory or fancy provide the objects for philosophical contemplation, but instead,

> He before his sight must place
> The Natural and Living Face;
> The real Object must command
> Each Judgment of his Eye, and Motion of his Hand. (sig. B2ʳ)

---

[152] Sprat, *History of the Royal Society*, sig. B1ʳ.

Those who had not turned to the material world for answers are described as being like the Hebrews wandering lost in the desert, until led forth out of it by a Baconian Moses.

Such ringing denouncement of earlier natural philosophers by Cowley and others connected to the Society led in turn to often scathing attacks on the new group, its members, and its methods. In turn, Thomas Sprat had begun writing the history of the Society shortly after it had received its first chapter in 1662, but was interrupted by both the Plague and the Great Fire in 1665 and 1666 (see CV 2.II). His *History of the Royal-Society of London for the Improving of Natural Knowledge* finally appeared in 1667. A former student of Willis's at Oxford in the 1650s, Sprat was a keen promoter of the new Society, but less a practitioner of experiments. In his opening, Sprat explains he was moved to chronicle the origins of this young endeavour 'in hope, that this Learned and Inquisitive Age, will either think their Indeavours, worthy of its *Assistance*; or else will be thereby provok'd, to attempt some *greater Enterprise* (if any such can be found out) for the Benefit of humane life, by the Advancement of *Real Knowledge*' (pp. 1–2). 'What can be more delightful', Sprat announces, than

for an *Englishman* to consider, then that notwithstanding all the late miseries of his Country; it has been able in a short time so well to recover it self: as not onely to attain to the perfection of its *former* Civility, and Learning, but also to set on foot, a *new* way of improvement of Arts, as *Great* and as *Beneficial* (to say no more) as any the wittiest or the happiest Age has ever invented? (p. 3)

The restoration of the monarchy, in Sprat's eyes, was not only a return to the civility of the pre-Commonwealth days, but also the opportunity to rebuild a new and even more robust intellectual culture. Making the same point as Hooke, Sprat declares that this new attitude towards learning will be one devoted to benefiting all walks of life, a claim for the pragmatic benefits of science that ironically echoes that made by writers in the 1650s on improvements in agriculture and mechanics for the benefit of the Commonwealth (see CV 1.II).

Sprat openly acknowledges that one of the purposes of writing his history is to defend the new science and its followers from those who might view its ideas and proceedings with suspicion, as undermining traditional education based on classical knowledge, leading to religious controversy, and being in general a distraction away from more serious pursuits and business. 'I doubt not then, but it will come into the thoughts of many *Criticks*, (of whom the World is now full)', Sprat observes, 'to urge against us, that I have spoken a little too sparingly of the Merits of former Ages; and that this Design seems to be promoted, with a malicious intention of disgracing the Merits of the *Antients*' (p. 46). Nothing could be further from the truth, he assures his reader, although he warns against a slavish devotion to the past and its dangers: 'They object to us *Tradition*, and the consent of all Ages. But do we not yet know the deceitfulness of such Words? Is any man that is acquainted with the craft of founding

Sects, or of managing Votes in *popular Assemblies*, ignorant, how easie it is to carry things in a violent stream?' (p. 48).

Among the supposedly idle and malicious detractors was Margaret Cavendish, Duchess of Newcastle. Her *Observations upon experimental philosophy to which is added The description of a new blazing world* (1666), appearing a year before Sprat's history, was reprinted in 1668. It is clear from her preface to the reader that she expects the new experimental science to have as disruptive effect on English thought as the war did on English life: 'I confess, there are many useless and superfluous Books, and perchance mine will add to the number of them', she opens her preface, 'especially is it to be observed, that there have been in this latter age, as many Writers of Natural Philosophy, as in former ages there have been of Moral Philosophy'.[153] The problem with this proliferation of philosophical books is that 'Natural Philosophers', 'who by their extracted, or rather distracted arguments, confound both Divinity and Natural Philosophy, Sense and Reason, Nature and Art, so much as in time we shall have rather a Chaos, then a well-order'd Universe by their doctrine' (sig. C1ᵛ). By tearing down the ancients, they are behaving like 'those unconscionable men in Civil Wars, which endeavour to pull down the hereditary Mansions of Noble-men and Gentlemen, to build a Cottage of their own' (sig. C2ʳ). She continues in an even more pointed fashion, 'for so do they pull down the learning of Ancient Authors, to render themselves famous in composing Books of their own'. 'But though this Age does ruine Palaces, to make Cottages; Churches, to make Conventicles; and Universities to make private Colledges', she concludes, with a direct reference to the recent conflicts, 'yet, I, hope God of his mercy will preserve State, Church, and Schools, from ruine and destruction' (sig. C2ʳ).

She also uses this preface to attack the Society's rhetoric of the social usefulness of experimental philosophy and its ability to advance trade and general English prosperity.[154] 'I cannot perceive any great advantage this Art doth bring us', she declares, 'the Ecclipse of the Sun and Moon was not found out by Telescopes, nor the motions of the Loadstone, nor the Art of the Card, nor the Art of Guns and Gun-powder, nor the Art of Printing, and the like, by Microscopes' (sig. C2ᵛ). 'If it be true', she says sceptically, 'that Telescopes make appear the spots in the Sun and Moon, or discover some new Stars, what benefit is that to us?' Indeed, in this celebration of new machines and technology, she fears, 'the truth is, most of these Arts are Fallacies, rather then discoveries of Truth; for Sense deludes more then it gives a true Information' (sig. C2ᵛ).

In spite of her invitation to visit the Society when she and her husband were in London in the spring of 1667 and her observation there of Hooke and Boyle performing experiments, she does not seem to have modified her views in the 1668 reprint. In the fictional part of this volume, *The description of a new*

---

[153] Cavendish, *Observations upon Experimental Philosophy*, sig. C1ᵛ.
[154] See Walters, *Margaret Cavendish*, chs 1, 4, and Lisa T. Sarasohn, *The Natural Philosophy*.

blazing world, which was also published separately in 1668 as *The Description of a New World, called the Blazing-World*, Cavendish imagines a parallel Arctic world, where the human cast-away who becomes its empress convenes a congress of her intellectual subjects (see CV 2.IV). The 'bear-men' use microscopes to investigate fleas, a favourite tool of Royal Society fellows, but, upon viewing the enlarged creature, the Empress demands 'whether their Microscopes could hinder their biting, or at least shew some means how to avoid them? To which they answered, That such Arts were mechanical and below that noble study of Microscopical observations'.[155] The bear-men are concerned: 'at her Majesties displeasure concerning their Telescopes, [they] kneel'd down, and in the humblest manner petitioned that they might not be broken; for, said they, we take more delight in Artificial delusions, then in natural truths'. 'Besides', they conclude ingeniously, 'we shall want imployments for our senses, and subjects for arguments; for were there nothing but truth, and no falshood, there would be no occasion for to dispute, and by this means we should want the aim and pleasure of our endeavours in consulting and contradicting each other' (p. 28).

Cavendish was hardly alone in her scepticism that the Society would be able to perform the multitude of tasks Sprat outlined for it, feeling that instead the members were simply inclined to a new form of debate, leading to pointless disputes and dissention. Henry Stubbe [Stubbes, Stubbs] (1632–76) was one of the most outspoken and persistent of the Society's critics, publishing four separate treatises in the early 1670s—*A Censure upon Certaine Passages Contained in the 'History of the Royall Society'*; *The 'Plus Ultra' Reduced to a Non-Plus*; *Legends no histories*; and *Campanella Revived, or, An Enquiry into the History of the Royal Society*—all attacking the glowing representations of the Society by Sprat and by Joseph Glanvill [Glanville] (1636–80), another of its most energetic supporters.

Stubbe's career at Oxford in the 1650s included not only serving as the deputy keeper of the Bodleian Library but also beginning his career as a polemicist. A friend of Thomas Hobbes by the mid-1650s, Stubbe began a Latin translation of *Leviathan* (see CV 1.I), which was never completed, and, although he himself never wrote in support of Hobbes's views directly, he aided in Hobbes's attacks on the future Royal Society fellow John Wallis (1616–1703). Wallis, who had been educated at Cambridge under the physician Francis Glisson, was engaged in a lively mathematical dispute with Hobbes for decades; during this time, Stubbe also wrote pamphlets under the aegis of the political theorist Sir Henry Vane, targeting Presbyterians, defending 'the good old cause' of republicanism, and attacking the moderate Richard Baxter. He also satirized Harrington's political writings (see MV 2.I), publishing in 1660 *The Rota, or, News from the Common-Wealths-Mens Club* and *The Common-Wealth of Oceana Put into the Ballance, and Found too Light.*

---

[155] Cavendish, *The Description of a New World, called the Blazing-World* (1668), 31–2.

Thus Stubbe was a well-seasoned polemicist when he turned his sights on the Royal Society. While practising as a physician in Warwick, Stubbe launched the first of his pamphlets against the London group. Published in Oxford by Richard Davis, the pamphlet's full title *A censure upon certaine passages contained in the history of the Royal Society as being destructive to the established religion and Church of England* suggests his main line of attack. Dedicated to Dr John Fell, Dean of Christ Church College, the pamphlet opens with a quotation from Sprat that Stubbe goes on to characterize as '*Impious, Blasphemous*, and *Offensive to all Protestant eares*'.[156] Stubbe accuses Sprat of being in sympathy with the Roman Catholic Church and rather tortuously argues that the new experimental philosophy is nothing less than a road back to Rome: 'how this *foundation* will be *sapped* and *undermined* by the project of our *Virtuoso*, I do submit unto the *serious* consideration of the *Church of England*' (p. 62). He concludes with a slap at Cowley's secular poetry in *The Mistress*, finding in its use of biblical allusions in romantic verse to be an 'application of *Sacred Writ*, to vulgar discourse, and . . . *Holy Raillery* deduced from *Scripture*': Cowley's lyrics appears to Stubbe's eyes as teetering on blasphemy in the pursuit of the style of wit approved of by these '*Virtuoso*', and he thus manages to merge poetic and scientific criticism, and finding in both romantic verse and science writings attacks on the Church of England.

In *Legends no histories, or, A specimen of some animadversions upon The History of the Royal Society* (1670) Stubbe expands his attack to include Joseph Glanvill's *Plus ultra, or, The Progress and Advancement of Knowledge since the Days of Aristotle* (1668), which Stubbe declares on his title page he will reduce to 'a NON-PLUS', as well as the early Society fellow Thomas Henshaw's (1618–1700) history of the invention of gunpowder and the making of saltpetre, papers he had presented there in 1662. In his 'Preface to the *Judicious* READER', Stubbe defends his attack on experimental philosophy as embodied in the Society as based on his concerns as a physician and what he sees as dangerous claims being issued by the Society's members: 'I speak not this out of *contradiction* I carry to these *Virtuosi*; it is the result of my thoughts after twelve years of *deliberation*, after *observations accurately made* in my *own practice*, and in that of other *antient* men.'[157] Stubbe asserts that he fears for the restored monarchy and the return of popery to the land through the undermining of university education and the experimental philosophy's attack on the received wisdom of the ancients:

The *Art of reasoning* by which the *prudent* are discriminated from *fools*, which *methodizeth* and *facilitates our discourses*, which informs us of the *validity of Consequences*, and the *probability of Arguments*, and manifests the *fallacies of Impostors* and *Comical Wits*; that *Art* which gives *life* to *solid Eloquence*, and which renders *States men, Divines, Physicians* and *Lawyers* accomplished, how is this *cried down* and *vilified* by the

---

[156] Stubbe, *A censure upon certaine passages*, 4.

[157] Stubbe, *Legends no histories*, 'Preface to the Judicious Reader'.

Ignoramus's of these days?…those *Moral* instructions which have produced the *Alexanders* and the *Ptolomeys*, the *Pompeys* and the *Ciceroes*, are now slighted in comparison of *day-labouring*! ('Preface')

Stubbe was not alone as seeing the practitioners of the new science as rejecting the arts of rhetoric. Sprat's history of the Society has been frequently cited by historians of science and literary historians alike for his ringing denunciation of rhetorical tropes and metaphorical language in the writings of science. Stubbe's attacks highlight the ways in which the new experimental mode of gaining knowledge also involved, in the view of many, a dismissal of the descriptive arts of metaphor and powers of rhetoric in favour of a more concrete and direct or 'artisan' style of expression.

Sprat's relationship with the arts of rhetoric and metaphor, of course, is complicated. He himself makes plentiful use of both in explaining the origins and nature of the new Society: 'We approach the Antients, as we behold their Tombs, with veneration: but we would not therefore be confin'd to live in them altogether: nor', he observes with some irony, 'would (I believe) any of those, who profess to be most addicted to their Memories' (p. 48). Elsewhere he compares experimental philosophy to Columbus's voyages of exploration and to weighing the dangers of putting to sea or staying always on shore.[158] A classically trained rhetorician himself, Sprat does not hesitate to employ it in his presentation of the new Society.

As scholars have noted, however, Sprat presented the Society as being particularly scrupulous in matters of their own use of language in conveying their experiments:

There is one thing more, about which the *Society* has been most sollicitous; and that is, the manner of their *Discourse:* which, unless they had been very watchful to keep in due temper, the whole spirit and vigour of their *Design*, had been soon eaten out, by the luxury and redundance of *speech*. The ill effects of this superfluity of talking, have already overwhelm'd most other *Arts* and *Professions*; insomuch, that when I consider the means of *happy living*, and the causes of their corruption, I can hardly forbear recanting what I said before; and concluding, that *eloquence* ought to be banish'd out of all *civil Societies*, as a thing fatal to Peace and good Manners. (p. 111)

No doubt, Sprat concurs, that the ornaments of eloquence were 'an admirable Instrument in the hands of Wise Men: when they were onely employ'd to describe *Goodness, Honesty, Obedience*; in larger, fairer, and more moving Images' (pp. 111–12). In days following the Restoration, however, perhaps harking back to the days of the Parliamentary debates and the fiery evangelical preachers exhorting their congregations, 'who can behold, without indignation, how many mists and uncertainties, these specious *Tropes* and *Figures* have brought on our Knowledg? How many rewards, which are due to more profitable, and difficult *Arts*, have been still snatch'd away by the easie vanity of *fine speaking*?' (p. 112).

---

[158] See Skouen, 'Science versus Rhetoric?', 27–9, and Vickers, 'The Royal Society'.

The Society's awareness of the dangers posed by 'this vicious abundance of *Phrase*, this trick of *Metaphors*, this volubility of *Tongue*, which makes so great a noise in the World' has led them according to Sprat to resolve 'to reject all the amplifications, digressions, and swellings of style: to return back to the primitive purity, and shortness, when men deliver'd so many *things*, almost in an equal number of *words*'. Sprat continues, 'they have exacted from all their members, a close, naked, natural way of speaking; positive expressions; clear senses; a native easiness: bringing all things as near the Mathematical plainness, as they can: and preferring the language of Artizans, Countrymen, and Merchants, before that, of Wits, or Scholars' (p, 113). Echoing Bacon's dismissal in *Novum Organum* of 'juggleries of words' and insistence on description that is brief, concise, and 'nothing less [*sic*] than words', Sprat's declaration maps out the linguistic ambitions of the Society.[159] In short, the language of science was to be vernacular English and the language of the working man, not that of the bookish Oxford don, even though the practitioner might indeed be a leading light at one of the universities.

As historians of science and critics have noticed, there was from the beginning a deliberate and careful attention paid by the early fellows to the ways in which they recorded their experiments.[160] Sprat describes the goal of the Society to record its experiments 'as reduc'd its principal observations, into one *common-stock*; and laid them up in publique *Registers*, to be nakedly transmitted to the next Generation of Men; and so from them, to their Successors' (p. 115). Boyle's experiments published in the early 1660s might appear to pull away from this standard, as he announces in *New experiments physico-mechanicall, touching the spring of the air . . . written by way of letter to the Right Honorable Charles, Lord Vicount of Dungarvan* (1660). The treatise at over 300 pages is rather more 'prolix' than expected for a letter considered as an epistolary genre. However, Boyle is at pains to explain the logic behind his choice of the epistle as the correct format for conveying his experiments: some of the experiments described within, 'being altogether new, seem'd to need the being circumstantially related, to keep the Reader from distrusting them'.[161] Furthermore, 'that in divers cases I thought it necessary to deliver things circumstantially, that the Person I addressed them to, might without mistake, and with as little trouble as is possible, be able to repeat such unusual Experiments' ('To the Reader').

Boyle clearly understands the significance of the expense of creating the experimental apparatus he employs and realizes that few of his readers will actually have the means to duplicate his experiments. It becomes, therefore, even more essential that his conveyance of the information permits them to visualize it while reading. He observes:

That foreseeing that such a trouble as I met with in making those tryals carefully, and the great expence of time that they necessarily require, (not to mention the charges of

---

[159] Quoted in Bradbury, 'New Science', 38.   [160] See Nate, 'Rhetoric'.

[161] Boyle, *New experiments*, 'To the Reader'.

making the Engine, and imploying a man to manage it) will probably keep most men from trying again those Experiments, I thought I might doe the generality of my Readers no unacceptable peice of service, by so punctually relating what I carefully observ'd, that they may look upon these Narratives as standing Records in our new Pneumaticks, and need not reiterate themselves an Experiment to have as distinct an Idea of it, as may suffice them to ground their Reflections and Speculations upon. ('To the Reader')

As historians of science have noted, Boyle is through the stylistic choices in his writing seeking to give the reader the impression of having actually witnessed the experiment, the impression of verisimilitude and truth.[162]

Interest in the nature of language as it pertains to the practice of scientific observation and the literary nature of the transmission of it had been a topic of discussion in the late 1630 throughout the 1640s. Hartlib's correspondence network had already brought together many of the early members of the Royal Society, including Petty, Boyle, and Evelyn in the late 1640s and 1650s (see *MV* 1.VI). There were also shared interests in the goals of Hartlib's network and the new Society that focused on the ways in which knowledge was organized and circulated among readers. Long before the formation of the Royal Society, Hartlib and Comenius in educational writings in the 1640s had urged a reform of the way in which knowledge was collected and distributed: Comenius advocated a theory of 'Pansophia' or universal knowledge to be made available to all through universal books and a universal language to be created by a college of learned scholars from around the world.[163] When *Via Lucis* was finally published in 1668, it was dedicated to the Royal Society 'the Torch-Bearers of this Enlightened Age... now bringing real philosophy to a happy birth'.[164]

In 1668, John Wilkins (1614–72), one of the first fellows and most influential members of the Society, published an *Essay towards a Real Character and Philosophical Language*, building from his 1641 publication *Mercury, or, The secret and swift messenger: shewing how a man may with privacy and speed communicate his thoughts to a friend at any distance*, which explored the idea of a 'universal character', which would be intelligible to readers of many different languages. Wilkins's interest in the power of language and its uses was long-standing, and it is debated what influence Comenius' writings might have had on his: before becoming Warden of Wadham College, Oxford, in 1648, he had achieved acclaim as a preacher in Gray's Inn, London, and had published *Ecclesiastes, A Discourse Concerning the Gift of Preaching* (1646). His interest in communicating science to a wider audience was also long-standing: in the late 1630s, he published two works attempting to present the ideas of Copernicus, Kepler, and Galileo to a more general audience, including in 1638 *The discovery of a new world, or, A discourse tending to prove, that ('tis probable) there may be another habitable world in the moon*—a popular work he

---

[162] See Shapin and Schaffer, *Leviathan and the Air-Pump*, ch. 2, 'Seeing and Believing: The Experimental Production of Pneumatic Facts', in particular, pp. 60–76.

[163] See Syfret, 'Origins', 110.   [164] Quoted in Syfret, 'Origins', 116.

expanded and one that enjoyed a fourth edition in 1684. Wilkins speculates on the possibilities of humans travelling to the moon and imagines them residing there.

As with literary pursuits (see *MV* 1.VI), science in the 1650s and 1660s was frequently loosely configured by networks of sociability held together by blood, location, and epistolary circulation. Wilkins, before leaving for Oxford in 1648, had been a member of a London group convened by Theodore Haak to study chemistry, mechanics, magnetism, geometry, and medicine. When he became Warden at Wadham, he began to hold scientific meetings at the college, which drew Lawrence Rooke and Seth Ward from their positions at Cambridge and caused Robert Boyle to move to Oxford along with Jonathan Goddard, Petty, Ralph Bathurst, and Thomas Willis; students during this period included Wren and the future chronicler of the Royal Society, Thomas Sprat. When in 1656 Wilkins married the Lord Protector's youngest sister Robina Cromwell, he became even more closely tied to the interests of the Commonwealth; in 1659, the fellows of Trinity College, Cambridge, petitioned that he be made master there, a post he would hold until the return of Charles II.

Wilkins was also quick to make use of a new means of circulating scientific information, the *Philosophical Transactions* published by the Society's secretary Henry Oldenburg, which Oldenburg produced starting in 1665 through 1678. In that first volume, Wilkins contributed a letter that had been sent to him 'Lately Written from Venice, by the Learned Doctor Walter Pope, to the Reverend Dean of Rippon, Doctor John Wilkins, Concerning the Mines of Mercury in Friuli; And a Way of Producing Wind by the Fall' (1 (1665), 21–6). Although obviously connected to the Society and its members and published by the Society's printers, it was not yet an official publication of it; Oldenburg made clear in his correspondence about it that it was his own editorial project, undertaken at his expense and his profit. Describing them as 'Rude Collections', the 'Gleanings of my *private* diversions in broken hours', Oldenburg in his dedicatory epistle to the first volume assures the members of the Society that the intent is 'to spread abroad Encouragements, Inquiries, Directions, and Patterns, that may animate, and draw on *Universal Assistances*'.[165]

Many of the articles within those early volumes deal with matters that would not today be considered experimental science.[166] In that inaugural volume, Robert Boyle contributed news of a 'Very Odd Monstrous Calf' and Captain Silas Taylor offered 'Of the way of Killing Ratle-Snakes' in Virginia by burning the leaves of the Penny Royal plant under the snake's nose, a piece that he had presented initially at a meeting of the Society, 'which he afterwards was pleased to give in writing, attested to by two credible persons in whose presence it was done' (1. 43). Likewise, there was a report of 'the nature

---

[165] Oldenburg (ed.), *Philosphical Transactions*, vol. 1, 'Epistle Dedicatory'.
[166] Daston and Park, *Wonders and the Order of Nature*, ch. 6; Da Costa, *The Singular and the Making of Knowledge*.

of a certain stone, found in the *Indies*, in the head of a *Serpent*', which had been sent by Sir Phileberto Vernatti in '*Java major*' to Sir Robert Moray to be preserved in the 'Repository' of the Royal Society; it supposedly was an anti-dote to any venomous poison (1. 101–3) and could release the poison when soaked in milk.

As can be seen in these few examples, from its beginning the *Philosophical Transactions* served to connect English natural scientists with those in Europe and in the New World. Several other items in the first volume were excerpts of correspondence from Paris, Rome, and Zurich. There were exchanges between English scientists and continental ones, such as 'Considerations of Monsieur *Auzout* upon Mr *Hook's* New Instrument for Grinding of *Optick-Glasses*' and '*Mr Hook's* Answer to Monseiur *Auzout's* Considerations, in a Letter to the Publisher of These *Transactions*' (1. 57–69). In the 1660s and early 1670s, the *Transactions* carried accounts from sea captains and merchant explorers as well as those who conducted their observations in their backyards or college rooms. While in Cambridge, Isaac Newton (1642–1727) would publish his first paper in the *Transactions*, 'A Serie's of *Quere's* Propounded by Mr *Isaac Newton*, to be Determin'd by Experiments, Positively and Directly Concluding His New Theory of Light and Colours', better known now as Newton's 'New Theory about Light and Colours' (7 (1672), 4004–5007, pagination error in original). This paper, along with his description of his newly invented reflecting or 'Catadioptrical' telescope, provoked both admiration and attack. Hooke, who felt challenged as the Society's expert in optics, was dismissive, which in turn drew an angry and sarcastic reply from Newton; the Dutch scientist Christiaan Huygens (1629–95) entered into an extended exchange with Newton, all conveyed through the pages of the *Transactions*.

In the creation and early years of the Royal Society of London, one sees the continuation of intellectual discussions that had begun in the Commonwealth period. Many of these same thinkers and writers would with the Restoration find new audiences through the publication of its experiments and even in the disputes that it created among its supporters and those who deplored it. The Society from its start had its critics: it was parodied by Thomas Shadwell in his 1676 comedy *The Virtuoso*, with its characters Sir Formal Trifle and Sir Nicholas Grimcrack, whose experiments include transfusing sheep's blood into a human with unfortunate results (he grew a tail) and bottling air from different parts of the country to be stored like fine wines. Nevertheless, it remained the most important nexus for the creation and dissemination of natural and pure science throughout the century. The arguments over the nature of scientific enquiry it provoked were matched by an interest in the appropriate nature of scientific writing and the means for its transmission: through its publications and its extensive domestic and international correspondence networks, it both created and sustained a passion for shared information and fostered a standard for scientific 'truth' that relied on experiments that could be reliably replicated and whose results would always be the same.

VI. 'Adventurous Song': Samuel Butler, Abraham Cowley, Katherine Philips, John Milton, and 1660s Verse

> For why I made these *rambles*, I can give no other accompt then a poor
> man does why he gets *children*; that is his pleasure, and this mine.
>
> Alexander Brome, *Songs and other Poems* (1661)

> Sing Heav'nly Muse, that on the secret top
> Of *Oreb*, or of *Sinai*, didst inspire
> That Shepherd, who first taught the chosen Seed,
> In the Beginning how the Heav'ns and Earth
> Rose out of *Chaos*: Or if *Sion* Hill
> Delight thee more, and *Siloa's* Brook that flow'd
> Fast by the Oracle of God; I thence
> Invoke thy aid to my adventurous Song,
> That with no middle flight intends to soar
> Above th'*Aonian* Mount, while it pursues
> Things unattempted yet in prose or Rhime.
>
> John Milton, *Paradise Lost* (1668)

The dozen or so years following the return of Charles II and his court saw a continuation of the 1650s practices of publishing single-author volumes of verse as well as popular collections of songs and drolleries. During this decade and a half, however, the majority of published volumes were by living authors, although there were also notable posthumous collections of poets from the early seventeenth century, such as that of the alchemist and philosopher Edward Herbert, Lord Herbert of Cherbury (1582?–1648), and the friend and biographer of Sir Philip Sidney, Fulke Greville, Lord Brooke (1554–1628). Readers outside older social manuscript networks could in the 1660s and early 1670s also become acquainted with the poems of John Donne (1572–1631), which were gathered and reprinted as a collection in 1669, as well those of Sir William Herbert, Earl of Pembroke (1506/7–70); there were reprints of volumes of verse by Thomas Deloney (1543?–*c.*1600), Francis Beaumont (1584/5–1616), Thomas Carew (1594/5–1640), Richard Corbet (1582–1635), and George Herbert (1593–1633). Other posthumous collections included an almost yearly publication in the early 1660s of the poems of the Royalist satirist John Cleveland (bap. 1613–58), and a new edition of Richard Crashaw's (1612/13–48) *Steps to the Temple* with additions. As an older generation of publishing poets began to pass away in the 1660s, including the prolific William Davenant and George Wither, a new generation of writers, including John Dryden, who would succeed Davenant as Poet Laureate on Davenant's death in 1668, and John Bunyan, who would do most of his writing while in prison for illegal preaching, begin establishing their publishing practices as poets. Volumes also began appearing in London more frequently from New England poets.

George Wither (see *MV* 1.I), the indefatigable poet prophet of the war and Interregnum, continued to publish his verses on the condition of England, nearly a pamphlet or a volume per year until his death in 1667. Wither, born during the reign of Elizabeth I, supported and then lamented Cromwell's rule, and greeted Charles II with *Speculum Speculativum, or, A Considering Glass*. Wither hopes that the poem by some chance may come to Charles's attention and 'If *Providence* hath brought this to your hand', he urges,

> Give up to REASON straight, the sole command
> Ov'r all your *Passions;* Make her of your *Isle,*
> (Your Isle of MAN) *Queen-Regent,* all the while
> You are perusing it.[167]

Comparing Charles to a woman prudently using her looking glass to make sure that she is appropriately and attractively attired rather than relying on her husband's assurances, Wither urges him to beware court flatters:

> So, by this *Glass,* you may have by reflection
> A sight of what pertains to your perfection.
> See, not with others, but, with your own eyes,
> Whether true *Ornaments,* or some *Disguise.* (sig. A3^r)

The popular poem, written early in 1661, went through three editions before Wither, ironically, was imprisoned in Newgate for seditious libel against the new Parliament and, upon his conviction in 1662, sent to the Tower. Somehow, in spite of supposedly being denied pen and paper, he published several pamphlets as well as verses, including *A proclamation in the name of the King of kings, to all inhabitants of the isles of Great Brittain* (1662), *Verses Intended to the King's Majesty* (1662), along with a prose pamphlet, *A Declaration of Major George Wither* (1662), the last 'Writ on three fair Trenchers, with a Piece of Char-Coal'. Upon his release from prison in 1663, he almost at once published a poetic warning against going to war with the Dutch, *Tuba-pacifica* (1664). Wither, in using verse in his pamphlet proclamations, was continuing the practice of earlier petitioners of Cromwell and Charles I (see *CV* 1.III), and we find him using his published writings as a means of gaining the notice of Charles II himself but also, he hoped, a sympathetic reading public. In *Verses intended to the King's Majesty*, whose subtitle indicates they were confiscated while he was imprisoned—'found Written with his own Hand, among his loose Papers, since his Commitment close prisoner to the TOWER; Are now Published, as pertinent both to his MAJESTY, and to Him'—and *A proclamation in the name of the King of kings* (1662), Wither declares that he has been imprisoned based on false evidence:

> This *Case of mine* concerneth now and then,
> Not me alone; but other honest men.

---

[167] Wither, *Speculum*, sig. A2^r.

Such like *false brethren,* in all Ages were
Among the *Saints,* and such-like still there are.[168]

He was in trouble with the authorities again in 1666 for *Sigh for the Pitchers,* another anti-Dutch war prophecy continuing *Tuba-pacifica*; also imprisoned with him were Henry Eversden, Sarah Anderston, Elizabeth Goslin, and Margaret Hickes, who had distributed it. Wither's final published work appeared that same year, *Ecchoes from the Sixth Trumpet* (1666), which would be republished by his children in *Nil ultra, or, The Last Works of Captain George Wither* (1668) and *Fragmenta prophetica, or, The Remains of George Wither* (1669).

As Wither passed away, another prisoner publishing poetry was at the beginning of his long writing career. John Bunyan, who had been a successful and popular preacher in the 1650s (see *MV* 1.IV; *CV* 2.V), had been imprisoned in 1661 in Bedford county gaol for preaching and also for denouncing the Church of England during his trial. Bunyan's first published volume of verse, *Profitable meditations fitted to mans different condition* (1661), is a short pamphlet in verse framed as nine conversations between Christ and a sinner. In his epistle to the reader, Bunyan explains why he chose verse for his message, foreshadowing his epistles prefacing *Pilgrim's Progress*. He opens:

Take none offence, Friend, at my method here,
Cause thou in Verse simple Truth dost see,
'Tis not the Method, but the Truth alone
Should please a Saint, and mollifie his heart:
Truth in or out of Meeter is but one;
And this thou knowst, if thou a Christian art.[169]

'Man's heart is apt in Meeter to delight', Bunyan declares, 'Also in that to bear away the more'. Bunyan uses simple, popular rhyme schemes that would be familiar to any reader or listener of broadside ballads and inexpensive chapbooks to convey the Gospel to a wide audience, although some critics have seen evidence of Sternhold's and Hopkin's settings of the Psalms in them. If the reader's only interest in poetry is the writer's 'wit', however, Bunyan warns, 'You will not by them edified be; | You see only the back-side of the Book'.

Robert Wild (1615/16–79), a Huntingdonshire man and nonconformist minister, but one educated at St John's College, Cambridge, had published early in 1660 his *Iter boreale, attempting somthing upon the successful and matchless march of the Lord General George Monck, from Scotland, to London, the last winter, &c. Veni, vidi, vici. By a rural pen,* reissued with more of Wild's poems in 1661. The pamphlet poem compares Monck to a modern-day St George and urges him, having delivered the country from the dragon of Parliament, next to bring back the King:

---

[168] Wither, *Proclamation,* 30.   [169] Bunyan, *Profitable meditations,* 4.

> One English *George* out-weighs alone (by odds)
> A whole Committee of the Heathen Gods;
> Pronounce but *Monck*, and it is all his due
> He is our *Mercury, Mars,* and *Neptune* too.[170]

The enlarged edition includes several elegies to departed friends and also a poetic 'tragedy' based on the trial and imprisonment of Christopher Love (1618–51). Love had been arrested and tried for involvement in Charles II's attempt to return to Scotland in 1649 and was beheaded on Tower Hill in 1651; Love's final letters to his wife and scaffold speech had been widely republished. Wild's 'Act I' of his verse tragedy opens:

> The *Philistins* are set in their High Court,
> And *Love*, like *Sampsons,* fetch'd to make them sport:
> Unto the Stake the smiling Prisoner's brought. (p. 23)

Act V concludes '*Love* lyes a bleeding, and the World shall see | Heaven Act a part in this black Tragedie', and all nature laments the passing of '*Love*' from the world (p. 27).

The poem foreshadows Wild's later poetic targets as he attacks Cromwell and members of Parliament responsible for the political trial and godly ministers who place politics above faith. Wild would be ejected from his living in 1662, and he moved to Oundle in Northamptonshire, where he launched satiric broadside attacks on both the bishops and those ministers who had conformed to the Restoration church, such as Richard Lee, the father of the dramatist Nathanial Lee, in *The Recantation of a Penitent Proteus* (1663); Wild also went after the royal licenser Roger L'Estrange (see *MV* 2.II) in *The Grateful Non-Conformist* (1665). Poetically sparring with the minister Nathaniel Wanley (1632/3–80), the father of the future librarian Humphrey Wanley, Wild had an ongoing exchange of poetic broadsides and pamphlets, including *The Fair Quarrel* (1666, reprinted 1668). Wild observed of the legislation forbidding nonconforming ministers to remain within a 5-mile radius of their former living that it could hardly be said to encompass all aspects of 'living':

> Nor is there any Statute of our Nation
> That sayes, *in five miles* of a *Corporation*
> If any *Outed-man* a Fart should vent,
> That you should apprehend the *Innocent.*[171]

Writing not only in a dramatically different poetic style but also from a continent away, the Yorkshire-born New England minister Michael Wigglesworth (1631–1705) created his very popular long poem on the apocalypse, *The Day of Doom*, which was published first in Massachusetts in 1662 and subsequently in London in 1666. Enjoying several editions between its initial London

---

[170] Wild, *Iter boreale*, 14.
[171] Quoted in Richard L. Greaves, 'Wild, Robert (1615/16–1679)', *ODNB*.

appearance and 1673, in New England alone the book sold out the 1,800 copies of the first edition within a year. The poem is dedicated to 'Christ the *Judge* of the World', and asks him for poetic inspiration:

> Oh, guide me by the sacred Sprite
> So to indite, and so to write,
> That I thine holy Name may praise,
> And teach the sons of men thy ways.[172]

Written in ballad-style metre, the opening of the poem sounds more like a nativity ode than the coming of Judgement Day: 'Still was the night, serene and bright, | when all men sleeping lay; | Calm was the season' (p. 1). The stanza concludes ominously, however:

> Soul take thine ease, let sorrow cease,
>   much good thou hast in store;
> This was their song their cups among
>   the evening before. (p. 1)

At midnight a light suddenly appears 'which turn'd the night to day: | And speedily an hideous cry | did all the world dismay' (p. 2). Twenty-two cantos later, the sinners are cast into hell to dwell forever, and this realization that it will be for all eternity 'makes Hell's fiery flakes | much more intolerable' (p. 79). Wigglesworth concludes his volume with a lengthy 'Postscript unto the Reader', a more complex verse form but still a conversational plea to remember that 'Thou hast a Soul, my friend, and so have I, | To save or lose a soul that cannot die', and 'A *song* of EMPTINESS, to fill up the *Empty Pages* following. VANITY OF VANITIES':

> Go boast thy self of what thine heart enjoys,
> Vain man! Triumph in all thy worldly Bliss:
> Thy best Enjoyments are but trash and toys;
> Delight thy self in that which worthless is. (p. 95)

Alexander Brome (1620–66), in sharp contrast, was named 'the English Anacreon' for his celebration of cavalier drinking songs. Brome, who was the older brother of Henry Brome, the bookseller who published his *Songs and other Poems* (1661), was a practising lawyer in London, married to another bookseller's widow, Martha Whitaker. He had entered Gray's Inn in 1648 and Lincoln's Inn in 1659 and while there made the acquaintance of Thomas Stanley and his circle (see *MV* 1.VI). During the 1650s, individual poems by Brome appeared in various miscellanies and as commendatory verse in collections, including Moseley's edition of Beaumont and Fletcher and Isaac Walton's *The Complete Angler* published in 1655 (see *MV* 1.III), but he did not gather his own poems together until 1661. Brome would issue an enlarged

---

[172] Wigglesworth, *Day of Doom*, sig. A2ᵛ.

edition of it in 1664 and a further edition with more poems was published in 1668 after his death and reissued in 1671 and 1680. Just prior to his death he issued his collection of *The Poems of Horace*, twenty-five of which he trans-lated while the others were done by friends and acquaintances.

Perhaps not surprisingly given his family and background, Brome's epistle to his reader shows a sophisticated appreciation of both the ways of social authorship and the business of print. 'To the Collection of these papers two accidents have concur'd', he opens, 'a *lazie disease*, and a *long vacation*; the one inclining me to do nothing else, and the other *affording* me nothing else to do'.[173] While he might claim numerous reasons for printing his poems, 'namely, *gratification* of Friends, importunity, prevention of spurious impres-sions', none of these is true, nor is it 'an ambition to be in print; to have a *face* cut in copper, with a *lawrell* about my head; a motto and verse underneath made by my self in my own *commendation*', he declares, not even 'to be accompted a *wit*, and call'd a *Poet*' (sigs A2ᵛ–A3ʳ). Indeed, he was warned against it by friends, saying that by printing he would expose himself to 'the new Generation of *judge-wits* who, like *Committee-Men* or *black-witches* in *Poetry*, are created only to do mischief' (sig. A3ʳ). However, Brome continues, 'for why I made these *rambles*, I can give no other accompt then a poor man does why he gets *children*; that is his pleasure, and this mine' (sig. A3ᵛ). With a commendatory verse written by Isaac Walton, some of the volume's poems strongly call to mind Walton's other friend, John Donne, such as 'Song II. The Indifferent':

> Mistake me not, I am not of that mind
> To hate all *woman kind*;
> Nor can you so my *patience* vex;
> To make my *Muse* blaspheme your sex. (p. 3)

Another poet with a more direct connection to Donne published his collected poems the following year in 1662, Sir Aston Cokayne (1608–84). Educated at Cambridge and residing for a time in London at one of the Inns of Court, Cokayne claimed the friendship of numerous pre-war court poets and drama-tists: '*Donne, Suckling, Randolph, Drayton, Massinger, | Habbington, Sandys, May*, my acquaintance were', he announced in *Small poems of divers sorts* (1658). This text he only published, he informs his readers, because, on his leaving London, papers that he had given to a friend to keep fell into the hands of the printer William Godbid, who published his play *The Obstinate Lady* without Cokayne's knowledge. The 1662 volume, published by Philemon Stephens, junior, incorporates the 1658 title pages for the poems *The Obstinate Lady* and *Trappolin* (the source for Nahum Tate's popular comedy *A Duke and No Duke*, 1684), and repeats the same author's apology but adds to this the 1662 title page of Cokayne's *The Tragedy of Ovid* 'intended to be acted

---

[173] Brome, *Horace*, sig. A2ᵛ.

shortly'. Cokayne, who had been imprisoned for his Royalist sympathies throughout much of the late 1640s, never did stage his dramas, with the exception of a masque performed in 1639 at the house of his uncle, the Earl of Chesterfield, for Twelfth Night celebrations.

The year 1663 gave the reading public works by two of the most widely read poets of their generation, Abraham Cowley's *Verses* and Samuel Butler's satire *Hudibras*, part 1. Although each was frequently reprinted, Cowley became a literary icon for the period, and his collected *Works* were published in 1668 after his death, while Butler (bap. 1613–80), even though his book had five editions in the first year and four more that were pirated, struggled with poverty at the end of his life. Unlike Cowley in exile in France with the royal family, Butler was in England during the war and Commonwealth period and was a servant in some capacity to the Countess of Kent until she died in 1651. According to John Aubrey, Butler must then have migrated to London, where he and the satirist John Cleveland '&c. of Grayes Inne, had a Clubb every night' (Aubrey, *Brief Lives*, 1. 175) and perhaps during this time he began *Hudibras*, whose protagonist Butler described as 'a West Countrey Knight then a Coll: in the Parliament Army & a Committee man, with whome I became Acquainted Lodging in the same house with him in Holbourne'.[174] After the Restoration, Butler was briefly steward for the Earl of Carberry at Ludlow Castle, but left in 1662 before publishing the first part of *Hudibras* in late December of that year, although the title page shows 1663.

Hudibras. The First Part. Written in the time of the late Wars is written in a mock epic, burlesque style divided into cantos, and its verse form of octosyllabic couplets generated the term 'Hudibrastick'. It chronicles the adventures of the thick-headed Presbyterian knight 'Sir Hudibras' in mock heroic terms, styled in the manner of Cervantes's *Don Quixote*:

> A wight he was, whose very sight wou'd
> Entitle him *Mirrour of Knighthood;*
> That never bow'd his stubborn knee
> To any thing but Chivalry.[175]

The name is derived from a minor figure in Spenser's *The Faerie Queene*, book two, a knight 'more huge in strength, then wise in workes he was | And reason with foole-hardize ouer ran'.[176] Like all good romance knights, Sir Hudibras is accompanied by a loyal squire, Ralpho, but in this burlesque story the servant's possession of the 'new-light' of inspired religion causes him to fall into endless quarrels with his master.

The opening of the poem quickly establishes the cause of the recent wars to have been nothing more than people falling out over matters they do not actually comprehend, and Sir Hudibras epitomizes this obstinate quarrelsomeness.

---

[174] Quoted in Hugh de Quehen, 'Butler, Samuel (*bap.* 1613, *d.* 1680)', ODNB.
[175] Butler, *Hudibras*, 2.   [176] Spenser, *Faerie Queene*, II. ii, st. 17.

> For his *Religion* it was fit
> To match his Learning and his Wit:
>
> .   .   .   .   .
>
> Such as do build their Faith upon
> The holy Text of *Pike* and *Gun*
> Call Fire, and Sword, and Desolation,
> A *Godly-thorough-Reformation.* (p. 8)

Setting forth on their bony steeds, the two encounter a number of adventures, all leading to physical mayhem, from breaking into a bear-baiting contest, being captured by the irate crowd and imprisoned, to being assaulted with rotten eggs by a group of women, and falling into a quarrel with an astrologer Sidrophel while asking for advice for winning a wealthy widow. The third part digresses for a complete canto to describe the chaos after Cromwell's death and the quarrels among the sectarians to seize power. The plot is episodic, with frequent digressions and numerous epigrammatic maxims in couplet form, and they all depict senseless conflict and muddled motivations.

Some critics have seen close affinities between Butler's mock heroic and Spenser's allegorical masterpiece, with Spenser's knights each embodying a particular virtue and Hudibras representing the vice of hypocrisy.[177] In *The Fairie Queene*, the knight Hudibras woos the eldest of three sisters, the youngest of whom cares for nothing but pleasure, the middle who chooses moderation, and the eldest, Elissa, who views all forms of pleasure as 'base', resulting in a company in constant turmoil: 'Still did they striue, and dayly disagree.' In Butler's satire, the Puritans as a group are relentlessly depicted as hypocritical zealots, whose principal form of pleasure is in creating discord. Part 2 followed in 1664, but the third part did not appear until 1678, and it was not until 1684, four years after Butler's death, that the three parts were united in a single volume.

Contemporaries were also quick to conclude that Butler was including satiric portraits of actual people in his tale, and Roger L'Estrange is credited with creating a 'key' published in 1709 so that readers could more easily identify these figures from the war years. In his 1674 edition of the poem, Butler himself added helpful notes identifying various members of the Parliamentarian party, but, as critics have noted, it is not only specific sects that are targeted for satire, but indeed all fanaticism that leads to blind, unthinking actions or romantic self-delusions.[178] 'But as for our part, we shall tell | The naked truth of what befell; | And as an equal friend to both', Butler opens the second canto of part 1 'With neither faction shall take part, | But give to each his due desert: | And never coyn a formal lye on't' (p. 36).

The popularity of *Hudibras* was such that there were several pirated editions and also a hastily thrown together continuation of part 1 before Butler printed his own part 2. Abraham Cowley's publisher, Henry Herringman, likewise

---

[177] See Jack, *Augustan Satire*, ch. 1.   [178] See Yadav, 'Fractured Meanings'.

warned readers in the 1663 edition of *Verses, Written upon several Occasions* that Cowley's popularity had led to spurious publications and damaged poems. 'Most of these Verses, which the Author had no intent to publish, having been lately printed at *Dublin* without his consent or knowledge, and with many, and some gross mistakes in the Impression', Herringman asserts in an advertisement following the title page, 'He hath thought fit for his justification in some part to allow me to reprint them here'.[179] Like Butler, however, Cowley's reputation was at its height during his lifetime and a decade after but faded rapidly in succeeding generations. In 1675, John Milton's own nephew Edward Phillips declared that Cowley was the most admired poet 'of our nation both the present and past ages'.[180] Although he was praised at his funeral as being the English equal of the finest of the classical poets, remembered by John Evelyn as 'that incomparable Poet, & Virtuous Man, my very deare friend' (Evelyn, *Diary*, 3. 489–90, 1 August 1667), Cowley's fame as a poet began to diminish, and by 1711 Joseph Addison, writing in *The Spectator* (see *MV* 5.III), declared that '*Homer*, *Virgil*, or *Milton*, so far as the Language of their Poems is understood, will please a Reader of plain common Sense, who would neither relish nor comprehend an epigram of *Martial*, or a poem of *Cowley*' (no. 70, 21 May 1711).

The contents of the 1663 volume include one of Cowley's most popular poems, 'The Complaint', several odes to individuals including Katherine Philips, an ode on the return of Charles II, and paraphrases and translations from Horace and Virgil. There are two poems that specifically address Cowley's representation of himself as a poet, 'Upon occasion of a Coppy of Verses of my Lord *Broghills*', and 'Mr *Cowley's* Book presenting it selfe to the University Library of *Oxford*'. Cowley opens to the ode to Broghill (Roger Boyle, 1st Earl of Orrey; see *MV* 1.VI; *MV* 2.III) with a complaint to the Muse, 'Ingratefull Mistress', that

> Thou bad'st me write, and write, and write again;
> 'Twas such a way as could not miss.
> I like a Fool, did thee Obey,
> I wrote, and wrote, but still I wrote in vain.[181]

To her response that she has given him 'Fame', he retorts, 'Who now, what Reader does not strive | T' invalidate the gift whilst w' are alive?' The harshness of his readers angers the poet so much he angrily throws his copies of Ovid and Horace out of the window and 'I my own Off-spring, like *Agave* tore' (p. 9). The Muse calms him with his 'reward', a poem by Boyle praising Cowley: 'Nothing so soon the Drooping Spirits can raise | As Praises from the Men, whom all men praise' (p. 10). His book, on being presented to the Bodleian, likewise pleads 'Will you into your Sacred throng admit | The meanest Brittish Wit?':

---

[179] Cowley, *Verses*, 'Advertisement'.
[180] See Nethercot, 'The Reputation of Abraham Cowley'.   [181] Cowley, *Verses*, 8.

> You Gen'ral Councel of the Priests of Fame,
> Will you not murmur and disdain,
> That I place among you claim,
> The humblest Deacon of her train? (p. 13)

If only, his book laments, his author had been kept safely at Oxford rather than being forced into 'Business which the Muses hate, | He might have then improv'd that small Estate, | Which nature sparingly did to him give' (p. 14). As with the poem to Boyle, this one concludes that the merits of the poet and his poetry are best seen in the company that they keep.

Cowley's ode to Katherine Philips, 'On *Orinda's* Poems. ODE', is also about poetry and poets, in particular women poets. He praises her as a conquering figure, one whose poetry now claims what other women's beauty before had won. 'Where e're I see an excellence', Cowley declares, he must praise it in Philips's verses: 'I must admire to see thy well knit sense, | Thy numbers gentle, and thy Fancies high':

> 'Tis solid, and 'tis manly all,
> Or rather 'tis Angelical,
> For as in Angels, we
> Do in thy Verses see
> Both improv'd Sexes eminently meet,
> They are than Man more strong, and more than Woman sweet. (p. 6)

Philips's poems on honour and friendship inspire him for her 'inward virtue is so bright' that 'It through the paper shines where she does write'.

Critics have pointed out that Cowley's paraphrases and translations from the classics made him a particular favourite and model for women readers and poets.[182] In his poems in praise of rural retirement based on Horace, Virgil, and Martial, Cowley celebrates the classical vision of the contemplative man removed from the strife of cities and courts and well situated: 'Oh happy (if his happiness he knowes) | The Country Swain, on whom kind Heav'n bestowes | At home all Riches that wise Nature needs' (p. 44). In his poem 'The Complaint', Cowley depicts himself as 'Melancholy *Cowley*' who is visited in a dream by his muse, who rebukes him: 'Art thou return'd at last, said she, | To this forsaken place and me?' she demands, 'Thou Prodigal, who didst so loosely waste | Of all thy Youthful years, the good Estate; | Art thou return'd here, to repent too late?' The muse accuses Cowley of having been 'bewicht with noise and show, | Wouldst into Courts and Cities from me go' to see the world and 'forsooth, be something in a State' (p. 53). She points out that, although he may have believed that 'once the publick storm were past' his remaining days would be happy, even with the return of Charles and the exiles to England,

---

[182] See King, 'Cowley among the Women', 43–60.

But whilst thy fellow Voyagers, I see
All marcht up to possess the promis'd Land,
Thou still alone (alas) dost gaping stand,
Upon the naked Beach, upon the Barren Sand. (p. 54)

'Melancholy Cowley' rebukes the muse, however, for having from his cradle stolen him away and kept him captive. And, he concludes the poem and the volume, his poetic muse should hardly dare criticize Charles II for being tardy in rewarding his faithful servant, since 'Kings have long hands (they say) and though I be | So distant, they may reach at length to me' and the only reward bestowed upon him by poetry for his life of service is 'but with popular breath, | And that too after death' (p. 58).

The following year, 1664, saw the legitimate publication of part 2 of *Hudibras* and also the unauthorized edition of Katherine Philips's *Poems*. If Cowley lamented that fame and appreciation of one's poetry came only after death, Philips was annoyed and dismayed by the attention drawn to her verses by an unauthorized version published by Richard Marriot and took immediate steps through her London friends to have it recalled. Philips, as we have seen, was not averse to publishing some of her verse (see *CV* 1.V) and had just enjoyed a successful production of her translation of *Pompey* at the new Theatre Royal in Dublin in 1663 (see *MV* 2.III), whose text also was published in 1663 by London publisher John Crook. *Poems by the incomparable Mrs K.P.* was advertised by Marriott in the *London Newes* on 14 January 1664, where he stated her full name as 'Madam Catherine Phillips'. He had registered it with the Stationers on 25 November 1663, and the licenser Roger L'Estrange had approved the octavo volume on 25 November. On 18 January, Marriot announced in the *Intelligencer*, another periodical publication published by L'Estrange along with the *London Newes*, that Marriot had been deceived about the origin of the manuscript he had published, 'both of the Correctnesse of the Copy and of that Ingenious Lady's Allowant to have them Printed'. Marriot declares that he 'intends to forbeare the sale of them, being not without hope, that this false Copy, may produce the true One'.

The 1664 volume opens with Cowley's ode to Philips that had appeared in his 1663 collection and a second set of verses by 'H.A.'. Like Cowley, this poet praises Philips in the context of her superiority to all previous women poets (Cowley dismisses Sappho, since 'the shame | I'th' manners soil the lustre of her fame'), declaring awkwardly that 'We may t'your Sex (though not to you) apply: | For now we've seen from a Feminine Quill | Poetry good as e're was, and as ill'.[183] The first poem by Philips in this unauthorized volume is 'Upon the double Murther of K. *Charles I*. in Answer to a Libellous Copy of Rimes made by *Vavasor Powell*', followed by her poems on the Restoration and the return of the royal family, thus highlighting her political as well as poetic allegiances.

---

[183] Philips, *Poems by the Incomparable Mrs K.P.*

In 'To Her Royal Highness the Duchess of *York*, on her commanding me to send her some things that I had written', Philips makes it clear that she herself would never have offered her verses to the Duchess (although she did dedicate *Pompey* to her), these 'humble Papers', the 'blushing tribute of an artless Muse' (pp. 22, 23) but for Anne Hyde's specific request to read them. Her more personal occasional poems directed to those in her 'Circle of Friendship' (see *MV* 1.VI) do not begin until page 29.

Philips had been notified of the volume's appearance by John Jeffries ('Philaster' in her poetry; see *MV* 1.VI). She wrote to her friend Lady Dorothy Temple that she needs advice how to suppress the volume and that 'I shall need all my friends to be my champions to ye Criticall & malicious'.[184] She sent two letters to her friend Sir Charles Cotterell ('Poliarchus'), one repeating her desire to have the volume suppressed and another that he might circulate publicly to show 'to any body that suspects my Ignorance and Innocence of that false Edition of my verses' (2. 125). She complains in this public letter that Marriot's publication has cause her to be 'expos'd to play the Mountebanks and dance upon the Ropes to entertain the Rabble . . . to be the Sport of some that can, and Derision of others that cannot read a Verse' (2. 144). Furthermore, the volume is riddled with errors, she declares, characterizing it as 'careless blotted Writing', and 'abominably printed', even including verses that were not by her.[185] Philips travelled to London from Wales in March of 1664 and apparently, like many other poets who had been printed without their advance knowledge, began preparing a true copy of her poems for the press. Unfortunately, she died in June from smallpox; a posthumous volume was published in 1667 by Henry Herringman, most believe seen through the press by Cotterell, which will be discussed later in this chapter.

Another volume that appeared in 1664 was Margaret Cavendish's *Poems and Phancies*, a corrected and revised version of her 1653 volume *Poems and Fancies* (see Figure 2; see also *CV* 1.V), which was again reissued with revisions in 1668, which suggests a completely different approach to both women's verse and publication. The most notable change in the 1664 edition is the commendatory verse from her husband William Cavendish that opens the volume: 'I Saw your *Poems*, and then Wish'd them mine', it opens:

> Your *New-born*, *Sublime Fancies*, and such store,
> May make our *Poets* blush, and Write no more:
> Nay *Spencer's Ghost* will haunt you in the Night,
> And *Johnson* rise, full fraught with *Venom's Spight*.[186]

Even 'Gentle *Shakespeare*' will join Chaucer in the dust because of her display of 'Such *Metaphors*, such *Allegories* fit' and 'Drawing all things to all things, at your Pleasure'. Newcastle applauds his wife's 'freshness' of expression combined

---

[184] Philips, *Collected Works*, 2. 142.   [185] See Hageman, 'Treacherous Accidents'.
[186] Cavendish, *Poems and Phancies*, sig. A2r.

with 'Similizing to the *Life* so like', declaring that her verses display 'the *Quintessence* of *Wit*' (sig. A2ᵛ). These nearly 300-page folio volumes, with their elaborate paratexts of dedications, epistles, and commentary by the poet on her own poetry, highlight not only her awareness that she is a 'female pen' publishing in a format typically used for 'works' by male writers, but that she wishes her poetry to be seen as being unorthodox, original, and experimental.

The 1667 version of Katherine Philips's poems, in contrast, while celebrating the unique status of the poet, clearly does so by embedding her in classical conventions. *Poems by the most deservedly admired Mrs Katherine Philips*, which was reprinted again in 1669 and 1678, includes the poems published in the unauthorized edition with the addition of forty-one more, and her translations of the dramas *Pompey* and the unfinished *Horace*. This handsome folio includes a portrait of her by William Faithorne (see *MV* 1.III) as a restrained classical bust (in contrast to Margaret Cavendish's full-length portrait of herself atop a pedestal), a copy of her public letter denouncing the earlier edition, and numerous dedicatory poems in praise of her and her verses, 'the English Sappho', including those by Roger Boyle, the Earl of Orrery, the Earl of Roscommon, the 1663 ode by Abraham Cowley as well as a new one on her death, an unknown Irish woman 'Philo-Philippa', who had written to Philips after the performance of *Pompey* in Dublin, the historian James Tyrrell (1642–1718), and Thomas Flatman, the poet and painter.

The posthumous volume and the poems to and about Philips established one model of critical discourse about female authorship that would persist for the next several centuries, that of the chaste, virtuous matron whose writing is marked by Platonic love and purity, where the personal life of the poet is inextricably tied to the quality of her verse. As Cotterell states in his preface to the reader, 'we might well have call'd her the English *Sappho*, she of all the female Poets of former Ages, being for her Verses and her Vertues both, the most highly to be valued'. In this, Cotterell concludes, '*Orinda's*' virtues 'they as much surpass'd those of *Sappho* as the Theological do the Moral, (wherein yet *Orinda* was not her inferiour)'.[187]

In all the commendatory verses, Philips is eulogized as a woman poet and an English one. 'In me it does not the least trouble breed, | That your fair Sex does Ours in Verse exceed', declares Boyle, but 'Philo-phillippa' observes:

> Thou glory of our Sex, envy of men,
> Who are both pleas'd and vex'd with thy bright Pen
>
> .   .   .   .   .
>
> But mens sore eyes cannot endure its rayes;
> It dazles and suprizes so with light,
> To find a noon where they expected night.[188]

[187] Philips, *Poems by the most deservedly admired Mrs Katherine Philips*, 'Preface'.
[188] Philips, *Poems by the most deservedly admired Mrs Katherine Philips*, sig. dʳ, 'To the Memory of the Excellent Orinda'.

Tyrrell mourns the loss of both her and Cowley, who passed away in 1666, noting 'For were not Nature partial to us Men, | The World's great Order had inverted been' (sig. er), and furthermore:

> Has she such Souls plac'd in all Woman-kind,
> Giv'n 'um like wit, not with like goodness join'd,
> Our vassal Sex to hers had homage pay'd
> Woman had rul'd the World, and weaker Man obey'd. (sig. e^r)

Thomas Flatman's ode on Philips, 'To the Memory of the incomparable *Orinda*', opens with a salute to her as the epitome of female virtue:

> A Long Adieu to all that's bright,
> Noble, or brave, in Womankind,
> To all the wonders of their Wit,
> And Trophies of their mind. (sig. f^r)

As other critics have observed, apart from her poems on political occasions and addressing members of the royal family, Philips's verse is noted for its exploration of the personal occasion, in particular poems describing her friendship with other women.[189] As Philo-Philippa begins 'To the Excellent *Orinda*', 'Let the male Poets their male *Phoebus* chuse, | Thee I invoke, *Orinda*, for my Muse':

> Fearless she acts that friendship she did write:
> Which manly Vertue to their Sex confin'd,
> Thou rescuest to confirm our softer mind;
> For there's required (to do that Virtue right)
> Courage, as much in Friendship as in Fight. (sig. d^r)

She concludes this stanza: 'The danger we despise, doth this truth prove, | Though boldly we not fight, we boldly love' (sig. d^r). Cowley, in his second ode on Philips, declares that 'No violent passion could an entrance find | Into the tender goodness of her mind', but he also praises her capacity for friendship, 'which so long had told | Of three or four illustrious Names of old': in Philips's verses there is 'A new, and more suprising story | Of fair *Lucasia* and *Orinda's* glory' (sig. g^r).

Philips's poems of friendship directed to Lucasia and Rosiana borrow both from Donne's metaphysical merging of true lovers' souls and cavalier motifs of male friendship as offering the only stability in a hostile, volatile world (see *MV* 1.VI).[190] Recent critics have also found in her friendship poems not only expressions of Platonic love and political ideology but also a prototype for closeted lesbian discourse.[191] In addition to her poems to her husband,

---

[189] See Andreadis, *Sappho in Early Modern England*, ch. 3; Stiebel, 'Subversive Sexuality'.

[190] See Chalmers, *Royalist Women Writers*, ch. 2; Scott-Bauman, *Forms of Engagement*, ch. 4.

[191] See Robinson, *Closeted Writing*, preface and ch. 2, pp. 19–36; for an extensive overview, Loscocco, 'Inventing the English Sappho'; and, for a more recent reconsideration, Lanser, *The Sexuality of History*, ch. 4.

James Philips (Antenor), and to her friends on the occasions of their marriages, the poems to Lucasia and Rosiana, including 'Friendship's Mystery', 'Parting with *Lucasia*', 'To my *Lucasia*', and 'To Mrs *M.A.* upon Absence', are very much dramatizations of a passionate attachment between women, including the motifs of the lover scorned, the pain of the separation of the lovers, and the complete, all-encompassing satisfaction of the ideal relationship: 'For thou art all that I can prize, my Joy, my Life, my Rest'.

> No Bridegrooms nor Crown-conquerors mirth
>   To mine compar'd can be:
> They have but pieces of this Earth,
>   I've all the World in thee.
> ('To my Excellent Lucasia, on our Friendship' p. 52)

That Philips was interested in the nature of intense friendships, between women and men and between members of the same sex, is manifest in her earlier exchanges with Jeremy Taylor (see *MV* 1.VI). In his discourse on friendship, he seems to cast doubt on women's ability to engage in a level of friendship that men can attain. Philips's response in her letter to him and in the poem 'A Friend' suggests otherwise:

> If Soules no Sexes have, for Men t'exclude
>   Women from Friendship's vast capacity,
> Is a Design injurious or rude,
>   Onely maintain'd by partiall tyranny. (p. 95)

She begins this poem by declaring that friendship is indeed

> Nobler then Kindred or then Marriage-band,
>   Because more free; Wedlock-felicity
> It self doth only by this Union stand,
>   And turns to Friendship or to Misery. (p. 94)

The same year that Katherine Philips's posthumous edition appeared also saw the publication of John Milton's *Paradise Lost*. Milton, in contrast to Philips, had been leading a restricted and retired life since the Restoration, having narrowly escaped lengthy imprisonment and trial for his part in defending the regicide in the early 1650s and his pamphlets written on the eve of Charles II's return urging the retention of the Commonwealth. An order for his arrest had been issued in June 1660, and in July copies of his books had been burned by the public executioner. *Paradise Lost* is believed by some critics to have been begun in the early 1640s as a tragedy, and Milton's nephew Edward Philllips recounted in his life of his uncle hearing Satan's soliloquy from book 2 in this context; some drafts for a drama exist in the Trinity manuscript. Most believe it was completed during the 1658 to 1663 period, its publication delayed first by the outbreak of the plague in London, which Milton and his family fled, and then by the Great Fire in 1666 (see *CV* 2.II). Milton had shown a manuscript of the text to his Quaker friend Thomas Ellwood in August 1665; Ellwood had secured the cottage in Chalfont St Giles, Buckinghamshire, to which Milton and his family had retired during the plague and where he would write *Paradise Regained*. Completely blind by this time, Milton composed the epic by using an amanuensis, to whom he would dictate the lines he had composed, with his nephew and former pupil Edward Phillips overseeing the corrections to the text.[192]

Milton in his invocation to the heavenly muse Urania in book 7 points to this difficult period in his life during which the text had been composed and refined:

> More safe I Sing with mortal voice, unchang'd
> To hoarce or mute, though fall'n on evil dayes,
> On evil days though fall'n, and evil tongues;
> In darkness, and with dangers compassed round,
> And solitude.[193]

His hope is not literary fame or worldly acclaim but that his work will 'fit audience find, though few' (p. 175). He returns to the haunting image he had employed in *Lycidas* of the death of Orpheus, the poet whom the muses loved but failed to protect when he was attacked by the Bacchantes: he urges Urania for his sake to do what the classical muse could not and to

> …drive farr off the barbarous dissonance
> Of *Bacchus* and his Revellers, the Race
> Of that wilde Rout that tore the *Thracian* Bard
> In *Rhodope*, where Woods and Rocks had Eares
> To rapture, till the savage clamor dround
> Both Harp and Voice. (7. 32–7)

The original format of the poem was in ten books, which would be expanded in the 1674 edition into twelve by dividing the lengthy books seven and ten to bring it further in accord with classical epic structure, although, as recently argued, Milton could have been basing his ten-volume format on that of Lucan.[194] Published by a minor London printer, Samuel Simmons, whose father had published some of Milton's earlier prose pieces, it appeared in a quarto format and sold for three shillings.[195] As commentators have observed, Simmons appears to have been an active collaborator with Milton in producing the second edition; Simmons explains to the reader of the second edition that, 'for the satisfaction of many that have desired it, I have procur'd [the Argument], and withal a reason of that which stumbled many others, why the Poem Rimes not'.[196] The first edition had three impressions, the first of 1,300 copies and the

---

[192] See Gordon Campbell, 'Milton, John (1608–1674)', *ODNB*.
[193] Milton, *Paradise Lost*, 175, 7. 24–8.
[194] Norbrook, *Writing the English Republic*, ch. 10.
[195] Lindenbaum, 'Milton's Contract'.
[196] Milton, *Paradise Lost*, sig. A2r, S. Simons; Dobranski, *Milton, Authorship, and the Book Trade*, ch. 1.

others of 1,500; Milton received £5 initially with the guarantee of a future £5 if the initial impression sold out and £5 for any subsequent ones. After Milton's death in 1674, his third wife, Elizabeth Minshull (1638–1727), sold the remaining rights of the poem to Simmons for £8, sums that may seem paltry but in fact were consistent with publishing practices of the period.

Paradise Lost has been considered by later generations of readers and critics as Milton's masterpiece, and it has held an assured position in the canon of English literature, although not without controversy. Imagined by Milton first as a tragedy, it retains its dramatic impact on readers. It has subsequently generated an enormous body of secondary critical commentary, both on its artistic merits and on its historical and theological contexts, from its depiction of a charismatic Satan and a distant God to its representation of the creation of Adam and Eve, 'He for God only, she for God in him'. Many of the issues Milton dramatizes for readers to grapple with were present in his earlier prose works. Readers of Milton's political treatises from the 1640s and 1650s find the issues of freedom and servitude retold first in the fall of Satan from heaven and then of Adam and Eve, as God explains to Christ in book 3:

> Sufficient to have stood, though free to fall.
> Such I created all th' Ethereal Powers
> And Spirits, both them who stood & them who faild;
> Freely they stood who stood, and fell who fell.
> Not free, what proof could they have giv'n sincere
> Of true allegiance, constant Faith or Love (3. 99–104)

Likewise, passages from his divorce tracts on the nature of marriage and the necessity of husbands and wives to be more than bedmates but helpmeets underlie his depiction of the relationship of Adam and Eve before the Fall in 'thir blissful Bower': 'Haile wedded Love, mysterious Law, true sourse | Of human ofspring, sole proprietie, | In Paradise of all things common else.'

> Founded in Reason, Loyal, Just, and Pure,
>
> .   .   .   .   .
>
> Farr be it, that I should write thee sin or blame,
> Or think thee unbefitting holiest place,
> Perpetual Fountain of Domestic sweets,
> Whose bed is undefil'd and chaste pronounc't,
> Present, or past, as Saints and Patriarchs us'd.
> Here Love his golden shafts imploies, here lights
> His constant Lamp, and waves his purple wings,
> Reigns here and revels. (4. 750–65)

In *Paradise Lost*, Milton draws on all his vast accumulated knowledge of classical, biblical, and contemporary verse, creating a dazzling and audacious retelling of Satan's temptation of man and man's Fall, incorporating the conventions from multiple genres including pastoral, epic, allegory, and, in book 9, tragedy.

Although there was an immediate response to the publication of *Paradise Lost* in 1667, it was no overnight sensation or bestseller for either Milton or Simmons. The Christian epic justifying the ways of God to men through the retelling of the Fall of man is an extremely complex text for multiple reasons, and it has provoked conflicting interpretations from its first appearance. There is an oft-repeated anecdote found in Jonathan Richardson's *Explanatory Notes and Remarks on Milton's Paradise Lost* (1734) that Sir John Denham (1614/15–69) appeared in Parliament with a sheet 'wet from the press' declaring that it was from 'the noblest poem that was ever wrote in any language or any age',[197] but there are few other printed records of responses to the poem. The extensive surviving correspondence between John Evelyn and John Beale (bap. 1608–83), a clergyman and writer on natural philosophy and member of the Royal Society residing in Yeovil, Somerset, suggests that Milton's reputation as a poet could outweigh his involvement with the government of the Interregnum.

Beale suggested to Evelyn that, with the death of Abraham Cowley, Milton could be usefully employed to serve as a laureate for the new Society and new philosophy (see *MV* 2.V). Beale argued that there is a 'potent efficacy of the true spirit of good poesy, yea and of common balladry to modell the Genius of the people' and he wished that force to be employed for the good of the Society.[198] Milton's ability to serve as a type of national poet, Beale claims, lies in his gift for Pindaric forms, and he hopes that Milton will be invited to offer an ode in memory of the late Cowley. When *Paradise Lost* was issued in the autumn of 1667, Beale and Evelyn were soon discussing it in their letters in that November.

In Beale's opinion, *Paradise Lost* shows a poet declining in age, but still skilled; he states that, in comparison with his earlier poetry, it is 'excellent, but the other more wonderful'.[199] Because it is an epic, 'men will be apt to expect great things from the adventure'.[200] Beale is concerned with Milton's use of blank verse, a concern that was sufficiently widespread that Milton would write an explanatory note for the 1668 edition, but more so with Milton's politics. In a letter to Evelyn Beale he acknowledges the irony of thinking about Milton as a national poet: 'You will Joyne with mee to whisper in a smile, that he writes so good verse, that tis pity he ever wrote in prose.'[201] Beale continued his preference for Cowley over Milton, troubled over Milton's representation of Satan in contrast to Cowley's in his *Davideis*, writing in 1679 that Milton 'mistakes the maine of Poesy, to put such long & horrible Blasphemyes in the Mouth of Satan, as no man that feares God can endure to Read it, or without a poisonous Impression'.[202]

---

[197] The standard source for such materials about Milton's life is Masson, *The Life of John Milton*, 6. 628; see also the recent collections of essays giving an overview of the expanding scope of Milton biographical and critical studies in Corns (ed.), *A Companion to Milton*, and McDowell and Smith (eds), *The Oxford Handbook of Milton*.

[198] Quoted in von Maltzahn, 'Laureate', 183.   [199] Quoted in von Maltzahn, 'Laureate', 185.

[200] Quoted in von Maltzahn, 'Laureate', 183.   [201] Quoted in von Maltzahn, 'Laureate', 189.

[202] Quoted in von Maltzahn, 'Laureate', 194.

Beale thus anticipated the nature of critical debate about the text that has continued throughout the centuries, Milton's handling of genre and poetics and the republicanism views seemingly infusing and instructing its themes and characters. The licenser Thomas Tomkins, the Archbishop of Canterbury's domestic chaplain, was concerned over potentially inflammatory sentiments contained in a passage in book 1 lines 594–9; the passage compares Satan's alteration after the Fall:

> As when the Sun new ris'n
> Looks through the Horizontal misty Air
> Shorn of his Beams, or from behind the Moon
> In dim Eclips disastrous twilight sheds,

concluding that with eclipses 'and with fear of change | Perplexes Monarchs', a reference to the popular belief that eclipses typically predicted the downfall of an emperor or king. Charles II had need to be concerned in 1665–7, with a sequence of disasters both natural and political, including the plague, the Great Fire, the military loss to the Dutch coming in the summer of 1667, and the dismissal of the Earl of Clarendon from the court (see CV 2.II). In spite of this offending passage, the book did indeed receive its licence.

More recent commentators have been less concerned by metaphors suggesting the decline and fall of monarchs than with the representation of heavenly civil war involving the Satanic invention of gunpowder, a crabbed and unapproachable God, and a charismatic rebel leader, Satan. Many have noted that the language of the debates staged in book 2 of the fallen angels in Hell whether to establish a commonwealth or an empire closely resembles that of the radical sectarians; the charges made by Satan and his followers of tyranny levelled against an omnipotent God challenge concepts of monarchy as an institution.[203] That is not to say that there is critical agreement on the significance of such rhetoric being given to the fallen angels. Furthermore, to add to the complexity of the text, although the narrative is biblical and thus timeless, as critics have pointed out, the initial audience of *Paradise Lost* could not but have read it as being a product of England's own very recent history. It is likewise engaging the Bible using a classical, pagan genre, epic, specifically that of Virgil, who used it to immortalize and legitimate the founding of empires, and in Spenser's English epic, *The Faerie Queene*, the celebration of Elizabethan monarchy through layers of allegorical meaning, while recent studies draw our attention to the importance of Lucan and Homer.[204]

While the government and Beale may have been distressed by the antimonarchical sentiments found in the piece, other early readers embraced *Paradise Lost* as an antidote to the libertine court and the attacks by those such as Butler in *Hudibras* on Puritan dissenters. Sir John Hobart (bap. 1628–83),

---

[203] See King, *Milton and Religious Controversy*, ch. 1, and Worden, 'Milton's Republicanism'.
[204] See Martindale, *John Milton*, Burrow, *Epic Romance*, and Hopkins, 'Milton and the Classics'.

a Norfolk MP and staunch Presbyterian, wrote enthusiastically to his cousin on reading *Paradise Lost* in the following January that he had 'never read any thing more august, & withal more gratefull to my (too much limited) understanding'.[205] Like Beale, Hobart rejects Milton's Commonwealth politics—he describes Milton as 'a criminall & obsolete person'—but he also acknowledges Milton's powers as a poet and a scholar. Hobart finds no problem with the use of blank verse, seeing in it a classical model, and sees Milton's use of archaic words as in keeping with the nature of epic, 'this continued (& sure extreordinary) Peice may purchase him soe high a plase amounge our eminent Poets, That hee may use the liberty of Homer or Virgil, who resussitated many words'.[206] Hobart also directly links Milton with Spenser, assuring his cousin that, 'in the opinion of the impartiall learned', the epic was 'not only above all the modern attempts in verse, but equall to any of the Antient Poets'.[207] But what particularly pleased Hobart was that this was a biblical narrative, a heroic Christian epic brought forth during a period in which many despaired of the general immorality and secular nature of the culture engendered by the Restoration (see *MV* 2.IV; *CV* 2.II).

Paradise Lost was followed by the publication of *Paradise Regain'd* in 1671 in conjunction with *Samson Agonistes*. *Paradise Regain'd* tells in four books the story of the temptation of Christ in the wilderness by Satan and the reversal of the losses incurred by Adam and Eve. Milton had shown this manuscript to Ellwood in London in 1666 after he had returned from Ellwood's house in Chalfont St Giles, and the text supposedly was Milton's answer to Ellwood's request to write of paradise 'found' as well as lost. 'I Who e're while the happy Garden sung, | By one mans disobedience lost, now sing | Recover'd Paradise to all mankind', the poem opens in a Virgilian style,

> By one mans firm obedience fully tri'd
> Through all temptation, and the Tempter foil'd
> In all his wiles, defeated and repuls't,
> And *Eden* rais'd in the wast Wilderness.[208]

Jesus resists the temptations of the world suggested by the demons and offered to him by Satan after his forty days in the wilderness, declaring in book 2: 'For I esteem those names of men so poor | Who could do mighty things, and could contemn | Riches though offer'd from the hand of Kings' (2. 447–9):

> Yet he who reigns within himself, and rules
> Passions, Desires, and Fears, is more a King;
>
> .   .   .   .   .
>
> And who attains not, ill aspires to rule

[205] Quoted in von Maltzahn, 'First Reception', 490.
[206] Quoted in von Maltzahn, 'First Reception', 492.
[207] Quoted in von Maltzahn, 'First Reception', 493.
[208] Milton, *Paradise Regained*, 1, 1. 1–7.

Cities of men, or head-strong Multitudes,
Subject himself to Anarchy within. (p. 2, 2. 447–9)

'To know, and knowing worship God aright', Milton concludes, 'Is yet more Kingly, this attracts the Soul, | Governs the inner man, the nobler part, | That other o're the body only reigns' (54, 2. 466–78).

The imperative need to reign within oneself is also at the heart of *Samson Agonistes*. Critics are not in agreement over when it was composed, and even Edward Phillips declared he was not certain when Milton wrote it. In the past, some critics argued, based on stylistic traits, that it was written before the Restoration, but others more recently have seen it as Milton's response to his situation in the Restoration and the defeat of the Commonwealth, even being directly allusive to the public trials of the regicides in 1661–2.[209] A so-called closet drama intended to be read rather than staged, *Samson Agonistes* observes the classical unities, taking place within a twenty-four-hour span, with Samson shorn of his strength and a blinded captive held by the Philistines in Gaza. Like Jesus in *Paradise Regained*, Samson is offered various temptations, to be ransomed by his father, to be taken into Dalila's house as an object of charity, and to be provoked by the taunts of the giant Harapha of Gath. Throughout the poem, the drama is primarily internal, as Samson struggles to understand how he, of whom it had been foretold by signs even before his birth that he would be the saviour of his people, has become helpless and enchained. Playing on the notions of 'seeing' and being blind, of understanding and ignorance, Milton moves Samson through a series of tortured reflections on who he thought he was and what heroism really is. Physically debarred from his role as the unbeatable warrior on the battle field, the blind captive recognizes,

O impotence of mind, in body strong!
But what is strength without a double share
Of wisdom, vast, unwieldy, burdensom,
Proudly secure, yet liable to fall (12, ll. 52–5)

Near the end of the poem, the Chorus commenting on Samson's new insights observes that

...patience is more oft the exercise
Of Saints, the trial of thir fortitude,
Making them each his own Deliverer,
And Victor over all
That tyrannie or fortune can inflict. (p. 77, ll. 1287–91)

To complete Milton's return to public attention as a poet rather than a political writer was the reissuing of his 1645 *Poems* in 1673 as *Poems, &c. Upon Several Occasions . . . With a small Tractate of Education to Mr Hartlib*. It was published by Thomas Dring, the son of the Thomas Dring who had published

---

[209] See Worden, 'Milton, *Samson Agonistes* and the Restoration'.

numerous literary works in partnership with Humphrey Moseley and who had published Robert Baron's *Pocula Castalia* (1650), which had attempted to pass some of Milton's verse off as Baron's.[210] During the early 1670s, the younger Thomas Dring was publishing dramas by Aphra Behn, William Wycherley, and Buckingham's *The Rehearsal* as well as Milton's poetry. In addition to reprinting the contents of the 1645 *Poems*, the 1673 version includes seven other occasional poems and a translation of Horace as well as Milton's sonnets and translations of the Psalms. While the volume still opens with 'On the Morning of Christs Nativity', the ordering of the 1645 edition has been changed, with 'On the Death of a fair Infant dying of a Cough', which Milton dates as being written when he was 17 (a claim disputed hotly by critics and editors), coming before 'The Passion'. Several topical poems, such as 'On the late Massacher in *Piedmont*', and 'On the new forcers of Conscience under Long PARLIAMENT', are inserted after '*L'Allegro*' and '*Il Penseroso*', thus coming before his courtly entertainment 'Arcades'.

The political poems interestingly situate Milton as having been at odds with Parliament and the forces in power in the 1640s and 1650s, as well as reminding readers of Milton's collaboration in the 1630s with Royalist poets and musicians. Sonnet 11, 'A Book was writ of late call'd *Tetrachordon*', and Sonnet 12', 'I did but prompt the age to quit their cloggs', pointedly ridicule the critics of his divorce tracts, while Sonnet 13, 'To Mr *H. Lawes*, On his Aires', was written to celebrate the court musician's *Ayres and Dialogues*. Sonnet 16, 'When I consider how my light is spent', on his blindness, is now dated to the early 1650s and resonates with the striving for patience to be God's instrument found in *Samson Agonistes*:

> But patience to prevent
> That murmur, soon replies, God doth not need
> Either man's work or his own gifts, who best
> Bear his milde yoak, they serve him best.[211]

Sonnets 20 and 21 seem to resist the Puritan condemnation of sports and recreations:

> What neat repast shall feast us, light and choice,
> Of Attick tast, with Wine, whence we may rise
> To hear the Lute well toucht, or artfull voice
> Warble immortal Notes and *Tuskan* Ayre? (p. 60)

Milton declares to Edward Lawrence, to whom the poem is addressed: 'He who of those delights can judge, And spare | To interpose them oft, is not unwise' (p. 60).

---

[210] See Ustick, 'The Courtier and the Bookseller'.
[211] Milton, *Poems, &c. Upon Several Occasions*, 59.

The other notable trend in the publication of verse during the 1660s and early 1670s directly responds to such appeals for recreation and such delights among the reading public, whose titles emphasized their light-hearted nature, wit, and variety. Starting in 1661, Henry Brome published a series of entertaining volumes of verse, starting with *Choyce Poems being songs, sonnets, satyrs and elegies by the wits of both universities*, Alexander Brome's collection, *Rump, or, An exact collection of the choicest poems and songs relating to the late times by the most eminent wits from anno 1639 to anno 1661* (1662), and Henry Bold's *Poems Lyrique, Macaronique, Heroique, &c* (1664). Richard Flecknoe would contribute two volumes, *A Farrago of several pieces* (1666) and *Epigrams of all sorts* (1669). Thomas Jordan (*c*.1614–85) published two collections, *A Royal Arbor of Loyal Poesie* (1663) and *Poems and Songs* (1664).

Collections of verses by multiple hands begin appearing almost yearly in the early 1670s. Clearly indebted to the 'Academies' of the 1640s and 1650s (see CV 1.II), the collections look forward to the popular format of the miscellany that writers such as Aphra Behn and John Dryden would edit in the 1680s and 1690s (see CV 4.V), an important venue for young writers seeking to appear in print and a supplemental source of income for dramatists. The universities provided the materials for a second collection in 1671, *The Oxford drollery being new poems and songs* in part by William Hicks and in part by his friends. The reopening of the theatres also meant that there was a new market for collections of verse featuring the songs from the new plays, and, in 1671, the same year as *Paradise Regained*, the *Westminister Drollery* appeared. Part 2 of it followed in 1672, and its title page assured the prospective buyer that it was *The Last, and now only, compleat collection, of the newest and choiest songs and poems, that are now extant both at courts theatres and elsewhere*. Likewise, *A Collection of Poems written upon several occasions by several persons, with many additions, never before in print* (1673) assured its buyer not only of the newness of its contents, but also of a promise of access to materials previously available only to a select few, such as *The Holborn-drollery, or The beautiful Chloret surprised in the sheets…to which is annexed, Flora's cabinet unlocked* (1673).

Verses published in the 1660s and early 1670s were a mixture of old and new, poetic ambition and delightful recreation. Verse was still the preferred medium for transmitting didactic encouragement to live a better life, as well as recording the popular tastes of the time; poetry was still used to chronicle the news, to satirize contemporary people and events, and to commemorate joyful public events (see CV 2.II). Poets who had been read and respected prior to the war continued to publish, and new editions of early seventeenth-century poetry were available for Restoration readers. Genres in favour prior to the war and Commonwealth, especially lyrics, continued to delight, while the outpouring of translations during the 1650s (see MV 1.VI; CV 1.I, 1.V) brought the works of classical authors to an audience that could read only English, as well as giving pleasure to the cultivated patrons who made the volumes possible. Two women were among the most publicly recognized publishing poets: Margaret

Cavendish, for her unflinching self-display and experimental verse forms, and Katherine Philips, for her matronly disdain for print readers who probably would not understand her poems. Cowley, at the height of his powers and popularity, completely reimagined the form of the classical ode, but lamented the poor treatment of poets, while John Milton, blind and in poverty, produced his epics blending the Bible and classical epic formulas in ways that would ensure his place in the English literary canon.

3

Reading and Writing for Profit and Delight, 1674–1684

I. 1674–1675

Whilst all *Europe* besides, lies now groaning under the Weight of a
Cruel War, and sees on every side her Cities sack't and spoilled…
England alone, by Your Royal Care, does now injoy a happy Tranquility
and sees Peace and Justice raign in all her Borders. One would think,
this Fortunate Isle were by heaven set apart to prove a New Ark; a most
safe Harbor still ready to receive and shelter all the shatter'd remains of
the Wreck't Universe…An Earthly Paradise, inviron'd round about
with Sandy Desarts; and, in fine, that *England* were, as indeed she is,
above all others in the World, Heaven's-Darling, the Earths Delight, the
Seas Soveraign Queen; the Eye, the Heart, the Pearl of the whole World.

'Your Royal Academy of Music To the Kings Most Excellent Majesty',
Ariadne, Or The Marriage of Bacchus (1674)

I Shall not, like too many of our modern Pamphleteers, nauseate the
Reader with a tedious, or Impertinent Preamble, let it therefore (to
awake his attention) suffice to say, that the sad and Tragical Relation,
I am hear to give him, is no less remarkable for its certainty, then its
Bloody Cruelty, and equally most true, and most Barbarous…

Anon., *The Bloody Inkeeper, or Sad and Barbarous News from
Glouster-shire: Being a True Relation how the Bodies of
seven Men and Women were found Murthered in a Garden belonging
to a House in Putley near Gloucester* (1675), 1–2

Lady Fidget: Ay, he's a base rude Fellow for't; but affectation makes
not a Woman more odious to them, than Virtue.

Horner: Because your Virtue is your greatest affectation, Madam.

Lady Fidget: How, you saucy Fellow, wou'd you wrong my honour?

Horner: If I cou'd

William Wycherley, *The Country-Wife* (1675), Act One

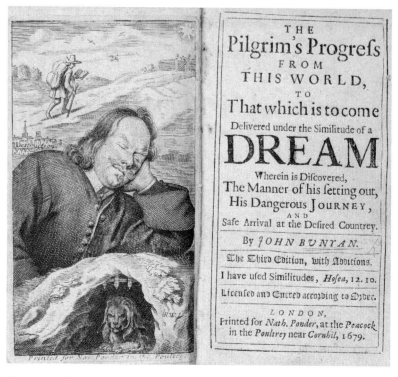

Figure 4. John Bunyan, *The Pilgrim's Progress*, third edition (1679). © The British Literary Board. Shelfmark C.70.aa.3.

The year 1674 was marked by the death of several public figures and literary notables whose lives and writings helped to define the multiple aspects of their generations—Edward Hyde Lord Clarendon, John Milton, Robert Herrick, and Thomas Traherne all passed away. Clarendon (1609–74), the adviser to kings who had lived the latter part of his life in exile, after death was brought back to London to be buried in Westminster Abbey. Milton (1608–74), who had lived his last years under a regime he considered fraudulent and immoral, died from gout and was buried next to his father in St Giles, Cripplegate, in November 1674. In July of 1674, a new edition of *Paradise Lost* in twelve books had been published, with a verse preface by Andrew Marvell, and, before his death, Milton had surprisingly given John Dryden, Poet Laureate, permission to convert his blank verse epic into rhyme for a theatrical opera. Robert Herrick (bap. 1591–1674), one of the last surviving poets from among the group known as the 'Sons of Ben', had returned in the early 1660s to his ministry in rural Dean Prior in Devon, where he quietly passed the final twenty-five years of his life after the publication of his only book of verse, *Hesperides*. Thomas

Traherne (*c*.1637–74), for nearly twenty years the rector of the tiny parish of Credenhill in Herefordshire, was preparing the second of his published works, *Christian Ethicks*, for the press, but he died before finishing the proofs of it. He left it in his will to his brother Philip, then with the Levant Company in Smyrna in Turkey, along with his best hat and the handwritten volumes of verse and prose meditations that he, his brother, and their friends had written over the 1660s, volumes that would not be recovered and printed until the twentieth century.

What topics were being written about, read, and discussed in the years 1674 and 1675? Religious treatises and works of divinity continued to dominate the printed page, with government proclamations and ordinances running a strong second. The Quakers alone, for example, printed sixty-seven titles in 1674 and eighty-six in 1675, for a total estimated 883 pages.[1] Texts on religious matters in general made up over 30 per cent of the total offerings during these years. London, as it had since after the Civil War, continued to dominate the English publishing market: of the 1,123 items now known to have been printed in 1674, 920 of them were done in London; the publication numbers increased in 1675 to 1,281, of which 1,059 originated in London.[2]

The other most numerous printed texts of the period included broadside ballads, pamphlets describing wonders, marvels, and unusual natural phenomena, and accounts of sensational crimes and criminals. There were more than a dozen pamphlets featuring 'bloody' and 'barbarous' in their titles—for example, *Bloody news from Chattam, or, A true and impartial account of a most barbarous murther, committed upon the body of a widow, and her son.* As a counterpoint to this, 'love' was a part of over 100 titles, along with 'delight' in some two dozen, ranging from the dramatist and poet Thomas Shadwell's (*c*.1640–92) broadside *The Delights of the bottle, or, The town-galants declaration for women and wine being a description of a town-bred gentleman with all his intregues, pleasure, company, humor, and conversation,* to 'William Shakespeare's' *Cupids cabinet unlock't, or, The new accademy [sic] of complements Odes, epigrams, songs, and sonnets, poesies, presentations, congratulations, ejaculations, rhapsodies, &c. With other various fancies. Created partly for the delight, but chiefly for the use of all ladies, gentlemen, and strangers, who affect to speak elegantly, or write quaintly* (1674).

The links between reading, speaking 'elegantly', and writing are highlighted on many title pages, suggesting readers' appetite for a means to acquire a better style of self-presentation. Dictionaries, guides, and entertaining 'academies' offered the growing number of literate readers glimpses of the manners that were supposedly practised in a sophisticated elite society, in part as they were

---

[1] See Raven, *The Business of Books*, 92–3; Peters, *Print Culture*, ch. 2; and Barnard, McKenzie, and Bell (eds), *The Cambridge History of the Book in Britain*, 4. *1557–1695*, 790, table 6.

[2] Barnard, McKenzie, and Bell (eds), *The Cambridge History of the Book in Britain*, 4. *1557–1695*, 783, table 1.

manifest by modes of speech and appreciation of witty turns of phrase. This same cultivated mode of self-presentation was represented on stage in popular comedies set in contemporary London, with references to actual places and people, who discussed 'fashion' and the 'mode', drawing distinctions between the 'true' sophistication practised by the witty libertine characters, the laughable excesses of the fops, and the awkward manners and speech of country visitors. In addition to the public theatres, by 1675 the nearly 3,000 London coffee houses such as Will's, Lloyd's, and the St James also brought people together for conversations about politics, literature, and business opportunities, circulating the latest reports, shipping news, and gossip: as the anonymous *The Coffee-Houses Vindicated* (1675) declared, 'it is older than Aristotle, and will be true, when Hobbes is forgot, that man is a sociable creature, and delights in company'. For readers and listeners in 1674 and 1675, everyday life itself was a performance waiting to be polished and improved.

All responses to contemporary life, however, were not couched in tones of approval. In April 1675, John Taylor, a member of a radical sect 'The Sweet Singers of Israel', also called the 'Family of Love', travelled to Guildford and announced to several outraged listeners that 'Christ . . . is a Whore-master, and Religion . . . is a Cheat, and Profession . . . God damn and confound all your Gods'. After being arrested, he repeated his beliefs before the House of Lords, was sent to Bedlam, and would be tried in the King's Bench Court for blasphemy in 1676.[3] The witty libertine style of some poets likewise pushed some readers too far. Around the author's name on the title page of the Folger Shakespeare Library copy of the 1674 edition of *Poems and Essays with A Paraphrase on Cicero's Laelius* (1673) by Edward Howard (bap. 1624–1712), an irate reader has added the inscription 'a depraved unblushing shameless profligate . . . A disgrace to his name',[4] a charge that is repeated in the blank space between the end of the author's letter to the reader and the errata list.[5] Howard admits in the preface to his mildly erotic verse that perhaps 'I have been too airy or wanton in some of my Poems' (sig. A3ᵛ), but he continues by encouraging his women readers to 'manage accordingly their blushes before their Servants and Admirers; not doubting, (where I have hit their fancies) they may as much smile when alone'. He concludes that he sincerely pities 'the Artificial Constraints of the fair Sex, in being oblig'd to dissemble (with no small trouble to themselves) their soft Inclinations' (sig. A3ᵛ). Several of his verses do depict women enjoying a variety of sensual pleasures, from 'Fricatrices: Or, a She upon a She', which begins 'Two Females meeting, found a sportful way | Without Man's help a Tickling game to play' (p. 10) to an unexpected amorous encounter while 'Bathing in a River' (p. 8). Howard, a struggling playwright (*The Usurper* (1664); *The Change of Crownes* (1667) and younger brother of the

---

[3] *Journal of the House of Lords*, 12 (1666–75), 687–8, 11 May 1675. See Apetrei, 'The "Sweet Singers" '.

[4] Howard, *Poems and Essays*, sig. A3r.   [5] FSL, call no. H2973A.

much more successful Sir Robert Howard (1626–98), was clearly aware that his small volume might meet with a mixed reception: he opens his volume of verse with the advice 'To his ensuing Poems' that they should 'Stand on your Feet now, Verses, if you can, | And face the Critick, and Censorious man' (p. 1).

As Howard had already experienced with his comedy *The Womens Conquest* (1670), which was ridiculed on stage in Buckingham's satire *The Rehearsal* (see *MV* 2.III), to publish one's verse, drama, or essays in this developing age of literary criticism and competition was to risk an assessment not only of your metre, but also of your lifestyle and your patrons, especially if your writings could in any way be connected to court or party politics. John Dryden's (1631–1700) and Elkanah Settle's (1648–1724) literary quarrels in 1674 and 1675 had their origins in the success of Settle's drama *The Empress of Morocco*. It had first been performed at court in the 1672–3 season, with Charles's courtiers taking parts and John Wilmot, Earl of Rochester (1647–80), and John Sheffield, Earl of Mulgrave (1647–1721), writing prologues; it was subsequently staged for the public in 1673 at the new Dorset Garden Theatre, taking full advantage of its new stage machinery. The play featured heroic rhymed drama, intrigues in the exotic court of Morocco, spectacular scenes and special effects, captive princesses, and bloody assassinations. In the printed version that appeared in 1673 dedicated to the Earl of Norwich (Henry Howard, who in 1669 had been ambassador to Morocco), the expensive text was lavishly illustrated with six engravings showing the most spectacular scenes and a view of the outside of the theatre itself (Figure 3). The excesses in the plot and characters of the play had already been satirized in *The Empress of Morocco A Farce*, the first of Thomas Duffett's [Duffet] (fl. 1673–6) so-called travesties acted by the King's Company that parodied productions at the rival Duke's Theatre, Dorset Garden. The elaborate printed edition drew forth a caustic response from John Dryden, Thomas Shadwell, and Thomas Crowne, *Notes and Observations on The Empress of Morocco* (1674).

Describing Settle's play as a 'Rapsody of non-sense', which could hold the attention even of the indiscriminate paying public audience only because of 'the help of Scenes and Habits, and a Dancing Tree', the author of the preface states that initially he would have been willing to let the young poet go unmolested in the hope that his style would mature. However, as the preface to Settle's printed edition arrogantly dismissed the Poet Laureate (Dryden) and other established dramatists, Dryden, Shadwell, and Crowne believed they had cause to feel that 'he should be made an Example, to the discouragement of all such petulant Ill Writers'.[6] 'Never did I see such a confus'd heap of false Grammar, improper English, strain'd Hyperboles, and downright Bulls', the critics announce: 'his Plot is incoherent and full of absurdities...every one Rants and Swaggers, and talks Non-sense abundantly'. If his plot and character are not enough to

---

[6] Dryden, *Notes and Observations*, 'Preface'.

damn the play, 'he steals notoriously from his Contemporaries; but he so alters the property, by disguising his Theft in ill English, and bad Applications, that he makes the Child his own by deforming it'. Finally, as for the author himself, 'he's an Animal of a most deplor'd understanding, without Reading & Conversation...for want of Learning and Elocution, he will never be able to express any thing either naturally or justly' ('Preface').

Settle responded with a pamphlet of his own, *Notes and Observations on The Empress of Morocco Revised*. Settle accuses Dryden of not having been content to attack another writer's style, but in addition to cast aspersions on the audiences as well. 'Now the calling all Mankind Fools, one would think were the boldest Drydenism that e're came in Print...there's worse behind, this Rude, unmannerly, ill-bred, sawcy and over-grown Rayler cannot forbear calling the Ladies Fools too', he observes.[7] This last he points out, is particularly egregious, as 'I am not ignorant that his admirers, who are most commonly Women, will resent this ill' (p. 1). Settle describes Dryden's style in attacking him as 'Billingsgate', referring to the vulgar and raucous part of London with its fishwives and street hawkers, and Settle declares that he will turn this style back on him by going through Dryden's recent heroic drama *The Conquest of Granada* and picking out passages to ridicule for bombastic heroics, as had been done to *The Empress*.

Settle was not the only writer to attack Dryden's style and manner. In the scribal version of 'An Allusion to Horace', which was circulating among the courtiers, John Wilmot, the Earl of Rochester, to whom Dryden had dedicated his comedy *Marriage à la Mode* in 1673, opens conversationally, 'Well Sir, 'tis granted, I said Dryden's Rhimes, | Were stoln, unequal, nay dull many times' (*POAS* 1. 358). Although Dryden may surpass 'Crowne's tedious scenes for poetry and wit', Rochester labels him 'Poet Squab', but allows that 'nor dare I from his sacred temples tear | That laurel which he best deserves to wear' (*POAS* 1. 362). Speaking of his own writing and reputation, Rochester concludes:

> I loathe the rabble: 'tis enough for me
> If Sedley, Shadwell, Sheppard, Wycherley,
> Godolphin, Butler, Buckhurst, Buckingham,
> And some few more, whom I omit to name,
> Approve my sense. I count their censure fame. (*POAS* 1. 363)

In conjunction with printed pamphlets and the broadsides, handwritten texts during these years circulated satires and libels attacking the court and the perceived lifestyle of its members, the troubling nature of political relationships with France, and the tension between religious practices and perceived government policies. These tensions were also recorded sometimes in a more neutral fashion by numerous diary-writers and memoirists, including John Evelyn (1620–1706), the Yorkshire MP Sir John Reresby (1634–89) and Bishop Gilbert

---

[7] Settle, *Notes and Observations on The Empress of Morocco Revised*, 1.

Burnet (1643–1715), as well as the lively if suspect accounts of the French diplomat and adventurer Philibert, comte de Gramont (1621–1707), whose *Mémoirs de la vie du comte de Grammont contenant particulierement histoire amoureuse de la cour d'Angleterre sous la régne de Charles II* would be translated into English by Abel Boyer in 1719.

To discover what events and people were considered newsworthy, one also has in 1674–5 several handwritten commercial news periodicals, compiled by a series of mostly unknown London scribes and mailed to subscribers outside London. One such was the tri-weekly Newdigate Newsletters sent to Sir Richard Newdigate in Warwickshire between 1674 and 1715 (Folger Library) and another the Bulstrode Newsletters, sent to Sir Richard Bulstrode between 1667 and 1687 (University of Texas at Austin). The most famous was without doubt that of Henry Muddiman (bap. 1629–92), who in 1660 had been granted the sole privilege of publishing newsbooks, and who oversaw the official government newspaper, the *London Gazette*. His handwritten news reports to private subscribers often contained information, such as Parliamentary proceedings, that until the lapse of the Licensing Act in 1679 would be illegal to print; references to Muddiman and his newsletters appear in the period's correspondence as well as in Etherege's comedy of the times, *The Man of Mode* (1676). The scribal newsletters consisted of information collected from printed gazettes and pamphlets as well as information sent by individual correspondents living abroad; they conveyed to the subscriber up-to-date accounts of royal events, interesting trials, important marriages and deaths, shipping matters, foreign battles, and notable debuts on the London stage as well as transmitting the latest society scandals.

The stage dramas that were both performed and printed in 1674 and 1675, whether tragicomedies, comedies, or tragedies, display conventional characters and stock plots that were enjoying popularity, from the exotic middle Eastern settings in romances and dramas, to the clashes between courtiers and 'wits' and their imitators, the aspiring fops and the potentially encroaching middle-class merchants and their families. Opera, with its Italian and French musicians and composers complemented by the newly designed stage machinery, was beginning to make an impact on the commercial theatre (see *MV* 4.IV); the commercial success of Shadwell's and Dryden's musical rewriting of Shakespeare's *Tempest* for Dorset Garden in 1674 with songs and special scenery perhaps lay in part behind Dryden's desire to convert Milton's *Paradise Lost* into a semi-operatic form, although it would not be published until 1700 and never performed.

Peace, prosperity, and the blessed state of being English were prominent themes for official celebration. The Third Dutch War, England's attempt to blockade Holland as part of its secret agreement with France in the 1672 Treaty of Dover, was concluded at the beginning of 1674 with the Treaty of Westminster. Out of this negotiation, England gained New Amsterdam, which would in time become New York; in 1674–5, the attention of 'old' England was again to be engaged by reports of life in the colonies and their unfamiliar plants and animals. Such reports, however, would soon be sensationally unsettled by the accounts of bloody conflicts during the Indian wars that broke out in 1675.

Private letters from English settlers in Jamaica and the Barbados likewise contained news not only extolling the expanding commercial opportunities in the sugar plantations, but also of the complexities faced by English colonial society shaping itself around the relatively new reliance on African slave labour. William Whaley, who was managing Bybrook, the sugar plantation of Colonel William Helyar in Jamaica, wrote in 1674 thanking Heylar for sending 'the sheets of lead and the ratsbane, also the book you sent me the *Gentlemans Calling*, in which you advice me to study, which you need not doubt'.[8] In January 1675, he writes that 'our main and greatest want is some 40 negroes more and 2 or 3 coppers [barrel makers] ... Thanks be to God that our negroes are in good health and all things in pretty good order, we have had a very sickly year of it amongst our white people, but thanks have not lost any'.[9] Later in the year he is forced to describe a more delicate matter: 'When your brother was living he being as indeed in these hot countries most men are a little venerial given, he in order thereunto did keep in the house a mullato that is one that is begotten between a negro and a white man and by her he had two boys'. On his marriage, Heylar pensioned off his mulatto mistress, but after his death, on the advice of her present mistress, 'she this last court sued me for £140, whereof £128 was for four years past and the remainder for damage she sustained by not receiving the money as it because due, pretending that Mr Heylar had promised her before witnesses to allow her £32 per annum as long as she should live'.[10] A lively court exchange followed, with some of the jurors finding for the woman, and some for the plantation, to the great embarrassment of the overseer.

Nearer to home, politics itself provided much material for writers and readers of all types. Charles called Parliament to assemble again in spring 1675, having prorogued (adjourned) it in 1673. Following the Duke of York's decision to resign all his public offices rather than take the Test Act in 1673 (which would have obliged him to take an oath denying the Catholic tenet of transubstantiation) and the recent arrangement of the Duke's marriage to the Catholic Princess Mary of Modena, many in Parliament had been bitterly estranged from the court in its positions on matters of religion, finances, and relationships with France. In April of 1675, the writer of the Bulstrode newsletter recorded that 'Ye King went by land in his chaise in much greater state then ever I saw him, & made twice as long a speech as he us'd to doe, ye greatest part of which concerned religion'.[11] Charles announced that 'The principal End of My calling you now is, to know what you think may be yet wanting to the securing of

---

[8] See SRO DD/WHh 1090/2/27, and Amussen, *Caribbean Exchanges*.
[9] SRO DD/WHh 1009/2/61.   [10] SRO DD/WHh 1090/2/1.
[11] *Catalogue of the Collection of Autograph Letters and Historical Documents*, 284.

Religion and Property, and to give Myself the Satisfaction of having used the uttermost of My Endeavours to procure and settle a right and lasting Understanding between us'. 'I have done as much as on My Part was possible', he declared, 'to extinguish the Fears and Jealousies of Popery, and will leave nothing undone that may shew the World My Zeal for the Protestant Religion as it is established in the Church of *England*, from which I will never depart'.[12] He then drew attention to the need for money from Parliament to restore the fleet, 'which I am not able to put into that State it ought to be; and which will require so much Time to repair and build, that I should be sorry to see this Summer (and consequently a whole Year) lost, without providing for it'.[13]

As the Bulstrode correspondent noted, the reception by the Parliament of the King's rhetoric was a mixture of polite scepticism and political theatre. When a motion was made to thank the King for 'his gracious speech', 'some were against giving thankes for it in general, but for taking it in pieces & thanke his M. for wt they lik'd & letting the other alone, wch was carried in yt House'.[14] Thus 'the humble thanks of yt House should be given his Ma: for yt part of his speech in which he assures tm of his resolution to preserve their religion & propertie & for his calling them together now; this they did to prevent anybody's believing yt they like ye matter of ye ships too well'. The House of Lords likewise decided on a qualified thanks: showing a fine distinction in their own choice of words, they voted to 'not to thanke his Ma. for his gracious speech but for ye gracious expressions in his speech'. At this point the House of Commons revived the bills from the previous session, including 'one furious one against Popery' (p. 284).

Thus 1674–5 found Charles II securely on the throne, but still at odds with Parliament. He was still without a child from his marriage to Catherine de Braganza, still deeply in debt, and still adroitly balancing the very public demands and charms of his three principal mistresses, Barbara Palmer (Lady Castlemaine), Louise de Kéroualle (Duchess of Portsmouth), and the actress Nell Gwyn (1651?–87). The royal family, its many amours and intrigues, and the tensions between its members and between it and Parliament, was itself a type of ongoing public spectacle, with characters and events rivalling any drama or romance. Doings and sayings were avidly reported by newsbooks, commented on and circulated in manuscript satires and lampoons, and recorded in the memoirs and diaries of the period. There were so many of these texts in circulation that, in 1675, the Surveyor and Licensor Roger L'Estrange (1616–1704) suggested to the newly created Libels Committee that the legal term 'libel' should be extended to include handwritten materials, since 'not one in 40 libels ever comes to Presse, though by the help of MS, they are well nigh as public'.[15]

---

[12] *Journal of the House of Lords*, 12 (1666–75), 652.
[13] *Journal of the House of Lords*, 12 (1666–75), 652.
[14] *Catalogue of the Collection of Autograph Letters and Historical Documents*, 284.
[15] Quoted in Kitchin, *Sir Roger L'Estrange*, 198.

Newsletters likewise carried the gossip out into the countryside and overseas. In 1675, when the King created his young illegitimate son by the Duchess of Portsmouth the Duke of Richmond and Lennox, the Bulstrode newsletter suggested that this led to 'Mrs Gwinn's son...to be made Earl of March to pacifie her a little & to ease her in some measure of the mighty disquiets wch ye other promotions caused her'.[16] The comedienne, who had been born into poverty and the dark side of London theatre life, unlike Charles's other principal mistresses, apparently never asked for an aristocratic title and sinecure for herself, but Nell Gwyn was as determined to secure the future of her children. The newsletter concludes, 'but it is said that the honour does not quite content her, shee looking upon her son as fit to be made a Duke as any of ye other' (p. 307).

The antics of members of the royal family provided a variety of material, from politics to religious practices to public morality, for a broad range of fascinated or outraged readers in a variety of media. John Freke's (1652–1717) lampoon 'History of the Insipids' begins promisingly, 'Chaste, pious, prudent Charles the Second', but quickly moves to an ironic comparison between him and the 'reformer' Henry VIII:

> Our Romanish bondage-breaker Harry
> Espoused half a dozen wives:
> Charles only one resolves to marry,
> And other men's he never swives.
> Yet hath he sons and daughters more
> Than e'er had Harry by threescore. (*POAS* 1. 244)

The song continues:

> New upstarts, pimps, bawds and whores
> That locust-like devour the land
>
> .   .   .   .   .   .
>
> Have render'd Charles, thy restoration
> A curse and plague unto the nation. (*POAS* 1. 244)

The poem was sufficiently over the limits of satire to cause a warrant for Freke's arrest to be issued and in 1676 for him to be tried before the King's Bench for high treason, where he was let off for insufficient witnesses.

The households of the royal family members also proved excellent sources for scandalously entertaining stories. The Bulstrode correspondent reported archly on 13 July 1675 that 'we have had a little mischance this morning at St James' in the Duchesse's court'. It appears that Mary Kirke, one of the maids of honour, had the 'ill fortune to become a mother of a brave boy. It is suppos'd ye poore lady, being unskillfull in such affaires, mistook her reckoning & was

---

[16] *Catalogue of the Collection of Autograph Letters and Historical Documents*, 307.

surprised, for shee had design'd many month to retire to a monastry'.[17] Apparently behaving much like heroines in future fictions by Aphra Behn and Delarivier Manley, Mistress Kirke,

so soone as shee discovered the condition her frailty had brought her to, shee became a catholick, ye apprehension of her shame giving her either a sincere remorse for her fault, or suggesting to her a convenient way of concealing it, & from ye houre yt shee was so, she declared her resolution of leaving the world & becoming a nun. (p. 303)

Persuaded by well-meaning friends to stay at the court in order to attempt to preserve her reputation, she stayed a further five months but 'overstrained ye argument & spoilt it all'. Her mother, on learning the news, fell into a swoon from which she could hardly be recovered. What is not mentioned in this report but which was a widely recorded scandal the proceeding September, also sounding more like a passage in a romance novel than real life, was that when John Sheffield, the Earl of Mulgrave (1647–1721), attempted to win her away from her then current lover, James Scott, the Duke of Monmouth (1649–1685), Monmouth had him waylaid and locked up; on the birth of the child, Kirke's brother accused Mulgrave of being the father and challenged him to a duel.[18]

Even more serious aristocratic misbehaviour is reported only a few days after the Kirke birth. In an entry for 24 July, the scribe details the imprisonment and trial of Thomas Rivers, Viscount Colchester in Surrey, 'condemn'd to be hang'd for murther, burglary & some other such small faults'.[19] In the account, the writer remarks that 'several poore people came in agst him and prov'd yt he had broken open their houses & bound several of ym and I think ravish'd one woman' (p. 308). Colchester pleaded drunkenness for the murder, 'the other with geast and & frolick; but he will certainly die in earnest', concludes the correspondent, punning grimly: 'this is the second time at least, if not ye third, yt he has been catch'd in such sports as some of these' (p. 308). Colchester, along with his brother Richard (aka 'Tyburn Dick', who would become one of the most notorious rakes of the period), and three others had already in early 1674 been implicated in the death of one William Cole in a brawl—on 26 December 1674 Charles II granted pardons to all of them. Nor does it appear that Colchester was executed in 1675, but died of more or less natural causes in 1680, at which point his brother Richard succeeded to the title.

The lifestyles of Charles's courtiers were, as critics have argued, themselves a kind of performance, both for the entertainment of the King and the other wits of the court, but also to command the attention of the 'other' world, first through scandalizing it, and then by providing materials through the stories of their exploits circulating in gossip, ballads, satires, and even on stage in the

---

[17] *Catalogue of the Collection of Autograph Letters and Historical Documents*, 303.

[18] HMC Rutland MS II. 27, quoted in Wilson, *Court Satires*, 258–9.

[19] *Catalogue of the Collection of Autograph Letters and Historical Documents*, 308.

popular comedies set in contemporary London as part of a celebrity culture. John Wilmot, the Earl of Rochester, is an obvious example of such a life performed, written about, and in circulation. Having been banished in December 1673 when he supposedly by accident handed the King his obscene and derisive lampoon, 'Scepter-Prick', Rochester, at least according to the account in Gramont's memoirs, returned to London in early 1674. There he amused himself with masquerading as a common citizen before returning to Parliament in February in his own identity. The period 1674–5 was also one of his most prolific and engaged periods as a poet and social critic, including the composition of 'Tunbridge Wells', a version of 'The Disabled Debauchee', and an early version of 'Satyr on Mankind', which had begun to circulate in handwritten copies in London.[20] He acted as patron for the young dramatist Nathaniel Lee (1645x52–92) and as John Crowne's promoter at court; simultaneously, he supplied an epilogue mocking Crowne, Shadwell, and Dryden for the comedy dedicated to him, *Love in the Dark*, by Sir Francis Fane (d. 1691), performed in the spring of 1675. He continued his affair with Elizabeth Barry (1656x 58–1713)—'So much wit and beauty as you have should think of nothing less than doing miracles, and there cannot be a greater than to continue to love', opens one letter to her in 1675—and also apparently dallied with an attractive French musician James [Jacques] Paisible (c.1656–1721), whom he would recommend to the King as a court musician and who would eventually marry Moll Davis, one of Charles's early mistresses from the theatre. Rochester's growing disenchantment with the court and the King, however, is clear in the short lampoons attributed to these years:

> God bless our good and gracious King
> Whose promise none relies on
> Who never said a foolish thing
> Nor ever did a wise one. (p. 292)

Rochester repeatedly found himself needing to retire from the court to his country estate at Woodstock on account of his very public and publicized antics. The first occasion was for a drunken assault on Charles's sundial in the Privy Garden that was chronicled by John Aubrey and Sir Francis Fane (the grandson of the poet and dramatist Sir Mildmay Fane, 2nd Earl of Westmorland); this allegedly phallic object was completely destroyed, including, symbolically, its glass portraits of the King, Queen, the Duke of York, the Queen Mother, and Prince Rupert.

Another popular, spectacular, and often controversial public figure in 1674 and 1675 was the King's oldest illegitimate son, James Scott, Duke of Monmouth (1649–85). As the 1673 Test Act began to remove prominent Catholics, including his uncle the Duke of York, from office, Monmouth had begun to acquire more and more public titles and responsibilities: he quickly became an Admiralty

---

[20] See Wilmot, *Works*, ed. Love, 369, 373, 591.

commissioner, followed in 1675 by a series of appointments including master of the horse, a Scottish privy councillorship, and a commission to make a treaty with Sweden. In 1674, Charles, who styled Monmouth in official documents in 1674–5 as 'our dearest and most entirely beloved son' (*CSPD, 1673–75*, 327–8; *1675–76*, 200), decreed that all orders relating to the armed forces would pass through Monmouth before being sent for royal approval, and thus it was Monmouth who oversaw the troops that subdued the rioting London weavers in 1675. When he was appointed chancellor of Cambridge University in 1674, an anonymous poet celebrating this event declared of the young man (who had not learned to read or write until he was 9 and struggled with literacy his entire life):

> You are not ours but *Learning's Chancellour*.
> Now drooping Arts, raise your afflicted head,
> And view that Blessing, which your Pray'rs have bred
>
> .   .   .   .   .
>
> Heaven has eternal happiness in store,
> And *Learning* now shall be despis'd no more.[21]

In 1674 Monmouth switched his attentions from Mary Kirke to Eleanor Needham (1650–1707?), with whom he would subsequently have four children.

The Queen, the childless Catholic Catherine of Braganza, was also a public figure who absorbed the attention of everyday English people. She had weathered the political pressures for Charles to divorce her in 1674, but the Venetian ambassador writing of her in 1675 noted that 'the customary freedoms of the king and even more the flaunting of his mistresses dispirit her and render her incapable of disguising her sorrows' (*CSPV, 1673–5*, 305). In 1675, Charles even managed to find time for one of his earlier loves, the dashing Hortense Mancini, the Duchess Mazarin (1646–99), who appeared in London in December 1675, attired in men's clothing, 'riding astride, booted and spurred', according to one contemporary pamphlet account, as she fled from her notoriously abusive husband, Armand-Charles de la Porte, duc de La Meilleraye.

Mazarin had supposedly come to visit her friend, the Duke of York's second wife, in her fashionable new court, a complicated setting where politics, drama, and religion could hardly be separated. The young Mary of Modena (1658–1718), married at age 15 and only four years older than James's daughter Mary, was alleged by some panicked Englishmen to be the daughter of the Pope himself; her arrival in London in September of 1673 had been preceded by crowds burning effigies of him. It was high treason 'to absolve, persuade, or withdraw any subject from their obedience to the King, or to reconcile them to the Pope; or to draw them to the Popish Religion' and the *News from the Sessions at the Old-Bayly, 12*[th] *December, 1674* records the trial and sentencing of William Burnet

---

[21] *To the Most Excellent and Illustrious Prince James*, 6.

for being a 'Romish Priest'.[22] He did not deny the charge, but argued that 'if it were a Crime so Capital in him to persuade People to the Roman Catholique Religion, (which he was verily persuaded was the onely true one) then it must be the same offence in Quakers and other different persuasions, since they as well as he made it their endeavour to draw people from the Church of England to their particular party' (p. 2). The jury, however, pointed to the specific identification of 'popish' religion in the law and sentenced him to be hanged, drawn, and quartered, 'which he received with a modest Generosity, saying these words, *Gloria in Excelsis deo*' (p. 3).

James had not yet in 1674–5 publicly stopped attending Anglican services, as he would in 1676, but his religious beliefs and practices were key issues in political discussions in 1675. The discourse of the day made little distinction between 'popery' and 'arbitrary government' or absolutism. Freke's 'History of the Insipids', for example, warns 'Then, Charles, beware thy brother York, | Who to thy government givens law; | If once we fall to the old work, | You must again both to Breda' (*POAS* 1. 250). A short anonymous satire entitled 'A Passionate Satyr on a Devilish Great He-Whore who lives yonder at Rome', printed in 1675, concludes:

> Who in Parliament time subscribed to the Church:
> Must We all be undone by a damn'd Popish Crew,
> Some that is about us, and some We ne're knew?
> Must the King and his Friends foe and know this
> And yet be advised that nothings a miss?[23]

Perhaps to counter this alarming and self-destructive image of the profligate royal household, one highly successful event was the specially commissioned masque from John Crowne (bap. 1641–1712), *Calisto*, described by several contemporaries as a 'celebration' of the royal family. Members of the court began public rehearsals in September 1674 with the young daughters of the Duke of York, Princesses Mary and Anne, then aged 13 and 11, taking the central roles along with members of the court and professional actors and singers such as Mary Wright. The cast highlights the virtues and splendours of the young princesses in particular and the English nation as a whole; interestingly, the cast included not only the young princesses and their ladies in waiting, but also Monmouth, Mary 'Moll' Davis (*c.*1651–1708), who was Charles's former mistress with whom he had had a daughter in 1673, Lady Anne Fitzroy (1661–1722), who was Charles's eldest daughter with Lady Castlemaine, and Lady Henrietta Wentworth (1660–86), who would in the future become the mistress of Monmouth and use her jewels to help support his rebellion.

The Harvard-educated John Crowne had been assisted in securing the royal commission by Rochester (the future literary critic John Dennis believed Rochester had done it to spite the then Poet Laureate John Dryden). Crowne

---

[22] *News from the Sessions at the Old-Bayly*, 2.   [23] *A Passionate Satyr*, 2.

noted apologetically in his dedication to Princess Mary that the circumstances of his creation of this courtly entertainment were irregular and not auspicious. 'Being unexpectedly called out of my Obscurity, to the Glory of serving your Highness, (and indeed the whole Court) in an Entertainment so considerable as this', he writes, 'my fears and amazements were such as (I believe) Shepherds and Herdsmen had of old, when from their Flocks and Herds they were call'd to Prophesie to Kings'.[24] The 'few Abilities I have', Crowne notes of himself, were strained beyond his abilities by the limited amount of time given him to compose the piece, 'scarce a Month', and the strict dictates of the casting, 'but seven allow'd me, neither more nor less: those seven to be all Ladies, and of those Ladies, two onely were to appear in Mens Habits'. Realizing he could not possibly create a new story, Crowne says that he resolved to 'choose the first tolerable Story I could meet with', but unfortunately, while he was attracted to the character of Calisto, the chaste nymph, the details of her story from Ovid placed him in the position of having to write quickly 'a clean, decent, and inoffensive Play, on the Story of a Rape' (sig. A2).

Nevertheless, Crowne succeeded in creating a spectacular entertainment for the princesses and the court in Sir Christopher Wren's remodelled New Hall Theatre at Whitehall, a production costing more than £3,500.[25] John Evelyn saw it twice, commenting 'my deare friend Mrs *Blagg*, who having the principal part, perform'd it to admiration: They were all covered with *Jewels*' (Evelyn, *Diary*, 4. 49–50). Interestingly, unlike the fanciful masquing costumes designed by Inigo Jones for the court of Anne of Denmark at the start of the century, the descriptions of the costumes found in the 'Accounts of the Master of the Robes' closely resemble Restoration court attire in general: although the cupids had ostrich feather wings, they wore doublets and breeches made of white satin, albeit trimmed with 20 yards of 3-inch-wide silver lace.[26] Likewise, Margaret Blagge's dress as Diana resembled a lady's court dress, requiring 24 yards of gold brocade and 146 yards of gold and silver lace in addition to a quiver with sixteen arrows.[27] Perhaps the most fanciful costume of the production was given to the professional male actor, Mr Ford, playing 'America', featuring '30 doz. Jewels, several colours, 36 doz. Spangles', and '6000 swan's feathers of several colours'.[28]

Crowne notes in his epistle to the printed edition of *Calisto* that the mere text falls far short of the performance, 'the Dancing, Singing, Musick, which were all in the highest Perfection, the most graceful Action, incomparable Beauty, and rich and splendid Habit of the Princesses, whose Lustre received no moderate encrease from the Beauties and rich Habits of the Ladies who had the

[24] Crowne, *Calisto*, sig. A2.
[25] See, in particular, Boswell, *Restoration Court Stage*, pt III on the staging of *Calisto*.
[26] Boswell, *Restoration Court Stage*, 332.
[27] Boswell, *Restoration Court Stage*, 323–4.
[28] Boswell, *Restoration Court Stage*, 315–16.

Honor to accompany 'em'.[29] One of these ladies was the maid of honour Sarah Jenyns (1660–1744), who played Mercury, one of the breeches roles, and it is said that her performance may have then caught the attention of her future husband, John Churchill (1650–1722). He would become the 1st Duke of Marlborough and the leader of England's successful armies, but in 1674 he was Lady Castlemaine's lover and a needy courtier.

Theirs was not the only complicated romantic situation behind the scenes of the idyllic masque. Margaret Blagge (1652–78), the epitome of womanly virtue for John Evelyn whom he would immortalize after her early death in *The Life of Mrs Godolphin* (first printed in 1847), would leave after this performance without telling anyone, to marry her long-time suitor, Sidney Godolphin (1645–1712), who would become a trusted statesman, lord treasurer, and 1st Earl of Godolphin. She portrayed a central character, the chaste goddess Diana, but Blagge, who had performed in private theatrical productions before as a maid of honour in the household of Queen Catherine, was reluctant to return to the court, having left it in 1673 to pursue what she hoped would be a life of religious devotion. To add to her distress, in the crowd after the performance, she had the misfortune to lose a jewel worth £80 lent by the Countess of Suffolk to complete her outfit (valued at some £20,000 in jewels alone), but Evelyn records in his life of her that the Duke of York gallantly covered its cost.

Calisto opens with a prologue performed by several nymphs, representing the river Thames, Peace, and Plenty, who are approached by nymphs representing Europe, America, Asia, and Africa, bearing gifts. The princesses then danced several 'Sarabrands with Castanets' and the Duke of Monmouth, a noted dancer, performed a minuet. The 'Genius of England' then appears, and the Thames (Charles's former mistress Moll Davis, who would double as a shepherdess), declares 'Pleasure, Arts, Religion, Glory, | Warm'd by his propitious Smile, | Flourish there, and bless this Isle'. The stage direction states that the Genius of England then, 'Turning to the King & Queen', declares: 'But stay! What wonder does my spirit seize? | See! Here are both the great Divinities.' The Thames confirms: 'The God and Goddess too of this bless'd Isle!',[30] thus drawing the whole court within the pastoral world of peace, prosperity, and heroic virtues as the other parts of the world pay tribute.

In the main part of the play, the two young princesses firmly maintain their innocence and chastity: 'Divinest power!' exclaims Calisto, announcing her devotion to the goddess Diana and her rejection of the world: 'Can any pleasures be | Compar'd to Innocence and Chastity?' Playing her younger sister 'Nymph', Princess Anne declares:

> How am I pleas'd my Sisters praise to hear,
> Though like a little Star I near appear,

[29] Crowne, *Calisto*, 'Epistle'.   [30] Crown, *Calisto*, sig. b2[r].

> Nature and Friendship do enough prefer
> My Name to Honour, whilst I shine in her. (I. ii, p. 7)

The virtues of the princesses raise the jealousy of another nymph in Diana's court, Psecas, and Calisto's beauty attracts the lust of Jupiter. Jupiter, a breeches role played by Lady Wentworth, then disguises himself/herself as the goddess Diana to attempt to seduce Calisto, and mischief and malice are promoted by the envious nymph Psecas. This role was played by Lady Mary Mordaunt (1658/9–1705), the future Duchess of Norfolk, whose own notorious divorce proceedings brought before the House of Lords by her husband in the 1690s for adultery would not be settled until 1700 (see *MV* 5.I). After fending off Jupiter and being falsely accused by Psecas of unfaithfulness to Diana and of having lovers, the two young nymphs are brought on stage in veils to be revealed as heroines: 'Come Princesses!' urges Diana,

> …this posture is not due!
> Truth has unvail'd it self, and so may you.
> Your Beauties are not brighter than your Fame,
> Falshood and Malice you have put to shame.
> For the Rewards of Virtue now prepare,
> And scorn the utmost which your Foes can dare. (V. i, p. 75)

Outside the world of the masque, however, so much gossip was circulating in London about court life and politics that Charles briefly passed an edict closing all coffee houses, viewed by many as a site for potentially inflammatory gatherings. A proclamation was issued on 29 December 1675, forbidding the sale of 'any Coffee, Chocolet, Sherbett, or Tea', in the 'Multitude of Coffeehouses of late years set up and kept within this Kingdom'.[31] Coffee houses were described as being 'very evil and dangerous', and 'the great resort of Sore and disaffected persons', a distraction for honest tradesmen from their labours, and a means for 'divers false, Malicious and Scandalous Reports [to be] devised and spread abroad, to the Defamation of his Majesties Government, and to the Disturbance of the Peace and Quiet of the Realm'.[32] Apparently, as with the theatres in the 1640s and 1650s, this proclamation proved unenforceable; another proclamation lifted the ban after only three weeks early in January 1676, with the provision that the proprietors of coffee houses were to report to authorities any derogatory or inflammatory discourse within forty-eight hours.

This association of the coffee house with both business and politics had already been noted by the pamphlet-writers in a series of humorous satires and mock petitions. Pamphlet and broadside debates also existed about the virtues of coffee itself. One such broadside, featuring a woodcut of a well-dressed gentlemen seated around a table, *A brief description of the excellent vertues of that sober and wholesome drink, called coffee* (1674), extols it as a

---

[31] Charles II, *A proclamation for the suppression of coffee-houses.*
[32] Charles II, *A proclamation for the suppression of coffee-houses.*

heaven-sent cure for many ailments created by 'the sweet Poison of the Treacherous Grape' and effects of 'Foggy Ale', when 'Drink, Rebellion, and Religion too, | Made Men so Mad they knew not what to do'. It concludes with 'The Rules and Orders of the Coffee-House', most of which concern the nature of polite conversation and civil exchange, which include a twelve-pence fine for swearing:

> Let Noise of loud Disputes be quite forborn,
> No Maudlin Lovers here in Corners Mourn,
> But all be Brisk, and Talk, but not too much
> On Sacred things, Let none presume to touch,
> Nor Profane Scripture, or sawcily wrong
> Affairs of State with Irreverent Tongue.

On the other hand, the health benefits of coffee-drinking had been robustly attacked by the 1674 satiric pamphlet by 'a Well-willer', *The Women's Petition against Coffee*. Englishmen's reputations as being the '*Ablest Performers in Christendome*' had become sadly diminished as they had become '*Frenchified…meer Cock-sparrows*' that can only talk of fashionable love rather than '*stand* to it, and in the very first Charge fall down *flat* before us'.[33] The cause of this national disaster is the 'Excessive use of that Newfangled, Abominable, Heathenish Liquor called *coffee*, which Riffling Nature of her Choicest *Treasures*, and *Drying* up the *Radical Moisture*, has so *Eunuch'd* our Husbands, and *Crippled* our more kind *Gallants*' (p. 2). As for the atmosphere created by the coffee houses themselves, the writer charges they encourage the production of 'a thousand Monster Opinions and Absurdities' (p. 4). *A Satyr Against Coffee* (1675) opens even more resolutely: 'Avoid, Satanick Tipple! hence | Thou Murtherer of Farthings, and of Pence; | And Midwife to all false Intelligence!' Connecting it directly with dangerous politics, the song observes: 'Bak'd in a pan, Brew'd in a pot, | The third device of him who first begot | The Printing Libels, and the Powder-plot.'

In 1673, an anonymous pamphlet entitled *The Character of a Coffeehouse, with the Symptomes of a Town-Wit* had enumerated the ways in which the coffee house as public meeting space amplified many of the general consumer's issues and anxieties over relationships between court and city, Englishmen and foreigners, and the possibility of another rebellion growing out of the discontent of Londoners. The writer merges lower-class radical politics and the physical consequences of sexual misbehaviour, concluding: 'A *Coffee-House* is a *Phanatique Theatre*, a *Hot-House* to flux in for a *clapt understanding*, a *Sympathetical* Cure for the Gonorrhea of the Tongue, or a *refin'd Baudy-House*, where *Illegitimate Reports* are got in close *Adultery* between *Lying lips* and *Itching Ears*.'[34]

This pamphlet provoked in 1675 *The Coffee-houses Vindicated in Answer to the late Published Character of a Coffee-House*. The long title asserts that

---

[33] *The Women's Petition against Coffee*, 1–2. [34] *The Character of a Coffeehouse*, 1.

'Reason, Experience, and good *Authours*' demonstrate 'the Excellence *Use*, and *Physical Vertues* of that *Liquor*, With The grand *Conveniency* of such civil places of *Resort* and Ingenious *Conversation*'. Speaking of the writer of the original pamphlet, the defender of the coffee house dismisses him as a 'little *Fop* whose spungy Brain can but coyn a small drossy *Joque*, or two, [who] presently thinks himself priviledg'd to *Asperse* every Thing that comes in his way though in it self never so *Innocent*, or *beneficial* to the Publick', and a 'Pamphlet-monger...[who] will needs take upon him to be dictator of all Society' and whose snooping and spying on honest citizens in coffee houses should have been stopped by the royal proclamation.[35] Not only is drinking coffee remarkable for its benefits; coffee houses themselves provide an alternative for businessmen to meeting in taverns and alehouses, so that, rather than becoming tipsy, 'take each Man a dish or two (so far from *causing* that it *cures* any dizziness or disturbant Fumes) and so dispatching their business, go out more *sprightly* about their affairs than before' (p. 4). Well-regulated coffee houses, this writer concludes, are

> The Sanctuary of Health.
> The Nursery of Temperance.
> The Delight of Frugality.
> An Accademy of Civility AND
> Free-School of Ingenuity. (p. 4)

It is in the coffee house, mingling with a variety of persons, that we '*civilize* our manners, Inlarge our *understandings*, [and] refine our *Language*' (p. 5). Coffee houses were for the men of the merchant and businesses classes what the courts traditionally had been for the courtiers—a place for the cultivation, refinement, and display of the self, a public space for the establishment of authority through adroit and polished social performances.

The commercial stage was offering examples of virtuous civic behaviour and heroic valour in its dramas. In addition to the public spectacles provided by the lives of the King and court, on the commercial stage, the now seasoned professional John Dryden offered his last heroic rhyming drama *Aureng-Zebe* in late 1675. Both acted and registered for print in 1675, it is set in exotic India in 1660, and its plot concerns the strife between the old Emperor, played by Michael Mohun, and his favourite son Aureng-Zebe, played by Charles Hart, over possession of the captive queen Indamora, played by Mrs Cox. Aureng-Zebe is presented as the exemplary son and prince, but he refuses his father/ king's unjust demand that he hand over his beloved and equally exemplary Indamora; in a rage, the Emperor turns to his other ambitious son, Morat, played by Edward Kynaston, and Aureng-Zebe is imprisoned. To add to the amorous complications, Aureng-Zebe has attracted the incestuous passion of the Empress Nourmahal, played by one of the veteran sister actresses, Rebecca

[35] *The Coffee-houses Vindicated*, 1, 4.

Marshall, who, when he spurns her advances, attempts to have him poisoned. In a moment of despair, the betrayed hero observes:

> When I consider Life, 'tis all a cheat;
> Yet, fool'd with hope, men favour the deceit;
> Trust on, and think to morrow will repay:
> Tomorrow's falser than the former day.[36]

In the end, however, the evil characters die through various sensational means, and in the closing speech the old Emperor gives his virtuous son both the throne and a perfect queen, declaring: 'The just rewards of Love and Honour wear. | Receive the Mistris you so long have serv'd; | Receive the crown your Loialty preserv'd' (V. i, p. 86).

The character of the ambitious and bloodthirsty Morat was viewed by some as being based in part on Monmouth, given his part in leading forces to put down the London weavers' riot, and the constant talk regarding the King's lack of a legitimate Protestant heir. Regardless of the identification with contemporary figures, the play also serves as a type of public declaration by Dryden of his lessening ties to the world of the theatre. Although he was still under contract with the King's Company to write plays, in the dedication to the Earl of Mulgrave in the printed version he states that, 'if I must be condemn'd to Rhyme, I should find some ease in my change of punishment. I desire to be no longer the *Sisyphus* of the Stage; to rowl up a Stone with endless labour … which is perpetually falling down again' (sig. A4^r). The Poet Laureate admits that 'I never thought myself very fit for an Employment, where many of my Predecessors have excell'd me in all kinds [of plays]', he observes, 'and some of my Contemporaries, even in my own partial Judgment, have out-done me in *Comedy*' ('Dedication').

One of his contemporaries who enjoyed the premiere of a successful comedy that season was William Wycherley (bap. 1641–1716). At the start of 1675, William Wycherley had staged *The Country-Wife* on 12 and 15 January at the newly opened Theatre Royal in Drury Lane with the King's Players. It also appeared in print that year, giving the original cast list. While it has the young romantic couple, Alithea and Harcourt, struggling to overcome being kept apart by a greedy relative and arranged financial marriage to a classic fop character, Sparkish, the young lovers are not the centre of the action of the play. The principal attention is on the rake and the ingénue from the country. The rake/hero Horner was played by Charles Hart, noted for his portrayals of manly, larger-than-life heroes, including, as we have seen, Aureng-Zebe and Marc Antony in Dryden's *All for Love*; his contemporary John Downes reported of him that those who saw him in tragic parts declared: 'That *Hart* might Teach any King on Earth how to Comport himself.'[37] Along with Nell Gwyn, with

---

[36] Dryden, *Aureng-Zebe*, IV. I, p. 49.   [37] Downes, *Roscius Anglicanus*, 16.

whom he had frequently acted in the 1660s, Hart has been credited by critics for helping to create the witty couple so characteristic of Restoration comedies, and was unquestionably one of the period's most acclaimed male leads.

Set in fashionable contemporary London and utilizing references to popular social gathering places such as Hyde Park and the theatres, *The Country-Wife* in some ways offers to hold up to its audiences a mirror of the worst of modern manners and morals. Posing as a eunuch to gain easier access to bored wealthy wives, Horner lectures them on hypocrisy, even while supposedly rummaging through their very fashionable 'china closets', an implied sex scene that apparently both scandalized and titillated early audiences. He also successfully seduces the virtuous but extremely naive young country wife, Margery Pinchwife. In this play, which many critics feel owes some of Horner's attitudes to Rochester, the rake figure is not, as in previous comedies, reformed at the end with marriage to a virtuous young woman. Instead, he successfully commits adultery with the citizens' wives, seduces an innocent and sheltered bride from her elderly, brutal, formerly libertine husband, and leaves her at the end of the play, sadder but wiser.

Wycherley would have been writing these parts with specific members of the King's Company in mind. Sparkish, the fop, was played by a promising young comedian noted for his graceful dancing and stage presence, Joseph Haines. Margery Pinchwife was portrayed by Elizabeth Bowtell, whose previous roles, according to the 1741 *History of the English Stage* (attributed to fellow actor Thomas Betterton by the bookseller Edmund Curll (see *MV* 5.IV)), were all those of a 'young innocent lady whom all the heroes are mad in love with'.[38] Her elderly husband, Pinchwife, featured the veteran character actor Michael Mohun, more known for his roles as villains such as Iago, Volpone, and the unjust Emperor in *Aureng-Zebe*. Samuel Pepys's much admired former mistress Elizabeth [Mary] Knipp played the sprightly and lascivious Lady Fidget, who happily collaborates with Horner, while the romantic couple Alithea and Harcourt showcased a very new actress, Elizabeth James, and a seasoned veteran, Edward Kynaston. Kynaston, who in earlier times had specialized in playing women's roles on stage—'the prettiest woman in the house' according to Pepys—before actresses took the stage in 1660, thus would have provided a contrast to the two other rake figures as the romantic male lead.

Thomas Shadwell's (*c.*1640–92) play *The Libertine* was staged by the Duke's Company in June 1675. Unlike Wycherley's use of contemporary London for the setting, *The Libertine* is set largely in Seville, but its central character, Don John, sounds remarkably like the Earl of Rochester and his companions (see *MV* 2.IV):

> Thus far without a bound we have enjoy'd
> Our prosp'rous pleasures, which dull Fools call Sins;
> Laugh'd at old feeble Judges, and weak Laws;

---

[38] Betterton, *The History of the English Stage*, 21.

And at the fond fantastick thing, call'd Conscience,
Which serves for nothing but to make men Cowards.[39]

As Shadwell states in his address to the reader in the printed text, it is based loosely on the Don Juan stories; it is difficult to define the genre of the play, as it mixes comedy, song, and terror. Along with broad physical comedy provided by the servant Jacomo, every act contains either a murder or a rape, occasionally both. Act Four, scene ii, begins in 'a delightful Grove' with shepherds and nymphs describing the joys of simple pastoral life and concludes with a musical chorus. This musical idyll is interrupted by Don John and his friends who immediately decide that 'We'll serve 'em as the *Romans* did the *Sabines*, we'll rob 'em of their Women; onely we'll return the Punks again, when we have us'd them'. 'I am not in Love', he informs the crowd, 'but in Lust, and to such a one a Belly-full's a Belly-full, and there's an end on't' (IV. ii, p. 120). Continuing to the end his career of libertinism, Don John closes the play by being dragged to hell by a chorus of singing devils.

In addition to veteran writers for the commercial stages such as Dryden and Shadwell, a group of new playwrights made their public debuts, some having first tried their talents as actors. The year 1674 notably saw the first commercial dramatic productions by Nathaniel Lee, with *Nero* (1674) and *Sophonisba* (1675) written in heroic couplets, which even his then patron, John Wilmot, Earl of Rochester, described as 'fustian' writing. Newcomer Thomas Otway (1652–15), also with the help of Rochester, made his debut with a sensational rhyming tragedy *Alcibiades*. It has as its Greek hero a worthy man wrongly dispossessed of power, in exile, surrounded by treachery and murder, who goes insane. Alcibiades was played by Thomas Betterton, the leading actor of the Duke's Company. The lustful Queen of Sparta who murders her husband to be free to pursue the hero featured Mary Lee, the future Lady Slingsby (fl. 1670–85), who had starred in several of Elkanah Settle's plays, including *The Empress of Morocco*. Lee would go on in 1675 to play a breeches part in Settle's *The Conquest of China by the Tartars*, which includes a scene with her fighting a duel with the man she loves, and in 1676 she would become the violently passionate Mrs Loveit in the comedy *Man of Mode* by Sir George Etherege (1636–91/2). In addition to the veteran actors, *Alcibiades* also featured the 17-year-old actress Elizabeth Barry appearing as Draxilla, Alcibiades's naive sister, who tells him of the suicide of his fiancée (who is actually concealed nearby as a test of his love), resulting in his madness and death. Barry had, at least according to report, been carefully prepared for this role since 1673 by the personal attentions of Rochester, who, although in disgrace at court at that moment, supposedly nevertheless attended *Alcibiades*'s first night performance, along with the King, Queen, and maids of honour.[40]

---

[39] Shadwell, *The Libertine*, I. i, pp. 1–5.
[40] For the complexity of the issues surrounding the anecdotes concerning Barry's early acting career and Rochester's part in it, see Hume, 'Elizabeth Barry's First Roles'.

Otway, along with Lee, offered a new style of spectacular, affective tragedy, a style that critics have referred to as 'the couplet bloodbath', with scenes of rape, murders, lingering deaths, and ghosts.[41] Another relative newcomer to the stage, Aphra Behn, a friend of both Lee and Otway at this time, would follow in 1676 with her one attempt at tragedy, *Abdelazar*, which, like those of her friends Lee and Otway, featured an unrepentant evil queen and much spectacular horror. Such plays, along with the new style of 'semi opera' productions, relied heavily on the ability of this theatre to contrive special effects, including numerous trap doors, quickly changing scenes, and machines to 'fly' up to four individuals across the stage.

The two newly built theatres, Dorset Garden Theatre (1671), home to the Duke's Company headed by Davenant's widow Mary, with Betterton and fellow actor Henry Harris seeing to the running of it, and the Theatre Royal at Drury Lane (1674) were designed to meet new audiences' expectations for entertainment. The King's Company had chosen to open its new Drury Lane Theatre Royal with the opera *Ariadne* in 1674, featuring French musicians. In response, the Duke's Company at Dorset Gardens offered Shadwell's musical adaptation of Dryden's and Davenant's revision of Shakespeare's *The Tempest* with music by Mathew Locke (*c.*1622–77). Using twenty-four violins along with harpsichords, oboes, and singers placed between the audience in the pit and the stage, the opening scene represented 'a Tempestuous Sea in perpetual Agitation...[with] many dreadful objects in it, as several Spirits in horrid shapes flying down amongst the Sailers, then rising and crossing in the Air'. To finish the dramatic opening, 'when the Ship is sinking, the whole House is darken'd, and a shower of Fire falls upon 'em. This is accompanied with Lightning and several Claps of Thunder'.[42]

In addition to the conventional stage features, the Dorset Garden Theatre could 'fly' a cloud spanning the width of the stage carrying musicians, as featured in the 1675 performance of *Pysche*. With music again by Matthew Locke, libretto by Thomas Shadwell, and dances by the Italian musician Giovanni Battista Draghi (*c.*1640–1708), whom Charles II had brought to London to help establish opera, it was a major theatrical event. John Downes recorded that 'the long expected Opera of *Psyche* came forth in all her Ornaments; new Scenes, new Machines, new Cloaths, new *French* Dances. This opera was also splendidly set out, especially in Scenes; the Charge of which amounted to some £800'.[43] It ran for eight days, but, Downes notes, it took in less than Locke's earlier opera attempt with Shadwell, *The Tempest*. Because of the high cost of staging, even with ticket prices raised to three and four times the normal price, such spectacular productions were always risky business. *Psyche*'s epilogue reminds the audience that they are seeing not a typical entertainment, but a

---

[41] See, e.g., Hume, *The Development of English Drama*, 200–1.
[42] See the account of this production in Hume, *The Development of English Drama*, 206–7.
[43] Downes, *Roscius Anglicanus*, 75.

spectacle that rivals what in previous times was restricted to royal masques and a courtly audience:

> What e'r the Poet has deserv'd from you,
> Would you the Actors for his faults undo,
> The Painter, Dancer, and Musician too?
> For you those Men of skill have done their best:
> But we deserve much more then all the rest.
> We have stak'd all we have to treat you here,
> And therefore, Sirs, you should not be severe
>
> .   .   .   .   .   .
>
> Poor Players have this day that Splendor shown,
> Which yet but by Great Monarchs has been done.[44]

The Dorset Garden Theatre with its more elaborate stage machinery could seat 850, and the new Theatre Royal designed by Christopher Wren, which opened in 1674, could hold an equivalent audience.[45] The Theatre Royal on Drury Lane offered spectators nine rows of backless benches on the floor, ringed by boxes on three sides and two upper galleries, which 'ordinary' people frequented. It also featured a prominent 'apron' acting stage at its front, with the middle portion of the stage housing the grooves and shutters for the new sliding scenery, while the very back portion could offer 'vistas'.[46] The thrilling scenes on the stages and the daylight performance times, however, did not prevent unruly audience behaviour, even among the 'Gentlemen' present. The Newdigate Newsletters report in March and April 1674 that 'His Majesty has also been pleased to Order ye Recorder of London to examine ye Disorders & disturbances on Tuesday last at ye Dukes Theatre [Dorset Garden] by some persons in drink, to proceed agt ym according to law for ye Ryot'.[47] The area of London around Dorset Garden, Alsatia, was also considered unsafe, and, with the Dorset Garden's front access to the Thames, patrons frequently preferred to arrive by boat.

Matthew Locke, who wrote the music for the successful productions of *The Tempest* and *Psyche*, attempted to explain the changing developments in the theatre in his dedication of *The English opera, or, The vocal musick in Psyche* (1675). Opera, he informs the dedicatee, the Duke of Monmouth, is derived from the Italian and involves

industry and pains for splendid Scenes and Machines to Illustrate the Grand Design, with Art are composed in such kinds of Musick as the Subject requires...which variety (without vanity be it said) was never in Court or Theatre till now presented in this

---

[44] Locke, *Psyche*, 72.

[45] The exact number of seats in Drury Lane in the 1670s is problematic, with some critics speculating that it ranged as high as 2,000 while others find better evidence for 800. See 'Drury Lane', in Hartnoll (ed.), *The Oxford Companion to the Theatre*, and Langhans, 'The Theatres'.

[46] See, for further details of the construction, Hartnoll (ed.), *Oxford Companion to the Theatre*.

[47] Wilson, 'Theatre Notes', 79.

Nation: though I must confess there has been something done, (and more by me than any other) of this kind. ('Preface')

This text also contains Locke's music composed for *The Tempest*, and music lovers were able to buy the songs and masques from that opera also in separate publications.

The response of the Theatre Royal, which could not successfully compete in terms of special stage effects, was to offer burlesque performances of the Dorset Garden's spectaculars. Thomas Duffett, who had parodied Settle's *Empress of Morocco*, likewise quickly staged in 1674 *The Mock-Tempest, or, the Enchanted Castle* (1675), which in addition to Prospero and Ariel has characters named 'Quakero', 'Beantosser', 'Mousetrappa', and 'Drinkallup'. Instead of the Dorset Garden's dramatic storm at sea, Duffet's opens with the directions, 'A great noyse heard of breaking Doors, and breaking Windowes, crying A Whore, a Whore, etc'.[48] At the end of the opening, the whores battle constables and 'It Rains Fire, Apples, Nuts' over the audience (p. 9). In the next scene, Prospero and Miranda are discovered in Bridewell rather than on an exotic island. Duffet also quickly obliged with *Psyche Debauch'd* in May of 1675.

In addition to the stage wars over special effects, there was also a strong market for printed versions of earlier popular comedies and farces. Edward Ravenscroft (fl. 1659–97) printed his first comedy, a close remodelling of Molière's *Le Bourgeois Gentilhomme* to suit a London setting, *Mamamouchi: Or, The Citizen Turn'd Gentleman*. It had a spectacular run of nine straight days of full houses when it premiered in 1672 at the Dorset Garden Theatre; when it was issued in 1675 with a dedication to Prince Rupert, Ravenscroft claimed 'of thirty times it has been acted, you seldom failed to honour it with your presence'.[49] The play had been a showcase for two of the troupe's senior male comic actors, and involves the folly of social ambitions, the clash of generations, comic foreigners, and what money cannot buy.

As with its source, the principal character, Mr Jorden, is an older London citizen attempting to pass himself off as a gentleman; this role went to the acclaimed comic actor James Nokes. The play opens with the efforts of his dancing master, French valet, and music master to transform him into a 'gentleman' by changing his speech, clothes, and recreations. His goal is to marry the well-born Marina, the daughter of an elderly and poverty-stricken knight, but unfortunately she is also the beloved of his son, Young Jorden. His daughter Lucia—whom, unknown to her, he wishes to marry to a country gentleman sight unseen that very day—upbraids him for disturbing the neighbourhood with his noisy self-improvements. She bluntly responds to his assertion that he must learn French because it is spoken in court: 'The Court, Sir, is no fit place for you, nor you no fit man for it' (I. i, p. 6). Jorden's answer to his daughter is the triumph of the self-blind man who has come into his hard-working alderman

---

[48] Duffett, *The Mock -Tempest*, 1.   [49] Ravenscroft, *Mamamouchi*, sig. A2.

father's fortune: 'I was born a Courtier, only I was spoil'd in the bringing up' (I. i, p. 6). The unravelling of this complicated set of ambitious matches and the reuniting of the correct young lovers requires the intervention of characters with names Cleverwit, Trickmore, and Dr Cureal. Following closely on Molière's original plot but without the stabilizing presence of the citizen's sensible wife, which Molière's version includes, Cleverwit (in love with Lucia) pretends to be a vastly wealthy Turkish Sultan to cut out Sir Simon's Softhead's suit for Lucia; Sir Simon, played by another established comic, Cave Underhill, is in turn distracted by Betty Trickmore, Lucia's maid in disguise. With a band of dancing Turks and an elaborate musical scene performed in stage Turkish, Jordan, who has happily agreed to change his religion and become a Mahometan in exchange for a Turkish royal title, is crowned a 'Mamamouchi', and Trickmore's sister, Betty, is married off to Sir Simon as a royal Turkish princess. Once all is revealed, social order is restored, but with some twists: the young lovers are all appropriately sorted out and the son has tricked his father into giving him his fortune and Lucia's dowry, while Betty Trickmore announces pertly to Sir Simon that 'My Dowry is my brain'. Sir Simon, on the discovery of the deceptions, announces that he will return to Suffolk whence he came, for in the country, 'there people either have more honesty, or less wit' (V. i, p. 72).

Country versus city also supplies the energy in John Crowne's third production during this period, *The Countrey Wit*, performed at the Duke's Theatre and published in 1675. Once again he is clearly writing for the comic skills of Nokes and Underhill, and, in this comedy, making use of the romantic charms of Thomas Betterton and Mrs Leigh. Although derived in part from Molière's *Le Sicilien, ou l'Amour Peintre*, the scene is announced to be 'The Pall-Mall in the year 1675'; the play introduces the character of Sir Mannerly Shallow, a 'foolish Countrey Knight', a type of character that Crowne will continue to adapt and revise in his later plays, and 'Lord Drybone', an 'old debauched Lord'. Christina's father Sir Thomas Rash has pronounced views on marriage, and announces to his daughter at the start of the play that she will be married on the following day. Urged by all to consider that more carefully, he retorts, 'why what had I to consider of that requir'd time? Here's my daughter *Christina* and 5000£ Portion; there's Sir *Mannerly Shallow*, a young Baronet, and 2000£ a year' (I. i, p. 2). The hero, played by Betterton, is Ramble, 'a wild young Gentleman of the Town', whom Christina loves, even though she knows that he has been unfaithful but excuses as being the result of the 'Ayriness and Gayetie of his temper' (I. i, 7). Not a model romantic lover by any means, by Act Three Ramble glumly concludes:

now am I discover'd in all my Rogueries, and Intrigues, and Falshoods; and must never hope to enjoy the sweet pleasure of Lying and Forswearing any more; I must now either repent, and become a down right plodding Lover to *Christina*, or in plain terms lose her … Well, I cannot bear the loss of Mrs *Christina*, I had rather endure Marriage with her, than injoy any other Woman at pleasure (IV. iii, p. 56)

In his dedication, Crowne asserts that this play was a favourite of Charles II. But, when one turns to the majority of the printed texts being produced in these two years, in contrast to the libertine sentiments expressed by Ramble, one is struck by the degree to which texts aimed at the average city-dweller's desire for self-improvement, the dissemination of new discoveries in science and the natural world, and concern over establishing codes of public moral conduct dominated the titles offered by the booksellers. While attending the theatre and observing the court were clearly popular entertainments, in 1674–5, texts on religious subjects and didactic advice were still the most numerous types found among the printed volumes and pamphlets for sale.

Although fewer in number, there was also a significant group of texts being published that were aimed at a small but influential intellectual readership. The years 1674 and 1675 saw several important publications of a more abstract nature from members of the Royal Society (see *MV* 2.V), some based on experiments performed at Gresham College, some the published versions of papers that had been circulated in manuscript among close associates for several years. Robert Hooke's (1635–1703) 1675 treatise *An Attempt to Prove the Motion of the Earth by Observation* highlights the importance of scientific instrument design on discovery; in it he describes the telescope he had created in his rooms in the college to attempt to measure any changes in position of the constellation Draco over the course of a year. His colleague, the natural philosopher Robert Boyle (1627–91), who had suffered a severe stroke in 1670 that limited his direct participation in the activities of the Royal Society, nevertheless continued to publish numerous treatises based on his earlier work. Residing with his sister Katherine, Lady Ranelagh (1615–91), in fashionable Pall Mall, London, he published several volumes of short tracts, including *Suspicions about the Hidden Realities of the Air* (1674), which considers the agency of air in the process of various chemical reactions based on previously performed experiments, *An Account of a Statical Hygroscope and its Uses*, *A Fragment about the Natural and Preternatural State of Bodies*, and *A Sceptical Dialogue about the Positive or Privative Nature of Cold*. In the 'advertisements' of these short tracts, he laments the loss of his experimental observations: 'Impediments made him more than once break off his work...such unwelcome Accidents happen'd since the foregoing Tract was sent away, that he could not seasonably recover any competent number of Observations, and fears he shall never recover some of them';[50] notably, his sister would commission Robert Hooke in 1676 to add a laboratory to her house for her brother's use, suggesting her continued optimism about her brother's experiments.

He also published *The Excellency of Theology Compar'd with Nature Philosophy (as both are Objects of Men's Study) Discours'd of in a Letter to a Friend*. The publisher informs the reader that the work was composed in 1665,

---

[50] Boyle, *An Account of a Statical Hygroscope*, 'Advertisement'.

when its author was travelling away from London to avoid the plague; the Author, in his preface, explains the delay in publication due to 'the Temper of this Age'. Knowing it as he does, he realizes that 'Some will ask, For what Reason a Discourse of this Nature was written at all; and that Others will be displeas'd that it has been written by Me'.[51] In 1675, Boyle would publish another of his theological treatises balancing natural philosophy with religious belief, *Some Considerations about the Reconcileableness of Reason and Religion, with a Discourse about the Possibility of the Resurrection*. In a letter to the secretary of the Royal Society, Henry [Heinrich] Oldenburg (*c*.1619–77), the German mathematician and philosopher Leibniz declared of Boyle that 'I esteem him as much as virtue and knowledge can be esteemed in any man. Recently I read his discourse on "Not despising the Study of Theology". It affected me amazingly.'[52]

Isaac Newton (1642–1727) had likewise found himself in the 1670s turning his thoughts towards theology, but his studies took him further and further from orthodox belief. This would jeopardize his posts as the Lucasian professor of mathematics and his Fellowship at Trinity College, Cambridge, which at the time required the holder to be or to become an ordained minister. The loss of his position, however, was halted by a royal mandate exempting the Lucasian professorship. As his notebooks show, these years were also being devoted to the serious study of alchemy and its principles.[53] The year 1675 also found Newton once again involved in public controversy with other important scientists, although not over his interest in alchemy, a field of enquiry shared by many other intellectuals. His experiments in the early 1670s on colour involved the use of prisms, the results of which he communicated in a letter to Henry Oldenburg; these were subsequently printed in the Royal Society's *Philosophical Transactions* (6 (1671–2), 3075–87), edited by Oldenburg, the most important publication for the circulation of scientific knowledge among English and continental scientists.

The publication of Newton's work on optics began a series of controversies that burst forth in 1674–5. Francis Hall, also known as Father Linus (1595–1675), an English Jesuit priest residing in Liège, wrote to Oldenburg that he himself 'neere 30 yeares agoe showed the same together with divers other experiments of light to that worthy promotour of Experimentall Philosophy, Sr Kenelme Digby', except with different results from Newton's. 'It is farre from my intent, that the mistake here mentioned doe any way derogate from that learned person', he concludes, but 'the Theory of light grounded upon that experiment cannot subsist'.[54] Newton's initially temperate response from Cambridge dated 5 December 1674 was that he had no desire to engage the elderly scientist: 'I have long since determined to concern my self no further about ye promotion

---

[51] Boyle, *The Excellency of Theology*, sig. A4ʳ.
[52] For the complete letter, see Newton, *Correspondence*, 1. 396–403.
[53] See Westfall, *Never at Rest*, ch. 8.
[54] See Newton, *Correspondence*, 1. 317–64, for the sequence of letters.

of Philosophy' (1. 328) and once again in December of 1675, 'I desire to decline being involved in such troublesome & insignificant disputes' (1. 364).

In the midst of this controversy, Newton was officially admitted as a Fellow of the Royal Society in February 1675 when he was visiting London. This positive reception seems to have brought Newton briefly back into the London world of scientific collegiality. He visited Robert Boyle and discussed 'trepanning ye common Ether', an apparently encouraging exchange which Newton mentioned in a letter to Oldenburg, noting Boyle 'was pleased to entertain it with a smile', and Newton expressed the hope that Boyle himself would be conducting related experiments with his air pump apparatus (1. 393).

In late 1675, Newton is writing again to Oldenburg: 'I had some thoughts of writing a further discourse about colours to be read at one of your Assemblies, but find it yet against ye grain to put pen to paper any more on yt subject', but Oldenburg was successful in persuading him to submit his 'Discourse of observations', and 'Hypothesis explaining the properties of light', which were read aloud at the Royal Society meetings in December 1675 and then published in the *Philosophical Transactions*. In his 'Hypothesis explaining the properties of light' Newton declares, 'whitenesse is a dissimilar mixture of all colours, & that light is a mixture of rays endowed with all those colours. This I believe hath seemed the most paradoxicall of all my assertions, & met with the most universall & obstinate Prejudice', he observes (1. 385). Newton's work would be eventually be published in English under the title *Opticks* in 1704.

Against this background of duelling intellectuals and concerns over the rival claims of religion and science, practical applications of new inventions, popular circulation of new discoveries about the natural world, and improvements in the technologies of everyday life had an eager reading public in the 1674–5 years. Aimed at a wider readership and more general audience, numerous vernacular domestic improvement guides and manuals appear to have found a ready market. Some were clearly created for women readers, while others offered information with which either sex could advance their skills and even make a better impression in their society. Writers offered women readers advice on household management (although the signatures on many of the surviving ones suggest that men were reading them as well), which ranged from household medical matters to letter-writing, care of delicate fabrics, and cookery. There were also books for young clerks, aspiring lawyers, and surgeons; there were several dictionaries and conduct books aimed at improving the reader's understanding of 'hard words' they might encounter in this new reading matter. Other texts offered systems for teaching spelling, penmanship, and grammar (some directed towards those who have no access to teachers), in addition to dealing with taking down speeches and sermons using shorthand or 'speedy writing'.

Perhaps the ending of the war with the Dutch also permitted readers to contemplate once again foreign lands as sources of entertainment, investment, and curiosity. The period 1674–5 was also one in which several accounts of voyages and exploration were published. Joshua Barnes, the scholar of Greek and passionate Royalist who in 1670 gave forth in verse *The Life of Oliver Cromwell the Tyrant* and who would be best known for his poems to the royal family on state occasions in the 1680s, published *Gerania: A New Discovery Of A Little sort of People Anciently Discoursed of, called Pygmies* imagining a peaceful and harmonious culture based on Homer's account of them in the *Iliad*. John Josselyn's *An Account of Two Voyages to New England* printed in 1674 attracted enough readers to require a second edition in 1675.

But violence and warfare also figured in the travel accounts of these years. Eyewitness reports of the Indian wars in North America were also prominent among 1675 publications. Unlike Barnes's peaceful pygmies, the native dwellers of New England in 1675 declared war on the settlers, starting the so-called King Philips War, a conflict involving half of the New England's colonies in which ninety settlements were attacked and casualties were extremely high on both sides. The anonymous account published in London in 1675, *The Present State of New-England, With Respect to the Indian War*, told Londoners about the assassination of the Native American John Sassamon, a Christian convert who had attended Harvard University, supposedly killed for warning the colonists of possible attacks by Metacom's followers; accounts quickly followed of the resulting trial and execution of his killers and the retaliation by Metacom's allies.

This was picked up by pamphlet-writers in England, who produced polemical and highly coloured accounts of the conflicts, such as *A Brief and True Narration Of the Late Wars Risen In New-England: Occasioned by the Quarrelsom disposition, and Perfidious Carriage of the Barbarous, Savage and Heathenish Natives There*. This text ascribes the source of the conflict to the Indians attempting to retake lands they had sold to the English, 'who by their great industry, have of a howling Wilderness improved those Lands into Cornfields, Orchards, enclosed Pastures, and Towns inhabited; which hath considerably advanced the value of the Lands'.[55] The Quaker deputy governor of Rhode Island, John Easton, however, circulated in manuscript in both New England and old a very different account in his 'A Relation of the Indian War', placing the blame squarely on the colonists.

The appeal of cultivating the wilderness whether in the New World or at home was a marketing feature of a number of publications in 1675. Of the eight works featuring 'husbandry' as a title word, the prize for the longest title certainly goes to John Worlidge for the page-long version of *Systema Agriculturae, The Mystery of Husbandry Discovered*... The oddly but appropriately named Samuel Strangehopes offered a work with an interesting if much shorter title, *A Book of Knowledge In three Parts. The first, containing a brief Introduction to Astrology: The second, A Treatise of Physick...: The*

---

[55] *A Brief and True Narration*, 3.

Third, the Country-mans Guide to good Husbandry. The connection to 'husbandry' and recipes as remedies is continued in Joseph Blagrave's two 1675 titles, *The Epitome of the Art of Husbandry Comprizing all Necessary Directions for the Improvement of it* and *New Additions to Epitome of the Art of Husbandry. Comprizing a new way of Enriching Meadows, Destroying of Moles, making Tulips of any Colour: With an approved way for ordering of Fish and Fish-ponds...With directions for Breeding and Ordering all sorts of Singing-Birds; With Remedies for their several Maladies not before publickly made known.* Such books and their titles highlight the expanding interests and new tastes of landowners for cultivating colourful tulips and decorative songbirds as well as practical ways to rid oneself of agricultural pests. Even in the countryside, it appears, there is time for the cultivation of pleasures.

For those readers who wished improvement not only of their lands but also of themselves to step up the social ladder, 1675 offered a strong selection of what in later times might be called 'self-help books'. 'A Person of Honour' offered *The Courtier's Calling: Shewing the Ways of making a Fortune, and the Art of Living at Court, According to the Maxims of Policy & Morality* addressed to 'Noblemen' and 'Gentlemen'. Charles Cotton (1630–87), the prolific translator and writer of fiction about whom more will follow, in 1674 provided the male reader with *The Compleat Gamester: Or, Instructions How to play at Billiards, Trucks, Bowls, and Chess.* In addition to these social pastimes, there is a section on the 'arts and mysteries' of riding, racing, archery, and cock-fighting. 'Recreation', notes Cotton in his epistle to the reader, 'is not only lawful but necessary'.[56] The design is not to create a new generation of gamesters, he assures his reader, but to 'inform all in part how to avoid being cheated by them'. As he observes, the game billiards is shaped in part by whether it is played by candlelight or during the day and in all cases 'All controversies are to be decided by the Standers by, upon asking judgment' (p. 33).

Appealing to a different category of reader but also using the allure of the court and genteel pastimes, a broadside featuring the royal seal advertised the establishment of an 'Academy' by John Wells, confirmed by royal letters of patent to protect 'the most curious and profitable Engine that ever was invented'. At Wells's academy, through the use of 'artificial horses', and for the price of a shilling, 'all Persons may learn with great facility to hold themselves steady on Horse-back, to carry the Lance, to run at the Ring, to lace the Javelin, to shoot a Pistol with evenness with one Bullet onely...which are the Noble Employs of a true Gentleman'. In addition, 'the Ladies will receive as great pleasure and satisfaction as the Gentlemen, and may learn the same Exercise as they; which they shall perform either upon Horses or in Chariots drawn by the same Horses'.

In a more elevated style, it is interesting to consider the apparently expanding audience of various dictionaries published that year. Thomas Blount's

---

[56] Cotton, *The Compleat Gamester*, 'Epistle to the Reader'.

(1618–79) *Glossographia: Or, a Dictionary, Interpreting Hard Words* enjoyed a fourth edition in 1674, and the potential purchaser is assured on the title page that it will prove 'very useful for all such as desire to understand what they read'. In contrast, John Ray (1627–1705), the naturalist and lexicographer, published his *Collection of English Words Not Generally used* in 1674, a collection of 'local words' and English dialects, which also contained catalogues of English birds, fish, and metals. The Oxford scholar Christopher Wase's Latin–English dictionary *Dictionarium Minus: A Compendious Dictionary, English–Latin & Latin–English* had its second edition for the 'studious and less accomplish'd persons', in which he also explained the names of plants and herbs, different proverbs and identified antiquities. Likewise, J. G. Van Heldoren provided for 'lovers of the English tongue' *An English and Nether-dutch Dictionary, Composed out of the best English Authors*, noting in his address to the reader that 'little Books are convenient for young schollars and travellers, seeing they are easie to be carried therefore I have composed a Dictionary very brief, good and useful'.[57]

For students of any age, Samuel Botley (1640/1–77) expanded on Jeremiah Rich's system of shorthand in *Maximum in minimo* (1674/5), adding a section on legal terms for scholars in 'London, Bristol, and Exeter'. Elisha Coles (*c*.1640–80) informed his reader that through his twelve years' experience as a schoolteacher he had arrived at *The Compleat English Schoolmaster. Or the Most Natural and Easie Method of Spelling English*, according, as the title page states, 'to the present proper pronuntiation of the Language in Oxford and London'. Coles, who also published *The Newest, Plainest and the Shortest Short-Hand* in 1674, a copy of which was owned by Samuel Pepys, produced two further educational titles in 1675, *Nolens volens, or, You shall make Latin Whether you Will or No* and *Syncrisis*, which features Latin texts with facing English translations.

The changing language of business and credit also required guides to help the reader negotiate the expanding world of financial discourse. Although not technically a dictionary in format, *Debitor and Creditor Made Easie: or, A Short Instruction for the attaining the Right Use of Accounts* was described by Stephen Monteage as having been written some dozen years before 'for the use of my Children and Friends' with 'no thought of making it publick', but he decided to print it at the urging of those who found his style more suited for 'Youths, young Scholars, men of Ordinary reach or employment'.[58] He notes, however, that such studies are 'not unworthy of Gentlemen, Noble-men and Princes, who in forreign Countries have not disdained to manage Transactions in this Method': 'all Sorts and Conditions, in Court, City or Countrey, from the Supreme Potentate to the meanest Cottager, may make use of with delight and advantage' (sig. A3ʳ).

---

[57] Van Heldoren, *An English and Nether-dutch Dictionary*, sig. A2.
[58] Monteage, *Debitor and Creditor*, sigs B2, A3.

Books dealing with recipes and cookery also fit nicely into this company of volumes offering both delight and advantage. If one was looking to buy a printed cookery text in 1675 rather than compile one's own manuscript volume, there were a number from which to choose that catered to a wide range of domestic circumstances. While the 1670s did not match the most prolific decade for the publication of recipe books—the 1650s—in terms of numbers of authors, it nevertheless saw the issue and reprinting of a perhaps surprising array of books offering recipes and advice concerning household management. There were six books produced in 1675 that fit our concept of cookery recipe books and several more that include medicinal recipes for both humans and animals. These are: the anonymous *The Gentlewoman's Cabinet Unlocked* in its seventh edition done for 'EC'; William Rabisha, the former royal cook, *The Whole Body of Cookery Dissected,* in its second edition (printed interestingly by the radical sectarian printer Elizabeth Calvert); Gervase Markham's *The English Housewife*, in its eighth edition from George Sawbridge; and three texts attributed to Hannah Wolley—the first edition of *The Accomplisht Ladys Delight* printed by Benjamin Harris, *The Queen-like Closet or Rich Cabinet . . . with Supplement*, third edition done by Richard Lowndes, and *The Gentlewoman's Companion; Or a Guide to the Female Sex*, second edition by Andrew Maxwell for Edward Thomas.

The numerous publications of Hannah Wolley or Woolley (1622?–74), with their revealing autobiographical sections scattered through them, offer 'all Ingenious Ladies, and Gentlewomen' instructions for the handling of household matters, from cooking, preserving, making cordials, and cleaning silk fabrics and gold and silver lace, to cures for common ailments for humans and livestock, to creating appropriate embroidery patterns and writing appropriate letters. 'The twelve years past since first in print I came | More for my Countries good, than to get fame', she tells her female readers in *A Supplement to the Queenlike closet* (1674). 'My study was to impart to others free, | What God and Nature hath informed me'.[59] Some of her medicinal recipes seem more remote in their application than others—for the Falling Sickness, the reader is advised to 'take a live Mole, and cut the throat of it into a Glass of White wine, and presently give it to the party to drink at the New and Full of the Moon . . . this will Cure absolutely, if the Party be not above forty years of Age' (p. 18)—while others feature more simple herbal mixtures and frequently also serve as cosmetic applications to improve the skin and eyes.

In the autobiographical interludes that are interwoven with the recipes, she tells her readers that she acquired her skill from both her mother and her elder sisters, who were 'very well skilled in Physick and Chirurgery' (p. 10). As a young woman, she went into the service of Anne, Lady Maynard, who gave her the task of caring for the local poor. Her patron 'bought many Books for me to

---

[59] Wolley, *A Supplement to the Queenlike closet*, sig. A2r.

read', as well as having her consult with her own physicians (p. 11). At around age 24, she married Jerome Wolley and they kept a school near Saffron Walden; 'we having many Boarders my skill was often exercised amongst them' (p. 12). On her husband's passing away, she turned her household and medicinal talents into *The Ladies Directory* (1661), the contents of which she enlarged and recycled through the 1660 and early 1670s.

There are additional recipes for both cookery and medicine to be found in places we might not expect them. In John Josselyn's *New England's Rarities Discovered*, his accounts of the animals and plants are followed by their medicinal application—for example, raccoon fat as being good for healing bruises and the habit of the Indians to boil and mash water lily roots to treat wounds. While one could argue that the reader of this text would be less interested in practical 'recipes' or 'remedies', since few of them would have access to raccoon fat, and that the contents are more of the nature of exotic information for one's reading pleasure, equally one could argue that very few people would have the means or ability to prepare William Rabisha's bill of fare for 'a flesh dinner in Autumn' whose first course proposes twenty-two possible dishes and twenty-two different ones for the second. In both, one could argue, the pleasures of aspirational or escapist reading are being invoked in the guise of improvement and cultivation.

Lovers of more openly fantastic adventures done in prose had several to choose from during these years, but lovers of poetry had very few new volumes by a single author to peruse. *Iter Boreale* by Robert Wild (1615/16–79) was in its eighth edition in 1674, a long poem celebrating General Monck's march from Scotland and taking over of Parliament (see *MV* 2.I). Likewise, Abraham Cowley's *The Four Ages of English*, written in 1648, was reprinted in 1675. George Herbert's collection of religious verse *The Temple* was reprinted in 1674 in its tenth edition. At the opposite end of the poetic spectrum, an early version of Rochester's *A Satyr Against Mankind* found its way from circulated scribal copy into print in 1675, with its sardonic opening declaration,

> Were I, who to my cost, already am,
> One of those strange, prodigious creatures Man;
> A Spirit free, to choose for my own share,
> What sort of Flesh and Blood I pleas'd to wear,
> I'd be a Dog, a Monkey or a Bear:
> Or any thing, but that vain Animal,
> Who is so proud of being rational.[60]

Much of the 'new' verse in print in 1674 and 1675 was contained in anthologies, such as *Mock Songs and Joking Poems...With other New Songs, and Ingenious Poems Much in use at Court, and both Theatres* (1675), which announces in bold type on the title page 'NEVER BEFORE PRINTED'. *The*

---

[60] Wilmot, *A Satur Against Mankind*, 1.

Westminster-Drollery. Or, A Choice Collection Of the Newest Songs & Poems Both at Court and Theatres was in its expanded third edition in 1674. Closely related in terms of contents, but by a single author, 'C.F.', *Wit at a Venture: Or, Clio's Privy Garden* appeared in 1674 along with Thomas Flatman's elegant Pindarics in *Poems and Songs* and Edward Howard's libertine *Poems and Essays*, which as we have seen drew much ire from one of its readers. The young Oxford poet Richard Leigh (1649/50–1728), who had previously boldly attacked Dryden's style in *The Conquest of Granada*, issued his own volume of verse, *Poems upon Several Occasions and to Several Persons* in 1675, perhaps most noticeable for his interest in science, optics, and what some critics have referred to as his 'metaphysical' style.

As a companion to such volumes of contemporary verse, Edward Phillips (1630–96?), the nephew of John Milton, published his useful catalogue of ancient and modern poets, both English and continental, under the title *Theatrum Poetarum, Or, A Compleat Collection of the Poets, Especially The most Eminent, of all Ages, The Antients distinguish't from the Moderns in their several Alphabets: With Some Observations, and Reflections upon many of them, particularly those of our own Nation: Together with a Prefatory Discourse of the Poets and Poetry in Generall* (1675). Phillips, living in London and surviving as a hired commercial writer, prefaced his compendium of poets, which is alphabetized according to the writer's first name, with an essay on the nature of poetry and its 'native' genius. 'Wit, Ingenuity, and Learning in Verse, even Elegancy it self, though that comes neerest, are one thing, true Native Poetry is another; in which there is a certain Air and Spirit; which perhaps the most Learned and judicious in other Arts do not perfectly apprehend, much less is it attainable by any Study or Industry', he observes. It is this 'poetic Energie' he declares that can shine through even 'unpolish't and antiquated Language, and may happly be wanting, in the most polite and reformed'.[61] On this basis he makes his claims for the poetic greatness of both Spenser and Shakespeare:

> *Spencer*, with all his Rustie, obsolete words, with all his rough-hewn clowterly Verses; yet take him throughout, and we shall find in him a gracefull and Poetic Majesty: in like manner Shakespear, in spight of all his unfiled expressions, his rambling and indigested Fancys, the laughter of the Critical, yet must be confess't a Poet above many that go beyond him in Literature some degrees. ('The Preface')

Fiction was a distant third in terms of numbers found in booksellers' catalogues, and many of the titles were translations of French works. Nevertheless, in the fiction of 1674–5, clear conventions of the genre are appearing, and market strategies are being developed by booksellers. One finds interesting overlaps between the narrative techniques found in the advice and conduct literature and these early forms of the novel, as well as with those used to relate

---

[61] Phillips, *Theatrum Poetarum*, 'The Preface'.

criminal confessions and trial narratives from the various law courts. It seemed as though there was a market for both extremes of lifestyle, from the romance of exotic court life to criminal misconduct and its rewards.

Charles Cotton, who also published *The Compleat Gamester* in 1674, has been credited with the translation from French of *The Fair One of Tunis: or The Generous Mistress. A new piece of Gallantry* (1674). Cotton, who had first appeared in print in 1649 in the same volume as Dryden and Marvell, *Lacrymae musarum*, had already achieved literary success with both his poetic burlesques of the classics, notably the popular and often reprinted *Scarronnides*, and his prose translations, including Du Vair's *Morall Philosophy of the Stoicks* (1664). The translator of *The Fair One of Tunis* assures his readers that no stoicism will be required in this volume, announcing in his advertisement to the reader that 'my first and principal design was to divert my self; my next (Dear Reader) to please thee, in saying here and there some things, that I thought were pleasant and rational enough'.[62] As is customary in epistles to the reader by this time, he resolutely declares that what follows 'is really a true History', and that the reader must 'not look upon it as a meer piece of Invention, for it is no such thing' ('Epistle to The Reader'). The plot concerns the adventures of a prince, Albirond, who, bored with peace in France, becomes a wandering knight errant or 'Cavaleer' throughout Europe, until a 'suddain whymsy took him, wholly to throw himself into the arms of Fortune', which leads him to board the first ship which he encounters (p. 3). This takes him to Tunis, the principal city of the Barbary Coast, where the remainder of his adventures take place.

In addition to romance and intrigue, the tale offers the curious reader fanciful information about foreign customs and in particular the seraglios, although Cotton firmly declares that 'grave Sir *Politick Woodbees*' (a reference to the character in Ben Jonson's *Volpone*) will seek in vain that level of information in a text designed only 'to entertain the amorous with a new piece of Gallantry' (p. 5). The 'Turks' as a group are represented as rude-mannered by European standards of courtesy, but whose accessories are luxurious and sensual, and 'it is not to be believed how naturally gallant the Women are in that Country' (p. 36). The garden of the palace is particularly luxurious; Albirond wastes little time before carving love poems on trees and, when moved, to 'break into this suddain Rapture' in song. Not surprisingly, his activities attract the attention of a mysterious beauty in the window overlooking the gardens, very much forbidden fruit (p. 13). The Sultaness, the 'beautiful *African*', has her equally beautiful Spanish slave, Donna Isabella, shoot arrows bearing messages to attract his attention; once his attention has been gained, the lovers spend their time singing a duet and exchanging gallant dialogues ('I have no mind to repeat all that these new Lovers said to one another in their first ardor...what I have said is sufficient to let you see that they were already advanc'd pretty far in their affairs') (pp. 27, 39). Although their courtship is brief, their time in Tunis is

---

[62] Cotton, *The Fair One of Tunis*, 'Epistle to The Reader'.

filled with incidents, and through many adventures Albirond acquires a friend in Don Pedro, who falls in love with the captive slave Donna Isabella. This complicates the plot, as two sets of lovers must escape from the seraglio by sea, pursued and harassed by the Turks.

Enjoyment of *The Fair One of Tunis* in part depends on the reader's preparation by other tales of exotic ladies in seraglios and their rescue by gallant Europeans to accept the formula of romance fiction. *The Fair One of Tunis* contains the standard plot and pace of the large folio French romance narratives, but in a more compact form: Donna Isabella, not surprisingly, turns out to be of a noble family, and she and Don Pedro quickly wed once they reach safety. By page 299 of this smaller quarto volume, 'after so many dangers; griefs, and fears, did joy in torrents come tumbling in upon our fair Lovers' and 'nothing now remain'd to perfect their happiness, but the conversion of the fair *African*, which also was no hard matter to do, and she had not run such and so many hazards to stick at any thing' (p. 299). She simultaneously converts to Christianity and weds Albirond, and both couples travel to Spain to claim Donna Isabella's rightful inheritance. Having made a 'mutual protestation of perpetual Friendship', the couples part, and Albirond and the Sultana 'by easy and pleasant Journeys retired into their own Country' to end the narrative on page 302.

The French also gave the English readers another edition of a well-known tale from Boccaccio through Chaucer, *The True and Admirable History of Patient Grisel, A poor Mans Daughter in France, and Noble Marquess of Salus. Shewing How Maids by her Example in their good and virtuous Behaviour may Marry Rich Husbands* (1674). It features a new title page with woodcut illustration and an old-style black-letter font. This favourite apparently continued to hold appeal for readers and could be marketed as offering good advice for maids and wives.

In the fiction *Beraldus, Prince of Savoy, A Novel. In Two Parts* translated from French by an anonymous 'Person of Quality' in 1675, which is less didactic in its appeal, the foreign setting is an important feature. Also for this text, there is an imagined audience of 'Ladies' awaiting adventures; they are addressed in the opening epistle, and, as with *The Fair One of Tunis*, these readers are not urged to take the characters as role models, but instead to enjoy them as types. The hero Beraldus is renowned for arms and unlucky in love, resulting in ten years of wandering around Europe. In this tale, the villains are rapacious Bandetti 'who infest the Alps', led by the mysterious Hedemont.[63] The key female character in the plot is the 'severely virtuous' Cunegond, who spurns the advances of Beraldus's King Otho and, to discourage his attentions, announces she secretly loves Beraldus (p. 15). Beraldus, however, spurns women who too easily show their hearts: 'If *Cunegond* loves me, said I, and has the weakness to tell me so, and to forget her virtue for me, she is not worthy to be treated better than the others, and I shall have an equal contempt for her as for all those who

[63] *Beraldus*, 4.

strive to make themselves belov'd, rather than esteemed' (pp. 20–1). This clash-ing set of agendas binds the couple together to deceive Otho in what they describe as mutual sacrifices of their principles. Rather than songs, the two exchange tortured letters. This complicated relationship becomes even more so when Cunegond falls into the hands of Hedemont, who falls in love with her and to whom she feels the ties of obligation. Unlike in *The Fair One of Tunis*, much more time is spent displaying the interior thoughts and emotions of the characters, as they struggle to uphold their virtuous principles, than on the physical adventures they experience or the strangeness of the foreign setting.

The most prolific writer of entertaining fiction during 1674–5 was without dispute Richard Head (*c.*1637–86?). The Irish writer and bookseller had launched his long career with *The English Rogue* (1665), a fictional autobiography of a professional thief, Meriton Latroon, loosely based on incidents in his own father's life; this work went through several editions and generated several additional parts. The title page for part three, issued in 1674, features a series of woodblock vignettes in a panel, illustrating the various adventures inside. Working in the 1670s as a bookseller and a hack writer at what his acquaintance John Aubrey states was a fee of 20*s* per sheet, Head was no doubt in tune with popular tastes in reading, and his productions for these two years highlight many of the conventions used to present fiction as 'true history' and fact.

In 1674, Head produced three titles. *The Western Wonder: Or O Brazeel, An Inchanted Island discovered*, formed around a legend about an island north of Ireland, serves as the vehicle for allegorical social satire, complete with frontis-piece illustrations to lend verisimilitude. *Jackson's Recantation* is a fictional first-person criminal narrative, and the contents of Head's third offering, *Nugae Venales*, are captured in its long title, *Or, The Complaisant Companion: Being New Jests, Domestick and Forreign, Bulls, Rhodomontados, Pleasant Novels, And, Miscellanies*. This last is a compilation that had several editions but that makes no attempt to claim itself as 'real history', although Head asserts in the epistle to the reader that the 'novels' that 'are acted in our own Country are new, true and pleasant, as to what are translated, out of French; if their Plot be bad, impate the blame to the sterility and dullness of *Monsieur's* fancy, and not of him, who is your Countrey-man'.

The year 1675 was equally prolific for Head. *O-Brazile Or The Inchanted Island Being A perfect Relation of the late Discovery... Of An Island On the North of Ireland* (1675) also concerns an island off Ireland, but presents itself as a letter from a merchant cousin in Ireland describing how, on 2 March 1674, a Captain Nisbet, along with his crew of eight named sailors, happened upon the island after a night of fog. *The Miss Display'd, With all Her Wheedling Arts And Circumventions... By the Author of the First Part of the English Rogue* (1675) announces itself to be the 'true History of a late famous or Infamous Whore'.[64]

---

[64] Head, *The Miss Display'd*, 1.

In both *Jackson's Recantation* and *The Miss Display'd* the narrators assure the reader that these 'true' life stories of criminals are being provided in order that the reader can arm him- or herself against cunning. Jackson, whom the title announces is 'now Hanging in Chains at Hampstead', has his story told in the first person, having supposedly dictated it to a 'friend' shortly before he was executed. In addition to repenting his evil deeds, the 'Notorious High-Way-Man' also offers an insider's guide as to how to recognize highwaymen when one is travelling and 'truly discovered the whole Mystery of that Wicked and Fatal Profession of Padding on the Road'.[65] Likewise, 'this true History of a late famous or infamous Whore, laying open her cunning contrivances, Intrigues, Cheats, Plot and Projects... is made publick to no other end then to the Reformation of Vice'.[66]

The narrator of *The Miss Diplay'd* states his views succulently: 'doubtlessly there are good Women in the World, but they are so few, by reason of the spreading Contagion of their vicious inclinations, that thereby some are induced to believe, that it is onely a supposed goodness' (p. 4). Cornelia is the beautiful daughter of an English father and an Irish mother of good family; she is, unfortunately, 'haughty, proud and disdainful, so averse and impatient in the encountring any thing that opposed, or withstood her roving fancy, and beloved cogitations, that she would yield to no other power but her own, and acknowledge no *God*, but her own *Will* and *Pleasure*' (p. 8). She is seduced in the big city of Dublin by the devilish Ignatos, who regales her with stories of women of humble birth obtaining wealth and power (thus superficially resembling the popular patient Griselda). However, in Cornelia's story, women do this by becoming courtesans to great men. The story of Cornelia is not one of the repentance of a fallen woman. Instead, at the end, sounding much like the ambiguous heroines in Daniel Defoe's future fictions, or indeed the mistresses of Charles II, Cornelia

is now Arrived to a great height of unexpected glory... she glitters in the Boxes of the *Play-houses*, she draws all eyes after her whereever she comes, to the amazement of vertuous Women, and encouragement of the Vitious, who delight only in Finery, costly Treats, Dancing, Singing, Balls, Masks, Masquerades, Plays, Frolicks, Rambles Assignations, and all manner of Idleness, in imitation of such a thriving Example. (pp. 132–3)

Against the backdrop of the highly visible, real-life successes of the royal mistresses of Charles and his courtiers and the fictionalized ones of popular writers such as Head, little wonder that authors addressing Christian readers lament the moral condition of the country in 1674 and 1675. John Bunyan (bap. 1628–88), who had composed his allegorical masterpiece *Pilgrim's Progress* while in prison in the late 1660s and which was in limited circulation in manuscript during this period, did not publish it until 1678 (see *MV* 3.V).

[65] Head, *Jackson's Recantation*, title page.
[66] Head, *The Miss Display'd*, 2.

Instead, he issued a fourth enlarged edition of *Sighs from Hell: Or, The Groans of a Damned Soul* and *Instruction for the Ignorant* (1675). It takes the form of a dialogue, designed, Bunyan says in his opening for members of his congregation, 'to put you again in remembrance of first things, and to give you occasion to present something to your carnal relations that may be (if God will) for their awakening and conversion'.[67] As Bunyan calls it, the volume is a 'little book', suitable for carrying in one's pocket, and 'in a plain and easie dialogue, fitted to the capacity of the weakest' (sig. A2^{r-v}).

In 1674, however, Bunyan was himself involved in public scandal involving a member of one of his congregations, the trial of Agnes Beaumont (bap. 1652–1720). The 20-year-old woman, who lived alone with her father on a farm in Bedfordshire, was charged with his murder when he forbade her to attend services Bunyan held at nearby Gamlingay. He locked her from the house in the snow after learning from neighbours that Bunyan had let her ride behind him on his horse to the meeting. Beaumont herself records her pride at being seen in such a familiar way with this famous preacher: 'But to speak the truth I had not gone far behind him, but my heart was puffed up with pride, and I began to have high thoughts of myself, and proud to think I should ride behind such a man as he was; and I was pleased anybody did look after me as I rode along.'[68]

Beaumont was accused by a rejected former suitor of poisoning her father, but cleared by a coroner and jury trial. She recorded the events of her trials of faith and of law in a manuscript narrative that enjoyed circulation in multiple manuscript copies among the Baptist congregations, eventually appearing in print in 1760 in Samuel James's collection of narratives of the persecution and trial of seventeenth-century nonconformists. Bunyan himself was also under legal threat again for preaching without a licence, and in March of 1675 a warrant for his arrest was issued: his refusal to appear in the archdeacon's court on the charge led to his excommunication from the Church of England. In the midst of these controversies, Bunyan continued his pamphlet war with 'false Preachers', 'the crafty Children of darkness', in *Light for Them that Sit in Darkness* (1675) ('Preface to the Reader'), primarily targeting Quakers and latitudinarians whom he believed were misleading well-intentioned Christian readers.

On a less controversial level, among the most popular devotional texts printed in 1674 and 1675 were the new editions of two texts now attributed to the provost of Eton College, Richard Allestree (1621/2–81), *The Whole Duty of Man, Laid down In a Plain and Familiar Way for the Use of All, but especially the Meanest Reader* (first printed 1658) and *The Gentleman's Calling. Written by the Author of the Whole Duty of Man*. The latter, a copy of which, as we have seen, had been sent to Barbados in 1674 for Richard Whaley's edification, discusses the ways in which a 'Gentleman', through his advantages of education, wealth, time, authority, and reputation, has the duty to use his

---

[67] Bunyan, *Sighs from Hell*, sig. A2^{r-v}.
[68] Beaumont, *Narrative*, 43–4.

God-given advantages and not pursue a life of idleness and pleasure. Printed in a small octavo and thus easily carried, the book, which first was printed in 1660, attacks contemporary attitudes concerning piety and wealth: it laments, 'GENTILITY has long since confuted Jobs Aphorisme, Man is born to labour, and instead thereof, has pronounced to its Clients the Rich mans Requiem, Soul take thine ease, eat drink and be merry. *A Gentleman* is now supposed to be onely a thing of pleasure'.[69]

This call for readers of all social classes and of both sexes to be active and engaged Christians in the secular world permeates many of the texts published in 1674 and 1675. James Janeway (1636–74), a popular London evangelical minister, published *Saints Incouragement to Diligence in Christs Service* in 1674 shortly before his death. Like his earlier publications, most notably *A Token For Children: Being An Exact Account of the Conversion, Holy and Exemplary Lives, and Joyful Deaths of several young Children* (1672; pt II, 1673), viewed by some as being the first 'children's book' written specifically for that market, this text exhorts Christians to persevere in their faith, 'quit you like men, be strong; behold the cross, win it and wear it'.[70]

Saints Incouragement relies heavily on biographical anecdotes of everyday people for exemplary stories. Featured on the title page, for example, is the promise of 'the Deathbed experiences of Mris B. which were taken from her own Mouth in Short-hand'. In the preface, Richard Baxter (1615–91), the former chaplain in the Parliamentary army in the 1640s and author of the frequently reprinted book of devotion *The Saints Everlasting Rest* (1650) (see *MV* 1.IV), notes that 'the Treatise before you is so weighty, serious, spiritual, and well cloathed, that to me it is as savoury as any he hath yet published'.[71] It is commendable, he believes, to include the '*triumphant* Express Expressions of a dying woman...for these lively workings of the Faith of others, is a great help to confirm the Readers faith' (sig. a4ʳ). In this section, Janeway recounts the final days of one of his parishioners. In her extreme physical distress, she receives comfort from Janeway, who prays with her, and he recalls: 'Oh, at what rate did she praise the Lord! Her joys increased wonderfully.' On her final night, he concludes: 'she judged that she heard Sweet Musick, and could not be satisfied, but that I must be sent for to hear that Melody; but before I could come to her she was joined in the glorious Consort above. HALLELUJAH' (pp. 116–17).

Richard Baxter also published his own text created specifically for families of the less well-to-do, *The Poor Man's Family Book...In plain familiar Conferences between a Teacher and a Learner* (1674), a popular work that would be frequently reprinted during the next two decades. Under the author's name on the title page, the potential purchaser is greeted 'with a request to

---

[69] Allestree, *The Gentleman's Calling*, sig. A4ʳ⁻ᵛ.
[70] Janeway, *A Token For Children*, 59.
[71] Baxter, 'Preface', in Janeway, *Saints Incouragement*, sig. a3ᵛ.

landlords and Rich men to give to their Tenants and poor Neighbours, either this or some fitter book'.[72] Opening the book with 'A request to the Rich', Baxter discloses that, in order to include the necessary instructions in a method that 'the ignorant' will be able to grasp, he has had to write a book of a size they could not afford to buy. Therefore, he urges that 'you will bestow one Book (either this or some fitter) upon as many poor families as you well can' (sig. A3^r). 'I hope rich Citizens, and Ladies, and rich Women, who cannot themselves go talk to poor families, will send them such a messengers as this, or some fitter Book, to instruct them, seeing no Preacher can be got at so cheap a rate' (sig. A3^v).

In his epistle to the reader, Baxter owns that his inspiration was Arthur Dent's *The Plain Mans Path way to Heaven*, a book he himself had owned for over forty years. While he will begin his book 'in the language of the Vulgar', he will not continue it, however, throughout, supposing that 'riper Christians need no so loose a stile or method as the ignorant and vulgar do' (sig. A4^r). The style of the 'conversation' features a very well-spoken sinner, Saul, who freely admits 'being Ignorant and unlearned, I am loath to talk with such a man as you, about high matters, and things of Religion, which I do not well understand', but, unlike many of John Bunyan's fictional sinners, a listener who is very amenable to the teacher Paul's observations concerning salvation. Paul translates the concept of salvation into the language of family relationships and everyday ownership practices: when God 'converteth a Sinner', Paul explains, 'he sets his *name* and *mark* upon him, not outwardly only as you do on your Sheep or goods; but *inwardly*, as the Parents convey their own nature and likeness to their Children … [he] turneth them to a new life' (p. 5).

It was not only through a simple, conversational style that devotional writers sought to hold their audience's attention. After Janeway's own early death at age 38, his admirers soon published *Mr James Janeway's Legacy to his Friends, Containing Twenty Seven Famous Instances of Gods Providences in and about Sea Dangers and Deliverances, with the Names of Several that were Eye-witness to many of them* (1674). In addition to this work, published by Janeway's usual publisher, Dorman Newman, Anne Purslow (fl. 1675–7) printed a single page broadside *Mr Janeways sayings not long before death*, which includes among the numbered observations that 'Many are carried very quietly to Hell, and fear nothing till they fell and are not brought to their senses, till unspeakable horror and anguished doth it'. A more expensive and imposing volume appeared later in 1674, *Saints Memorials: Or Words fitly spoken, Like Apples of Gold in Pictures of Silver*, a collection of memorable sayings by four deceased ministers, Edmund Calamy, Joseph Caryl, Ralph Venning, and James Janeway, also using a panel of woodblock portraits of the departed divines for its frontispiece. The end of the volume offers the reader a catalogue of books sold by Dorman Newman, sorted by size, mostly

[72] Baxter, *The Poor Man's Family Book*, title page.

devotional texts and dictionaries and grammars, with a special notice for Thomas Sternhold's frequently reprinted metrical translation of the Psalms, with a list of ministers who recommend it for its 'fluent Sweetness'.

The use of compendia of examples drawn from Scripture, history, and contemporary life to impress the reader with the active presence and judgements of God in everyday life is a common feature in the didactic writings of 1674 and 1675. The diligent and prolific anthologist of such examples both good and bad, the Revd Samuel Clarke, addressed the reader 'from my Study in Hammersmith, April 14, 1674', and offered *A Looking-glass for Persecutors: containing Multitudes of Examples of God's Severe, but Righteous Judgments upon bloody and merciless Haters of his Children in all Times, from the beginning of the World to this present Age.* Under Clarke's engraved frontispiece, showing him seated with paper and writing pen, the engraver Walter Binneman urges:

> View here his Shadow whose Laborious Quill
> By Sacred Chymistry doth Balm Distill
> to Calm ye Persecuting Spirits Rage
> and mixe Delight with Profitt in each Page.

Whether in religious devotions, guides to self-improvement, accounts of criminals' confessions and repentance, coffee-house conversations, or witty dialogues on stage, a pervasive thread in what was being written, read, sung, and performed in 1674 and 1675 suggests an emphasis on the combination of profit and delight. Of course, the libertine courtiers pursued different paths to pleasure and profit from those followed by the industrious Christian merchants, and the readers of popular fiction explored different worlds in addition to those visited by English travellers to the New World and their new plantations, but it was a literary discourse infused with the pursuit of both happiness and profit, whether worldly or heavenly.

Writers and their readers were harshly critical of the excesses of the times, but they also celebrated the bonds of friendship and the comparative prosperity of an England not actively engaged in war. Thomas Flatman (1635–88), a painter of miniatures, chose to open the first edition of his frequently reprinted *Poems and Songs* (1674) with a Pindaric ode 'To the memory of the incomparable Orinda' (Katherine Philips), which in part is a lament for what he felt was the death of the type of English poetry represented in the poems by her and Abraham Cowley. In his opening epistle, he describes the contents as the results of 'my many Idle hours', which he exposes 'to the mercy of the wide World, quite guiltless of Address or Ceremony',[73] but the pages that follow record no fewer than five formal verse epistles from his literary friends. The volume, while paying tribute to the past, celebrates their present vigorous poetic comradeship. Summarizing this attitude of mingled praise for the individual and laments over the excesses of their times, his fellow writers congratulate the

---

[73] Flatman, *Poems and Songs*, sig. A4ᵛ.

poet on appearing in print 'in a Debauch'd, and a Censorious Age', but applaud in particular his being able to bring readers to a place of calm and serenity in spite of the times, those 'who sometimes will unbend their care | And steal themselves out from the busie Throng' and join in friendship to appreciate 'Your pleasant Songs in solemn Comfort Sung'.[74]

II. Laws Regulating Publication, Speech, and Performance, 1674–1684

Because of the publicly visible tensions between the court and rival parties in Parliament, soon to be commonly known as the Whigs (in opposition to the court) and the Tories (in support of monarch and court policies), the need for the government and the Church of England to control what was published and performed between 1675 and 1685 was acute. There were inflammatory opposing points of view over the government's finances and the looming threat of the succession to the throne by a Catholic, resulting in the Exclusion Crisis occurring between 1678 and 1681, as Whig supporters led by the Earl of Shaftesbury attempted to pass legislation blocking the succession of James, Duke of York.

The early and mid-1680s were marked by a series of spectacular treason trials. Even members of the royal family faced scrutiny for involvement in treasonous politics, with Charles II's eldest illegitimate son, James, Duke of Monmouth, becoming a central figure in rumoured conspiracies against the throne. The 'Rye House Plot', which erupted in 1683 on the heels of the Popish Plot (see CV 3.II), was supposedly a plan created by a secret cabal of Whig extremists to assassinate Charles and his brother James as they returned to London from the Newmarket races, to raise a general insurrection, and to place the Protestant Monmouth on the throne. Monmouth was not brought to trial, but he was forced to leave England by his father. As historians have noted, since neither the assassination nor the insurrection actually occurred, the details of the plot came from charges laid by informers, beginning with Josiah Keeling, a London merchant and nonconformist. Sir John Reresby in his memoirs observed of the events and what emerged at the trials that those involved were 'such as had been disappointed of preferments at Court, and of protestant dissenters' (Reresby, *Memoirs*, 304).

The resulting show trials and the executions of prominent public figures were widely described in the popular press and also in the writings of those accused, which circulated in both print and manuscript copies. These included the well-known alderman and sheriff of London Henry Cornish (d. 1685), who was described by Bishop Gilbert Burnet in his history of the period as an innocent

---

[74] Richard Newcourt, 'To his Esteemed Friend Mr Thomas Flatman upon the publishing of his poems', in Flatman, *Poems and Songs*.

man falsely accused and wrongly executed, likewise by the Quaker William Penn, who was present at the execution and declared his dying words were those of 'an outraged man'. The former Lord Warden of the Cinque Ports, Algernon Sidney [Sydney] (1623–83), who had published his *Discourses Concerning Government* between 1681 and 1683, defending armed rebellion against tyranny and in defence of Protestants against unjust persecution, republican positions echoing earlier ones of John Milton, continued to defend beliefs in his dying words speech from the scaffold, a text that was quickly widely circulated and read. Finally executed in this group was William Russell, Lord Russell (1639–83); his wife Rachel (bap. 1637–1723) helped prepare his defence, took notes during his trial, unsuccessfully petitioned Charles II for a pardon, helped to craft his scaffold speech, and ensured its wide circulation, resulting in his posthumous reputation as a Whig martyr.

The last woman to be executed for treason in England, Elizabeth Gaunt (d. 1685), was executed the same day as Cornish by being burnt alive. The London shopkeeper and her husband, who may have been Anabaptists, had been actively involved in the early 1680s assisting radical dissenters to travel between London and Amsterdam, including, it was believed, the Earl of Shaftesbury when he fled in 1682; as with Cornish, there was little evidence of her direct involvement with the Rye House group.[75] Her dying speech, *Mrs Elizabeth Gaunt's last speech, who was burnt at London, Oct 23 1685* (1685), moved many in the audience to tears, and its publication in both English and Dutch established her as a martyr for the Protestant faith. To counter such accounts, Charles himself commissioned the historian of the Royal Society, Thomas Sprat, to write the official account of events, *A True Account and Declaration of the Horrid Conspiracy Against the Late King, His Present Majesty, and the Government: As it was Order'd to be Published by His Late Majesty* (1685) (see MV 4.1).[76] Under the Sedition Act of 1661, as demonstrated in the Popish Plot trials between 1679 and 1681, it was high treason even to speak of imagining harm to the King ('within the realm, or without, [to] compass, imagine, invent, devise or intend death or destruction or any bodily harm' to the monarch[77]), much less to take action to do so: there was no shortage of controversial topics during this volatile period, and speaking, preaching, performing, or writing about any of them was to open oneself up to scrutiny by government and religious authorities.

Under pressure from Parliament, Charles had rescinded the Declaration of Indulgence in March 1673; the Test Act passed by Parliament further required that all office-holders receive Anglican Communion, swear allegiance to the King, and affirm the King as the head of the Church of England. These measures put dissenting ministers such as the popular writer and preacher John

---

[75] See Melinda Zook, 'Gaunt, Elizabeth (d. 1685)', *ODNB*.
[76] See Zook, *Radical Whigs and Conspiratorial Politics*, ch. 5.
[77] Charles II, *An Act for Safety and Preservation of His Majesties Person and Government*.

Bunyan once again under threat of arrest for preaching without a licence and violating the second Conventicle law of 1670 (see MV 2.II). For Quakers in particular, who refused to swear any oaths, the years between 1675 and 1685 saw renewed prosecution by local magistrates across the countryside; more than fifty members of the Society of Friends were imprisoned between 1682 and 1684 alone.[78] William Penn (1644–1718) argued in the aftermath of the Rye House trials in *Reasons Why The Oaths Should not be made A Part of the Test To Protestant Dissenters* (1683) that such practices designed to find out treasonous Catholic plotters should not be administered to Protestants, declaring that 'Let it be consider'd, that such Dissenters will be of all People the most Miserable: For being expos'd to the Punishment of *Papists* and the Punishment of *Protestant-Dissenters* too, they must needs be in a worse Condition, than the *Papists*; for they will be at this rate ground between two *Mill-stones'*.[79] So widespread was the persecution that in 1676 the London Quakers instituted a 'Meeting for Suffering' to record and publicize the gaoling and fining of their members and to offer advice and comfort to those in the provinces who reported local accounts of suffering.

The prominent Quaker writer William Dewsbury addressed words of comfort to the persecuted believers who refused on principle to take the required oaths, *To all the Faithfull and Suffering Members in all Holes, Prisons and Goals for the Word of God and Testimony of Jesus Christ; with the rest of the Faithful where-ever scatter'd upon the face of the Earth* (1684), declaring at the pamphlet's end that the words were what God had spoken to him while he was incarcerated in the Warwick gaol. Joseph Harrison in *The Lamentable Cry of Oppression Or, The Case of the Poor, Suffering & Persecuted People called* Quakers *in and about fakenham in norfolk* (1679) warns the reader that 'it may make the Heathen to question the Christian Religion',

when they hear of those Rending, Tearing and Devouring Dealings amongst the Professors thereof. Certainly the Papists may Laugh at the great Victory they have gotten by their under-hand accomplishing such a Law, as sets one Protestant against another, In such a Day as this; and that for no other Reason, but for their Sincerity to God-ward; not for any Vice, but for Virtue.[80]

In spite of these laws passed primarily to control the activities of Catholics, there was nevertheless a widespread public belief in Catholic conspiracies that climaxed in the Popish Plot in 1678 (see CV 3.II), highlighting the connections between religious and political practices as well as the increasing efficiency of popular circulation of information, whether valid or fictitious. The Exclusion Crisis of 1679–81, a series of three bills introduced by the Whig party led by the Earl of Shaftesbury to bar the Catholic James, Duke of York, from succeeding to the throne, likewise demonstrates the ways in which party politicians

[78] See Davies, *The Quakers*, 181–90, table 13. [79] Penn, *Reasons Why The Oaths*, 4.
[80] Harrison, *The Lamentable Cry of Oppression*, 'To the Reader'.

utilized a printed pamphlet and broadside campaign reminiscent of the pamphlet deluge of the 1640s to attempt to shape public sentiments (see *CV* 1.III). The resulting prosecutions for seditious libel highlight the court and the church's efforts to contain dangerous opinions, whether preached, sung, or published in a pamphlet and read in a public coffee house.

As a result of the nearly continuous political and religious disputes between 1675 and 1684, witty satires, crude lampoons, earnest pleas for toleration, polemics against absolutism and popery, and history plays with obvious links to contemporary crises all helped to create discourses of dissent, whether circulated in handwritten copies, sold on the streets in cheap pamphlets and illustrated prints, sent to provincial booksellers, or acted on stage. To attempt to control the multiple discourses of opposition, the government relied heavily on licensing. The Act passed by Parliament in June of 1662, 'An Act of Preventing the frequent abuses in printing Seditious, Treasonable, and unlicensed Books and Pamphlets; and for the Regulating of Printing and Printing Presses', which has been variously referred to by historians as 'the Printing Act', 'the Licensing Act', and 'the Press Act', would remain in effect until May 1695, although permitted to lapse between 1679 and 1685 (see *MV* 2.II). Uniting the interests of the Stationers' Company to control printing rights with those of the government to control potentially inflammatory texts through licensing, the Act placed Sir Roger L'Estrange (1616–1704) in the position of being 'surveyor of the imprimery and printing presses', and the official licenser for all books except those on law, divinity, philosophy, physic, and heraldry. L'Estrange would perform these roles from 1662 until 1688, with the exception of the secretary of the Royal Society Henry Oldenburg's very brief tenure in the post between February and April 1675. This post gave him, along with members of the Stationers' Company, the right to obtain a warrant to enter and search premises even suspected of having seditious publications, with only the home of peers of the realm being exempt; L'Estrange oversaw the activities not only of the authors and printers, but also of page correctors and hawkers or vendors. Government agents called 'Messengers of the Press' were empowered to investigate where one could obtain seditious or scandalous materials and to gather evidence against writers, publishers, and booksellers.

While the terms of the Act are clear, the extent to which it was consistently enforced up to its lapse in 1679 is less so. While historians and critics agree on the high level of zeal L'Estrange showed in pursuing individual seditious texts and those who created and distributed them, they disagree as to how effective L'Estrange was in controlling the printed press in general.[81] Robertson estimates that during his tenure, 1660–5, L'Estrange and his agents suppressed nearly 3 per cent of total publications, excluding serials and periodical publications, or approximately 1,000 items in the 25-year period and he points

---

[81] See Siebert, *Freedom of the Press*, ch. 12. See Walker, 'Censorship of the Press', and Robertson, *Censorship and Conflict*, for contrasting points of view.

tellingly to the fates of the dissenting printers and distributers such as Brewster, Calvert, and Dover who died in prison or shortly after release (see *MV* 2.II).[82] Clearly, however, many books and pamphlets were printed that were not licensed by L'Estrange or the other licensers. Contemporary comments throughout his tenure strongly suggest that L'Estrange was open to financial persuasions, from interested individuals, or indeed, as the bookseller and memoirist John Dunton (1659–1732) alleged, if the wife of the printer smiled kindly upon him. A complaint against L'Estrange brought in 1676 and directed to Secretary of State Williamson declared that L'Estrange received £50 per year 'besides presents' from the two playhouses, while 'Quacks Bills and Books' brought in £500, and a not inconsiderable income for 'winking at the numerous spawn of nonconformity books [and]…his seizing arbitrarily without conviction of fact the goods of such as act contrarily to his pretended power'.[83] In 1681, after the lapse of the Act, the broadside *News from Parnassus* summarized his career: 'he was Arch-oppressor of the Press [and] he had taken as a bribe from a certain Society every New Year's Day for many years 100 guineas'.

After 1675 and until the Act lapsed in 1679, numerous additional official proclamations were issued attempting to control the circulation of politically sensitive materials in a variety of media, and several independent committees were formed from the House of Lords to investigate libels. In addition to inconsistencies in the licensing of texts, by 1675, there were at least ten unlicensed printers who had set up trade, thus exceeding the number of London presses set by the Stationers' Company (*CSPD, 1675/6*, 43) (see *MV* 2.II). The Coffee House proclamations in 1674 and 1676 urged coffee-house owners to report any seditious speech they overheard, and pressure was put on them not to keep any possibly seditious pamphlets, whether printed or in scribal copy, in their businesses. Several printers and booksellers had their shops next to coffee houses, such as Nathaniel Crouch, senior, who sold his books at the Bell, next to Kemp's coffee house in the 1680s, and many coffee houses were located near St Paul's and Covent Garden, centres for numerous booksellers and printers, which made a convenient link between the coffee-house patrons and the writers of the period. In addition to providing printed materials for their customers, of course, the coffee houses were important social meeting places for poets, politicians, scribes, and publishers, in effect forming an informal network of literary exchange outside print publication.[84] This was officially noted in 1675, when L'Estrange suggested to the newly created Libels Committee that the legal term 'libel' should be extended to include handwritten materials, since 'not one in 40 libels ever comes to Presse, though by the help of MS, they are well nigh as public'.[85] In 1681, this connection between poets, coffee houses, and seditious talk would be highlighted in the trial of Stephen College

---

[82] Robertson, *Censorship and Conflict*, 198.   [83] Kitchin, *Sir Roger L'Estrange*, 201.
[84] See Harris, 'Captain Robert Julian'; Love, *Scribal Publication*, ch. 6, and Love, *English Clandestine Satire*, ch. 8.   [85] Quoted in Kitchin, *Sir Roger L'Estrange*, 198.

[Colledge] (*c*.1635–81), to be discussed later, who was described as 'bawling against the government', reciting his poems in London coffee houses and taverns.[86]

Informers were crucial in tracking down authors of seditious or scandalous texts in the years leading up to 1679. 'Against the Spreading False News' and 'For the Discovery of Libellers' offered significant rewards to informers to turn in either the printer (£20) or the author (£50); by 1679, the bounty on printers was increased to £40. In March 1676, L'Estrange was issued with a warrant to search for three libels: *Letter from a Person of Quality*, arguing for the passage of an exclusion bill to block Catholics from the throne, attributed by some to John Locke and others to Shaftesbury; *The Naked Truth. Or, The True State Of The Primitive Church* by Bishop Herbert Croft (1603–91), urging accommodation rather than persecution and prosecution for nonconformists; and Andrew Marvell's response to attacks upon Croft, *Mr Smirke; Or, The Divine in Mode*, published under the pseudonym Andreas Rivetus. Marvell's publisher, Nathaniel Ponder, who was also John Bunyan's, was briefly imprisoned for publishing it without a licence, a charge brought apparently to appease the offended Bishop of London and the church hierarchy in general.[87]

In February 1677, Charles II finally recalled the prorogued Parliament. A quickly published pamphlet, *Some Considerations Upon the Question, Whether The Parliament is Dissolved By it's Prorogation for 15 Months*, was deemed libellous, and a committee was formed to discover its author and printer, and to make enquiries concerning 'any other printed books that are of that nature'.[88] Suspicions fell on the Whig party leaders, but authorship was never proven. A Dr Cary was brought to the bar to answer to the charge that he had given the manuscript to the press; he refused to identify the author or who had employed him to convey the manuscript and was convicted of contempt, fined £1,000 and sent to the Tower. Andrew Marvell, in one of his last polemics, *An Account of the Growth Of Popery, And Arbitrary government* (1678), a text reprinted frequently in the eighteenth century under his name, used the case as an example of the government's turn towards arbitrary authority: 'Doctor *Cary*, a Commoner, was brought to the Barre before them . . . under that new Notion of Contempt, when no other crime would do it.'[89] For the discovery of the author and publisher of *An Account of the Growth Of Popery*, which bluntly declared that 'There has now for diverse Years, a design been carried on, to change the Lawfull Government of *England* into an Absolute Tyranny, and to convert the established Protestant Religion into down-right Popery' (p. 3), a notice in the *London Gazette* (21 February–5 March 1678) states that the government will

[86] *A Complete Collection of State Trials*, 8. 610.

[87] See Nicholas Murray, *World Enough and Time: The Life of Andrew Marvell* (St Martin's Press, 2000), ch. 26, and Smith, *Andrew Marvell*, 300–13.

[88] See Kitchin, *Sir Roger L'Estrange*, 209 and *passim*.

[89] Marvell, *An Account of the Growth Of Popery*, 82.

award £50 for information about the printer and author and £100, an enormous sum, for the 'Hander of it to the Press'.

The Licensing Act lapsed in 1679 after the Popish Plot scare had started (see CV 3.II). Parliament was fully engaged in examining the details of the supposed Catholic conspiracy to assassinate the King and to take over the government, in addition to the Whig party's growing efforts to block the succession of the Duke of York to the throne. The Lord Chancellor on 6 March 1679 declared mildly that 'it may not be amiss to think of some better remedy for regulating the press, from whence there daily steal forth Popish Catechism, and Books of Controversy' and that it would be better to prevent libels and propaganda being published in the first place than to arrest the distributors after the fact.

The resistance to renewing the Act, however, came from a variety of sources. Charles Blount argued eloquently in *A Just Vindication Of Learning: Or, An Humble Address to the High Court of Parliament In behalf of the Liberty of the Press. By Philopatris* (1679) that learning and the spread of knowledge had been venerated since ancient times, but that

> Learning hath of late years met with an obstruction in many places, which suppresses it from flourishing or increasing, in spight of all its other helps, and that is, the *Inquisition upon the Press*, which prohibits any Book from coming forth without an *Imprimatur*; an old Relique of Popery, only necessary for the concealing of such defects of Government, which of right ought to be discover'd and amended.[90]

Citing with admiration 'Mr Milton', Blount declared that reading books teaches and enhances the reader's understanding to the greater benefit of government, while 'no Vocal Learning is so effectual for Instruction, as Reading; for that written discourses are better digested, and support themselves better on their own weight, than words disguised by the manner of expression, cadence or gesture, which corrupt the simplicity of things' (p. 2).

Both the court and the Whigs in Parliament had more immediately pragmatic reasons for not wishing to impose a stricter licensing Act. The court, which was accused by its opponents of having a design to impose arbitrary rule, had no interest in appearing to want to stifle publication by renewing licensing; the Whig party, as historians have noted, for its part 'made every effort to ensure that as many people as possible throughout the kingdom were apprised of the threat of popery and arbitrary government and educated about the things that might need to be done in order to avoid it. This was achieved through a brilliant exploitation of the media.'[91] Certainly, once the Act had lapsed, as had happened in the 1640s with the collapse of the Star Chamber, the amount of printed reading material in circulation in London and throughout the country increased dramatically: the numbers of books and pamphlets increased from about 1,081 in 1677 to 1,730 in 1679, 2,145 in 1680, and 1,978 in

[90] Bount, *A Just Vindication of Learning*, 2.
[91] Harris, *Restoration*, 142. See also Harris, *London Crowds*, ch. 5.

1681, which means that, given typical print runs, between 5 million and 10 million pamphlets were in circulation between 1679 and 1681.[92]

As before the passage of the 1662 Act, prosecutions to control the press after 1679 were based on royal prerogative and the issuance of judicial warrants to discover seditious libel (see *MV* 2.II).[93] Control by the government after 1679 was enforced by regulating the distribution of printed materials, this time typically targeting the poorest link in the publishing chain, the street hawkers. Authors, if known, also faced increased scrutiny. Thomas DeLaune (d. 1685) was charged with 'Not regarding his due *allegiance*, but contriving and intending to disquiet and disturb the peace and common Tranquillity of this Kingdom of *England*' for his reply to a sermon published by Dr Benjamin Calamy, *Discourse About A Scrupulous Conscience* (1683). DeLaune's pamphlet, *Plea For The Nonconformists* (1683), refutes Calamy's characterization of dissenters as being 'over nice' in their refusal to participate in elements of Anglican worship services by asserting that the current Church of England is closer to the Church of Rome in its love for ceremony and DeLaune compares the present-day dissenters to the Protestant martyrs who suffered under the reign of 'Bloody Mary', Mary I. The indictment against DeLaune also declares that his publication works to 'bring the said Lord the *King* into the greatest hate and contempt of his subjects—Machinating and farther intending to move stir up and procure *Sedition* and *Rebellion*, and to Scandalize the Book of *Common Prayer*'.[94] DeLaune, a translator and schoolteacher born in Ireland who had converted from Catholicism, probably had no such inclinations in mind, given that he signed his pamphlet 'Your Friend and Servant, *Thomas De Laune*'. Nevertheless, he was found guilty, the pamphlet was burned in front of the Royal Exchange, and he was fined 100 marks (just under £70). Unable to pay the fine, DeLaune was kept imprisoned in Newgate; as he was unable to support his family in London, his wife and children were eventually forced to join him there. He published a plea in 1684, *A Narrative Of The Sufferings Of Thomas DeLaune*, but no relief resulted, and, by 1685, all of the family had died in Newgate. DeLaune's *Plea For Nonconformists* was frequently reprinted after his death well into the nineteenth century; in 1706, Daniel Defoe, identifying himself on the title page as the author of the political periodical *The Review* (see *CV* 5.III), would publish another edition including DeLaune's narrative of his imprisonment, stating in his preface that the treatment of DeLaune 'will for ever stand as a Monument of the Cruelty of those Times'.[95]

Particular attention was paid to the activities of publishers for the Whig opposition, especially those offering topical 'news' papers and journals. These included the printers of many of the key documents in the Popish Plot and its trials, Benjamin Harris, Francis Smith, Henry Care, and Langley Curtis. Henry

[92] Harris, *Restoration*, 142. [93] Crist, 'The Expiration of the Printing Act'.
[94] Delaune, *A Narrative Of The Sufferings Of Thomas DeLaune*, 22.
[95] Defoe, 'Preface', in DeLaune, *Plea For The Nonconformists*, p. i.

Care (1646/7–88), who had previously published such innocuous titles as *The Female Secretary* (1671), a letter-writing guide for ladies, and translated texts on medicine, was in 1679 publishing an anti-Catholic newsletter, *The Weekly Pacquet of Advice from Rome*, which included in each issue a section called the *Popish Courant*, a satiric commentary on contemporary events aimed at what he described as 'middle or meaner Rank' of readers; he was also publishing allegorical satiric short fictions, *The Snotty-Nose Gazette* and *Poor Robin's Intelligence, Newly Revived*, for the same readership. Historians have estimated that Care was among the most active of the Whig publishers between 1678 and 1683.[96] He was brought in for examination for seditious libel on five occasions between 1679 and 1685; in 1679, he was accused of libelling Lord Chief Justice Sir William Scroggs and found guilty in July 1680. Scroggs, who presided at the trial, informed the jury in his summing up that 'So fond are Men in these Days, that when they will deny their Children a penny for Bread, they will lay it out for a Pamphlet', and he concluded the likes of Care cater in their writings to this sort of reader, who is 'only pleased when they discover writings against the government, for which their appetite is ravenous'.[97]

Perhaps the most notorious prosecution of a Whig publication, however, took place in Oxford, where the London artisan joiner and coffee-house poet Stephen College was tried for his ballad *A Ra-Ree Show* (1681), which was reportedly sung publicly in Oxford and at various Whig private gatherings, describing the King as a puppet master, who was repeating his doomed father's practices of 'Fleecing *Englands* Flocks', with the same result threatened—'the *Hunts* begun... Like Father, Like Son'. The song inspired two published cartoons, one showing Charles II being pushed over by Parliament while the Anglican bishops and courtiers are put into a 'bag of tricks', and a second depicting the Duke of York as the devil and the bishops as Jesuits. Although College denied writing this poem during his trial, supposedly on his way to his execution he did admit that he had 'uttered some words of Indecency... concerning the King' and warned his son about the dangers of writing verse.[98] Much in the same way as Sir Edmund Godfrey's bloody body became a popular representation of a Whig martyr to Catholic and court intrigues (see CV 3.II), Stephen College's image was sold in the streets of London and he was described as a 'martyr for the people's privileges' (*CSPD, July–Sept. 1683*, 309). On the other side, loyalist dramatists including Aphra Behn in *The Roundheads* (1682) and John Crowne in *City Politiques* (1683) included characters based on him as warnings about what happens when 'mechanicks' meddle in politics.

Licensing for all professional theatrical performances on stage still came under the eye of the Master of the Revels. The theatre manager Thomas

---

[96] See Lois G. Schwoerer, 'Care, Henry (1646/7–1688)', ODNB.

[97] Quoted in Auchter, *Dictionary of Literary and Dramatic Censorship*, 367. See also Greene, *The Trouble with Ownership*, 80–8.

[98] College, *A true copy of the dying words of Mr Stephen Colledge*.

Killigrew (1612–83) held this office briefly from 1673 to 1677, followed by his son, Charles Killigrew (1655–1724/5), who served from 1677 until his death in 1725 (see *MV* 4.II; *MV* 5.II). During Charles Killigrew's lengthy tenure, the office was under the direct control of the Lord Chamberlain, who was during this period Henry Bennet, Lord Arlington. As a result of the political turmoil of the late 1670s and early 1680s, there were a number of plays that were censored or even refused licences.[99] The 'very Scandalous Expressions and Reflections upon ye government' (*RETD* I. 218) caused Nathaniel Lee's historical tragedy *Lucius Junius Brutus* to be banned by the Lord Chamberlain after only a few performances in December 1680, although Lee was able to print it in 1681 with a dedication to the Earl of Dorset. The play features a character named Vinditius, who describes himself as 'a true Commonwealthsmen, and do not naturally love Kings', and a rebuke of a ruler who ignores a national crisis 'to lye at home and languish for a Woman!'[100] During that same month, Nahum Tate's version of Shakespeare's *Richard II* was suppressed and did not appear until 1682 in an obviously heavily revised version with the title *The Sicilian Usurper*. In his dedication in the printed 1681 version, Tate protests that 'why a History of those Times shou'd be supprest as a Libel upon Ours, is past my Understanding'.[101] When Thomas Shadwell printed his suppressed play, *The Lancashire-Witches* (1681), he included the censored parts of it in italics and denied any design to write a 'Satyr upon the Church of *England*', although the play does feature an Anglican chaplain named Smerk, probably an allusion to Marvell's controversial satire. It has also been described by critics as being largely written as a pro-Whig play mocking foolish Tory gentry, who superstitiously follow the dictates of the Crown and Anglican Church, thus potentially offending a large group of interested individuals.[102]

John Crowne, who had written the commissioned royal masque *Calisto* (see *MV* 3.1), nevertheless fell foul with two of his later plays, one an adaptation of Shakespeare's *2 Henry VI*, which was performed under the title *Henry the Sixth, The First Part* (1681), and a satiric comedy *City Politiques* (1682). Interestingly, the first of the plays offended for precisely the opposite reason that Shadwell's had—namely, for its hostile representation of Catholic characters, which caused it to be suppressed. The second was a sharp-edged attack on the events surrounding the Popish Plot and the Whig party's involvement dramatized under the guise of an exposé of Neapolitan political corruption. The central character, Paulo Camillo, is elected to be the 'Podesta' of Naples through the aid of Dr Panchy (Titus Oates) and the Bricklayer (Stephen College). A character named Craffy labours to write poems in response to Dryden's satires on Shaftesbury's manipulation of the Duke of Monmouth to

---

[99] See White, 'The Office of Revels and Dramatic Censorship'.
[100] Lee, *Lucius Junius Brutus*, II. i, pp. 14, 27.   [101] Tate, *The Sicilian Usurper*, 'Dedication'.
[102] See Slagle, 'Thomas Shadwell's Censored Comedy'.

raise a rebellion in *Absalom and Achitophel* and *The Medal*.[103] The topical allusions would have been unlikely to be missed by the London theatregoer, and the Whig Parliamentarians were successful in having it suppressed until Charles himself stepped in and permitted it to be staged again.

History plays in particular during this period seem to have raised official concern. Characters and events in Dryden and Lee's *The Duke Of Guise* (1682) were felt to be too close to contemporary ones to be staged. In the preface to the printed version that appeared in 1683, the authors deny any intention of portraying living figures in their characters, but the similarities between the recent acts of Duke of Monmouth and the historical Duke of Guise (both shown plotting to gain control of the government, both being sent away from court by the respective kings) is not hard to see. The King, when appealed to by Dryden, did permit the play to be staged, and it was performed before the Queen in December 1682. The same fate did not befall John Bank's *The Innocent Usurper* (1682?) and *The Island Queen* (1684). The first deals with the tribulations of Lady Jane Gray and the second with those of Mary Stuart, Queen of Scots. Killigrew refused licences for them both, and it was not until 1693 that *The Innocent Usurper* was printed and not until 1704 that *The Island Queen* was finally performed under the title *The Albion Queens* (see CV 5.II).

Not only authors came under the control of the Master of the Revels and the Lord Chamberlain, but also the actors themselves. The comic actor Joseph Haines was arrested on 8 June 1677, 'for reciteinge...a Scurrilous and obscoene Epilogue' (*RETD* 1. 197–8). The Theatre Royal itself was ordered closed by the Lord Chamberlain for ten days in January 1681. In 1682, *The True Protestant Mercury* for 12–16 August reported that Aphra Behn's epilogue for *Romulus And Hersilia; Or, The Sabine War*, spoken by the actress Lady Slingsby, 'reflected on the D. of Monmouth [and] the Lord Chamberlain has ordered them both in custody to answer that affront for the same' (*RETD* 1. 229). The epilogue in question was spoken by the character Terpeia—who has perjured herself for love in the play—and certainly seems a clear reference to Monmouth's recent fall from favour in 1681:

> Of all Treasons, mine was most accurst;
> Rebelling 'gainst a KING and FATHER first.
> A Sin, which Heav'n nor Man can e're forgive;
> Nor could I *Act* it with the face to live—

but there are no records of whether Behn, the loyal Tory writer, was indeed taken into custody or what excuse she might have offered. Likewise, the response of the actress to the charge has been lost.[104]

It was not only professional entertainers and politicians whose words were carefully scrutinized. Blasphemy cases were tried in the King's Bench Court as a common law offence after the case of *Rex v. Taylor* in 1676. In this ruling,

---

[103] See White, *John Crowne*, 123–37.   [104] See Todd, *The Secret Life of Aphra Behn*, 288–9.

Lord Chief Justice Sir Matthew Hale proclaimed that 'such kinds of blasphemous words were not only an offence to God and religion, but a crime against the laws, State, and Government, and therefore punishable in that Court'. He concluded that 'Christianity is parcel of the laws of England and therefore to reproach the Christian religion is to speak in subversion of the law'.[105] Londoner John Taylor had travelled to Guildford to preach in the streets that Christ 'is a Whore-master, and Religion... is a Cheat, and a Profession... God damn and confound all your Gods' and had been brought before the House of Lords to be examined.[106] He was initially sent to Bedlam and later tried and convicted for blasphemy, fined and sentenced to stand in a pillory both in Westminster and in Guildford with a paper on his head stating 'For Blasphemous Words tending to the Subversion of all Government'.[107] An anonymous pamphlet, *The Sweet-Singers of Israel, Or, The Family of Love* (1678), elaborated on the unorthodox nature of the religious observances of Taylor's fellow worshippers in London, alleging that they 'Sing obscene Songs in Psalm-Tunes; and Divine ones, in Ballad-Tunes'.[108]

Lodowicke Muggleton (1609–98) was tried and convicted at the Old Bailey on 17 January 1677 for blasphemy and also watched his books burn as he stood in the pillory with a paper stating his crime pasted on his head. The account of his trial explicitly connects preaching and the publishing of blasphemy, noting that, 'as all Hereticks covet to be Authors and Ring-leaders to a Sect, so by divers printed Books and Corner conferences, he easily seduced divers weak and instable people (especially of the Female-Sex) to become his Proselytes, who from him call themselves *Muggletonians*'.[109] When his house was searched in August 1676, 'a great quantity of his books were seized' which he had authored; in the indictment, specific passages from these books were included, but the contents are 'so horrid and blasphemous, that we think fit to spare the Christian modesty of each pious ear, by not repeating the same here, where there is no necessity for it' (p. 3).

The literary activity least likely to be censored or punished was the production of pornography, especially after the lapse of the Licensing Act in 1679. Trials for obscenity were less common than for political or religious speech transgressions (see *MV* 3.V), and the punishments and fines much less severe. In 1677, L'Estrange attempted to close down the shop of a bookseller named Wells for having unwittingly in his stock from a lot of books purchased from Amsterdam the scandalous *Escole des Filles* along with several other erotic titles 'which he did not conceive in any way prohibited in England'. This effort by L'Estrange was complained about to Secretary Williamson, and there is no record of further action taken.[110]

---

[105] *The King Against Taylor*, in *Pleas of the Crown*, 1. 226–8.
[106] Taylor, *Full and True Account*, 3.   [107] See Apetrei, 'The "Sweet Singers"'.
[108] *The Sweet-Singers of Israel*, 4.   [109] *Proceedings of the Old Bailey, 17th January 1677*, 3.
[110] See Foxon, *Libertine Literature*, 9–10.

In 1683, the printer John Wickins faced only a 40 shilling fine for printing *The Whores Rhetorick*, while at the same session bills were brought against Joanna Broom for publishing the political newsletter *The Observator* and Francis Smith was fined £10 for *The Irregular Account of Swearing the Two Pretended Sheriffs*. In 1684, the stationer William Cademan was indicted for 'exposing, selling, uttering and publishing the pernicious, wicked, scandalous, vicious and illicit book entitled *A Dialogue between A Married Lady, and a Maid Tullia Octavia*' (see MV 3.V). Unfortunately, whatever action against him was taken by the Westminster magistrates has not survived. Indeed, these pornographic titles had sufficiently wide circulation among readers to be found copied into a commonplace book and to be referenced by Edward Ravenscroft in his comedy *The London Cuckolds* (1682), where a character lamenting the precocity of young girls declares 'the other day I catcht two young wenches, the eldest not above twelve, reading the beastly, bawdy translated book called *the Schole of Women*'.[111] In the years between 1675 and 1684, what drew the attention of the law were issues about politics and matters of religious practice, not, as would be the case in the 1690s, what was read in the bedroom (see MV 4.II, 4.III).

III. Poets and the Politics of Patronage and Literary Criticism

> We are fallen into an Age of Illiterate, Censorious, and Detracting people, who thus qualified, set up for Critiques.
>
> John Dryden, 'The Authors Apology for Heroique Poetry; and
Poetique Licence', The State of Innocence, and Fall of Man (1677)

> My Lord,
>
> It was not without a great deal of debate with my self, that I could resolve to make this Present to Your Lordship: For though Epistles Dedicatory be lately grown so Epidemical, that either sooner or later, no man of Quality (whom the least Author has the least pretence to be troublesome to) can escape them; yet methought Your Lordship should be as much above the common Perplexities that attend Your Quality, as You are above the common Level of it, as well in the most Exalted Degrees of a Noble Generous Spirit, as in a piercing Apprehension, good Understanding, and daily ripening Judgment, all sweetned by an obliging Affability and Condescention.
>
> Thomas Otway, 'To the Lord Eland, Eldest Son to the Right
Honourable the Marquiss of Hallifax', The Atheist; or,
The second part of The soldiers fortune (1684)

---

[111] See Foxon, *Libertine Literature*, 4–6, and Thompson, 'Two Early Editions'.

Two figures feature prominently in the dedications and prologues written in the second part of the century: the critic and the patron. The first is typically characterized as a tasteless, self-aggrandizing commentator, typically depicted as holding forth in the pit of the theatre during a performance or later in a coffee house; lacking literary skills himself, this type of critic seeks to entertain those around him at an author's expense. The second is the late-seventeenth-century version of Maecenas, the revered patron of Virgil and Horace, whose good judgement, wit, and generosity ensure that great works of literature are created and preserved. A professional author in the latter part of the seventeenth century in England could not expect to live solely on sales to the booksellers and the theatre: competing for patrons and fending off damaging critics were part of the work of a commercial writer. While Charles II had reinstituted royal patronage in the form of royal appointments, in reality it was often hard to claim those wages: Dryden during his time as Poet Laureate (see CV 4.V) was often out of pocket, and, at the time of Charles's death in 1685, he was owed some £1,075.[112] Public approval by a prominent member of court could be the making of a play and playwright's fortunes, while a dismissive sneer could speed its demise.[113] Fortunately, during this period as well, many of the most prominent of the literary patrons, such as the Earls of Mulgrave and Roscommon, performed the role of the discerning critic as well, contributing to the growing body of texts reflecting on the characteristics of good and bad writing, and establishing the criteria by which works of translation and literary forms should be evaluated (see CV 4.III).

Literary historians have observed that, over the course of the eighteenth century, the older system of patronage—a wealthy, powerful individual who in a variety of ways supports others' careers—was gradually replaced for authors by the developing commercial marketplace for literary products.[114] During the 1670s and early 1680s, however, it was very much part of literary life, as testified to in prefaces and dedications in a variety of texts, from plays and volumes of verse to translations and sermons. Also during this period we see an expansion of published literary criticism, some of it by the same figures who served as patrons, and some by professional writers done with the conscious design of defining standards for English vernacular literature. In 1668, for example, Dryden had offered his *Essay of Dramatick Poesie* in the form of a conversation among four gentlemen, Eugenius, Crites, Lisdideius, and Neander, who hold differing views on the merits of classical and modern drama; in the use of dialogue to convey multiple critical perspectives, Dryden thus mimics the conventions of polite social exchange in his fictionalized critical discourse.[115] On

---

[112] Foss, *The Age of Patronage*, 48, 62. See also Korshin, 'Types of Eighteenth-Century Literary Patronage', 457.

[113] See Payne, ' "And Poets shall by Patron-Princes Live" '.

[114] See also Griffin, *Literary Patronage in England*, chs 1, 2.

[115] Trolander and Tenger, *Sociable Criticism*, ch. 4.

the other hand, the published responses to it and other works attempting to shape public literary taste often displayed an aggressive attack on the writer as well as the critical models they presented to the reader.

Some of the most prominent and powerful of the literary and artistic patrons of the later part of the seventeenth century were themselves highly regarded poets, and several of them also published works exploring literary merit and practice. Some of the patron–critics associated with Dryden include the Earl of Rochester, to whom Dryden had dedicated the libertine tragicomedy *Marriage à-la-Mode* (1673); an early supporter of Dryden, Rochester would become a mocking antagonist later on, apparently either tiring of what he perceived as Dryden's social ambitions or taking offence at Dryden's other chief patron in the 1670s, John Sheffield, Earl of Mulgrave. In Rochester's poem 'An Allusion to Horace', which circulated widely in manuscript from around 1675, Rochester not only attacks Dryden, but also passes judgement on other contemporary writers. Imitating loosely Horace's tenth satire, Rochester's poem opens with the bland assertion that,

> Well, Sir, 'tis granted I said Dryden's rhymes
> Were stol'n, unequal, nay dull many times.
> What foolish patron is there found of his
> So blindly partial to deny me this? (*POAS* 1. 358)

thus dismissing the taste of Dryden's patrons as well as the poet. He attacks Dryden's critiques of earlier writers, including Ben Jonson as being 'dull', Beaumont and Fletcher 'incorrect and full | Of lewd lines (as he call them)', and

> Shakespeare's style
> Stiff and affected, to his one the while
> Allowing all the justness that his pride
> So arrogantly had these deni'd. (*POAS* 1. 362)

While he admits that Dryden deserves the poet laureateship and 'His excellencies more than faults abound', nevertheless, Rochester declares that he will hold Dryden up to the same standard and try to determine 'If those gross faults his choice pen does commit | Proceed from want of judgment or of wit' (*POAS* 1. 362).

Rochester's dissection of another poet he had patronized, John Crowne (see *MV* 3.I), is almost as unflattering. If the amount of writing produced justified literary merit, Rochester observes, 'by that rule I might as well admit | Crowne's tedious scenes for poetry and wit'.[116] Likewise, Thomas Otway, who thanked Rochester for drawing royal attention to his play *Don Carlos, Prince of Spain* (1676) and dedicated *Titus and Berenice* and *The Cheats of Scapin* to Rochester when they were printed in 1677, also fell under Rochester's displeasure. Rochester sneeringly describes the young dramatist as labouring 'in vain' to 'divert the

---

[116] Rochester, 'An Allusion to Horace', *POAS* 1. 358.

rabble and the court'. Nathaniel Lee, who had secured Rochester for his patron for his early play *Nero* (1674), had lost favour with Rochester by *Sophonisba* (1675); in his satiric critique Rochester describes Lee as 'the hot-brain'd fustian fool' (*POAS* 1. 358) (see *CV* 3.I). What Rochester admires in contemporary writing, he declares, is Shadwell's 'force of nature, none of art. | With just, bold strokes he dashes here and there, | Showing great mastery with little care', and Wycherley, who 'wants no judgment nor he spares no pains' (*POAS* 1. 360–1). Edmund Waller, 'by nature for the bays design'd', Rochester applauds for 'force and fire and fancy unconfin'd'. He concludes his poem with a general recommendation to those who wish to write 'what may securely stand the test' to 'Scorn all applause the vile rout can bestow | And be content to please those few who know' (*POAS* 1. 362–3). Rochester specifically contrasts the 'poor praise | Of fops and ladies' with the 'shrewd judges in the drawing room'. 'I loathe the rabble', he concludes,

> 'tis enough for me
> If Sedley, Shadwell, Sheppard, Wycherly,
> Godolphin, Butler, Buckhurst, Buckingham,
> And some few more, whom I omit to name,
> Approve my sense. I count their censure fame. (*POAS*, 1. 363)

Conspicuously absent from Rochester's list of poet–patrons is one figure closely associated with Dryden from the mid-1670s until the poet's death in 1700: John Sheffield, Earl of Mulgrave (1647–1721) (who would be styled the Marquess of Normanby after 1693 and after 1703 the Duke of Buckingham). Mulgrave combined the roles of both patron and critic, as well as those of court wit, soldier, Lord Chamberlain, Privy Councillor, poet, and essayist.[117] Although Mulgrave had, along with Rochester, contributed a prologue to Dryden's rival in the theatre, Elkanah Settle's *The Empress of Morocco* (1673), he never wavered in his support of Dryden. Dryden dedicated his tragedy *Aureng-Zebe* to him in 1675 (see *CV* 3.I) and modelled the character of Adriel in *Absalom and Achitophel* (1681) on Mulgrave: 'Sharp-judging Adriel, the muses' friend. | Himself a muse: in Sanhedrin's debate | True to his prince, but not a slave of state.'[118] The two would remain closely associated for the rest of Dryden's life, with Dryden dedicating his final great translation of *The Aeneid* (1697) to his patron and literary collaborator (see *CV* 4.III).

In 1679 Mulgrave's own *An essay upon satyr* was circulating widely in manuscript copy. This verse is sometimes called the 'Rose Alley satire', which was widely attributed to Dryden at the time and perhaps resulted in the beating Dryden received in December 1679 at the hands of hired bullies in Rose Alley, supposedly hired by Rochester, although little evidence remains to prove that.[119] In his poem, Mulgrave touches on the multiple ways in which the times

---

[117] Margaret D. Sankey, 'Sheffield, John, first duke of Buckingham and Normanby (1647–1721)', *ODNB*.   [118] Dryen, *Absalom and Achitophel*, 29.
[119] See Gelber, *The Just and the Lively*, 157, and Winn, *John Dryden and his World*, 325–9.

are ripe for the satiric lash: *An essay upon satyr* castigates the King, his mistresses, and courtiers such as Rochester, Dorset, and Buckingham and presents to a limited extent Mulgrave's views on the art of satire.

Poetry, Mulgrave begins by striking a traditional note, has always been designed both to please and to instruct:

> Satire has always shone among the rest,
> And is the boldest way, if not the best,
> To tell men freely of their foulest faults;
> To laugh at their vain deeds, and vainer thoughts. (*POAS* 1. 402)

But its opening declares that the goal of satire is laughter and 'men aim rightest when they shoot in jest', and that, unlike the 'loose-writ libels of the age', to strive 'with sharp eyes those nicer faults to find | Which lie obscurely in the wisest mind' (*POAS* 1. 403). After Mulgrave's death, the young satirist and critic Alexander Pope (1688–1744) (see *MV* 5.V) edited his papers, revising this poem and suggesting that it had been in circulation since 1675. If this is so, Mulgrave was composing his satire on the moral failings of the courtiers during the period when he himself was conducting an affair with Moll Kirke, the mistress of both the Duke of York and the Duke of Monmouth and was subsequently wounded in a duel by her brother Captain Percy Kirke.

Mulgrave's critique is particularly venomous towards Rochester and his writings, testifying to a long-standing hostility between the two competing courtiers. Rochester had been challenged by Mulgrave to a duel in 1669, and, in various accounts, was declared by Mulgrave to be a coward as a result. A poet's character and his verse are inextricably linked: speaking of Rochester's reputation as a court wit and as a poet, 'Rochester I despise for want of wit, | (Though thought to have a tail and cloven feet)', Mulgrave begins, 'For while he mischief means to all mankind, | Himself alone the ill effects does find' (*POAS* 1. 412).

> False are his words, affected is his wit;
> So often he does aim, so seldom hit;
> To every face he cringes while he speaks,
> But when the back is turn'd, the head he breaks,

the poet charges; sneeringly he continues, 'I'd like to have left out his poetry; | Forgot by all almost as well as me', but 'So lewdly dull his idle works appear, | The wretched texts deserve no comments here' (*POAS* 1. 412).

Another of the courtiers who took Horace for his starting point to discuss contemporary poetry and morals was Sir Carr Scrope (1649–80). He contributed his thoughts on the topic in his 'In Defense of Satire' (1677), using Horace's fourth satire, book one, as its starting point. A minor figure at court and man of the town, Scrope contributed songs and prologues to several plays by Lee, and also provided translations to several printed miscellanies, including 'Sapho to Phaon' in Dryden's collection of *Ovid's Epistles* (1680) and two more for Dryden and Tonson's *Miscellany Poems* (1684) (see *CV* 3.III; *CV* 4.V).

Scrope, whom some believe may have been the model for Etherege's Sir Fopling Flutter in *Man of Mode*, was frequently himself the target for satiric lampoons by Rochester and other court wits; he was also mocked in Mulgrave's *Essay on satire*. In spite of this, like Mulgrave, Scrope defined the function of satire as moral: 'Nothing helps more than satire to amend | Ill manners, or is trulier virtue's friend' (*POAS* 1. 364). Satire, in Scrope's vision of literary modes, is to act as the medicine to cure societal illnesses: 'Look where you will and you shall hardly find | A man without some sickness of the mind' (*POAS* 1. 364). Like Mulgrave, he targets Rochester in particular, again tying the poet's perceived character with his limitations as a writer. He points witheringly to Rochester's involvement in a drunken 'frolic', in which Rochester drew his sword on a constable, and in the resulting scuffle one of his companions was killed as the rest fled: 'Yet him a witty, pleasant man you call. | To whet your dull debauches up and down, | You seek him as top fiddler of the town' (*POAS* 1. 367).

As seen in the response to this poem, patronage, literary criticism, and personal attack all mingle in the critical discourses in circulation in the late 1670s and 1680s. Rochester quickly retaliated to this use of him in Scrope's piece with 'On the Supposed Author of a Late Poems "In Defense of Satire"'. 'To rack and torture thy unmeaning brain | In satire's praise to a low unturned strain', he retorts, 'In thee was most impertinent and vain' (*POAS* 1. 371). Scrope countered with 'The Author's Reply': 'Rail on, poor feeble scribbler, speak of me | In as ill terms as the world speaks of thee' (*POAS* 1. 373), but Rochester had the final word, targeting Scrope in 'On Poet Ninny'. As critics have pointed out, 'Ninny' is a character in Shadwell's comedy *The Sullen Lovers* who bores the true wits in the play by reciting his own poetry and giving his views on the work of others.

On a more positive note, Dryden and his patron Mulgrave also collaborated on several other projects, such as the translation of the letter from Helen to Paris in Dryden's edition of *Ovid's epistles translated by several hands* (1680). Shortly thereafter, in 1682 Mulgrave published *An Essay upon Poetry*, a work much admired by his future editor, Alexander Pope, to whom he later would also act as a patron (see *MV* 5.III, 5.V). Based on Horace's *Ars Poetica*, the long verse essay establishes many of the themes that will be present in Pope's *Essay on Criticism* (1711) (see *MV* 5.V). 'Of Things in which Mankind does most excell, | Nature's chief Master-piece is writing well', opens Mulgrave's poem.[120] What makes good poetry is its genius rather than a strict adherence to form:

> A Spirit which inspires the work throughout,
> As that of Nature moves this World about;
> A heat that glows in every word that's writ,
> That's something of Divine, and more than Wit. (1. 130)

'True Wit' is 'everlasting, like the Sun, | Which though sometimes beneath a cloud retir'd, | Breaks out again, and is by all admir'd', while 'Number, and

---

[120] Sheffield, 'An Essay on Poetry', in *Works*, 1. 129.

Rime, and that harmonious sound, | Which never does the Ear with harshness wound, | Are necessary, yet but vulgar Arts' (1.130).

In Mulgrave's essay 'On Criticism' published in Pope's revised edition of Mulgrave's works, he observes that 'there have been always Criticks', some good, but more bad, and 'I believe there was never such an age and nation for that humour as our is at present'.[121] The criticism found in the 'eating-houses, coffee-houses, and play-houses...is nothing in the world but a mixture of ill-nature and ignorance' (2. 237); the danger of this sort of criticism is that 'these bleak winds are ever blasting all our hopeful blooms; for they hinder the modestest and best wits from writing'. 'Our Town-sparks think it consists in nothing but finding fault, which is but the least half of their work', Mulgrave asserts; indeed he admits, 'when I came first abroad into the world, being extremely young, I thought it a fine thing to laugh at ever body, to shew my wit; and fancied my self the better, as I represented others to be worse' (2. 238–9). Reflecting on his own writing, Mulgrave declares he 'seldom find[s] any thing worth commending, because of those great Idea's I have of the Antients: which make me yet more unsatisfied with my self than with any body else'. When he encounters merit in others works, 'I approve it gladly' (2.239).

As has been seen in the examples of the essays on satire modelled after the writings of Horace, the classics were the shared ground among the critics and patrons. Another of Dryden's patrons, Wentworth Dillon, 4th Earl of Roscommon (1637–85), had praised Katherine Philips's play *Pompey* (1663) and written a prologue for its Dublin performance (see *MV* 2.III). In 1679, now in London, he published a blank verse English translation of Horace's *Ars Poetica* as *Horace's Art of Poetry*, openly demonstrating his admiration for Milton's *Paradise Lost*; a few years later, Roscommon printed his highly praised *Essay on Translated Verse* (1684) with commendatory verses by Dryden and members of his informal 'academy'.

Like Mulgrave's essay, Roscommon's is written in couplet form, and, like his, it stresses the moral and didactic function of literature more than the specific the technical aspects of translation. ''Tis true, *Composing* is the *Nobler* Part, | But good *Translation* is no *easie* Art', Roscommon admits, 'by *Improving* what was writ *Before*; | *Invention* Labours *Less*, but *Judgment*, *more*'.[122] Roscommon urges the English translator to choose carefully an author not only for his merits as a writer, but also for the individual's character:

> Examine how your *Humour* is inclin'd,
> And which the *Ruling Passion* of your Mind;
> Then, seek a *Poet* who *your* way do's bend,
> And chuse an *Author* as you chuse a *Friend*.
>
> .   .   .   .   .   .
>
> Your *Thoughts*, your *Words*, your *Stiles*, your *Souls* agree,
> No Longer his *Interpreter*, but *He*. (p. 7)

---

[121] Sheffield, *Works*, 2. 237.   [122] Dillion, *Essay on Translated Verse*, 5.

Regardless of the poet selected for translation, '*Immodest words* (whatever the Pretence) | Always *want* Decency, *and* often, Sense' (p. 8); however, Roscommon warns, 'Yet 'tis not all to have a Subject, *Good* | It must *Delight* us when 'tis *understood*' (p. 9) and 'Be not too fond of a Sonorous Line; | Good Sence *will through a* plain expression *shine*', sentiments that will again be found to resonate in Pope's *Essay on Criticism* (1711) (see MV 5.V).

Literary historians have drawn attention to the informal literary academy centred around Roscommon that focused its energies on the arts of translation and its informal ambitions to create a British Academy to refine and fix the English language, as the French Academy had done for that literature.[123] Its members included Dryden, Rochester's correspondent George Savile, marquess of Halifax, the Earl of Dorset, Lord Cavendish, who would become the Duke of Devonshire, Richard Maitland, later the Earl of Lauderdale, Sir Charles Scarburgh, Colonel Heneage Finch, the husband of the poet Anne Finch and future Earl of Winchilsea (see MV 5.V), and Knightly Chetwood (bap. 1650–1720), whose manuscript memoir establishes the existence of this group of poet–patrons.[124] Chetwood, who would later become the Dean of Gloucester, while a student at Cambridge had contributed both English and Latin verses to *Letters and Poems in Honour of ... Margaret, Duchess of Newcastle* (1676) and published *An Ode in Imitation of Pindar on the Death of ... Thomas, Earl of Ossory* (1681). On coming to London, he entered Roscommon's circle and provided Dryden and Tonson with translations for *Plutarch's Lives* (1683) and from Virgil for *Miscellany Poems* (1684). According to Chetwood, the members of this group, in addition to translating individual authors—George Savile translating Tacitus and Maitland Virgil—undertook a critical assessment of English texts and 'they purposed severally to peruse our best writers, & mark such words, as they thought vulgar, base, improper, or obsolete'.[125]

Other powerful patron–poets in this group were Charles Sackville, 6th Earl of Dorset and 1st Earl of Middlesex (1643–1706), and William Cavendish, Duke of Newcastle (bap. 1593–1676). Dorset, whose libertine antics with companions Sir Charles Sedley and Sir Thomas Ogle so scandalized Samuel Pepys in the 1660s (see MV 2.IV), had gained an early reputation as well for his part in the translation of Corneille's *La Mort de Pompée* (1663) and for his ballad 'To All ye Ladies now on Land' (1664); Dryden included him in his *Of Dramatick Poesy* in the character of Eugenius, who argues for the merits of contemporary English drama and poetry as superior to the Elizabethans and even the classics.[126] He continued that pattern of patronage found in the long life of William Cavendish, Duke of Newcastle, who had been one of the principal patrons of Ben Jonson in the 1630s to the war, and who had continued to

---

[123] Niemeyer, 'The Earl of Roscommon's Academy'.   [124] CUL MS Mm.1.47
[125] Chetwood MS, in Considine, *Academy Dictionaries*, 102.
[126] Harold Love, 'Sackville, Charles, sixth Earl of Dorset and first Earl of Middlesex (1643–1706)', *ODNB*.

support poets and dramatists after the Restoration, collaborating with Dryden in the 1660s on the successful comedy *Sir Martin-Mar-All*. Cavendish also supported Thomas Shadwell's career, frequently having him to stay at Welbeck Abbey; Shadwell dedicated four plays to him, including *The Libertine* (1676), and after the Duke's death supervised the publication of some of Cavendish's plays. George Etherege likewise had sought patronage from the Newcastle family, offering a poem 'To her Excellence the Marchioness of Newcastle after the Reading of her Incomparable Poems' (see *MV* 2.VI).

Both Shadwell and Etherege enjoyed Dorset's patronage, with Etherege engaging in a poetic correspondence in 1663–4 and dedicating his first play *The Comical Revenge* to him. Like Cavendish, Dorset frequently entertained writers and musicians at his country home at Thole, which had its own room devoted to the poets' portraits, including poets and men of letters he admired in addition to those he supported. The gallery included such notables as John Locke, John Milton, and Sir Isaac Newton.[127] Over his long career, Dorset supported many of the leading literary figures of the day, as well as numerous ones largely faded from literary history. In addition to supporting Dryden, Etherege, and Shadwell, he served as patron for many of the most active dramatists throughout the end of the century including D'Urfey, Lee, Otway, William Congreve, Nahum Tate, whom he supported for the poet laureateship, and Matthew Prior, whom he made his protégé while Prior was still at school and who would dedicate to Dorset his *Satire upon the Poets* (1694) (see *MV* 4.V). A former member of his household, Robert Gould, dedicated three of his satires to Dorset: *Satyr against Woman*, *The Playhouse*, and *Satyr against Man*, noting apologetically in the dedication of the *Satyr against Man* that 'the best Excuse the Author of a Dedication can make his Patron, is, in my Judgment, to Assure him he shall not be troubl'd with his future Impertinence'.[128]

In the 1690s and early 1700s, Dorset had plays dedicated to him by Catherine Trotter (*Agnes de Castro*, 1696) and Susanna Centlivre (*Love's Contrivance*, 1703). Dorset also offered his support even without poem or a play being dedicated to him—for example, when in 1679 he came to the financial rescue of theatre manager William Killigrew when the King's pension failed to materialize.[129] While Aphra Behn never solicited his patronage with a dedication, she, like so many other hopeful writers, celebrated his second marriage with *A Pastoral Pindarick. On the Marriage of the Right Honourable the Earle of Dorset...to the Lady Mary Compton* (1685). In *A pindarick poem on the happy coronation of His Most Sacred Majesty James II and his illustrious consort Queen Mary* (1685) she describes Dorset as

> A *Hero* more than half a God,
> Whom all the Graces and the Charms Adorn;

[127] Harris, *Charles Sackville*, pt IV, 'Patron of Literature', 196.
[128] Gould, *Poems*, 'The Epistle Dedicatory'.   [129] Harris, *Charles Sackville*, 180.

Whom ev'ry Muse, and Vertue do's inspire,
Whom all the Witty, Great, and Good, admire.[130]

Dryden and Dorset enjoyed a harmonious working relationship from the mid-1660s until Dryden's death in 1700; when Dryden was forced to resign the poet laureateship in 1689 with the crowning of William III, it was Dorset who paid up his salary (see CV 4.V). Dryden frequently sent Dorset copies of his plays before they were staged; in the preface of *Don Sebastian* (1690), dedicated to Philip Sidney, 3rd Earl of Leicester (1616–98), Dryden dismisses those critics who had condemned parts of its actions because 'the Earl of Dorset was pleased to read the tragedy twice over before it was acted, and did me the favour to send me word, that I had written beyond any of my former plays, and that he was displeased anything should be cut away'.[131] Dryden concludes, 'if I have not reason to prefer his single judgment to a whole faction, let the world judge' (p. 13).

Over his long literary career, Dryden printed many works of literary criticism in a variety of formats. As we have seen, his first efforts used literary forms such as dialogues and epistles to friends and patrons. In the 1670s he also began engaging directly with literary critics such as Thomas Rymer (1642/3–1713); Dryden wrote to Dorset, who was a patron of Rymer's, in 1678 from the country that 'Mr Rymer sent me his booke, which has been my best entertainment hitherto...'tis certainly very learned & the best piece of Criticism in the English tongue; perhaps in any other of the modern'.[132] Although Dryden concedes that he is not always in perfect agreement with Rymer's views (see CV 3.I), he jests that he is happy, 'that he has not fallen upon me, as severely and as wittily as he has upon Shakespeare, and Fletcher' (p. 13). Rymer's *The Tragedies of the Last Age Consider'd* (1678), printed by Richard Tonson, Jacob Tonson's brother (see CV 3.III), was written as a letter to his friend, the courtier Fleetwood Sheppard (1634–98), who was closely connected to Dorset; upon Dorset's being appointed by William III to be the chamberlain of the royal household, Sheppard became the avenue of patronage from Dorset.[133]

In his letter to Sheppard, Rymer examines 'the choicest and most applauded *English Tragedies* of that last age; as *Rollo*; *A King and No King*; the *Maid's Tragedy*, by *Beaumont and Fletcher*; *Othello*, and *Julius Cæsar*, by *Shakespeare*; and *Cataline* by Worthy Ben'.[134] (pp. 1–2). Reflecting on the earliest classical dramas, Rymer muses that 'I had heard that the *Theater* was wont to be call'd the *School* of *Vertue*; and *Tragedy* a *Poem* for *Kings*', but 'surely (thought I) mens brains lye not in the same place as formerly; or else Poetry is not now the same thing it was in those days of yore' (p 2). Rymer purposes to make an examination of 'what *difference* might be in our *Philosophy* and *Manners*; I found that our *Philosophers* agreed well enough with theirs, in the *main*;

[130] Behn, *A pindarick poem on the happy coronation*, 13.
[131] Dryden, *Don Sebastian*, 'Preface'.   [132] Dryden, *Letters*, 13.
[133] Frank H. Ellis, 'Sheppard, Sir Fleetwood (1634–1698)', *ODNB*.
[134] Rymer, *The Tragedies of the Last Age*, 1–2.

however, that our Poets have forc'd another way to the *wood*; a *by-road*, that runs directly cross to that of *Nature, Manners* and *Philosophy* which gain'd the *Ancients* so great veneration' (p. 3). Comparing the classical dramas and the modern, he observes that, while '*Nature* is the same, and *Man* is the same, he *loves, grieves, hates, envies,* has the same *affections* and *passions* in both places, and the same *springs* that give them *motion*. What mov'd *pity* there, will *here* also produce the same effect' (p. 8).

Thus it is not necessarily the problem of the temperament of the two nations, for 'the *English* want neither *genius* or *language* for so great a work' (p. 11). If modern dramatists would have followed the models of Sophocles and Euripides in composing the plots of their tragedies, 'we might e're this day have seen Poetry in greater perfection, and boasted such *Monuments* of wit as *Greece* or *Rome* never knew in all their *glory*'. Tragedy, Rymer insists, is not history and should be tied not to facts but to ideals.

Unlike Rymer, who, even though he wrote dramas, took a strictly historical perspective on criticism using the classical past and the dramas of the Elizabethans to establish the criteria for evaluating literary merit, Dryden throughout his long and prolific career frequently turned to his own works as the occasion to ponder both literary history and the nature of genre. While the 1690s saw Dryden's critical attentions at their peak, simultaneous with his most important translations of Virgil and Aesop (see CV 4.V), in the 1670s and 1680s he was critiquing his own earlier writings. In the 'Prologue' to *Aureng-Zebe* (1676) he explains his decision to stop writing plays in rhyme in preference for the 'natural' language of blank verse. In the epilogue he laments the failings of his very successful *The Conquest of Granada* (1672): 'He thought in hitting these, his bus'ness done, | Though he, perhaps, has fail'd in ev'ry one.'[135] In 'The Authors Apology for Heroique Poetry; and Poetique License' that prefaces *The State of Innocence* (1677), his opera treatment of *Paradise Lost*, Dryden analyses how the classical past can provide rules for writing that have proved true throughout time but also provide 'Hypercritiques', which use the strict adherence to all rules as the standard of judgement as an artificial measure with which to degrade authors: 'they wholly mistake the Nature of Criticism, who think its business is principally to find fault. Criticism', asserts Dryden, 'as it was first instituted by *Aristotle*, was meant a Standard of judging well. The chiefest part of which is to observe those Excellencies which should delight a reasonable Reader'.[136] Speaking of those critics who find epic and heroic verse to be less 'perfect' in its form than tragedy, 'I do not dispute the preference of Tragedy; let every Man enjoy his tast', Dryden observes, 'but 'tis unjust, that they who have not the least notion of Heroique writing, should therefore condemn the pleasure which others receive from it, because they cannot comprehend it' (sig. b2ᵛ). 'Let them please their appetites in eating what they like', he

---

[135] Dryden, *Aureng-Zebe*, 87.   [136] Dryden, *The State of Innocence*, sig. b1ᵛ.

concludes, 'but let them not force their dish on all the Table'. Recognizing and responding to the power of the work to move its listeners and readers as opposed to judging merely its formal correctness, Dryden, while defending the classical unities, nevertheless declares: 'those Springs of humane Nature are not so easily discover'd by ever superficial Judge: It requires Philosophy as well as Poetry, to sound the depth of all the Passions; what they are in themselves, and how they are to be provok'd: and in this Science the best Poets have excell'd' (sig. b3ʳ).

Shakespeare's rather than Dryden's own works provided him with the occasion to reflect on English literary tradition and to attempt to rewrite Shakespeare. Following classical models of Aristotle, Horace, and Longinus, Dryden offered his reworking of Shakespearean tragedy in *All for Love or, the World Well Lost* (1678) and *Troilus and Cressida* (1679). The appeal of the story of Antony and Cleopatra, Dryden notes, is that it is a profoundly moral one: 'For the chief persons represented were famous patterns of unlawful love; and their end accordingly was unfortunate'.[137] Dryden observes that his version of the tragic love story succeeds in preserving the unities of time, place, and action 'more exactly observed, than perhaps the English theatre requires' (sig. B1ʳ). While embracing Aristotle, he rejects the sterile classicism of the French academy: 'French poets, I confess, are strict observers of these punctilios', with the result that the manners of French heroes 'are the most civil people breathing; but their good breeding seldom extends to a word of sense; all their wit is in their ceremony; they want the genius which animates our stage' (sig. B1ᵛ). Likewise, although rejecting Shakespeare's vast and rambling plot, 'in my style, I have professed to imitate the divine Shakespeare; which that I might perform more freely, I have disencumbered myself from rhyme. Not that I condemn my former way, but that this is more proper to my present purpose' (sig. B1ᵛ).

The issue of secondary plots arises again in his reworking of *Troilus and Cressida*. He prefaces the printed version with an essay, 'The Grounds of Criticism in Tragedy'. In this he is more critical of Shakespeare and his play. He opens by observing that *Troilus* surely must have been one of Shakespeare's earliest efforts at tragedy: 'many of his words, and more of his Phrases, are scarce intelligible. And of those which we understand some are ungrammatical, others coarse; and his whole stile is so pester'd with Figurative expressions, that it is as affected as it is obscure'.[138] Dryden is aggressive in his critique of the original play's faults: 'the later part of the Tragedy is nothing but a confusion of Drums and Trumpets, Excursions and Alarms', he notes, and, contrary to Aristotelian theory, Troilus and Cressida do not die in the end and, worse, 'Cressida is false, and is not punish'd'. 'Because the Play was *Shakespear's*, and that there appear'd in some places of it, the admirable Genius of the Author', Dryden concludes, 'I undertook to remove that heap of Rubbish, under which many excellent thoughts lay wholly bury'd' (sig. a1ʳ). This involved extensive

---

[137] Dryden, *All for Love*, sig. B1ʳ, 'Preface'.
[138] Dryden, *Troilus and Cressida*, sig. a1ʳ, 'Preface'.

reorganization of the plot—'no leaping from *Troy* to the Grecian Tents, and thence back again in the same Act' for Dryden (sig. a1ʳ).

Turning from his revision of Shakespeare, Dryden examines the grounds of tragedy as found in Aristotle and the development of the double plot by Terence in Rome. Aristotle's definition of tragedy as involving 'one intire, great, and probable action', as he notes, disqualifies all of Shakespeare's historical plays as chronicles. Concerning character or what he calls 'manners', which motivate action, Dryden is adamant that the hero of a tragedy must be admirable, not a villain, in order to move the audience to pity, and, as for 'a perfect character of virtue, it never was in Nature; and therefore there can be no imitation of it: but there are allays of frailty to be allow'd for the chief Persons, yet so that the good which is in them, shall outweigh the bad'.[139]

He then turns to an analysis of the tragedies of Shakespeare and Fletcher as representing the English lineage of the genre. ''Tis one of the excellencies of *Shakespear*, that the manners of his persons are generally apparent; and you see their bent and inclinations. *Fletcher* comes far short of him in this, as indeed he does almost in every thing: there are but glimmerings of manners in most of his Comedies.' Citing Longinus on the sublime, Dryden maintains as a principal rule of tragedy that 'passions be Artfully employ'd', and the discourse must match it. 'There is nothing more ridiculous than a great passion out of season', Dryden notes, pointing to Longinus's criticism of Aeschylus,

who writ nothing in cold blood, but was always in a rapture, and in fury with his Audience: the Inspiration was still upon him, he was ever tearing it upon the Tripos; or (to run off as madly as he does, from one similitude to another) he was always at high floud of Passion, even in the dead Ebb, and lowest Watermark of the Scene. (sig. b1ᵛ)

While Shakespeare clearly understood the passions, 'he often obscures his meaning by his words, and sometimes makes it unintelligible' (sig. b1ᵛ). 'I will not say of so great a Poet', Dryden concedes, 'that he distinguish'd not the blown puffy stile, from true sublimity; but I may venture to maintain that the fury of his fancy often transported him, beyond the bounds of Judgment', resulting in 'coyning of new words and phrases, or racking words which were in use, into the violence of a Catachresis' (sig. b2ᵛ). Even given these failings, Dryden concludes, '*Shakespear* had an Universal mind, which comprehended all Characters and Passions; *Fletcher* a more confin'd, and limited … he either touch'd not, or not *Masterly*. To conclude all; he was a Limb of *Shakespear*' (sig. b2ᵛ).

This desire to understand what gives a literary work lasting merit and acclaim would inspire Dryden, his patrons, and his critics throughout his long career. Patronage, which was so important to Dryden and his contemporaries, could take a variety of forms and formats, from polite social dialogues and imitations of the classics, to personal satires attacking the merits of a rival poet's character as well as his writings. Professional writers such as Dryden,

---

[139] Dryden, *Troilus and Cressida*, sig. a2ʳ.

Shadwell, Behn, Congreve, Rymer, and Wycherley were able to be commercially successful in part due to the support and promotion by their amateur patron–critics, who, in turn, were also helping to shape the emerging discourse of English literary criticism.

IV. Theatrical Entertainments Outside the London Commercial Playhouses: Smock Alley, Strollers, School Plays, and Private Performances

The decade between the staging of Wycherley's *The Country-Wife* (1675) at the King's Theatre and the reduced London theatre season of 1685, which staged only three dramas with the United Company, was nevertheless rich in opportunities for Londoners and those living outside the capital to enjoy and to participate in a variety of theatrical entertainments (see CV 3.I). The city of London provided free civic pageants such as those by the veteran actor and writer Thomas Jordan (*c*.1614–85), including *London in Luster* (1679) and *London's Joy* (1681). Students at Oxford and Cambridge, as well as at schools including Merchant Taylor's and various 'dancing schools', performed original dramas written for special occasions. Smock Alley in Dublin staged the tragicomedy *Belphegor, Or, The Marriage of the Devil* in 1677, and its troupe of actors several times performed in Oxford. Drolls, short comic sketches with titles such as *Love lost in the Dark, or, the Drunken Couple*, were performed at Newmarket when the court was visiting in 1680. In August of every year Bartholomew Fair entertained its crowds with titles such as *The Irish-Evidence* and *The Humours of Teague, or The Mercenary Whore* (1682). Twice a year the Inns of Court offered its guests the entertainment of a banquet and a play performed by one of the London companies. Finally, dramas preserved in manuscript copies, such as that written by Anne Wharton (1659–85), *Love's Martyr, or Witt Above Crowns*, (*c*.1679),[140] preserved in a fair copy dedicated to Mrs Mary Howe, may have offered friends and family occasions for private readings and performances.

There were numerous groups of travelling performers who staged events in private homes as well as in provincial cities. The group of Italian comedians who had arrived in England in June of 1675 performed before the King at Whitehall that summer, and the troupe, which included the famous comic Scaramouch (Tiberio Fiorilli), gave public performances there as well. In 1677, a troupe of French actors arrived, whose costumes and materials were directed to be landed free of Customs and subsequently exported in '70 Bales' of their belongings, also free of Customs (*RETD* 201, 204). On that occasion, Sir Christopher Wren was ordered to make the Whitehall stage 'as it was for

---

[140] BL Add. MS 28693.

Scarmouch's Acting and his Majesty's seate to be placed & made as then it was... also to make such boxes & partitions as the ffrench Comeadians shall desire you' (*RETD* 193). The Duke of Modena's company toured in 1678–9, as did the Prince of Orange's troupe in 1683–4. Charles and his courtiers so enjoyed these visiting foreign performers that, in 1684, money was paid from 'secret service' funds for players to accompany the court to Windsor and Winchester (*RETD* 250). He also patronized the English players while away from London: *The True Protestant Mercury* (17 October 1682) reports that, while Charles was in Newmarket, 'His Majesty every morning recreates Himself upon the Heath, and in the evening (after Horse racing) to see a Play acted by his Majesty's Servants'.

We have scattered references to performances during this period in Dublin and more to the Duke of Ormond's troupe, which frequently toured in England and thus required licences (see *MV* 3.II). *The Loyal Protestant*, for example, reported in its 13 August 1681 issue that 'From Dublin we hear, That a Play was lately acted there, which lively described a Subborner, and Malice against Innocence. But as guilty Conscience always discovers it self that one of the Spectators... seeing himself thus drawn to life, tho' not intended by the Poet, began to sweat and blush'. The account concludes humorously when the mortified spectator 'all in a rage... went to the Lord Lieutenant, and complained that the Actors had abused him, and the Play was made purposely to expose him to the world'.

More modest groups of entertainers, sometimes identified as 'Strollers', were also required to obtain a licence to perform from the Master of the Revels (see *MV* 2.III). The manager of the future United Company of actors, Charles Killigrew (see *CV* 3.1), held the office between 1677 and 1725, after a brief legal skirmish with his father Thomas, who reluctantly released it.[141] Both Killigrews issued frequent notices in the *London Gazette* reminding the performers and justices of the peace of the need for the entertainers to have a current, valid licence. The Mayor's Court Book for Norwich suggests a lively interest in dramatic entertainment in that city.[142] John Coysh and his company and Cornelius Saffery and associates were licensed in 1672 to perform 'Comedies tragedies pastorall & interludes' and made a contribution to the 'hamper' for the city's poor in the amount of 20 shillings.[143] Over December and January of 1673–4, 'Mr Perin' of the Duke of Monmouth's company also played there, but was refused a request for a third extension of his time in the city. In November 1676, it is recorded that Mr Robert Parker 'had lycence to act Pieces of plaies & drolls according to a Lycence under the Sale of the Office of Revells for Tenn days from Monday nxt at ye Redd Lion in St Stevens' (*RETD* 190) and his name reappears frequently for this venue as his licence to perform was extended.

---

[141] See White, 'The Office of Revels and Dramatic Censorship'.
[142] See Rosenfeld, 'Players in Norwich', and her *Strolling Players and Drama*.
[143] Quoted in Rosenfeld, 'Players in Norwich', 131.

Norwich was such a successful venue for Parker, it appears, that he returned in the autumn of 1678 as 'Master of the Players' with a licence to perform full-length 'plaies Comadies & Tragedies' as long as he observed 'good orders & Howres and not to act or Keepe Companie together after 9 at night' (*RETD* 190, 207). In December 1680, Parker's original licence was extended for ten days because of poor weather, 'they absteyning every day next weeke except monday next' (*RETD* 218).

In addition to plays, short interludes, and drolls, the Norwich Mayor's Court Book also records various other forms of dramatic entertainment. Robert Austin's licence to 'make shew of a Motion of Poppetts' was incorrectly titled and had to be amended to read 'Edward ye Fourth & Jane Shore', not 'Henry ye Fourth' (*RETD* 235). Likewise, rope-dancing such as performed by the celebrated Jacob Hall (fl. 1662–81)—also celebrated for his affair with Lady Castlemaine and frequently mentioned in contemporary songs and verses—was among the entertaining performances that amused visitors at Bartholomew and Southwark fairs, as well as Sturbridge Fair in Cambridge. *The Loyal Protestant* for 7 September 1682 announced that 'the famous Indian Water Works, adorned with several new additions…together with Masquerades, Songs and Dances', can be seen at the Bartholomew Fair at 'the Old Elephant's Ground near Osier Lane', while Cornelius Saffery's troupe would perform *The Irish-Evidence* at a booth near the Greyhound Inn.[144] A poem published in the 1683 edition of *The Compleat Courtier: or, Cupid's Academy* nicely summarizes the variety of entertainments and spectacles offered at Bartholomew Fair:

> Here's the woman of Babylon, the Devil and the Pope,
> And here's the little girl just going on the Rope;
> Here's Dives and Lazarus and the World's Creation,
> Here's the Tall Dutch Woman, the like's not in the Nation.
> Here is the Booths where the High Dutch Maid is,
> Here are the Bears that dance like any Ladies;
> Tat, tat, tat, tat, says little penny Trumpet;
> Here's Jacob Hall, that does so jump it, jump it.[145]

The Oxford colleges were a popular destination for visiting acting companies, in addition to hosting plays written and performed by the fellows and students themselves. In the 1670s a new theatre was built, and the City Council Book entry for June records that orders had to be issued to stop irate parishioners of St Mary Magdalen, who were threatening 'to disturb his royal highnesse the Duke of York's servants…in building their play-house in Broken Heys where the City have gave them leave to build'.[146] These players apparently gave several performances of Elkanah Settle's first tragedy *Cambyses, King of Persia*, the prologue for the Oxford performances being preserved in two manuscript

---

[144] See Morley, *Memoirs*, 220–5, and *London Stage*, pp. xliv–xlvii.
[145] *The Compleat Courtier*, 128.   [146] See Rosenfeld, 'Some Notes on the Players', 367.

versions. In addition to the playhouse at Broken Hays, in 1671 there were performances at the New Tennis Court near St Aldates, an apparently spartan
playing space described in Settle's prologue as lacking in 'ornament and Scene
| Which the chiefe grandeur of a Play Maintain'.[147] A decade later, in 1681, *The
True Protestant Mercury* of 19–23 March records that the King on his visit to
Oxford 'was pleased to be present at the first Play here, being Tamerlane the
Great, where also was the Dutchess of Portsmouth and Madam Guin'. No
doubt the presence of the King and two of the royal mistresses made the performance even more memorable for the citizens of Oxford.

In Oxford in 1677, the Duke of Ormond's Irish 'Players who were with us at
the Act and twenty days after' earned £600–700 'clear gains' while charging
'much at the same rate the Kings and Dukes used to do' (*RETD* 199). The
comic actor Joseph Haines (d. 1701), who had begun his career with John
Coysh's strolling players in Cambridge, wrote the epilogue to one of their productions, which makes reference to the apparent misbehaviour of members of
the King's Company in previous visits: 'The Town Shee Players that lead such
merry lives', it opens,

> She was both seen, felt, heard and understood;
> She was understood so well—
> That if she had stay'd, I'm told to her renown,
> She 'ad civilly been carted out of Town.[148]

In 1680, both the King's Company and the Duke of Ormond's visiting
Smock Alley Irish players applied to the Vice-Chancellor of the University for
permission to perform, which appears to have caused local consternation.
Timothy Halton wrote that he hoped the King's Company would not be
granted a longer extension to their playing dates, as 'several young Gentlemen
of good Estates & fortune are undone by them, and the poorer sort of scholars
spend that money on these Plays wch should support them for a considerable
space…& when yt small stock fails them they sell their books'.[149] There are
also records during this period of plays being written and performed by scholars
in the various colleges at both Oxford and Cambridge as well as by students in
private schools. Joshua Barnes (1654–1712), a fellow of Emmanuel College,
Cambridge, and author of *Gerania* (1675) based on Homer's *Iliad*, had several
of his dramas performed there. These ranged from the comedy *The Academy
or The Cambridge Dons* on 28 June 1675, *Englebert*, an operatic tragedy, in
1680, and *Landgartha, or The Amazon Queen of Denmark* in 1683.[150] Younger
students were also involved in performing dramas. *Musick; Or A Parley Of
Instruments*, a short and much simpler mixture of pastoral dialogues and

[147] Rosenfeld, 'Some Notes on the Players', 367.
[148] Rosenfeld, 'Some Notes on the Players', 369.
[149] Rosenfeld, 'Some Notes on the Players', 370.
[150] Harbage, *Annals of English Drama*, rev. Schoenbaum, 180–1, 184–5.

instrumental music, was performed by an unnamed music school and licensed for print by Roger L'Estrange in 1676.

The same year, 'The Scholars of Mr Jeffery Banister, AND Mr James Hart, At their New BOARDING-SCHOOL for Young Ladies and Gentlewomen, kept in that House which was formerly Sir Arthur Gorges, AT CHELSEY', performed Thomas Duffett's masque *Beauties Triumph*, printed in 1676. The prologue, 'spoken by a young Lady', welcomes the audience but warns that

> This was intended for our selves alone,
>
> .   .   .   .   .
>
> —and beg a kind excuse,
> For straiten'd time, and a disorder'd House[151]

and hopes that 'the want of practice, fitting dress, | And glorious Scenes, may make our failings less'. Even with this declaration of modest ambitions, the complicated opening scene displays 'Fate' sitting on a throne, '*dress'd in a dark-colour'd Robe, powder'd with Swords, Stars, Daggers, Books, Flames and Crowns, &c.—a Crown on his head, a Globe at his feet, and a great Book open before him: near his feet sit the Three Fatal Sisters, one holding a Distaff, another Spinning and drawing out Threads, and the third cutting them*'. In addition to this striking tableau,

> On the Stage stand a King and Queen crown'd, and richly habited; a Hero crown'd with Laurel, and a Slave chain'd:—near him a beautiful Lady, and a despairing Lover:—a man and woman, whose dress express Poverty and Misery: in the midst of all stands Death, threatning with his Dart and Hour-glass.—Thus all continue, while a solemn Ayr is play'd by Violins, Rechorders, &c. (p. 1)

Parents must have been pleased indeed to see their daughters so elegantly displayed.

On the other hand, William Johns, a schoolmaster, penned *The Traitor To Himself, Or, Mans Heart his greatest Enemy*, a 'Moral Interlude In Heroic Verse', performed in 1678 'by the Boys of a Publick School at a Breaking up, And Published as it may be useful, on like occasion', printed and sold in Oxford and Evesham. In his epistle to the reader, Johns explains that 'I am not ignorant of the multitude of Plays that are already extant, but I could never find any that in my apprehension was suitable to such an occasion, being either full of Vanity and so apt to corrupt young Minds, or with Women's Parts, which I never thought fit to put on Boys'.[152] He also defends the choice of English heroic verse over Latin or Greek, noting that the performance is designed 'chiefly for the entertainment of the Governours of the School, who with a fatherly care yearly honoured us with their presence' ('To the Reader'). In a similar didactic vein, the prolific author and educator Samuel Shaw (1634/5–96) printed in 1683 his

---

[151] Duffett, *Beauties Triumphant*, 'Prologue'.
[152] Johns, *The Traitor To Himself*, 'To the Reader'.

Minerva's Triumph: Or, Gramar and Rhetorick In all the Parts of them, Personated by Youths In Dramatick Scenes In A Country School. Presented to the View of all that Love Learning, but especially Recommended to the Perusal of Young Schollars, and the use of Schools at their Breakings up. The play had been staged in 1678/9 at the school at Ashby-de-la-Zouch, in Leicestershire, the former Royalist stronghold during the war. In the preface, Shaw describes the scenes as 'innocent Satyre to promote Morality, and by a surprizing kind of raillery Tax the grave fopperies and beloved vice of the doting world'.[153]

In contrast to these serious, didactic entertainments, the poet 'Ephelia' published the prologue, epilogue, and two songs from her comedy *Pair of Royal Coxcombs* described as 'Acted at a Dancing-School' in her volume of collected verse, *Female Poems On several Occasions* (1679).[154] In the prologue, the author urges the males in the audience 'to give it your Applause', 'Though not for Wit, nor Worth, but yet because | A Woman wrote it; though it be not rare', she concludes, 'It is not common'. Because it is also a school play, her audience, male and female, should hold it to a different standard from the commercial theatre whose authors 'write for a Third day' benefit performance,

> For She protests, She had no other ends
> In writing this, than to divert her Friends:
> Like, or dislike, She's careless, bid me say,
> That you shou'd Censure only when you Pay. (p. 17)

In addition to such public performances by amateur groups of actors, surviving manuscript copies remind us of the popularity of private theatricals and play reading among families and friends (see *MV* 1.VI). 'R. Carleton' contributed a pastoral, *The Concealed Royalty, or the May Queen*, to be acted by the family of Lord Bruce in 1674, and the following year a tragedy, *The Martial Queen*.[155] The founder of the Oxford Chair of Poetry, Henry Birkhead (1617–96), who had previously published a slim volume of Latin verse, was at work in the early 1680s composing *The Female Rebellion*, preserved in two manuscripts.[156] In the quarto fair copy version held at Glasgow, there are stage directions in brackets in the outer margins, suggesting to some that Birkhead's drama was privately performed. In the Tanner MS, which is a working draft with corrections, the performance aspects are even more in evidence, as the text gives precise directions for the side of the stage from which the characters enter and exit as well as sound effects ('a Kettle drum and trumpeters sound triumph within'[157]). The Tanner manuscript also has a revealing epigram on the title page and

---

[153] Shaw, *Minerva's Triumph*, 'Preface'.

[154] 'Ephelia', *Female Poems*, 16. Maureen E. Mulvilhill has made a spirited argument for the identity of Ephelia as being Mary Stewart, Duchess of Richmond (1622–85). See her 'Introduction', to *Ephelia*.

[155] Bodl., MS Eng.Poet.d.2. See Harbage, *Annals of English Drama*, rev. Schoenbaum, and Avery and Scouten, *The London Stage*, 1. 210, 221.

[156] Bodl., MS Tanner 466; UG Hunter 635.   [157] Bodl., MS Tanner 466, fo. 175ʳ.

a dedication on the inside flyleaf: under the title, 'The Female Rebellion, A Tragicomedy', is inscribed *'Principis est virtus maxima, nosse Sous. Mart:'*, which is a reference from Martial 8.15.8, 'it is the greatest virtue of a prince to know his own [subjects]'. The Dedication is to 'Your Majesty' and is signed by Birkhead; in it, mixed with the usual compliments, is a warning. Charles's reign 'has vindicated from imputed pride the reputation of Monarchy', Birkhead observes, but the story of the 'good Soveraigne' in the play which is 'couched' in the form of the Amazonian Queen whose generals rebel against her, might 'through a crystal Cover', permit the better viewing of challenges to the authority of a divine right monarch in the present times (fo. 1ᵛ).

Birkhead, who was at the time the Registrar of Norwich, initially seems an unlikely person to write this drama about strife among the Queen of the Amazons and her generals over divine right monarchy and the erosion of traditional bonds of loyalty in the face of popular cries for liberty. Birkhead's half-sister, however, was the celebrated singer and court performer Mary Knight (bap. 1631–in or after 1698). Knight was herself a poet, and is recorded as receiving a pension from Charles starting in 1672, suggesting a close and perhaps personal relationship. Because of this connection, some critics believe she is responsible for the Hunter fair quarto version and perhaps its private staging.[158] Certainly the dedication and epigram make it clear that Birkhead anticipated this being presented to Charles, either as a private entertainment or as an allegorical text.

Anne Wharton (1659–85) crafted her blank verse drama, 'Love's Martyr; or Witt above Crowns: A Tragedy', in the late 1670s or early 1680s. Although entered in the Stationers' Register in 1685, there is no evidence of it having been printed. Wharton, who had been raised by her grandmother, the Countess of Rochester, drew on her familiarity with the epistles of Ovid. She created her tragedy about the poet's love for Julia, daughter of the emperor Augustus, and the political machinations of those around Caesar. Although she declares in her dedication to her friend Mary Howe that the piece was not intended for the 'public', it does contain specific stage directions in the margins, and certainly the readers of this carefully produced manuscript text at the very least would have been able to imagine it as a staged drama. As the play opens, Caesar declares

> I am by Princes lov'd and Poets serv'd—
> Poets who can alone exalt the fame
> Of conquest or of power—Poets alone
> Can make a Conquering Monarch truly great.[159]

Caesar is determined to marry Julia to Marcellus—'She is yet young and has not learnt to Love | but doubtless you will quickly teach her th' art | of giving through her yielding eyes her heart' (fo. 6ʳ). Brief stage directions in the left

---

[158] See Pittock, *Henry Birkhead*, 87–105, and the privately printed edition of the play by Alexander Smith (1872). [159] Wharton, 'Love's Martyr', fo. 5ʳ.

margin have Marcellus turning to Julia to ask her to 'own' what Caesar has spoken, but Julia instead kneels at her father's feet declaring:

> May Caesar ever find obedient hearts
> as mine by double tyes is bound to be
> both to a father and an Emperour
> But yet Dread Sr upon my knees I begg
> (though I admire Marcellus vertues much)
> I may not be too quickly made a Bride. (fo. 6ʳ)

Julia and Ovid, in a series of asides to each other, confirm that Julia has her reasons for wanting to delay any marriage:

> Doubt not my Ovid but I'l still be true
> no Monarch ere possess's such charmes as you
> Let meaner souls the Diadem admire
> 'tis witt not crowns can set my heart on fire. (fo. 7ʳ)

The play ends with the banishment of Ovid by Caesar for presuming to love Julia, who in response stabs herself, but commands Ovid to live on after her (fo. 51ʳ), and Ovid weeps over her body as it is carried off stage.

Perhaps the most notorious of the surviving manuscript plays of this decade is *Sodom, or The Quintessence of Debauchery*, published in 1684 and frequently ascribed to the Earl of Rochester, Anne Wharton's beloved and admired uncle, although this attribution has been strongly challenged by Harold Love, Rochester's most recent editor.[160] The play itself exists in numerous versions and in eight manuscript texts in English, including a 1689 version done after Rochester's death with contributions from other writers. Written in heroic rhyming couplets, the five-act play (1678–80) is generally considered to be a misogynistic, pornographic fantasy, as well as a thinly veiled satire on Charles's court originating around 1673.

The plot concerns the edict of King Bolloximian (Charles II) to shun sexual relationships with women, who have infected the men with venereal disease, and to couple only with other men; critics have pointed to the parody of the language found in Charles II's Declaration of Indulgence (1672) promoting toleration of Catholicism.[161] The mock heroic style describing grossly crude sex acts seems likewise to parody the inflated ways in which the court painters represented the persons and acts of the royal family and their associates, such as when titled mistresses were painted as chaste shepherdesses and, in the case of Lady Castlemaine and Charles Fitzroy, her illegitimate son by Charles, painted by Sir Peter Lely as a Madonna and child. Some critics have argued that versions of the play were actually performed. They base their argument largely

---

[160] Johnson, 'Did Lord Rochester Write *Sodom*?'; Love, 'But Did Rochester Really Write *Sodom*?'. In his recent edition of Rochester's collected works, Love includes it, but under the category of 'attributed to'.   [161] Elias, 'Political Satire in *Sodom*'.

on the prologue and the similarity of the conclusion of Act Two, where 'six naked men and six naked women appear and dance' as they fondle each other's genitals, with the recorded activities in the 1670s of the drinking and sex society 'the Ballers', of which Rochester was a founding member. Others contend that the satiric content, with its clear attacks on Charles and his mistresses, would have simply been too dangerous to stage, even privately.

While London would continue to be the centre of theatrical energy during the 1670s and 1680s, audiences in provincial towns, the universities, and at popular fairs were well provided with theatrical entertainments brought to them by travelling companies and strolling entertainers. From the number of references to plays written for performance in both boys' and girls' schools during this period, it seems clear that being able to sing and to recite was considered part of a proper education, and that parents then as now must have enjoyed seeing their offspring perform in these academy offerings. Professional actors and actresses entertained everyone from the King and his courtiers at court and in Newmarket to casual visitors at Bartholomew Fair and the Red Lion at Norwich; the taste for writing and reading dramas within private circles as found in manuscripts of plays staged in colleges and homes suggests that both sexes enjoyed participating in theatrical culture beyond simply paying for a seat in the audience.

V. Fictions: *The Pilgrim's Progress*, the New 'Novels', and Love and Erotica

The most successful work of English fiction in the late seventeenth century was written in prison by the Baptist minister John Bunyan (see CV 2.V): *The Pilgrim's Progress from This World to That which is to come Delivered under the Similitude of a Dream* (1678) (see Figure 4). A Christian allegory using motifs from romance narratives as well as everyday provincial English life, it went through eleven editions during Bunyan's lifetime and has never been out of print since, having also been translated into over 200 different languages.[162] In contrast, the popular fictions written during this period calling themselves 'novels' on their title pages have mostly disappeared, except in scholarly bibliographies.

In the epigram on the title page, Hosia 12:10, 'I have used Similitudes', Bunyan alerts his readers that the dream narrative will challenge and delight them to understand his allegorical narrative and figurative language. In his verse 'Apology for his Book', Bunyan explains that he had not intended to write using allegory but 'Fell suddenly into an Allegory | About their Journey, and

---

[162] See Hill, 'Bunyan's Contemporary Reputation', 15; Hofmeyr, *The Portable Bunyan*.

the way to Glory'.[163] Debating whether he should print it or not, he says that he showed the manuscript to friends, some of whom urged him to publish it, others objecting to the 'dark' language as opposed to plain, direct admonition and instruction. Bunyan defends his book, arguing that the Scriptures use parables and metaphor.

> This Book will make a Travailer of thee,
> If by its Counsel thou wilt ruled be;
> It will direct thee to the Holy Land,
> If thou wilt its Directions understand. (sig. A6ᵛ)

Bunyan concludes:

> This Book is writ in such a Dialect,
> As may the minds of listless men affect:
> It seems a Novelty, and yet contains
> Nothing but sound, and honest Gospel-strains. (sig. A6ᵛ)

'As I walk'd through the wilderness of this world, I lighted on a certain place, where was a Denn; And I laid me down in that place to sleep', the story begins:

And as I slept I dreamed a Dream. I dreamed, and behold I saw a Man cloathed with Raggs, standing in a certain place, with his face from his own House, a Book in his hand, and a great burden upon his back. I looked, and saw him open the Book, and Read therein; and as he Read, he wept and trembled: and not being able longer to contain, he brake out with a lamentable cry; saying, what shall I do? (p. 1)

The right-hand margin contains glosses to particular Scripture passages, inviting the reader to have their Bible open as they read to amplify the message of the story and place it the appropriate context.[164] This is the first step of the journal of the hero, Christian, who must leave his family: they reject him and mock his fears of damnation, thinking him ill or perverse, but he sets out for the Kingdom of Heaven, even though the path there is not clear to him and often dangerous.

On the way, Christian is accompanied at times by fellow pilgrims who bring their own strengths and weaknesses to the journey. His neighbour 'Obstinate' urges another neighbour in the City of Destruction, 'Pliable', not to listen to Christian, warning that '*Come then, Neighbour* Pliable, *let us turn again, and go home without him; There is a Company of these Craz'd-headed Coxcombs*', but Pliable muses, 'if what the good *Christian* says is true, the things he looks after, are better then ours: my heart inclines to go with my Neighbour' (p. 5). Pliable's resolve lasts until the first obstacle, the 'Slow [slough] of Dispond', a miry bog created by the doubts and fearful apprehension of sinners who have recognized their sinful nature and sink into despair; Pliable finds this all too

---

[163] Bunyan, *The Pilgrim's Progress*, sig. A3ʳ.
[164] See Luxon, *Literal Figures*, ch. 6; Seidel, '*Pilgrim's Progress* and the Book'.

difficult and soon escapes, returning the way he came, but Christian, who is throughout his journey tormented by doubts, needs the assistance of 'Help' to set him back on the right path.

Throughout Christian's journey, as critics have pointed out, the rural land-scape of Bedfordshire, with its real bogs, village fairs, wicket gates, and inns, is transformed into spiritual allegory.[165] Likewise, Bunyan is drawing on his own youthful reading of romance fictions, which he lamented in his spiritual auto-biography, *Grace Abounding the Chief of Sinners* (see CV 2.V). Christian and his travelling companions encounter giants, are locked up in castle dungeons, face down lions, and don armour to battle Apollyon; on the other hand, they also are confronted with everyday obstacles such as steep hills and deep rivers. His companion Faithful will lose his life at the hands of angry townspeople inhabiting 'Vanity Fair', based on Sturbridge Fair, Cambridge.

The Pilgrim's Progress was also a triumph for Bunyan's publisher, Nathaniel Ponder, and it also inspired multiple imitations.[166] The original octavo cost 1s. 6d.; the success of it supported more expensive subsequent editions that included illustrations. Unlike Bunyan's publications involving theological dis-putes with other ministers, *The Pilgrim's Progress* had pictures, appealing to readers familiar with reading with pictures in chapbooks and broadsides. The third edition published in 1679 contains the famous 'Dreamer' author's por-trait as a frontispiece, done by Robert White (see MV 1.III), incorporating the sleeping Bunyan into a narrative image highlighting stops in the allegorical journey. White would also produce the striking full-length author portrait of another of Bunyan's allegorical fictions, *The Holy War* (1682), published by Dorman Newman and Benjamin Alsop. Ponder explained in the 'Advertisement' to the 1680 fifth edition that the book, 'having found good Acceptation among the People' to justify more editions, that 'the Publisher observing, that many persons desired to have it Illustrated with Pictures, hath endeavoured to gratifie them therein'. Ponder offered thirteen 'Copper Cuts curiously Engraven for such as desire them' that could be purchased along with the book for a shil-ling.[167] By the time of the eleventh edition in 1688, Ponder was including the pictures inside the text.

Bunyan's *The Holy War*, whose full title contains the gist of the matter (*The Holy War Made by King Shaddai Upon Diabolus, to Regain the Metropolis of the World, Or, The Losing and Taking Again of the Town of Mansoul*), like-wise allegorizes the struggle between good and evil for man's soul and the ways in which evil can overcome mankind. The town of Mansoul was created perfect by King Shaddai but nevertheless is deceived by the charismatic Diabolus into rebelling against its creator and taking him as its ruler; Shaddai then sends his son, Prince Emanuel, to retake it. As critics have observed, the tone of the

---

[165] Turner, 'Bunyan's Sense of Place'; Davies, '"Stout and Valiant Champions for God"', and *Graceful Reading*, chs 4, 5. [166] See Brown, *John Bunyan*, 439–67. [167] See Collé-Bak, 'The Pilgrim's Progresses of Bunyan's Publishers and Illustrators'.

allegory is militaristic and apocalyptic, and many have interpreted it as a response to the unrest and anxieties provoked by the Popish Plot (see CV 3.II).[168] As with *The Pilgrim's Progress*, *The Holy War* opens with a long verse epistle from Bunyan to the reader, justifying his use of allegory ('Let no men, then, count me a fable-maker', he declares) and also including in later editions 'An Advertisement to the Reader' that confirms that, although 'Some say the "Pilgrim's Progress" is not mine', indeed both texts came from 'the same heart, and head, fingers, and pen'.[169]

Other fictions adopted different strategies to secure their audiences. The term 'novel' on the title page of printed fictions during this decade appears with increasing frequency. Typically, these texts are concerned with love and intrigue, sometimes set in foreign or exotic settings, but between 1675 and 1684 some writers were also beginning to use English settings and characters. The majority of them are still translations of popular French works, with a few done from Spanish. Notably several of the titles were also thinly veiled satires or fictionalizations of the exploits of Charles and his courtiers, which could cause their publishers to be investigated on charges of seditious libel.

The publishers James Magnes and Richard Bentley (bap. 1645–97) had an extensive list featuring these short fictions. Called 'novel Bentley' by fellow bookseller John Dunton, Richard Bentley would issue in 1692 his twelve-volume collection *Modern Novels*, a repackaging of ninety-two individual fiction titles from the 1670s and 1680s. They largely feature works translated from French, which were very often by contemporary writers, especially women, including Mme La Fayette, Mlle La Roche-Guilhen, and Madeleine de Scudéry. Typically, the women's identities are not revealed on the title pages; La Roche-Guilhen's *Almanzor and Almanzaida* (1678) is announced to be a 'novel written by Sir Philip Sidney, and found since his death amongst his papers' and Mme de La Fayette's *Zayde A Spanish History being a pleasant and witty novel* is attributed to Monsieur Segray.

It was not only the identity of the women novelists that became obscured in the translations. One of the most popular of the translated French novelists appeared under the name of Gabriel de Brémondor Saint-Bremond, but has been recently established as being Sebastien Bremond (*c*.1646–*c*.1705), a French librettist and writer who was for a time part of Charles's court and who in 1679 would himself translate the Duchess of Mazarin's scandalous autobiography into English.[170] In 1677, Magnes and Bentley printed translations of Bremond's *The Cheating Gallant, or The False Count Brion* and *The Happy Slave A Novel*. The last was reprinted frequently through the 1680s and 1690s; in the advertisement of the 1685 second edition, the author of this 'trifle' and 'toy' nevertheless feels compelled to 'declare to the Publick, and especially to those who busie themselves in penetrating into other mens intentions, that under the literal sense

---

[168] Mackenzie, 'Rhetoric versus Apocalypse'; Runyon, *John Bunyan's Master Story*; for a contrasting view, see Zinck, 'From Apocalypse to Prophecy'.
[169] Bunyan, *The Holy War*, sig. A2ᵛ.   [170] See Grobe, 'Sebastien Bremond'.

of my Tales there is not hid any Allegorical meaning, that when I speak of the Turks and of Africk, I have not any Ideas in Europe or any other Nation'. 'If the Intrigues or Adventures I write of', he concludes, 'have some conformity to those of our times, I am not to answer for it: 'Tis the fault of Chance and not mine.'[171] Bremond's declarations aside, the content of his novel *Hattige, or, The Amours of the king of Tamaran a novel* was clearly a fictionalization of the affair between Charles II and Lady Castlemaine. As a result, Bentley, but not the author, was brought up on charges of seditious libel in 1676 for selling the French version; in 1680, it appeared in English with a false imprint on the title page, identifying it as printed in Amsterdam for 'Simon the African'.

This was also the imprimatur for another of Bremond's novels, *Homais, Queen of Tunis* (1681), which Bentley would also include within his twelve-volume collection in 1692. Identified as being by 'Sebastian Grenadine', the novel opens with a reference to *Hattige*:

Since the Amorous Adventurers have been beyond Sea, the Discoveries of Love they have made in Africa, have been so Successful, that that Country (as Barbarous as it is) does now seem to be become an inexhaustible source of Gallantry.... In a word, Barbary, which in all other things is rightly called by that Name, is the most refin'd part of the Universe, in point of Love.[172]

Apparently these exotic fictions winking at contemporary people and events were popular, and critics have pointed to Delarivier Manley's subsequent use of these novels in constructing her 1696 tragedy *Royal Mischief* and the political roman-à-clef attributed to her using the relationship between John Churchill and Castlemaine in *The Secret History of Queen Zarah and the Zarazians* (1705) to comment on the court of Queen Ann.[173]

In 1678, Roger L'Estrange, the official licenser for the press until the lapse of the Licensing Act in 1679 (see MV 3.II), published his translation of Marianna d'Alcoforado's *Lettres d'armour d'une religieuse* as *Five Love Letters from a Nun to a Cavalier*. This frequently reprinted story, which also inspired a continuation in 1683, *Five love-letters Written by a Cavalier in answer to the five love letters written to him by a nun* by Noël Bouton Chamilly, is narrated in the form of intimate letters sent by a Portuguese nun to the French cavalier who had seduced and then abandoned her. They chronicle her attempts to renew his affections, her growing realization of his betrayal, and her futile attempts to spurn him and to reconcile herself to his loss. The epistle to the reader sets out the nature of their appeal for the modern reader: 'you will find in them the Lively Image of an Extravagant, and an Unfortunate Passion; and that *a Woman may be Flesh and Bloud, in a Cloyster, as well as in a Palace*'.[174]

In her first two letters, she fears for his safety and pines for his company, but by the third letter she admits: 'Yes, yes; 'Tis now a Clear Case that your whole Address to me was only an Artificial disguise. You betray'd me as often as you

---

[171] Bremond, *The Happy Slave*, sig. A4v. [172] Bremond, *Homais*, 4.
[173] See Herman, 'Similarities'. [174] L'Estrange, *Five Love Letters*, 'To the Reader'.

told me, how over-joy'd you were that you had got me alone: and your Passions, and Transports were only the Effects of my own Importunities.' She sadly concludes, 'yours was a deliberate design to fool me; your business was to make a Conquest, not a friend; and to triumph over my Heart, without ever engaging or hazzarding your own' (p. 37). In the final letter, even as she is vowing never to have further to do with him, however, she closes pathetically, 'I must leave you, and not so much as think of you. Now do I begin to Phansie that I shall not write to you again for all This; for what Necessity is there that I must be telling of you at every turn how my Pulse beats?' (p. 117). In its stream of pure first-person emotion and the speaker's distracted attempts at self-understanding, the voice of the nun offers the reader the language not only of female passion but also of tormenting self-doubt, which will feature in later fictions revealing and revelling in passion, such as those by Aphra Behn.

Original novels in English were also appearing in this decade. Charles Blount or Blunt (no apparent relation to the freethinker or lexicographer) printed several of these. Alexander Oldys, who was once believed to have written *The London Jilt*, about which more will follow, offered *The Fair Extravagant, or, the humorous bride. An English novel* (1682), which describes the adventures of Ariadne, a 17-year-old heiress to £1,200 a year, who comes alone to visit London. Her house in St James is fashionable and her library rather surprising, as she delights in binding together authors who in their lives were opponents or rivals, such as Suckling and Denham, Shakespeare and Jonson, with only Rochester and Cowley on their own: 'in short, here lay a Play, there a Sermon; here an Academy, there a Prayer-Book; here a Romance, and there a Bible'.[175] She particularly favours 'romances, for she was a great lover of Knight Errantry, and was a little that way addicted' (pp. 3–4). Through various trials and confusions of identities, Ariadne at the end is happily wed to the long-suffering Polydor.

In 1684, Aphra Behn published the first part of her long, three-part epistolary fiction *Love Letters Between a Nobleman and his Sister*. Based on a true scandal, the elopement of Lord Grey with his wife's sister, Henrietta Berkeley, the work combines the appeal of the 'secret history' with an intense exploration of the expression of emotions, as seen in *Five Love Letters from a Nun to a Cavalier*. Although Behn declared in the dedication that she is merely translating a volume of French letters, *L'Intregue de Philander & Silvia*, no trace of such a title has been found, suggesting that, for fiction, having a French origin, even if fictitious, was an attractive feature for readers.[176] English readers, however, would have had little difficulty in placing the characters in the context of very recent public English events: in parts two and three, issued in 1685 and 1687, Behn only thinly veils Grey's involvement in the Rye House Plot and Monmouth's Rebellion.

---

[175] Oldys, *The Fair Extravagant*, 3–4,
[176] See Behn, *Love Letters*, in Behn, *Works*, 2. 3, n. b.

In part one, the then naive heroine Silvia elopes with Philander, who is married to her sister Mertilla. In her dedication to Thomas Condon, Behn describes the letters as 'soft and amorous'. The opening letter from Philander sets the tone for the first volume of passionate exchanges: it begins 'though I parted from you resolv'd to obey your impossible commands, yet know, oh charming Silvia! I found the God (too mighty for the Idol) reign absolute Monarch in my Soul'. Silvia still appears to him in the form of 'her unresistable Idea!'

With all the charmes of blooming youth, with all the Attractions of Heavenly Beauty! Loose, wanton, gay, all flowing her bright hair, and languishing her lovely eyes, her dress all negligent as when I saw her last, discovering a thousand ravishing Graces, round white small Breasts, delicate Neck and rising Bosome, heav'd with sighs she wou'd in vain conceal…Oh I dare not think on, lest my desires grow mad and raving. (2. 11)

Silvia, once she has succumbed to his passion and lost her virginity to him, writes with equal ardour and candour. When she surveys

the print where thou and I were last night laid…imagine over all our solemn joys, every dear transport, all our ravishing, repeated blisses, then almost fainting, languishing, cry—*Philander!* Oh, my charming little God! Then lay me down in the dear place you press'd, still warm and fragrant with the sweet remains that thou hast left behind thee on the Pillow. (2. 88)

'To love thee with all thy disadvantages, and glory in my ruine', she concludes, 'these are my firm resolves, these are my thoughts' (2. 89).

Other 'new' novels in English that appeared in the early 1680s all depend on foreign settings. Of them, only the anonymous *The Unsatisfied Lovers. A New English Novel* (1683) is truly 'new', while the other two, William Chamberlayne's (*c*.1619–89) *Eromena, or the noble Stranger* (1683) and Walter Charleton's (1620–1707) *The Cimmerian Matron, a pleasant novel shewing the wit and subtility of the female sex* (1684), are either retellings or repackagings of earlier works. Chamberlayne's *Eromena* is a short retelling in prose of his long verse romance *Pharonnida*, which had appeared in 1659 (see *MV* 2.1).

The literal repackaging of unsold copies of earlier texts, as Bentley would do in 1692 with his collection, highlights the aggregate nature of many publications aimed at a popular market for entertaining reading. The physician Walter Charleton's attack on Platonic love, which he had also first published in 1659 as *The Ephesian Matron*, had been combined with another fiction in 1668 as *The Ephesian and Cimmerian Matrons, two notable examples of the power of love & wit* published by Henry Herringman, who likewise reissued *The Cimmerian matron…to which is added the Mysteries and miracles of love* in 1684. In a separate letter to Charleton, the unknown author of *The Cimmerian Matron* explains:

behold a Second Matron, whose Amorous Adventure very neerly resembles that of the kind Ephesian. She in like manner falls into an Intrigue (as they now adays call it) with a Souldier, and at first sight too: and encountering no small difficulty in the pursuit of her love, is witty enough both to surmount that, and conceal her stoln pleasures, by a trick that pass'd for no less than a Miracle.

The 1668 version has separate title pages and page numbers for each novel; the 1684 edition simply omits the Ephesian story and opens with this letter.

Another new English novel had apparently a much shorter shelf life than the popular reprints and collected novels. *The Unsatisfied Lovers. A New English Novel Part I* (1683) is dedicated to the Earl of Ranelagh by its publisher James Patridge and is set in France during the time of Francis I in the sixteenth century. It features a beautiful, modest, yet witty Madam de St Maure, who attends the dauphine's wife; through her conversation she inflames the passions of Chastillon, who despairs of obtaining her. Many pages pass before either will confess their feelings. Their various virtuous passions, however, become intertwined with the amorous intrigues of Diane de Poitiers, the mistress of Henry II. Part I ends with the true lovers fearing exposure of their passions through Poitiers's indiscretions. The promise of a continuation or new part in the future is a common convention for this type of fiction, but, as no trace of part II has survived, what troubles they faced are left in mystery or yet to be written.

In stark contrast to the virtues of some of the heroines of these novels, after the lapse of the Licensing Act in 1679, the 1680s also saw the publication of a series of anonymous libertine erotic fictions. *The London Jilt or the Politick Whore, Shewing, All the Artifices and Strategems which the Ladies of Pleasure make use of for the Intreaguing and Decoying Men; Interwoven with Several Pleasant Stories of the Misses Ingenious Performances* (1683) is a first-person narrated picaresque story of Cornelia's life as a London whore. Her career begins as an only child of doting London parents, and she is 'brought up in some sort of Libertinism', meaning that all her wishes are gratified; she is sent to school, where she learns dancing and French, and, from an early age, 'I began to imagine, that there was nothing in the World more pleasant, than to sleep in the Arms of a Man'. When her family lose their money and the father dies, both the mother and eventually the daughter resort to labouring 'with their buttocks'. Although the preface is sternly didactic in its declaration that the narrative is intended to warn the reader about deceitful women, critics have noted that the voice of Cornelia herself creates a witty and entertaining account of her 'pranks' as she seeks to survive financially. Regardless of whether its readers viewed it as morally didactic or simply mildly pornographic, literary critics analysing the catalogues of book auctions from the period have found that, although surviving copies of erotica from this period in libraries are now extremely rare, during the late seventeenth century it was an extremely popular novel both in England and America, as well as being translated into French and German.[177]

Likewise, readers in the early 1680s happily bought English translations of *The School of Venus* (1680) (read by Samuel Pepys in its French original), the

---

[177] See Thompson, 'The London Jilt', and Vries, 'Literature of the Enlightenment', 303–4.

English canting slang of *The Whore's Rhetorick* (1683), *The London Bully...*
Displaying the Principal Cheats of our Modern Debauchees (1683), and *Tullia*
and Octavia (1684), a series of dialogues between two young women concerning different ways to enjoy sex, also translated from French. Publishers of such
works were occasionally prosecuted (see *MV* 3.II), but licensers during this
period were more concerned with political texts than erotic ones, except, of
course, when the erotic was used as a thinly disguised satire on members of the
court. *The Whore's Rhetorick*, for example, although loosely based on an
Italian fiction, included topical references, with the notorious and celebrated
London brothel madam Mrs Creswell, who had a sensational trial in 1681, as
the principal narrator, as well as allusions to the sexual escapades of the Duke
of Monmouth. Its publisher, John Wickins, however, was fined only 40s. at the
trial at the Guildhall on 16 April 1683, while, at the same session, the publisher
of *The Second Part of the Ignoramus Justices* and *The Growth of Popery*,
Eleanor Smith, was fined £10, suggesting the relative harmlessness of the erotic
fiction in balance with that of the political.[178]

Sometimes erotic fiction might slip by the gaze of the censors because of its
anti-Catholic nature (see *CV* 3.II). An example is the extremely rare and
obscene *The Adamite, or, The Loves of Father Rock and his intrigues with the*
nuns a famous novel translated out of French published by the well-known
bookseller Dorman Newman in 1683, the year after he had published Bunyan's
The Holy War.[179] This 'famous novel' was based on actual events in France in
which a mentally unstable Jesuit priest, Father Rock, founded his own convent
of naked 'Adamites'. In a similar vein, *The Nunns Complaints against the*
Fryars was based on the real complaints of the nuns of St Clare in France in the
1660s, published in French in 1667, and suppressed there by order of Louis XIV.
The English translation appeared in 1676 with a preface explaining that the
text is valuable in that it will prevent English Catholics from sending their
daughters to French convents and revealing the true antics performed in nunneries. Texts such as these thus form part of the background against which
Aphra Behn wrote her short fictions during the 1680s, such as *The Fair Jilt* and
The History of the Nun set in continental nunneries.

The connection between Catholicism and sexual excess by both sexes but
particularly in the female is pervasive in the fiction of this period, perhaps
fuelled by the near universal unpopularity of the royal mistress, the French
Catholic Louise de Kéroualle, Duchess of Portsmouth. Richard Head's *The*
Miss Displayed (1675) likewise involves a Catholic 'heroine' who is easily led
into the paths of vice (see *MV* 3.I), and the provocatively entitled anonymous
Eve Revived, or The Fair one Stark Naked (1684), another translation from
French, also features a Catholic female protagonist, this time a former nun

---

[178] For accounts of trials for pornographic texts, see Foxon, *Libertine Literature*, 7–10.
[179] For further information concerning anti-Catholic pornographic fiction during this period, see
Thompson, *Unfit for Modest Ears*, ch. 8.

named Angelica. *Venus in the Cloister* was translated from French in 1683 and sold by Henry Rhodes, also the publisher of *The London Jilt* that same year. This text is a series of dialogues between Sister Angelica and an inexperienced novice Agnes, who is 'an Enemy to all Restraint', and whom the older woman introduces to the range of sexual pleasures, including lesbianism. As critics have pointed out, it owes much to the dialogues of Aretino and Chorier, and texts such as *L'Escholle des Filles* and *Satyra Sotadica*, both of which feature as favourite reading matter in Sister Angelica's convent.[180]

The 'new' novels of the decade 1675–85 appealed to readers not only for their exotic settings and plot-driven adventures, but also because the fictions often hinted at the 'secret' lives of public figures and events. While translated novels from the French still dominated the market, there is a clearly developing English style for conveying stories of passions, ranging from displays of the language of intense emotions, male and female, to the bawdy celebration of sexual adventures in everyday London.

VI. Foreign Parts: English Readers and Foreign Lands and Cultures

> Although my skin be black, within my veins
> Runs bloud as red, and Royal as the best.
>
> Aphra Behn, *Abdelazer, or, The Moor's Revenge* (1677)

> *I* went along that day mourning and lamenting, leaving farther my own Country, and travelling into the vast and howling *Wilderness*, and I understood something of *Lot*'s Wife's Temptation, *when she looked back* ... The *Indians* were as thick as the trees: it seemd as if there had been a thousand Hatchets going at once: if one looked before one, there was nothing but *Indians*, and behind one, nothing but *Indians*, and so on either hand, I my self in the midst, and no Christian soul near me, *and yet how hath the Lord preserved me in safety? Oh the experience that I have had of the goodness of God, to me and mine!*
>
> Mary Rowlandson, *The soveraignty and goodness of God, together with the faithfulness of his promises displayed* (1682), 20–1

English readers and audiences in the mid-1670s through the 1680s were confronted with an increasing range of descriptions of and interactions with people not like them. On stage, London theatregoers enjoyed watching the dramas about foreign princes and queens, such as seen in Elkanah Settle's *The Conquest*

---

[180] See Foxon, *Libertine Literature*, chs 2, 3.

of China by the Tartars, Nathaniel Lee's historical representation of Alexander the Great in *The Rival Queens* with its murderous queen Roxana (1677), and Behn's captive Moor *Abdelazer* wreaking havoc as he seeks his revenge (1677), to Thomas Southerne's *The Persian Prince, or the Loyal Brother* (1682), based on a popular novel (see *MV* 3.V).

This fascination with exotic settings would be continued in the 1680s and 1690s, with multiple plays such as Delarivier Manley's tragedy *The Royal Mischief* (1696) and later *Almyna; or, The Arabian Vow* (1707) competing for audiences with Mary Pix's *Ibrahim, the Thirteenth Emperor of the Turks* (1696) and Southerne's adaptation of Aphra Behn's fiction *Oroonoko* (1695) for the stage (see *MV* 4.IV).[181] In 1704, the first volume of the English translation of Orientalist Antoine Galland's twelve-volume *Les Mille et une nuits* (1704–17) based on a collection found in a Syrian manuscript, appeared under the title *The Arabian Nights Entertainments*, and its stories narrated by the heroine Scheherazade would generate a passion for Oriental tales on stage and in fictions well into the nineteenth century.[182]

As critics have noted, however, most of the foreigners represented on stage were merely Europeans dressed in exotic costumes with appropriate cosmetic make-up.[183] Although there was a growing population of dark-skinned peoples in England in the 1670s and 1680s, some the servants of returning West Indian planters and some serving as free seamen on English ships, the plays of the 1670s such as Elkanah Settle's *Love and Revenge* (1675) and Aphra Behn's *Abdelazer: The Moor's Revenge* (1676) featured actors wearing blackface as exotic villains.[184] As critics have noted of the tragedies of this period, which frequently emphasize bloody spectacle and violence (see *CV* 3.I), perhaps in reaction to the unsettled political climate and the anxieties raised by the Popish Plot and the Exclusion Crisis (see *CV* 3.II), these tragedies with their menacing dark protagonists threatened not only to wreak political upheaval within the plays but also to push the boundaries of sexual transgression. Their foreignness is exotic fantasy, but it is also alarming and titillating.[185]

In real-life encounters, the 1670s saw a series of violent conflicts between Europeans and foreign non-European powers, many of which were chronicled in first-person narratives, histories, ballads, and news reports. In New England, King Philip's war, also known as Metacom's Rebellion or the First Indian War, began in 1675 between a union of several Native American tribes and the Puritan English colonists (see *MV* 3.I). In Europe, across what is today Poland, Hungary, Serbia, and Austria, the Great Turkish War or the War of the Holy League (1667–83) continued to play out, pitting the Islamic Ottoman Turks

---

[181] See Ballaster, *Fabulous Orients*, ch. 3.
[182] See Dobie, 'Translation in the Contact Zone'.
[183] See Matar, *Turks, Moors, and Englishmen*.
[184] See Fryer, *Staying Power*, ch. 2; Vaughan, *Performing Blackness on English Stages*, chs 8, 9.
[185] See Orr, *The Empire on the English Stage*.

against the Christian Habsburg Empire, culminating in the attack on Vienna. In September of 1683 Vienna endured a two-month siege prior to the rescue of it by the combined forces of the Holy Roman Empire and the Polish–Lithuanian Commonwealth, who defeated the forces of Sultan Mehmed IV (1642–93). Further east, English merchants with the East India Company experienced losses and disruptions during the Deccan Wars in India, pitting the forces of the Marantha Empire against those of the Islamic Mughal Empire ruled by Aurangzeb (the hero of Dryden's last rhymed heroic tragedy *Aureng-zebe* in 1675) (see CV 3.I) between 1680 and 1707, which ended the Mughal reign. Accounts of these far-away battles on both continents as well as the behaviour of the foreign princes and their armies were chronicled in official published dispatches, letters from observers, as well as memoirs and diaries of those who lived through them; these images permeated the popular imagination of the exotic and the foreign, both as dangerous but also as luxurious and alluring.

The 1670s and early 1680s offered English readers with sufficiently deep pockets the opportunity to buy richly illustrated folio geographies that included maps and plates depicting native dress as well as foreign plants and animals. John Ogilby's 1670s massive geography *Africa* with fifty-two plates of illustrations and maps promised its reader on its lengthy title page not only a description of that continent and its inhabitants, but also '*an accurate description of the regions of Aegypt, Barbary, Lybia, and Billedulgerid, the land of Negroes, Guinee, Aethiopia and the Abyssines: with all the adjacent islands, either in the Mediterranean, Atlantick, Southern or Oriental Sea*' as well as '*their wonderful plants, beasts, birds and serpents: collected and translated from most authentick authors and augmented with later observations*'. This was followed in 1671 by Ogilby's *America*, with its thirty-two pages of plates, and in 1673, his translation of Johannes Nieuhof's *An Embassy from the East-India Company of the United Provinces, to the Grand Tartar Cham, Emperor of China*. English translations of the French gem merchant Jean-Baptista Tavernier's (1605–89) extensive travels conducted between 1630 and 1668 appeared in 1677 and again with additions in 1680. *The six voyages of John Baptista Tavernier, Baron of Aubonne, through Turky, into Persia and the East-Indies, for the space of forty years giving an account of the present state of those countries…to which is added, a new description of the seraglio* was published in multiple formats over the decade, and offered maps as well as adventures. As its author informed his readers:

if the effect of Education may be liken'd to a second Birth, I may truly say, that I came into the World with a desire to travel…I was with much delight attentive, inspir'd me betimes with a design to see some part of those Countries, which were represented to me in the Maps, from which I never could keep off my Eyes.[186]

Many English readers appear to have shared that desire to see, if only on the page, the countries delineated in the maps.

---

[186] Tavernier, *The six voyages*, 'The Design of the Author'.

Additionally, foreign places were news, written about in pamphlets and broadsides and publicized in ballads (see *CV* 2.II). In terms of contemporary events rather than histories or geographies, readers in England, Scotland, and Ireland as well as New England were kept abreast of what was to be the bloodiest conflict in the New World, as Native American Indians from several tribes united in the southern part of the colonies and made every effort to dislodge the settlers, rejecting the sovereignty of the English monarch over them. Few among the settlers were unaffected by the fighting: Plymouth Colony alone is estimated to have lost 8 per cent of its adult male population, while, by the end of the conflict, the Native American tribes in the area were decimated, having lost between 60 and 80 per cent of their population.[187]

The spark for the war was the death of the Harvard-educated Christian Indian John Sassamon (also sometimes called Sausaman), who was killed in January 1675, apparently at the urging of Metacom or Metacomet, the chief of the Wampanoag known as 'King Philip' to the English. This was followed by the speedy trial and execution of his alleged murderers in June of that year in Plymouth, the events of which were widely published in pamphlets and broadsides (see *MV* 3.I). Historians have debated why Sassamon, who was an adviser and translator for Metacom, was ordered to be killed; the Boston congregational minister Increase Mather (1639–1723), writing about the event, had no doubt it was Sassamon's conversion that had led to the events that triggered his death.[188] Mather published *A brief history of the war with the Indians in New-England* (1677), first in Boston and in December of the same year in London under the title *A brief history of the war with the Indians in New-England, from June 24, 1675 (when the first Englishman was murdered by the Indians) to August 12, 1676, when Philip, alias Metacomet, the principal author and beginner of the war, was slain.* Mather opens with the flat declaration:

That the Heathen People amongst whom we live, and whose Land the Lord God of our Fathers hath given to us for a rightful Possession, have at sundry times been Plotting mischievous Devices against that part of the *English Israel*, which is seated in these goings down of the Sun, no man that is an Inhabitant of any considerable understanding, can be ignorant.[189]

As for the death of Sassamon, 'no doubt but one reason why the Indians murdered John Sassamon, was out of hatred against him for his Religion…because he discovered their subtle and malicious designs' (p. 2). Indians served on the jury that convicted Sassamon's killers; most of the Native Americans who had converted to Christianity, the so-called Praying Indians, sided with the settlers or remained neutral. This, however, did not prevent the settlers from sending

---

[187] See Pulsipher, *Subjects unto the Same King*; Schultz and Touglas, *King Philip's War*; and Mandell, *King Philip's War*, esp. 134–7.

[188] See Lepore, *The Name of War*, 10.   [189] Mather, *A brief history of the war*, 1.

them to confinement camps, such as the one on Deer Island in Boston Harbor, and they were also taken captive and killed by the hostile forces.

Accounts of the battles and the atrocities were quickly published both in Boston and in London. The minister William Hubbard (1621/2–1704) opens his account with the settlement of New England by the colonists and their various treaties with the Native groups. His *A Narrative of the Troubles with the Indians in New-England* does not always paint a flattering portrait of the earliest European settlers, but the hero of his narrative is without a doubt Captain Benjamin Church (1639–c.1717). Church was a settler who commanded a small regiment, and was one of the first of the colonists to adopt the Native American style of fighting, guerrilla warfare or 'ranging', as opposed the European military formations, and of forming units integrating Native Americans and settlers.[190]

Hubbard, for example, recounts Church's capture of one of King Philip's principal warriors, Annawan, not as the result of a direct military confrontation but instead by surprise and the charms of English courtesy.

Capt. *Church* by direction got up to their Wigwams before they were aware: and pleasantly told *Annawan*, that he came to sup with him that night; whereat the said *Annawan* (who had fallen flat upon the Earth, expecting to have his head cut off) looked up and cried *Taubut*, in their Language; *thank you*, as one being much affected with the generosity of our English Captain.[191]

Church questioned Annawan as they shared the stolen 'English Beef boyling in their Kettles'; to prevent his captive's escape that night, 'they lay down to sleep together in the Wigwam: Capt. *Church* laying one of his legs upon *Anawans* Son, and the other upon himself, that he might have notice, if any of them offered to stir' (p. 108). Apparently overcome by Church's treatment of him, Annawan confessed that 'he did believe by all those late occurrents, that there was a great God, that over-ruled all; and that he had found, that whatever he had done to any of those, whether Indians or English, the same was brought upon himself in after time' (p. 108).

Church's observations about those involved in the war and on his innovative tactics were compiled and edited by his son Thomas under the title *Entertaining Passages relating to Philip's War* (1716), which enjoyed numerous editions. In his preface to the reader, Church declares that 'seeing that every particular of historical Truth is precious; I hope the Reader will pass a favourable Censure upon an Old Souldier, telling of the many Ran-Counters he has had, and yet is come off alive'.[192] Church, who had lived with no animosity with the Native Americans in his area, was convinced that many would be happy to cease hostilities, and in his memoir he highlights his extensive negotiations with the female sachem of the Wampanoag, Awashonks.

---

[190] Mandell, *King Philip's War*, 53–7.   [191] Hubbard, *A Narrative of the Troubles*, 108.
[192] Church, *Entertaining Passages*, 'To the Reader'. See also Gould, 'Reinventing Benjamin Church'.

Awashonks had signed articles of agreement in 1671 with the English but came under pressure from King Philip to join him. She requested Church to come to her, and he advised her to put her tribe under the protection of the English. As tensions mounted over the escalating clashes between settlers and King Philip's followers, Awashonks again requested a meeting. The events of this meeting are told in a dramatic narrative fashion, complete with dialogue: as the two walked together alone,

where at once a-rose a great body of Indians, who had lain hid in the grass...and gathered around them, till they had clos'd them in; being all arm'd with Guns, Spears, and Hatchets &c with their hair trim'd and faces painted, in their Warlike appearance. It was doubtless some-what surprising to our Gentleman at first. (p. 23)

Undaunted, Church requested that they lay down only their guns, 'for formality sake', and to sit and share 'Occapechees', rum, with him. She agrees but suspects him of offering her poison and insists that he drink first, 'he then told her, *There was no poison in it*, and pouring some into the Palm of his hand, sup'd it up, and took the Shell and drank to her again, and drank a good Swig which indeed was no more than he needed'. She then 'ventured a good hearty dram, and pas'd it among her Attendants' (p. 24). Subsequent historians of events attribute the unravelling of King Philip's army to the decisions of sachems such as Awashonks not to fight against the British.

Another narrative of the war, which had numerous reprints in both Boston and London was Mary Rowlandson's captivity narrative, published as *The soveraignty and goodness of God, together with the faithfulness of his promises displayed* (1682) in New England and the same year in London as *A True History of the captivity and restoration of Mrs Mary Rowlandson*. Rowlandson (*c*.1637–1711) had emigrated to Salem, Massachusetts, in 1639 with her parents and married Joseph Rowlandson, the minister at Lancaster. In February 1676, Lancaster was attacked, and Rowlandson and three of her children were taken captive until ransomed three months later. She wrote down and subsequently published her spiritual memoir, as the running title of the work explains, for 'all that desires to know the Lords doing to, and dealings with her. Especially to her dear children and relations, written by her own hand for her private use, and now made publick at the earnest desire of some friends, and for the benefit of the afflicted'.[193]

In the preface to the reader in the Cambridge edition, believed by many critics to be by Increase Mather, the male writer explains that 'this Narrative was penned by the Gentlewoman her self, to be to her a memorandum of Gods dealing with her, that she might never forget, but remember the same, & the severall circumstances thereof, all the dayes of her life' (sig. A3ʳ). Others who read the handwritten version felt it too important in its revelations of God's providence, and 'though this Gentlewomans modesty would not thrust it into

---

[193] Rowlandson, *The soveraignty and goodness of God*, title page.

the Press, yet her gratitude unto God made her not hardly perswadable to let it pass, that God might have his due glory' (sig. A3ʳ). The initial edition published in Cambridge was extremely popular, selling out quickly and requiring further editions; historians believe that this initial text enjoyed such extensive circulation among families and friends that 'only a few stained and dog-eared pages' have survived.[194]

Rowlandson recounts in simple language the terror of 10 February 1675 when, while her husband was away, the Indians attacked Lancaster. Watching from the window as their neighbours' houses were attacked and the occupants killed or taken captive, Rowlandson initially attempts to flee with her children and one of her sister's, 'but as soon as we came to the dore and appeared, the *Indians* shot so thick that the bulletts rattled against the House, as if one had taken an Streme of stones and threw them, so that we were fain to give back' (p. 3). As fire forces them back out of the house, her brother-in-law is killed, 'wherat the *Indians* scornfully shouted, and hallowed, and were presently upon him, stripping off his cloaths, the bulletts flying thick, one went through my side, and the same (as would seem) through the bowels and hand of my dear Child in my arms' (p. 3). As Rowlandson and her children were taken away as captives, she reflected 'Oh the dolefull sight that now was to behold at this House! *Come, behold the works of the Lord, what dissolations he has made in the Earth.* Of thirty seven persons who were in this one House, none escaped either present death, or a bitter captivity, save only one' (p. 4).

Rowlandson calls the stages of the journey she took with her Indian captors 'removes'. 'It is not tongue, or pen can express the sorrows of my heart, and bitterness of my spirit, that *I* had at this departure', she recalls, walking alongside a horse bearing her wounded child, who was 'moaning all along, I shall dy, I shall dy. . . . At length I took it off the horse, and held it in my armes till my strength failed, and *I* fell down with it: Then they set me upon a horse with my wounded Child in my lap' (pp. 7–8). The child soon died, and, as Rowlandson's series of 'removes' take her further from the land of the English colonists into the forests of the Native Americans, her determination to retain what is English merges with scriptural allegories for comfort. '*I* went along that day mourning and lamenting, leaving farther my own Country, and travelling into the vast and howling *Wilderness*, and I understood something of *Lot*'s Wife's Temptation, *when she looked back*', she remembers (p. 20).

She comes to view her captors as God's scourge to the English. Of her captivity, she writes:

Before I knew what affliction meant, I was ready sometimes to wish for it. When I lived in prosperity; having the comforts of the World about me, my relations by me, my Heart chearfull: and taking little care for any thing; and yet seeing many, whom I preferred before my self, under many tryals and afflictions, in sickness, weakness, poverty, losses,

---

[194] Colley, *Captives*, 150–1.

crosses, and cares of the World, I should be sometimes jealous least I should have my portion in this life, and that Scripture would come to my mind, *Heb.* 12.6. *For whom the Lord loveth he chasteneth, and scourgeth every Son whom he receiveth.* (p. 20)

'But now I see', Rowlandson concludes, that

the Lord had his time to scourge and chasten me. The portion of some is to have their afflictions by drops, now one drop and then another; but the dregs of the Cup, the Wine of astonishment: like a sweeping rain that leaveth no food, did the Lord prepare to be my portion Affliction I wanted, and affliction I had, full measure (I thought) pressed down and running over. (p. 72)

After three months, Rowlandson was ransomed and reunited with her surviving children.

English readers were already familiar with captivity narratives, but less so from the New World. Charles II had gained possession of Tangiers in 1661 as part of Catherine de Braganza's dowry. Long before that, however, English readers and listeners had been horrified and entertained by first-person narratives of encounters with the famed Barbary pirates; English captives had been providing first-hand accounts of the customs and behaviour of Moorish peoples since accounts published in Richard Hakluyt's *Principal Navigations* (1589) and Richard Hasleton's *Strange and Wonderful Things Happened to Richard Hasleton...in his Ten Years' Travails in Many Foreign Countries* (1595). Early seventeenth-century captivity and rescue accounts include John Rawlins's *The Famous and Wonderful Recovery of a Ship of Bristol, Called the Exchange, from the Turkish Pirates of Argier* (1622) and *News from Sally* [Salle] *of a Strange Delivery of Four English Captives from the Slavery of the Turks* (1642), and Francis Knight's *A Relation of Seven Yeares Slaveries Under the Turkes of Argeire, suffered by an English Captive Merchant* (1640). Operating from the North African port cities of Tunis, Algiers, and Tripoli, these pirates under the control of the Ottoman Empire raided not only in the Mediterranean, but as far north as Iceland and west to South America, capturing merchant and passenger ships and raiding towns to obtain Christian slaves for the Ottoman market.

In 1676, Dorman Newman published *A True narrative of a wonderful accident which occur'd upon the execution of a Christian slave at Aleppo in Turky being a remarkable instance of divine providence, attesting the acceptableness of the Christian religion, and the virtue of chastity to Almighty God.* The anonymous pamphlet was 'written at first for the Satisfaction of a Friend only; and since made publick for the strengthening of Virtue'. The validity of the contents is authorized by the confirmation of several 'Eminent and Worthy Gentlemen (Turky-Merchants), who gather at Elford's Coffee House in the George-yard in Lombard Street'.[195] The pamphlet details how 'a handsome

---

[195] *A True narrative of a wonderful accident*, 1.

French Slave, a young man of eighteen years old', inspired the lust of his household's Steward, 'that horrid and unnatural sin (too frequent with the *Mahumetans*) Sodomy' (p. 2). After attempts to bribe the young slave fail, the Steward 'took up a resolution to pollute the chast Youth by force', and in the struggle the slave sliced off his attacker's head. As he attempted to flee the city, the Frenchman encounters his Turkish master on the road and is eventually executed for the killing. However, even though his naked body and head were left exposed on the execution ground, none of the carrion dogs that swarmed the field would touch his body, and it 'did neither stink, corrupt, nor (which is somewhat odd) did it change its colour, but remain'd as fresh and vivid, as if he had been but asleep' (p. 5). So astonished were the Turks that at last they dug a grave to 'intomb this Chast Martyr'.

Less romanticized first-person accounts of the treatment of prisoners taken by pirates and sold into slavery published in the 1670s offered tales of suffering and the persecution of Christians, including William Okeley's *Ebenezer; or, A Small Monument of Great Mercy, Appearing in the Miraculous Deliverance of William Okeley* (1675, repr. 1676, 1684) and Thomas Phelps's *A True Account of the Captivity of Thomas Phelps* (1685).[196] Okeley's popular text was published by John Bunyan's publisher Nathaniel Ponder; its frontispiece shows vignettes of prisoners being executed, burned, 'divers Cruelties', and ultimately their daring escape in a canvas boat. Okeley was a captive in Algiers between 1639 and 1644; he had been a crew member on a ship commissioned by the Earl of Warwick, Lord Saye, and Lord Brooke, Puritan leaders in Parliament, and John Pym, the future Parliamentary leader, to establish a godly new colony in the West Indies off the coast of modern Nicaragua. In the opening verses, 'Upon this Book, and its Author', Okeley declares:

> This Author never was in Print before
> And (let this please or not) will never more
>
> .   .   .   .   .
>
> He should as soon another Voyage take,
> As be Oblig'd another Book to make.[197]

The poem goes on to declare 'This Book is Protestant, and hates a Lye' and repeatedly stresses its anti-Catholic stance, which would have been attractive to many readers during the Popish Plot years in which it first appeared (see *CV* 3.II). In the 1684 edition, it makes direct allusion to Bunyan's *Pilgrim's Progress* (1678) (see *MV* 3.V), declaring that

> If Gentleman and Christian may avail,
> If Honour and Religion can be bail
> For this poor Pilgrim's Truth and Faithfulness,
> It may with Leave and safety past the Press.[198]

---

[196] Potter, 'Pirates and "Turning Turk"'.   [197] Okeley, *Ebenezer*, 'Upon this Book'.
[198] Okeley, *Ebenezer* (1684 edn); subsequent quotations are from this edition.

The text was 'drawn out many years with my own hand', he informs the reader in the preface, 'yet till I could prevail with a Friend to teach it *to speak a little better English*, I could not be perswaded *to let it walk abroad; The Stuff and Matter is my own, the Trimming and Form is anothers*, for whom I must vouch, that he has done the *Truth, my self, and the Reader Justice*' (sig. B4ʳ). 'Let him know, that he shall meet with nothing *in Fact* but what is *precisely true*; what of *wonderment* he may Encounter, was of *God's own working*, not of *Man's inventing*', the author of the preface avows, and throughout his narrative the reader is exhorted to see the hand of Providence at work (sig. A2ᵛ).

Appended to the 1684 edition was an account of the enslavement of another seaman and his comrades, one James Deane, captured in June of 1679. Deane, in his account, highlights again 'the detestable sollicitations of their most unnatural Lusts, to which they were not wanting in their cursed Importunities' (p. 91). If that were not sufficient to harrow the reader, Deane recounts that 'our very *Souls* were not free from their Tortures; They being so filthy as to mix with *Brute Beast*, having seen such Evidences of their abominations in that kind, with some Creatures that were on Board, as fill'd our Hearts with horror, and are not fit to be named amongst Christians' (p. 91). Once on land and sold, he and his fellow European slaves contrived to build a boat, only to have it discovered; fortunately, within a few weeks of that disappointment, James Deane's ransom, 400 pieces of eight, arrived from England and he was freed.

Phelps, who was held captive in Meknes in 1684–5, dedicated his account to Samuel Pepys, who had introduced Phelps at James II's court to tell his story to the King. Phelps had been used as a slave to construct the new royal city of Meknes in Morocco, and he intended his account to be less a record of divine intervention in human lives than a pragmatic warning to those sailing in the Barbary waters, although dutifully grateful to God's benevolence. Phelps declared that he had been brought to publish it to educate 'my fellow Sea-men; as well as satisfying the curiosity of my Country-men, who delight in Novel and strange Stories'.[199] Describing in his preface to the Christian reader that he had experienced a slavery 'worse than *Egyptian* Bondage ... to the most unreasonable and Barbarous of Men', Phelps draws a larger patriotic point to the attention of his readers about the rights enjoyed by Englishmen: 'now I know what Liberty is, and can put a value and make a just estimate of that happiness, which before I never well understood' (p. 8). Phelps declares that 'I have been several times in the *West-Indies*, and have seen and heard of divers Inhumanities and cruelties practised there, I have also read in Books, and have heard Learned men discourse of the *Sicilian* Tyrants and Roman Emperours, but indeed I forget them all, they are not to be named in comparison with this Monster of *Africk*, a composition of Gore and Dust, whom nothing can attone but humane Sacrifices' (pp. 8–9).

---

[199] Phelps, *A True Account*, 'To Samuel Pepys'.

Phelps and several companions escape and are rescued by a passing English man-of-war. Phelps offers to lead them back into the harbour at Mamora, where they are successful in setting fire to two of the pirate ships. In his conclusion, Phelps apologizes for his writing style as 'rough and unpolish'd, which the courteous Reader I hope will a little excuse, expecting no other from a blunt Seaman, acquainted with nothing so much as Dangers and Storms', but he proudly proclaims that 'I have Penn'd this Narrative with all the sincerity and truth, that becomes a plain-dealing *English-man*', and he urges his readers to have compassion for the English captives still in slavery (p. 26).

Although the number of attacks had declined by the latter part of the seventeenth century, the figure of the Christian slave in the hands of the Muslim pirate remained a potent one for an English audience. Pirates in the fictions of the 1670s and early 1680s are essentially part of the foreign settings and foreign customs providing the background for the adventures of the protagonists both male and female. They also function as an important plot device to move the characters from one adventure into the next, unlike the degrading and impoverished slavery described in the real captives' narratives. The male protagonist in Roger Boyle's *Parthenissa* (1676) is captured by a 'Cilician Pyrate' but so impresses his captor that 'I had nothing of a Slave, but the name, and whose affection I gain'd so entirely, that he often protested 'twas that only which hinder'd my liberty'.[200]

The combination of ladies in distress and threatening pirates creates opportunities not only for a heroic rescue, but also for several ingenious and independent heroines. In one novel translated from French, *Zelinda* (1676), as the African pirates attack, the intrepid and chaste heroine cuts her hair and dons male attire to escape. In *Evagoras* (1677), the heroine Alcandra repeatedly is captured, imprisoned, and confronted with immediate death, including being captured by a pirate who takes her to Rhodes, where 'I escaped narrowly losing my Life there; for these Pirates have a Custom to Sacrifice a Virgin to the God *Neptune* every time they go to make some Voyage, and as bad luck would have it, the lot fell upon me: but as if Fate would seem to contradict it self, the Priest became deeply in Love with me', and preserves her for further adventures.[201] Likewise, in *Diana, Dutchess of Mantua, or, The persecuted lover a romance* (1679, 1681), by Rowland Carleton, the hero Frederick, having escaped the Moors, is then taken by Turkish pirates, 'a Captive among the rest, and stripped both of all his Cloaths, and what was dearest to him in the World, next your self, the Picture was taken from him'.[202]

In terms of the real dangers faced by ordinary seamen, the 1670s saw increased military action being taken against the pirates. Charles II's

---

[200] Boyle, *Parthenissa*, 290.

[201] *Evagoras*, 136.

[202] Carleton, *Diana*, 105. For attribution, see Morgan, *The Rise of the Novel of Manners*, 41, 189, 191.

Ambassador, Heneage Finch, 3rd Earl of Winchilsea (1627/8–89), had an account of his earlier diplomatic mission in 1660 and his residence in Constantinople published in 1661 by his secretary Paul Rycaut (1629–1700) as *A Narrative of the success of the voyage of the right honourable Heneage Finch, earl of Winchelsea*, which was frequently reprinted in the 1670s. Rycaut himself became the Consul at Smyrna. Rycaut's *The Present State of the Ottoman Empire*, which was published shortly before the Great Fire of London in 1666, had become by the late 1670s the standard work on the subject, translated into French, Dutch, German, Italian, and Polish. Containing accounts of the nature of government, the education of the ruling classes, the military forces, and accounts of Islam as a religion, the volume was also illustrated with drawings of native costumes and architecture. This was followed in 1679 with *The History of the Turkish Empire* [in later editions *History of the Turks*] *from the year 1623 to the year 1677* with the period from 1660 to 1677 based on his own experiences and observations, 'some part of those fruits arising from my vacant hours of eighteen Years residence in *Turky*, seven whereof I compleated at *Constantinople*, in quality of Secretary to the Lord Ambassadour, and for eleven Years I exercised the Office of Consul at *Smyrna*'.[203]

Writing around the year 1677, Rycaut gives an account of the effect of Mehmed IV's declaration of his intention to return to the capitol throne at Constantinople after sixteen years' absence: 'the humour which then possessed *Constantinople* appeared like that of *London* at our Kings Restauration, all joy, even to transport, for this unexpected Return; the people in the streets congratulating their mutual happiness, thanked God, that they had lived to see that happy day and blessed hour' (p. 328). However, instead of a grand formal entry into the city, the Sultan camped outside its gates, visited it incognito, and upon visiting a Dutch resident in Therapea, liked his house 'so well, that he took it from the Proprietor, and conferred it without any consideration of money on one of his Courtiers, giving out a Proclamation, That no Christian Minister should possess any Seat or Habitation on the side of the *Bosphorus*'. 'A strange thing', Rycaut concludes temperately, 'and what is not to be paralleled in any part of the World' (p. 329).

Rycaut's account also includes episodes that resemble those found in contemporary fictions, involving the beautiful women of the seraglios. One of the former concubines of Sultan Iharhim, having obtained her freedom, gave herself the title *Soltana Sporcha*, which Rycaut rejects, declaring 'for she was no other than a Bawd, or something worse, making it her Profession to buy young Girls, and to educate them in singing, dancing, and in all the ways which best accomplish Courtisans' (p. 331). With the new Sultan's court now in close proximity, she pinned her hopes on a girl

[203] Rycaut, *The History of the Turkish Empire*, sig. J1^r.

more brisk and aery than the others which could sing, and dance, and prate incomparably, and was so quick in her Reparties, that she greatly delighted the Pasha's and Lords, whose pleasures she attended, bringing from them considerable Gifts and Presents to the enriching of her self and Mistress; and became so much the talk of the Court, that at length the report of her arrived the ears of the Grand Signior, (p. 331)

who requests that she be sent to him. Sporcha agrees, but 'consigned her with great submission into the hands of the Messenger; but with this caution, that she humbly desired the Sultan not to make any attempt on her Chastity, in regard she was both a Virgin and a Free-woman' (p. 331). The Sultan, although attracted, found her resistance to his advances more frustrating than rewarding and returned her. However, while 'exercising her Arts', she was viewed by 'one *Chesmé* Aga, a Bosnian by Nation, Captain of the Great Viziers Guard, a stout and valiant man' (p. 331), eventually leading to the couple eloping for love. The fate of the star-crossed lovers was as quick as in any fiction: 'it was not long before the fatal Decree came for putting *Chesmé* Aga to death, and sending the Woman to the Seraglio, which was immediately executed' (p. 323). Rycaut explains: although the Sultan's act

might seem to denote a natural cruelty in the Sultan, being in reality very severe, though the whole course of his Reign hath been more gentle and mild than of any of the Ottoman Emperours; only this fact proceeded rather from disdain than thirst of blood, being angry that this Girl should prefer the Love of one of his Vassals before the Honours of the Seraglio. (p. 323)

In general, Rycaut's portrait of the Sultan is a positive one, at least as he stands in comparison to the conduct of his father and earlier rulers. 'There is none but must judge him to have deserved the Character of a prudent and politick Person' (p. 333), Rycaut summarizes after the death of 'the Grand Signior' in September of 1677. 'Certainly he was not a Person who delighted in bloud, and in that respect of an humour far different from the temper of his Father', Rycaut notes. Of particular praise in Rycaut's eyes was Mehmed IV, who was 'educated in the Law, and therefore greatly addicted to all the Formalities of it, and in the Administration of that sort of Justice very punctual and severe', leading him also to be 'very observant of the Capitulations between our King and the Grand Signior, being ready to do Justice upon any corrupt Minister, who pertinaciously violated and transgressed them' (p. 333).

As the invading Ottoman Turk armies moved further into Europe, English translations of foreign accounts gave eyewitness accounts not only of the battles but also of the person of the Sultan and his retinue. The account by the French captive Georges Guillet de Saint-Georges (1625–1705), held in slavery in Barbary for four years, went through an estimated thirty-six editions in English and French between 1675 and 1676: *An Account of a late Voyage to Athens...also the most remarkable passages in the Turkish camp at the siege of Candia and divers other particularities of the affairs of the port.* The Siege of Candia in Crete had lasted from 1648 to 1669, with the Turks ultimately defeating the Venetians. In the 1680s, readers learned of the steady progress of Turkish forces moving from Belgrade towards Vienna. Battles between Turkish forces and members of the Habsburg Empire were reported in the *London Gazette* and described in letters home from Englishmen engaged in the fighting. In the 1680s the threat to Vienna was seen as an attack on the stability of Christian Europe. A multinational European force including numerous English soldiers ultimately defeated the attacking Turks, but battles between the European forces and the Turks over Hungary and Transylvania would continue for another sixteen years.

While narratives of the New World, North Africa, and the Levant in the 1670s and 1680s are permeated with both a fascination for the exotic and a horror of Christians in captivity, English writers' accounts of the Far East, China, Japan, India, and the Spice Islands, on the other hand, focused on trade, luxury, wealth, and potential greatness. As critics have noted, John Milton in book X of *Paradise Lost* (1667) has Michael point out to Adam the 'Mightiest Empire[s]' of the future, including '*Cambalu*, seat of *Cathaian Can* | ... | To *Paquin* of *Sinean* Kings'.[204] Josiah Child, director of the East India Company, observed in 1681: 'Foreign Trade produceth Riches, Riches Power, Power preserves our Trade and Religion; they mutually work one upon and for the preservation of each other'.[205] English readers had had translations of earlier Spanish, Dutch, and Portuguese accounts of the Far East since the sixteenth century, and in the 1670s there were several new editions of texts by Juan de Palafox y Mendoza (1600–59), *The History of the Conquest of China by the Tartars* (1676, 1679), Lorenzo Magalotti (1637–1712), *China and France, or, Two treatises the one, of the present state of China as to the government, customs, and manners of the inhabitants thereof ... from the observation of two Jesuites lately returned from that country* (1676), and Michel Baudier (1589?–1645), the historiographer to the court of France's *The History of the Court of the King of China* (1682).

Baudier's account was based on a narrative recorded by a Jesuit visitor to China and published in French in 1626; the first English version appeared in 1682, and it was also included in Awnsham and John Churchill's *Collection of Voyages and Travels* (1704, 1732, 1744–6, and 1752). Unlike the hardships endured by Turkish and Moorish subjects at the hands of their capricious rulers, the Chinese are applauded for their stability, for 'we find in their Histories, that for above two thousand years they have conserved and maintained their Monarchy against the Troubles, which might be stirred up within and about the vast Extent thereof';[206] this had come to an end with the collapse of the Ming dynasty in 1644 and the subsequent Manchu conquest, which culminated with the seizure of Taiwan in 1683. Writing of the earlier Ming period, however,

[204] Milton, *Paradise Lost*, bk X, ll. 389–92. See Markley, *The Far East*, ch. 2.
[205] Child, *A Treatise*, 29.   [206] Baudier, *History of the Court of the King of China*, 81.

Baudier's narrator recounts that 'the Vertue of the *Chineses* is not without Divertisement', and, thanks to 'abundance of Riches, brings forth Delights amongst them, and conducts their Life in the Charms of Pleasures', especially that of feasting (p. 82). There follows a detailed description of the elaborate dining practices, highlighting the skills of Chinese arts, which 'bear the Bell from all other people of the World' and the elegance and refinement of the manners of the court:

They cover not these Tables with any Table-clothes, the Cleanliness and Neatness of the *Chineses* in their Eating has no need thereof: They spread upon them Carpets of Damask, or like Stuff, hanging down to the ground: They place upon the four Corners of the Table severall little open Baskets, woven with Threds of Gold and Silver, some full of divers Flowers of Sugar, represented to the Natural...In the middle of the Table are placed exquisite Viands...ordinarily all sorts of Fowl and Venison in Plates of Silver and fine Porcelane: They eat neatly, and take their Meat with Forks of Gold or Silver, not touching it any way with their Hands. (p. 82)

The English East India Company, founded in 1600, had successfully established a trading post on the island of Taiwan in 1672 and in the next decade began trading directly with Canton, Amoy, and Chusan, although the great expansion of trade between England and China would occur after 1700, and Canton became the key port in 1715. As part of the initial agreement, the English merchants were granted permission to create a factory in Taiwan and to purchase silk, sugar, Japanese copper, and deerskins in exchange for gunpowder, matchlock guns, and iron, in addition to providing a blacksmith to make guns and gunners to train the Chinese in the use of them.[207] Simon Delboe and an eight-person staff managed the Taiwan trading house. English ships such as the *Experiment*, the *Return*, and the *Camel* were sailing in the 1670s between India, Thailand, Macao, and Taiwan, much the same route as Daniel Defoe would have Robinson Crusoe travel in his continuation *The Farther Adventures of Robinson Crusoe Being the Second and Last Part of his Life and Strange Surprizing Accounts of his Travels Round three Parts of the Globe Written by Himself* (1719). Prior to the defeat of the Ming dynasty by the Qing dynasty of the Manchu, Taiwan had been an important port of call for foreign trade with Japan; the ships carried home tea, silver, and silks such as damask, and red and white brocades. Such rich cargoes tempted pirates, so the merchant ships were typically escorted by men-of-war, such as the frigate *Formosa*, which was active in 1676 and 1677.

Japan itself, however, was closed to foreigners by the Emperor's policy of *sakoku* in 1638. Nevertheless, in 1677, the East India Company sent ships to Nagasaki in an attempt to sell English cloth to the Japanese and to offer 'other English Manufacture, and for the procuring of Gold, Silver & Copper for the

[207] Tsai, *Maritime Taiwan*, 64. See Morse, *Chronicles*, vol. 1, and Shepherd, *Statecraft and Political Economy*.

supply of our other Factories in East India yt wee may not send Gold & Silver' there from England.[208] The English ships were simply refused permission to land. Robert Ferguson (d. 1714), who would twenty years later attempt to justify the establishment of the Darien Scheme in Panama by the Scots, which effectively bankrupted that country (see CV 5.I), wrote in 1677 that the East India trade would prove to be the most profitable for the English, and commented on the desirability of securing both China and Japan as markets for English goods in exchange for silver. He also admitted the high cost of the failed expedition to Japan: 'though they have met with very great difficulties and disappointments in the attempts they have made, one undertaking about three years since for the gaining of that Trade, though designed with all the care and circumspection possible, proved ineffectual, to the Companies loss of at least 50 thousand pounds'.[209]

The expanded edition of Tavernier's voyages published in 1680 included his travels in India, China, and Taiwan, and includes reports of earlier travellers' experiences of Japan. In Tavernier's narrative, the culture of the elite Japanese epitomized both refinement and arbitrary violence. 'There is no Nation under Heaven that fears Death less than this, or that is more enclin'd to cruelty', he observes, noting the custom of requiring loyal retainers to demonstrate their allegiance: 'If any Prince or great Lord makes a Feast for his Friends, at the end of the Feast he calls his principal Officers, and asks 'em, if there be any that has so much love for him as to kill himself before the Guests for his sake. Presently there arises a dispute among them who shall have the Honour; and who ever the Prince is pleas'd to name, rips up his Belly with a *Cric*, which is a kind of Dagger, the poynt whereof is Poyson'd'.[210]

Tavernier relates encounters he had with earlier Portuguese merchants who recounted the determination by the Japanese to expel Christianity: 'In sixteen years, that is, from 1613 to 1629, the Christians were so multiply'd, that there were above 400,000; but in the year 1649, the same *Hollander* relates, that those *Japonners* who were brought from thence by the Company's Ships to *Amsterdam*, affirm'd, that Christianity was utterly extirpated out of the Island' (p. 11). Such accounts would form the background for Jonathan Swift's use of Japan in *Gulliver's Travels* (1726), as well as his unfinished satire on English court corruption, *An Account of the Court and Empire of Japan*.[211] The accounts of foreign parts emerging in the 1670s and 1680s will thus help to form the imagination of the exotic and the luxurious as well as the nature of barbarity and inhumane well through the first half of the eighteenth century.

---

[208] Quoted in Massarella, *A World Elsewhere*, 356.   [209] Child, *Treatise*, 22.
[210] Tavernier, *The six voyages* (1680 edn), 4.   [211] See Markley, *The Far East*, chapter 7.

4

The End of the Century, Scripting Transitions, 1685–1699

I. 1685–1686

I am never to forget the unexpressable luxury, & prophanesse, gaming, & all dissolution, and as it were total forgetfulness of God (it being Sunday Evening) which this day sennight, I was witnesse of; the King, sitting & toying with his Concubines Portsmouth, Cleaveland, & Mazarine: &c: A french boy singing love songs, in that glorious Gallery, whilst about 20 of the greate Courtiers & other dissolute persons were at Basset round a large Table, a bank of at least 2000 in Gold before them...and surely as they thought would never have an End: six days after was all in the dust.

John Evelyn, *Diary*, 4. 413–14, 6 February 1685

Now may this little Book a blessing be,
To those that love this little Book and me,
And may its buyer have no cause to say,
His Money is but lost or thrown away,
Yea, may this Second Pilgrim yield that Fruit,
And may with each good Pilgrims fancie sute,
And may it perswade some that go astray,
To turn their Foot and Heart to the right way.

John Bunyan, *The Pilgrim's Progress. From This World to that which is to come The Second Part*, 2nd edn (1686)

In February 1685, Charles II died unexpectedly following a sudden apoplexy. His brother James, Duke of York, ascended the throne as James II amidst intense speculation and fears over his religious faith and his political philosophy. The death of Charles would have an immediate simple effect on the literary culture of the period: the London theatres of which he had been patron and

Figure 5. John Milton, *Paradise Lost* (1688). RB 139965. The Huntington Library, San Marino, California

a devoted attendee were closed; the professional poets and dramatists were occupied in crafting public documents of mourning, on the one hand, and creating a new coronation spectacle, on the other. Cromwell's government had melted down the earlier crowns of the English queens, so a set had to be designed for Mary of Modena's coronation as the Queen of England. The general public watched and waited to see what the newly crowned King James would change, as he publicly attended Catholic mass for the first time with his Italian Catholic wife.

Among the first and most obvious of the changes happened in the courtier lifestyle that had so intrigued and scandalized commentators since the 1660s, set the tone for the fashionable London comedies on stage, and provided the plots for scandalous 'secret histories' and allegorical fictions and lampoons. Unlike his brother Charles, in his maturity James became less a friend to drunken wits, regardless of their literary abilities or amusing natures. James dismissed from court his own mistress, Catherine Sedley (only to recall her later), attempted to ban the aristocratic practice of duelling, and attempted to increase taxes on wine. Observers reported that, 'On Sunday last, the King going to Mass told his attendants he had been informed that since declaring against the disorder of the household, some had the impudence to appear drunk in the Queen's presence . . . he advised them at their peril to observe his orders, which he would see obeyed'.[1]

Charles died asking that his mistress Nell Gwyn would be looked after; the former celebrity comedienne on the London stage received a handsome pension and a house in St James's. The Duchess of Portsmouth, the much-disliked French Catholic mistress of Charles, was told by James that, as long as she settled her debts in England, she was free to return to France with all her accumulated titles and wealth, which she did. Broadside ballads such as 'A pleasant dialogue betwixt two wanton ladies of pleasure; or, The Dutchess of Portsmouths woful farwel to her former felicity', and 'The Dutchess of Portsmouths farewel: the Dutchess holds a dialogue, yea, doth relate the wretched state, and talks with Madam Gwin', quickly spread the news. Barbara Palmer, Duchess of Cleveland, Charles's first and most powerful *maîtresse en titre*, had returned from France a converted Catholic in 1682, but had not returned to the court to reside. Her influence could still be felt there, however: in January 1685, the ailing Charles rescinded the fine keeping her current lover, the actor Cardell Goodman, in prison, and in October of that year James II pardoned Goodman completely, permitting him to return to his roles with the United Actors Company, recently formed in 1682.

After Charles's death, the court would slowly cease to be the glittering spectacle on display for all viewers. It would during James's brief reign remain a chief patron of the arts, especially the visual ones; plays were performed there frequently after the mourning for Charles was over, and the court of Mary of Modena produced several notable poets from among her maids of honour. In 1685 and 1686, the court of James II was of necessity more occupied with the transition to power and with the almost immediate challenge issued to it by Charles's Protestant, illegitimate son, the Duke of Monmouth.

London remained the centre of the English publishing world in 1685–6. Of the estimated 2,034 titles published in 1685, 1,625 of them were published in London; production declined in 1686 down to 1,084 works, the lowest number since the period between 1665 and 1670, but of those 853 appeared with a London imprint.[2] The subject classifications in the Term Catalogues, 1685–9, reveal that, as before, 'divinity' was still the leading topic for publication, with 'history' and 'poems' being the other large categories along with 'miscellaneous' (table 4). Jacob Tonson (1655/6–1736) (see *CV* 3.III) was one of the leading London publishers of literary materials, having become Dryden's only publisher after 1679. He would eventually pick up the copyrights of many of the literary authors such as John Donne and of the plays of Ben Jonson, which Henry Herringman (bap. 1628–1704) had previously purchased on the death of Humphrey Moseley in 1661 (see *MV* 1.III; *CV* 3.III). Tonson and Dryden

[1] Quoted in Haile, *Queen Mary of Modena*, 122.
[2] Barnard, McKenzie, and Bell (eds), *The Cambridge History of the Book in Britain*, 4. *1557–1695*, table 1.

would collaborate on several lengthy editorial projects during these two years, including the second volume of Tonson's series of miscellanies, *Sylvæ* (1685), to be discussed later in this section, which comprised mostly commissioned verse translations. Herringman had changed his focus from acquiring the copyrights of living writers, to bringing out collected editions of famous dead ones, and in 1685 he produced his edition of Shakespeare.

Other presses active in these years included the one at Edinburgh, where the royal patent was zealously held by the heirs of Andrew Anderson, notably Agnes Campbell, and the presses in Dublin and York. In Dublin, the King's Printer, Benjamin Tooke, was less successful in controlling trade, and Joseph Ray set up a flourishing rival press. In York, although most of the texts produced were by Quaker writers, J. White published an expanded second edition of the local interest book by the attorney George Meriton (1634–c.1711), *The Praise of Yorkshire Ale* (1685), cataloguing drinks and 'the Humors of most sorts of Drunkards', featuring a 'York-shire dialogue, in pure natural Dialect, as it is now commonly spoken in the North parts of York-shire'. Meriton, interestingly, would go on in 1698 to publish *Immorality, Debauchery, and Profaneness Exposed* specifically targeting drunkenness and the profanity of the stage (see *MV* 4.IV). Authors and booksellers in the provinces were also commissioning London printers to produce texts specifically for their areas: *Miscellany Poems and Translations By Oxford Hands* (1685) was printed in London for Anthony Stephens, a 'Bookseller near the Theatre in OXFORD'. Likewise, the minister John Lougher had his *Sermons on Several Subjects* (1685) printed by 'T.S.' in London for Edward Giles, 'Bookseller in *Norwich*, near the Market-place'. In his epistle to the reader, Lougher dedicates the volume to 'my esteemed Christian Friends in and about *Southrepps* and *Alby* in *Norfolk*': 'they were once delivered to your Ears, they are now in your Eye, the Lord writ them in all your hearts'.[3]

In 1685, three young poets also died, and their lives, writings, and posthumous publications offer a window into some aspects of the literary culture of their time. Mary Evelyn (1665–85), Anne Killigrew (1660–85), and Anne Wharton (1659–85) all participated in the female side of court culture or moved near it through their parents, with Anne Killigrew serving as a maid of honour in the court of Mary of Modena, Mary Evelyn having numerous social contacts through her parents with the maids of honour, and Anne Wharton having been raised by Anne, Countess of Rochester, the mother of the poet and court satirist John Wilmot, Earl of Rochester, and along with her sisters having accompanied the Countess to the court of St James. All three writers were accomplished in several genres, and, although their writings were in circulation among friends and family, their works were not printed until after their deaths. As case studies, the numerous poetic responses to the deaths of Killigrew and Wharton highlight their active presence in the literary culture of

---

[3] Lougher, *Sermons*, sig. A2^r.

their generation, while Mary Evelyn's death, deeply lamented by her parents, also reveals her engagement with matters both spiritual and worldly.

We have the most complete record of the education and literary activities of Mary Evelyn through her father's diary and her mother's correspondence. She read widely in devotional texts in English, French, and Italian: her father records that she spent 'a considerable part of every day in private devotion, reading and other virtuous exercises, she had collected & written out aboundance of the most useful and judicious period of the Books she read, in a kind of Commonplace' (Evelyn, *Diary*, 4. 421). She occasionally went to see public plays, 'but since the stage grew licentious, tooke greate scandal at them', although she herself had 'the talent of rehearsing any Comical part or poeme, as was to them she might decently be free with, more pleasing than the Theatre' (Evelyn, *Diary*, 4. 422). 'No body living', in her grieving father's view, 'read prose, or Verse, better & with more judgement, & as she read, so she write not onely most correct orthography, but with that maturitie of judgement, and exactness of the periods, choice expressions, & familiarity of style' (Evelyn, *Diary*, 4. 423). In her father's study, 'she had read aboundance of History, & all the best poets, even to Terence, Plautus, Homer, Vergil, Horace, Ovide, all the best Romances, & modern Poemes'; he adds, she 'could compose very happily, & and put in her pretty Symbol, as in that of the *Mundus Mulierbris*, wherein is an enumeration of the immense variety of the Modes & ornaments belonging to the Sex' (Evelyn, *Diary*, 4. 423–4).

Mundus Muliebris: or, The Ladies Dressing-Room Unlock'd, and her toilette spread In burlesque was subsequently published in 1690 (see MV 4.V). The anonymous preface highlights the poem's theme, the ways in which modern young ladies demand the spoils of the world to ornament the personal space of their dressing room. Foreshadowing Alexander Pope's description of Belinda's dressing table in *The Rape of the Lock* (1714) (see MV 5.V), the poet describes:

> Tea-Table, Skreens, Trunks, and Stand,
> Large Looking-Glass richly Japan'd,
> And hanging Shelf, to which belongs
> Romances, Plays, and Amorous Songs.[4]

Mary Evelyn devoted a considerable part of her day to the practice of reading critically, making commentaries on what she read, and creating her own mild satire of fashionable female life. Like many cultivated readers both male and female of that time, she was fully engaged with the literary culture of her day, both as a reader and as a commentator on it, although never seeking publication.

Among the papers of her mother's family has recently been found a manuscript copy of some of the verses by Anne Killigrew.[5] Killigrew was the daughter of Dr Henry Killigrew, the chaplain of the Duke of York and prebendary of Westminster; her uncles Thomas Killigrew (1612–83) and Sir William Killigrew

---

[4] Pope, *The Rape of the Lock*, 8.   [5] BL Add. MS 78233.

(bap. 1606–95) were both intimates of Charles II and his courtiers, and Thomas Killigrew had received one of the first patents for the new theatres in 1660 (see *MV* 2.III). Her mother, Judith, and various other female relatives all served members of the royal family, and Anne herself is listed as one of the maids of honour of Mary of Modena in 1683. Thus Killigrew grew up in a vibrant if often clashing mixture of literary, court, and clerical domains. She was known during her lifetime, not only as an accomplished poet, but also as a painter, making portraits of James as the Duke of York and Mary of Modena in addition to pastoral landscapes and biblical scenes. After her death from smallpox, her grieving father published the manuscripts he collected as a monument to her life, *Poems by Mrs Anne Killigrew* (1686).

The frontispiece is a mezzotint engraving of her self-portrait, showing a solemn, but fashionable, young woman with a direct gaze. The twenty-nine poems in the volume include pastoral dialogues, epigrams, occasional verse exchanged between her and her literary friends ('To my Lord Colrane, *in Answer to his Complemental Verses Sent Me under the Name of* CLEANOR'), and a fragment of an unfinished epic on Alexander the Great, at whose end the editor notes, 'this was the first Essay of this young Lady in Poetry, but finding the Task she had undertaken hard, she laid it by till Practice and more time should make her equal to so great a Work'.[6] In her own 'An Epitaph on her Self', Killigrew makes clear her dedication to art: 'When I am Dead, few Friends attend my Hearse, | And for a Monument, I leave my VERSE' (p. 82).

In an interesting occasional poem, 'Upon the saying that my VERSES were made by another', she describes her dedication to the muse of poetry: 'Next Heaven my Vows to thee (O Sacred *Muse!*) | I offer'd up, nor didst thou them refuse' (p. 44). However, 'Embolden'd thus, to Fame I did commit, | (By some few hands) my most unlucky Wit' (p. 46). However, rather than the hoped-for fame, Killigrew asserts,

> My Laurels thus an Others Brow adorn'd,
> My Numbers they Admir'd, but Me they scorn'd:
> An others Brow, that had so rich a store
> Of sacred Wreaths, that circled it before. (p. 46)

The next stanza is a tribute to Katherine Philips, '*Orinda*, (*Albion's* and her Sexes Grace)', and a contrast between her reception and Killigrew's:

> Nor did her Sex at all obstruct her Fame,
> But higher 'mong the Stars it fixt her Name;
> What she did write, not only all allow'd,
> But ev'ry Laurel, to her Laurel, bow'd! (p. 46)

It is not clear to whom the readers of her circulated manuscripts ascribed her poems, other than that it was an already well-established poet, but the piece

---

[6] Killigrew, *Poems*, 5.

raises interesting questions in terms of the dynamics of social literary exchange where pieces frequently circulated in copies with no author attribution.

Regardless of her perception in this piece that she was not viewed as a poet, the epitaphs on her death, both published in the volume and several known manuscript ones, suggest the range of her readership and literary links. Dryden's ode 'To the Pious Memory of the Accomplisht Young Lady Mrs Anne Killigrew, Excellent in the two Sister-Arts of Poesie and Painting' is the only one signed in the posthumous edition and is certainly the best known by later generations, declared by the eighteenth-century critic Samuel Johnson to be the finest example of the Pindaric form. In his ode, Dryden uses the virtuous young maid of honour and her brief artistic career to comment on what he increasingly viewed as the decline of public literary culture.

> O Gracious God! How far have we
> Prophan'd thy Heav'nly Gift of Poesy?
> Made prostitute and profligate the Muse,
> Debas'd to each obscene and impious use,
> Whose Harmony was first ordain'd *Above*
> For Tongues of *Angels*, and for *Hymns* of *Love*? (sig. a³ʳ)

For Dryden, Killigrew's life and writings stand against 'This lubrique and adult'rate age'. Apparently sharing Mary Evelyn's growing distaste for the commercial theatre, Dryden questions why we applaud the efforts of popular writers that 'T'increase the steaming Ordures of the Stage? | What can we say t'excuse our *Second Fall*? | Let this thy *Vestal*, Heav'n attone for all!' (sig. a³ʳ).

The other two elegies in the volume are not signed, an anonymous one in English, one in Latin by her uncle Henry Killigrew with its translation, part of which served as her epitaph on her funeral monument.

> Who her, *so Great*, can paint beside,
> The Pencil her own Hand did guide?
> What Verse can celebrate her Fame,
> But such as She herself did frame?[7]

the poem opens. 'Court Glory she did not admire; | Although it lay so neer and faire.' In addition to the printed tributes, there are at least two others never published that have survived. One, signed 'E.E.' and dated 1685, is written on the flyleaf of the volume now in the Turnbull Library in Wellington, New Zealand: 'On the Death of the Truly Virtuous Mrs Anne Killigrew who was Related to my (Deceased) Wife'. It declares that 'I cannot Mourn thy Fate, Sweet Mayd, but Joy | That Thou are gone from all this Worlds Annoy', and concludes:

> My all the Virtuous Celebrate thy Name;
> All Poets Hearts Partake of thy Great Flame

---

[7] Killigrew, *Poems*, 'The Epitaph Engraved on her Tomb'.

> That all their Ardors & their Flights may be
> The Flames that Fly up to the *Deitie*.[8]

The other surviving unpublished tribute is found in the 280-page manuscript compilation volume entitled 'Poems', assembled by a young Cambridge scholar, John Chatwin.[9] Chatwin matriculated at Emmanuel College in 1682, and was a contemporary of the poet Matthew Prior then at St John's; he took his BA in 1685 and then basically vanished from the records. There is no indication that Chatwin, who was raised in Leicestershire, ever met Killigrew; his poem 'To the Pious Memory of Mrs Ann Killigrew' is divided between his admiration for her poems, 'Till she appear'd' all Poetry lay dead', and that for Dryden's ode (fos 149–50).

The final one in this trio of young poets to die in 1685 was Anne Wharton, the niece of John Wilmot, Earl of Rochester. Only one of her poems was published during her lifetime, her elegy on Rochester, under the name 'Urania'; Nahum Tate reprinted it in *Poems by Several Hands* (1685). 'Deep waters silent roll, so grief like mine | Tears never can relieve, nor words define', the poem opens, and highlights Rochester's role as her guide and teacher:

> He civiliz'd the rude and taught the young,
> Made fools grow wise; such artful music hung
> Upon his useful kind instructing tongue.[10]

Critics have commented on the extent to which Wharton's elegy drew forth praise from its readers, including the poet Edmund Waller and the rising politician John Grobham [Jack] Howe [How] (1657–1722), which were published much later in *Examen Miscellaneum* (1702). Aphra Behn wrote a verse letter to Wharton on reading her elegy and Rochester's good friend, Robert Wolseley (1648/9–97), who would write the preface to the printed text of Rochester's play *Valentinian* (1686), likewise praised her. In her 1688 collection, *Lycidus*, Behn would gather together texts relating to Wharton and the performance of Rochester's *Valentinian* (to be discussed later in the section) and published 'To Urania in Mourning', along with her own poem to Wharton, Wharton's response to Wolseley's preface to *Valentinian*, and Behn's own first day prologue for the 1684 performance of *Valentinian*.

Later, in 1693, several more of Wharton's poems appeared in *A Collection of Poems by Several Hands*. The titles of her poems make it clear that initially she wrote as part of a network of correspondents: Gilbert Burnet, who had been Rochester's spiritual adviser before his death and had published his deathbed confessions in 1680, for example, wrote his 'Paraphrase on the Fifty-third Chapter of Isaiah in Imitation of Mrs Anne Wharton', and sent numerous of his poems to her. Edmund Waller likewise wrote 'Cantos of Divine Poesy' upon his reading of her 'Paraphrase of the Fifty-second Chapter of Isaiah'. When she showed her 'Lamentations of Jeremiah' to Samuel Clark, he wrote

---

[8] Repr. in Killigrew, '*My Rare Wit Killing Sin*', 110–11.
[9] Bodl., MS Rawl. poet. 94.   [10] Tate, *Poems by Several Hands*, 393–4.

that they 'would afford more comfortable reflections at a dying hour, than conversing with what belongs only to, or is fit for the Theater'.[11] She also circulated her rhymed heroic drama, *Love's Martyr, or Witt Above Crowns* (*c.*1679),[12] preserved in a fair copy dedicated to Mrs Mary Howe, John Howe's wife (see *MV* 3.IV).

The first collected edition of her works, twenty-four poems and the play, was not made until 1997. In 2004, however, another manuscript volume was discovered that contained further poems by Wharton and one by Edmund Waller, of which eleven of Wharton's were previously unknown.[13] In short, like many poets of the period, Anne Wharton had an extensive critical readership, male and female, of her writings in manuscript; she had a literary network that included professional writers Aphra Behn and Edmund Waller as well as some of the leading Presbyterian and nonconformist ministers of the day. Not unlike the posthumous literary publication of her uncle's poems, some of Wharton's texts circulated singly in letters and also survived to be copied into fair manuscript volumes preserved in libraries; other individual items appeared in print over the next few decades in popular verse compilation volumes.

These three young poets were lamented by friends and family, private losses in a time of public grief and concern. The events in the news of the country at large leading up to Charles's death in early 1685 had created a general atmosphere of uncertainty and alarm. The 1670s and 1680s had been punctuated by a series of widely reported conspiracies and plots to assassinate members of the royal family as well as archbishops and Members of Parliament. These events were followed by highly publicized trials and executions. They ranged from Bacon's rebellion in Virginia, which would serve Aphra Behn as a backdrop for her drama *The Widdow Ranter*, to the domestic Popish Plot invented by Titus Oates and spread by zealous publishers, the Meal Tub Plot to block James's ascension, and the Rye House Plot to murder both Charles and James (see *CV* 3.II).

In the spring of 1685, Thomas Sprat (bap. 1635–1713), the historian of the Royal Society (see *MV* 2.V), published the Rye House narrative, *A True Account And* DECLARATION OF *the Horrid Conspiracy Against the Late* KING, *His Present* MAJESTY, AND THE GOVERNMENT: *As it was Order'd to be Published by His late Majesty* (1685), a text apparently approved and also amended by both Charles and James. Sprat also separately published many of the original documents of the case: *Copies of the information and original papers relating to the proof of the horrid conspiracy against the late king, his present Majesty, and the government*, which includes testimony that led to the trials and executions of William, Lord Russell, and Algernon Sidney [Sydney].

Despite this climate of fear and suspicion, initially, the transfer of power from Charles to James in early 1685 went smoothly. This was much to the surprise of some who believed that the Parliamentarians of the 'Country Party',

---

[11] Bodl., MS Rawl., letters 53, fos 351–2, quoted in *ODNB*.
[12] BL Add. MS 28693.   [13] Beinecke, MS Osborn b408.

now commonly referred to as Whigs, who had attempted to pass the exclusion bills in the late 1670s and 1681, would once again challenge James's title because of his overt practice of Catholicism. The leader of the Whigs during that earlier time, Anthony Cooper, Earl of Shaftesbury, had died in exile in 1683, but many anticipated civil unrest on a local level. Sir John Reresby in Yorkshire noted in his diary that upon hearing the news of Charles's illness he wrote to the officers based in York to tell them to double the watch and that 'a strict watch and ward should be kept in every town for the stopping and apprehending of such as did appear dangerous' (Reresby, *Memoirs*, 350, 4 February 1685). Upon James being declared king, acting on orders from Lord Sunderland, Reresby then had the garrison's great guns fired to salute the new monarch, recording with satisfaction that 'all this being done with all the signs of peace and satisfaction that could be, not only in Yorke, but afterwards throughout the country, and indeed the whole kingdome' (Reresby, *Memoirs*, 352). Christopher Wyvill (1651?–1711), the chaplain of the Duke of Ormond and future dean of Ripon, published in York, at the urging of his listeners, his sermon, whose long title summarizes the feelings of many: THE DUTY OF *Honouring the King, And The Obligations we have thereto: Delivered in a* SERMON *Preached at* RICHMOND *in* York-shire, *on the* 6th. *of* February, *1685/6. Being the Day on which His* MAJESTY *began His happy Reign. At a general Assembly of the Loyal Gentry of those Parts, held there on purpose to celebrate the* KING'S *quiet and peaceable* Succession *to the* Throne *of His* Ancestors.

In Reresby's opinion, the peaceful succession was due in part to James's immediate publication of his principles and plans. 'In a great measure did quiet the minds and apprehension of people was the declaration made by King James to the Privy Councill immediately after the breath was out of the body of his brother, that he would defend the government of England both in Church and State as by law established' (Reresby, *Memoirs*, 353). Also issued as a royal proclamation, James's speech delivered to his Privy Council announced that he was well aware that 'I have been Reported to be a Man for Arbitrary Power, but that is not the onely Story has been made of Me' (Reresby, *Memoirs*, 353). James clearly intended to publish widely his own story—his discourse of monarchy acknowledges the fears of those he governed and reassures in terms of pledging the continuation of rule by law.

I know too, That the Laws of *England* are sufficient to make the King as great a Monarch as I can wish; And as I shall never Depart from the Just Rights and Prerogative of the Crown, so I shall never Invade any mans Property. I have often heretofore ventured My Life in Defence of this Nation, and I shall still go as far as any Man in Preserving it in all its Just Rights and Liberties.[14]

James likewise affirmed to his listeners and readers that 'I know the Principles of the Church of *England* are for Monarchy, and the Members of it have

---

[14] James II, *An Account of what His Majesty said.*

shewed themselves Good and Loyal Subjects, therefore I shall always take Care to Defend and Support it'.[15] While not declaring his own faith, James is clearly signalling to his audience his intentions to be a king who rules by law rather than a personal agenda. It would be in the interpretation of the law, however, that the future rupture between king and Parliament and eventually king and country would arise.

The coronation of James and his wife, Mary of Modena, had to strike a balance between the country's grief over the sudden loss of Charles, and the need to make a new royal image. William Sancroft, the Archbishop of Canterbury, created the order of the service, which is preserved in manuscript, which took place on St George's Day, 23 April 1685, in Westminster Abbey. Henry Howard, 7th Duke of Norfolk, acted as the 'Chief Butler', overseeing the arrangements for the coronation, such as publishing in a broadside the very specific details of the attire for ladies, as determined by their rank, who would be in the Queen's train: a baroness's train would trail a yard upon the ground and be edged for one inch around with ermine, while a countess's train would fall a yard and a half on the ground, her cape would have three rows of ermine, and all would wear crimson velvet, scalloped and fringed with either gold or silver, and their 'Petticoats to be Cloath of Silver, or any other White Stuff, either Lac'd or Embroider'd, according to every ones Fancy'.[16] Ironically, he would serve this same function at the coronation of William and Mary in 1688. The music was orchestrated by Henry Purcell and John Blow, who also conducted the royal choir as it marked the entrance of the royal pair with the anthem 'We are glad'.

Numerous accounts of the journey of the new king and queen from the stairs at Whitehall along the Thames to the stairs at Parliament, the procession to Westminster Abbey, the coronation, and the evening's fireworks were published for the benefit of those unable to attend or who wished for a memento of the occasion. Francis Sandford, the Lancaster Herald, published a highly detailed account of the day later in 1687. A contemporary anonymous broadside published by George Croom at the Blue Ball seems particularly good value: at the top, it has an illustration of the procession forming a three-loop serpentine beginning with the royal trumpeters and followed by the various ranks of clergy, civil leaders, and nobility, and it described the procession below in six columns of text.

The death of Charles and the crowning of James also produced a large outpouring of poetic responses attempting to capture the royal image left by Charles and to welcome the new king. Popular dramatists including John Dryden, Aphra Behn, Thomas Otway, Thomas D'Urfey, and Elkanah Settle, as well as lesser-known writers, published odes lamenting Charles and celebrating James. Bibliographers of the period have described seventy-eight pieces printed on the death of Charles alone (*POAS* 3. 584). An anonymous broadside

---

[15] James II, *An Account of what His Majesty said.*   [16] *An Account of the ceremonial.*

formatted with a heavy black border and tombstone-like *memento mori* motif at the top, *An Elegy on the Death of his Sacred Majesty King Charles the II of Blessed Memory*, offers the conventional praise of Charles as 'A Worthy SON of His Great FATHERS Name', and himself 'A King! whose *Vertues* onely to Rehearse, | Rather requires a VOLUMN then a VERSE'. His endurance in exile and his willingness to forgive—'Never did Person so much *Mercy* Breath'—are highlighted, but perhaps more of a stretch for readers, given Evelyn's depiction of life at his court a mere week before his death, is the assertion that 'His *Actions* may our *Pattern* be, | His *Godly Life*, the *Christian Diary*'.

The dramatist Thomas Otway chose to write about Charles in *Windsor Castle, in a Monument To our late Sovereign K. Charles II*. The tone of the poem seems more personal than many of the other numerous tributes: while praising Charles as 'the Royal Dove', for 'when this Land in Blood he might have laid, | Brought Balsam from the Wounds our selves had made', Otway also touches on the qualities of his personality 'Mercifull, just, good-natur'd, lib'ral, brave, | Witty, a Pleasure's Friend, yet not her Slave',[17] although subsequent generations might disagree. Otway chooses to remember Charles as being embodied by Windsor, seeing in its historic buildings and noble paintings all the elements of what made him a great king and 'father' to his people. Otway concentrates on Charles and his relationship with historical kings, not bringing in references to his court until the very end, and there concentrating entirely on the relationship between Charles and James. He closes with imagining Charles on his deathbed and

> ...the Wonders of Fraternal Love;
> How mourning *James* by fading *Charles* did stand,
> The Dying grasping the Surviving Hand;
> How round each other's Necks their Arms they cast,
> Moan'd with endearing Murm'rings, and embrac'd,
> And of their parting Pangs such Marks did give,
> 'Twas hard to guess which yet cou'd longest live. (p. 26)

The years 1685 and 1686 were prolific for Aphra Behn, with the publication of part two of her successful fiction *Love-Letters Between a Nobleman and his Sister* (see MV 3.V), the performance of her comedy *The Luckey Chance*, and the publication of her anthology of verse *Miscellany*, which included her translation of La Rochefoucauld's cynical *Maximes* as *Reflections on Morality or Seneca Unmasqued*. Her three poems marking the passing of one monarch and the crowning of his successor claim her place as a poet commenting on national public events; they were published by the music printer Henry Playford and were reprinted in Dublin by the printers Andrew Crook and Samuel Helsham.

Behn's poem on the death of Charles, *A pindarick on the death of our late sovereign: with an ancient prophecy on His Present Majesty*, dramatically

---

[17] Otway, *Windsor Castle*, 3, 6.

enacts the first-person speaker's response to awakening to the initial news of Charles's illness, his seeming to rally, and his final demise. Waking from 'Ominous *Dreams*', the narrator receives the initial reports of Charles's death with disbelief, 'That such a *Monarch*! Such a *God* should dye! | And no *Dire Warning* to the World be giv'n: | No *Hurricanes* on Earth! no *Blazing Fires* in Heav'n!'.[18] The news that Charles temporarily rallied permits the speaker to imagine, as does Otway, the final meeting between royal brothers. The dying Charles is described as

> Like *Moses*, he had led the Murm'ring Crowd,
> Beneath the *Peaceful Rule* of his Almighty Wand;
> Pull'd down the *Golden Calf* to which they bow'd,
> And left 'em safe, ent'ring the promis'd Land. (p. 5)

The poem is nearly as much about the succession as it is about Charles. 'To good JOSHUA, now resigns his sway, | JOSHUA, by *Heaven* and *Nature* pointed out to lead the way' (p. 5). James, in this biblical analogy, is depicted as 'Full of the *Wisdom* and the *Pow'r* of God, | The *Royal* PROPHET now before him stood: | On whom His Hands the Dying MONARCH laid'. Behn chose to describe the royal brothers as dearest friends as well as blood kin, 'Not God-like *Jonathan* with greater pain, | Sigh't his last Farewell to the *Royal Swain*', perhaps to highlight the natural succession of the crown from one to the other. Her Pindaric concludes with 'an Ancient Prophecy on His Present MAJESTY', highlighting how 'ev'ry *Miracle* | Preserv'd for *Universal Rule*' through his tumultuous younger days in exile and as a soldier, and how more recently 'In *Patience, Suffering*, and *Humility*, | Your *Condescention*, and Your *Banishment*' were displayed by James, 'Then let the *Obstinate* (convinc'd) agree, | *You only* were preserv'd, and fit, for *Sacred Government*' (p. 5). Behn's second poem, to the dowager queen Catherine, *A Poem on her Sacred Majesty Catherine Queen Dowager* (1685), concentrates on the figure of the virtuous Queen in her grief. It combines both intense religious imagery—Catherine imagined by the speaker as 'like the *Queen* of *Heav'n*' receiving Christ's body—with pastoral,

> As the Chast Goddess of the silent Night,
> You Reign alone, retir'd from Gaudy Light;
> So Mourning Cinthia with her Starry Train,
> Wept the sad Fate of her Lov'd sleeping Swain,[19]

and thus imagines the royal couple as both divine figures but also pastoral lovers.

Behn's final contribution, a lengthy pindaric on the coronation, *On the Happy Coronation of his most Sacred Majesty James II*, begins with a command to her 'muse' to throw off mourning in order to celebrate the coronation

---

[18] Behn, *A pindarick on the death of our late sovereign*, 4.
[19] Behn, *A Poem on her Sacred Majesty Catherine Queen Dowager*, 4.

day. The lengthy thirty-stanza poem follows the events of the day starting with the awakening of James and Mary and their dressing for the coronation—Mary is described with pastoral enthusiasm, as the 'Young waiting *Cupids* with officious care | In smiling order all attend: | This, decks Her *Snowy Neck*, and that her *Ebon Hair*'.[20] 'Oh, Blest are they that may at distance gaze, | And *Inspirations* from Your *looks* may take', this section concludes, and switching to a biblical metaphor laments that the speaker is not close enough to hear her speak, but realizes that it is enough to be able to gaze on her; like the Israelites 'It was enough for them below to *view* the Heav'nly flame' (p. 7).

Their journey on the Thames likewise moves fluidly back and forth between the participation of pagan sea gods and river nymphs, who watch in awe as they 'pay their Tributes to the *Greater* DEITY', and Christian iconography of kingship. While the Nereids sing praises of James as a warrior hero and Mary as

> The President of Vertuous Wives,
> The bright example of the fair,
> Whence Virgins learn their modest lives;
> And Saints their pure Devotion there, (p. 11)

along the banks of the river, the people of London have gathered and

> all the Banks with Acclamations rung,
>
> .   .   .   .   .   .
>
> The different shoutings of the Throng,
> The Female Treble, and the Manly Base,
> The dead flat Notes of the declining race,
> Tun'd to the sharp ones of the young,
> Compleats the noblest Musick of the Day. (p. 12)

'Great Prince of *wonders*, and welcome to that *Throne*', the verse loyally concludes, 'both to Your *Vertues*, and Your *Sufferings* due, | By *Heav'n* and *Birthright* all Your own, | You shar'd the *Danger*, share the *Glory* too' (p. 20).

Dryden's offering *Threnodia Augustalis* also mixes classical and Christian allusions attempting simultaneously to praise Charles for bringing peace and mercy to England while admiring the new warrior king, James. Dryden firmly grounds his verse in Latin precedents, with an epigram from *The Aeneid*, 'O happy friends! For, if my verse can give | Immortal life, our fame shall ever live'.[21] Dryden's tribute did not appear until early March, and he observes in the opening stanza that

> Thus long my Grief has kept me dumb:
> Sure there's a Lethargy in mighty Woe,
> Tears stand congeal'd, and cannot flow;
> And the sad Soul retires into her inmost Room. (*POAS* 4. 585)

[20] Behn, *A pindarick poem on the happy coronation*, 7.
[21] Dryden, *Threnodia Augustalis*, in *POAS* 4. 585.

As with Otway's and Behn's poems, the presence of James next to the throne as the rightful heir is insistently highlighted. 'Our Atlas fell indeed, but Hercules was near' (*POAS* 4. 585), Dryden asserts, introducing the metaphor he will develop for James as the semi-divine warrior.

The second stanza dramatically narrates Charles's final hours from James's point of view. Being awakened with 'ill-omen'd rumor', James, 'Half unarray'd he ran to his Relief, | So hasty and so artless was his Grief' (*POAS* 4. 587). This is a seemingly odd detail, unless one is aware of the other rumours in circulation that the King had possibly been poisoned, rumours that Monmouth would subsequently publish identifying James as the villain. Dryden then narrates the efforts over the five days to restore the King, and Charles's acceptance of his coming death,

> Kind, good, and gracious to the last,
> On all he lov'd before, his dying beams he cast.
> Oh truly good, and truly great,
> For glorious as he rose benignly so he set! (*POAS* 4. 594)

Dryden, like Behn, makes it clear that Charles passes the throne willingly to his brother, 'To whom both heav'n | The right had giv'n | And his own Love bequeathe'd supreme command'. In a section that might be read obliquely as a rebuke to Charles's son, the exiled Duke of Monmouth, Dryden describes James as

> A prince who never disobey'd:
> Not when the most severe commands were laid;
> Nor want, nor Exile, with his duty weigh'd;
> A Prince on whom (if Heav'n its Eyes could close)
> The Welfare of the World it safely might repose. (*POAS* 4. 595)

While applauding the period of peace that Charles brought to England, Dryden looks forward to the change in England's standing with the rulers of rival powers, '*Gaul* and *Batavia* dread th' impending blow; | Too well the Vigour of that Arm they *know*' (*POAS* 4. 595).

Finally, Dryden abandons the classical allusions and addresses more directly than Otway or Behn the contemporary political strife over the succession that had marked the politics of the 1680s. In the final stanza, the poet pleads that 'Heav'n, unfold thy Adamantine Book' to convince those who had fought to exclude James from the throne of the divine intention that James should rule.

> Let them not still be obstinately blind,
> Still to divert the Good thou hast design'd,
> Or with malignant penury,
> To starve the Royal Vertues of his Mind. (*POAS* 4. 604)

'Oh, give them to believe, and they are surely blest!' and with these 'amended Vows of English Loyalty', a prosperous reign will result, with a conquering navy spreading prosperity even to 'the remoter Shores'. 'The British Cannon formidably roars', and the gods of the sea once again acknowledge the domin-ion of England over the waves.

Dryden had also been at work on a major theatrical spectacular when Charles passed away, the allegorical opera *Albion and Albanius*. As with the earlier royal masque *Calisto* in 1675 (see *MV* 3.I), public rehearsals of parts of *Albion and Albanius* had been performed at Charles's request at the court. In the postscript to the printed version, Dryden recorded that Charles had found the first and third acts particularly pleasing and 'publicaly declar'd more than once, That the composition and Chorus's, were more Just, and more Beautiful, than any he had heard in England'.[22] Dryden added a scene for the apotheosis of 'Albion' to complete the allegory and was finally able to present it to the public on 3 June. The production, however, seemed to be cursed by occasions of national crises: John Downes commented that it was finally performed on a 'very unlucky day, being the day the Duke of Monmouth landed in the West. The nation being in a great consternation, it was performed but six times, which not answering half the charge they were at, involved the company very much in debt'.[23]

This spectacular piece, whose run-up costs were rumoured to be £4,000, featured music by one of Charles's favoured composers, the Frenchman Louis Grabu. It was performed for the paying public at the Queen's Theatre in Dorset Garden by the United Company then headed by Thomas Betterton. The sets were elaborate, ornate, symbolic tableaux. Interestingly, they featured represen-tations of both actual contemporary scenes such as monuments and triumphal arches in London and Windsor and the town and cliffs of Dover as well as purely mythological scenes such as 'Poetical Hell' showing Sisyphus rolling his boulder up a hill, Prometheus chained to a rock with a vulture eating at his liver, and an 'abundance of Figures in various Torments'.[24] (II. i). The printed stage directions for the appearance of Iris on a 'very large Machine' stressed the reality behind the fantasy: 'this was really seen the 18th of March 1684 by Capt. *Christopher Gunman*, on Board his R.H. Yacht…He drew it as it appear'd, and gave a draught of it to us. We have only added the Cloud where the Person of *Iris* sits' (I, i, p. 8). English records of natural phenomena become blended with classical imagery, merging the symbolic past with the concrete details of the immediate present.

Other characters descend and ascend the stage in equally complex machin-ery, such as the initial entry by Mercury 'in a Chariot drawn by Ravens' at the start and at the end, Venus and Albanias rise from the sea 'sitting in a great Scallop-shell, richly adorn'd…drawn by Dophins. It moves forward while a Simphony of Flutes-Doux, &c is playing till it Lands 'em on the Stage, and then it closes and sinks' (III. i, p. 27). The Ascension of Albion into the heavens requires a 'very large, and a very glorious Machine' in the form of gilded clouds

---

[22] Dryden, *Albion and Albanius*, 'Postscript'.   [23] Downes, *Roscius Anglicanus*, 40.

[24] Dryden, *Albion and Albanius*, II. i, p. 10.

with Apollo sitting in a golden throne at its centre. After Albion has ascended, the scene is then changed to the final one, representing a walk opening on to a view of Windsor facing Eton and showing the castle, while in the air above it are a 'Vision of the Honors of the Garter; the Knights in Procession, and the King under a Canopy'. The character of Fame rises from centre stage while standing on a globe resting on a pedestal decorated with an image of thin man with 'Fiends Wings and Snakes twisted round his body . . . imcompast by several Phanatical Rebellious Heads, who suck poison from him, which runs out of a Tap in his Side' (III. ii, p. 30). The scenes themselves are so clearly to be read interpretatively that in some sense the spoken or sung words are merely confirming the message of the image.

The plot, such as it is, is an allegorical telling of the restoration of Charles II to the throne. The opera opens with Augusta and Thamesis lying on couches in attitudes of despair, being oppressed by the characters Democracy and Zeal. Lamenting the ruin brought on by these two and their Commonwealth, Thamesis and Augusta sing together 'A Commonwealth's a Load | Our old Imperial Flood | Shall never never never bear again' (I. i, p. 5) as news comes that Albion is to return. In the second Act, Democracy and Zelota, the mother of Zeal, driven out by Mercury, are now in classical Hell, where they create a plot to assassinate Albion. The devilish chorus sings:

> 'Tis a Jubilee here when the World is in trouble:
> When People rebel
> Wee frolick in Hell;
> But when the King falls, the pleasure is double. (II. i, p. 13)

Act Three, Charles's favourite, features Albion landing at Dover, singing that

> To rule by Love,
> To shed no Blood,
> May be extol'd above;
> But here below,
> Let Princes know
> 'Tis fatal to be good. (III. i, p. 21)

Of course, in the following battle between Democracy, Zeal, and Albion, the gods come to Albion's aid and the character of Innocence declares 'Kings they made, and Kings they love, | When they protect a rightful Monarch's Reign, | The Gods in Heav'n, the Gods on Earth maintain' (III. i, p. 27). The character of Albanius, presented as the 'Warlike Loyal Brother', is brought by Venus to the stage to witness Albion being called back to the Heavens, leaving Albanius to continue the legacy and 'shall with fraternal virtues Reign' (III. i, p. 28).

To help cover the costs incurred before the opening, Betterton had doubled the price of box seats to one guinea, and Dryden had prepared for the press an edition of the libretto to be released with its premiere. Dryden had modified the original, including quite recent political events, such as the fall from power of the instigator of the Popish Plot Titus Oates and his subsequent public flogging in May 1685 (see CV 3.II). To ensure a good crowd, the opera's debut was scheduled to coincide with the return of the new Parliament.[25] All seemed poised for a literary success until the news reached London of Monmouth's landing in the west with the intention to take the throne in the name of Protestantism.

Monmouth's rebellion was not the first challenge, however, to the new king. In part triggered by James's public display of Catholicism during a period preceded by highly publicized conspiracies to overthrow the crown, in June 1685 the Scots Presbyterians had risen again under Archibald Campbell, the 9th Duke of Argyll, fighting under the awkward banner 'For God and Religion against Poperie, Tyrany, Arbitrary Government and Erastianisme'.[26] In two declarations issued in Scotland in May 1685, Argyll's supporters pointed to the harsh treatment of Scottish nonconformists, especially after the Rye House Plot (which included the forfeiture of Argyll's estates), actions described as 'Tyranny and Popery twisted together'.[27] However, Argyll's declaration failed to unite the Scots, as Argyll himself was viewed as being a 'malignant' by the more radical Presbyterian Covenanters, and his forces were quickly defeated.

Sometimes referred to as 'the Killing Time'—the years between 1685 and 1688 in Scotland when James II declared that preaching in the fields, or conventicles, was high treason—this period features heavily in the increasing literature of martyrology of the Scottish Covenanters. With the royal monopoly for printing being firmly held by the heirs of Andrew Anderson in Edinburgh, who thus served as the voice of the government and Scottish Council, most of these accounts were not printed until after 1700 and even then were sometimes forced to find their printers in Amsterdam. In 1685, the Argyll and Monmouth rebellions focused the government's attention even more sharply upon groups in opposition to institutions of the government and Anglican Church, the Covenanters as well as the dissenters in London.

In Scotland, large numbers of men and women were imprisoned in the tiny cells at Dunnottar Castle. Alexander Peden (1626?–86), the most charismatic of the many conventicle preachers who travelled southern and central Scotland and Ireland, and who had himself narrowly escaped transportation to Virginia, sent a public letter, subsequently printed, 'The exact Copy of a Letter from Mr Alexander Peden to the Prisoners in Dunnottar Castle, in the Month of July 1685, being above Eightscore, being Sixscore and two men, and Forty-six Women, all driven into one vault'.[28] In his characteristic conversational style, Peden urges the prisoners to consider their own speech carefully: 'let your expressions of Christ be suitable to your experience of him. If ye think Christ's house be bare, and ill provided, harder than ye looked for, assure yourselves, Christ minds only to diet you, and not to hunger you; our steward kens, when

[25] Winn, *John Dryden and his World*, 416.   [26] Quoted in Harris, *Revolution*, 77.
[27] Quoted in Harris, *Revolution*, 77.
[28] Peden, 'The exact Copy of a Letter', quoted in Walker, *Six Saints of the Covenant*, 110.

to spend and when to spare', he urges. 'He's the easiest merchant ever the people of God yoked with', Peden declares, turning to the language of everyday, 'if ye be pleased with the wares, what of his graces makes best for you, he and ye will soon sort on the price; he'll sell good cheap, that ye may speir [ask] for his shop again, and he draws all the sale to himself'.[29]

Peden's biographer, Patrick Walker, in the 1720s and 1730s would publish his accounts of the lives and deaths of leaders of the Covenanting movement, which were eventually gathered together as *Six Saints of the Covenant* (1901). Walker was himself as a young man imprisoned for much of 1684 and in 1685, having been repeatedly tortured for information about weapons; he was sentenced to transportation, but managed to evade it. Among the faithful, much as with the early Quakers chronicling their persecution by the government, careful records were kept of the unfortunate people who were executed by the military without trial under the Act 'Against Preachers at Conventicles, and those present at Field Conventicles' issued in May 1685. The frequently reprinted *A Cloud of Witnesses for the Royal Prerogatives of Jesus Christ* (1714), by John Henderson Thomson, records 'a list of those Killed in the Fields' during 1685 and 1686.[30] One of the most frequently cited stories was the fate of John Brown of Priesthill, 'known in the district as the Christian carrier', who in May of 1685 was shot outside his home before his wife and children on the charge of preaching (pp. 537–9).

A Cloud of Witnesses also offers an anthology of the epitaphs of those killed in this fashion, a compendium of the simple verses and political defiance engraved in stone and carved in wood. Brown's epitaph, forming an acrostic of his name, was set on his gravestone isolated on the moor:

> B utchered by Claverse and his bloody band,
> R aging most ravenously over all the land,
> O nly for owning Christ's supremacy.
> W ickedly wronged by encroaching Tyranny,
> N othing how near soever he to good
> Esteemed, nor dear any truth his blood. (p. 574)

Similarly, equally simple lives were briefly noted for the manner of their deaths within the faith. James Algie and John Park lived their short lives in Kenniswood, a small village near Glasgow; in February 1685, they were hanged for refusing the Oath of Abjuration, and later a marker at Paisley admonishes travellers:

> Stay, passenger, as thou goes by,
> And take a look where thos do ly;
> Who for the love they bare to truth
> Were deprived of their life and youth. (p. 570)

---

[29] Peden, 'The exact Copy of a Letter', quoted in Walker, *Six Saints of the Covenant*, 110.
[30] Thomson, *A Cloud of Witnesses*.

The epitaph continues that their trial was a mockery and that 'At ten condemn'd, at two to die. | So cruel did their rage become, | To stop their speech, caus'd beat the drum'. It concludes, as do many of the stones, 'This may a standing witness be | 'Twixt Presbytery and Prelacy' (p. 570).

Argyll's May 1685 rebellion in the north was supposed to coincide with that launched in the west of England by Charles's illegitimate son, James, Duke of Monmouth, but failed to do so. Monmouth instead landed with a small force in Dorset in early June. The once popular and glamorous courtier, who had danced with the royal princesses in the masque *Calisto* celebrating the unity of the royal family and who was the hero of Baronne D'Aulnoy's *Memoirs of the Court of England in 1675*, was quickly defeated and executed in July. His followers were tried in what became known as the 'Bloody Assizes' presided over by Judge Jeffreys, in which 320 were executed and 800 more transported, clearly demonstrating, as did the continuing treatment of the Scottish Covenanters and Argyll's followers, the new monarch's uncompromising response to rebellion.

The first to be tried by Jeffreys was a 70-year-old widow, Lady Alice Lisle (*c*.1614–85). She was initially sentenced by Jeffreys to be burned alive for giving shelter to fugitives from Monmouth's army, one a well-known nonconformist minister, John Hickes, and his friend, who was a member of Monmouth's army. In the published accounts, Lady Alice acknowledged giving shelter to the Presbyterian minister and his friend but steadily denied the charge of treason or of knowing that they were fugitives. Herself being nearly deaf, she had a friend stand next to her to repeat all that was said loudly in her ear; after a six-hour trial, she was reluctantly condemned by the jury, but Jeffreys is reported to have declared: 'I would have condemned her had she been my mother.'[31]

In her final speech before her sentence was carried out, which James had commuted to beheading, she spoke from the market square in Winchester, addressing 'Gentlemen, Friends & Neighbours'. In her brief speech, she began by acknowledging that 'it may be expected, that I should say something at my Death, my Birth and Education being near this place. My *Parents* instructed me in the Fear of God; and *I* now Dye of the Reformed Religion; always being instructed in that Belief, that if *Popery* should return into this Nation, it would be a Great Judgment'[32] 'The Crime was, my Entertaining a Non-Conformist Minister, which is since sworn to have been in the Duke of Monmouth's Army', she confirmed. 'My Defence was such, as might be expected from a Weak Woman; but such as it was, I never heard it repeated again to the Jury' (p. 3). She closed by acknowledging James's alteration of the means of her execution, 'and I pray God he may long Reign in Mercy as well as Justice, and that he may Reign in Peace, and that the True Religion may Flourish under him' (p. 3). Others found guilty who were hung, drawn, and quartered had their parboiled heads and body parts displayed through the towns of the western region where the rebellion had begun.

---

[31] *A Complete Collection of State Trials*, 7. 373.   [32] *The last words*, 3.

The accounts of the formation of the rebellion, the landing, and Monmouth's own subsequent execution are striking and dramatic. Pawning the jewels of his mistress Henrietta Wentworth and her mother, Monmouth returned with an army of eighty-two men from Holland, where he had been staying with William and Mary of Orange after the Rye House Plot. On 13 June at a market cross in Lyme in the west of England, Monmouth had read aloud, *The Declaration of James, Duke of Monmouth, and the noblemen, gentlemen and others now in arms for the defence and vindication of the Protestant Religion, and the Laws, rights, and priviledges of England from the Invasion made upon them; and for delivering the kingdom from the usurpation and tyranny of James, Duke of York.* Written by the radical Scottish dissenting pamphleteer and spy Robert Fergusson, aka 'The Plotter', immortalized by John Dryden as 'Judas' in *The second part of Absalom and Achitophel* for his part in the foiled Rye House Plot, the declaration simultaneously lays out the view that government was ordered by God for the 'Peace, Happiness, and Security of the Governed, and not for the private Interest and personal Greatness of those that Rule'.[33] It also demonizes James as an individual on every possible charge: James is asserted to have been personally responsible for the Great Fire of London, the Popish Plot, and hiring an 'execrable villainess to assassinate the late Earl of Essex' while in the Tower awaiting trial for his part in the Rye House Plot (p. 2). Later in the document James is even charged with having poisoned Charles II to gain the throne:

in order to the expediting the Idolatrous & bloody designes of the Papists, the gratifying of his own boundless ambition after a Crown, and to hinder enquiry into his Assassination of *Arthur Earl of Essex, hath poisoned the late King,* and there in manifested his ingratitude, as well as Cruelty to the world, in murdering a *Brother,* who had almost ruin'd himselfe to preserve and protect him from punishment. (p. 7)

Sandwiched between the blood-curdling accusations against James are appeals for the vindication of English legal and religious rights, calling for the '*penal Laws* against *Protestant Dissenters* [to] be repealed, and legal provision made against their being disturbed by reason of their *Consciences,* and for their enjoying an equall Liberty with *other Protestants*' (p. 5). Ultimately, Monmouth is figured as the wronged son fighting to avenge his father's unnatural death: 'deeply sensible of that Barbarous and horrid parricide committed upon his *Father,* doth resolve to pursue the said James Duke of Yorke, as a mortall and bloody Enemy, and will endeavor as well with his own hand, as by the assistance of his Friends, & the Law, to have justice executed upon him' (p. 7).

Despite this dramatic pronouncement, Monmouth's rebellion was short-lived and ended ingloriously with him being captured lying in a ditch two days after the defeat of his small forces at Sedgemoor. His close collaborator Ford Grey, the future Earl of Tankerville, who in 1684 had figured in the scandal that

---

[33] Monmouth, *Declaration,* 1.

had provided Aphra Behn with the materials for her *Love Letters Between a Nobleman and his Sister*, was likewise quickly captured. Unlike Monmouth, Grey was ultimately pardoned on the grounds of offering a full confession implicating others and later testifying at their trials. Quickly published broadsides with songs and verses about the rebellion kept London audiences seemingly up to the minute with the fighting and its aftermath and were also quickly reprinted in Dublin by the official printers, Andrew Crook and Samuel Helsham.

The first popular broadside ballads called loyal citizens to respond to the threat. *Monmouth Degraded Or James Scot, the Little King in Lyme* urges its listeners or readers to arm against the invasion:

> Such a Fop-King was ne're before
> Is Landed on our *Western* shore,
>
> . . . . .
>
> Let us assume the Souls of *Mars*
> And March in Order, Foot and Horse,
> Pull down the Standard at the Cross,
> Of *Perkin* King in *Lyme* Boyes.

A new song, to the tune of, the granadeers march, a broadside ballad printed in Dublin, likewise urged its listeners to enlist: 'We'l drown Argile in the raging Sea | Bring Rampant Monmouth to his Knee | and Cuckold Grey to the Triple tree.'

The Countreys advice to the late Duke of Monmouth and Those in Rebellion compared him to Lucifer, Absalom, and Icarus and warned followers of their similar fates. In *Monmouth Routed, and Taken Prisoner. With his Pimp the Lord Gray*, which was printed before Monmouth's execution, he is depicted ironically as 'True *Protestant* Prince of which *Presbiters* brag | Is catch'd under a Hedge in a lousie rag', concluding 'A fair Conclusion o' th' King in the *West*'. Grey figures as an unsavoury coward, who had shared his wife's bed with Monmouth, and, echoing *Monmouth Degraded*, the verses highlight 'This was the success of our fine Fop-Things, | That came for to conquer the greatest of Kings'.

The pamphlet press also issued numerous accounts of Monmouth's capture, letters, and his execution. Monmouth's final moments before his execution were frequently reprinted with the title *An account of what passed at the execution of the late Duke of Monmouth on Wednesday the 15th of July, 1685, on Tower-Hill* (1685). The account is presented as a transcript of what passed between Monmouth, the ministers, and the executioner, including in parentheses Monmouth's physical gestures at certain points; after the prayers for the King are begun, the minister asks 'Sir, do you not pray for *the* King with us? (The Versicle was again repeated) . . . M. (After some pause he answered) *Amen*'.[34] The pamphlet offers the reader a vivid image of the demeanour and actions of all of those gathered on the scaffold, from the clerics anxious that he make a full confession, to the seemingly disordered and distracted Monmouth, and

---

[34] *An account of what passed*, 3.

the axe man, who assured him the blade was sharp (it took multiple blows, however, to sever his head from his neck).

Up until his final moments, the ministers were still encouraging him publicly to acknowledge his crimes and to warn others of the inevitable end of rebellion: 'My Lord, It is fit to be Particular; and considering the Publick Evil you have done, you ought to do as much good now, as possibly you can, by a Publick acknowledgment' (p. 3). Monmouth, however, appeared to have been more concerned with clearing the reputation of his mistress, Henrietta Wentworth, '*I declare, That she is a very Vertuous and Godly Woman. I have committed no Sin with her; and that which hath passed betwixt Us, was very Honest and Innocent in the sight of God*', and one of his final acts was to ask that his private belongings—believed by the observer to be 'something like a Tooth-pick-Case'—be taken to her. When he was entreated again to speak to the soldiers and urge all citizens to be loyal to the King, his response was simply, 'I have said I will make no Speeches; I will make no Speeches; I come to die' (p. 3).

After his death, black-edged broadside elegies were quickly printed, pondering the ways in which ambition and flattery combined to cause the fall of a once popular Duke.

> Led only by Thy Visionary Dreams;
> Till in persuit of Crowns and Diadems,
> With many a Restless Night and tugging Groan,
> They mount a *Scaffold* whilst they seek a *Throne*.
> (*An Elegy on James Scot, late Duke of Monmouth*, 1685)

Another broadside elegy with the same title printed by Elizabeth Mallet, known during this period for her publication of criminal narratives and confessions, emphasized the role of politics and politicians in his ultimate fate:

> So the late Monmouth, giving way to Pride,
> A mighty Ruin pull'd upon his Head;
> Debauch'd by Faction, Those that sought our Woe,
> And Studied Brittains empires overthrow.

It concludes with an epitaph for Monmouth focusing on his mythic qualities:

> Soaring upon Icarian Wings he fell,
> Who durst against the best of Kings Rebell.
> Now silent is he whose late restless Mind,
> Ambition swell'd, till a Grave did find.

Charles Allestree (1653/4–1707) published his sermon given before the mayor in Oxford to celebrate the defeat of Monmouth, comparing Monmouth to the defeated Canaanite general Sisera killed by Jael in the Old Testament. He concludes by reminding his listeners 'what Load and oppression of Grief must there needs have been upon the Spirits of the present Generation of Men in the late REBELS success? In that nothing that was *Sacred*, nothing that was *Dear*, nothing that was *innocent*, could have been suppos'd to have remain'd inviolated in his prosperous and Triumphant Rebellion'.[35] For readers and listeners, what emerged in the accounts of Monmouth's rebellion was not only how pride leads to the downfall of a promising individual but also how the politics of the period used terms such as 'liberty' and 'religion' to validate their actions. The black-print broadside ballad, *The Late Duke of Monmouth's Lamentation* (1685), complete with its woodcut of Monmouth on the scaffold, beheaded and gushing blood, concludes with the warning, 'take warning you Traytors | and all you Crown Haitors | Your cunning designs your Heads shall not save'.

On 24 June 1685, Parliament restored the Licensing Act (1662), 'An Act for preventing the frequent Abuses in Printing Seditious Treasonable and Unlicensed Bookes and Pamphletts, and for Regulating of Printing and Printing-Presses', which had been permitted to lapse in 1679.[36] The accounts of Monmouth's rebellion, the broadsides describing his execution, and the elegies reflecting on his sad end all prominently bear the phrase 'This may be printed' with the date and the initials 'R.L.S.'. Roger L'Estrange returned to his post as licenser, and the *London Gazette* was again the only officially permitted newspaper (see *MV* 3.II).

Those critical of the government again turned to Amsterdam for their printing needs. Gilbert Burnet (1643–1715), who had been outspoken against Catholicism and had been removed from his royal posts, asked James's permission to leave the country, departing for Paris just before Argyll's rebellion. During 1685 and 1686 he journeyed through Switzerland and Italy, publishing his letters to his friend the scientist Robert Boyle as *Some LETTERS, Containing An account of what Seemed most remarkable* (Amsterdam, 1686) along with *Reflections on Mr VARILLAS'S HISTORY of The Revolutions that have happened in Europe in Matters of Religion*. As he recounts in his autobiography, 'my chief design was to lay open the misery of those who lived under an absolute government and a devouring superstition' (Burnet, *Supplement*, 251). In May 1686 he was invited to visit the court of William, Prince of Orange, and his wife, Mary, James's daughter, in The Hague, an invitation that offended James strongly. This relationship would eventually result in a charge of treason and outlawry in 1687, as Burnet continued publishing treatises arguing against the repeal of the Test Act in England ,which James was hoping to secure.

Among the nearly 3,000 men who answered Monmouth's call to arms and thus faced charges of treason was the young, newly married Daniel Defoe (1660?–1731). Raised in London as the child of dissenters and educated in a dissenting academy at Stoke Newington, Defoe had been barred from attending university or holding military or public office by the increasingly strict enforcement of the Test Act, laws requiring ministers and office-holders to take Communion in the Church of England and to swear allegiance to the monarch

---

[35] Allestree, *A sermon*, 33.
[36] Statutes of the Realm, 6. 20. BHO <http://www.british-history.ac.uk>.

as the head of the Church (see *MV* 4.II). So apprehensive was the government of the dissenters rising to challenge the new monarch, on the news of Monmouth's landing, some 200 known dissenters were arrested in London as a preventative measure. Defoe, who fought on Monmouth's side at the final battle of Sedgemoor, managed to avoid being captured, and, although he remained a visible supporter of dissenting causes, posting bail for two widows arrested for attending a conventicler meeting, he would eventually be pardoned for his part in the uprising in 1687.

English Protestants had numerous reasons for alarm during this period apart from the overt Catholicism of their new king and the treatment of the Scottish radical Covenanters and English dissenters. During late 1685, English readers learned with horror of the treatment of the French Huguenots as the French king ruthlessly reimposed Catholicism as the only official religion of France. In his diary on 3 November 1685, John Evelyn described what news was coming from France, describing the French 'persecution of the Protestants, raging with utmost barbarity, exceeding what the very heathens used':

The Fr[ench] Tyrant, abrogating the Edicts of Nants…without any Cause on the suddaine, demolishing all their Churches, banishing, Imprisoning, sending to the Gallies all the Ministers: plundering the common people, & exposing them to all sorts of barbarous usage, by souldiers sent to ruine & prey upon them; taking away their children; forcing people to the Masse, & then executing them as Relapsers: They burnt the libraries, pillag'd their goods, eate up their fields & sustenance, banish'd or sent to the Gallies the people & seiz'd on their Estates. (Evelyn, *Diary*, 4. 484–5)

It was against this backdrop of an absolute monarch enforcing Catholicism on an entire nation that James's actions were observed by his countrymen. By the end of 1685 and throughout 1686, seeming to confirm people's worst fears, James made no secret of his religion, openly attending mass and appointing English Catholic priests at court. Documents were produced suggesting that the former King Charles had died in the Catholic faith.

In seeming opposition to the public's hostile welcome and the pope-burning pageants that greeted the arrival of Mary of Modena in the 1670s and the frenzy of anti-Catholic propaganda generated by Titus Oates and the Popish Plot (see *CV* 3.II), under James, Catholicism soon began officially to be infused into public culture. Evelyn notes with dismay that 'Popish pamphlets & Pictures sold publiqly: no books or answers against them appearing &c [till long after]' (Evelyn, *Diary*, 4. 489, 20 November 1685). James also ignored the Test Act and began to appoint Catholics to public offices. Texts explaining Catholic practices to English Protestant readers started becoming available in spite of numerous Parliamentary acts, much to the dismay of John Evelyn, who in his office as one of the Commissioners of the Privy Seal recorded his refusal to seal a lease to a printer who styled himself 'his Majesties Printer' for the printing of 'Missals, Offices, Lives of Saints, Portals, Primers &c' (Evelyn, *Diary*, 4. 504, 12 March 1686). Readers could now purchase texts with titles such as *The Method Of Saying the* ROSARY *of our* BLESSED LADY *... As it is said in Her* Majesties *Chappel at St JAMES's* (1686), *An Exposition of the* Holy Ornaments *and Ceremonies which the* CHURCH Uses at MASS *... now publish'd for the common good of all* Catholicks, *and others* (1686), and Serenus Cressy's I. Question. WHY ARE YOU A CATHOLIC? *The* ANSWER *follows.* II. Question. BUT WHY ARE YOU A PROTESTANT? *an* ANSWER *Attempted (in vain.)* (1686) (see CV 4.IV).

Initially, after the thwarted rebellions, Protestant nonconformists benefited from James's attempts to expand the tolerance of Catholic practices starting in 1686. John Bunyan was finally free from the constant threat of fines or imprisonment. The years 1685–6 were prolific ones for the popular author and preacher, and he frequently preached in London and engaged in controversies that divided different Baptist denominations. His writings from this period still show a desire for theological disputation, but also his mission as a pastor to engage his lay readers. In 1684, he published the second part of the very popular *Pilgrim's Progress*, telling the story of Christian's wife, Christiana, and their children as they travel to the City of Light (see *MV* 3.V). Bunyan's printer, Nathanial Ponder, had reprinted the first part of *Pilgrim's Progress* in 1685, and he reissued the second part in 1686. Whereas the first part of *Pilgrim's Progress* focuses on the individual, the second part, the story of Christiana and her friends and family, not only addresses the topical 1680s issue of women's participation in worship services—Bunyan was not in favour of separate women's worship meetings, even though women made up a large part of the Baptist congregations, seeing the practice as too like that of the Quakers—but is also a story of Christian community in the face of adversity. It highlights the need for strong leaders such as 'Mr Great-heart' to assist the congregation along the way and the ultimate triumph of the believers over the worldly.

Bunyan's dramatic 1684 work *Sighs from Hell* had its eighth edition in 1686; the Folger Shakespeare Library copy shows by its inscriptions in the flyleaves that it was a text that preserved its value through multiple generations of readers, being owned once by 'Sarah Jevon' and ultimately making its way to 'Thomas Hopkins' by 1723.[37] In the same year as *Sighs from Hell*'s reissue, *Come and welcome to Jesus Christ* showed readers the blessings of salvation as opposed to the terrors of damnation. In *A Discourse Upon the Pharisee and the Publicane* (1685), Bunyan, identified with an author portrait and on the title page as 'author of the *Pilgrims Progress*', tells his readers that 'in reading this little Book thou must needs read thy self'.[38] 'Though the Publicane seemed to be far behind, yet in running he got the prize from the lofty Pharisee' ('To the Reader'). The Pharisee is identified on the title page, the 'Hypocritical and Self-righteous Man', the smug religious formalist who is pleased with his careful observance of the conventions, while the Publicane feels his sins so heavily, all he can do is beg for mercy.

---

[37] FSL, Wing / 2454:05.   [38] Bunyan, *Come and welcome*, 'To the Reader'.

Bunyan's other lengthy text from 1686 was *A Book for Boys and Girls: Or Country Rhimes for Children* also printed by Nathaniel Ponder, and done entirely in verse, as had been his earliest publications (see *MV* 2.VI). Bunyan explains in his epistle to the reader that the intended audience is 'Boys and Girls of all Sorts and Degrees, | From those of Age, to Children on the Knees'.[39] However, the primary audience is very young children, and Bunyan explains the idea of syllables in 'An help to Chil-dren to learn to read Eng-lish', which also introduces several styles of alphabet. The first lesson is for children to learn to spell their own names and to master figures and the roman numbers; 'I shall forbear to add more', he concludes, being 'perswaded this is enough for little Children to prepare themselves for Psalter, or Bible' ('To the Reader'). The following rhymes are simple in their diction and rhymes, but contain Bunyan's basic teachings: 'Meditations upon an Egg' opens 'The Egg's no Chick by falling from the Hen; | Nor man a Christian, till he's born agen' (p. 7). Bunyan uses dialogues in some of his poems and to emblems to make his points. 'XXIII: Upon the Lark and the Fowler' makes use of simple country metaphors of the 'simple Bird' who is lured into the net by the hunter in spite of the narrator's warnings. It concludes with a 'comparison', which explains:

> This Fowler is an Emblem of the Devil,
> His Nets and Whistle, Figures of all evil.
> His Glass an Emblem is of sinful Pleasure,
> And his Decoy, of who counts sin a Treasure. (p. 31)

The admonisher is the 'true Teacher' whose job it is to 'shew the Soul the snare and bliss, | And how it may this Fowler's net escape' (p. 31).

The didactic appeal of Bunyan's writing for a broad general readership is, of course, made manifest in many other types of writing during the period. Most 'true account' publications describe their offerings as being of benefit to readers in that they reveal the wickedness of the world and the necessity to follow a godly life. The phrases 'true account' or 'true history' feature as key elements in the titles of many of the cheap pamphlet publications and broadside ballads in 1685 and 1686 whose function is to help the reader to see the moral lesson in average, working people's crimes and circumstances, and they foreshadow the later fictions of Daniel Defoe such as *Moll Flanders*. The years 1685 and 1686 were particularly strong for didactic works from the printer and bookseller Elizabeth Mallet (fl. 1672–1706) before she turned her business over to her son David. She published not only the proceedings of the commissioners of the peace at Old Bailey court, but also, using two presses at her shop in Black Horse Alley, the true accounts of horrid crimes and repentant criminals. *A True Account of the Behavior, Confession, and Execution of William Charley and Ann Scot* (4 September 1685), for example, opens with a typical general admonition: 'still it appears, notwithstanding the many precedent

---

[39] Bunyan, *A Book for Boys and Girls*, 'To the Reader'.

Examples Justice has made of Offenders, that divers are besotted to that degree, or deluded by the wiles and Temptations of the Enemy of mankind; that regardless of their Safety, Lives, or Reputations, they will rashly run themselves to Ruin and Disgrace'.[40] The narrator continues that the stories that follow 'will more evidently appear in the following Relation…more especially the Crimes, Manner of Behaviour and Confession of two Persons cut off by the Hand of Justice, in the prime and strength of their days, as it was observed and taken from themselves in *Newgate*, &c' (p. 1).

During this session, Anne Scot was sentenced to death for having 'Feloniously taken a Flower'd Mantua-Gown, a Sattin-Petticoat and other Goods out of the House of *James Marmion*' (p. 3). 'Upon her return to *Newgate* [she] became sad as the former, being frequently observed to wring her Hands and Sigh, saying, she was the unhappiest Woman alive wishing she had never been Born.' She had been raised in Ireland and 'brought up there to work divers curious Works with the Needle', but having a desire to see England, she found employment in London living as a single woman working with embroidery. Unfortunately, like Charley, she fell into 'loose and idle Company, who encouraged her in Leudness and altogether took her off from her Employment to follow unlawful Courses, as well Debauchery and Prostitution, as pilfering and many other Matters tending to Defraud'. Like William Charley, she, too, had been formerly arrested for theft, but, because of lack of evidence, she was acquitted, 'yet was not so wise as to lay that narrow escape to her Heart, nor to take up, and rest her self satisfied therewith' (p. 3).

Sad and Dreadful news from Dukes-place near Aldgate: Or, a True Account of a Barbarous and Unnatural Self-Murther Committed by Dorcas Pinkney (1686) begins ominously: 'Many and Strange are the Delusions and Evil Suggestions of the Prince of Darkness, that Implacable Enemy of Mankind, to undermine and overthrow the Felicity of Mortals.'[41] Dorcas Pinkney was another single woman, aged around 40, who worked successfully as a child's coat maker in 'divers Eminent Shops in and about London'. She had been observed to be 'much dejected with Melancholly' by the concerned family with whom she lodged, but could not be brought to answer their questions. Retiring one evening to her chamber to read and meditate, she did not answer summons in the morning; when they opened the door, they found that through repeated efforts she had succeeded in hanging herself with a piece of string. 'How she came by it (all Mischievous Things of that, or any other kind, being as carefully as possible laid out of her way) is as yet altogether unknown' (p. 2). The verdict was self-murder with the notation that she was 'distracted': 'and though she had often suggested a fear of Wanting e'r she died, which was thought to discompose her Mind', when her room was searched, 'they found Money and other Things in her Chamber, which shew'd she was not in so great Necessity as she imagin'd' (p. 2). Such narratives, dwelling on the lives of common men

---

[40] *A True Account*, 1.   [41] *Sad and Dreadful news*, 1.

and women in hard times making bad choices, offer both 'true' lessons to be learned and small interior dramas played out in settings that allowed the reader to engage with the emotional states of those facing the gallows or of those who took their own lives.

At the opposite scale of publication, desiring to establish scientific truth as opposed to moral, the presentations to the Royal Society and the pieces recorded in its *Philosophical Transactions* demonstrate the wide-ranging fields of enquiry and developing styles of scientific discourse (see *MV* 2.V). As in the 1660s after the founding of the Royal Society, many of these pieces were part of a vast scientific correspondence network, communicated to the editor of the *Philosophical Transactions* by letters from across England, the colonies, and Europe and subsequently published. Other pieces were accounts of presentations and experiences done before the fellows and reviews of recent publications. Richard Waller (*c.*1660–1715), a translator, artist, and natural philosopher who would go on to serve as the Society's secretary and to edit the *Philosophical Transactions* at the turn of the century, contributed articles on 'flying glow-worms' (1685) and a 'catalogue of Simple and Mixt Colours, with a Specimen of Each Color Prefixt to Its Proper Name' (1686). The astronomer Edmond Halley (1656–1742) contributed numerous pieces during these years concerning barometric pressure, gravity, and the origins of trade winds in the tropics, while the linguist Francis Lodwick (bap. 1619–94) attempted 'an essay towards an universal Alphabet' (1686). 'A Voyage of the Emperor of China into the Eastern Tartary, Anno 1682' (1686) required two publications and was accompanied by an article by 'R.H.' on Chinese language and its characters. Samuel Pepys (1633–1703), the Society's President in 1686, contributed an article on 'the most seasonable time of felling of trees' (1686), and the newly elected fellow Hans Sloane (1660–1753), the future secretary of the Society, offered 'a description of the Pieminta or Jamaica Pepper-Tree' (1686).

Nehemiah Grew (bap. 1641–1712), a botanist and secretary of the Royal Society, had been commissioned in 1678 'at his leisure' to make a catalogue of the rarities held by the Society. He eventually published *Musaeum regalis societatis, or, A catalogue and description of the natural and artificial rarities belonging to the Royal Society and preserved at Gresham College* (1681, 1686). In his record of the collection and his descriptions of the objects, one sees both the wide range of scientific topics of interest and the quest for a direct language of scientific description that does not waste the reader's time with 'fruitless and endless Disquisitions and Contests', but instead offers 'a cleer and full Description of things'.[42] He proceeds with a descriptive catalogue of Egyptian mummies, 'the entire SKIN of a MOOR', 'The WOMB of a WOMAN blown up and dried', the foot of a white Greenland bear, a beaver's tail, stalks and roots, seeds, gem stones, salts, antique coins, and 'things relating to Chymistry'.[43]

---

[42] Grew, *Musaeum regalis societatis*, 'Preface'.
[43] Grew, *Musaeum regalis societatis*, 'A Prospect of the Whole Work'.

The frail natural philosopher Robert Boyle (1627–91) continued his prolific publication during these years, concentrating mostly on medical matters, including *Of the Reconcileableness of Specifick Medicines to the Corpuscular Philosophy* (1685), but also continuing his theological explorations in titles such as *Of the high veneration man's intellect owes to God, peculiarly for his wisedom and power by a Fellow of the Royal Society* (1685). He describes this latter as written at various times and places, 'hastily tack'd together', 'a rough Draught, the Nobleness, Sublimity and Sacredness of the Subject, not allowing the Authour to presume, that the first thoughts he committed to Paper about it, might be for good and all parted with by him, till he shall have heedfully revis'd and corrected them'.[44] He opens the discourse with the observation that 'I shall take leave to declare, that 'tis not without some Indignation, as well as Wonder, that I see many men, and some of them Divines too, who little considering what God is, and what themselves are, presume to talk of Him and his Attributes as freely and as unpremeditately, as if they were talking of a Geometrical Figure, or a Mechanical Engine' (p. 1).

Isaac Newton (1642–1727), the man who would become the dominant scientific thinker of his age, had become a member of the Society in 1672 (see *MV* 2.V). In 1684, he was approached by Edmund Halley to solve a problem that Halley, Robert Hooke, and Christopher Wren had debated concerning the nature of the orbit of planets around the sun. Newton's response was to return to earlier work on orbits under an inverse square law of attraction, and the result was that, in 1686, he wrote to Halley with the manuscript of the book forming *Philosophiae naturalis principia mathematica* to the Royal Society through the agency of one Dr Vincent, a fellow both of Clare Hall Cambridge and the Royal Society.[45] Halley announced in April 1686 to the Society that Newton's work, dedicated to the Society, was ready to be printed; in May, a second vote was recorded that it 'be printed forthwith in quarto in a fair letter; and that a letter be written to him to signify the Society's resolution, and to desire his opinion as to the print, volume, cuts &c'.[46]

Between the national dramas of the succession and the rebellions, the domestic dramas of the true crime narratives, and new scientific discoveries, Londoners had plenty of material to read and hear, but it was a very limited season on the London stage itself in 1685 and 1686. The theatres would close for three months at the death of Charles II, leaving actors and dramatists to shift for themselves. Especially compared to the 1670s before the combining of the two acting companies into the United Company headed by Betterton (see *CV* 3.I), these two years have fewer new contributions, and, of those that did reach the stage, some, such as Dryden's ill-fated *Albion and Albanius*, lost the theatre nearly catastrophic amounts of money.

---

[44] Boyle, *Of the high veneration*, 'Advertisement'.
[45] See Westfall, *Never at Rest*, 443–6, for an account of the publication of this text.
[46] Westfall, *Never at Rest*, 445.

Many of the dramatists who dominated the stage in the 1670s fade from sight. Thomas Otway died in 1685 in debt and in misery; Lee was confined to Bedlam in 1684, Wycherley was languishing in debtors' prison. Otway, whose most critically well-regarded tragedy *Venice Preserv'd* had been staged in 1682 and whose last comedy *The Atheist* was printed in 1684, had printed an ode on the death of Charles, *Windsor Castle*, and there is some evidence that he was at work on another play, as Betterton offered a reward in the November and December issues of the *Observator* for 'Four Acts of a Play' written before Otway's death. At the age of 33, he died under obscure circumstances, but all agree in extreme poverty.

His close contemporary Nathaniel Lee, who had made his theatrical debut during the same years as Otway, had had two plays performed in 1683, *Constantine* and *The Princess of Cleve*, but neither had been a success. In late 1684, he was admitted to Bedlam, the hospital for the insane, where he would stay, supported by a royal pension from James II, until 1688. William Wycherley, whose comedies including *The Country-Wife* and *The Plain-Dealer* had helped to set the tone for the stage in the 1670s, found himself a widower in 1685, as his wife, the Countess of Drogheda, passed away; instead of inheriting a fortune from her, as he had imagined, he inherited her extensive debts and was arrested in July 1685 and put into Fleet Street prison. His friends organized a performance at Whitehall of *The Plain-Dealer* to attempt to bring Wycherley back into favour at court; eventually James did settle Wycherley's debts, and he would be released in April 1686 and be given a pension by James of £200.

Dramatists who did succeed in having plays performed during these two years included John Crowne reprising his popular character *Sir Courtly Nice* from *The Countrey Wit* (1675) and the indefatigable Thomas D'Urfey (see CV 3.I). D'Urfey chose to adapt a comedy by Fletcher as *A Commonwealth of Women* (performed 1685, published 1686) and also wrote a new comedy *The Banditti, or, A Ladies Distress* (1686) staged at the Theatre Royal and also printed that year. Less overtly about contemporary politics than his previous plays in the early 1680s, *A Commonwealth of Women*, which was staged in August 1685, does have Joseph Haines in the prologue bringing on stage a 'western scythe' he says was used by Whigs to 'cut down Monarchy like Grass', but on this occasion, it will be used to mow down any 'fools' and critics who might not like the play.[47] The play exploited the multiple talents of the combined acting company, requiring over twenty-two actors, nine of whom are women, and it has numerous musical and dancing scenes.

The opening scenes are set at Covent Garden with the rakes abusing their womenfolk, but the action moves quickly to an Amazonian community that burlesques pastoral conventions. The community of young virgins may begin by praising their celibate life, but, when a shipwrecked young Marine is cast on their shores, they demand their queen take in all the men. By Act Five, the men

---

[47] D'Urfey, *A Commonwealth of Women*, 'Prologue'.

are the Amazons' slaves and the former 'wild Fellows' of London are set to washing the women's clothes, sewing, and tending their pets. The epilogue was spoken by the 13-year-old future leading lady, Anne Bracegirdle.

According to the dedication to 'Sir Critick-Cat-call', the source for *The Banditti* was suggested to D'Urfey by none other than 'the Late Blessed King of ever glorious Memory',[48] a Spanish translation of an Italian romance. The heart of the plot is babies swapped at birth: Don Diego seems impervious to all attempts to educate him as a gentleman of rank and Don Fernando dislikes his ignoble bandit parents' ways so much that he runs off to become a soldier. The distressed ladies are Elvira and Laura, who are in turns pursued by the womanizing Antonio, who ends the play as the conventional husband of Laura. Perhaps as notable as the plot revolving around one's birth being one's destiny is that assertion in the prologue that one reason that the critics in the audience will not like it is because it is not a 'Bawdy Rout'. Instead, this play is for the ladies:

> A Pretty Tale with Art and Labour wrought
> Calm as their Passions, Modest as each Thought;
> Upon my Credit no Lewd Word is there,
> If you dare trust the Credit of a Player. ('Prologue')

Certainly, compared to the comedies of the 1670s such as *The Country-Wife*, *Man of Mode*, or D'Urfey's own *The Fond Husband*, there is a distinctly lower level of sexual language and of sexual peril for the female characters; indeed, the bandit mother Megaera was played by James Noakes as a comic 'dame' part. In addition to this softening of the sexual edge of the comedy, D'Urfey, who was also a popular song-writer during this period, included three songs in this play, with music by Samuel Ackroyde.

Perhaps the most intriguing original play of this period for modern readers was Aphra Behn's London comedy, *The Luckey Chance, or, An Alderman's Bargain*, performed in the spring of 1686 and printed in 1687. Behn was in hard financial straits during this period, although not yet in so much debt as Wycherley, and there is some evidence to suggest that she borrowed £6 from Zachary Baggs, a London money-lender, based on the completion of this play.[49] It is a play very much about money, who has it, who deserves it, and women's relationship to it. The plot involves three love triangles where young men in pursuit of true love are impeded by old men who possess both the money and the women. The young men were played by the not-so-young leading actors of the company: 'Mr Gayman A Spark of the Town, Lover of Julia', was Betterton, 'Belmour', who is contracted to Leticia but who had been forced to flee the country for duelling, was Kynaston. The old men of the play, Sir Feeble Fainwould, 'an old Alderman to be married to Leticia', was done by Anthony Leigh, while Sir Cautious Fulbank, husband of Julia, was played by

---

[48] D'Urfey, *The Banditti*, sig. a3[r].   [49] Todd, *The Secret Life of Aphra Behn*, 356.

James Nokes. Elizabeth Barry played the married Julia, described in the cast list as 'in love with Gayman, honest and generous', Sarah Cook, who had performed Behn's prologue for *Valentinian* in 1684, played the 'young and virtuous' Leticia, and the newly married Susanna Mountfort played Diana, Sir Feeble's daughter, who, seeing the fate of May–December marriages made on money, elopes with her true love, Bredwell.

The Luckey Chance has a fairly complicated plot, with multiple pairs of lovers. Belmour has returned incognito on the morning of Leticia's marriage to Sir Feeble, in hiding because of having killed a man in a duel. Unknown to him, Sir Feeble has told Leticia that Belmour was killed in a fight abroad, and she, being in financial difficulties, finally gave in to Sir Feeble's aggressive, persistent advances and agreed to marry him. In this triangle, the problem is bringing the two true lovers back together, which requires the unravelling of Leticia's marriage to Sir Feeble by avoiding consummating it and securing Belmour's pardon for duelling, which Sir Feeble is suppressing. In the plot of Julia, Sir Cautious, and Gayman, it is less clear why Julia married the unpleasant elderly man, but Gayman, undaunted, has mortgaged his estates to Sir Cautious and at the start of the play has even pawned his clothes and sword in order to continue to give impressive presents to Julia to demonstrate his love. As the play begins, he is living in Alsatia, a notorious thieves' den, and making love to his landlady 'Old Nasty', in order to get his clothes out of pawn. He is also quite willing to sleep with an unknown woman in disguise who sends him a gift of money to redeem his estate, although he is sure she must be old and ugly.

While both the romantic leads are 'gentlemen', neither has money or any position or authority; they are not courtly rakes, as in Behn's earlier plays, but 'men of the town'. Unfortunately, 'the town' seems to be firmly in the power of the old city men who use their wealth to buy young marriageable women, pervert the law, and in general oppress younger males. Sir Feeble contracts his daughter without her consent to Bearjest, a nephew of Sir Cautious, in a mercenary deal between the families, even though he has previously promised her to the virtuous but poor brother of Leticia, Bredwell. This is perfectly acceptable to Bearjest because of the money, even though he has made promises to Pert, Julia's waiting woman. Through a series of disguises, ruses, and masked meetings, Julia steals the money from her husband to give to Gayman to redeem his estate; rather than give up the mortgage too easily, Sir Cautious then strikes a bargain with Gayman to wager it all against permitting Gayman to have sex with his wife, the 'bargain' and the 'lucky chance' of the title, which Gayman wins. By the end, the old men admit they are wrong to try to monopolize young women, and the young couples are all reunited. The exception to this happy ending is Julia, whom Sir Cautious announces he will leave to Gayman in his will, but she refuses to agree to such terms after Gayman's collusion in the sexual interlude that night.

The actor Thomas Jevon (1651/2–88) not only performed in fellow actor William Mountfort's farce discussed later in this section, but also created his own, a comedy, *The Devil of a Wife, or, A Comical Transformation*, where a cobbler's wife and a country-house fine lady magically change places. It was staged in March 1686 at the Queen's Theatre in Dorset Garden, and he dedicated the printed version that year to 'My Friends and Patrons at Lockets Ordinary', a famous dining house at Charing Cross mentioned in numerous plays, from Wycherley's *The Country-Wife* to William Congreve's *The Way of the World* (1700). In his prologue, which he himself performed, Jevon asks his audience, 'How long is't since you saw I pray | That strange old fashion'd thing call'd a New Play?'[50] In the play he takes the role of Jobson, a 'psalm-singing Cobler', who is the tenant of Sir Richard Lovemore, whose wife, Lady Lovemore, is 'A Proud Phanatick, always canting and brawling. A Perpetual Fixen [vixen] and a Shrew' (sig. a2ᵛ) played by Sarah Cook. In contrast, Jobson's wife Nell is 'a simple innocent Girl' played by Mrs Percival (Susanna Mountfort before her marriage). She spoke the epilogue, which made the point to the audience that this piece is the 'first address of a young tender muse', which does not aim to reach comedy's level but 'Farce is her aim, the persons low and mean, | Humble the language homely it the seene'. The farce proved so popular that the printed text had eight editions by 1735, and it was transformed in 1731 into a one-act 'ballad opera' by Theophilus Cibber.

In November 1685, James gave the order that 'playes should be Acted at Court every Weeke', requiring repairs and refurbishing of the theatre at Whitehall (*RETD* 1. 257). Among the plays performed there were popular plays from the 1670s including Lee's *The Rival Queens*, Behn's *The Rover*, Etherege's *Man of Mode*, Wycherley's *The Plain-Dealer*, and Dryden's *All for Love* and *The Maiden-Queen*.[51] Shakespeare's *Othello* and *Hamlet* were also performed. Crowne's *Sir Courtly Nice* was a favourite, being done once in 1685, the year it first appeared on the commercial stage, and again in 1686. There were also Jacobean plays staged for the court's entertainment, such as Fletcher's *The Humorous Lieutenant*, which was performed twice, Webster's *The Dutchesse of Malfi*, and Beaumont and Fletcher's *A King and No King*.

The other staged performances in London these years were more farces, civic pageants, school plays, and drolls at Bartholomew Fair. The translator and future Poet Laureate Nahum Tate (*c.*1652–1715) offered his farce adaptation of Ben Jonson's *Eastward Ho!* under the title *Cuckold's Heaven, or An Alderman No Conjuror* (1685). The dedication of the printed version, which also appeared that year, highlights the importance of writing for a known group of actors and how much the success of a play might depend on the presence of the right actor in the right role. Tate apologizes for offering a piece that had little success on stage: 'The principal Part (on which the Diversion depended) was by Accident, disappointed of Mr Noke's Performance, for whom it was designed'.[52]

---

[50] Jevon, *The Devil of a Wife*, sig. a1ᵛ.   [51] See Boswell, *Restoration Court Stage*, app. C.
[52] Tate, *Cuckold's Heaven*, sig. Aʳ.

Another farce, *Doctor Faustus, with the Humours of Harlequin and Scaramouche*, loosely based on Marlowe's play, was created by the actor William Mountfort (*c*.1664–92) and performed in 1686. Mountfort, who had made the step to leading man in 1685 playing Sir Courtly Nice in Crowne's comedy, was also becoming popular in London as an entertainer on his own; Sir John Reresby recorded in his diary how, at a dinner given by the Lord Mayor of London, Sir Robert Jeffreys, Mountfort was called in to imitate 'all the principal lawyers of the age, in their tone of voice, and action or gesture of body' (Reresby, *Memoirs*, 408). In his farce, Mountfort mixes lines taken directly from Marlowe—'A sound Magician is a Demi-God: | Here tire my Brains to get a Deity' with the good and bad angels at the ready to fly down—with comic interludes featuring the well-known clown figures of Scaramouch as Faustus's servant and Harlequin as his sidekick.[53]

The drolls performed at Bartholomew Fair were probably equally well-known stories with popular allusions. In 1685, one could have little doubt about what one would see in the drolls with titles such as *The Whore of Babylon, the Devil, and the Pope* (1685), *St George and the Dragon* (1686), and the topical *Vienna Besieged* (1686). Advertisements suggest that there were other forms of popular entertainment: notices in the *London Gazette* from the Master of the Revels Charles Killigrew reminded all 'rope dancers, Prizefighters, players, Strollers, and other persons showing motions and other sights, are to have Licences' (*RETD* 1. 258). An unknown entrepreneur was ordered to be arrested for failing to secure a licence to display an elephant in September 1685 (*RETD* 1. 255). Another 1686 advertisement, a broadsheet *There is lately come to the Famous City of London*, featuring the royal coat of arms at its top, made it known that 'there is lately come...the Rarity of the World, viz A Man of the Least Stature that has been seen in the memory of any; being but two Foot and seven Inches in Height'. This gentleman was Swiss, speaks high Dutch, sings well, 'has a very large Beard...[and] has been seen by the King and Nobility at White-hall'. The curious could see him daily at 'the Plume of Feathers, over against the King on Horseback in Stock-Market every hour of the Day', and for a small consideration, if 'Persons of Quality have a desire to see him at their Houses or Lodging, he is willing to wait upon them'.

In addition to these public entertainments, there was also the annual civic pageant in October for the installation of the Lord Mayor of London. Matthew Taubman (d. 1690?), who succeeded Thomas Jordan in this role, was laureate for the Lord Mayor of London between 1685 and 1690. Taubman's main interests throughout his writing career were clearly political. The October 1685 *London's Annual Triumph* was performed the same year his collection *Loyal Poems and Satyrs upon the Times, since the Beginning of the Salamanca Plot*, to be discussed later in this section, appeared. The function of these yearly pageants was to install the new Lord Mayor and to reaffirm the prominence of

---

[53] Mountfort, *Faustus*, 1.

London as the centre of civilized Europe. The title 'LONDON's Triumph', he announces in the preface to the 1685 publication describing the pageant, 'is appropriate to the Solemnities of this Illustrious day...for the Antiquity of its Institution, the Grandeur of the Preparations, the Splendor of the Pageantry, and the Magnificence of the Entertainments'.[54] For those who cannot attend the procession or view the allegorical pageants, he writes, 'Nor is the Book the least Addition to the Luster of this Day, which is read by those who see not the Pageantry; and when all the rest is over, remains a lasting and visible Monument to Posterity'.[55]

If new offerings were sparse on the leading London stages, readers of drama fared much better in 1685 and 1686. Titles ranged from reprints of popular favourites such as Dryden's *Marriage a-la-Mode* and Etherege's *Man of Mode*, which had first been printed in the 1670s, to texts of plays performed in the 1685–6 seasons. The publisher Henry Herringman, along with Richard Bentley and Edward Brewster, produced the fourth folio edition of Shakespeare's *Comedies, Histories, and Tragedies* (1685). This edition also included seven plays attributed to Shakespeare, including *Pericles*, now generally accepted as being at least in part by Shakespeare, but also plays now not generally ascribed to him, including *The London Prodigal*, *The History of Thomas Lord Cromwell*, *Sir John Oldcastle*, *The Puritan Widow*, and *The Tragedy of Locrine*.

Several living authors also published dramas which were not performed, including a pastoral drama by the future author of the controversial polemic *The Foreigners* (see *MV* 5.I), John Tutchin's (1660x4–1707) *The Unfortunate Shepherd. A Pastoral*. This was published with its own title page as part II of his volume of verse, *Poems on Several Occasions* (1685). Tutchin, an ardent Whig, as his poems show, published this volume before joining Monmouth's rebels, a fact that drew the attention and ire of Judge Jeffreys at his trial.

Sir Francis Fane's (d. 1691) *The Sacrifice* (1686) was never performed, the author, as he explained in the preface, 'having long since devoted himself to a country life and wanting patience to attend the leisure of the stage'.[56] Nahum Tate, in a prefatory poem 'To the Author', applauds Fane for writing a reforming and refining tragedy,

> Whose happy Muse...
> And temper *Shakespeare's* Flame with *Johnson's* Art.
> Whose Characters set just Examples forth;
> Mix Humane Frailties with Heroick Worth. ('To the Author')

Tate concludes:

> Accept our Thanks, tho you decline the Stage,
> That yet you condescend the Press t'engage:
> For while we thus possess the precious Store,

---

[54] Taubman, *London's Triumph*, 'Preface'.
[55] Taubman, *London's Yearly Jubilee*, 'Preface'.   [56] Fane, *The Sacrifice*, dedication.

Our Benefit's the same, your Glory more;
Thus, for a Theatre the World you find,
And your Applauding Audience, All Mankind. ('To the Author')

The following commendatory piece signed by John Robins names Fane as Rochester's poetic heir, and begs him 'once more to send a Pattern to the stage' ('To Sir Francis Fane'). It also ties the piece firmly to the political dramas of the times:

Shou'd Traiterous *Whiggs* but view the lasting Dress
That you've put on *Ragalzan*'s Wickedness,
Tho hatred to the best of Kings they wear,
Yet all designs against him they'd forbear,
Lest you shou'd make them your next Character.
('To the Honorable Sir Francis Fane')

Aphra Behn's poem 'To the Honorable Sir Francis Fane, On his Excellent Play, The Sacrifice', which concludes the prefatory material, likewise returns to the sad state of contemporary theatre, 'a forsaken, self-declining Stage'. Her poem concludes:

Live, mighty Sir, to reconcile the Age
To the first Glories of the useful Stage:
'Tis you her rifled Empire may restore
And give her Power she ne're could boast before.
('To the Honorable Sir Francis Fane')

Fane's comedy *Love in the Dark* (1675) (see MV 3.I) had been dedicated to his friend the Earl of Rochester, and his other contribution to the drama in 1685 was the masque he wrote for *Valentinian*, which was published in Tate's *Poems by Several Hands* (1685). The Earl of Rochester's adaptation of Fletcher's revenge tragedy *Valentinian* was staged in 1684 and subsequently printed in 1685. This posthumous production and publication was very much a collaborative effort among Rochester's friends, admirers, and relatives. Rochester's 1679 manuscript version of the play included an appropriate cast of actors from the King's Theatre for the play. By the time it came to be staged in 1684, a new group had to be formed, and most of those involved in the promotion of the performance had personal ties to Rochester, including Behn and Wharton. Elizabeth Barry played the raped innocent Lucina, Behn wrote a new prologue for the first night spoken by Sarah Cooke, and Ann Wharton appears to have been a key figure in having the play staged and its text printed in 1685.[57]

Like *The Sacrifice*, *Valentinian* is about a king who lets sexual appetite rule him. Valentinian becomes obsessed with Maximus's wife, Lucina, who, unlike the other women of the court, will not part with her virtue to serve her king.

---

[57] See Todd, *The Secret Life of Aphra Behn*, 334–5.

Tricked into coming to his court, Lucina is betrayed by the other women and servants. The emperor decides instead of persuasion

> 'Tis nobler like a Lion to invade,
> Where Appetite directs, and seize my Prey,
> Than to wait tamely like a begging Dog,
> Till dull Consent throws out the Scraps of Love.[58]

After her rape, the emperor warns her to stay silent to protect her own reputation, and her response is uncompromising: 'As long as there is Life in this Body, | And Breath to give me words, I'le cry for Justice' (IV. iii, p. 48). After she is discovered weeping by her husband and sent home, she kills herself, setting in motion the revenge plot, where Valentinian is killed by his own soldiers.

The printed text appears to have been taken from a manuscript of a stage copy, including as it does prompter's notes in its margins. In addition to Behn's prologue applauding the results of combining the talents of 'Great *Fletcher*, and the Greater *Rochester*', the edition offers another verse prologue by the satirist and friend of Wharton, John Grobham Howe, and a lengthy prose preface by a friend of both Wharton and Rochester, Robert Wolseley (1648/9–97). Wolseley describes the condition of the manuscript on which the staged version was based as 'an unfinished Piece'. Rochester, he asserts, 'intended to have alter'd and corrected this Play much more than it is, before it had come abroad' ('Preface').

One of Wolseley's primary tasks in the preface was to defend Rochester's posthumous reputation from the attack launched against it by the Earl of Mulgrave in his *An Essay on Poetry* (1682), targeting Rochester for obscenity:

> Here, as in all things else, is most unfit
> Bawdry barefac'd, that poor pretence to Wit;
> Such nauseous Songs as the late Convert made,
> Which justly call this censure on his Shade. (p. 6)

'Obscene words, too gross to move desire', Mulgrave charges, may pass for wit with some, but, for Mulgrave, 'that Author's Name has undeserved praise' (p. 6). Wolseley makes no attempt to deny the presence of obscenity or 'bawdry' in Rochester's writings, but takes exception to it being described as a poor attempt at wit, seeing it instead as wit in the service of satire. 'He had a Wit that was accompanied with an unaffected greatness of Mind, and a natural Love to Justice and Truth', Wolseley wrote, 'a Wit that was in perpetual War with Knavery, and ever attacking those kind of Vices most, whose malignity was like to be most diffusive, such as tended more immediately to the prejudice of publick Bodies' ('Preface'). 'If he did not take so much care of himself as he ought', Wolseley declared, 'he had the Humanity however to wish well to others, and I think I may truly affirm, he did the Worlds as much good by a right application of Satyre, as he hurt himself by a wrong pursuit of Pleasure' ('Preface').

---

[58] Wilmot, *Valentinian*, IV. ii, p. 46.

More recent critics have agreed that Rochester's adaptation of *Valentinian* turns the tragedy at least partially into a commentary on Charles's court. In a passage added by Rochester not found in Fletcher, the character of Maximus, whose wife, Lucina, Valentinian raped, on being banished by Valentinian, confronts him with a portrait of his crimes. Who would not, he demands,

> kill this luxurious Worm,
> Ere yet a thought of Danger has awak'd him.
> End him even in the midst of night-Debauches,
> Mounted upon a *Tripos*, drinking Healths
> With shallow Rascals, Pimps, Buffoons and Bawds,
> Who with vile Laughter take him in their Arms,
> And bear the drunken Caesar to his Bed,
> Where to the scandal of all Majesty,
> At every grasp he belches Provinces,
> Kisses off Fame, and at the Empires ruine,
> Enjoy his costly Whore. (V. v, p. 78)

Wharton, who was gravely ill, wrote a verse letter to Wolseley thanking him for defending her uncle as a poet and a man:

> To you, the generous task belongs alone
> To clear the injur'd and instruct the Town:
> Where, but in you is found a mind so brave
> To stretch the bounds of Love beyond the grave?[59]

Not all contemporaries viewed the stage as a vehicle for social satire in its representation of corruption and immorality. As we have seen, Dryden, Mary Evelyn, as well as Mulgrave and others all expressed their aversion to the licentiousness of the plays, their songs, and often of their performers. One of the most vitriolic of these critics of the stage was the satirist Robert Gould (1660?–c.1709). Having begun his working life in London as a servant, he published an attack on women's characters in *Love Given O're or, a Satyr against the Pride, Lust, and Inconstancy, &c of Woman* (1683) (see MV 4.V), which would provoke the young Sarah Fyge to respond with *The Female Advocate* (1686). In 1685, *Love Given O're* was reprinted, and Gould was at work writing 'The Play-House. A Satyr', which he would publish in 1689 in his *Poems*.

> Of all the things which at this guilty time,
> Have felt the honest Satyr's wholsome Rhime,
> The Play-house has scap't best, been most forborn,
> Though it, of all things, most deserves our scorn.[60]

The separate title page for the long satire states that it was 'writ in the Year 1685' and in his poem dedicating it to his patron, the Earl of Dorset, he states that 'Deny'd the *Press*, forbid the *Publick* view, | This *Trifle* for a Refuge flies to

---

[59] Wharton, in Behn, *Lycidus*, 95.   [60] Gould, *Poems*, 161.

You' and he concludes that in the satire 'Buffoons and Bullys equally despis'd: | *Strumpets* not spar'd, whate'r is their degree; | If bad, what is their *Quality* to me?' Unfortunately, his honest portraits, he feels, 'for the *Publick* thought too fit a Dress; | For to write *truth* is one sure way to be deny'd the *Press*'.

The satire directs its attention first to the members of the audience, then to the content of the plays being staged, then to the writers of these plays, and concludes with an attack on several of the most popular actors of the United Company. Few of the popular dramatists of the 1680s and the players escape some withering comment, whether on their lack of wit, their poor compositions, or their general unfitness as moral spokesmen. As for the audience, especially the women, in Gould's representations of the different sections of the theatre, it seems mostly composed of whores of various social ranks and prices, and the male members of the audience, fops, fools, or tasteless critics eager to impress their listeners.

As far as the plays themselves are concerned, in Gould's assessment, compared to the works of Shakespeare, Jonson, and Beaumont and Fletcher,

> ... our *Plays* are now so loosely writ,
> They've neither *Manners, Modesty,* or *Wit.*
> How can those things to our *Instruction* lead
> Which are unchast to see, a Crime to read?' (p. 174)

When he singles out Behn for example, he ironically dissects what pleases this 'nice age':

> ... for Instance, that clean piece of wit,
> The *City Heiress,* by *chast Sappho* writ,
> Where the lewd *Widow* comes, with brazen face,
> Just reeking from a *Stallion*'s rank embrace,
> T' acquaint the *Audience* with her slimy case. (p. 173)

Even Dryden, whom he admires for his retelling of Antony and Cleopatra in the tragedy *All for Love,*

> ... but when his *Limberham* I name,
> I hide my Head and almost blush with shame,
> To think the Author of both these the same:
> So bawdy it not only sham'd the Age,
> But worse, was ev'n too nauseous for the *Stage* (p. 176)

Dryden's *The Kind Keeper, or Mr Limberham* (1678), is indeed a sex comedy, but it was one whose satiric portraits apparently so offended some of its targeted 'keepers' and their actual mistresses that it lasted only three performances. Sounding much like Mulgrave's criticism of Rochester's songs, Gould declares that:

> If Witty 'tis to be obscene and lewd,
> We grant for Wit in some esteem it stood;

But what is in it for *Instruction* good?
And that's one end for which our *Bards* shou'd write. (p. 184)

It is only '*Fools* and *Women*', Gould concludes, who admire Dryden's rhyming tragedies.

Concerning actors as a group, he summarizes,

> To speak 'em all were tedious to discuss,
> But if you'l take 'em by the Lump, they're thus:
> A pack of idle, pimping, spunging Slaves,
> A Miscellany of Rogues, Fools and Knaves;
> A Nest of Leachers, worse than *Sodom* bore,
> And justly merit to be punish't more:
> Diseas'd, in Debt, and every moment dun'd;
> By all good Christians loath'd, and their own Kindred shun'd. (p. 184)

The women actors as a group are epitomized by Gould as '*Goats* are *more sweet*, and *Monkeys* are *more chast*' (p. 181). Elizabeth Barry is not named directly, but, through alluding to the sad death of his friend Thomas Otway and his passion for her, Gould portrays her as

> …a ten times cast off *Drab*, in *Venus* Wars
>
> .   .   .   .   .
>
> she'l prostitute with any,
> Rather than wave the getting of a penny. (p. 181)

Even Betterton, traditionally referred to with respect by his contemporaries, is lampooned for setting himself up as 'th' only Judge of *Wit*', although, in Gould's opinion, 'No Parts, no Learning, Sense, or Breeding' make him a poor choice as a dictator of modern taste. Gould, in short, was just one of a growing chorus of voices complaining about the decline of the commercial theatre in these years.

Dramatists and actors, however, also had other formats in which to publish their work. Thomas D'Urfey frequently republished the songs from his plays as broadside ballads. The broadsides also frequently mention songs from the plays that provide the music ('to the tune of') creating space for still further new ballads (see *MV* 4.III). There were increasing numbers of collections of songs printed with their musical scores. *A Collection of Twenty Four Songs, Written by Several Hands and set by several Masters of Musick* includes copperplate engravings of the music for them, 'most of them within the Compass of a Flute' (1685). In 1685, D'Urfey issued *A Third Collection of New Songs, Never Before Printed* with settings by Purcell, Blow, Ackeroyde, and others and copperplate engravings of the scores for oboe and bass-viol.

Songbook compilations were joined by the popular miscellany format for publishing occasional verse, songs, and short translations. Some of the miscellanies are organized around a topic and others around a group of writers. Matthew Taubman, the creator of the Lord Mayor's London city pageants, compiled *Loyal Poems and Satyrs Upon the Times, Since the beginning of the Salamanca Plot* (1685). With its epigram from Dryden's *Absalom and Achitophel* ('Plots true or false are necessary things | To set up Common-Wealths, and Ruin Kings'), the collection features poems about personalities and events of the Popish Plot (see *CV* 3.II) as well as more recent events including 'Shaftsburys farewell, or the Association' on Shaftesbury's flight from England and 'On the Kings Deliverance at Newmarket' in reference to the Rye House Plot.

The Oxford bookseller Anthony Stephens had printed for him *Miscellany Poems and Translations by Oxford Hands* (1685), and, in his letter to the reader, he explains the logic behind this poetic miscellany. Poetry has become 'the favourite of the Age', he declares, and that, since his design as a bookseller is to 'divert and please', he finds that 'a Miscellany must needs yield more delight then one continued Poem'.[61] Most readers, he believes, are in search of 'entertainment', and 'most People are pleas'd with variety of Courses, when a standing Dish would not at all gratify their Appetites' (sig. A2^r). In his Oxford miscellany, he has included only those poems that have been read and approved by knowledgeable critical readers: 'I admitted no Copy but what had stood this Tryal, and came of with reputation' (sig. A2^v). The contents include several translations by Francis Willis, a fellow of New College, as well as translations and poems ranging from lyrics to Pindaric odes from several authors identified only by their initials, 'T.B.', 'Mr C.S. of Wadham College', 'H.W.', and 'J. Glanvil of Trinity College'.

Several other significant collections of verse were printed in 1685, including Dryden's *Sylvæ: Or The Second Part of Poetical Miscellanies*, Nahum Tate's *Poems by Several Hands and on Several Occasions*, and Behn's *Miscellany, Being a Collection of Poems by Several Hands*. In *Sylvæ* Dryden opens the preface with the admission that 'for this last half Year I have been troubled with the disease (as I may call it) of Translation'.[62] Inspired he says by reading the Earl of Roscommon's *Essay on Translated Verse* (1684) (see *MV* 3.III), Dryden wished to see if he could follow the Earl's rules for translation. The result, for Dryden, is to highlight the role of the translator 'to make his Author appear as charming as possibly he can, provided he maintains his Character, and makes him not unlike himself' (sig. A3^r). 'Translation', states Dryden, 'is a kind of Drawing after the Life', and the translator must maintain those elements of the original author's character 'which distinguishes him from all others, and makes him appear that individual Poet whom you wou'd interpret' (sig. A3^r). The contents of *Sylvæ* are mostly Dryden's translations from parts of Virgil's *Aeneid*, several odes of Horace, three idylls of Theocritus, and sections from Lucretius. Tonson himself included his own poem on the death of the young satirist whom he had published, John Oldham; other contributors include the obscure William Bowles, H.D., 'a Person of Quality', and Mr Stafford along

---

[61] Stephens, *Miscellany*, sig. A2^r.   [62] Dryden, *Sylvæ*, A2^r.

with completely anonymous translations from contributors including Virgil's fourth Georgic, 'Englished by an unknown hand', and selections from Horace and Ovid. There are also several songs and Dryden's prologue for Tate's play *Duke and no Duke*.

Nahum Tate's collection has some English translations from classical texts, but the majority of its contents are original English verse. There are several pieces attributed to the deceased Earl of Rochester, including 'Upon Nothing', 'Love and Life: a Song', and 'Upon Leaving his Mistress'. There are also poems to and about Rochester, including 'Elegy on the Earl of Rochester', by 'Mrs Wh—' [Wharton]. There are several pieces from Sir Francis Fane, either to or about Rochester, including his dramatic 'mask' created for Rochester's *Valentinian*. There are older poems by Abraham Cowley, and some specific occasional verse such as 'Occasioned by a sight of his *Majesty*, walking near the *River* in the time of the *Oxford Parliament*'. William Bowles, who is here identified as a fellow of King's College, Cambridge, has his imitation of Theocritus; Mr Ballow, another fellow of King's, translated a series of Ovid's elegies. There are linked poems included: 'Of Divine Poesies', by Edmund Waller, 'Occasioned upon sight of the Fifty-Third Chapter of *Isaiah* turn'd into Verse by a Lady' (Anne Wharton), as well as her 'Answer to Mr Waller'. The 444-page volume concludes with a poem on the death of Charles I. In the letter from 'The Publisher to the Reader', Tate explains that he has gathered these poems with 'some pains and trouble'. He asserts that little of the content is by him and also that 'I am certain, none that can give offence to the chastest Ear'.[63]

Behn's verse collection includes several of her own poems, including her elegy on the death of Rochester and paraphrase on the Lord's Prayer. *The Miscellany, Being a Collection of Poems by Several Hands*, frequently identifies contributors by their initials: Behn is 'Mrs A.B.', there are numerous occasional verses by 'T.B.' or Thomas Brown (bap. 1663–1704), several songs by 'Mr J.W.', and songs by the Earl of Dorset, George Etherege, and a Mrs Taylor. Many of these songs are taken from popular plays; Behn's 'Selinda and Cloris' is described as 'made in an Entertainment at Court'. There is a 'Lady of Quality', who translated 'Verses made by Sappho, done from the Greek by Boileau and from the French'. The universities also contribute their share; H. Crisp, another literary fellow of King's College, Cambridge, contributed translations from Catullus and Tibullus. There are also references to pieces published in other miscellanies that year; Behn includes her 'A Pastoral to Mr Stafford, under the name of Silvio, on his Translation of the Death of Camilla: Out of Virgil', which had appeared in *Sylvæ*.

Unlike Dryden and Tate in their miscellanies, Behn includes prose in hers. Her translation of La Rochefoucauld's maxims concerning the presence of self-interest even in acts of charity—'Our Vertues are for the most part but

---

[63] Tate, *Poems by Several Hands*, 'The Publisher to the Reader'.

Vice disguised'[64]—is offered under the title *Reflections on Morality, or Seneca Unmasqued*. The secondary title apparently was derived from the frontispiece of the 1675 edition of *Maximes* showing Cupid removing a mask from a bust of the Stoic philosopher Seneca, who believed that virtue was founded in reason. Dedicated to 'Lysander', Behn's text includes the original preface to the reader in the 1665 edition of *Maximes*, which Behn translates and gives more specifically English overtones and references to recent events. She personalizes several of the maxims and in doing so changes the sex of the speaker from the original Frenchman into an Englishwoman: '338. The more I love Lysander, the readier I am to hate him', she writes, then in the following maxim, she reverts to a more universal form of address, '339. If we can resist our Passions, 'tis more from the weakness of them than our own Vertues' (p. 368). By inserting Lysander's name and suggestions about their personal relationship, *Seneca Unmasqued* often reads more like a romance narrative than a collection of moral observations, and, obviously, the preface does not function, as do most of hers, as an attempt to attract the interest of a wealthy patron.

Along with the printed editions of popular plays, songs, and miscellanies in 1685 and 1686, bookshops would have had a ready stock of the now clearly established fictional form of the 'novel', which had continued its growing popularity in the late 1670s. Still conveniently sized in octavo or duodecimo and usually under 200 pages and thus easily carried in one's pocket, these literary 'trifles', as their publishers often referred to them, offered both male and female readers stories of complicated love affairs and nefarious political conspiracies set in exotic foreign countries, but now also in English settings with English protagonists.

Translations of novels from French, Italian, and Spanish continued to be popular. Printers Richard Bentley and Simon Magnes (see *MV* 3.V) had thirty-five novels listed in their catalogue. The anonymous *The History of Nicerotis*, which supposedly had its origin in 'an antient Greek Manuscript', is dedicated to an unnamed Duchess and her friends, who commanded the translator to put it 'into a Language intelligible to persons more concerned in affairs of that nature, than acquainted with the Tongue in which before now it was only extant'.[65] Nathaniel Noel produced *The Politick and Heroick Vertue of Love Displayed in Agreeable Conversations* (1686) and dedicated it to the newly widowed Duchess of Monmouth. The conversations that supposedly took place in the French court are translated into English, and they include 'several new Songs set to Music', which Noel acknowledges is not typical in books of this type, but he hopes will be much appreciated by the female readers. France is also the setting for the anonymous *Love's Posie: Or, a Collection of* Seven *and* Twenty LOVE LETTERS, *both in* VERSE *and* PROSE; *That lately pas'd betwixt a* GENTLE-MAN *and a* very Young LADY *in* FRANCE (1686). Finally, the influential Spanish

---

[64] Behn, *Miscellany*, 301.   [65] *The History of Nicerotis*, 'To the Dutchess'.

picaresque novel *The Spanish Rogue, Or The Life of Guzman de Alfrache* (1685) by Mateo Alemán, which first appeared in 1599 and was translated into English in 1622, was reissued in 1685, reintroducing a new generation English readers to the exploits of the dashing rogue and his friends.

Two other self-identified novels published in 1685 represent the breadth and development of the genre's appeals: *The Gallant Ladies or the Mutual Confidence* and *Delightful and Ingenious Novells*. The first, *The Gallant Ladies or the Mutual Confidence. A Novel* was a translation of a French text by Raymond Poisson in which two aristocratic French ladies who had been childhood friends encounter each other in the Tuilleries and exchange stories of their various amorous adventures since they had parted. Although it is a translation, the publisher is at pains to connect it to an English audience. Amusingly, the volume is dedicated to a 'Mr Horner, Esquire'—this makes more sense when one discovers in the advertisement at the end that the publisher Richard Baldwin also offers for sale in his shop William Wycherley's *The Country Wife*. In the dedication, Horner is lauded for his contributions to English notions of matrimony: 'I think it necessary to let all Married Women know, how vigorous as Asserter you are of their Liberties; I mean not only in your Personal Performances, but in the Character you bestow upon the whole Herd of Husbands, whom you so generously call Tyrants over their Ladies.'[66] The novel should indeed be dedicated to him by 'the Fair Sex, in having so unparallel'd an Heroe to deliver them from the Insolence and Barbarity of their most Tyrannical, Arbitrary Cuckolds'.

In contrast, *Delightful and Ingenious Novels* is a purely English product. Published by Benjamin Crayle, it offers a slightly different form of entertainment for its readers, where virtue is usually triumphant, although a little conniving is never held against the characters. Its full title points to its innovative narrative technique and suggests that readers will find a new variety of stories told in a 'novel' way: *Delightful and Ingenious Novels: Being Choice and Excellent Stories of Amours, Tragical and Comical. Lately Related by the most Refin'd Wits. Under Borrowed Names. With* INTERLUDES *between each novel. I. The Lucky Throw, or A Wife by Chance II. The Frustrated Intentions Or Love's Martydom. III. The distressed Traveller. Or Fortunate at last. IV. The Generous Gallant, or The Intrigues of Love. V. The Unhappy Counterfeit, Or Fortunate Gipsy. VI. The Champion of Honour. Or, Vertue Preserv'd*. Miniaturizing the popular romance convention of a group of friends gathered together to tell stories, this collection of tales features all English characters, whose names, the reader is informed, have been changed to protect their rank and families, as well as the names of the 'wits', male and female, telling these stories.

It is immediately obvious that the reader is entering a different literary landscape than *The Gallant Ladies*. The heroes tend to be the sons of wealthy English merchants and are typically connected to the Inns of Court in London;

---

[66] Poisson, *The Gallant Ladies*, 'Epistle Dedicatory'.

the young law students fall in love with local gentry beauties and battle greedy uncles and gypsies rather than pernicious eunuchs or rival emperors. The conventions of the romance—the youth and beauty of the protagonists, their difficulties in their romantic lives, the conflict of parents and children over money and matrimony, the characteristically pastoral romance names—are all present, but, in addition to the English, middle-class settings in many the stories, there are also further interesting additions. There are scenes of frightening supernatural events and significant dreams requiring interpretation, impoverished younger sons triumphing through their wits to win the girl and her money, and young Londoners encountering and besting local country bumpkins and provincial magistrates. Only one of the pieces ends unhappily, with the separated lovers dying from grief. Even here, however, their deaths break romance conventions—Orinthea dies of grief brought on by the false news of her lover's marriage, but as a ghost she acknowledges her mistake. The unmarried and innocent young man is haunted for months by the lurid, blood-dripping ghost of his beloved Orinthea and goes mad, but he does not actually die until he is killed in a duel while playing bowls with his friends. In another story, a man is unjustly hanged for the murder of his niece, which he did not commit (she had voluntarily run off with the gypsies as a child); when, at the end of her happy tale, the listeners complain on the wronged uncle's behalf, they are told by the story's narrator that 'Sir, sayes Parmenio, I could have wish'd it had not been true, but as it is so under unquestionable Evidence, I durst not give my Hand the Liberty of one Sweetning Stroke'.[67]

The insistence on verisimilitude in the midst of romance trappings, the deliberate blurring of the lines between fictional events and lived experience of the reader, is a characteristic of many different types of texts available for readers and viewers during this period. Aphra Behn had printed for herself the second part to *Love-Letters between a noble-man and his sister: Mixed with the History of their Adventures* (1685) (see MV 3.V). Although her name is not included on the title page, she signs the dedication as 'A.B.' and identifies herself as the author of the first part. In part two, Behn changes from the primarily epistolary mode of the first part to include a narrator telling of Philander and Silvia's arrival in Holland and their discovery of new friends and affairs there. Once they have arrived, with Silvia disguised as a boy, they fall into agreeable company with a group of Hollanders, including Octavio, to whom Philander reveals his conflicts with his king. Octavio urges him to flee the country, which he does, saying he will send for Silvia when she is well. As her sister, Philander's wife, had warned Silvia in part one, what Philander has done to one woman, he will do again. Philander abandons the pregnant Silvia. As Philander writes to his servant Briljard (in real life, Ford Grey's servant William Turner, who married Henrietta Berkeley as a cover for his master's affair), 'be careful of Silvia, and observe her with diligence, for possibly I should not be extravagantly afflicted to find she were inclin'd to love me less for her own ease and mine, since Love is troublesome when the height of it carries it to jealousies, little quarrels, and eternal discontents'.[68] Silvia eventually recognizes in Philander's letters 'that never failing mark of a declining Love, the coldness and alteration of the Stile of Letters, that first Symptom of a dying flame' (p. 182). Eventually, he develops a new passion, another innocent and naive girl from a convent, Calista.

Initially, Silvia's response is that of the innocent betrayed and she seems as if she will die from her lost love, even attempting to kill herself with a penknife. However, her maidservant Atonett, like many of the maidservants in Behn's dramas, is made of more pragmatic stuff. She comforts her mistress with an analogy one of her own former lovers told her: 'a Woman was like a Gamester, if on the winning hand, hope, int'rest, and vanity made him play on, besides the pleasure of the play it self; if on the losing, then he continu'd throwing at all to save a stake at last...so either way they find occasion to continue the game' (p. 186). Silvia, who has already found herself attracted to Philander's friend the handsome Octavio but refuses to admit it, retorts, 'what shall that Gamester set, who has already play'd for all she had, and lost it at a cast?' '"Oh Madam," reply'd Antonett, "the young and fair find Credit every where, there's still a prospect of a return...I am indeed of that opinion, that love and int'rest always do best together, as two most excellent ingredients in that rare Art of preserving of Beauty"' (p. 186). Fortunately for the despairing Silvia, there is no shortage of handsome young men quite willing to take Philander's place. Enraged with Philander's infidelity, Silvia plots revenge through Octavio; she neglects to tell Octavio, however, that she is still legally married to Philander's servant Brilljard, who in the course of part two has fallen violently in love with his in-name-only wife. Philander writes to Octavio to say he has lost all feelings for Silvia, and, in the final scene, Silvia and Antonett leave for a nearby church where waits the unsuspecting Octavio.

The 'real' Sylvia, Henrietta Berkeley, apparently returned quietly to England, alone, in 1685. Lampoons describe her as having 'ugly grown; and 'tis our Natures | When Beauty's gone, to think 'em nauseous Creatures'.[69] The anonymous 1684 verse *A Letter to Ferguson* imagines the meeting of the conspirators who fled into Holland after the collapse of the Rye House Plot: Grey is there and '*Good enough* brings grizly T—ner in, | And his fair Spouse, that lately sick had bin, | And scap't great danger her last Lying-in'.[70] Ford Grey would remain abroad until he returned as part of Monmouth's army, the events of which Behn would shape into part three.

While fervent passion and tormented lovers ruled in fiction, it is not the dominant topic in the volumes of verse by single authors during these two

---

[68] Behn, *Love Letters*, in Behn, *Works*, 151.
[69] Quoted in Todd, *The Secret Life of Aphra Behn*, 496, n. 13.
[70] *A Letter to Ferguson*, 3.

years. The ageing Edmund Waller (1606–87) published his *Divine Poems* (1685) celebrating divine love over worldly passions. He includes his poem written in response to reading Anne Wharton's poem on the 53rd chapter of Isaiah: 'Not Love which Brutes as well as Men may know, | But Love like his, to whom that Breath we owe' and lauds her paraphrase of the Lord's Prayer.[71] At the opposite end of poetic tone, John Oldham's (1653–83) *Satyrs Upon the Jesuits* (1685) was given its third edition. Oldham's previous publications had been gathered together and published under the title *Works* in 1684. In the 1685 edition of *Satyrs Upon the Jesuits*, his translation from Ovid of 'The Passion of Byblis' is given a separate title page and ends with 'A Satyr Upon a WOMAN, who by her Falshood and Scorn was the Death of my Friend'. To continue with a more light-hearted collection, Samuel Wesley (bap. 1662–1735) (better known for his later career as a clergyman and as father of the founders of Methodism John and Charles Wesley), while an Oxford student entitled his volume of verse *Maggots: Or Poems on Several Subjects Never Before Handled. By a Schollar* (1685). Published by his brother-in-law John Dunton, the volume does indeed open with a poem on maggots:

> The *Maggot* Bites, I must begin:
> *Muse!* pray be civil! enter in!
> Ransack my addled *pate* with Care,
> And *muster* all the *Maggots* there![72]

Other topics include 'On Two Souldiers killing one another for a Groat', 'On a Supper of a Stinking Ducks', and 'A Pindaricque on the Grunting of a Hog'.

Thomas Flatman's *Poems and Songs* (1686) enjoyed its fourth edition with additional poems and a gently mocking preface by Flatman. Saying that his friends warned him that 'without a Preface the Book would be unfashionable', Flatman describes his efforts at poetry as being 'a very near Resemblance of the Ambling-Saddle; It's a good Invention for smoothing the Trott of Prose... [and] physically it gives present Ease to the Pains of the Mind, contracted by violent Surfeit of either good or bad usage in the World'.[73] 'When any Accident hath either pleas'd or vex'd me beyond my power of expressing either my Satisfaction or Indignation in downright Prose, I found it seasonable for Rhiming', he confesses and concludes that he never had any design to be considered as a 'poet' but 'my utmost End was merely for Diversion of my self and a few Friends whom I very well love' ('To the Reader').

In contrast, *Female Advocate: or an ANSWER to A Late Satyr against The Pride, Lust, and Inconstancy, &c. of WOMAN* (1686), 'Written by a Lady in Vindication of her Sex', clearly felt vexed beyond the expression of mere prose. Sarah Fyge (1670–1723), who signed the opening epistle with her initials S.F., states that she was only 14 when Robert Gould's *Love Given O're: Or, A Satyr*

---

[71] Waller, *Divine Poems*, 24.   [72] Wesley, *Maggots*, 1.
[73] Flatman, *Poems and Songs*, 'To the Reader'.

Against the Pride, Lust and Inconstancy of Women (1683) was published and had felt herself compelled to respond to it publicly. Fyge's was one of several spirited rebuttals of Gould's satire, which enjoyed popularity well into the early 1700s and which states as its mission to 'Discover all their [women] various sorts of Vice, | The Rules by which they ruine and intice, | Their Folly, Falshood, Lux'ry, Lust, and Pride'.[74] It had been reprinted in 1685, and a revised version of Gould's satire was reissued in 1686 in which several extremely coarse sections had been removed.

Fyge's response is largely on the grounds of theology, that God made both sexes and made them as helpmeets, not to ruin one another. Libertine men, she observes, can hardly be fit judges of the characters of women in general. 'In Lust perhaps you others have excell'd', she charges, 'And made all Whores that possibly would yield; | And courted all the Females in your way'. Then, when rebuffed by a pure virgin or chaste wife, 'Therefore you call what's Virtuous, Unkind: | And Disappointments did your Soul perplex. | So in meer spight you curse the Female Sex'.[75] Fyge published an expanded and corrected version of *The Female Advocate* in 1687: 'when I found I could not hinder the Publication, I set a resolution to bear patiently the Censures of the World, for I expected its Severity, the first Copy being so ill writ, and so much blotted, that it could scarce be read; and they that had the Charge of it, in the room of blots, writ what they pleas'd and much different from my Intention'.[76] Verses published in Fyge's later collected volume, *Poems on Several Occasions together with a Pastoral* (1703), provide more context for the writing of *The Female Advocate*. In 'To the Lady Campbell, with a Female Advocate', Fyge describes it as her 'fatal book', whose public appearance caused her father to send her to live with relatives in the country, and she declares that it was hastily written, 'less time than fourteen days', and 'Without Design of Publication writ, | And Innocence supply'd, the want of Wit'.[77]

In the late 1690s and early 1700s, Mary Astell and other women writers would ably continue and expand the debates between the sexes over domestic politics that Gould and Fyge represented in the 1680s (see *MV* 4.V). However, in national politics, the decade following the transition years encompassing with the change from Charles II to James II, the 1688 'Glorious Revolution' (see *CV* 4.1), and subsequent crowning of William and Mary, English readers and writers were attempting to come to grips with shifting court cultures, a brief infusion of Catholic practices into religious and political life, followed by an almost bloodless revolution, and the creation of a new court in exile in France. There would be a change of government within three years of the death of Charles; there would be a new Poet Laureate to replace John Dryden; and the literature of party politics begins to find new venues for expression. At the same time, in London and other cities, there would be a growing movement in the late 1680s

---

[74] Gould, *Love Given O're*, 2.   [75] Fyge, *Female Advocate*, 'An Answer to a late Satyr'.
[76] Fyge, *Female Advocate* (1687), 'To the Reader'.   [77] Fyge, *Poems*, 22.

and 1690s to reform manners and a desire for a less libertine public culture. In the 1690s, a new generation of dramatists and fiction-writers would begin to replace the Restoration pioneers. Behn dies in 1689, but a new group of writers, most notably Thomas Southerne, Catherine Trotter, and Susanna Centlivre, would be poised both to invoke her memory and to take her place.

II. Laws Regulating Publication, Speech, and Performance, 1685–1699

James II renewed the Licensing Act in 1685 for seven years, and it was continued for another two years under William and Mary, but opposition to it was growing in Parliament. The events of the 1680s had clearly revealed the problems with having a chief licenser who was associated strongly with one party or another; one finds in both the pamphlets and the political discourse of the early 1690s a renewed opposition to the Act. In 1692, James Fraser, a Whig, was removed from the post for licensing *A True Account of a book Entitled Eikon Basilike*, viewed by Tory politicians as an attack on Charles I. The Tory Edmund Bohun (1645–99) became the next chief licenser in September 1692. He was himself a political author, who had written a defence of Sir Robert Filmer's theory of the divine right of monarchy against the republican Algernon Sidney's attacks on it after the Rye House Plot (see CV 3.II) and who in 1685 had produced an edition of Filmer's classic political text *Patriarcha, or, The Natural Power of Kings*. His position was controversial because of his perceived shifts in loyalties between James II and William III, seeming at first to favour William's triumphant entry into London in his *History of the Desertion* (1689), juxtaposed with Bohun's supposed alterations to the second edition of his own *Geographical Dictionary* (1688) to favour James.

In early January of 1693, Bohun licensed a tract subsequently attributed to the freethinker Charles Blount (see MV 3.II), *King William and Queen Mary, Conquerors, or, A discourse endeavouring to prove that Their Majesties have on their side, against the late king, the principal reasons that make conquest a good title*. The Commons reacted strongly to the title, which implied that the English people had been defeated in battle, and ordered the book burnt and Bohun imprisoned. He was fired from the position of licenser shortly thereafter on 24 January.

Bohun's behaviour as a licenser came under severe scrutiny again with his treatment of a 1693 tract whose contents are dated 17 January, and which has in the past been attributed to Blount, although signed 'J.M.'. It was entitled *Reasons Humbly Offered for the Liberty of Unlicens'd Printing to which is subjoin'd the just and true character of Edmund Bohun, the licenser of the press in a letter from a gentleman in the country to a member of Parliament.* While the bulk of the pamphlet is taken without attribution from Milton's

Areopagitica (unlike Blount's treatise in 1674, which acknowledges 'Mr Milton' as its source), the section devoted to Bohun offers excerpts from his publications seeming to support absolutism. Concerning Bohun's character, the author reminds readers that 'Bohun, as a Justice in Suffolk, was for many Years the common Disturber of the Peace of that County, in the time of King Charles the Second; and that not only by a rigorous Execution of the Laws against Protestant Dissenters, but by encouraging and upholding most villainous Informers'.[78] 'Being now fix'd in his Libelling Post, he exerts himself according to his bigoted Principle', the writer asserts, 'and licenses many Pamphlets on the side of the *suspended Bishops*, and other *Non-jurors*, and highly favouring the *Jacobite Interest*' (p. 22). In terms of particular acts that Bohun has done since obtaining the post as licenser, the writer asserts that he also refused to license pro-William texts such as 'the Revered and highly-meriting Mr [Samuel] Johnson's late excellent *Argument upon the Abrogation of the Late King James by the People of England from the Throne*, which sets the Government upon its true Basis', and that 'he refused to allow the printing of a Book called *A New Martyrology*, which gives an Account of the Cruelty and bloody Practices of *Jeffries* in the *West*' (p. 26). Furthermore, Bohun supposedly 'told Mr *Dunton* the *Bookseller*, who carried it to him, that *he would not License it for its Weight in Gold*'.

Following Bohun's exit, his successor, Daniel Poplar, was threatened with prosecution in 1694 for licensing Robert Molesworth's seemingly innocuous *An Account of Denmark*, a work, however, that the King of Denmark found so offensive he complained to the Privy Council.[79] When in early 1695 the Act again came up for renewal, there were further scandals: the licenser Roger Altham got into trouble for licensing a book that accused the bishop of Salisbury, Gilbert Burnet, of being sympathetic to heretics, and there were complaints that the Archbishop of Canterbury and the bishop of London, who oversaw the licensing of religious texts, demanded that sermons conform to their own particular views of church orthodoxy.

Several anonymous pamphlets urged that the Act not be renewed. *Reasons Humbly offered to be considered before the Act for Printing be renewed* (1693) argues that the Act as it existed hindered honest tradesmen from pursuing their professions for the public good. Pointing at the figure of Roger L'Estrange, the author asserts that the 1662 Act, in addition to attempting to control seditious libel, is also about the creation of unfair monopolies, especially for publishing the most lucrative texts, bibles, books of psalms, grammars, and common-prayer books. The author highlights the scandal of having the majority of reasonably priced and well-produced English Bibles printed in Holland 'by one Athias a Jew' because of the stranglehold of the English patent holders. When these well-made and reasonably priced foreign books are brought over, they are

---

[78] *Reasons Humbly Offered for the Liberty of Unlicens'd Printing*, 21.
[79] See Astbury, 'The Renewal of the Licensing Act', 298.

confiscated by the licenser and his agents, the seller fined, and the books then resold to the profit of others. The threat of seditious publications is dismissed as 'their old Stalking-horse', as the patent holders attempt to monopolize trade in books. 'They are now Zealous to get that Act renewed, that they may be enabled to continue these Practices, and to tax the Publick, as they have done for 30 years past', it concludes.[80]

In addition to keeping honest English printers from work, 'many learned Authors have been defrauded of their Rights', because of fraudulent entries into the Stationers' Register. 'By a bare delivery of their Books to be Licensed or Transcribed' they apparently run the risk of having another's name attached to their work (p. 3). Furthermore, along with such crimes against living English scholarly authors, 'the works of *Homer, Hesiod, Horace, Ovid, Virgil, Caesar, Lucan, Plautus, Tully*… and Multitudes of other ancient Classick Authors, which were always free to all Printers and Booksellers to Print, before the making of said Act… are since got into Patents, and by that Act prohibited from being Printed' (p. 4). According to this anonymous author, it was the mercenary machinations of Roger L'Estrange, then a Member of Parliament, that got the Act renewed after its lapse during the Popish Plot.

It is not so much the rights of the author, however, that concerns this writer, but instead the condition of the trades of printing and bookselling as a 'manufacture' like other English goods. 'If the Manufacture of Printing were left free, as other Trades', the writer observes, 'it would employ above double the number of Printers that are in England and that on Lawful Work, too' (p. 2). 'Freedom of Printing here', he continues, 'would soon produce a Manufacture to export as well to our Plantations as to those very Countries who now furnish us and them, whereby the King's Customs would be advanced by Paper imported and Books exported' (p. 2). 'These Books being prohibited are always imported by Stealth', he concludes pragmatically, 'so that the King is always defrauded in his Customes' (p. 4). If books 'Mechanical, Mathematical, Trade, Cookery, Husbandry, Phisick, Surgery, Geography, and the like, were not required to be Licensed', he observes cheerfully, 'the Bishops Chaplains would be so much the less disturbed from their Studies; and it is humbly presumed', he concludes, that 'the Government can scarcely be harmed thereby' (p. 4).

A two-sided broadsheet, *A supplement (to the paper called, Reasons humbly offered to be considered…)*, again focuses its attack on L'Estrange's persuasion of James II to renew the lapsed Act in 1685 in the name of controlling sedition, but in reality to enable him to benefit from the fines and from the resale of confiscated books. The price of having a book licensed, this text alleges, is also oppressive, booksellers and printers having to pay '20£. 30£. 40£ a piece, *per Annum*' to license what they print. 'There is no authorized Licenser to Talk, Preaching, Writing, but Men may Speak, Preach and Write, at their Peril', the tract points out; 'why should not Print and Publish at their Peril

---

[80] *Reasons Humbly offered to be considered before the Act for Printing be renewed*, 3.

too…it is humbly presumed, the Law will reach all the Offenders alike'.[81] It concludes strongly that as the nation itself 'lately rescued it self from Slavery and Oppression (*to the introducing whereof that Act was used as a main Instrument*) The Traders in the Ancient Manufacture of Printing, &c may not be the only Persons that have no Inheritance in the free Priviledges and Laws of *England*' (p. 2).

In his observations on the Act, the political philosopher John Locke (1632–1704) likewise was less concerned about the rights of the author than the needs of the scholarly or professional reader. In his memorandum to his friend in Parliament Edward Clarke, Locke added his voice to the crowd of objectors when it came before Parliament again in 1694. Locke himself disliked the bill on several grounds, finding the language so vague ('wherein anything contrary to Christian faith or the doctrine or discipline of the Church of England is asserted; or which may tend to the scandal of religion, or the church, or the government, or governors of the church, state, or of any corporation, or particular person, are prohibited to be printed, imported, published, or sold'), that 'it is impossible any book should pass but just what suits their humours'.[82] Locke continues: 'I know not why a man should not have liberty to print whatever he would speak; and to be answerable for the one, just as he is for the other' (5. 785–6). He declares the licensing of the press to be similar to 'gagging a man, for fear he should talk heresy or sedition'. Locke targets the Company of Stationers as being the primary beneficiaries of licensing, especially regarding classical texts and the Bible. Instead of licensing, Locke advocates, as did the earlier pamphlets, prohibiting materials from being printed and sold without the bookseller or printer's name, to be 'answerable for whatever is against law in it, as if he were the author, unless he can produce the person he had it from, which is all the restraint ought to be upon printing' (5. 785–6).

The lapse of the Act in 1695 was an end to the government's official control of the censorship of printed materials and the beginning of the deregulation of the print trade. It also meant that printing was no longer restricted in terms of numbers of presses permitted to operate and that printing was no longer restricted to London and the university towns. In London there were approximately forty-five presses operating in 1695 and nearly seventy in 1705.[83] After 1695, one finds printers once again, as they had during the war years, setting up small shops in provincial cities, such as Bath. Newspapers also revived: the Act lapsed on 3 May with the closing of Parliament, and independent newspapers appeared on 7 May.[84]

Some aspects of literary publishing, however, remained the same: London still remained the centre of English publication after the lapse of the Act,

---

[81] *A supplement to the paper called, Reasons humbly offered …), 2.*
[82] Locke, *Correspondence*, 5. 785–6.
[83] See Treadwell, 'The Stationers and the Printing Acts'.
[84] See Sommerville, *The News Revolution*.

publishers still enjoyed the right of perpetual copyright, authors were still selling their works outright, and the law of seditious libel was rigorously invoked to control what could be viewed as potentially dangerous materials during a dangerous time. William III was particularly sensitive to the power of propaganda, and, with the threat of a possible invasion led by the supporters of James II, the Jacobites, combining with the French, there was no 'freedom of the press' in any modern sense.[85]

As recent historians have observed, the lapse of the Licensing Act meant the freedom to print, perform, or say what you would, but also to pay the consequences, sometimes fatal. In terms of religious expression and practice, the Act of Toleration (1689) meant that Protestant dissenters such as Baptists and Congregationalists were at last free to hold public meetings and teach their beliefs without being fined or imprisoned: James Renwick (1662–88) would be the last of the prominent Scottish Covenanters to be executed in the final days of James II's reign. Renwick went to the scaffold in February 1688, announcing as he heard the beating of the drums to prevent the crowds from hearing his final speech that 'Yonder is the welcome warning to my marriage; the Bridegroom is coming: I am ready, I am ready'.[86] The long title 'An Act for Exempting their Majestyes Protestant Subjects dissenting from the Church of England from the Penalties of certaine Lawes' makes it clear that toleration did not extend to English Catholics and that there were still limits imposed on dissenters. Dissenters were still barred from attending the universities, could only be legally married using the Anglican service, and could not hold public office or enter into a corporation without receiving Anglican Communion. In the case of Quakers, who refused to take oaths of any sort, special negations led by George Whitehead were required to find acceptable substitute expressions that would confirm their loyalty to the Crown.[87] In spite of that, records show that, between the passage of the Act in 1688 and 1690, there were 108 licences taken for new permanent places of Quaker worship, of which 64 were clustered in Lancashire, and 131 licences issued for temporary sites.[88] In 1695, an Act was passed that permitted Quakers to make a solemn affirmation in the presence of God rather than take an oath in legal cases, which finally permitted a measure of legal security for their lands and property.

Although the Act of Toleration (see CV 4.IV) and its subsequent additions greatly relieved the penalties for nonconformity, other laws were soon devised to control public expression. Sir John Philipps (c.1666–1737), Member of Parliament for Pembroke, introduced several bills whose intent it was to suppress 'vice and profaneness', including the Blasphemy Act of 1698 and the unsuccessful 'immorality bill' of 1699. The first made it illegal for a person who had been

[85] See Astbury, 'The Renewal of the Licensing Act', 298.
[86] Quoted in Carslaw, *James Renwick*, 89.
[87] See Evans, *Friends in the Seventeenth Century*, 558–9.
[88] See Lecky, *A History of England*, 1. 255.

educated as a Christian or made a profession of Christian faith to write, preach, or teach a denial of the persons of the Holy Trinity as being God, to assert there is more than one God, to deny the truth of Christian religion, or to deny that the Holy Scriptures were created by divine authority. Philipps's bill was written in part in response to the young freethinker John Toland (1670–1722), whose *Christianity not Mysterious* (1695) argued that no tenet of Christianity should be contrary to or above human reason, an argument that drew the attention of the grand jury of Middlesex and was denounced from the pulpit in Dublin and condemned by the Irish House of Commons. The blasphemy law was seldom enforced, but its existence signals a shift in public attitudes towards acceptable speech and behaviour. The second bill was intended to strengthen the laws against public prostitution, but expanded to include adultery; Parliament deemed this to be unenforceable, and it was dropped.

Philipps's bills had been preceded by several royal proclamations. In 1692, a proclamation was issued against vice, debauchery, and profanity, and in 1698 and again in 1699, William issued proclamations for 'preventing and punishing immorality and profaneness'.[89] On 10 May 1698, *Dawkes's Newsletter* reported that at the Old Bailey, 'the grand jury of London delivered a presentment against all stage-plays and lotteries'. Narcissus Luttrell recorded in his diary that 'the justices of Middlesex have presented the playhouses to be nurseries of debauchery and blasphemy' (*RETD* 1. 331). The presentment objected to 'the frequenting of the Theatres by women in Masks' as their presence encouraged 'very much to debauchery and immorality' (*RETD* 1. 330). Singled out in the presentment were the printed versions of William Congreve's *The Double-Dealer* and Thomas D'Urfey's *The Comical History of Don Quixote* for 'profane and immorall expressions'. The grand jury condemned the booksellers Samuel Briscoe and Jacob Tonson (see *CV* 3.III) for publishing and selling the plays as well as the playhouses for performing them.

Censorship of the content of stage plays during this period was, as before, in the hands of the Master of the Revels, Charles Killigrew, and the Lord Chamberlain, the Earl of Sunderland (see *MV* 3.II). In April 1692, the journal compiled by Anthony Motteux, the *Gentleman's Journal*, reported that 'the Town was big with the Expectation of the performance' of Dryden's tragedy *Cleomenes* but that 'Orders came from her Majesty to hinder its being Acted; so that none can tell when it shall be play'd' (*RETD* 1. 292). It was finally performed on 16 April, 'the reflecting passages upon this government being left out' (*RETD* 1. 292). The Earl of Sunderland, the Lord Chamberlain, in June of 1697 issued an order to the actors in Lincoln's Inn Fields, Dorset Gardens, and Drury Lane that all new plays must be presented to the Lord Chamberlain's secretary for approval before performance, given that 'many of the new Plays Acted by both Companies…are scandalously lew'd and Prophane, and Contain Reflections against his Majesty's Government' (*RETD* 1. 324).

---

[89] William III, *A proclamation, for preventing and punishing immorality and prophaneness.*

This order was reported in the newspaper the *Post Man* as an attempt to curb entertainments 'contrary to good Government and good manners', thus directly linking public morality and political stability (see CV 4.IV). The theatre in particular was to be held to strict standards, although, as with the effect of many literary censorship laws, evaluating the extent to which the stage was indeed 'reformed' by them requires careful delineation between the rhetoric of the law and the popularity of the plays and players.

III. Heard in the Street: Broadside Ballads

> And so having ended I wish you all well
> each youngman & maid to the place where you dwell
> But yet I would have you one penny bestow
> & that is the price of this Ballad you know
> You know it is good to learn Children to Read,
> it's fit for a Youngman to sing to a Maid
> It is good for pastime on each holy day,
> and here be the Ballads come buy them away.
>
> 'Tobias Observation; a Youngman came unto a fair, by
> chance he met his true Love there, by Tobias Browne' (1687)

Both a performance and a text, an account of topical news and of traditional lore, the inexpensive one-sheet ballad broadside was ubiquitous in the streets of London and provincial areas throughout the seventeenth century. Critics have speculated that there were more copies of ballads in print in the seventeenth century than any other type of writing, although relatively few of them have survived; some have estimated that by 1660, a year with much to celebrate and commemorate, as many as 400,000 were sold.[90] As well as being printed, of course, ballads were sung on street corners, in taverns and inns, at fairs and festivities, and at public executions. Printed broadsides, often featuring woodcut pictures, were posted on walls, doors, and posts, and in public spaces such as the doors of St Paul's Cathedral as well as within the home for decoration. Traditional ballads were also the markers of oral performance culture, many of which might never be written down, or were written down in multiple, often regional, forms; so-called journalistic ballads and literary ones were composed for particular occasions about specific people and events, and, while they, too, were intended to be performed, such ballads were also composed to be printed and circulated as texts.

---

[90] Capp, 'Popular Literature', 199; see also Watt, *Cheap Print,* for an account of the early development and popularity of the form. There are several digital repositories of ballads, including the University of California at Santa Barbara, which has created a digital archive of English broadside ballads at <http://ebba.english.ucsb.edu/> and the Bodleian Library Broadside Ballads catalogue <http://www.bodley.ox.ac.uk/ballads/> (both accessed 23 April 2017).

Ballads on subjects ranging from forsaken love to the adventures of Robin Hood, the dangers of drink, the dying man's repentance, and recent military victories were sung and sold by men and women called hawkers or mongers as they walked the streets and by chapmen and peddlers carrying their miscellaneous wares from town to town.[91] Unlike other forms of cheap theatrical entertainment such as that found at the fairs, ballads required no licence to be sold by hawkers, and they were sung or cried by their sellers to engage a crowd and persuade them to part with their pennies. For these readers, by the final two decades of the seventeenth century, the traditional black-letter, gothic type that had characterized the broadside ballad during the sixteenth and early seventeenth centuries was giving way to roman type or so-called white letter, still typically including a woodcut picture but sometimes, instead, bars of music, especially if the song was originally sung on stage.

The ballad trade, as historians have noted, was a specialized one for printers and booksellers, often associated with particular families. In the earlier part of the seventeenth century, the printed ballad trade was largely controlled by the so-called Ballad Partners, a 'conger', or a type of business syndicate, which created a warehouse from which peddlers and hawkers could purchase copies, the site of which was rebuilt after the Great Fire in 1666 (see CV 2.II). As critics have discovered, printers from the ballad's earliest appearances in broadside form in the sixteenth century would buy 'futures', betting that the ballad they registered with the Stationers' Company for a sixpence fee would become popular enough in wholesale terms to recover production costs and earn a profit.[92] During the last two decades of the seventeenth century, a limited number of figures still controlled the production and distribution of ballads. The printer Thomas Passinger in his 1688 will left his nephew Thomas 'all my share in the Ballad warehouse of all the stocke and Copyes of books and ballads which I now have in partnership with Mr William Thackeraye in a Warehouse in Pye Corner'. There was a specific request that the ballads be kept in print 'as formerly in the said Warehouse' during young Thomas Passinger's apprenticeship, which was finished in 1693.[93] Thackeray apparently continued as the sole London ballad printer until 1689, when an agreement was formed between Thackeray, John Millet, and Alexander Milbourn to take over the remaining stock, as well as 'jointly interested in several Reams of Paper, and quantities of ye said Books, Ballads, Songs &c, already printed, being ye Stock belonging to the Ballad-Ware-house', near the bookseller at the Angel in Duck Lane.[94] When Millet died in 1692, his widow, Elizabeth, continued the partnership.

The ballads that the hawkers and peddlers obtained from the ballad warehouse might be traditional stories, the most popular during this period dealing

---

[91] See Spufford, *Small Books*, ch. 5.

[92] See. Rollins, *Analytical Index*; Würzbach, *The Rise of the English Street Ballad*; Smith, 'Afterword'.   [93] Quoted in Blagden, 'Notes on the Ballad Market', 173.

[94] Blagden, 'Notes on the Ballad Market', 174.

with the exploits of Robin Hood, or journalistic ones, telling of sensational news of the day, such as marvels, monsters, crime, and executions. Such topical ballads had fuelled popular attitudes during the Popish Plot (see CV 3.II) and political figures clearly understood the importance of them in reaching a wide public.[95] *Englands Deliverance, Or, God's Gracious Mercy at the time of Misery*, for example, celebrates the departure of the Catholic King James II and his replacement with the Protestant William and Mary in 1688 (see CV 4.I):

> The People of God then was all to have dy'd
> To gratifie *Hammond's* most insolent Price,
> Which we by the Romans was promis'd our Doom,
> Which was to be sacrificed to Rome.

> This grieved the Princes[s] in another Land
> When as our ruin she did understand,
> This *Hester* from *Holland* sent her General,
> Who through God's Mercies redeem'd us from Thrall.

> True Love the did flow like a Fountain or Flood,
> And Con quer'd without the effusion of Blood;
> The strong Arm of Heaven this Battel did fight,
> And put our most absolute Foes to the flight.

Ballads reporting the marvellous, even if satirically, typically opened with an invitation and declaration of authenticity: 'Come listen a while, and I here will unfold; | A wonder as strange now as ever was told | By persons of Credit the truth is well known', begins 'A Fair Warning for PRIDE: By a Foal which is lately said to come into the World with a Top-Knot on its Head of Several Colours', a 1691 ballad collected by Pepys ridiculing women's extravagant headdresses. The opening lines of another 1691 ballad, *The Distressed Gentlewoman, a True Relation*, likewise begins with the hawker's invitation to

> Good People all, I pray you now draw near,
> Unto these Lines lend an attentive Ear;
> While I a dismal story do unfold,
> Which is as true as ever Mortal told.

Instead of a mocking satire on popular fashion, the ballad tells the sad plight of a godly young woman living near Lincoln's Inn Fields possessed by an evil spirit that refuses to let her take Communion and through her mouth curses the pious ministers who attempt to help her. It concludes:

> No Tongue is able to express her Grief,
> While thus she does remain, void of relief:
> Let sober Christians pray to God above,
> That he will manifest his tender Love.

---

[95] See McShane, ' "*Ne Sutor ultra Crepidam*" '.

Secular love was an even more popular topic, whether celebrating the happy marriage of William and Mary in 'The Royal Salutation, OR, The Courtly Greeting between K. William and Qu. Mary at his Return from the Wars in Ireland to his Royal Pallace' (1690) or telling the story of simple country folk and their courtship. *Tobias Observation* (1687) tells of the young man who meets his sweetheart at a fair, offers her a beer, and is dismayed to discover that she does not have any desire to become a wife. The young man declares:

> For night nor day I can take no rest,
>   for Love that lies harbour'd within my Breast
> And thou art she that canst ease my pain,
>   then grant me love for love again,

only to have the young woman reply:

> Good Sir, I do fancy you jeer at me,
>   your Riches and mine will never agree,
> For I am a poor Mans daughter its known
>   I work for my Living abroad & at home.

When he protests this is no obstacle, she declares forthrightly that

> For I have no fancy to be made a Wife
>   nor ne'r was concern'd with no man in my Life
> And for to live single it is my delight
>   and so honest youngman I wish you good night.

In contrast, the country suitor overhead by the ballad narrator in *Love without Measure: Or, the Young Man's Delight, and the Maiden's Joy* (1693–5?) has a happier ending and

> The Maiden she hearing what he had spoken,
> She had no power to [sa]y him nay,
> But gave him a kiss in love as a token,
> As he unto Church should take her away.

Other ballads served to spread the news of battles, crimes, and unusual natural phenomena, as well as communicating political ideologies. The legal scholar John Selden (1584–1654), an enthusiastic collector of ballads, held the opinion about earlier ballads that 'more solid things do not show the complexion of the times so well as Ballads and Libels'.[96] The literary historian Hyder Rollins records that James, while Duke of York, had hired a ballad-maker as part of the retinue that he took with him to Scotland to write ballads praising him and his actions. Ironically, the ballad 'Lillibullero', which was sung during the English Civil War, took on a whole new meaning during the war in Ireland in 1689–91. Its lilting tune, a favourite with William's army, became a satire of Irish Catholic Jacobites, in particular of Richard Talbot, 1st Earl of Tyrconnell,

---

[96] Pepys, *The Pepys Ballads*, I, p. ii.

who had been appointed by King James as the Lord Deputy of Ireland in 1687, the first Irish Catholic to hold that post in centuries (see CV 4.I). The lyrics, supposedly written by Whig Politician Thomas Wharton (1648–1715), feature two Irish peasants celebrating the prophecy 'found in a bog' that 'The country'd be ruled by an ass and a dog'; according to Bishop Gilbert Burnet's *History*, the tune with its new lyrics became wildly popular across England, some claiming it helped in expelling King James.[97]

Other journalistic ballads reported details of gruesome crimes and the criminals' repentant dying words, the latter sometimes being performed in front of the person standing at the gallows. These ballads typically combine details of the crime from the trial and are written in the first person as a confession. *The Murthers Lamentation* (1694) is the story of John Jewster and William Butler, found guilty of robbing and murdering Jane Legrand and executed at Spittlefields on 19 July:

> Alas, let me do what I can,
>> declare the truth I must,
> I Butler was the very man,
>> that stopt her breath at first;
> By violence I seiz'd her throat,
>> oh horrid villany;
> My soul on seas of grief does float,
>> as being brought to dye.

Nearly all of these gallows ballads conclude with the repentant criminal imploring God's mercy and declaring:

> Let others a fair warning take,
>> by this our distany,
> Who must in shame the world forsake,
>> as being brought to dye.

This ballad was sung to the tune of 'Russels Last Farewell', a tune commonly associated with gallows ballads, and a reference to the execution of Lord Russell for treason in 1683 for his part in the Rye House Plot. The tune featured in forty-three ballads subsequently, twenty-two of which were gallows ballads.[98] The tune applied equally well to female criminals: *The Midwife of Poplar's Sorrowful Confession and Lamentation in Newgate* (1693), also sung to it, offers an account of a woman named Compton who was condemned to death for performing abortions and infanticide. The sensational lyric recounts how the midwife and her assistant would leave infants in their care alone to starve. Neighbours were horrified when

---

[97] J. Kent Clark, 'Wharton, Thomas, first marquess of Wharton, first marquess of Malmesbury, and first marquess of Catherlough (1648–1715)', *ODNB*.

[98] Dragstra, 'The Last Farewell', 178.

> The Boy he told unto them then,
>   that they might find two more,
> Young Infants in a basket dead,
>   upon a shelf below.

Critics have argued that the combination of formulaic presentations and familiar tunes nevertheless does not negate the autobiographical and biographical elements of such ballads, offering instead a framework for perhaps semi-literate first-person speakers to address the audience while reviewing their own lives and explaining their motives.

While the first-person speaker's identity is thus of considerable importance and interest in these journalistic ballads, it is notable that an individual author's name rarely appears on late-seventeenth-century ballads. Few towards the end of the century were attributed to a known poet, unlike the earlier ballads by Thomas Deloney (d. *c.*1600), who had published a frequently reprinted collection of his ballads *The Garland of Good Will* (1593) or those of Martin Parker (fl. 1624–47), who also wrote chapbooks, in the 1630s and early 1640s. Instead, the texts are identified with a printer or bookseller, the information about where they could be purchased being more important it appears than who wrote the lyrics. While William Congreve's song 'Buxom Joan of Lymas's Love to a jolly Sailor', from *Love for Love* (1695) ended up being published as a separate broadside ballad, featuring instead of a woodcut picture the music score, his name does not appear on the broadside. Aphra Behn's song 'The Lover's Invitation', anthologized in contemporary volumes as 'Love in fantastic triumph sat' from *Abdelazar* (1676), likewise appeared as a broadside ballad a decade later with no attribution to her.

Ballads and ballad-writers in general are represented in the more elite literature of the period as clichéd and naive literary forms written by mercenary hack writers for a mere pittance. While Dryden might point to the noble origins of the ballad form, 'Thespis, the first professor of our art, | At country wakes sung ballads from a cart' (see CV 3.I),[99] other literary figures were much more withering, notably Shakespeare and Ben Jonson in earlier generations. Thomas D'Urfey, whose songs included in his plays were very popular (see MV 4.IV), supposedly responded to such sneers robustly: 'the town may damn me for a poet, but they sing my songs for all that'.[100] On the other side of the matter, to become the subject of a ballad was viewed as the equivalent of being targeted by modern paparazzi. William Congreve's jilted protagonist Heartwell in *The Old Bachelor* (1693) (see MV 4.IV) laments midway through the play that 'I shall be the jest of the town. Nay, in two days I expect to be chronicled in ditty, and sung in woeful ballad, to the tune of "The Superannuated Maiden's Comfort," or "The Bachelors Fall"'. He concludes gloomily, 'Upon the third I shall be hanged in effigy, pasted up for the exemplary ornament of necessary-house and cobblers' stalls'.[101]

---

[99] Dryden, 'Prologue', in Lee, *Sophonisba*.   [100] D'Urfey, *Songs*, 39.
[101] Congreve, *The Old Bachelor*, III. ii, p. 20.

Although they were inexpensive compared to other types of printed texts, the appreciation and enjoyment of ballads was not confined to the lower end of the social scale and because of that significant numbers of them were preserved. One of the reasons modern readers and critics have been able to work with these printed ephemera is the enthusiasm of late-seventeenth-century collectors. Samuel Pepys began by acquiring John Selden's collection in the 1680s, and by his own death in 1703 had in his library some 3,000 of them bound in five special volumes. His inscription on the title page of the first declares, 'My Collection of Ballads. Vol. I. Began by Mr Selden … continued to the year 1700. When the Form, till then peculiar thereto, viz of the Black Letter with Pictures, seems (for cheapness sake) wholly laid aside'.[102] Dryden and the Earl of Dorset were credited with having assembled collections that have subsequently disappeared.[103] Anthony Wood was successful collecting from Oxford, annotating some 400 of them with the date of purchase and notes on historical occurrences mentioned in them, ranging from 1640 to his death in 1695; unlike Pepys, he did not cut up the ballads and paste them into volumes, but preserved them intact. Narcissus Luttrell collected three volumes' worth of contemporary ballads, held now at the Houghton Library; the antiquarians John Aubrey and Edward Lhuyd (1659/60?–1709), the Welsh linguist and naturalist, both collected ballads that now form part of the Ashmole collection at the Bodleian Library.[104] John Bagford (1650/1–1716) collected ballads as part of his research for a history of printing and also collected Restoration period ballads for Robert Harley and what would become the Roxburghe Collection.[105] The portion of the Roxburghe Collection assembled by Harley, like Pepys's, stops at 1700 with the change in ballad formatting and style. Collections such as these were the forerunners of attempts by scholars to preserve and analyse popular, traditional literary forms such as Thomas Percy's *Reliques of Ancient Poetry* (1765) and the massive ten-volume collection assembled by Francis James Child published between 1882 and 1898 as *The English and Scottish Popular Ballads*.

The broadside ballad, its performance, its texts, and its conventions, continued to be a shared experience of everyday life throughout the country in towns and villages as well as London into the nineteenth century. It would feature in the world of the *Spectator* essays (see *MV* 5.III) as well as the engravings of the satirist William Hogarth, and the ballad and the ballad-monger remained important in the literary lives described in the nineteenth-century novels of Charles Dickens. Mingling as it does traditional stories and tunes with topical journalistic narratives, the ballad would provide the perfect vehicle for one of the most famous of the early eighteenth-century theatrical events, John Gay's

---

[102] Quoted in Shepard, *The Broadside Ballad*, 65.

[103] Blagdon, 'Notes on the Ballad Market', 164.

[104] See <http://hcl.harvard.edu/libraries/houghton/collections/hyde/broadsides.cfm> and <http://www.bodley.ox.ac.uk/ballads/help/contents.htm> (both accessed April 2017).

[105] Theodor Harmsen, 'Bagford, John (1650/51–1716)', *ODNB*.

The Beggar's Opera (1728). This showcase of the balladeer's art ran for an unprecedented sixty-two straight performances, attacking corruption and greed at all levels of society, set to tunes that the audience had probably grown up hearing and singing.

IV. Seen on Stage: English Operas, the Female Wits, and the 'Reformed' Stage

The merger of the original two patent companies into the United Company in 1682 meant that the talents of all the performers from both were available for dramatists to create new roles, but with the ending of competition between the companies there was a sharp decline in the number of new plays being offered. James II, like his brother before him, remained an ardent supporter of the theatre, both attending the public theatre and having plays staged at court by the United Company. After the departure of his court for exile in France in 1688, however, the new court of William and Mary was significantly less interested in the London theatre than had been their predecessors. The long-time patron of the stage George Villiers, Duke of Buckingham, died in 1687, and many of the prominent dramatists of the 1670s and 1680s, including Aphra Behn, George Etherege, and Thomas Shadwell, died in the late 1680s and 1690s, as well as the prolific composer for the stage, Henry Purcell. John Dryden, whose heroic plays and tragicomedies had dominated the stage in the 1670s, worked with Purcell in shaping the emerging form of the English dramatic opera, but Dryden in the 1680s had begun devoting more of his time to political satires, editing poetical miscellanies, and translating, returning reluctantly in 1689 to writing for the stage when he lost the post of Poet Laureate (see CV 4.V). Another prolific writer, Thomas D'Urfey, likewise began to concentrate his commercial talents on producing collections of songs and drolls.

Nevertheless, a new generation of dramatists continued to provide the London stage with its comedies and tragedies. After stability was restored in 1688, the rate of new plays being performed goes from an average of only three in the early 1680s to twenty-one in 1696 and 1697.[106] New writers, including William Congreve, Thomas Southerne, John Vanbrugh, Abel Boyer, Charles Gildon, and Colley Cibber, faced the challenge of attempting to please audiences whose tastes were no longer primarily identified with those of the court. The United Company under the control of Christopher Rich was weakened in 1695 when some of its most important actors, Thomas Betterton, Elizabeth Barry, and the young star Anne Bracegirdle, broke away to form their own London company as an actors' cooperative, based at Lincoln's Inn Fields. This split did have the effect of rekindling the rivalry between companies for audi-

---

[106] Hume, *The Development of English Drama*, 380.

ences and plays. The new Players Company, as opposed to Rich's Patent Company, opened on 30 April with a great success, a new comedy *Love for Love*, by William Congreve.

A group of women dramatists, satirically christened 'The Female Wits' in a play of that name in 1696, Delarivier Manley, Mary Pix, and Catharine Trotter, also wrote prolifically for the stage in the 1690s thanks to the formation of two companies, but they also combined drama with writing fiction to make ends meet (see CV 4.II). Perhaps the most significant factor in terms of what was being performed on the London and provincial stages in the 1690s and the first part of the eighteenth century, however, was the growing public concern over the moral decadence of the theatre and its entertainments, which culminated in the attack by the minister Jeremy Collier in *A Short View of the Immorality and Profaneness of the English Stage* in 1698.

For the more general popular theatrical entertainments in London during this period, Matthew Taubman (d. 1690?) continued supplying the city with its annual civic pageant until Elkanah Settle took over that task in 1691, staging *The Triumph of London*. Prior to that, Taubman produced *London's Triumph, or, the Goldsmiths Jubilee* on 29 October 1687, when James II attended the Civic Banquet: the *London Gazette* of 31 October recorded that 'the Pageants, which make a great part of the Shew, are chiefly designed to express the benefits the City enjoys of peace and plenty under his Majesties happy government, and for the many advantages of that liberty which his Majesty has been pleased so graciously to indulge to all his subjects'. In 1689, with William and Mary on the throne, Taubman's praise for the new Lord Mayor of London Sir Thomas Pilkington, who had been imprisoned during James's reign, highlighted Pilkington's defiance. In the dedication of *Londons Great Jubilee* printed by the Whig publisher Langly Curtis, Taubman declared: 'when Arbitrary Force, and the Lawless Usurpation had Unreasonably Imposed upon us New Lords, and New Laws, contrary to the Practice, and known Customs, of this City. Then did You, in Defence of our Just Rights and Liberties, stand in the Gap, and Bravely Oppos'd the Violence of the Impetuous Torrent'.[107]

The entertainment itself consisted of four allegorical pageants with splendid costumes and music. It began with the procession of barges on the Thames landing the new Lord Mayor at Westminster Stairs, where he takes his oath of office before proceeding through the streets to Cheapside, where the pageants are staged. The second of these featured an 'Imperial Throne gloriously Adorn'd with all manner of Jewels, Pearls, and Topaz...On the top of this Pedestal sits a *Masculine* Warlike Person, stiled *Monarchy*, drest in the Habit of a *Caesar*, with a Scepter in his Hand, and a Lawrel about his Head, holding a Globe in his Hand, with this Inscription, *(Britannia.)* It seems to slip out of his Hands, which he, timely recovering, Kisses, and hugs it in his Arms' (p. 7).

---

[107] Taubman, *Londons Great Jubilee*, sig. A2 ʳ⁻ᵛ.

Figures representing Fortitude, Temperance, England, Scotland, France, and Ireland surround the throne as the figure of Majesty salutes the Lord Mayor and the crowd, paying tribute to William, '*Sent by Indulgent Heav'n to set us Free | From* Arbitrary Force *and* Slavery' (p. 8). The pageantry continued through the streets of London, finally finishing at the Guildhall Banquet with songs of tribute for both the new monarchs William and Mary as well as the new Lord Mayor.

This mingling of music, elaborate costuming, and spectacle was also popular in the theatres proper with the English operas. Italian and French opera were entirely sung performances, while the English version included spoken dialogue, elaborate theatrical staging such as machines for 'flying performers', and expensive costumes and scenes, leading some critics to refer to it as a type of 'hybrid' semi-opera. The term 'opera' had been applied to the elaborate spectacle productions in the 1670s (see *MV* 3.I; *CV* 3.I), such as Dryden and Shadwell's musical version of Shakespeare's *Tempest* (1674) and Shadwell's *Psyche* (1675); Dryden in the preface of the printed version of *Albion and Albanius* (1685) (see *MV* 4.I) defined it as 'a poetical Tale or Fiction, represented by Vocal and Instrumental Musick, adorn'd with Scenes, Machines, and Dancing', which, as critics have noted, was said to cost the astonishing sum of £4,000 to stage.[108] The subject matter is larger than life, and the plot 'admits of that sort marvellous and surprising conduct, which is rejected in other Plays'. Peter Motteux's 1699 opera adaption of Nahum Tate's reworking of a play by John Fletcher, *The Island Princess*, likewise had notable success.[109] Furthermore, the late 1680s and 1690s offered audiences the music of Henry Purcell (1659–95) in works such as Nahum Tate's *Dido and Aeneas* (1689), which was first performed as a school entertainment at Josias Priest's (d. 1734/5) Boarding School in Chelsea before appearing on the London stage. Purcell contributed music to over forty theatrical productions between 1690 and 1695, including Thomas Betterton's *The Prophetess, or, The History of Dioclesian* (1690), Dryden's *King Arthur, or, The British Worthy* (1691), and the musical adaptation of Dryden and Howard's *The Indian Queen* (1695).

Not all playgoers found the extensive inclusion of music suitable, especially in heroic or tragic dramas. An anonymous critic writing in 1702 observed of Betterton and Purcell's *The Prophetess*, 'How ridiculous is it in that Scene… where the great Action of the Drama stops, and the chief Officers of the Army stand still with their Swords drawn to hear a Fellow Sing—*Let the Soldiers rejoice*'.[110] John Dennis (1658–1734) was determined to avoid that pitfall in his second offering on stage, *Rinaldo and Armida* (1698) with music by John

---

[108] See Milhous, 'The Multi-Media Spectacular'.

[109] Sprague, *Beaumont and Fletcher*, 82–6, 123; *The Island Princess: British Library Add. MS 15318, a Semi-Opera*, ed. Curtis Alexander Price and Robert D. Hume.

[110] *A Comparison Between the Two Stages*, 50. See also Kathryn Lowerre, *Music and Musicians on the London Stage, 1695–1705*, ch. 2.

Eccles (*c*.1668–1735), the director of music for Betterton's company at Lincoln's Inn Fields. The original cast included the ageing Betterton as Rinaldo, Elizabeth Barry as Armida, Elizabeth Bowman as Urania, and it is probable Anne Bracegirdle as Venus.[111] Described on the printed title page as a tragedy, *Rinaldo and Armida* is Dennis's reworking of the 1562 poem by Torquato Tasso of the enchantment of the Christian knight Rinaldo on his way to liberate Jerusalem by the sorceress Armida, who, having fallen in love with him, keeps him with her on a magical island.

In his preface to the printed text of the play, Dennis declares that 'As the Action is Great, the Characters are Illustrious, and the Scene is extraordinary. All the Objects that appear to the Agents are almost intirely new; ev'ry thing they see in Nature, being wonderful, and surprising; ev'ry thing that they see in Art, being Terrible, and Astonishing'.[112] In the preface to the separately published *The musical entertainments in the tragedy of Rinaldo and Armida all compos'd by Mr John Eccles and writ by Mr Dennis*, also published in 1699 by one of the leading publishers of literary texts Jacob Tonson, Dennis is at pains to make clear that, although it was presented as 'an Opera; yet is neither the Dramatical Part of it, like the Drama of our usual Opera's, nor the Musical part of it like that which is Sung and Play'd in those Entertainments'.[113] The function of the music is to 'move as many Passions as I could successively without doing violence to my subject'. Neither of the main characters Rinaldo or Armida sings, and the instrumental music and songs serve to create atmosphere, to summon supernatural spirits, and to be part of the seductions practised by those spirits. As found in Purcell's operas, each act has musical interludes, but they are typically a masque scene directly tied to events of the plot.

As critics have pointed out, comedies incorporating this level of song were much less concerned with preserving the coherence of the plot.[114] Elkanah Settle, during the same time he was creating civic pageants, also produced *The World in the Moon* (1697), which, like the civic pageants, has explicit stage directions for the presentation of the musical portions with allegorical scenes, and it is clear that the action of the plot is suspended during them. In Peter Motteux's adaptation of John Fletcher's comedy *The Island Princess* (1699) he explains in his 'To the Reader' of the printed version, 'it wou'd hardly have been relish'd now on the Stage. As I found it not unfit to be made what we here call an Opera, I undertook to revise it, but not as I wou'd have done, had I design'd a correct Play.'[115] While the music for *Rinaldo* was solely by Eccles, Motteux engaged the services of Henry Purcell's brother Daniel, Richard Leveridge, and Jeremiah Clark (1673?–1707) to contribute songs and dance music. Instead of the music being particularly composed for the play, some of the pieces had been composed earlier, and, unlike the music of *Rinaldo*, the

[111] Plank, 'Introduction', p. xiv.   [112] Dennis, *Rinaldo and Armida*, 'Prologue'.
[113] Dennis, *The musical entertainments*, 'Preface'.   [114] See Lowerre, 'Dramatick Opera'.
[115] Motteux, *The Island Princess*, 'To The Reader'.

individual songs were reprinted and apparently frequently performed outside the play.

English semi-opera even made it to provincial stages. Thomas Doggett, who had become the head of the troupe previously led by Coysh (see *MV* 3.IV), under the patronage of the Duke of Norfolk, advertised in *The Flying Post* of 20–23 January 1700 his staging of Betterton's *The Prophetess, or, the History of Dioclesian* as 'being the first that ever was attempted out of London'.[116] The rival strolling company in the 1690s was led by John Power, who had taken over the Newmarket Company; it, too, received permission to stage 'playes, drolles, ffarces and interludes with Musicke and Sixteen Servants att the Red Lion' (*RETD* 1. 340) in Norwich, but only for restricted periods of time, and on agreeing to give the profits of one play selected by the mayor to the poor of the community. A comedy entitled *The Critics*, which scholars have suggested was a version of the early satiric comedy *The Rehearsal*, is recorded as having been 'acted privately at Norwich', suggesting that those living outside London were becoming interested in more challenging entertainments than drolls and farces.[117] Doggett continued to work in Cambridge and in Bath after 1700 (see *CV* 5.II). Power's company continued to travel the provinces, including Bristol, Bath, and Oxford in the early 1700s, and it would provide a home for the young actress Susanna Caroll, who, after her marriage, would become one of the most performed playwrights in the eighteenth century after Shakespeare, Susanna Centlivre (see *CV* 5.II).

The ageing Aphra Behn, Sir Charles Sedley, and Thomas Shadwell made their contributions to the stage in the years immediately preceding the 'Glorious Revolution' and after it, offering a farce, an adaptation of a Latin comedy set in contemporary London, and a comedy of humours in the style of Ben Jonson critiquing mercenary contemporary morals. Behn's *The Emperor of the Moon A Farce* (1687), derived from an Italian source and previously performed in France, successfully integrated music and pleasing scenic effects to make it a highly successful play for her. Behn explains that, for the English taste, she has attempted to 'bring within the compass of Possibility and Nature'.[118] The cast of characters includes 'Twelve Persons representing the Figures of the twelve Signs of the Zodiak', as well as 'Negroes, and Persons that Dance', and 'Musick, Kettle-Drums, and Trumpets'. Set in Naples, the play's plot features the rivalry between the servants 'Harliquen' and 'Saramouch' for the unattractive governess 'Mopsophil', and an eccentric father who is concerned with the state of affairs on the moon, which he gazes at obsessively through his oversized telescope, while forbidding his daughter and niece, Elaria and Bellemante, to venture out of the house. 'Doctor Baliardo', played by veteran comedian Cave Underhill, is tricked by two suitors, Don Cinthio and Don Carmante, into believing that they are actually 'Inedonozar', the Emperor of

---

[116] Quoted in Rosenfeld, *Strolling Players and Drama*, 44–5.
[117] Harbage, *Annals*, 186–7.   [118] Behn, *The Emperor of the Moon*, sig. A2ᵛ.

the Moon, and the 'Prince of Thunderland', and he happily surrenders his daughter and his niece to them.

The play is perhaps more notable for the frank sexuality of its songs than for the situations of the plot or characters. In her dedication to the marquess of Worcester, Behn suggests that the piece was originally written for Charles II, 'that Great Patron of Noble Poetry, and the Stage, for whom the Muses must for ever mourn' (sig. A3ʳ), and perhaps not surprisingly its opening song announces that women as much as men by nature seek sexual conquest and variety:

> Born free as Man to Love and Range,
> Till Nobler Nature did to Custom change.
> Custom, that dull excuse for Fools,
> Who think all Vertue to consist in Rules. (I. i, p. 1)

Recalling the libertine badinage of earlier comedies, the song concludes:

> Than she that Constancy Profest,
> Was but a well dissembler at the best;
> And that imaginary sway
> She feigned to give, in seeming to obey,
> Was but the height of Prudent Art,
> To deal with greater Liberty her Heart. (I. i, p. 2)

Sedley's *Bellamira, or, The Mistress* (1687) continues this libertine posture, while, in contrast, Shadwell's *The Squire of Alsatia* (1688) and his *Bury-Fair* (1689), which was presented after the Revolution, suggest that something is broadly amiss in the morals of contemporary London. The comic heroine of *Bellamira* is the daughter of a bankrupt who turns to profitable prostitution, successfully manipulating her lover Keepwell, while Isabella, the young virtuous heroine in peril, is an orphan who has been repeatedly kidnapped, sold, and given in payment for debt, trafficked between England, Jamaica, and Spain. The language and cynicism hark back to Charles's courtiers, the ageing libertine Merryman invoking Hobbes in his declaration that 'in the matter of women, we are all in a state of nature, every man is hard against every man'.[119] Lionel, who had fallen in love with Isabella on seeing her in Spain, announces: 'Cou'd I but get this Divine Creature into my hands, by Fraud, Force, Price, Prayer, any way so that I enjoy her, I care not' (II. i, p. 15). He succeeds by pretending to be a eunuch to gain access to the girl, who is placed in Bellamira's care, and by the end of Act Three, as Isabella is preparing to bathe, Lionel takes the opportunity to take 'her by Storm, having no leisure for a Siege' (III. i, p. 35). When his shocked companion asks whether or not she cried out and objects ''Twas something a harsh way', Lionel retorts dismissively: 'No Woman ever

---

[119] Sedley, *Bellamira*, III. i, p. 33.

heartily fell out with a Man about that Business.' The play ends with Lionel and Isabella married, but Bellamira remains happily a courtesan.

Shadwell, who was one of the supporters of Sedley's final comedy, also turned to Sedley's source for his very popular comedy *The Squire of Alsatia* (1688), which takes a very different view of London society and its values. Adapting the Roman playwright Terence's *Adelphoe*, Shadwell's comedy transports the original into contemporary English politics and London's criminal culture. Alsatia was an area in Whitehall Chapel that historically served as an area of sanctuary from arrest, and thus was mostly inhabited by criminals of every description. Shadwell in the printed version of the play helpfully includes a dictionary of thieves' canting language used in the play, including 'bowsy' (drunk), 'clear' (very drunk), 'coale, ready, rhino, darby' (ready money), and 'rhinocerical' (full of money). The plot revolves around Sir William Belfond's education of his two sons; Sir William had been a 'Spark of the Town', but had retired into the country with his fortune and become 'rigid, morose, most sordidly covetous, clownish, obstinate, positive and forward'.[120] He brings up his eldest son, Belfond Senior, in the country with him, educating him only in utilitarian matters of farming and estate management and treating him with rigour and severity. As a result, the young man is goaded into open rebellion and, when his father is out of the country, runs off to the city to 'become leud, abominably vicious, stubborn and obstinate' and falls into the hands of Captain Hackum, a notorious cheat.

His younger son, Belfond Junior, was adopted by Sir William's brother in London, a merchant who, having amassed a fortune in trade, 'lives single with ease and pleasure, reasonably and virtuously. A man of great humanity and gentleness and compassion towards mankind; well read in good Books, possessed with all Gentlemanlike qualities.' Sir Edward raises the younger son 'with all the tenderness, and familiarity, and bounty, and liberty that can be; instructed in all the Liberal Sciences, and in all Gentlemanlike Education'. This young man is admittedly 'Somewhat given to Women, and now and then to good fellowship; but an ingenious, well-accomplish'd Gentleman; a man of Honour and of excellent disposition and temper' ('Dramatis Personae').

The play suggests a confrontation between lifestyles and values, but reverses the usual stereotypes that offer the country as being the site of pastoral innocence and the city as the cradle of vice. The characters of the two young men and the play's conclusion, however, offer an ambiguous moral vision, one complicated by contemporary politics.[121] The country represents a refuge for Tory short-sightedness and heavy-handed authoritarianism personified in Sir William's rigid and punitive treatment of his son, his 'Natural Care of him … whom by my strictness I have form'd according to my heart … When ever he

---

[120] Shadwell, *The Squire of Alsatia*, 'Dramatis Personae'.
[121] See Berman, 'The Values of Shadwell's *Squire of Alsatia*'; Hughes, *English Drama*, 325–8; and Hume, *The Development of English Drama*, 81–6.

committed a fault, I maul'd him with Correction' (I. i, p. 15). The naive and boorish rustic is immediately duped in the city and barely escapes marriage to a prostitute.

In contrast, Junior (Ned) has been raised to be a 'Compleat Gentleman, fit to serve his Country in any Capacity' (II. i, p. 29), although Sir Edward is forced to admit, 'What if he does Wench a little; and now and then is somewhat extravagant in Wine? Where's the great Crime? All young fellows that have mettle in em will do the first' (I. i, p. 14). However, the classically educated Ned is discovered at the start of Act Two attempting to comfort a young woman, Lucia (Anne Bracegirdle, to be discussed later in this section, in one of her first roles), whom he has just deflowered, and to fend off the attack of his previous mistress, Termagant, with whom he has a 3-year-old child; this combination results in a female cat-fight in front of his father and uncle. Fortunately, the love of Isabella, a virtuous and wealthy young woman, appears to put Ned on the path to reform: when she states flatly in Act Five that ''Twould be much for my honour, to put myself into the hands of a known Wencher', Ned responds that she should trust herself to 'the hands of one, who has abandon'd all the thoughts of Vice and Folly for you' (V. i, p. 74).

The play concludes with Sir William admitting repeatedly that his methods of raising his oldest son were wrong and have resulted in not only a stupid and dissolute heir, but one who wishes his father dead. Sir Edward declares: 'You, that would breed your Children well, by Kindness and Liberality endear em to you: And teach em by Example' (V. i, p. 87). Ned concludes: 'Farewel for ever all the Vices of the Age: | There is no peace but in a Virtuous Life, | Nor lasting Joy but in a tender, Wife' (V. i, p. 87). Shadwell's comedy thus seems to assert that it is Ned's education that has enabled him to overcome youthful indiscretions and folly to achieve a mature moral vision that returns him to the world of civilized and ethical behaviour and that rakes indeed can be reformed by love. So appealing was this message that the play ran for thirteen nights, making it, according to Downes, the most profitable third night (the night the author received the profits) of the period.

Both Shadwell's plays were dedicated to his patron, the poet Charles Sackville, the 6th Earl of Dorset. In the dedication to *Bury-Fair* (1689), Shadwell also thanks him for assisting him to the position of Poet Laureate after Dryden's ouster (see CV 4.V). In both the dedication and the prologue of *Bury-Fair*, Shadwell reminds his readers and audience that he was for many years 'then opprest, would have you know it, /Was Silenc'd for a *Nonconformist* Poet'.[122] The didactic strain in *The Squire of Alsatia* is even more pronounced in *Bury-Fair*, with Lord Bellamy, played by Thomas Betterton, instructing Mr Wildish, played by William Mountfort, on the dangers of libertinism. In this play, the country reverts to being the more conventional site of virtue against the corruption of city vices; the country life also offers a protective

---

[122] Shadwell, *Bury-Fair*, 'Prologue'.

buffer against affected French notions. Staged only a year after James II and his followers' departure for an exile court in France, the play concludes with solid English good sense putting foreign encroachments and fashions to flight back to the Continent where they belong: the fraudulent French count, La Roch, who flaunts his contempt for 'peasants' as being mere slaves, is revealed to be himself merely a barber, and he is forced to flee along with his patroness, the irritatingly affected and unpleasant Mrs Fantast.

While Shadwell at the end of his career was turning to exploring the philosophy of self-restraint, younger playwrights were experimenting with reworking some of the more successful early Restoration materials. Thomas Southerne (1660–1746) had left Dublin to try his fortune in London in 1680; having not found the study of law there to his taste, in 1682 his first play was staged at Drury Lane, *The Loyal Brother*, followed in 1684 with *The Disappointment, or, The Mother in Fashion*. This play proved to be disappointing to audiences and its author, even though borrowing heavily from Cervantes's interpolated story in *Don Quixote* of the husband who tests his wife's chastity by asking his best friend to seduce her as he spies on them, a plot Aphra Behn had also used in *The Amorous Prince, or, the Curious Husband* in 1671 and Thomas Crowne would revisit in *The Married Beau, or, The Curious Impertinent* (1694).[123] Southerne, whose *The Loyal Brother* celebrated James, Duke of York, joined Princess Anne's army in 1685 and served as a lieutenant until 1688. After the Revolution, Southerne apparently abandoned any Jacobite tendencies and, returning to London, wrote his first successful comedy, *Sir Anthony Love, or, The Rambling Lady* (1690), quickly followed by the much less popular *The Wives Excuse, or, Cuckolds Make Themselves* (1692), and *The Maids Last Prayer, or, Any, Rather than Fail* (1692). He concluded this prolific period with two tragedies adapted from Behn's fictions, *The Fatal Marriage, or, The Innocent Adultery* (1694) and *Oroonoko, or, The Royal Slave* (1696).

The period's leading actors continued to have roles created specifically for them in their new plays. Southerne's plays provided the rising star Anne Bracegirdle (bap. 1671–1748) with roles showcasing her youth and vivacity, in addition to roles confirming Elizabeth Barry's continued dominance as the queen of pathetic she-tragedy (see CV 3.I). Southerne declared in the dedication of *The Fatal Marriage* that 'I had no occasion for the Comedy, but in the three first Acts, which Mrs *Bracegirdle* particularly diverted, by the beauty, and gayety of her Action', that he wished it could remain a comedy; however, 'I could not, if I would, conceal what I owe Mrs *Barry*…I made the Play for her part, and her part has made the Play for me'.[124] Southerne simplifies Behn's more complex characters and motivations (see CV 4.II), while acknowledging his debt to her story: in Southerne's version, believing that her husband is dead and facing poverty, Isabella marries again after seven years' waiting, only to

[123] See Snider, '*The Curious Impertinent*'.   [124] Southerne, *The Fatal Marriage*, sig. A2ᵛ.

have her first husband return. Instead of murdering her husband, as in Behn's story, Isabella becomes mad and closes the play by stabbing herself, offering the pathetic spectacle of female innocence and suffering at which Barry excelled.

Anne Bracegirdle, who would eventually rival Barry for fame and who would frequently herself play opposite Barry, the innocent victim to Barry's villains, had literally grown up in the London theatres. Apparently apprenticed at a very early age, she had been raised by Thomas Betterton and his wife Mary and may have played child roles as early as age 6, appearing in Thomas Otway's *The Orphan* (see CV 3.I). Her first season being listed as a member of the United Company was 1688, and she played small supporting roles, including the wronged Lucia in Shadwell's *The Squire of Alsatia*, Emmeline in Dryden's opera *King Arthur*, and Atelina in the actor and dramatist William Mountfort's tragedy *The Injured Lovers*. Her first breeches part was Behn's posthumously produced tragicomedy *The Widdow Ranter, or The History of Bacon in Virginia* (1689), and, given her attractive figure, she frequently delivered prologues wearing men's attire. Her first notable success as a tragic heroine was her Statira in Nathaniel Lee's *The Rival Queens* (1690) with William Mountfort playing Alexander the Great; she also portrayed Desdemona in a revival of *Othello*.

Her career is closely connected to Mountfort's and that of his wife, Susanna, and she acted roles in Mountfort's plays such as Biancha in *The Successful Strangers* (1690), also and spoke its prologue. Susanna Mountfort (bap. 1666–1703) was, like Bracegirdle, known for her comic roles, but hers tended to be resourceful young women, often 'jilts' or coquettes, such as the role of Lady Froth in Congreve's *The Double-Dealer* (1693), or women comfortable with flouting social norms, such as the breeches role in *Sir Anthony Love* (1690) by Southerne, Berinthia in Vanbrugh's *The Relapse*, to be discussed later, and the title role in Thomas Jevon's comedy *The Devil of a Wife* (1686).[125] She frequently played opposite her husband, reviving the style of 'witty couple' in plays such as Mountfort's *Greenwich Park* (1691), a style originally popular in the 1660s and 1670s with Nell Gwyn and Charles Hart (see MV 2.III). She was also not averse to playing 'low' characters, such as D'Urfey's 'Mary the Buxom', a crude young country 'wench' or hoyden in *The Second Part of the Comical History of Don Quixote* (1694), or old sour maids, as in Southerne's *The Maid's Last Prayer* (1693). Colley Cibber recorded in his memoir that she was 'so fond of Humour, in what low Part soever to be found, that she would make no scruple of defacing her fair Form, to come heartily into it'.[126]

Cibber, whose memoir *An Apology for the Life of Colley Cibber* (1740) has served as an important source for literary historians, highlighted the contrast between the two actresses. Bracegirdle's talents were such that, as Cibber notes, 'the most eminent Authors always chose her for their favourite Characters, in which she acquitted herself with uncommon Applause', and she was also noted

---

[125] See Howe, *The First English Actresses*, 82–90. [126] Cibber, *Apology*, 95.

for her fine singing voice (p. 98). Among these writers was Nicholas Rowe, who in the early 1700s wrote roles in which Bracegirdle was the suffering innocent heroine, such as Lavinia in *The Fair Penitent* (1703) and Selima in *Tamerlane* (1701), and William Congreve, with whom her career is most closely associated. Congreve, whom gossip held was her lover although that has never been clearly documented, created for her leading roles in *The Old Batchelor* (1693), *Love for Love* (1695), and *The Mourning Bride* (1697), culminating in what many see as the finest comedy of the period, *The Way of the World* (see MV 5.I). Bracegirdle's comic heroines were typically refined, attractive young women, the ones pursued rather than the ones desperate for marriage or money. Indeed, characters associated with Bracegirdle such as Fulvia in D'Urfey's *The Richmond Heiress* (1693) and Mrs Sightly in Southerne's *The Wives Excuse* (1691) view men as fortune-hunters and would prefer to remain single than marry a rake. Unlike an earlier generation of actresses, Bracegirdle had no children out of wedlock, never married, and retired from the stage at a relatively young age.

The role of the aloof beauty who scorns to be held cheaply was also part of her public persona and appeal to her audiences. Cibber describes how 'she had no greater claim to Beauty than what the most desirable Brunette might pretend to. But her Youth and lively Aspect threw out such a Glow of Health and Chearfulness, that on the Stage few Spectators that were not past it could behold her without Desire. It was even a Fashion among the Gay and Young to have a Taste or Tendre for Mrs Bracegirdle.'[127] This infatuation with Bracegirdle by the male portion of the audience had fatal consequences, as her friend William Mountfort was killed in 1692 in an exchange with Lord Mohun and Captain Richard Hill over their attempt to kidnap her. The Captain was obsessively in love with her, and, with his companion Charles Mohun, 4th Baron Mohun (1675?–1712), apparently viewed Mountfort as a rival; the encounter ended with Mountfort's death, Hill's flight, and Lord Mohun being charged with murder. He was subsequently acquitted by the House of Lords in a sensational trial to rival any theatrics on stage.

Southerne's adaptation of Behn's *Oroonoko* (1695) in this context is notable for its focus on the tragic aristocratic male who is an isolated figure in a corrupt and debauched world. In his dedication, Southerne again acknowledges Behn as his source, commenting on her attitude towards its hero:

I have often wonder'd that she would bury her Favourite Hero in a *Novel*, when she might have reviv'd him in the *Scene*. She thought either that no Actor could represent him; or she could not bear him represented: And I believe the last, when I remember what I have heard from a Friend of hers, That she always told his Story, more feelingly, than she writ it.[128]

John Verbruggen (1670?–1708) took on the task of representing the romantic African prince, and the young actress Jane Rogers appeared as Imoinda in one

---

[127] Cibber, *Apology*, 97–8.   [128] Southerne, *Oroonoko*, sig. A2ᵛ.

of her first leading roles.[129] Verbruggen had by this time married Mountfort's widow, Susanna. Verbruggen, whom later theatre historians describe as a 'rough diamond', was noted for being able to 'touch tenderly the finer feelings, as well as excite the wilder emotions of the heart'.[130] Susanna Mountfort, now Verbruggen, played the breeches role of Charlot Welldon in a comic subplot added by Southerne of two sisters in the colony in search of husbands and financial security.

Although Behn's novel and Southerne's play feature an African repeatedly betrayed by dishonourable Christians, slavery is not the central concern of the play, but instead the sad fate of the heroic nobleman in a crass, commercial environment. Even Oroonoko himself observes as he refuses to lead a slave revolt in Surinam:

> If we are slaves, they did not make us slaves,
> But bought us in an honest way of trade
> As we have done before 'em, bought and sold
> Many a wretch and never thought it wrong. (III. ii, p. 39)[131]

Another striking change is Southerne's reconfiguring of Behn's heroine Imoinda as being not an African princess, the perfect female counterpart of Oroonoko with whom he falls in love at first sight, but instead the daughter of a European general who commanded Oronooko's father's army. She is repeatedly threatened with rape by the planters, and it is she in the final act who suggests the only solution for them is suicide.

> O! that we cou'd incorporate, be one,
> One Body, as we have been long one Mind:
> That blended so, we might together mix,
> And losing thus our Beings to the World,
> Be only found to one anothers Joys,

cries Oroonoko, embracing her before he takes up the dagger to kill her, and, as his resolution falters, she seizes the dagger and stabs herself (V. ii, p. 81). In contrast to the heroic couple who cannot live in this world, the mercenary English colonists use whatever means they must to survive and prosper. As in Behn's fiction (see CV 4.II), they are represented as mostly lower-class riff-raff and criminals, and the women of the comic subplot are resourceful, both clever and conniving, with Charlot Welldon in disguise as a man cheating the Widow Lackitt out of her fortune and persuading an impoverished Jack Stanmore to sleep with the Widow as part of the deception. Southerne's tragedy suggests that what survives in the 'modern' world are not the heroic virtues associated with nobility of birth and character, but instead resilience, quick wits, and a lack of ethical sensibility.

---

[129] Howe, *The First English Actresses*, 189.
[130] Doran, *'Their majesties' servants'*, 1. 62.
[131] See Dodds, *Thomas Southerne*, 140 ff.; Rich, 'Heroic Tragedy'.

Southerne's comedies were in general not as successful as these tragedies, with *Oroonoko* notably being steadily performed through the eighteenth century. *The Wives Excuse* failed to draw much of an audience, but, as critics have observed, it shares with several other 1690s comedies an exploration of the state of marriage and the causes of unhappiness.[132] Plays by Southerne, Crowne, the first efforts of Colley Cibber, who had acted in Southerne's *Sir Anthony Love*, and John Vanbrugh explore martial tensions between neglected wives and untrustworthy husbands. Rather than cuckold their husbands, as the male figures in these plays assume they will, the wives in these 1690s plays instead remain chaste; in upholding their own honour, they protect their families and maintain their marriages, even if their husbands are left looking less than heroic. Southerne's Mrs Friendall, Crowne's Mrs Lovely in *The Married Beau*, Cibber's Mrs Amanda Loveless, the abandoned wife in his debut play *Love's Last Shift, or, The Fool in Fashion* (performed in January 1696), and Vanbrugh's continuation of it, *The Relapse, or, Virtue in Danger* (performed in December 1696), are all offered more than ample reasons in terms of earlier Restoration comedies to be unfaithful to their husbands. As Amanda declares in *Love's Last Shift*, 'All the Comfort of my Life is, that I can tell my Conscience, I have been true to Virtue'.[133]

John Vanbrugh (1664–1726), who would become one of the leading architects in England in the early eighteenth century, had turned to the stage after a series of unsuccessful business endeavours, including an appointment in the East India Company, a series of military posts, and a period of imprisonment in France, apparently caught up with espionage activities surrounding the exiled court of James II. His first play was *The Relapse*, quickly followed by *The Provok'd Wife* (1697), both of which were immediately successful and frequently performed; he also produced two translations of French plays, *Aesop* and *The Country House*. Cibber, who gained acclaim for playing Vanbrugh's character Lord Foppington in *The Relapse*, noted that 'he not only did me Honours, as an Author, by writing his *Relapse*, as a Sequel, or Second Part, to *Love's Last Shift*, but as an Actor, too, by preferring me, to the chief Character in his own Play'.[134] Vanbrugh's ability to capture contemporary turns of phrase in an elevated style was, according to Cibber, a key element in his plays' successes: 'from its new, and easy Turn of Wit, [*The Relapse*] had great Success, and gave me, as a Comedian, a second Flight of Reputation along with it'.[135]

Both plays represent modern marriage with an edge: in *The Relapse*, the married rake proves unreformed and has an affair with his wife's friend, while in *The Provok'd Wife* the question is raised of what happens when a husband and wife mutually loathe each other. Elizabeth Barry played Lady Brute in the latter, who married Sir John Brute strictly for his money; he turns out to epitomize his name, having married her only because she will not have sex with him

---

[132] See Cordner, 'Marriage Comedy'.   [133] Cibber, *Love's Last Shift*, I. i, p. 9.
[134] Cibber, *Apology*, 120.   [135] Cibber, *Apology*, 120.

without marriage. Brute fills his days with drinking and during the course of the play beats a man in a street brawl to the point where he is reported dead. Thomas Betterton took on the repellent role of the husband who senselessly abuses his wife, and, as he announces in the opening soliloquy, 'What cloying meat is Love,—when Matrimony's the Sauce to it. Two years Marriage has debauched my five Senses. Every thing I see, every thing I hear, every thing I feel, every thing I smell, and every thing I taste—methinks has Wife in't',[136] He concludes grimly: 'Sure there's a secret Curse entail'd upon the very Name of Wife. My Lady is a young Lady, a fine Lady, a Witty Lady, a Virtuous Lady— and yet I hate her' (I. i, p. 1).

Anne Bracegirdle, who played the romantic young lead, spoke the prologue, announcing the satiric intent of the play:

> Since 'tis the Intent and Business of the Stage,
> To Copy out the Follies of the Age;
> To hold to every Man a Faithful Glass,
> And shew him of what Species he's an Ass. ('Prologue')

The question posed by the opening of the play is whether an abused wife has the right to leave the marriage or take a lover. In her opening soliloquy, Lady Brute admits: 'The Devil's in the Fellow I think—I was told before I married him, that thus 'twoud be; But I thought I had Charms enough to govern him; and that where there was an Estate, a Woman must needs be happy; so my Vanity has deceiv'd me, and my Ambition has made me uneasie' (I. i, p. 2). 'I never lov'd him, yet I have been ever true to him', she muses, although besieged by her admirer Constant, 'Let me see—What opposes?—My Matrimonial Vow?—Why, what did I Vow: I think I promis'd to be true to my Husband. Well; and he promis'd to be kind to me. But he han't kept his Word—.' 'Lord what fine notions of Virtue do we Women take up upon the Credit of old foolish Philosophers', she concludes, 'Virtue's it's own reward, Virtue's this, Virtue's that;—Virtue's an Ass, and a Gallant's worth forty on't' (I. i, p. 3).

In 1696, an as yet still unidentified female dramatist calling herself 'Ariadne' adapted the fiction by Alexander Oldys, *The Fair Extravagant, or The Humorous Bride* (1682) (see MV 3.V), as *She Ventures, and He Wins*.[137] Performed by the Players' Company with Anne Bracegirdle in the leading role of Charlotte, the play concerns the adventures of a witty and independent young heiress who is seeking a husband who 'loves my Person as well as Gold': 'I'm not obliged to follow the World's dull Maxims', she announces, 'nor will I wait for the formal Address of some Ceremonious Coxcomb, with more Land than Brains…or else some gay young fluttering Thing, who calls himself a Beau, and wants my Fortune to maintain him in that Character'.[138] Along with her cousin Juliana, the two young women dress as men and strike out to find suitable mates; in the comic

---

[136] Vanbrugh, *The Provok'd Wife*, I. i, p. 1.   [137] Bush-Bailey, *Treading the Bawds*, 114–20.
[138] 'Ariadne', *She Ventures, and He Wins*, I. i, p. 2.

subplot, Elizabeth Barry's role was as Urania, a vintner's wife keeping a tavern who must rid herself of the troublesome advances of Squire Wouldbe and preserve her good name. The prologue, spoken by Elizabeth Bowman, who played Juliana in her male attire, makes it clear that 'This is a Woman's Treat y'are like to find; | Ladies, for Pity; Men, for Love, be Kind': 'You will not think, though charming Aphra's dead, | All Wit with her, and with Orinda's fled', she declares. 'We promised boldly we would do her Right' (I. i, p. 2).

Continuing to draw attention to contemporary women dramatists, the anonymous play *The Female Wits* (1696) was staged by the rival Patent Company at the Theatre Royal, with Susanna Verbruggen playing Marsilia, a 'Poetess, that admires her own Works, and a great Lover of Flattery', and Colley Cibber her suitor Mr Praiseall. Other women characters include Mrs Wellfed, 'One that represents a fat Female Author, a good sociable well-natur'd Companion', and Calista, 'A Lady that pretends to the learned Languages, and assumes to her self the Name of a Critick' (see *MV* 4.V). That same year saw the staging of two plays by Delarivier Manley (*c.*1670–1724), an unsuccessful comedy *The Lost Lover, or The Jealous Husband* performed in March by Rich's Patent Company and *The Royal Mischief*, a tragedy staged by Betterton in May, and two by Mary Pix (*c.*1666–1709) by the Patent Company—*The Spanish Wives* and *Ibrahim, the Thirteenth Emperour of the Turks*—both of which were performed into the next century. The previous year, the young Catherine Trotter (1674?–1749) had adapted Behn's fiction *Agnes de Castro* as a tragedy, and it was performed in December 1695 by the Patent Company at the Theatre Royal and printed in 1696.

Trotter declared in the dedication of her second play, *The Fatal Friendship* (1698), that *Agnes de Castro* was her attempt to write a reformed tragedy for the London stage, with the intent to 'discourage vice, and recommend a firm unshaken virtue'.[139] Contemporaries pointed to these two plays as exemplars: 'A celebrated Female in use, has lately convinc'd you, in her *Fatal Friendship*, that 'tis possible to entertain, with all the Judgment, Wit and Beauty of Poetry; without *shocking our senses*, with intollerable prophaness or obscenity'.[140] Mary Pix, who, unlike Trotter and Manley, was a mature woman in her thirties when she turned to commercial authorship, produced popular and entertaining farces and dramas set in exotic locales, exploring gender politics at a distance as part of an increasing body of orientalist writings contrasting the restraint imposed on Eastern women with the freedom offered by European customs. Manley, whose exotic tragedy *The Royal Mischief* was staged shortly before Pix's, in contrast, had as its central and most memorable character a woman who openly challenges all norms, has multiple sexual partners, connives in the assassination of many of the other characters, and dies completely unrepentant of her actions.

The published version of Trotter's *Agnes de Castro* features a prologue by Wycherley and a poem to the author by Manley, announcing that Trotter has

---

[139] Trotter, *The Fatal Friendship*, sig. A2ᵛ.   [140] *A Letter to Mr Congreve*, 36–7.

recaptured the poetic laurels for women writers that Katherine Philips and Aphra Behn had initially won and in essence throwing down the gauntlet to rival male dramatists. 'O! How I long in the Poetick Race, | To loose the Reins, and give their Glory Chase', Manley declares, 'For thus Encourag'd, and thus led by you, | Methinks we might more Crowns than theirs Subdue'.[141] It is also notable that both Pix and Trotter contributed laudatory verses to the printed version of *Royal Mischief* that highlight women's abilities as poets and dramatists. Trotter declared that Manley was 'our Champion, and the Glory ours. | Well you've maintain'd our equal right in Fame, | To which vain Man had quite engrost the claim', while Pix described her hyperbolically as 'You the unequal'd wonder of the Age, | Pride of our Sex, and Glory of the Age', and an unknown male poet concluded 'What, all our Sex in one sad hour undone, | Lost are our Arts, our Learning, our Renown'.[142] In her preface to the reader, Manley defends herself against the charge that the character played by Elizabeth Barry, the evil queen Homais, is too 'warm' in her passions; like Behn before her (see CV 3.I). Manley suggests that those upset with her rendition of female sexuality had no problems when such women were created by male writers, pointing to Dryden's representation of female passion in *Aureng-Zebe*, and declaring 'the Pen shou'd know no distinction. I should think it but an indifferent Commendation to have it said she writes like a Woman' ('To the Reader').

Manley had created a disturbance when she pulled her tragedy *The Royal Mischief* out of rehearsals at the Theatre Royal and gave it to the rival company, which is paralleled in *The Female Wits* by Marsilia, who at the end storms out of the rehearsal cursing the actors, 'your damn'd ill Humour began my Misfortunes. Farewel, *Momus*; farewel, Ideots: Hoarse be your Voices, rotten your Lungs, want of Wit and Humour continue upon your damn'd Poets, and Poverty consume you all'.[143] *The Female Wits* in its preface pays homage to the satire on the bombastic heroic satirized in *The Rehearsal* (see MV 2.IV).[144] Like that earlier satire on heroic excesses in drama, *The Female Wits* may also have been a composite piece, with some suggesting that the disgruntled actors of the Patent Company created it as a way of striking back at Manley and at Betterton's company; the Patent Company at that time had several established actor–writers, including the comedian Joseph Haines, Cibber, Hildebrand Horden, and George Powell, who had by 1696 himself created four plays and two operas.[145] The play is clearly a spoof of both the contents and the production of *The Royal Mischief*, whose excesses are not hard to spot, and *The Female Wits* paints a portrait of Marsilia/Manley as an imperious and rude author who constantly talks over her friends and harangues the actors, boasting, for example, that 'I think I may say, without a Blush, I am the first that

---

[141] Manley, 'To the Author', in Trotter, *Agnes de Castro*.
[142] Pix, 'To Mrs Manley', in Manley, *The Royal Mischief*.   [143] *The Female Wits*, V, p. 66.
[144] See Hook, 'Introduction'; Bush-Bailey, *Treading the Bawds*, 122–6; Morgan, 'Introduction', in *The Female Wits*; Andrea, *Women and Islam*.   [145] Hook, 'Introduction', p. xiii.

made Heroick natural'. Mrs Wellfed, supposedly representing Pix, is a pleasant if ineffectual sidekick, and Calista, or Trotter, a rather conceited and pretentious young lady.

In Manley's actual play, as critics have noted, the heroic themes of love and death are played out to the utmost extremes. The elderly, impotent Prince of Libardian enacted by the veteran Edward Kynaston, has secured his young and lusty wife, Homais (Elizabeth Barry), in the castle while he is off at war; the sexually frustrated Homais, who was initially seduced by Ismael, the cousin of her current love interest, the nephew of her husband, Levan Dadian, schemes with her eunuch Acmat how best to enthral him. Levan, meanwhile, has been married to the unwilling captured Princess Bassima (Anne Bracegirdle), who is in turn loved by Osman, the chief Visier of the court (Thomas Betterton), unhappily married to the sister of the Prince of Libardian, Selima. In a highly charged erotic scene, Homais successfully seduces Levan Dadian, and they retire behind a curtain on stage to make love. Bassima, who is persecuted on all sides, resists all temptations to passion, and for her pains is poisoned; Osman continues to beg for her favours even as she is dying, but she remains chaste, and he is found with her by her titular husband Levan and Homais. Osman is carried away to be executed by being fired out of a cannon, which is heard offstage. Bassima dies slowly and elegantly from the poison. The play concludes with the Prince of Libardian discovering Homais and Levan embracing and stabbing her with his sword; her response is 'Thou Dotard, impotent in all but Mischief, | How could'st thou hope, as such an Age, to keep | A Handsome Wife?' (V, p. 45). She then lists all the men with whom she has made love, and in her final act attempts to strangle Levan 'my Darling Evil', so they will always be together. Selima, the jealous wife, is described as 'distracted' and wandering around outside the castle picking up the 'smoaking Relicks of her Lord', Levan commits suicide, and the Prince of Libardian exclaims, 'O horrour, horrour, horrour! | What Mischief two fair Guilty Eyes have wrought' (V, p. 47).

Jeremy Collier (1650–1726) did not reference Manley's play in his initial attack on the immorality of the stage, but, interestingly, one of his supporters, Revd Arthur Bedford, would cite *The Female Wits* in his 1706 *The Evil and Danger of Stage-Plays*, as displaying all the categories described by Collier of wickedness promoted by the theatre at the end of the century.[146] Collier, who had been occupied in the late 1680s and early 1690s with urging for the restoration of James II, argued that the invasion of William was an attack on divine authority and thus served to undermine public morality (see *CV* 4.1). Collier was hardly alone in his concern over what was viewed by many clergy and laymen alike as the general decline of moral order and authority. John Tillotson, Archbishop of Canterbury, often cited to support William and Mary's call in 1689 for a reformation of manners starting with the stage, preached in a frequently reprinted sermon that 'as the Stage now is, [the plays] are intolerable,

---

146 Hook, 'Introduction', p. xv.

and not fit to be permitted in a *civilized*, much less in a *Christian* Nation … by the prophaness of them, they are apt to instill bad Principles into the Minds of Men … by their lewdness they teach vice'.[147] The 1690s also saw the establishment and spread of Societies for the Reformation of Manners, the first of which was founded in London in 1691 with the goal of eradicating profanity and prostitution, with others at Canterbury, Leicester, Coventry, Shrewsbury, Hull, Edinburgh, and Portsmouth by the end of the decade.[148]

The publisher John Dunton (see *MV* 5.IV) printed for them *A Proposal for a National Reformation of Manners* (1694), which urged that 'the publick Play-Houses may be suppressed'.[149] Describing public theatres as '*Nurseries* and *Seminaries* of *Vice*', the pamphlet charges that those who attend the theatres are 'allured hereby into the love of, and delight in *Idleness*, excessive *Vanity*, *Revellings*, *Luxury*, *Wantonness*, *Lasciviousness*, *Whoredome*, and such *Debaucheries* (by *Oaths, looseness of conversation, corrupt Atheistical princples*, touching *God* and *Religion* …)' (p. 14). In 1697, William targeted the theatres with a proclamation against 'Prophaneness and Immorality' of the theatre. Collier's 268-page *A Short View of the Immorality and Profaneness of the English Stage, together with the Sense of Antiquity upon this Argument*, which appeared in 1698, can be seen as the culmination of popular and clerical dismay at the picture of society being performed on stage and went through four editions in approximately eighteen months.

Collier's view of what the stage should do is simple: 'The business of Plays is to recommend Virtue and discountenance Vice; to shew the Uncertainty of humane greatness, the suddain Turns of Fate, and the Unhappy Conclusions of Violence and Injustice: 'Tis to expose the Singularities of Pride and Fancy, to make Folly and Falsehood contemptible and to bring every thing that is Ill Under Infamy and Neglect'.[150] What it actually is doing, he charges, is to promote vice in four distinct ways—'the immodesty of the stage', 'the profaneness of the stage', 'the clergy abused by the stage', and 'the stage-poets make their principal persons vicious and reward them at the end of the play' (p. 1). Rather than condemning the theatre in general terms, Collier offers his reader specific quotations from Congreve's *Love for Love*, Vanbrugh's *The Relapse* and *The Provok'd Wife*, as well as many other contemporary plays, including Wycherley's *The Double-Dealer* and Dryden's *Amphitryon* and his opera *King Arthur*, to illustrate how plots, characters, and language all offend.

Vanbrugh comes under fire for *The Relapse* and *The Provok'd Wife* as promoting immorality and mocking religion. Berinthia in *The Relapse* incorporates language that typically would end a sermon in her speech when urging Amanda

---

[147] Tillotson, 'The Evil of Corrupt Communication', in *Fifteen sermons on several subjects*, 319, 320.

[148] Bahlman, *Moral Revolution*, 37–8; see also Curtis and Speck, 'The Societies for the Reformation of Manners'; and Hayton, 'Moral Reform and Country Politics'.

[149] *A Proposal for a National Reformation*, title page. [150] Collier, *A Short View*, 1.

to commit adultery, 'Heaven give you grace to put it in practice',[151] and in the passages between Lady Brute and Bellinda in *The Provok'd Wife* in Act Three the lines between fashion, flirtation, and devotion are deliberately blurred: 'were there no men in the world, o' my conscience I should be no longer a-dressing than I'm a-saying my prayers; nay, though it were Sunday'.[152] Collier sees Fashion's attempt to get money out of Lord Foplington as the main plot of *The Relapse*, and summarizes its moral as vicious and 'puts the *Prize* into the wrong Hand. It seems to make *Lewdness* the reason of *Desert*, and gives *Young Fashion* a second Fortune, only for Debauching away his First'.[153]

About the dialogue, Collier asserts: 'The Modern Poets seem to use *Smut* as the Old Ones did *Machines*, to relieve a fainting Invention':

Such Talk would be very affrontive in Conversation, and not endur'd by any Lady of Reputation. Whence then comes it to Pass that those Liberties which disoblige so much in Conversation, should entertain upon the *Stage*. Do the Women leave all the regards to Decency and Conscience behind them when they come to the *Play-House*? Or does the Place transform their Inclinations, and turn their former Aversions into Pleasure? Or were Their pretences to Sobriety elsewhere nothing but Hypocrisy and Grimace?...It supposes their Imagination vitious, and their Memories ill furnish'd: That they are prac-tised in the Language of the Stews, and pleas'd with the Scenes of Brutishness. (p. 7)

Swearing has also become as commonplace as immodest expression and behaviour:

the *English Stage* exceed their predecessors in this, as well as other Branches of immoral-ity. *Shakespear* is comparatively sober, *Ben Jonson* is still more regular; And as for *Beaumont* and *Fletcher*, In their *Plays* there are commonly Profligate Persons that Swear, and even those are reprov'd for't. Besides, the Oaths are not so full of Hell and Defiance, as in the Moderns. (p. 57)

Needless to say, with charges being brought before the magistrates even against booksellers publishing and selling plays as well as actors performing in them (see *MV* 4.II), authors including Vanbrugh and Congreve published defences of their work, while others, such as John Dennis, Elkanah Settle, and Edward Filmer (1651/2–1703), published treatises praising the public benefits of the theatre in general. Vanbrugh attempted to minimize the charges against him with a pamphlet *A Short Vindication of The Relapse and The Provok'd Wife From Immorality and Prophaneness* (1698), suggesting that Collier was more offended by the portraits of comic clergymen than the supposed blas-phemy implied. Congreve issued *Amendments of Mr Collier's False and Imperfect Citations* (1698), a more lengthy rebuttal published by Tonson. Congreve acknowledges that there were expressions in some of his plays that in hindsight might be offensive to some, but 'Least of all, would I undertake to defend the Corruptions of the Stage; indeed if I were so inclin'd, Mr *Collier* has given me

---

[151] Vanbrugh, *The Relapse*, IV. ii, p. 69.   [152] Vanbrugh, *The Provok'd Wife*, III. iii, p. 40.
[153] Collier, *A Short View*, 209.

no occasion; for the greater part of those Examples which he has produc'd, are only Demonstrations of his own Impurity, they only savour of his Utterance, and were sweet enough till tainted by his Breath'.[154]

The first to reply was John Dennis with *The Usefulness of the Stage, to the Happiness of Mankind, to Government, and to Religion occasioned by a late book written by Jeremy Collier M.A.* (1698). It is more a defence of the theatre itself than of the individual playwrights or plays. Dennis admits that 'If Mr *Collier* had only attack'd the Corruptions of the Stage, for my own part I should have been so far from blaming him, that I should have publickly return'd him my thanks: For the houses are so great, that there is a necessity for the reforming them'. 'Not that I think that with all its corruptions the Stage has debauch'd the people', Dennis continues. 'I am fully convinc'd it has not, and I believe I have said enough in the following treatise to convince the Reader of it. But this is certain, that the corruptions of the Stage hinder its efficacy in the reformation of manners'.[155] In this treatise, as well as his *The Stage Defended* (1726), he argues that a well-regulated stage is in fact 'instrumental to the happiness of Mankind in general... [and] more particularly instrumental to the happiness of *Englishmen*' (p. 2). Likewise, tragedy is beneficial to both good government and the promotion of religion: 'it is proper to restrain a people from rebellion and disobedience, and to keep them in good correspondence among themselves: For this reason, the Drama may be said to be instrumental in a peculiar manner to the welfare of the *English* Government; because there is no people on the face of the Earth so prone to rebellion as the *English*, or so apt to quarrel among themselves' (p. 63).

Elkanah Settle's *A Defence of Dramatick Poetry being a review of Mr Collier's View of the immorality and profaneness of the stage*, also appearing in 1698, tackles Collier's representation of the purity of the classical theatre compared to the modern and his use of Scripture. Fundamentally, he suggests that Collier in fact cannot tell the difference between satire and the vice it condemns. Concerning the content of Congreve's dedication of *The Plain-Dealer* to a notorious bawd, Settle observes:

here's nothing but what, with a very Grave face of Truth, and in as earnest a Jest, might have been said upon any other Publick places of Meeting, *viz.* the *Dancing Schools*, the *Mall*, the *Parks*, the *Gardens*; and where not? And unless this Man of Morals, would have a Law made to suppress all Places of general Resort, and confine Mankind to Cells and Caves, I know not well how he will prevent all these Enormities that the *Plain-Dealer* has here rallied upon.[156]

Settle points out that the recently deceased Queen Mary was commended in her funeral sermon by William Payne for permitting dancing, card playing, and going to plays, 'Our Admirable QUEEN could distinguish here between Duty

---

[154] Congreve, *Amendments of Mr Collier's*, 3.
[155] Dennis, *The Usefulness of the Stage*, 'Introduction'.
[156] Settle, *A Defence of Dramatick Poetry*, 33.

and Prudence, between Unlawful and Inexpedient. She would not refuse those Common Diversions, nor use them too much: She would not wholly keep from seeing of Plays, as if they were utterly unlawful, &c' (p. 68). The piece ends with a spirited defence of Dryden, and concludes of Collier: 'I must say, to come up to all the Heights of that Christian Champion, he professes himself, undoubtedly he must have a double Portion of Faith and Hope, to make up for his Diminitive Talent of Charity' (p. 118).

Collier responded to these rebuttals with *Defence of the Short View* in 1699. The debate over the merits and dangers of public theatres would continue well into the first two decades of the eighteenth century (see *MV* 5.I). While Collier was certainly not the first to call for reform of the stage, his writings served to focus attention on it in ways that future dramatists and theatre managers, while they might continue to push the boundaries of taste, could not afford simply to ignore. Simultaneously, with the lurid excesses of spectacular tragedies of the 1680s and early 1690s, we find softening of the comic role of the rake into a reformed character and the safe containment of illicit passions such as found in Mary Pix's *The Innocent Mistress* along with the celebration of virtuous wives, suggesting the direction comedy and tragedy would move in the early 1700s. Likewise, the conditions under which the two companies were operating were such that, as the century ended, it was unclear whether London would continue to support two rival companies, with the ageing actors in Betterton's company and their cramped space in Lincoln's Inn Fields and the Patent Company's productions at Drury Lane and the Dorset Garden.

V. Debates between the Sexes: Satires, Advice, and Polemics

> A *Bad Woman!* Heav'n bless us, Sirs! Who dare
> Approach so near, to write her Character?
> Plagues owe their Birth to her envenom'd Breath;
> To *see* her's dangerous; to *touch* her, Death.
>
> *Mantuan English'd, and paraphras'd: or, The*
> *character of a bad woman (c.1679)*

> For Men being sensible as well of the Abilities of Mind in our Sex, as of the strength of Body in their own, began to grow Jealous, that we, who in the Infancy of the World were their Equals and Partners in Dominion, might in process of Time, by Subtlety and Stratagem, become their Superiours; and therefore began in good time to make use of Force (the Origine of Power) to compel us to a Subjection, Nature never meant...
>
> Judith Drake, *An Essay in Defence of the Female Sex* (1696)

The latter part of the seventeenth century certainly was not unique in the publications criticizing women and responses to them, but they seemed to increase in the late 1670s and to continue in popularity through the end of the century.[157] In addition to earlier generations' circulated satires and lampoons on court women and their promiscuous lives (see MV 4.V), women as a sex are the focus of a wide range of literary materials offering correction and entertainment, and sometimes both together. On stage in 1696, the comedy *The Female Wits* lampooned popular women dramatists Delarivier Manley, Mary Pix, and Catharine Trotter (see MV 4.IV). Broadsides and ballads depicted young men and women engaged in social guerrilla warfare, each sex wishing to exploit the other. In pamphlets and longer treatises, the disputes over the nature of women and their legal and moral roles within families and society at large ranged from arguments in favour of expanding education for girls to blaming the ills of society on women's inherently lascivious natures.

These longer debates sometimes took the form of an English version of the *querelle des femmes*, a term used to describe debates beginning in France in the fifteenth century, often conducted between male and female writers, over whether women are inherently inferior to men or whether their existing state of dependence and inferiority was the result of social conventions restricting women's access to education and spheres of activity. Other pieces in circulation in the 1680s and 1690s are more clearly modelled on classical attacks against women's lust and pride, such as those found in Juvenal and Martial, placing women's vices in the context of social corruption in general. A notable feature of the debates between the sexes occurring in the later decades in England is the reciprocal nature of the texts and the frequent pairing-off of male and female writers.

The anonymous *Mantuan English'd, and paraphras'd: or, The character of a bad woman* (c.1679), for example, was quickly answered in an anonymous broadside, *An Answer to the Mantuan, or, False character lately wrote against womankind* (1679), whose speaker demands 'who dare Presume to speak or write her Character? | Or what Pot-Poet dare attempt to vex | By cursed Libels this so glorious Sex?' As with many defences of women against satiric attacks, this rebuttal elevates women above men: 'A Sex that was by Heav'ns Decrees design'd | To be (and is) the best of Human kind'.[158] Women instead of being agents of moral chaos are represented as the agents who sustain and promote a civilized society.

We can see the basic motifs of the satiric attacks on women in another 1679 anonymous pamphlet text, *Female Excellence, or, Woman display'd in several satyrick poems | by a person of quality*, which has variously been improperly attributed to the Earl of Rochester and to Robert Gould, the latter of whom will be discussed later. It contains four satires: 'A General Satyr on Woman',

---

[157] See Perry, 'Writing the History'; McDowell, *The Women of Grub Street*; Weil, *Political Passions*.
[158] See Nussbaum, *On the Brink of All We Hate*.

'A Satyr upon Woman's Usurpation', 'A Satyr on Woman's Lust', and 'In Praise of a Deformed, but Virtuous Lady; OR, A Satyr on Beauty'. The general tenor of the four pieces is that women's natures are innately controlled by dangerous appetites—vanity, lust, and the desire for power, which they seek through their treacherous physical charms. ''Tis hard as 'tis impossible to find, | Virtue and *Venus* both together joyn'd', one satire concludes.[159] Eve's pride is the ultimate source of women's failings: in Eden before the Fall, 'The Legislative Power was solely in | Just *Man*, till *Woman* tempted him to sin', and

> Once she was happy, but her towring pride
> Could no Superiour, God or Man abide:
> *Man*'s now enslav'd, imperious *Woman* reigns,
> And governs Monarchs with her golden chains. (pp. 4–5)

The satire by Robert Gould (1660?–in or before 1709) *Love given O're, or, A Satyr against the pride, lust, and inconstancy &c. of woman* (1683) quickly ran through several editions. It appeared both as a separate, anonymous publication and in Gould's collected satires. As critics have noted, it is a deliberately crude and sharp-edged satire that focuses principally on women's cruelty to men who adore them: the speaker is a young man who has been betrayed by Silvia and now sees the duplicity of the sex's dealings with men in general, 'Come then my Muse, and since th' occasion's fair, | 'Gainst the lewd Sex proclaim an endless War'.[160] The speaker declares his intent to strip women metaphorically naked and to expose their sins and sinful flesh to all:

> Unvail 'em quite to ev'ry vulgar Eye,
> And in that shameful posture let 'em lie,
> Till they (as they deserve) become to be
> Abhorr'd by all Mankind, as they're abhorr'd by me. (p. 2)

Once again Eve is the origin of modern women's behaviour: 'The fatal Rib was crooked and unev'n, | From whence they have their Crab-like Nature giv'n; | Averse to all the Laws of Man, and Heav'n' (p. 2).

'How happy had we been, had Heav'n design'd | Some other way to propagate our kind?' the speaker continues and it becomes clear that female sexuality itself rather than a scriptural debate over the shape of Adam's rib is disgusting the rejected lover. Following Rochester's lead in his political satires, Gould deliberately deploys obscenity to increase the repulsive nature of ancient and modern women's insatiable lusts. In lines that will reverberate much more elegantly in Alexander Pope's *The Rape of the Lock* (1714) (see MV 5.V), Gould's speaker catalogues the extent to which women go to satisfy their sexual desire:

> How, when into their Closets they retire,
> Where flaming Dil[doe]—s does inflame desire,
> And gentle Lap-d[og]—s feed the am'rous fire:

---

[159] *Female Excellence*, 7.   [160] Gould, *Love Given O're*, 1.

Lap-d[og]—s! to whom they are more kind and free,
Than they themselves to their own Husbands be. (p. 5)

By the end of the poem it is also clear that it is female sexuality within marriage that is the goad, and the poem concludes: 'Trust me, the Man's as frenzical as he, | Who ventures his frail Bark out wilfully, | On the wild, rocky, matrimonial Sea' (p. 8). The success of the poem demanded several new editions in the 1680s, although, notably, several of the cruder sections were taken out.[161]

Such a provocative poem also generated multiple responses, some by men, and some by women. Richard Ames (bap. 1664?–92) created two responses using a female persona, Sylvia, to answer the attack in Gould's poem. *Sylvia's Revenge* (1688) was followed by *Sylvia's Complaint* (1692), with Gould's response coming quickly in 1691, *A Satyrical Epistle to the Female Author of a Poem, call'd Silvia's Revenge* (1691). *Sylvia's Revenge, or, A satyr against man in answer to the Satyr against woman* frames the conflict as no longer being a jilted lover/frustrated husband railing at the sex in general, but instead a part of 'a Warr betwixt our *Sex* and *Man*'.[162] '*Ye Gods!* how long shall injur'd *Virtue* groan? | How long shall *Innocence* be trampl'd on?' laments Sylvia in the opening, depicting the writer as 'a bold Scribling-*Fop* whose Head contains, | A Thousand *Maggots* for One Dram of *Brains*', whose title guarantees a particular type of male audience,

A pretty Title—sure the *Book* must sell,
Cries a *Clapt-Spark*, and likes it wondrous well,
Another Laughs, and *Snuffling* in the Nose,
E'gad *(says he)* the Subject's rarely chose. (pp. 1–2).

'Sylvia' gives a very different portrait of modern marriage:

Oh! she's a happy, too too happy Bride,
That has a *Husband* Snoring by her side:
Belching out *Fumes* of undigested *Wine*,
And lyes all Night like a good natur'd *Swine*. (p. 19)

The speaker points out grimly: 'She may indeed assume the Name of *Wife*, | But others know she's but a *Nurse* for *Life*' (p. 19). 'Are these ye Gods, the *Sov'raigns* we must own? | Must we before these golden Calves bow down?' the speaker demands (p. 20).

Ames, as the bookseller John Dunton recalled in his autobiography, was happy to embrace numerous personas and positions in his satires, including answering his own: 'you might engage him upon what Project you pleas'd, if you'd but conceal him' (Dunton, *Life and Errors*, 247). Thus, in addition to his exchanges with Gould, Ames also penned *The Female Fire-Ships: a Satyr Against Whoring* (1691) and *The Folly of Love: a New Satyr Against Women* (1691), answering the last with *The Pleasures of Love and Marriage* (1691). The

---

[161] See Marshall, *The Practice of Satire*, 130–9.   [162] Ames, *Sylvia's Revenge*, sig. A2^r.

ease of publishing and the proliferation of these satires suggest that the issues raised in these exchanges about women and marriage had settled into a conventional discourse of stereotypes and that the appeal surely must have been to see which poet could bring a new element, whether more obscene or more witty.

For the women who responded to Gould and the subsequent satires, however, more may have been at stake. Sarah Fyge (1670–1723) was a teenager when she first read Gould and felt compelled to answer with her *The Female Advocate* (1686) (see *MV* 4.I). Fyge attributes the crudity of the attack in Gould's original to being the result of the libertine nature of the speaker, who, given his own perverse and debauched sexual nature, can see others only through that lens. Fyge's defence returns to the biblical one, that God created both man and woman in his image, to be loving helpmeets rather than savage adversaries. Indeed,

> When Heaven survey'd the Works that it had done,
> Saw Male and Female, but found Man alone,
> A barren Sex, and insignificant;
> So Heaven made Woman to supply the want,
> And to make perfect what before was scant.[163]

Fyge published a second corrected edition of her poem in 1687 but then was sent by her family to live outside London, her father objecting to her poetic debut into the fray, and she did not to return to London until around 1700.

Publications attacking women for their sexual behaviour under the guise of excoriating prostitution fed into the discourse of satires against women and conflicts between the sexes. The Society for the Reformation of Manners (see *MV* 4.IV; *MV* 5.II) had concentrated on eradicating bawdy houses as well as cleaning up the theatres; several satirists such as Edward [Ned] Ward (1667–1731) have in their writings a very thin line between women who are prostitutes by trade and those who are so by nature. One of Ward's earliest publications, *Female Policy Detected. Or, The arts of a designing woman laid open In maxims proper to be observ'd by all* (1695), was dedicated to the apprentices of London, to 'serve as Armour to defend you from the Darts thrown from *Wanton and Designing Women*, whose evil Communication corrupts good Manners'.[164] While the mayors and justices of London have made it more difficult for 'a *Night-walking Strumpet* to strole through the City unpunish'd', they have not affected 'the Lust and Subtilty of those *private Madams*, whose gay Apparel, and false Pretence to Modesty, gives them Cover in reputable Families, where they heard with the Vertuous, declaim against the Vices of the Age, and seem to wonder at that Wickedness in others, which themselves do practice daily, to maintain their Pride' (sig. A3^r).

Chief among the dangers of these 'private Madams' is that, through their beauty, they drain young men's pockets. 'Be careful how you conceive too good

---

[163] Fyge, *Female Advocate*, [2].   [164] Ward, *Female Policy Detected*, sig. A2^v.

an Opinion of a Woman at first Sight, for you see not the Woman truly, but her Ornaments. Paint, Patches, and fine Dresses, are to hide Defects', Ward warns (p. 2). He suggests, foreshadowing Jonathan Swift's satires on women, 'If you like a Woman, and would discover if she be in Nature, what perhaps she may seem by Art, surprize her in a Morning undrest, and it is Ten to One, but you will find your Goddess hath shifted off her Divinity, and the Angel you so much admired turn'd into a *Magmallion*' (pp. 2–3). Likewise, the women that apprentices meet are 'sensible that Constancy is more priz'd than Beauty; but it is a Maxim among their Sex, to Deceive us most in what we most Value' (p. 10). Neatly summarizing the popular stereotypes, Ward declares that 'the Love of a Virgin is innocent and lasting, as her Vertue. The Love of a Just Wife friendly and delightful. The Love of a Widow politick and deceitful. The Love of a Lewd Woman lustful and revengeful' (p. 17).

Women were also popular targets in broadside ballads that reproved vanity and fashion. A 1691 topical ballad (see *MV* 4.III) dealt with a passing fashion in women's hairstyles, a conspicuous display of both wealth and vanity. In *Advice to the Maidens of London to forsake their fantastical top-knots* the singer rebukes 'young Females that follows the Mode' and that insist on wearing expensive and elaborate hair decorations in spite of their status.

> Here we may see what young Damsels will do,
>   before they will want of their pleasure,
> *Nancy* and *Nell* of the *Billings-gate* Crew,
>   they'l Mortgage their secret Treasure,
> For a *Top-Knot* be sure they'l have one.

The style also provoked another broadside account in 1691, *The Vanity of Female Pride a true relation of a sow that Pig'd seven monstrous pigs, at Highworth in Wiltshire, on Tuesday the ninth of June 1691, all with top-knots*. The pamphlet-writer attributes these strange deformities to 'our Jolly Dairy-Maid, being deck'd with those Ornaments, expecting the Company of her Dearly Beloved, and the Sow just then in the Act, her Eyes being fixed upon the Maid, and that (say some that would have it so) might be the occasion of this Monstrous Production'. The writer concludes with the warning to female readers that ''Tis not the High Top Knots, the Powder'd Hair, a Beautiful Face, a Clear Skin, a well-shap'd Body, and those, other Charming, Lineaments and Delusions' that create admiration, and that the wearing of them is only to 'ensnare and decoy the Wanton sort of Men to your Licure; or to speak more favourably, to Intice and Intrap the more Sober sort to a Confined State'.

A weightier publication on the connections between fashion and female vanity enjoyed its second edition in 1696, *Discourses and Essays, Useful for the Vain Modish Ladies and their Gallants* attributed to Francis Boyle, Viscount Shannon (1623–1699), the fourth son of Richard Boyle, 1st Earl of Cork and brother to the natural philosopher Robert Boyle and Roger Boyle, 1st Earl of

Orrery. Francis Boyle's wife, Elizabeth Killigrew, sister of the theatre manager and dramatist Thomas Killigrew, had given birth to one of the young Charles II's illegitimate offspring, Charlotte Jemina Fitz-Roy (*c.*1650–84), so discourses on topics such as 'Of the Inconstancy of most Ladies, especially such as are cry'd-up Beauties' and 'Of the French Fashions and Dresses' may have been understood as no mere theoretical reflections. 'Womens governing power, being so long and deep rooted an usurpation, possessed by so many Wives, and yielded to by so many Husbands, as long as Custom has made it a Disease in most Husbands minds', Shannon muses, to the point that in contemporary times very few husbands can be said to 'rule their wives'.[165] Speaking of women's fashions, Shannon observes, 'there belong[s] much more Rigging to set out a young Lady, than a Man of War; so hard 'tis to cast up the variety of parts, as now adays belong to compleat a great Modish Ladies Dress and Equipage' (p. 142). 'Pride is now turned into a Cancerous humor very apt to grow in all young handsom Womens brests', Shannon warns the reader, continuing the metaphors of disease: 'Pride is a distemper of the mind, which most young Ladies are naturally inclined to, and easily infected with' (pp. 186–7).

Men, of course, were not the only writers turning their gaze on the vanity induced in both sexes by fashion. Mary Evelyn (1665–85) (see *MV* 4.I) had written *Mundus Muliebris: or, The Ladies Dressing-Room Unlock'd, . . . Together with the fop-dictionary, compiled for the use of the fair sex* (1691) for the entertainment of her family and friends. It offers a whimsical voyage through the intricacies of modern fashionable attire for ladies:

> This is not half that does belong
> To the fantastick Female Throng:
>
> .   .   .   .   .
>
> *Mouches* for pushes, to be sure,
> From *Paris* the *tré-fine* procure,
> And *Spanish* Paper, Lip, and Cheek,
> With Spittle sweetly to belick:
> Nor therefore spare in the next place,
> The Pocket *Sprunking* Looking-Glass;
> *Calembuc* Combs in *Pulvil* Case,
> To set, and trim the Hair and Face:
> And that the Cheeks may both agree,
> *Plumpers* to fill the Cavity.[166]

After her death, her father John Evelyn had it published by Richard Bentley. It was answered quickly by the anonymous *Mundus Foppensis: or, the Fop Display'd Being the ladies vindication* (1691), rebuking the supposedly male detractor of female beauty secrets and detailing the ways in which fashionable male attire is designed merely to showcase 'Thighs and Groin'.

[165] Boyle, *Discourses and Essays*, 41.   [166] Evelyn, *Mundus Muliebris*, 5–6.

The common thread in printed satires, whether ballads and broadsides or admonitions about women's wiles, that women of all social classes are desperate to catch a good, in the sense of well-to-do, husband and will use any means available, is, of course, hardly unique to this period. The peculiar broadside *Mercurius Matrimonialis: or, Chapmen for the ladies lately offered to sale by way of auction Procured by one of their own sex* (1691) suggests that women themselves have organized a fair or sale to showcase their wares. It lists twenty-one men, ranging from 'A Milliner on the Royal Exchange, much admired for his Handsomeness and Gentility', 'A Coffee-man, well lin'd with Broad Pieces of Gold, and has a good Trade, a Widdower, wants a Bar-keeper', to 'A lusty, stout proportion'd Man, had a good Estate before the Fire, and is still fit for Womans Service', who proposed to bid on available females who put themselves up for auction, if such ladies 'prove clear Limb'd, and Members entire upon due Examination'. Richard Ames added his contribution, *A Continuation of a Catalogue of Ladies to be set up by Auction, on Monday the 6th of this Instant July* (1691), auctioned by 'E.Cl—r, Auctioneer, that sold the young Heiress in Q——street'. A series of ribald exchanges on the topic continued throughout the decade, seeming to reach the nadir of this joke in 1700 with the unabashedly obscene *The Cracks Garland Furnish'd with three excellent new songs. Song I. The weeping harlot….Song II. The female auction; or a curious collection of towncracks, to be sold by inch of candle, at Peticoat-Castle, near the sign of the furbelo lady, in Dildo-street.*

Perhaps in response to ubiquitous polemics against marriage and against women's desperate ploys to snag a husband, the former maid of honour to Mary of Modena, Anne Finch, Countess of Winchilsea (1661–1720), turned her satiric glance on the nature of matrimony from a female perspective. Writing during the 1690s from the countryside, where she and her husband had retired after the Glorious Revolution (see CV 4.I, 4.V), Finch worked steadily on her literary compositions, which were in the 1690s collected by her husband in fair copy volumes and read by friends and family. In her poem 'The Introduction', Finch confronts the imagined responses should she decide to publish her poems (which she did in 1713) (MV 5.V): 'Did I, my lines intend for publick view, | How many censures, wou'd their faults persue':

> True judges, might condemn their want of witt,
> And all might say, they're by a Woman writt.
> Alas! a woman that attempts the pen,
> Such an intruder on the rights of men,
> Such a presumptuous Creature, is esteem'd,
> The fault, can by no vertue be redeem'd.[167]

'Sure 'twas not ever thus, nor are we told | Fables, of Women that excell'd of old', Finch observes, concluding that, in her society:

---

[167] Finch, *The Poems of Anne, Countess of Winchilsea*, ed. Reynolds, 4.

How are we fal'n, fal'n by mistaken rules?
And Education's, more than Nature's fools,
Debarr'd from all improve-ments of the mind,
And to be dull, expected and designed. (p. 4)

Although she herself was very happily married and supported in her literary pursuits by her husband, Finch was acutely aware of the vulnerable position in which marriage placed other women by law. In 'The Unequal Fetters' she notes that 'Marriage does but slightly tye Men | Whil'st close Pris'ners we remain' (p. 150).

In addition to the satiric discourse surrounding women's natures, there were also a continuing series of works praising virtuous women as mentioned by Finch, and celebrations of women as a sex written by men, often clergymen, but also some done in the spirit of gallant defence of the fair sex. The year 1692 seemed particularly rich in these types of publications, with Theophilus Dorrington (1654–1715) responding in part to the satires on women with *The Excellent Woman described by her true characters and their opposites* (1692), declaring that 'I cannot chuse but think, that the Glory and Worth, and Happiness of any Nation depends as much upon them, as upon the Men'.[168] The same year the dramatist and Poet Laureate Nahum Tate offered *A Present for the Ladies being an Historical Vindication of the Female Sex: to which is added, the character of an accomplish'd virgin, wife, and widow, in verse*, and William Walsh (bap. 1662–1708) published a volume testifying to his enthusiasm for the female sex, *Letters and poems, amorous and gallant*.

In a more serious and sober vein, the minister Cotton Mather (1663–1728) published in 1691 in Boston, New England, a frequently reprinted treatise, *Ornaments for the Daughters of Zion. or, The character and happiness of a Vertuous Woman: in a discourse which directs the female-sex how to express, the fear of God, in every age and state of their life; and obtain both temporal and eternal blessedness*. Timothy Rogers (1658–1728) offered a defence of women in general in his funeral sermon on John Dunton's wife, Elizabeth, *The Character of a Good Woman* (1697); the published version of the sermon also included excerpts from her diary and a 'brief history of several excellent women'. Robert Russel published his wedding sermon *The Wedding Garment: or, The honourable state of matrimony* (1692), defending matrimony as a divine institution, with the husband's duty to be a 'Pattern of Piety to his Wife and Family, of whom he is the Head', and the Wife's duty to be willing to reprove her husband for sin to help him to heaven while still under obedience to him. Marriage, Russel concludes, is the earthly counterpart to 'the Union that shall betwixt the Saints hereafter in Heaven'.[169]

It is in this complicated context that more extended debates concerning how women should be educated were also appearing. Judith Drake (fl. 1696–1723)

---

[168] Dorrington, *The Excellent Woman*, p. ii.   [169] Russel, *The Wedding Garment*, 22.

offered a prose rebuttal to charges by satirists that contemporary women were governed by passions, making them vain, envious, and inconstant in their behaviour. *An Essay in Defence of the Female Sex* (1696) was at one time ascribed to Mary Astell, but it has subsequently been attributed to Drake, whose husband, Dr James Drake, saw to its publication and wrote an enthusiastic poem praising its contents.[170] The piece is dedicated to Princess Anne of Denmark, and in her preface Drake makes it clear that it was originally intended as an amusement for her friends, 'occasion'd by a private Conversation, between some Gentlemen and Ladies, and written at the request, and for the Diversion of one Lady more particularly, by whom with my consent it was communicated to two or three more of both Sexes, my Friends likewise'.[171] In addition to offering a rational polemic, Drake also includes satiric character portraits of men possessing the same failings attributed to women, 'a pedant, a squire, a beau, a vertuoso, a poetaster, a city-critick' (title page).

'I shall not enter into any dispute', Drake asserts, 'whether Men, or Women be generally more ingenious, or learned; that Point must be given up to the advantages Men have over us by their Education, Freedom of Converse, and variety of Business and Company' (p. 6). Nor will she debate which sex is more prone to virtue or vice, but instead merely the question, 'whether the time an ingenious Gentleman spends in the Company of Women, may justly be said to be misemploy'd, or not?' 'Our Company is generally by our Adversaries represented as unprofitable and irksome to Men of Sense', Drake continues, 'and by some of the more vehement Sticklers against us, as Criminal' (p. 8).

Issues relating to both social standing and national custom, Drake believes, are underlying the attacks on women's nature as inherently frivolous. If one looks at labouring men and women, 'the Condition of the two Sexes is more level, than amongst Gentlemen, City Traders, or rich Yeomen. Examine them in their several Businesses, and their Capacities will appear equal' (p. 16). Likewise, if one considers Dutch merchants' wives, 'There we shall find them managing not only the Domestick Affairs of the Family, but making, and receiving all Payments as well great as small, keeping the Books, ballancing the Accounts, and doing all the Business' (p. 16). In contrast, 'and I have often hear'd some of our considerable Merchants blame the conduct of our Country-Men in this point; that they breed our Women so ignorant of Business' (p. 17).

Likewise, '*State News, Politicks, Religion*, or private *Business* take up the greatest Part of [men's] Conversation, when they are amongst themselves only', Drake observes, but 'the Men look upon us to have very little Interest in the Publick Affairs of the World, and therefore trouble us very seldom with their grave, serious Trifles, which they debate with so much earnestness among one another' (p. 138). This leads to artificiality in conversation between the sexes as 'They look upon us as Things design'd and contriv'd only for their Pleasure, and

---

[170] Bridget Hill, 'Drake, Judith (fl. 1696–1723)', *ODNB*.
[171] Drake, *An Essay*, 'Preface'.

therefore use us tenderly, as Children do their Favourite Bawbles'. Men 'talk gayly, and pleasantly to us, they do, or say nothing that may give as any Disgust, or *Chagrin*, they put on their chearfullest Looks, and their best Humour, that they may excite the like in us'. This in turn leads to conversations between the sexes being unable to attend to matters of any substance and, where there might arise a difference of opinion, it is defused through male gallantry: 'They never oppose us but with a great deal of Ceremony, or in Raillery, not out of a Spirit of Opposition, (as they frequently do one another) but to maintain a pleasant Argument, or heighten by variety of Opinions an agreable Entertainment' (p. 138).

Exchanges between male and female writers over the position of women within the family and their education had been in circulation prior to Drake's publication. In the late 1670s and early 1680s, the painter Mary More (*c*.1633–*c*.1713) had engaged in a manuscript exchange with the Oxford don and early crony of the Earl of Rochester, Robert Whitehall (bap. 1624–85). She had addressed her essay, 'The Woman's Right, Or Her Power in a Greater Equality to her Husband Proved than is Allowed or Practiced in England', to her young daughter Elizabeth Waller, arguing in it that it was a lack of a proper education for women that permitted men to create laws that kept women in subordination. Familiar with both Greek and Latin, More argues correctly that the translators of the King James Version of the Bible rendered verbs differently when they were applied to women than to men, especially when referring to control of property. This deliberate translation strategy created an artificial subordination of women to men, whereas in truth, there was 'an equality in man & woman before ye fall, & not much difference after'. Robert Whitehall countered with 'The Woman's Right Proved False In which the True Right is easily discerned', which attacks the logical links More attempts to show in her argument.[172]

More and the educator and scholar Bathsua Makin (1600–in or after 1675) shared the belief that the way in which women were educated beyond the simple literacy found in dame schools had a profound impact on their standing within marriage and within society. Makin, who had been the tutor to the daughters of Charles I before the war, published in 1675 an advertisement for her school in London that was also a polemic advocating a more intellectually demanding curriculum for girls styled after that of Comenius (see *MV* 2.V) as well as a defence of learned women, *An Essay to Revive the Antient Education of Gentlewomen in religion, manners, arts & tongues with an answer to the objections against this way of education* (1673).[173] Like More, Makin sees women's inferior social and intellectual status as a direct result of social construction: 'Custom, when it is inveterate, hath a mighty influence: it hath the force of Nature it self. The Barbarous custom to breed Women low, is grown

---

[172] See Teague and Ezell, 'Introduction', in Teague and Ezell (eds), *Bathsua Makin and Mary More*; Erickson, *Women and Property*; and Ross, *The Birth of Feminism*, chs 6, 7.
[173] See also Teague, *Bathsua Makin*.

general amongst us, and hath prevailed so far, that it is verily believed (especially amongst a sort of debauched Sots) that Women are not endued with such Reason, as Men; nor capable of improvement by Education, as they are'.[174] In her dedication to 'Ingenious Ladies' and James's daughter the Princess Mary, Makin asks her female readers not to be offended that she will not '(as some have wittily done) plead for Female Preeminence. To ask too much is the way to be denied all', she concludes (p. 4). 'God hath made the Man the Head, if you be educated and instructed, as I propose, I am sure you will acknowledge it', Makin observes, and women should be 'satisfied that you are helps, that your Husbands do consult and advise with you (which if you be wise they will be glad of) and that your Husbands have the casting-Voice, in whose determinations you will acquiesce. That this may be the effect of this Education in all Ladyes that shall attempt it, is the desire' of the author (p. 4).

While More's text remained in a fair copy manuscript, Makin's is typically understood to have influenced the writings of Mary Astell (1666–1731), who began her series of publications on women, education, and marriage in the 1690s and whose writings clearly reflect the competing discourses surrounding debates over the inherent nature of women versus the social construction of it. Astell is believed by her biographers to have moved from Newcastle to London in 1687–8.[175] In 1694 she published her first book, *A Serious Proposal to the Ladies For the Advancement of their true and greatest Interest* (1694), with her correspondence with the Cambridge Platonist John Norris being printed under the title *Letters Concerning the Love of God* (1695) (see CV 4.IV). *A Serious Proposal* went through four editions by 1701 and was widely discussed, making its author a public intellectual, who created a network of female correspondents and patrons.

Astell's proposal to her female readers is a design 'to improve your Charms and heighten your Value, by suffering you no longer to be cheap and contemptible . . . to fix that Beauty, to make it lasting and permanent, which Nature with all the helps of Art, cannot secure: And to place it out of the reach of Sickness and Old Age, by transferring it from a corruptible Body to an immortal Mind'.[176] This, Astell assures her readers 'is a matter infinitely more worthy your Debates, than what Colours are most agreeable, or whats the Dress becomes you best? Your *Glass* will not do you half so much service as a serious reflection on your own Minds' (p. 7). Pointing to accomplished women of the recent past, including Katherine Philips and Mme Dacier in France, she chides her readers in terms that Mary Wollstonecraft will echo a century later, 'How can you be content to be in the world like Tulips in a Garden, to make a fine *shew* and be good for nothing'? (p. 11).

Concerning how the women of her generation had reached the state and status they have, Astell comments: 'One wou'd therefore almost think, that the

---

[174] *An Essay to Revive the Antient Education of Gentlewomen*, 3
[175] Ruth Perry, 'Astell, Mary (1666–1731)', *ODNB*.   [176] Astell, *A Serious Proposal*, 2–3.

wise disposer of all things, foreseeing how unjustly Women are denied opportunities of improvement from *without*, has therefore by way of compensation
endow'd them with greater propensions to Vertue, and a natural goodness of
Temper *within*, which if duly manag'd, would raise them to the most eminent
pitch of Heroick Vertue' (p. 21). The disadvantages that her contemporaries
labour under emerge from a faulty conception of what is appropriate for a
woman's education: 'Ignorance and a narrow Education, lay the Foundation of
Vice, and imitation and custom rear it up. Custom, that merciless torrent that
carries all before' (p. 44). 'When a poor Young Lady is taught to value her self
on nothing but her Cloaths, and to think she's very fine when well accoutered',
Astell alleges,

When she hears say, that 'tis Wisdom enough for her to know how to dress her self, that
she may become amiable in his eyes, to whom it appertains to be knowing and learned;
who can blame her if she lay out her Industry and Money on such Accomplishments,
and sometimes extends it farther than her misinformer desires she should? When she
sees the vain and the gay, making Parade in the World, and attended with the Courtship
and admiration of all about them, no wonder that her tender Eyes are dazled with the
Pageantry. (pp. 49–50)

Astell's proposal to rectify the prevailing customs of teaching young women to
value themselves only as objects competing for masculine approval with the
goal of marriage is to create a separate female space, an academy devoted to
serious intellectual and spiritual development. Retirement from the world into
a female community would enable women to avoid the pressures placed on
young women by social expectations and 'we shall find it does not only remove
all these, but brings considerable advantages of its own. For first, it helps us to
mate custom, and delivers us from its Tyranny, which is the most considerable
thing we have to do, it being nothing else but the habituating our selves to Folly
that can reconcile us to it' (p. 121).

The scheme for establishing a separate female intellectual community was
taken up by Daniel Defoe in his *Essay on Projects* (1697), although his version,
which included a moat to ensure that the young ladies were not disturbed, was
conceived, he said, prior to the publication of Astell's treatise.[177] Astell, who
had earlier secured the patronage of William Sancroft, Archbishop of Canterbury
(see CV 4.IV), now found new long-term patrons among aristocratic women,
including her near neighbour in Chelsea, Lady Catherine Jones, to whom Astell
dedicated *Letters Concerning the Love of God* (1695), Lady Elizabeth Hastings,
and Anne, Countess of Coventry. Princess Anne of Denmark was sufficiently
engaged by Astell's proposal that she permitted *A Serious Proposal to the
Ladies, Part II* (1697) to be dedicated to her.

Princess Anne was dissuaded from financially backing Astell's imagined
female community by her close adviser Bishop Gilbert Burnet (see MV 5.I),

---

[177] Perry, *The Celebrated Mary Astell*, 129, and Backscheider, *Daniel Defoe*, 68–72.

apparently because it too much resembled a Catholic nunnery.[178] The second part of the *Proposal* laid out in more concrete terms the vision of the establishment set forth in the first. The female institution as Astell imagined it, she believed, would not only benefit the individual women themselves, but also have significant impact on reforming the morals of the nation. This would be carried out in the family by having a wisely educated mother to rear her children in virtue and morality. In addition, she suggested, single women might also have an important role: 'perhaps the Glory of Reforming this Prophane and Profligate Age is reserv'd for you Ladies, and that the natural and unprejudi'd Sentiments of your Minds being handsomely express'd, may carry a more strong conviction than the Elaborate Arguments of the Learned',[179] suggesting that single women might take on the roles of reformer and even minister.

By the appearance of the second part of Astell's proposal in 1697, writings and performances highlighting debates over the nature of women, their places in society and the family, their education or lack of it, and their responsibilities within marriage permeated literary discourses. 'Philaretos' wrongly claimed in his 1697 treatise *The Challenge* that his collection was the first of its kind. The full title highlights the topicality of debate: *The Challenge sent by a young lady to Sir Thomas &c., or, The Female War wherein the present dresses and humours &c. of the fair sex are vigorously attackt by men of quality, and as bravely defended by Madam Godfrey and other ingenious ladies who set their names to every challenge: the whole encounter consists of six hundred letters pro and con on all disputable points relating to women, and is the first battle of this nature that was ever fought in England.* This volume appears to have been an offshoot of John Dunton's periodical the *Athenian Mercury* (see CV 4.II), an interactive periodical publication that invited its readers to submit questions, riddles, and verse for publication and discussion. The publisher 'Philaret' hopes that other well-known women writers, including Delarivier Manley, Mary Pix, and Elizabeth Singer '*will take up* Arms in this Litteral War; *in which all the* Dresses, Customs and Humours of the Fair Sex *will be boldly attact*'. Any young female readers who are interested are likewise urged 'to serve under Madam *Godfrey*, (their She-Champion) [and] are desired to send in their Names and place of Abode, and they shall be furnisht with Pen, Ink and Paper, and enter'd into present Service. The Place of Rendevouz is Mr *Darker*'s House in *Bull-head-Court* near *Cripplegate*, to whom all Letters must be directed'.[180]

From appropriations of the classics, biblical exegesis, popular broadsides, and cheap literary entertainments to impassioned polemics and plans for female academies, contemporary Englishwomen's lives in the 1680s and 1690s provided occasion for both serious reflection as well as satiric discourse. With the advent of popular periodical publications such as Dunton's encouraging young women to write their views, the debates over women's roles reached an ever-widening audience.

---

[178] See Apetrei, *Women, Feminism and Religion*, 15 and *passim*.
[179] Astell, *A Serious Proposal*, 211–12.   [180] *The Challenge*, sig. A3r, 'The Preface'.

5

Writing the New Britain, 1700–1714

I. 1700

> *Millamant*: . . . I hate Letters—No Body knows how to write Letters; and yet one has 'em, one does not know why—They serve one to pin up one's Hair.
>
> *Witwould*: Is that the way? Pray, Madam, do you pin up your Hair with all your Letters? I find I must keep Copies.
>
> *Millamant:* Only with those in Verse, Mr *Witwoud*. I never pin up my Hair with Prose. I fancy ones Hair wou'd not curl if it was pinn'd up with Prose.
>
> William Congreve, The Way of the World, Act II (1700)

> Speak, *Satyr*; for there's none can tell like thee,
> Whether 'tis Folly, Pride, or Knavery,
> That makes this discontented Land appear
> Less happy now in Times of Peace, than War:
> Why Civil Feuds disturb the Nation more
> Than all our Bloody Wars have done before.
>
> Daniel Defoe, 'Introduction' to
The True-Born Englishman (1700)

> For pray, what do Men propose to themselves in Marriage? What Qualifications do they look after in a Spouse? What will she bring is the first enquiry? How many Acres? Or how much ready Coin?
>
> Mary Astell, Some Reflections upon Marriage (1700)

In comparison with earlier decade beginnings after the Restoration, 1700 was a relatively uneventful year. There were no revolutions or attempted coups, no assassination attempts or the exiling of once prominent but lately fallen politicians, but there were still strong political tensions in play. Concerns over the granting of estates in Ireland by William III and his refusal to call the Scottish Parliament to meet caused tensions between King and subjects, and

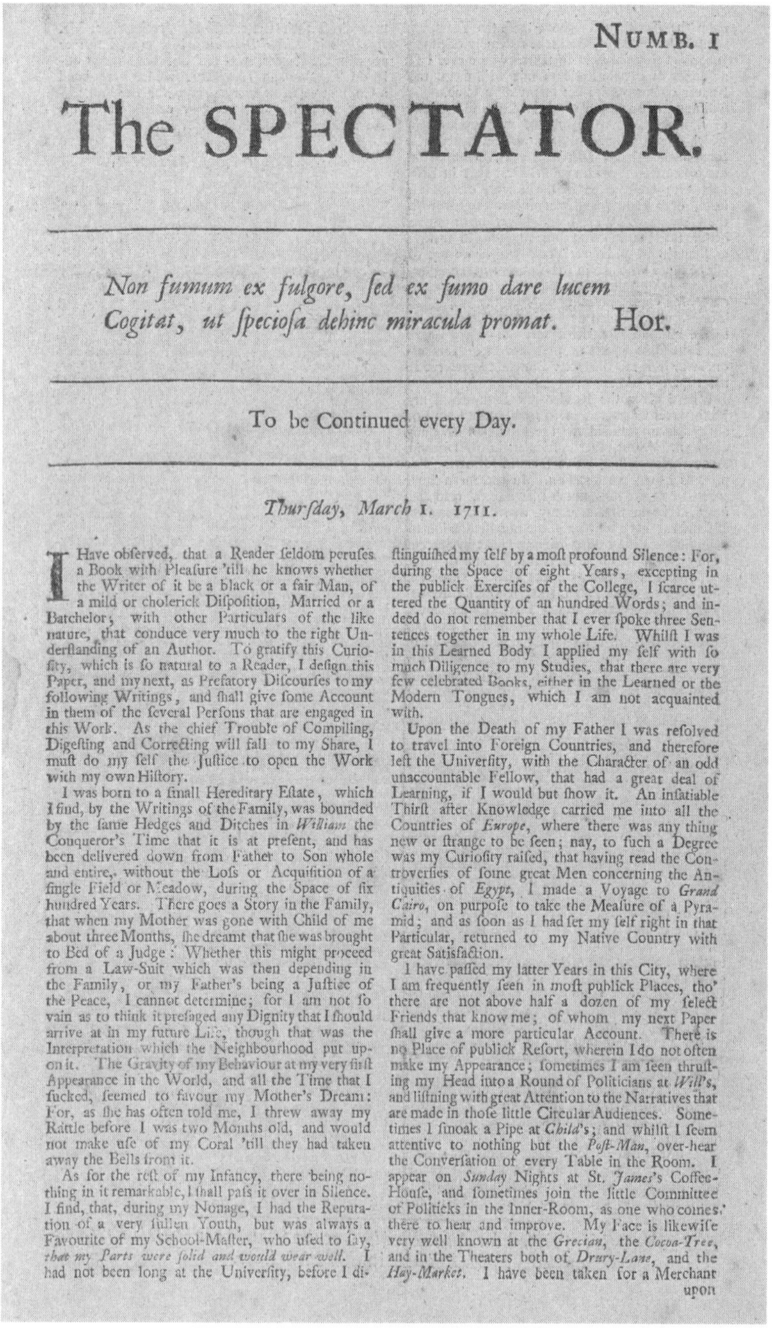

NUMB. I

The SPECTATOR.

Non fumum ex fulgore, fed ex fumo dare lucem
Cogitat, ut fpeciofa dehinc miracula promat. Hor.

To be Continued every Day.

Thurfday, March 1. 1711.

I Have obferved, that a Reader feldom perufes a Book with Pleafure 'till he knows whether the Writer of it be a black or a fair Man, of a mild or cholerick Difpofition, Married or a Batchelor, with other Particulars of the like nature, that conduce very much to the right Underftanding of an Author. To gratify this Curiofity, which is fo natural to a Reader, I defign this Paper, and my next, as Prefatory Difcourfes to my following Writings, and fhall give fome Account in them of the feveral Perfons that are engaged in this Work. As the chief Trouble of Compiling, Digefting and Correcting will fall to my Share, I muft do my felf the Juftice to open the Work with my own Hiftory.

I was born to a fmall Hereditary Eftate, which I find, by the Writings of the Family, was bounded by the fame Hedges and Ditches in *William* the Conqueror's Time that it is at prefent, and has been delivered down from Father to Son whole and entire, without the Lofs or Acquifition of a fingle Field or Meadow, during the Space of fix hundred Years. There goes a Story in the Family, that when my Mother was gone with Child of me about three Months, fhe dreamt that fhe was brought to Bed of a Judge : Whether this might proceed from a Law-Suit which was then depending in the Family, or my Father's being a Juftice of the Peace, I cannot determine; for I am not fo vain as to think it prefaged any Dignity that I fhould arrive at in my future Life, though that was the Interpretation which the Neighbourhood put upon it. The Gravity of my Behaviour at my very firft Appearance in the World, and all the Time that I fucked, feemed to favour my Mother's Dream: For, as fhe has often told me, I threw away my Rattle before I was two Months old, and would not make ufe of my Coral 'till they had taken away the Bells from it.

As for the reft of my Infancy, there being nothing in it remarkable, I fhall pafs it over in Silence. I find, that, during my Nonage, I had the Reputation of a very fullen Youth, but was always a Favourite of my School-Mafter, who ufed to fay, *that my Parts were folid and would wear well.* I had not been long at the Univerfity, before I di-

ftinguifhed my felf by a moft profound Silence : For, during the Space of eight Years, excepting in the publick Exercifes of the College, I fcarce uttered the Quantity of an hundred Words; and indeed do not remember that I ever fpoke three Sentences together in my whole Life. Whilft I was in this Learned Body I applied my felf with fo much Diligence to my Studies, that there are very few celebrated Books, either in the Learned or the Modern Tongues, which I am not acquainted with.

Upon the Death of my Father I was refolved to travel into Foreign Countries, and therefore left the Univerfity, with the Character of an odd unaccountable Fellow, that had a great deal of Learning, if I would but fhow it. An infatiable Thirft after Knowledge carried me into all the Countries of *Europe*, where there was any thing new or ftrange to be feen; nay, to fuch a Degree was my Curiofity raifed, that having read the Controverfies of fome great Men concerning the Antiquities of *Egypt*, I made a Voyage to *Grand Cairo*, on purpofe to take the Meafure of a Pyramid; and as foon as I had fet my felf right in that Particular, returned to my Native Country with great Satisfaction.

I have paffed my latter Years in this City, where I am frequently feen in moft publick Places, tho' there are not above half a dozen of my felect Friends that know me; of whom my next Paper fhall give a more particular Account. There is no Place of publick Refort, wherein I do not often make my Appearance; fometimes I am feen thrufting my Head into a Round of Politicians at *Will's*, and liftening with great Attention to the Narratives that are made in thofe little Circular Audiences. Sometimes I fmoak a Pipe at *Child's*; and whilft I feem attentive to nothing but the *Poft-Man*, over-hear the Converfation of every Table in the Room. I appear on *Sunday* Nights at St. *James's* Coffee-Houfe, and fometimes join the little Committee of Politicks in the Inner-Room, as one who comes there to hear and improve. My Face is likewife very well known at the *Grecian*, the *Cocoa-Tree*, and in the Theaters both of *Drury-Lane*, and the *Hay-Market*. I have been taken for a Merchant upon

Figure 6. The *Spectator*, no. 1 (1711). From the General Collection, Beinecke Rare Book and Manuscript Library, Yale University

heightened the jostlings of the two political factions, the Whigs and the Tories, who dominated Parliament.

The Parliamentarian, diarist, and book collector Narcissus Luttrell recorded for 11 April 1700 that, when the King came to the House of Lords, he passed thirty-seven of their private bills and twenty-three public ones, including some incorporating the old East India Company and the long delayed payment for the army, and others more varied and particular, for example, concerning the control of trade with bills prohibiting the wearing of East India silks and muslins, the divorce case of the Duke of Norfolk, and laws 'against popery; pyracy, &c' (Luttrell, *State Affairs*, 4. 633). The House of Commons, which was staunchly Tory in its agendas, voted in February 1700 to take back the Irish estates that William had given to his supporters, including the 90,000-acre estate from what had been the deposed James II's lands that William had given to Elizabeth Villiers, Countess of Orkney, his rumoured mistress in the 1680s. When the House voted that the King should be requested to remove all 'for-eigners' except for Princess Anne's husband, George of Denmark, from his councils, William prorogued Parliament, declaring in a letter that 'it is the ugli-est session I have ever had … it is impossible for anyone who has not been here to imagine the intrigues'.[1]

London by 1700 had reached a population of nearly 600,000 and thus rivalled Paris in terms of its size, but many writers were concerned about the ways in which the metropolis was shaping. Bishop Gilbert Burnet in his history reflects on 1700 that, 'though we were falling insensibly into a democracy, we had not learned the virtues that are necessary for that sort of government: luxury, vanity, and ambition, increased daily'. On the positive side, he records that 'the toleration of all the sects among us had made us live more quietly together of late than could be expected, when severe law were rigorously exe-cuted against dissenters'. 'No tumults or disorders had been heard of in any part of the kingdom these eleven years, since that act passed', he concludes, and 'yet much greater part of the clergy studied to blow up this fire again, which seemed to be now, as it were, covered over with ashes' (Burnet, *History*, 4. 444). John Evelyn also noted the changing climate both natural and spiritual of England in 1700 in his diary, describing in a May entry that 'there never had ben, in any mans memory, so glorious a Spring, such hope of aboundance of fruits of all kinds, & so propitious a yeare, & yet', he ends, 'never a more pro-fane, & atheistical age: most of the youth [& others] Atheists, Theists, Arians & Sectaries, which God of his mercy reforme' (Evelyn, *Diary*, 5. 911).

The court, which had played such a prominent role in shaping and sustain-ing literary culture in earlier years, was no longer the commanding stage for fashion or patronage. The widowed William III had been in his native country Holland for much of the previous year and only recently in the autumn of 1699

---

[1] Quoted in Van Der Zee and Van Der Zee, *William and Mary*, 457.

returned to England and begun entertaining again at Kensington Palace. Although Princess Anne acted as his hostess at such events, he still had a cool and distant relationship with his future successor, Anne and her court, although he appears to have been very fond of his nephew and namesake, the young William, Duke of Gloucester, the Protestant heir apparent. 'Hitherto', Burnet observed, 'the body of the nation retained a great measure of affection to him: this was beginning to diminish, by his going so constantly beyond sea, as soon as the session of parliament was ended; though the war was now over'. 'Upon this, it grew to be publicly said', Burnet noted, 'that he loved no Englishman's face, nor his company' (Burnet, *History*, 4. 431). As his never robust health worsened during the year 1700, on the advice of physicians, William left England again in July for Holland.

The talk in Parliament as well as in the streets highlights this concern over the presence of 'foreigners' in English life. Parliament entertained numerous petitions in 1700, specifically addressing the impact of importing 'foreign' labourers, materials, and manufactures on native English ones. The language of these petitions stresses the historical nature of the English trade, which is being threatened by recent concessions to 'foreigners and aliens'. Several of the petitions are directly tied to the changing English tastes in fashion and attire. The weavers' petition, *Reasons Humbly Offered, why the Importation of Foreign-wrought Figured, Flowered, Biassed, Stitched and Stripe Silks and Drugets, Tameenes and Estimenes, and other Stuffs made of Wool, should be prohibited*, opens with a reminder to Parliament that 'the Trade of *Weaving* is of great Antiquity and Usefulness, and for these Forty Years Past, hath exceedingly Improved, and been very advantageous to this Nation'. This happy arrangement, however, has been compromised by the 'frequent Importation of Foreign-wrought Commodities of Silk and Wool, especially from *France*', most of which, they allege, is smuggled in by small boats and avoiding His Majesty's Customs. Thus, the '*English* do maintain the *French* Kings Subjects at Work, whilst the Natives here are ready to starve and perish through want thereof'. English weavers, they point out, 'have been lately required by His Majesty and Council, to receive and imploy Aliens and Strangers', but the real damage has been caused by 'the Craft and Subtlety of a few *French Merchants* in *London*, about seven or eight in number, who to enrich themselves, care not how many thousands of the *English* (especially the poor Handicrafts) are ruined'.[2]

A very similar petition, *Reasons Humbly Offered to the Honourable the House of Commons, for laying a further Duty on all Forreign Paper, by which means the making of Writing and Printing Papers in England will be preserv'd and Encourged*, likewise stresses the former success of the craft of paper-making in England and the extent to which it 'Employs great numbers of Poor People, the Produce whereof is all clear gains to this Kingdom, being made

---

[2] *Reasons Humbly Offered ... Stuffs made of Wool.*

from *Raggs* Collected from the *Dunghills*, which would otherwise be useless and lost'. In the recent past, English paper had sold well, and this had encouraged the creation of 'many Mills, but since the War such Quantity's of *Foreign Paper* has been *Imported*, which has made it so Cheap', that, unless a penalty is applied, the English writing paper trade will fail (as it did).[3] Still another petition concerned itself with the impact of foreign events on everyday English people. The petition, which is represented as expressing the combined wishes of the clothiers, serge makers, silk and stuff weavers, merchants who traded with Italy and Turkey, shopkeepers, and 'by modest Computation above an Hundred Thousand Families of Poor employ'd by them ... the Starving Objects of Charity' declares that, unless Parliament acts in 'Regulating the *Publick* and *Frequent Mournings* for *Foreign Princes*', large sections of the labouring population will suffer. The heart of the petition, its fourth reason, is that shopkeepers specializing in fashionable attire and luxury items are required to have large stocks of merchandise 'against the usual Season of Trade', but, because of 'those unforeseen Accidents of Mourning, have all those Goods left on their Hands, the Channel of Trade turn'd from them, and the Demand being quite of another Nature, their Stocks lie dead 'till their Goods become unfashionable, by which they are unavoidably ruin'd'. The rituals of fashionable mourning associated with the demise of foreign princes, it is implied, are a luxury at the expense of English working people.

The 'foreignness' of William was the basis for one of most heated satiric exchanges that began in 1700 and would spill over into the next years. John Tutchin (1660x4–1707), who had been notoriously sentenced by Judge Jeffries for his participation in the Monmouth rebellion (see *MV* 4.I) to be whipped through the market towns of Dorset and who would in 1702 start the political journal the *Observator*, offered in August 1700 an anonymous short pamphlet satire, *The Foreigners. A Poem*. By 28 of August, the piece was brought before a grand jury to be declared a 'libel' (Luttrell, *State Affairs*, 4. 683). Like John Dryden's earlier political allegory, *Absalom and Achitophel*, Tutchin situates England as biblical Israel: its ill-conditioned natives, 'Kings of all sorts they ignorantly crav'd, | And grew more stupid as they were enslaved', and when they finally cast off their debauched rulers, they approach a neighbouring country, 'Where stormy Winds and noisy Billows roar; | A Land much differing from all other Soils, | Forc'd from the Sea, and buttress'd up with Piles'.[4] The inhabitants of this watery landscape (the Dutch) are equally unprepossessing and unnatural, 'From Nature's Excrements their Life is drawn, | Are born in Bogs, and nourish'd up from Spawn', and 'Their Land, as if asham'd their Crimes to see, | Dives down beneath the surface of the Sea' (p. 6), while their attempts to speak English result in 'the self-same Language the old Serpent spoke, | When misbelieving *Eve* the apple took' (p. 8). '*Bentir*', standing in for

---

[3] *Reasons Humbly Offered ... Duty on all Forreign Paper.*
[4] Tutchin, *Foreigners*, 3, 6.

William's favourite Dutch courtier, Hans Willem Bentinck, first Earl of Port-land, is depicted as enriching himself through 'lavish Grants whole Provinces he gains' and the poet angrily questions 'if we a Foreign Slave may use in War, | Yet why in Council should that Slave appear?' (pp. 7, 8). Perhaps even more shocking or irritating was the speaker's assertion at the end that 'When no Successor to the Crown's in sight, | The Crown is certainly the Peoples Right' (p. 9). 'Heaven allows', he continues, 'the People sure a Power | To chuse such Kings as shall not them devour: | They know full well what best will serve themselves' (p. 10).

The attorney-general Sir Thomas Trevor found that, since Tutchin had not used real but 'covert names' for his characters, he could not be prosecuted for libel, but other writers were quick to publish their condemnations of the poem and its writer. In a piece attributed to John Dennis (1658–1734) printed in late August, the author offered the reader *The Reverse: Or, The Tables Turn'd. A Poem Written in Answer, Paragraph by Paragraph, to a late Scurrilous and Malicious* Medly of Rhimes *Called the Foreigners*. This poem places the blame, not on the foreign William and his court, but on the native-born English religious fanatics, republicans, and conspirators: 'Fit for the Toil of one of O—s his Tribe, | Who Lash'd like *him*, like *him* could Snarl and Rail, | And shew his Malice, 'cause he shew'd his Tail' (*POAS* 6. 237). 'God first appointed Kings, and God ordain'd | That should be fix'd which He alone sustain'd', the poem firmly concludes. The anonymous *The Natives: An Answer to the Foreigners*, advertised in the *Post Boy* for publication in September and, like *The Reverse*, also printed by John Nutt, went line by line with its response on the left side of the page and the text of *The Foreigners* on the right; the author on the title page warns that he 'has taken Care to follow the Method of the Foreigner as near as reasonably he could, by which Means this Poem wants the Coherence that otherwise it might have had', including using the same line ending word as the original. Thus *The Natives* transforms *The Foreigners'* description of the Dutch as 'A Boorish, rude, and an inhumane Race' into a people who 'Does far transcend great part of *Jewish* Race', a faithful manipulation of text if not an inspired one.

Daniel Defoe was the last in this energetic series to respond in print with *The True-Born Englishman* published by a 'Capt. Darby'. In a 1715 pamphlet, Defoe wrote in hindsight that the contents and style of the 'vile abhor'd Pamphlet, in very ill Verse, written by one Mr *Tutchin*' affected him deeply, in particular the attack on 'his Majesty with Crimes, that his worst Enemy could not think of without Horror, he sums up all in the odious Name of FOREIGNER' (*POAS* 6. 259). Although Defoe himself had, like Tutchin, briefly taken part in the Monmouth rebellion, by 1700 those allegiances had passed: Defoe asserts that 'this fill'd me with a kind of Rage against the Book; and gave birth to a Trifle which I could hope should have met with so general an Acceptation as it did'. Critics studying Defoe believe that parts of the piece, which is considerably longer that Tutchin's, had apparently been in existence before Tutchin's appeared, such as Britannia's song praising William III, and that Tutchin's pamphlet provided Defoe with the topical occasion to enlarge and merge these fragments (*POAS* 6. 762). Although other writers immediately attacked Defoe for his own less than polished verse style, the demand from booksellers and readers meant that fifty editions of it were printed by 1750. Indeed, Defoe notes in a subsequent 1705 edition that, '*besides Nine Editions of the Author*', it was '*Twelve Times printed by other Hands, some of which have been sold for 1d, others 2d and others 6d, the Author's Edition being fairly printed, and on good Paper, and could not be sold under a Shilling. 80000 of the Small Ones*', he believes, were '*sold in the Streets for 2d or at a Penny*', suggesting the extent of the popular circulation of Defoe's rebuttal and his bookseller's losses owing to quick-acting literary pirates (*POAS* 6. 763).

'The End of Satyr is Reformation', Defoe opens his preface, 'And the author, tho he doubts the Work of Conversion is at a general Stop, has put his Hand to the Plow'. Defoe anticipates hostile comments about 'my *Mean Stile, Rough Verse*, and *Incorrect Language*', but 'the book is Printed, and tho I see some Faults, 'tis too late to mend them' (*POAS* 6. 763). 'An *Englishman*, who is so proud of being call'd *A Goodfellow*, shou'd be civil', Defoe observes, but it cannot be denied that, 'particularly to Strangers', the English are often 'the Churlishest People alive' (*POAS* 6. 286). Tutchin is portrayed by Defoe as a mercenary hack writer, '*Shamwhig*', who

> Burlesques his God and King in Paltry Rhimes:
> Against the *Dutch* turns Champion for the Times;
> And Huffs the King, upon that very score,
> On which he Panegyrick't him before. (*POAS* 6. 286–7)

'Unhappy *England*', Defoe laments, 'has thou none but such, | *To plead they Scoundrel Cause against* the Dutch?' The English supporters of Shamwhig are themselves burlesques, he charges, 'they scorn their Laws or Governors to fear; | So bugbear'd with the Name of Slavery, | They can't submit to their own Liberty'. '*Englishmen do all Restraint despise*', he concludes ironically, 'Slaves to the Liquor, Drudges to the Pots, | *The Mob are Statesmen, and their Statesmen Sots*' (*POAS* 6. 287).

In contrast, the character of Britannia lauds William in a separate song embedded towards the end of the piece:

> My Hero with the Sails of Honour furl'd,
> Rises like the Great Genius of the World.
> By Fate and Fame wisely prepar'd to be
> *The Soul of War, and Life of Victory.*
> He spreads the Wings of Virtue on the Throne,
> And ev'ry *Wind of Glory* fans them on. (*POAS* 6. 295–6)

Disdaining '*Hebrew* Stories' and covert names, Britannia declares 'Names and Things directly I proclaim. | 'Tis honest Merit does his Glory raise'. She encourages the virgin followers of the spirit of Britannia to 'Make him once a Lover and a King. | May he submit to none but to your Arms; | Nor ever be subdu'd, *but by your Charms*' (POAS 6. 296).

At the close of this song, Defoe returns to attacking Tutchin's text and tartly observes, 'we ne're complain'd | Of Foreigners, nor of the Wealth they gain'd | Till all their Services were at an End' (POAS 6. 297). 'Great *Portland* ne're was banter'd, when he strove | For Us his Master's kindest Thoughts to Move', he points out, and

> Ten Years in *English* Service he appear'd,
> And gain'd his Master's and the World's Regard:
> But 'tis not *England's* Custom to Reward.
> The Wars are over, *England* needs him not;
> Now he's a *Dutchman*, and *the Lord knows what*. (POAS 6. 299)

The conclusion of Defoe's poem turns to a larger issue—what true-born Englishmen actually inherit through lineage and families—and its conclusion to many must have seemed as radical as Tutchin's assertion that the people control the Crown:

> What is't to us, what Ancestors we had?
>
> .   .   .   .   .
>
> For Fame of Families is all a Cheat,
> *'Tis Personal Virtue only makes us great*. (POAS 6. 309)

This seeming dismissal of heredity 'true-born' privilege, of course, did not lessen the importance of establishing the childless William's successor to the throne, and in this matter the year 1700 was a significant moment. Princess Anne had lived retired from the world to a great extent and for her it was a tragic year. Her seventeenth pregnancy ended in January with her miscarrying a son; her only surviving child then was William, the Duke of Gloucester. Burnet, who had been overseeing the child's education, remembers that the child was to him a prodigy, already reading the Psalms, Proverbs, and the Gospels: 'I had been trusted with his education now for two years; and he had made an amazing progress...was often surprised with the questions that he put me, and the reflections that he made. He came to understand things relating to religion, beyond imagination' (Burnet, *History*, 4. 439).

The day after celebrating his eleventh birthday, the child complained of not feeling well. 'He had gone through much weakness, and some years of ill health', Burnet observed, 'the princess was with child of him, during all the disorder we were in at the revolution...this probably had given him so weak a constitution; but we hoped the dangerous time was over'. Unfortunately, the young Duke died after the fourth day, although Princess Anne herself nursed her only child 'with great tenderness, but with a grave composedness, that amazed all who saw it'. The boy's death 'gave a great alarm to the whole nation: the Jacobites grew insolent upon it' (Burnet, *History*, 4. 441).

In the public poetry lamenting the death of the child, grief is mixed with apprehension over the future of the throne. A tattered copy of an anonymous, cheaply printed broadside, 'In Tears: Elegy on the Death of his Grace Duke of Gloucester', opens with the observation that 'But tis our Sins, makes Fatal Stars Combine, | To snap in sunder *England's* Royal Line'.[5] It asserts that the child's death makes all who mourn him his countrymen, even while it underlines William's absence in Holland at this time: 'Our mighty Monarch, when this News he hears, | He will Lament, in sad and British Tears'. In several other poems, the figures of Albion and of Britannia are used to represent the loss of the future sovereign over the three kingdoms, not just an English prince, and while all agree that a heavenly crown is better than an earthly one, it is clear that the hoped-for future was a unified kingdom:

> Whilst Mourning *Albion* languishes in Tears,
> Sad with the Prospect of Succeeding Years:
> Sees her deluded Wishes render'd Vain,
> And all the Triumphs of thy promis'd Reign;
> Enjoy amidst the bless'd Angellick Host,
> A brighter Diadem, than *Britain's* lost.[6]

Thomas Yalden (1670–1736), a fellow of Magdalen College, Oxford, who had previously published verses in Tonson's *Miscellany Poems* in the 1690s and shown his loyalties to the Crown in the Pindaric ode *On the Conquest of Namur* dedicated to William's victory there in 1695, imagines Gloucester joining his recent relatives in heaven in a royal Temple of Fame. It is one of several poems that directly link the country's continuing grief over the recent death of his aunt, Queen Mary, to that for the loss of the child.

> Yes, GLOCESTER, our *summ'd Hopes* in THEE, weigh'd down
> The Lighter Jems in Fair MARIA's Crown.
> Stinted by Fate, her bounded *Glory* less,
> MARY the *present* Age could only bless.
> Convey'd thro' Thy *Rich* VEINS, what *Smiles of Heaven*,
> To *Endless Worlds*, thy Lengthned Life had given![7]

Still others of the printed laments offer the mother and the country the hope that there still is the possibility of a Protestant prince. 'And why shou'd *You* or *We* so much despair?' concluded James Gibbs's (bap. 1673–1724) poem, 'Heav'n kindly promises another Heir, | Which *You*, the *Country's Parent* yet shall bear'.[8] Gibbs, a physician who was working on his translation of the Psalms that would be published in 1701, shaped his consolation in terms of healing those left behind: 'If e're Harmonious Numbers can dispense | To Wounded Minds a Healing Influence', he opens, now is the time for poets. 'But vain's

---

[5] BL shelf mark C.161.f.2.(99).   [6] Yalden, *Temple*, 19.
[7] *Thrænodium Britannicum*, 5.   [8] Gibbs, *A Consolatory Poem*, 7.

th'Attempt, I fear, to bring Relief, | 'Tis hard to stop so Great, so Just a Grief' (p. 3). However, as great as the pain of the loss of the Prince, he urges the Princess,

> Think not on what so lately You have lost,
> The *Hopeful Prince*, Three Nations once could boast:
> When so much Danger in your Grief we view,
> How can we bear to mourn for *Him* and *You*!' (p. 3)

Wrapped in their own grief, the Princess and her husband did stay on at Windsor during the rest of 1700, refusing to see all visitors.

The year 1700 was one in which once private meditations and prayers as a form of spiritual healing were published by several authors. Jane Ward Lead (1624–1704), a follower of the German mystic Jakob Boehme and with Ann Bathurst one of the founders of the Philadelphia Society (see CV 4.IV), had published over a dozen of her visions of a loving and androgynous God since the 1680s. In 1700, she issued two, one a continuation of the publication of her spiritual diary, *A Fountain of Gardens*, which comprised her journal written in 1678, and the other *The Wars of David, and the Peaceable Reign of Solomon*. Lead wrote out her daily spiritual thoughts on small cards, which she gave to friends in spiritual need, and they were gathered together by Francis Lee, a former fellow of St John's College, Oxford, who had discovered her writings while in the Netherlands, her works having had much wider circulation there than in England. An international theosophical movement by 1700, the Philadelphia Society was centred in the ageing and nearly blind Lead's London household, the members of which oversaw the publication of her life's writings.

Lead's entry for 1 January 1678 in *A Fountain of Gardens* recounts how she saw a striking new vision of the creation story, a crystalline figure descending out of a 'sea of Glass'. Her imagery of the divine figures it as 'pure Light', which whispers its creation of a new world on earth.

On New Years-Day, upon the break thereof, this Figure was presented to me, as the Model of a new Creating power, and opened by an Image of transparent Glass, which descended from the Sea of Glass, and stood as upon a Mountain of Earth, which after a very little season mouldered all away, and became a plain. And then it was said, *Now observe, and see what will follow.* And out of the Belly of this Clarified Body did flow Water, that became as a great River, that covered all the plain, which soon drunk these Waters in. And then the Word, said, *Spring O Ground, and bring forth another Creation;* Then did there rise from the same figurative Body, a pure Light, which sprung within the case of Glass, from the Loyns upwards to the Head, and out of the Mouth a fiery Stream did proceed, which descended where the Waters were drunk in. And it was given immediately by the soft whisper of the Spirit, that this would be the sowing of the Holy Ghost, in a plain and leavened Ground, which would bring forth, after its own kind, as to Spirit and Body...[9]

---

[9] Lead, *Fountain*, 1–2.

This imaginative, spiritual eye in Lead's writings leads the reader to see past the material world and serves as a source for meditation upon the coming perfection.

The year 1700 also saw the passing of three figures representing very different aspects of the earlier century's literary culture. The minister Henry Killigrew (1613–1700), the brother of the dramatists William and Thomas Killigrew and father of the poet Anne Killigrew, had served after the Restoration as the chaplain and almoner to the Duke of York and master of the Savoy. Killigrew was well known for his Whitehall sermons, published in 1685. He had in his younger years written Latin poems as a college student, and created a tragedy in 1635 to be performed at the wedding of Charles Herbert, the son of the Earl of Pembroke and Mary Villiers, the daughter of the Duke of Buckingham, which was published as *The Conspiracy* (1638) and subsequently as *Pallantus and Eduora* from an uncorrected script in 1654 while its author was safely away in Italy. In 1695, he published anonymously his translation of Martial's *Epigrams*. Thomas Creech (1659–1700), the Oxford classics scholar whom Aphra Behn gave the sobriquet Daphnis in their poetic correspondence, committed suicide in 1700; his translation of Lucretius in 1682 had made him the darling of the London literary world, but his attempts at translating Horace published in 1684 became the butt of satire for his own and succeeding generations.

Creech's mentor, friend, and rival, the former Poet Laureate for Charles II and James II, John Dryden, also passed away in May 1700. He had been in ill health towards the end of 1699, but nevertheless in February he gallantly supplied his young kinswoman Elizabeth Stewart, who was living in Cotterstock, Northamptonshire, with copies of a recent London lampoon satirizing Bishop Burnet. In the lampoon, Burnet peevishly complains to Princess Anne that the court ladies are attending his sermons only to preen in front of the beaux:

> When Burnet perceiv'd that the beautiful dames
> Who flocked to the chapel of hilly St James,
> On their lovers the kindest of looks did bestow,
> And smil'd not on him, while he bellowe'd below. (*POAS* 6. 37–42)[10]

Written early in March and conveyed to her by the Oundle carrier, Dryden's letter was also accompanied by a copy of his recently published *Fables*. In his letter, Dryden ranges from the politics of religion to the politics of the London stage. He tells her that 'all Our hopes of the House of Commons, are wholly dash'd. Our Properties are destroyed', as a result of the statute passed as of September 1700 stating that all Catholics not taking the oath of allegiance and supremacy would be unable to inherit property. On this, he commented bitterly that 'they have made a breach in the Magna Charta; for which God forgive them' (p. 134). Literary news jostles with political as he also reported that

---

[10] Dryden, *Letters*, 133.

William Congreve's (1670–1729) latest comedy, *The Way of the World*, had enjoyed 'moderate success; though it deserves much better' (p. 134).

The former Poet Laureate's final letters give the impression of a writer still vitally engaged with many aspects of literary culture in London, from the point of view of both the audience and the author, including as we shall see engaging in literary feuds involving Sir Richard Blackmore. Writing on 11 April, Dryden reports that, like Elizabeth Stewart herself, 'the Ladies of the town…like my last Book of Poems, [*The Fables*] better than any thing they have formerly seen of mine';[11] in a later undated April letter he also notes that there will shortly be performed for his benefit a revised version of Fletcher's *The Pilgrim*, done by his friend the dramatist and architect John Vanbrugh, for which Dryden had written new a prologue, epilogue, and a secular masque. Dryden died only a few weeks after this letter and before the performance, which was staged at the Theatre Royal, Drury Lane.

In his prologue to the play, Dryden begins: 'How wretched is the Fate of those who write! | Brought muzled to the Stage, for fear they bite.'[12] Echoing sentiments he had written in the preface to *The Fables*, Dryden turns in the epilogue to refute Jeremy Collier's attacks on the immorality of the stage and its degrading effects on public morals (see *MV* 4.IV). Contrasting the courts of Cromwell and Charles II, he admits that, in the first, the ladies had been 'modestly conceal'd', while the Restoration court, 'the naked *Venus* first reveal'd' (ll. 21–2). However, the seeming modesty and morality of the 'Saints', he charges, ''Twas Chamber Practice all, and Close Devotion |…| Nothing but open Lewdness was a Crime', including the execution of Charles I, 'A *Monarch's* Blood was venial to the Nation | Compar'd with one foul Act of Fornication'. And now, Dryden charges, those same hypocritical Puritans speaking through Collier, 'Now, they wou'd Silence us' (ll. 26–31).

As critics have commented, Dryden's choice to add a secular masque to Vanbrugh's rewriting of *The Pilgrim*, an old-fashioned and explicitly courtly entertainment, seems to be a commentary on the end of the century, his life, and the earlier court cultures:[13] 'Weary, weary of my weight, | Let me, let me drop my Freight, | And leave the World behind', begs Chronos, 'I could not bear | Another Year | The Load of Human-kind' (p. 48). Momus, Diana, Mars, and Venus each appear to enact the changes in human life that have made Chronos sag. The age of Diana, devoted to sport and merriment, that of Mars devoted to war, and the age of Venus devoted to Love, have all passed and, as the final chorus declares,

> Thy Wars brought nothing about;
> Thy Lovers were all untrue.
> 'Tis well an Old Age is out,
> And time to begin a New. (p. 54)

---

[11] Dryden, *Letters*, 135.　　[12] Dryden, 'Prologue', in Vanbrugh, *The Pilgrim*, sig. A2ʳ.
[13] See Winn, *John Dryden and his World*, 509–12.

Indeed in 1700, with the passing of Dryden and the death of the young Prince, it must have seemed to many readers that it was 'time to begin a New', but that the direction to be taken was still in dispute.

With no real dramas occurring at the absent or mourning courts to occupy readers or spectators, conflicts within the theatre world and the continuing debates over the social implications of theatrical entertainments provoked lively discussions. A strong group of already successful and established drama-tists who were part of the new generation born following the restoration of the throne and the stage, including Congreve, George Farquhar (1676/7–1707), Abel Boyer (1667?–1729), one of Tutchin's rebutters John Dennis (who in the future would become better known as a literary critic and Alexander Pope's satiric target), and Mary Pix (*c.*1666–1709), all had new offerings on stage and in print. At the same time, the collected plays of the late Sir Robert Howard (1626–98) had their second edition printed (see *MV* 2.III), reminding readers of the origins of the social comedies these younger writers were producing. Public taste in comedies, however, was clearly changing from the racier 1670s and 1680s enjoyment of ageing cuckolds, rakish young men, and dangerous ladies. William Burnaby's (1673–1706) *The Reformed Wife*, where elderly Sir Solomon Empty blithely instructs a gallant young officer fresh from the war in Flanders how London women can be seduced, only to have the advice success-fully applied to his own wife (who describes her husband in the opening lines of the play as 'a conceited Fool'), failed to find an audience.

Many of these new plays and performances directly referenced Collier's attacks on the immorality represented on stage and defended the honour of playwrights and players alike. So numerous were the rebuttals to *The Short View of the Prophaness and Imorality of the English Stage* (1698), Collier himself published a second 'defence' of it in 1700, specifically as a reply to James Drake's (bap. 1666–1707) *The Antient and Modern Stages Survey'd* (1699). Drake, who was by training a physician and a member of the Royal Society and the Royal College of Physicians, was also a dramatist (although perhaps not a very suc-cessful one, as the title page of his comedy *The Sham-Lawyer*, 1697, announces, 'it was damnably ACTED at the Theatre-Royal in DRURY-LANE'). He was also in the late 1690s an enthusiastic literary historian, along with his wife, Judith Drake (fl. 1696–1723), the author of *An Essay in Defence of the Female Sex* (1696). Drake's 1699 critique of Collier's treatise had focused on Collier's motives for writing: 'Did Mr *Collier* contend only for the better Establishment of Virtue, and Reformation of Manners, I shou'd be asham'd to appear against him. But there is a Snake in the Grass', Drake asserted in his dedication to the Charles Sackville, Earl of Dorset, 'Mr *Collier* undertakes the Patronage of Virtue, as Cunning Men do the Guardianship of rich Orphans, only to make his Markets of it'.[14] Collier, Drake charged, deliberately misquoted and misrepresented the

---

[14] Drake, *Antient and Modern Stages*, sigs A3ᵛ–A4ʳ, 'Epistle Dedicatory'.

plays he used as his examples of immorality, his style 'fierce and bold, full of vehement exaggerations, and haughty menaces, he racks Sentences, and tortures Expressions, to extort a Confession from 'em of things to which they are absolute Strangers' (sig. A4^{r-v}). Collier responded in kind in 1700, also focusing his attention less on the stage than on Drake's own writing style. 'His Eagerness to Defend the *Stage,* has sometimes transported him into plain Rudeness: To this I shall only observe, That Railing is a scandalous Talent, and an Argument of an ill Undertaking. When a Man throws Dirt, 'tis a sign he has no other Weapon', Collier informed his reader: 'These are Unchristian and Ungentlemanly Sallies' (sig. A1^r, 'To the Reader').

All four of the dramatists named in Collier's original attack on the stage, William Congreve, Thomas D'Urfey, John Dennis, and John Vanbrugh, had plays in performance and printed in 1700. Vanbrugh's play, as seen before, was his revision of John Fletcher's comedy *The Pilgrim* with the additions from Dryden. It was performed at the Drury Lane Theatre and featured John Wilks, Colley Cibber, and Anne Oldfield in its cast. John Dennis's offering in 1700 was his translation of Eurpides's tragedy *Iphigenia*, performed at the Lincoln's Inn Fields theatre with Thomas Betterton as Orestes, the ageing Elizabeth Barry the Queen of the Scythians, and Anne Bracegirdle (bap. 1671–1748), Congreve's muse, as the tragic Iphigenia. 'My chief design is writing the following Poem', Dennis asserts in his preface, 'was to contribute my Mite towards the being serviceable to the publick....I thought I could not do that more effectually than by endeavouring to enflame the Minds of an Audience with the Love of so noble a Virtue as Friendship.'[15]

Congreve, too, continued the debate with Collier in the preface to his play. His 1700 drama is the best known and most highly regarded by subsequent generations, but, as mentioned in Dryden's letter, Congreve had initially only moderate success with the sparkling but disturbing social comedy *The Way of the World*. With Anne Bracegirdle as Millamant, the witty and self-possessed heiress sought by John Verbruggen's rakish Mirabell, Mrs Leigh as the ageing Lady Wishfort hindering their plans, Elizabeth Barry as the tempestuous plot spoiler Mrs Marwood, and the 66-year-old veteran comic Cave Underhill as Sir Willful Witwoud, the play boasted a seasoned cast in parts written specifically to highlight their talents. Congreve, in a long epistle touching the history of criticism as well as theories of comedy, dedicated the printed version of the play to the politician and patron of the arts Ralph, 1st Earl of Montagu (bap. 1638–1709). Montagu's house in Bloomsbury was described by contemporaries as the finest building in London, and the family seat, Boughton in Northamptonshire, was styled after Versailles, where he was famous for his convivial gatherings of artists, architects, writers, and diplomats, including Congreve.

---

[15] Dennis, *Iphigenia*, 'Preface'.

Congreve in his prefatory materials is clearly also still responding to Collier's criticisms. Given the 'general Taste' of the times, Congreve asserts, it is surprising that his comedy has succeeded at all on stage, since the majority of contemporary comedies provoke laughter by representing 'Fools so gross…they should rather disturb than divert the well-natur'd and reflecting part of an Audience'.[16] His design, in contrast, was to create characters who were ridiculous through their affected wit, 'a Wit, which at the same time that it is affected, is also false'. If, he asserts, 'it has hapned in any part of this Comedy, that I have gain'd a Turn of Stile, or Expression more Correct, or at least more Corrigible than in those which I have formerly written', he concludes, 'I must, with equal Pride and Gratitude, ascribe it to the Honour of your Lordship's admitting me into your Conversation, and that of a Society where every-body else was so well worthy of you' ('Dedication').

This comedy has many of the characteristics of the earlier comedy of manners from the 1670s and 1680s (see CV 3.I), and Verbruggen, for example, had also played parts such as the rake Wilmore in revivals of Aphra Behn's *The Rover*. Like the earlier plays of Wycherley and Etherege, Congreve's is set in fashionable contemporary London, with the first act taking place in a chocolate house, the second in St James's Park, and the final acts in the home of the wealthy widow Lady Wishfort. The central love plot revolves around the beautiful and witty heiress Millamant, who must gain her aunt's consent in order to marry and keep her fortune; Millamant is attracted to the dashing man of the town, Mirabell, but her aunt, Lady Wishfort, despises Mirabell, who had attempted to woo the older woman as part of his plan to obtain Millamant. Furthermore, Lady Wishfort has plans to marry Millamant to her nephew, the much older Sir Willful Witwoud, to keep control of the money. Complicating this are the subplots involving the former lover of Mirabell, Lady Wishfort's own unhappily married daughter Mrs Fainall, and her friend Mrs Marwood, who is engaged in an affair with the mercenary and unscrupulous libertine Mr Fainall, but who is also attracted to Mirabell. Mrs Marwood thus spends much of her time undermining Mirabell's schemes to secure Millamant, which include a plan to get Lady Wishfort's blessing by duping her into a sham marriage with Mirabell's servant and then blackmailing her to gain her consent to the other marriage.

Money is important to all the characters. Millamant has no intention of marrying without her dowry, and Mirabell must marry well in order to straighten out his tangled financial affairs. Fainall was only willing to marry his 'ruined' wife because of her fortune, and his goal is to secure all of her money in his hands, even if it means taking her through a public trial for adultery. The servant Mincing, a witness to Mrs Marwood and Mr Fainall's infidelity, reveals all at the end of the play to stop their plan to blackmail Lady Wishfort. Ultimately,

---

[16] Congreve, *The Way of the World*, 'Dedication'.

all the money ends up in the right hands, as Mirabell's skilful use of legal documents drawn up before her marriage to protect Mrs Fainall's fortune restores power to the women; out of gratitude, Lady Wishfort gives her consent for Millamant and Mirabell to marry with her dowry of £6,000 intact.

Notably, Millamant and Mirabell negotiate their own terms of marriage in Act IV. 'Ah! I'll never marry', Millamant declares, 'unless I am first made sure of my will and pleasure'. Her will and pleasures include sleeping in as late as she pleases, not to be called by familiar names such as 'Wife, Spouse, My dear, Joy, Jewel, Love, Sweet heart and the rest of that Nauseous Cant', and not to have her husband hanging on her in public: 'let us never Visit together, nor go to a Play together, But let us be very strange and well bred: let us be as strange as if we had been married a great while; and as well bred as if we were not marri'd at all'. Mirabell finds these demands, 'pretty reasonable', except for Millamant's determination to remain independent and to 'have my Closet Inviolate; to be sole Empress of my Tea-table, which you must never presume to approach without first asking leave'. With these conditions, she feels, she might 'by degrees dwindle into a Wife'. Mirabell in turn demands that there must be no female close confidante to come between them, that 'you continue to like your own Face, as long as I shall', forbidding such horrors and beauty masks worn at night 'made of oil'd–skins…Hog's-bones, Hare's-gall, Pig-water, and the marrow of a roasted Cat'. And when she is pregnant—a remark from which Millamant recoils ('Ah! Name it not. *Mirabell*: Which may be presum'd, with a blessing on our endeavours— | *Millamant*: Odious endeavours!'), there is to be no straitlacing lest 'you mold my boy's head like a Sugarloaf'. Finally, while she has dominion over her tea table and its conversations, Orange brandy and other 'strong Waters', which are favourites of Lady Wishfort, are banished. Millamant pretends to debate, 'what shall I do? shall I have him? I think I must have him', to which her friend Mrs Fainall urges, 'Ay, ay, take him', and she concludes, 'well, then—I'll take my death I'm in a horrid fright—*Fainall*, I shall never say it—well—I think—I'll endure you' (IV. i, pp. 59–60).

In marked contrast to Congreve's elegant if dark social comedy, Thomas D'Urfey (1653?–1723), the prolific writer of comedies and translations, offered one of his atypical tragedies, the second part of *The Famous History of the Rise and Fall of Massaniello*, both parts being printed together in 1700. The tragedy concerns a peasant uprising in Naples and the corruption of the noble fisherman Massaniello as he attempts to lead the people against the decadent and avaricious nobles. His unfortunately named wife Blowzabella and her attempts to become a fine lady while retaining the language of a fishwife make up a comic subplot: 'Well, Odsfish, 'tis a happy thing to be a Woman of Quality', she observes at the conclusion of the drama unaware of the fate that awaits her at the end.[17]

---

[17] D'Urfey, *Famous History*, pt 2, V. v, p. 47.

At the beginning of the tragedy, Massaniello defies the governor's orders concerning taxes on fish by smacking the Duke of Mataloni's steward across the face with a flounder, but, by the end, he has been seduced and destroyed by his passion for the Duke's virtuous wife. Initially, he defends his political acts eloquently, declaring that he is not a 'rebel' as charged, 'I love the King, and for him and my Country, have undertook this dangerous Enterprize; the People were opprest with loading *Gabells* [tax collectors], and in th'Oppression, the King's Honour tainted, which I resolve to abolish, tho I die for't'. 'It is the Times Distress that causes it', he announces, 'uncommon Crimes have forc'd down Heaven's Vengeance' (pt 1, IV. ii, p. 41).

However, Massaniello falls passionately in love with the Duchess of Mataloni. The noble Bellazaira spurns his love and even imprisonment and the threat of torture and rape fail to move her. Enraged, Massaniello threatens her 'you all my Power defie, | Then first I'll kill your Honour e're you die'. He orders her stripped and exposed to the guards; as she pleads for mercy he orders, 'strip her instantly; and when she's so disgrac'd, take off her Head, and send it to her Yoke-mate *Mataloni*' (pt 2, V. iii, p. 45). Fortunately, the Duke arrives and shoots him before this is carried out, completing the seeming reversal of character noted by critics, where the previously villainous aristocrat heroically rescues the innocent from the now debased peasant. Blowzabella also meets a savage end; she is seized during a masque she believes was given in her honour, dragged off, and hanged. As the play concludes, the audience is treated to a scene in which Massaniello's dismembered body is dragged behind horses with his head and hands stuck on a pole with Blowzabella and her friends hanging from gibbets. 'A dreadful Sight!', concludes the corrupt Cardinal,

> Yet bears it a good Moral,
> Discovering the vain state of Worldly Greatness;
> And what a slippery way he treads that chuses
> The Path of vain Ambition…
>
> .   .   .   .   .
>
> The Moral to all Rebels doth belong
> They may a while, but cannot prosper long. (pt 2, V. iii, p. 50)

Several of the songs from the two-part tragic spectacle, set by the actor Richard Leveridge (1670–1758) and Daniel Purcell (c.1670–1717), the brother of Henry Purcell, who had previously set several of D'Urfey's 'playhouse songs', were printed separately and sold with their musical scores (see *MV* 4.IV: *CV* 4.V). These inexpensive, engraved single sheets typically featured the name of the performer as well as the musical composer. Peter Motteux likewise had several songs from his plays, one from *The Mad Lover* set by John Eccles and performed by Anne Bracegirdle ('Must then a faithful Lover go, scorn'd & banish'd, banish'd like a Foe, | Oh! Let me Rave, Oh! Let me Rave, dispair, dispair') and one a two-part song between Cupid and Bacchus in *Timon of Athens* set by Henry Purcell, both conveniently presenting the lyrics and vocal score and the accompanying flute part on a single folio sheet. The largest publisher of bound volumes of printed music in 1700 continued to be Henry Playford (1657–1709), the son of John Playford, who had dominated the music publication business in the 1650s, but he now had competition from one John Young, himself an instrument-maker.

While lacking these commercially successful songs, Mary Pix unabashedly exploited the foreign origins of her play, *The Beau Defeated, or, The Lucky Younger Brother*. As her dedication to the Duchess of Bolton and the prologue and epilogue repeatedly state, this play is partly a translation from a French one, and Pix hopes with a slight nod to Collier that her additions 'had no Immodesty to offend' and her motive is to persuade 'the World to prize Desert, before the Gifts of Fortune', although she wryly admits defeat on that score.[18] In Pix's updated English version, as with earlier adaptation of popular French comedies, the comic tensions created by social climbers who with varying degrees of success seek to imitate the style and manners of the aristocratic mode are combined with a tremendously complicated mix of love intrigues. The beau who suffers defeat, Sir John Roverhead, appears to be an unintimidating version of earlier 1670s and 1680s rakish fortune-hunting males but who is revealed at the end to be a servant who has been dressed up and 'taught . . . the Modes and Manners' by a woman who is also revealed not to be the widow Lady Basset, but instead Sir Francis Basset's cast-off mistress. The romantic lead, played by Mr Verbruggen, is Younger Clerimont, the younger brother of the title, whose poverty, 'the detested Plague Poverty's upon me!' (IV. i, p. 25), places his marriage with Anne Bracegirdle's exemplary Lady Landsworth, 'A Rich Widow of the North', in danger. At the heart of the play, however, is the social education of the ambitious Mrs Rich, 'a Fantastick City Widow', played by Elizabeth Barry, seeking to become 'a Woman of Quality' with 'a great Name'. Her niece Lucinda, in contrast, wants to get married simply 'because I may have a little more freedom . . . and I have heard 'em say, Wives go where they will and do what they will' (III. i, p. 23), and in particular the young girl wants to go to plays, to stroll in the parks, and to have control over her own money.

As the play opens, Mrs Rich, a banker's widow, has just been humiliated when the carriage of a duchess has cut off her own carriage and forced it to give way, even though the duchess's coach possesses only 'two miserable starv'd Jades' and footmen in tattered rags. Its occupant tells her scornfully to 'hold thy peace, Citizen', even though, as her maid Betty exclaims, 'Citizen! Citizen! To a Lady in a gilt Coach, lin'd with crimson Velvet, and hung round with gold Fringe' (I. i, p. 1). In the end, it is the merchant Mr Rich, Lucinda's father, who has the final words: 'Now, Sister, and Daughter, to you I chiefly speak, let this days Adventure make ye for ever cautious of your Conversation; you see how near these pretenders to Quality had brought you to ruin: The truly Great are

---

[18] Pix, *The Beau Defeated*, 'Dedication'.

of quite a different Character' (V. iii, p. 47). The concluding verse negotiates the potential social precipice by announcing,

> The Glory of the World our *British* Nobles are,
>
> .   .   .   .   .
>
> But to our Citizens, *Augusta's* Sons,
> The Conquering Wealth of both the India's run

and reminds the audience that 'Honours alone, but empty Scutcheons are' (V. iii, p. 47).[19]

The veteran dramatist Thomas Southerne (1660–1746) returned to the stage after a five-year absence with a tragedy, *The Fate of Capua*, which, in spite of the acting efforts of Verbruggen, Betterton, and Elizabeth Barry, failed to move its audiences. In contrast, his friend Colley Cibber (1671–1757), the future theatre manager and Poet Laureate, staged and printed one of the period's most enduring tragedies. Cibber was acting in several of the 1700 productions, including, as mentioned, *The Pilgrim*, as well as a revival of Ben Jonson's comedy *Epicoene*, and the future Whig pamphleteer (see CV 5.III) John Oldmixon's (1672/3–1742) 'opera' *The Grove, or, Love's Paradice*, with music again by Daniel Purcell. Although celebrated for his comic 'fop' roles such as Sir Novelty Fashion and Lord Foppington, in 1700 Cibber performed the role of Richard III in his own loosely adapted version of Shakespeare's tragedy. Performed in February at the Theatre Royal, the play was also printed that year by Bernard (Barnaby) Lintot (1675–1736), who would soon rival Jacob Tonson as the leading publisher of literary materials in the early eighteenth century. In 1700, Lintott was still a young publisher in his first year free of his apprenticeship and was happy to use the title page of *Richard III* to advertise that, at his shop, '*Gentlemen and Ladies may have all sorts of Plays and Novels*'.

The play itself is a remarkable work, for its raising the wrath of censors and for its reworking of Shakespeare's plot. It continued to astonish later generations of critics by its success as a textual collage, combining just over 1,000 original lines by Cibber with only 800 from Shakespeare's original 3,600, but also mixing in over 100 lines taken from Shakespeare's other history plays, including *3 Henry VI*, *Richard II*, and *Henry V*.[20] Interestingly, for those reading the play, Cibber has had all the lines that are 'intirely *Shakespear's* to be Printed in this *Italick Character*' while 'those lines with this mark (') before 'em are generally his thoughts, in the best dress I could afford 'em'. All that is unmarked is 'intirely my own'. Cibber's version, which continued to be performed into the twentieth century, streamlined Shakespeare's plot and focused attention on the character of Richard, who is more motivated by love than by villainy, while drastically reducing the roles of the women in Shakespeare's version. Cibber lamented in the preface to the reader that, when it was first

---

[19] See Garcia, 'Female Relationships'.
[20] See Croissant, 'Studies in the Work of Colley Cibber'.

performed, the censor, Killigrew (see *MV* 5.II), insisted it be done without its first act, given that '*Henry* the Sixth being a Character Unfortunate and Pitied, wou'd put the Audience in mind of the late *King James*', an intention Cibber stoutly denies.

The year 1700 marked the debut of several important actresses, including Anne Oldfield (1683–1730), who was recommended by Vanbrugh to play Alinda in *The Pilgrim* staged in July. Cibber in his memoir recalls that he was not very impressed with her initially: 'I thought, she had little more than her Person, that appear'd necessary to the forming a good Actress; for she set out with so extraordinary a Diffidence, that it kept her too despondingly down, to a formal, plain (not to say) flat manner of speaking'.[21] Regardless of Cibber's caution about her, she would also perform this year the prologue to Susanna Centlivre's first drama *The Perjur'd Husband* (to be discussed later in this section), with whom she would form a lasting working friendship, and play in Catharine Trotter's only comedy, *Love at a Loss*, performed at Drury Lane in November.

For Susanna Carroll, soon to be better known as Susanna Centlivre (bap. 1669?–1723), one of the most produced playwrights in the eighteenth century after Shakespeare, 1700 could be said to be her breakthrough year in London.[22] Her first public poem was printed as part of the tribute to John Dryden, *The Nine Muses, Or Poems written by Nine Several Ladies Upon the Death of John Dryden Esq*; she contributed witty letters to printer Sam Briscoe's collection of *Familiar and Courtly Letters*; and her first dramatic production was staged in or about October.

It was also the debut year for several writers who would go on to considerable success in the early decades of the eighteenth century. Nicholas Rowe (1674–1718) offered his first blank verse tragedy, *The Ambitious Step-Mother*, with both Anne Bracegirdle and Anne Barry in the cast along with Thomas Betterton and performed at the 'new' theatre at Lincoln's Inn Fields. Rowe declares in his dedication published in 1701 how the plays of Thomas Otway were his model for the ending, which, per Rowe, some people have told him that 'the fifth Act is barbarous, and shocks the Audience'; Rowe defends the death of the innocent Amestris at the hands of the evil Mirza as essential to evoke the feelings of terror and pity tragedy requires.[23]

Carroll/Centlivre's first offering was a costume tragedy set in Venice during carnival, with the central characters being driven wild by passion. 'Why must weak mortals be expos'd to Passions, | Which are not in our Power to subdue, | And yet account for what they prompt us to?' laments Aurelia, who is promised to one man by her father and indeed bound to him by her own previous

---

[21] Cibbert, *Apology*, 165–6.
[22] Bowyer, *The Celebrated Mrs Centlivre*, p. v; Bratton, 'Reading the Intertheatrical'.
[23] Rowe, *The Ambitious Step-Mother*, 'Epistle Dedicatory'.

passion, but who suddenly falls in love with the married Bassino.[24] *The Perjur'd Husband, Or, the Adventures of Venice A Tragedy* was performed at the Theatre Royal in Drury Lane with Mr Mills playing the disingenuous false husband, Bassino, Mrs Kent his long-suffering wife, Placentia, and Anne Oldfield the rival love interest, Aurelia. Even the virtuous and wronged wife succumbs in the end to acting out of passion rather than her virtue or her reason: dressing as a young man to gain access to Aurelia, Placentia first reveals that Bassino is already married, and, when Aurelia refuses to believe her and give him up, Placentia stabs her just as Bassino enters and he, seeing this act, stabs the still disguised Placentia, only to have Bassino subsequently stabbed by Aurelia's fiancé. Their extended collective death scenes run for the entire last five pages of the play and conclude with the moral:

> Vengeance always treads on Perjury
>
> .   .   .   .   .
>
> A day waits, a Day' of general Doom,
> When guilty Souls must to an Audit come;
> Then that we may not tremble, blush or fear,
> Let our Desires be Just: our Lives unsullied here. (V. ii, p. 40)

It also has an interesting, if apparently controversial, comic subplot: while the heightened passions of the tragic characters require verse, the comic ones are in earthy prose. In her epistle to the reader, Centilivre answers 'Snarling Sparks', who in her view hide behind Collier's charges that the stage, in particular in its representations of immodest women characters, corrupts general morality. 'I cannot believe that a Prayer-Book shou'd be put into the hands of a woman, whose Innate Vertue won't secure her Reputation', she counters, 'nor is it reasonable to expect a person, whose Inclinations are always forming projects to the dishonour of her Husband, shou'd deliver her Commands to her Confident in the words of a Psalm' ('To the Reader'). Lady Pizalta is determined to enjoy the attractive visiting Frenchman Ludovico as long as carnival lasts, while her cunning maidservant Lucy profits handsomely through arranging assignations for her mistress, which become intertwined with her own artful and lucrative dealings with the elderly and lecherous husband Pizalto. While the tragic female Aurelia tells her maid 'Talk not of Reputation | When Lov's in t'other scale' (III. i, p. 18), Lady Pizalta declares robustly: 'Oh! Reputation, what several sorts of Slavery do we undergo to preserve Thee! For to be thought Virtuous, we are forced to be constantly railing against Vice, tho our Tongues and Maxims seldom agree' (II. i, p. 12).

From the few facts we know, Susanna Carroll/Centlivre had herself led a dramatic life before finally arriving in London. Although the details are not established, it would appear that, at some point in her early teens, she had left home, perhaps married a Mr Fox, perhaps joined a travelling theatrical troupe

---

[24] Centlivre, *The Perjur'd Husband*, III. i, p. 18.

playing breeches roles, and probably married an army officer named Carroll, who died shortly thereafter. Her publications in 1700 using this last name reveal that she was moving into the literary circles of professional writers such as the prolific Thomas Brown (bap. 1663–1704) and the multi-talented Abel Boyer (1667?–1729), whose *Royal Dictionary* had appeared in 1699 and whose translation of Racine's *Iphigénie* was performed at Drury Lane in 1700 under the title *Achilles*. Her inclusion in the volume *The Nine Muses, Or Poems Written by Nine Severall Ladies Upon the Death of the late Famous John Dryden, Esq* in September 1700, was as 'Polimnia' or the Muse of Rhetorick, who in the final poem of the collection laments the loss of Dryden 'the mortal Wonder', to whom the Muse had 'on his Brows fixt an Immortal Crown. | With Lovers hands, I lavisht all my Charms, | Gave up my self, to his more Lovely Arms').[25] Other writers in the collection introduced by the well-established printer Richard Basset include the dramatist and fiction-writer Delarivier Manley (*c*.1670–1724) as Melpomene, the muse of tragedy, the poet Sarah Fyge Egerton (1670–1723) as Erato, the amorous muse, and Mary Pix representing Clio the Muse of history, whose comedy *The Beau Defeated*, previously discussed, was performed at the New Theatre in Lincoln's Inn Fields in March and also printed by Richard Bassett that year.

Carroll/Centlivre's other known publication in 1700 is more difficult to characterize but it is also typical of popular commercial printing practices during the period. The full title of the collection in which it appears gives some sense of the volume's complexity and the marketing strategies of its publisher, Samuel Briscoe: *Familiar and courtly letters, written by Monsieur Voiture to persons of the greatest honour, wit, and quality of both sexes in the court of France. Made English by Mr Dryden, Tho. Cheek, Esq; Mr Dennis, Henry Cromwel, Esq; Jos. Raphson, Esq; Dr ——, &c. With twelve select epistles out of Aristanetus: translated from the Greek. Some select letters of Pliny, Jun. and Monsieur Fontanelle. Translated by Mr Tho. Brown. And a collection of original letters lately written on several subjects. By Mr T. Brown, Never before publish'd. To which is added, a collection of letters of friendship, and other occasional letters, written by Mr Dryden, Mr Wycherly, Mr —— Mr Congreve, Mr Dennis, and other hands.* Briscoe, who also published the posthumous edition of Aphra Behn's fictions, both as separate titles (see CV 5.IV) and in several volume collections throughout the 1690, had originally printed part of *Familiar and Courtly Letters* in 1696 as *Letters Upon Several Occasions . . . with a new Translation of select Letters of Monsieur Voiture by John Dennis.*

The 1700 compendium volume binds the new materials in with the old with a new title page and dedication, resulting in two independent sets of page numbers within the single volume, with seven separately titled sections altogether. In his dedication to the financier Sir Charles Duncombe, Sheriff of London,

---

[25] *The Nine Muses*, 13.

Briscoe praises his acts of charity and asks at the end that he pardon 'an unhappy Man, who has laboured under Afflictions, which he might have prevented if he wou'd have gone upon dishonest Methods, by which others have not only repaired, by improved their Fortunes'.[26] Briscoe describes the contents as letters given to him for publication by 'some of my Friends, who, in commiseration of my hard Circumstances, were willing to contribute something towards by Assistance' (sig. A3ʳ). The final section, 'LETTERS of *Friendship*', includes letters between Dennis and William Wycherley, John Dryden, and William Congreve, most touching on literary matters, ranging from gossip to discussions of the nature of comedy.

The short informal letters, with their references to unnamed mutual acquaintances, are demonstrating both the authors' sociability and epistolary skills and also the existence and nature of literary networks as they extended from London to those out in the countryside. 'Mr——' desires to know from Congreve 'all the ridiculous things that have happen'd at *Will's* Coffee-house since I left it, 'tis the merriest Place in the World'; he urges Congreve to tell 'the Lady, who was the Author of the *Hue and Cry* after me, she might have sent out a hundred *Hues and Cries* before she would have found a Poet' (p. 106). Letters between Congreve in Tunbridge Wells and John Dennis in London highlight the easy flow between fellow writers: 'Before I came to *Tunbridge*, I proposed to my self the Satisfaction of Communicating the Pleasures of the Place to you', but, he laments, Dennis's London letters are more entertaining (p. 88). Indeed, the spa setting has made Congreve idle, 'for Poetry is neither in my Head, nor in my Heart', and, rather than inspiring him to composition, 'I am half of the Opinion now, that this Well is an *Anti-Hypocrene*', the fountain on Mount Helicon sacred to the muses (p. 89). He urges Dennis to alert him to any new plays being staged, even though it is out of the season, 'yet I know there are now and then some Wind-falls at this time of Year' (p. 90). Congreve warns his friend that summer brings to London both 'Summer-flies and small Poets' and that the approaching St Bartholomew Fair serves to act like 'Days of Privilege, wherein Criminals and Malefactors in Poetry, are permitted to creep abroad' (p. 90). In a lengthy letter from Congreve to Dennis, he more critically describes the role of 'humour' in comedy: 'humor is from Nature', he observes, 'Habit from Custom; and Affectation from Industry' (p. 75). Humour, for Congreve, is the controlling aspect of character on finds in Ben Jonson's comedies, although as he concludes, 'there is more of Humour in our English Comick Writers than in any others … I look upon Humour to be almost of English growth' (pp. 84–5).

In the section titled 'Love-Letters, by Gentlemen and Ladies', the tone is flirtatious as well as satirical. Susanna Carroll responds to two letters addressed to 'Madam C—ll', and, as a married woman, wittily rejects the proposals of the suitor. The suitor complains that her rejection of him 'because you don't

---

[26] *Familiar and courtly letters*, sig. A3ʳ.

like me' leaves the door open for a renewed assault, since 'I am satisfied, your *Fortress* is not *Impregnable*, and though you won't *Capitulate* with me, though I offer your own *Terms*, I know the *Man*, to whom you would *gladly Surrender* upon his' (p. 234). Why do women, he complains, fall in love 'with the *Sons* of the *Muses*, those *poor Rogues* that can only pay with empty *Breath*, what I, with *substantial Gold*, wou'd *purchase*; and that used to be the most prevailing *Argument* with your *Sex*' (p. 234). 'Madam C——ll's Answer to ——', retorts, 'Cou'd I value a Man upon his *Fortune*, I shou'd condescend to Converse with a *Fool*, though by your *Assurance* and *Vanity*, one wou'd take you for a *Wit*' (p. 236). Noting that 'my *Husband* knows me so well by my *Company*, and you so well by your *Letter*, that he has given me leave to Answer it; nay, *commanded* me, else I had left you a Prey to your *Conceit* and *Vanity*; which in a little time, will make you fit for the *Stage*, and so make you good Company for *Women* of *Sence*' (p. 237). As a parting shot, she concludes: 'Sir, I advise you to make your *Valet* transcribe your Letters for you, for you own hand Spells worse than a *Whore*' (p. 237). Nothing daunted, the suitor replies that he hopes she appreciates the licence her husband gives her as much as he appreciates the wit and sense of her letter, a scarce '*Commodity* in your Sex', so much so that 'it ought to be taken into consideration by the *Parliament*, to prevent the Increase of Fools, that no one Man shou'd engross a *Person* of *Wit* to *himself*' (p. 237). '*Gold* is the *Womens God*', he repeats, 'there's scarce a *Dutchess* in this *Kingdom*, that can't find an use for a *superfluous* Sum' (p. 238). 'Look ye, Madam, I have no occasion to expose the *Product* of my *Brain*; the *Product* of my *Estate* is sufficient to afford me *Necessaries*; and that's more than your *Poetical Friends* can warrant from their spare *Diet* and hard *Study*' (pp. 238–9). 'And to answer the *Postscript*', he concludes, 'good *Spelling* is beneath a *Gentleman*' (p. 239).

Her answer suggests that, since he is a Member of Parliament, perhaps he can introduce a bill that would 'provide against the troublesome *Suit* of those we don't care for' (p. 239). Using a reference to the notorious bill of divorce brought by the Duke of Norfolk against his wife Mary for adultery, which after several attempts in the 1690s had finally passed through Parliament in February 1700, she warns that 'it may be of dangerous Consequence to all the *Husbands* in the *Nation*; for the Subjects will be for following the Example of higher Powers'. She taunts the suitor that 'I imagine you to be of the *Court* Party, you understand a Bribe so well', but that her husband 'falls not in your Road'. As for herself, 'I have *Wit* enough to distinguish the Arrogance of a Coach and Six from the Complaisance of a Man of *Sence*; I despise your *Price*, and *nauseate* your *Person*; and if you don't desist, I shall expose your Name in Print' (p. 240).

These probably fictitious letters highlight several interesting issues that recur during 1700: the language of love and courtship infused with that of economics and trade, the changing nature of how marriage as a relationship is perceived, and the voice of the financially and sexually independent woman. Such female figures, of course, were subject to comment, satire, and rebuke as well as earning the reputation for wit. Richard Ames's (bap. 1664?–1692) satire *The*

Folly of Love. A New Satyr Against Woman together with The Bachelors Lettany by the same Hand (1691) had its fourth edition, enlarged, printed in 1700. In it, he takes the contrary position to other of his own texts, including *Sylvia's Revenge, or, a Satyr Against Man* (1688), a refutation of Robert Gould's *Love Given O're* (1683), and even rebutted anonymously his own *The Folly of Love* with *The Pleasures of Love and Marriage* (1691): as John Dunton the bookseller observed of Ames as a professional commercial writer, 'you might engage him upon what Project you pleas'd' (Dunton, *Life and Errors*, p. 247).

As such, Ames's texts and their subsequent editions in 1700 suggest the nature of popular discourses and clichés about the wars between the sexes as well as the modish occupations and sought-after tone of young men on the town in search of wine and women. In his preface, Ames repudiates Dunton's representation of him as a write-to-hire author, declaring that 'these Papers, (the Effects of some leisure Hours in the *Country*) had never seen the Light, being Wrote only for my own Private Diversion'.[27] He was, he informs his reader, astonished to be asked to proof a fair copy of them for the press, knowing that 'I had the Original in my Closet, and wondred to find one so nearly like it in Manuscript' (sig. A2r). Although friends had asked for copies, he had always refused, and those to whom he had lent it promised never to transcribe a line; however, according to the bookseller requesting him to proof it, an individual had 'found it on the Road' and sent it to the bookseller, resulting in Ames being 'absolutely necessitated to Print it in my own Defence' (sig. A2v). There may be 'some Angry She' who might be offended with 'some biting Lines', but the author cares not 'for of all the Misfortunes Incident to Flesh and Blood, Heaven Deliver me from Love and Dotage'.

'Happy was Man, when first by Nature made', the satire opens, 'The welcome guest of *Eden's* blisful shade' (p. 1). In this version, however, it is Satan who first imagines Woman and it is not God who takes the rib from Adam but 'Some spirit came and stole his Rib away | And of that *crooked shapeless* thing did frame | The *Worlds great Plague* and did it *Woman* name' (p. 2).

> Oh! could we Live without that *cloven* Sex,
> Whose *only pleasure's* to torment and vex,
> Fate would, no doubt, some better method find,
> To propagate and multiply Mankind. (p. 2)

Speaking of modern Englishwomen, '*Lust's* the first *Lesson* which they always Learn, | 'Ere they the difference of the Sex discern' (p. 8). The satire focuses mostly on women's manipulation of men's sexual desires by the determined costuming of their own:

> But since the Name of *Lust* is too severe,
> Too harsh and rugged for the *Female Ear,*

---

[27] Ames, *The Folly of Love*, 'Preface'.

> We'll call it *Love*, and under that disguise,
> Observe their various *close Hippocrisies*. (p. 8)

Having surveyed the ways in which women satisfy their sexual nature, including professions of being a common street walker, a 'Lady *Abbess* of the *Fleet-street*', and a kept mistress who demands a coach and six before getting into bed, the satire concludes:

> Of all the Plagues attending human Life,
> The greatest sure is that we call a *Wife*;
> Nor is there a more pitied Wretch than he,
> That's doom'd to *Matrimonial* Slavery' (p. 14).

Wives are taught the secrets of intrigues and infidelity at the public theatres and the public parks—'(Places where Women teach their minds to sin)'—and they acquire there the 'fine Discourse' and 'pretty am'rous Chat, | Between the *Gallant* and the *Wife* is made' (p. 16).

The worst, however, of all relationships between men and women is that of 'a vertuous *Wife*; | She that with new Indearment ev'ry Night, | Provokes Desire and hightens Appetite'. Although she is faithful to her husband, 'like *Opium*' her very '*Female Fondness*' will destroy 'the choice delights of Love': 'For what we may at any time enjoy, | Does ev'n the relish of the Bliss destroy' (p. 17). While women apparently can be celibate only by being hypocritical, Ames argues, that is man's first and natural condition. Returning to the opening image of Eden, Ames ironically imagines the garden as overflowing with '*choicest Vines*' making 'the *Godlike Juice*', to be enjoyed 'with a Score of *Choice Selected Friends* . . . | We'd Live, and . . . Procreate like Trees' and never once be bothered with thought of womankind (p. 21).

Satire was the muse inspiring much of the verse published in 1700. Excluding the lyrics for popular songs from the playhouses, the collections dedicated to mourning the death of the young Prince and the passing of John Dryden, there were few published volumes of poetry and long poems printed in pamphlet form in that year. Playwright Charles Hopkins (1671?–1700), whose final play *Friendship Improv'd, or, the The Female Warriour* was published posthumously in 1700, produced a volume of verse *The Art of Love: In Two Books: Dedicated to the Ladies* based on his paraphrases of Ovid's *Ars Amatoria*. Another dramatist, Nahum Tate (*c*.1652–1715), offered his charming two-canto praise of tea and tea-drinking in *Panacea*, 'This is the Drink of Health, the Drink of Souls', with its mythological account of Chinese history. John Pomfret's (1667–1702) *The Choice*, advocating a life of country retirement and a good library over 'Intrigues of State', and *Reason* offer lovers of original English verse much diversion. His poem *Reason*, echoing John Locke's theories of *tabula rasa*, laments '*Custome*, the Worlds great Idol we Adore, | And knowing This, we seek to know no More':

> The Careful Nurse, and Priest is all we Need
> To Learn Opinions and our Country's Creed;

> The Parents Precepts early are Instill'd,
> And spoil the Man while they Instruct the Child.[28]

Both these poems were published by John Nutt in separate pamphlets, the first, *The Choice*, identifying the author only as 'a Person of Quality', while *Reason* identifies him only as the author of *The Choice*.

If volumes of verse by single authors were scarce in 1700, there was no shortage of satiric verses, many focused on the merits or lack thereof of other writers. William King (1663–1712), who had published his verses in Dryden's miscellany *Examen poeticum* (1693), took aim at Hans Sloane, the secretary of the Royal Society, in his *The Transactioneer with Some of his Philosophical Fancies*, spoofing the venerable *Philosophical Transactions*. Samuel Cobb (bap. 1675–1713), who had penned an ode in memory of Queen Mary while a student at Christ's Hospital (1694) and panegyric verses celebrating *Pax redux…on the Return of His Majesty and the Happy Conclusion of the Peace* (1697), in 1700 published *Poetae Britannici: A Poem, Satyrical and Panegyrical* on the character of English poets and poetry. Attacking contemporaries such as 'D—y' (D'Urfey) as 'In Comedy Immodest, and Prophane, | And Comick only in the Tragick strain, | Impertinent, indecent, hardned, vain', and 'Ry—r' (Thomas Rymer) 'Who only wants good Nature and good Wit',[29] Cobb ends his poem with praise of Roscommon, Oldham, Denham, Waller, and above all, 'Dr—n' (Dryden) whose

> Noble Rhyme
> For these, if well observ'd, can strictly shew,
> In charming Numbers what is false, what true,
> And Teach more good than *Hobbs* or *Locke* can do. (p. 24)

Richard Blackmore's (1654–1729) *A Satyr Against Wit* was part of an extended exchange of poetic insults begun by Sir Samuel Garth's attack on Blackmore's long poem *Prince Arthur* in *The Dispensary* (1699). Blackmore's opens with the indignant question 'Who can forbear, and tamely silent sit, | And see his Native Land undone by Wit?'[30] 'The *Mob* of Wits is up to storm the Town', he charges and identifies Dryden, D'Urfey, the Earl of Dorset, and Garth among many who are leading the charge against manly, native British good sense.

Defoe also felt drawn to this literary quarrel, although not himself directly named in it, and contributed *The Pacificator*, published shortly after Blackmore's *Satyr Against Wit*. Defoe frames the conflict as a mock battle between the 'Wits' 'Arm'd with *Burlesque, Bombast*, and *Bawdy-Song*', including even 'Some *Amazonian* Troops of Female Wit' against the men of sense and taste, among whom he includes Cowley, Milton, Waller, Rochester, and, interestingly, Aphra Behn, '*Giants* these were of Wit and Sense together'.[31] Defoe expands his satire away from the individual personalities involved, however, with his shrewd insight into the ways in which poetry is also political weapon:

---

[28] Pomfret, *Reason*, 7.   [29] Cobb, *Poetae Britannici*, 7.
[30] Blackmore, *A Satyr Against Wit*, 3.   [31] Defoe, *The Pacificator*, 5.

> The Pen's the certain Herald of a War,
> And Points it out like any Blazing Star:
> Men Quarrel first, and Skirmish with ill Words,
> And when they're heated then they draw their Swords. (p. 2)

Blackmore's satire was speedily met with Tom Brown's collection of *Commendatory Verses, on the Author of the Two Arthurs, and the Satyr against Wit* (1700), which was in turn answered by the anonymous *Discommendatory Verses, on those which are Truly Commendatory, on the Author of the Two Arthurs, and the Satyr against Wit* (1700). Brown's, which purports to contain some of Blackmore's 'particular Friends', manages to attack Blackmore both as a poet and a physician: 'Let the Quack scribble any thing but Bills, | His Satyr Wounds not but his Physick Kills'.[32] Echoing Dryden's MacFlecknoe, another squib declares:

> Well may'st thou think an useless Talent Wit,
> Thou who without it hast three Poems Writ:
> Impenetrably dull, secure thou'rt found,
> And can'st receive no more, than give a Wound. (p. 5)

Discommendatory Verses, in turn, attacked Brown, Garth, and numerous other contributors to the previous volume, including John Dennis, in 'To the Inviolably Dull Critick, on his Heroical Strains upon the *Satyr against Wit*', described as a 'crabbed piece of blustring Wit' who 'Labour'st to be thought intricate and dull'.[33] Thomas Rymer (1642/3–1713), who became most famous for his literary history and criticism *A short view of tragedy; its original, excellency and corruption, with some reflections on Shakespear, and other practioners for the stage* (1693), stressing Shakespeare's inability to observe the rules of decorum, and who contributed topical verses to friends' collections and Dryden's miscellanies, is addressed as 'To a *Rhimer*, who if he takes pains, Writes as if he did not', 'Who e're Thou art, to Me and Sense unknown, | Correct not others follies but thy own'. (p. 7). Likewise, 'To a Lady dignified and distinguish'd by the Name of Critick and Poet, on Her incomprehensible Raileries on the *Satyr against Wit*' opens 'Believe me, Madam, that your Muse has shown | So foul a Face, I beg you'd hide your own' (p. 8).

In addition to these highly personal satires and risqué picaresque fictions, readers in 1700 were reading and hearing about previously private quarrels and insults, and the intimate details of real marriages, which ended up in very public divorces. In 1700, the most prominent of these was the Duke of Norfolk's long-sought divorce obtained through an Act of Parliament. It was a confusing case, which had been proceeding slowly through Parliamentary hearings and published in the press since 1692. Henry, the 7th Duke of Norfolk, had served as the chief butler in James II's coronation in 1685 and was the first appointed Knight of the Garter under him; in 1688, he also served as the chief butler in

---

[32] Brown, *Commendatory Verses*, 3.   [33] *Discommendatory Verses*, 7.

the coronation of William and Mary. In spite of his obvious standing at court, he was plagued by financial difficulties, and his wife, Mary *née* Mordaunt, the Duchess of Norfolk, refused to give over her life interest in the estates, including Castle Rising settled on her at marriage by the Duke's father. In 1692, the Duke introduced a bill in the House of Lords requesting a divorce from her and the right to remarry, and he sued his wife's lover (and future husband) John Germain in the King's Bench court. Public sympathy seems to have been largely against him—the bill failed in Parliament, and he was awarded only 100 marks rather than the requested £100,000 for damages he had requested.

The Duchess had previously made excellent use of the press to rally support for her side of the case, publishing *A Vindication of her Grace Mary Dutchess of Norfolk* (1693). No stranger to the public gaze, she had as a young maid of honour performed in the royal masque *Calisto* in 1675 with Princesses Mary and Anne (see *MV* 3.I); her character in the piece was a not entirely pleasant one, the jealous nymph Psecas, who is wooed by Mercury, enacted then by the young Sarah Jennings, who in 1700 was the Duchess of Marlborough and still very much a power in Princess Anne's court. Two years after the masque, Mary Mordaunt married the Duke of Norfolk. The Duke was always quite public with his extramarital affairs: a letter from 1696 by Humphrey Prideaux concerning a party hosted by the Duke and his mistress Mrs Lane remarked that 'all that have any regard to their reputations think it scandalous to accept his invitations'.[34] The Duke, who had been raised a Catholic, had by 1688 declared himself Protestant, and his case to the House of Lords argued the necessity of the divorce and remarriage on the grounds of preventing the vast estates from passing into Catholic hands. Ironically, the Duchess had been reared a Protestant, but, after having been committed to a French Catholic nunnery by her husband in 1685 on the discovery of her affair with Germain, she then converted to Catholicism.

Her publications in defence of herself and answering the charges appeared several times in 1692 and in 1693 under the title of *A Vindication of her Grace, Mary Dutchess of Norfolk. Being a true Account of the Proceedings before the House of Lords (from Jan 7 1691 to Feb 17 following)…occasioned by several Libellous* PAMPHLETS *lately Published and Dispersed under the same Pretence and Title. A Vindication* takes the form of documentary reports of testimony made to the House of Lords and the petitions presented by both sides, accompanied by sections called 'Observations upon the foregoing Evidence' that invite the reader to make the conclusions. The Duchess informed the House of Lords that 'It is my Misfortune to be thus accused; I had rather stand charg'd for High Treason before your Lordships, than with this ignominious Crime'.[35] She resolutely declared her innocence, begged the Lordships' pardon for defending herself, and reminded them that 'I am not only the Duke of *Norfolk*'s

---

[34] Quoted in Rachel Weil, 'Howard, Henry, seventh duke of Norfolk (1655–1701)', *ODNB*.
[35] Howard, *A Vindication of her Grace*, 5.

Wife, but also born and descended from Parents and Ancestors of the Ancient Nobility; That your Lordship's Ancestors, and my Ancestors, who sat in this House, knew no such Proceeding' (p. 13). The witnesses against her are represented as disgruntled fired servants, 'a Jilting little Slut', 'a poor Roguy, Tricking Footman that was turned off for his ill Behavior', and 'a Street-Porter, brought in as a Witness to the Privacies of the Dutchess's Bed-Chamber' (p. 13).

In February 1700, the Duke again applied for a bill of divorce, this time with a long list of witnesses who testified to the Duchess's continuing adulterous affair with Germain. As one account of the proceedings, sympathetic to the Duke, observed: 'the Reputation which the *Dutchess* had maintained, of Wit and Discretion, made it difficult for many to believe, that she could be surprized in the very Act of Adultery, as had been formerly proved'.[36] Germain's steward Nicholas Hanseur provided further details: he had, he testified,

the opportunity of proving the Continuance of the same Adulterous Conversation at several Times and Places, from the Summer 1692 to 26*th* of *April* 1696. He swears he had after his return to Sir *John*'s Service, see them in Bed together at Sir *John*'s House, at the *Cockpit*, and at the *Dutchess*'s Houses at *Millbank*, and where she now lives. (p. 1)

William Bayly 'very unwillingly confirmed the Testimony' of other servants who had testified in the earlier attempts, that 'the Dutchess used to come mask'd to his *Master*'s House, that he has gone with him as far as the *Horse-ferry* towards her House and the *Millbank*; that then his Master sometimes *lay out all Night*, and the next morning he has *carried Linnens and Cloath* for his *Master*' at the Duchess's house (p. 1).

In April 1700, after the bill had been passed, John Nutt printed an advertisement to announce that on 15 April he would be publishing the complete proceedings of the divorce with depositions and all relevant papers by the Duke's order. In the same year, he also published Mary Astell's *Some Reflections Upon Marriage, Occasion'd by the Duke and Duchess of Mazarine's case, which is also considered*. Astell (1666–1731) was already established as an author commenting on contemporary issues concerning women and society; her *A Serious Proposal to the Ladies* (see MV 4.V) concerning women's education, which appeared in 1694, would go through four editions by 1701. Astell, supposedly retired in the country, 'thought an Afternoon wou'd not be quite thrown away in pursuing some Reflections' on the published account of the notorious Duke and Duchess of Mazarin's unhappy marriage, *The arguments of Monsieur Herard for Monsieur the Duke of Mazarin against Madam the Dutchess of Mazarin, his spouse and the factum for Madam the Dutchess of Mazarin against Monsieur the Duke of Mazarin, her husband by Monsieur de St. Evremont* (1699). Astell's reading of Hortense's marriage and wedded life pushed her to ask 'if Marriage be such a blessed State, how comes it, may you say, that there are so few happy Marriages?'[37]

---

[36] *The Duke of Norfolk's Case*, 1.   [37] Astell, *Some Reflections Upon Marriage*, 12.

For Astell, the initial answer can be found in the reasons that customarily govern why people marry: reminding one of the characters in Congreve's *The Way of the World*, she observes: 'For pray, what do Men propose to themselves in Marriage? What Qualifications do they look after in a Spouse? What will she bring is the first enquiry? How many Acres? Or how much ready Coin?' (p. 13). Marriage based on beauty or even love has shaky prospects, 'there's no great hopes of a lasting Happiness', she concludes (p. 21). And it is not only the men who marry for inappropriate reasons, although, as she points out, 'a Woman indeed can't properly be said to Choose, all that is allow'd her, is to Refuse or Accept what is offer'd' (p. 23).

In addition to pointing to the inadequacies governing why people marry, Astell charges that the institution itself is founded on principles of absolute authority, which England had rejected in its own government. A wife, she points out, put herself 'entirely into her Husband's Power, and if the Matrimonial Yoke be grievous, neither Law nor Custom afford her that redress which a Man obtains' (p. 28). Instead 'Patience and Submission are the only Comforts that are left to a poor People, who groan under Tyranny, unless they are Strong enough to break the Yoke, to Depose and Abdicate, which I doubt wou'd not be allow'd of here' (p. 28). Ironically, she highlights, 'for whatever may be said against Passive-Obedience in another case, I suppose there's no Man but likes it very well in this; how much so ever Arbitrary Power may be dislik'd on a Throne, Not *Milton* himself wou'd cry up Liberty to poor *Female Slaves*, or plead for the Lawfulness of Resisting a Private Tyranny' (p. 29). Grimly, she concludes: 'She then who Marrys ought to lay it down for an indisputable Maxim, that her Husband must govern absolutely and intirely, and that she has nothing else to do but to Please and Obey' (p. 59). In an appendix to the 1730 edition, she directly invokes again the rhetoric of the Civil War republicans, she demands: 'If *all Men are born free*, how is it that all Women are born slaves?... why is Slavery so much condemn'd and strove against in one Case, and so highly applauded and held so necessary and so sacred in another?'[38]

In his advertisement prefacing the first edition of Astell's polemic on marriage, the publisher explains the reason why there is no name on the title page. 'To name but one', he points out, '*Who will care to pull upon themselves an Hornet's Nest?*'. 'Bold Truths', he continues, 'may pass while the Speaker is *Incognito*, but are seldom endur'd when he is known' (sig. A2r). While many books were published without an author's name, it is clear, however, from other forms of advertising that in many instances the author's name and public recognition were featured prominently by booksellers in their marketing of new titles.[39]

Nutt's printing of an advertisement to announce the forthcoming publication of an item of interest also reflects the healthy market for readers who were willing and able to pay a penny for the news of the day in one of the three thrice-weekly

[38] Astell, *Some Reflections Upon Marriage* (1730 edn), 150.
[39] See Griffin, 'Anonymity and Authorship', and 'Introduction'.

newspapers that had begun publishing in the 1690s. The *Post Boy* (published by Abel Roper), the *Post Man*, and the *Flying Post* (published by the Scot George Ridpath) were still more concerned with happenings abroad, but also carried reports of the meeting of the Scottish Parliament and affairs in Ireland. John Dunton, writing in 1706 about 'the Secret History of the Weekly Writers', declares that the Huguenot M. Fonvive is the author of the *Post Man*, appearing Tuesday, Thursday, and Saturday, which brings him a living of £600 a year. 'His News is early and good, so his style is excellent', Dunton declares, 'his fancy is brisk and beautiful...Fonvive is the glory and mirror of News-Writers', he concludes, 'a very grave, learned, and orthodox man' (Dunton, *Whipping-Post*, 94–5).

Such notices are also a window into the publishing business and its rivalries as well as the vicissitudes of authorship. Dated London, 22 February, one advertisement asserts, 'Whereas *Advertisements* are This Day Printed in the *Post-Boy*, *Post-Man*, and *Flying Post*, That a Book Intituled, *The History of the Reign of* Lewis *the Thirteenth, King of* France *and* Navarre, *&c* by Mr *Michel le Vassor*, is This Day Publish'd by *John Nutt*; RICHARD WELLINGTON (the known Publisher) being asham'd to put this Name to it', and opens aggressively, 'this is to acquaint the World, That the same is a False and Spurious Edition of the said Book, the Translator having mistaken the Author's Sense, leaving out whole Paragraphs together; the Whole being slubber'd over by a Careless Hand'. Those desiring this book should know that 'a Translation is Printing, and will be Publish'd in a Fortnight; Every Sheet of which is Corrected and Revised by Mr. *Vassor* himself. Printed for *Thomas Cockerill*, Bookseller in the *Poultrey*'.

In addition to notices about forthcoming publications, auctions, and sales, advertisements appearing in 1700 also demonstrate their growing use to secure business for a variety of professions and the evolution of a rhetoric of marketing. From a reading of these advertisements, consumers in 1700 apparently desired a combination of the new and ingenious with practical application, a product that improved one's life in a wholesome fashion. An ingenious 'Swimming Girdle' is 'so portable that one will go into a Coat-pocket, or put on under a Surtoot-Coat cannot be discern'd', one advertisement enthused; in addition to being beneficial to sailors and ferry passengers, they can also be used to teach youth to swim '(& Ladys too if they please)', and, dramatically, when crossing rivers, 'a man may not only save his life, but his *Horse* too, without losing time'.[40] The virtues of the 'Jatropoton' enable it with just a few drops to be a 'most *Grateful* and *Wholesome Corrective* of all *Noxious Aigre*; too *Sharp* and *Flat Drink*': 'it makes all too *Thin, Sharp, Raking, Tartareous* Wines, to the *Palate, richer* and more *agreable* as well as more *wholesome*', and one bottle is sufficient '*to correct many Gallons of Drink*'.[41]

Medical practitioners in particular found advertisements and also broadsides to be profitable ways of letting the public know about their services.

---

[40] *Proposals for Selling the Swimming Girdles.*   [41] *Jatropoton.*

These advertisements were frequently designed to appeal to both the eye and the ear, even when the topic is somewhat unsavoury. In a handbill printed with an elaborate scene at the top of Venus in her chariot on the sea drawn by doves and surrounded by cupids, the advertisement wishes 'to give Notice unto all Persons whom it may concern, that hath been sporting in *Venus* Garden, to come unto me, and I will help them in as short a time as any one, to the admiration of all people'. The never named 'High Renowned Operator, Artist, Master, or Traveller' has recently come to England bringing with him an 'excellent, rare, specifick, amiable and cordial Remedy, prepared by a new invention against the POX' that has been 'approved of in many Nations by several Princes'. The attraction of his new cure is that 'the said Medicine if a Friend to nature, and easie to take, having no bad taste, and will Cure you, that none of your nearest Relation can take notice of it; you may walk, ride, sit, stand, or go abroad' while taking it. Ladies suffering from such complaints may also 'speak with his Wife, and she shall relieve them very secretly'.

One feels that the fiction printed in 1700 is not far removed from the wonderful abilities of 'Operator, Oculist, and Rupture Masters', from the real accounts of scandalous behaviour in aristocratic households, and the comedies set in real time, real world London. Even when, like Mary Pix's, the fictions boast their continental origins, they are nevertheless familiar to their English readers. Alonso de Castillo Solórzano's (1584?–1647?) picaresque tale *La garduña de Sevilla*, having been originally translated by John Davies of Kidwelly (1625–93), appeared in 1700 as it had been abridged by 'E.W.', Edward Waldron, who poses as the translator both on the title page ('*by the Ingenious Mr E.W. A known Celebrated* AUTHOR') and in the letter to the reader, as *The Life of Donna Rosina, A Novel*. Sold for a shilling by Benjamin Harris, it features a lurid frontispiece involving a night-time bedroom scene with two ladies in revealing dress; the novel promises 'a pleasant account of the Artifices and *Impostures* of a Beautiful Woman, who Jilted and Cheated the most Experienc'd *Sharpers*, and male all Persons Unhappy, that Thought her Handsome'.[42]

Likewise Aphra Behn's short fiction was enjoying its fourth edition in 1700, published by both Samuel Briscoe (printed by 'W.O.') as *History, Novels and Translations* and by Richard Wellington as *All the Histories and Novels Written by the Late Ingenious Mrs Behn*, which is based on earlier editions by Briscoe (see CV 4.V).[43] The 1700 edition done by Wellington includes, as did Briscoe's earlier versions, the 'LIFE and MEMOIRS' of Behn supposedly written by 'one of the Fair Sex', but whom critics have felt most likely to be Charles Gildon. Her memoir itself turns Behn into a comic heroine, describing her adventures in the Netherlands and her supposed witty exchanges and letters with her Dutch and London suitors. These later compilation editions of Behn's

---

[42] *The Life of Donna Rosina*, title page.
[43] For issues with the attribution of pieces in this volume to Behn, see Leah Orr, 'Attribution Problems'.

fiction by both printers include what many critics believe are Behn's genuine love letters to John Hoyle.

There were also comic fictions about love and romance where the emphasis was on the virtuous outcome of young lovers' disguises and intrigues. Congreve's short fiction *Incognita, or Love and Duty Reconciled* (1692), which had marked his debut as a professional writer, was reprinted in 1700 and also repackaged as one of three fictions included in the publisher Jacob Tonson's *A Collection of Pleasant Modern Novels* (1700). Congreve described this story of love found during a masquerade in Florence as being 'an essay begun and finished in the idler hours of a fortnight's time', and its themes and situations closely resemble a social comedy for the stage.

In addition to reprints of Behn and Congreve, 1700 also saw numerous cheap reprints of usually anonymous stories of adventure and romance, such as *The Famous and Delightful History of the Golden Eagle*, described in its long title as containing 'many other Adventures, both Pleasant and Profitable', the popular *The Famous and Renowned history of Valentine and Orson... containing their Marvelous Adventures in Love and War*, which first appeared in English in 1550 and, like *The Golden Eagle*, was also reprinted by 'W.O.', 'newly Printed and Abbreviated for the Benefite and [educ]ation of young Men and Maids, whose Impatience will [not suf]fer to read the larger Volume'. Likewise, Thomas Deloney's *c.*1612 short *The Pleasant history of Cawwood the Rook or the Assembly of Birds* includes *fit Morals and Expositions added to every Chapter in W.O.'s 1700 edition*. There was clearly a market for fiction, from inexpensive editions of favourite adventures and tales with their simple woodcut illustrations to collections of 'histories and novels' by prominent contemporary writers whose name on the title page could be expected to increase their sales.

There were also significant new versions of more weighty titles for fiction readers. Peter Anthony Motteux (1663–1718) published the first set of volumes of his edition of *The History of the most Ingengious Knight Don-Quixote de la Mancha*, with the remaining volumes appearing in 1703. Motteux, who also had several of his songs from various plays published in 1700, edited Thomas Shelton's translation, which had been revised by 'Captain John Stevens'; it was, the title page announced, a lavish volume with '33 Copper Plates curiously Engraved from the *Brussels* Edition'. It is also notable for incorporating the efforts of his friends and literary associates Wycherley, Congreve, Sir Samuel Garth, and Thomas Brown. As the advertisement explained, the translator and editor, not wishing to undertake the translation of the tale's verses, involved several others in the effort, and, while 'the true Turn and Design of the Author' is observed carefully, nevertheless 'Liberty is to be allow'd' in the translation of verses in order that 'they may appear with any Grace and Spirit'.[44]

---

[44] Motteux, *Don Quixote*, 'Translator's Preface'.

Brown's own *Amusements serious and comical, calculated for the meridian of London*, printed by Astell's printer John Nutt, was an altogether more affordable and topical fiction. Adopting his characteristic persona of the sophisticated man about town, Brown declares in his preface that 'I have given the following Thoughts the Name of *Amusements*; you will find them Serious, or Comical, according to the Humour I was in when I wrote them; and they will either Divert you, Instruct you, or Tire you, after the Humour you are in when you read them'.[45] 'I have a great mind to be in Print', he continues, but he wishes to be 'an Original', even though 'nothing will please some Men, but Books stuff'd with Antiquity, groaning under the weight of Learned Quotations drawn from the Fountains' (pp. 5, 7). In contrast, Brown announces, he will not ransack the ancients, 'but Pillage all I give you from the Book of the World' (p. 7). Foreshadowing some of Addison's and Steele's London essays, which would appear in the *Spectator* in the following decade (see MV 5.III), Brown offers lively descriptions of various public locations and characters of London: 'London is a World by itself', he opens one story, 'there are among the *Londoners* so many Nations differing in Manners, Customs, and Religions, that the Inhabitants themselves don't know a quarter of them' (p. 18). 'Thus I am resolv'd to take upon me the Genius of an *Indian*, who has had the Curiosity to Travel hither among us who had never seen anything like what he sees in *London*. We shall see', Brown declares, 'how he will be amazed at certain things, which the Prejudice of Custome makes to seem Reasonable and Natural to us' (p. 19).

The visiting Indian is immediately overwhelmed by the amount of traffic in the London streets, of chairmen calling to make way for their passengers, coaches, and hand carts all jostling for space as hawkers, tinkers, and peddlers shout:

Have you Brass Pot, Iron Pot, Kettle, Skillet, or a Frying-Pan to mend…Two a Groat, and Four for Six Pence Mackarel. One draws his Mouth up to his Ears, and Howls out, Buy my Flawnders, and is followed by an Old Burly Drab, that Screams out the Sale of her Maids and her Sole at the same Instant. (p. 21)

Stunned, the foreign visitor observes:

While I behold this Town of *London*, continues our Contemplative Traveller, I fancy I behold a Prodigious Animal. The Streets are as so many *Veins*, wherein the People Circulate. With what Hurry and Swiftness is the Circulation of *London* perform'd? You behold, say I to him, the Circulation that is made in the Heart of *London*, but it moves more briskly in the Blood of the *Citizens*, they are always in Motion and Activity. Their Actions succeed one another with so much Rapidity, that they begin a Thousand Things before they have finish'd one, and finish a thousand others before they have begun them. (p. 23)

Brown continues his tour through 1700 London's 'amusements' taking in the court and the public walks, coffee houses, 'the City Circle' or a lady's social

---

[45] Brown, *Amusements serious and comical*, 3.

assembly, and gaming houses, in addition to the amusements of the imaginary 'Countries' of London, 'Gallantry', 'Marriage', and 'Physick'.

In a similar fashion, Edward 'Ned' Ward (1667–1731), a writer whose publications in the late 1690s and early 1700s matched or outstripped those of the prolific Brown and who would over the next decade produce some 100 attributable satires, made good use of the first-person story of travels in England. Ward had his highly successful series of imaginary journeys published in the 1690s culminate with *The London Spy*, a tour of the criminal underside of London, which was published in eighteen monthly instalments starting in 1698 and concluding in 1700. His real life unsuccessful journey to make his fortune, *A trip to Jamaica with a true character of the people and island. By the author of Sot's paradise*, was also reprinted in 1700. He also offered 1700 readers 'tours' of Hell (a satire on dishonest wine merchants), Bath, and Stourbridge Fair, outside Cambridge. These short, typically sixteen-page, inexpensive pamphlets were sold for sixpence by his publisher J. How in Fenchurch Street. Ward's *Step to Stir-Bitch-Fair with remarks upon the University of Cambridge* includes a description of his stage ride there, his opinion of his fellow travellers, and the amusing songs they inspire. Arriving in Cambridge, he is less than impressed by the university—'in plain Terms is a Corporation of Ignorance, hem'd round with Arts and Sciences, a Nest of Fools, that dwell on the Superfluities of the Learned, an ingrateful Soil where the Seeds of Generosity are daily scatter'd, but produce nothing in return but the Wicked Weeds of Unthankfulness and Ingratitude'.[46] Leaving the town behind him, he strolls the mile to the next village to take in all the various sights, sounds, and smells from the booths and amusements to be found at Stourbridge Fair, offering a lively account of quacks with their medicines, madams with their willing girls, and merchandise of all kinds.

That same year, he offered the much more sensational and seamy travels of *The rambling rakes, or, London Libertines*, which recounts the fictional day and night of a fashionable young London male. 'Having spen the remainder of the day (when I had left you) after a Drunken and Libidinous manner, about Ten a Clock at Night, I stagger'd from my Company, and rambled about Streets, in quest of Common Game', he opens.[47] Not content with those pleasures, he hopes that 'the Wickedness of the Night, might Crown the Debaucheries of the Day; and that I might continue a Fashionable Libertine in a hot pursuit of Vice without any Cessation, lest an Interval should cool me into Sober reflecting on my past Lewdness' (p. 12). Finding what he believes to be an appropriate whore for his needs, he accompanies her back to her house, but in the morning is awakened by the landlord pounding on the door demanding rent, and finds himself naked and alone in a completely stripped household, except for 'the Dead Carcase of a Woman which marry'd men generally

---

[46] Ward, *Step to Stir-Bitch-Fair*, 14. [47] Ward, *The rambling rakes*, 12.

account to be their best Houshould stuff' (p. 14). The hungover hero hastily agrees to pay the rent in order that his father shall not hear of his 'Scandalous an Adventure' and disinherit him.

Such stories of London nightlife, whether Brown's well-born society gallantry or Ward's lurid and grotesque street scenes, are typically accompanied by a moral platitude:

> If such a Trick won't cool the Lust of Man,
> Sure nothing but Age, Death, or Sickness, can:
> Reader take Care of Jilts, for here you see,
> Living or Dead, they have been Plagues to me. (p. 15)

But to counter these fictionalized exploits of dashing young men in London's high and low society, there was also a steady production of conduct literature for both sexes specifically aimed at curbing such behaviours that 1700 fiction seems to foster. Brief pamphlet texts such as *The Apprentices Faithful Monitor* reminds young readers that God's eye is perpetually on them and urges them, in addition to honouring their parents as well as their masters or mistresses, particularly to 'carefully avoid all wicked Company, (that Snare of the Devil) whereby young Men are often drawn to the Commission of expensive Sins'.[48] One illustrated broadside ballad, *The Children's Example*, tells the story in verse of 'Mrs *Johnson's* Child' who was 'tempted by the Devil to forsake GOD, and follow the Ways of other wicked Children, who used to Swear, tell Lies, and disobey their Parents', but 'this pretty innocent Child resisting Satan, was comforted by an Angel from Heaven, who warned her of her approaching Death', sung to the tune of 'Bleeding Hearts'. *A Flaming Whip for Lechery: Or, the Whoremasters Speculum* offers adults a 'fearful Historical RELATION of such Wicked and unclean Persons, as have been made Publick and Private Examples of GOD's Divine Vengeance', and includes 'good Councel and Advice; With timely Warning, and serious Admonitions to Amendment of Life, and speedy Reformation of Manners'.[49]

The London-based Society for the Reformation of Manners, which had been formed in 1696 (see CV 4.IV) to check what their members saw as an alarming increase in sexual promiscuity, profanity, drinking, and gambling in society at large, was not identified with any one religious denomination or political position. Sermons that were given to the various Reformation of Manners societies in Portsmouth, London, and elsewhere in 1700 form a solid body of publications advocating action against the immorality of the times. They often invoked William III's own proclamations, as noted by the minister Robert Flemming in *Theokratia, or the Divine Government of Nations Considered and Approved* in its second edition in 1700: 'both in your Speeches to your Parliaments and Proclamations to your Subjects', Flemming observes,

---

[48] *The Apprentices Faithful Monitor*, sig. A1ʳ. [49] *Flaming Whip*, title page.

William's urging that existing laws 'might be put in due execution against open Wickedness, doth fully assure us, that it is none the least of your Regal Cares and Heroical Designs, to raise the Genius of your People by bettering their Morals'.[50] William and Mary in such sermons and accounts stand as iconic figures whose reigns, unlike those of Charles II and James II, symbolize piety and moral living. *An Account of the Societies for the Reformation of Manners in England and Ireland*, in its third edition by 1700, highlights the ways in which 'sincere Religion became the Jest and Scorn of our Courts in the late Reigns', when sin became 'fashionable'.[51]

To assist in their campaign against profanity, and against prostitution in particular, the societies published texts containing abstracts of all the penal laws against vice and blank forms of warrants to be issued for offences as well as suggestions for how to give evidence in cases before magistrates. *A Help to a National Reformation* (1700) was 'printed for the Ease of Magistrates and Ministers, and the Direction and Encouragement of private Persons, who, in any part of the Kingdom, are ingaged in the Glorious Work of *Reformation*' and also provides a guide for forming a Society for Reformation of Manners in 'any City, Town, or larger Village of the Kingdom'.[52]

Daniel Defoe, in the third edition of his *The Poor Man's Plea*, likewise points to William's endorsement of the cause as one reason why demand for his pamphlet has been so high as to require numerous reprintings. Defoe's argument is that, while laws and punishments can be enforced by magistrates to compel certain behaviours, 'Example is Persuasive and Gentle, and draws by a Secret, Invisible, and almost Involuntary Power'.[53] 'Immorality', he opens his text, 'is without doubt the present reigning distemper of the Nation: and the King and Parliament, who are the proper Physicians, seem nobly inclin'd to undertake the Cure' (pp. 1–2). Beginning in the court of James I, 'in the time of King *Charles* the Second, Lewdness and all manner of Debauchery arriv'd to its Meridian' (p. 4), Defoe asserts. It was the open example of the court that encouraged the general public decline in morals, 'an invincible Demonstration how far the Influence of our Governors extends in the Practice of the People' (p. 4).

This prompts the future author of *Moll Flanders* to issue his request to the 'Nobility, Gentry, Justices of the Peace, and Clergy' that they will 'be pleased either to reform their own Manners, and suppress their own Immoralities, or find out some Method and Power impartially to punish themselves when guilty' (p. 7). 'We find some People very fond of Monopolizing a Vice ... they must, as my Lord *Rochester* said of himself, *Sin like a Lord* ... they must be Lewd at a rate above the Common Size, to let the World see they are capable of it' (p. 16). The Poor Man, however, 'sees no such Dignity in Vice, as to study Degrees; we

---

[50] Flemming, *Theokratia*, p. iii.   [51] *An Account of the Societies*, 3.
[52] *A Help to a National Reformation*, title page.   [53] Defoe, *Poor Man's Plea*, sig. A2ᵛ.

are downright in Wickedness, as we are in our Dealings; if we are Drunk, 'tis plain Drunkenness; Swearing, and Whoreing, is all Blunderbus with us; we don't affect such Niceties in our Conversation' (p. 16). What is the common person supposed to believe, Defoe demands, when '*the Parson preaches a thundering Sermon against Drunkenness, and the Justice of the Peace sets my poor Neighbor in the Stocks, and I am like to be much the better for either, when I know perhaps that this same Parson and this same Justice were both Drunk together the Night before?*' (p. 25). The reformation of the coming century is essential, Defoe asserts, but it will not be achieved by the already wealthy and powerful condemning the behaviours of the poor. If a new Britain is to be formed in the decade following 1700, it would involve not only a moral reformation, but also the creation of a new nation, Great Britain, and a new perspective of the nature of English virtues.

II. Laws Regulating Publication, Preaching, and Performance, 1700–1714

The lapse of the Licensing Act in 1695 coincided with the passing of legislation ensuring elections would be held every three years, the Triennial Act. Daniel Defoe observed in his periodical the *Review* that 'the certainty of a new election in three years is an unhappy occasion of keeping alive the divisions and party strife among the people, which otherwise would have died of course'.[54] 'The Rage of Party' during this period was continually fed by an outpouring of political writings, pamphlets, newspapers, broadsides, and ballads. Historians such as J. A. Downie attribute the flourishing of the 'fourth estate' or the political press to the successful creation of political propaganda machines, complete with a distribution network for these texts throughout the country, and to the involvement of some of the most popular writers of the day, including Daniel Defoe, Jonathan Swift, Delarivier Manley, Joseph Addison, and Richard Steele.

Although it encouraged the creation of pro-government political propaganda literature, the government had not given up attempting to pass further licensing acts and attempting to control through various means what was printed, read, and performed. During the period up to the passage of the 1710 Act of Anne, the first concerning the concept of copyright enforced by the government and courts, the government made use of four avenues of censorship: prosecutions for high treason, Parliamentary prosecutions, general warrants, and seditious libel.[55] Concerning the definition of high treason, in a significant change from the turbulent times surrounding the Popish Plot (see CV 3.II) when to speak of even imagining harm to the King was legally treason, proof

---

[54] Quoted in Downie, *Robert Harley*, 1. [55] See Siebert, *Freedom of the Press*, ch. 18.

of an overt act was now required to convict for high treason. In 1707, an Act of Parliament did make it treason to print or write that the exiled son of James II, James Stuart (or, as he was called, James III, 'the Pretender') or any of his off-spring was the legitimate King of England.

The second means of control was exercised by both Houses of Parliament, which had the right to summon and examine individuals who were believed to be printing works considered to be 'breaches of privilege'. These were writings that were deemed libellous of a Member of Parliament, that contained negative reflections on Parliament, that cast aspersions on the monarch and his or her ministers, or that were particularly egregious cases of obscenity and blasphemy. The House of Commons was assiduous in defending its members and its own reputation, targeting primarily newspaper printers such as John Tutchin and the *Observator* and Samuel Buckley and the *Courant* (see CV 5. III). In 1701, the Commons issued a set of rules, one of which states that 'to print, or publish any Books or Libels, reflecting upon the Proceedings of the House of Commons, or any member thereof, for, or relating to, his service therein, is a high violation of the Rights and Privileges of this House of Commons'.[56]

This ruling extended to the writings of its own members. Richard Steele (bap. 1672–1729), while continuing to publish his political periodical the *Englishman*, was expelled from his newly won seat in Parliament in 1714 for the publication of a pamphlet entitled *The Crisis*. This piece of Whig political propaganda warned of the dangers of a Catholic successor to the ailing Queen Anne; the pamphlet by some estimates sold nearly 40,000 copies, and drew forth the Tory rebuttal branding it as seditious, *The Publick Spirit of the Whigs* by Jonathan Swift (1667–1745).

The third means of government control was the use of a general warrant for seditious libel.[57] Tutchin's verse satire on William III, *The Foreigners* (1700), resulted in him being taken by a warrant and brought before the Grand Jury in London for libel but acquitted because he had not used the actual names of William's ministers in it (see MV 5.I). In 1703, he was arraigned before the House of Commons for seditious libel published in the newspaper the *Observator*, 8–11 December, which was described as 'scandalous and malicious, reflecting upon the Proceedings of this House, and tending to the promoting Sedition in the Kingdom' (CJ 14. 269–79). Even though convicted on this occasion, Tutchin escaped punishment because an error in the procedure caused the proceedings to be declared null. This did not please those in power: Robert Harley (1661–1724), the employer of Daniel Defoe and future Prime Minister, received a letter from the Duke of Marlborough in which the Duke bluntly declared: 'If I can't have justice done me, I must find some friend that will break his and the printer's bones.'[58]

[56] Quoted in Siebert, *Freedom of the Press*, 371.
[57] See Treadwell, 'The Stationers and the Printing Acts'; Robertson, *Censorship and Conflict*, ch. 5.
[58] Quoted in J. A. Downie, 'Tutchin, John (1660x64–1707)', *ODNB*.

Defoe himself was heavily fined and sentenced to stand in the pillory for three days for his verse satire *Shortest Way with the Dissenters* (1702). It was written in response to the Occasional Conformity Bill debated in 1702, which would eventually be passed in 1711 as the Toleration Act, an Act that was designed to bar nonconformists and Catholics from taking 'occasional' part in the Church of England Communion in order to be eligible for public office. Defoe's poem parrots the language of High Church leaders demanding absolute conformity to the practices of the church, but with such heavy irony that both the dissenters and the churchmen were offended. However, the sentence was not popular with Defoe's reading public, who supposedly guarded him during his time in the pillory and sold copies of his *Hymn to the Pillory*: 'Hail hieroglyphic state machine, | Contrived to punish fancy in', it opens:

> But justice is inverted when
> Those engines of the law,
> Instead of pinching vicious men,
> Keep honest ones in awe.[59]

He concludes speaking of his own case:

> Tell them it was because he was too bold,
> And told those truths which should not have been told,
> Extol the justice of the land,
> Who punish what they will not understand. (p. 1)

Defoe's own contribution to the discussion of the ways in which the press could and should be controlled appeared in January of 1704, *An Essay on the Regulation of the Press*. Between the time of his being imprisoned and pilloried and the appearance of this essay, some of his own works had been published without his consent. The printer John How, capitalizing on Defoe's growing fame, produced *A Collection of the Writings of the Author of the True-Born English-man* (1703).[60] Six days after Defoe's publication calling for the regulation of the press, a Licensing Bill 'to restrain the Licentiousness of the Press' passed successfully through its first two readings in the House of Commons; however, in the push to pass the Occasional Conformity Bill, it failed to reappear.

In his essay, Defoe opens with the common-sense observation that 'all Men pretend the Licentiousness of the Press to be a publick Grievance, but it is much easier to say it is so, than to prove it or prescribe a proper Remedy'.[61] Although printing is 'own'd to be the most useful Invention ever found', Defoe notes, too many liberties are taken by 'Men of Wit in the World, the loose they give themselves in Print, at Religion, at Government, at Scandal' (pp. 3–4). However, he argues that a return to a licensing system 'makes the Press a slave to a Party; let

---

[59] Defoe, *Shortest Way*, 1.   [60] See Novak, *Daniel Defoe*, ch. 7.
[61] Defoe, *An Essay on the Regulation of the Press*, repr. with introduction by Moore (1947), 3.

it be which Party it will… whatever Party of Men obtain the Reins of Management, and have power to name the Persons who shall License the Press, that Party of Men have the whole power of keeping the World in Ignorance' (pp. 4–5). 'To Cure the ill Use of Liberty', Defoe argues, 'with a Deprivation of Liberty, is like cutting off the Leg to cure the Gout in the Toe' (p. 12). 'Licentiousness of all sorts ought to be Restrain'd, whether of the Tongue, the Pen, the Press, or anything else', he argues, but, as he would dramatize in his future criminal fictions such as *Moll Flanders*, 'Laws in their Original Design are not made to draw Men into Crimes, but to prevent Crimes… *Laws are Buoys* set upon dangerous Places under Water, to warn Mankind, that such Sands or Rocks are there, and the Language of them is, *Come here at your Peril*' (pp. 16, 19). Arguing much as John Locke had in his memorandum (see *MV* 4.II), Defoe urges that the law should make the 'last seller' of the text 'the Author' and that no book should be published without the names of the author, printer, and bookseller on the title page. Unlike Locke, however, Defoe's emphasis is on the author's role in these 'offences of the Pen'. First, he notes, it will finally link the crime and the punishment as opposed to the current system where authors are punished with 'such unequal Variety', some being fined minor amounts while others are forced to pay 1,000 marks. 'Writing of a Book has been punish'd with *Fines, Whippings, Pillories, Imprisonment for Life, Halters and Axes*', he notes, 'how 'tis possible the Guilt of the Pen can extend to merit all these several Penalties, is a thing I never met with a Lawyer yet that could resolve' (p. 25).

In addition, requiring all books to be published with the author's name might put a stop to 'a certain sort of Thieving which is now in full practice in England, and which no Law extends to punish, viz. some Printers and Booksellers printing Copies none of their own' (p. 25). This practice of literary piracy 'robs Men of the due Reward of Industry, the Prize of Learning and the Benefit of their Studies', he urges, and it robs the reader of having a text whose contents have been corrected and approved by the author (pp. 25–6). 'Some Mercenary Bookseller', he charges, 'employing a Hackney-writer' to abridge a popular work typically results in a mangled text, often at odds with the original author's intentions (see *MV* 5.IV). Another form of what Defoe calls 'Press-Piracy' is bringing out books in smaller print on poor paper to undercut the price of the original volume. If an author's name is required on the title page, he argues, the author has 'an undoubted exclusive Right to the Property of it' in terms of it being a patent to the author—if the law is to punish the author for the content of his book, then it should also protect his rights in it as being his property as a product of his labour.

In 1707, the Stationers' Company likewise was confronting the issue of pirated editions but from the point of view of the bookseller. They describe how pirated, cheap editions discourage authors who 'used to dispose of their Copies upon valuable Considerations, to be printed by the Purchasers… but of late Years such Properties have been much invaded, by other Persons printing the same Books'.[62] This bill failed in Parliament, some critics have argued, because it once again introduced licensing as the means of controlling what was printed. A second bill using language that focused exclusively on copyright or the concept of the text as property was successful in 1709, and in spring 1710 it was brought into law and became known as the Statute of Anne. Defoe wrote several articles in his periodical the *Review* expanding on the arguments made in the *Essay on the Regulation of the Press* and urging Parliament to 'secure the Authors of Books their Right of Property'.[63] In the 6 December 1709 issue, he argues passionately that, while we have 'Laws against House-breakers, High-way Robbers, Pick-Pockets, Ravishers of Women, and all Kinds of open Violence', authors have no protection.

During these public debates, Joseph Addison (1672–1719), writing in Steele's popular periodical the *Tatler* (see MV 5.III), took a similar position arguing for the preservation of the author's right to control his labour. 'All Mechanick Artizans are allowed to reap the Fruit of their Invention and Ingenuity without Invasion', he declares, but a scholar who has spent his entire life in the pursuit of useful knowledge 'has no Property in what he is willing to produce, but is exposed to Robbery and Want'.[64] He compares the writer's brain with a countryman's estate, land that must be carefully nurtured and tilled to produce. It is the skill of the farmer that creates the harvest, the labours of the mind that create the final text.[65]

The final version of the law, *An Act for the Encouragement of Learning, by vesting the Copies of Printed Books in the Authors or purchasers of such Copies, during the Times therein mentioned*, as its long title runs, was enacted in 1709 and became law in 1710. In it, the concept of a bookseller's having perpetual rights to a text such as had been enjoyed by printers in the seventeenth century was replaced by the notion of a limited copyright term. Publishers had the protection of law for fourteen years for newly acquired texts and twenty-one years for those already in print; copyright could be extended for a further fourteen years if the author was still living. Anyone other than the bookseller or printer holding the copyright who reprinted a text was subject to a fine, part of which went to the author and part to the Crown, and the pirated texts were to be destroyed. The statute continued the practice of requiring books to be registered with the Stationers' Company before publication as a means of identifying who held the copyright. Although the author is acknowledged as the original owner of this textual property, in this law authors were understood to have sold their products outright to the bookseller or printer. The language of the Act, as indicated in its long title, highlights not only the book in its original as the property of its author, but also the needs of the

---

[62] Quoted in Rose, *Authors and Owners*, 36.   [63] Defoe, *Review*, 6 December 1709.

[64] Addison, *Tatler*, 1 December 1709.

[65] See Rose, *Authors and Owners*, ch. 3, for a discussion of the changing metaphors of proprietorship.

public reading audience that desires useful literature to expand the general level of education.

This Act, therefore, had the effect of once and for all removing printed literary production from the grasp of pre-publication censorship by the means of licensing, which had been in force since the Restoration. 'The passage of the statute marked the divorce of copyright from censorship and the reestablishment of copyright under the rubric of property rather than regulation.'[66] It also broke the pattern of perpetual monopoly previously enjoyed by some publishers, such as Tonson's over Milton's texts. Some critics have argued that the inclusion of the author as having the original statutory copyright in this Act was less an affirmation of the rights of the author to control intellectual property but instead was simply a means of Parliament's divesting the booksellers of monopolies, and indeed in practice held little benefit for the authors.[67] Whether it was intended to do so or not, it did provide the initial language for future laws that would address more directly authorial proprietorship.

In addition to matters of copyright and piracy, other Acts had a direct effect on the publication of newspapers, pamphlets, and ephemeral literary materials. The Stamp Act of 1712, the statute for *Laying Down sever Duties upon all Sope and Paper made in Great Britain or imported into the same*, taxed not only paper itself, but also books and maps imported from abroad at the rate of £30 for every 100 pound weight; domestically made paper was taxed based on size and quality of the sheets.[68] It did have an exemption for paper used to print books in Latin, Greek, or 'Oriental or Northern Languages, within the two Universities of Oxford and Cambridge'; however, it was a heavy burden on other types of publication. There was a specific duty for 'Books and Papers commonly called Pamphlets, and for and upon all Newspapers or Papers containing publick News, Intelligence or Occurrences' (see CV 5.III). If the duty on any publication of more than one sheet was not paid, the author, printer, and publisher lost all title and every copy that was made, as well as having to pay a £20 fine.[69] While not a direct form of censorship, it did drive up costs for newspapers and pamphlets, and some historians have suggested it was a contributing factor in many, including the *Spectator* (see MV 5.III), ceasing to publish shortly before it came into effect.[70]

The spoken word, like the printed one, continued under government and church regulation. Although, compared to earlier times covered in this volume, in the first decade of the eighteenth century prosecutions of nonconformist and separatist ministers, dramatists, actors, and performers were low, censorship did not, however, vanish from the realm of preaching or performance. The

---

[66] Rose, *Authors and Owners*, 48.

[67] See Milhous and Hume, *The Publication of Plays*, 83–5, and Raven, 'Booksellers in Court'.

[68] See Deazley, *On the Origin of the Right to Copy*, 43.

[69] See Feather, 'The English Book Trade', chs 5, 6.

[70] Justice, *The Manufacturers of Literature*, 44.

Society for the Reformation of Manners and Jeremy Collier's attacks upon the immorality of the stage in the 1690s (see *MV* 4.II, 4.IV) were still having effects on what the public considered to be acceptable entertainment. Charles Killigrew, as he had since 1677, continued in his role as Master of the Revels, licensing strolling entertainers and watching for offensive content in the plays staged in London. However, in the atmosphere of public reformation of manners, strolling players were no longer made welcome in many of their former playing spaces (see *MV* 2.III; *MV* 3.IV): in August of 1701 plays were banned by the Lord Mayor from being performed at Bartholomew Fair, an edict that was repeated in August 1702, banning 'stage-plays, interludes, comedies, gaming, lotteries or musick meetings' there (*RETD* 1. 352, 362). The Court of Aldermen issued an order against posting playbills in public places in London. The Grand Jury at Bristol in December 1704 gave a presentment to suppress 'lewd and disorderly amusements', which included 'acting plays or interludes', and, in the summer of 1705, Cambridge University passed a resolution to prosecute stage players who attempted any performances there (*RETD* 1. 387, 395).

It was not only the strolling players and entertainers who were carefully watched for impropriety in their performances. In December 1700, the well-regarded comedians Thomas Doggett, Abigail Lawson, and Cave Underhill were charged with profanity for their performances in William Congreve's *Love for Love* (*RETD* 1. 350). In February 1702, Lord Chief Justice Holt found the actors of Lincoln's Inn Field Company guilty of 'most Abominable, Impious, Prophane, Lewd, and Immoral Expressions, contained in the Plays acted by them'; he hopes that by his sentence it will 'deter for the future such as shall write Plays from using any Lewd and Immoral Expressions' (*RETD* 1. 356). The actors, including the venerable Thomas Betterton, Elizabeth Barry, and Anne Bracegirdle, petitioned Queen Anne, arguing that they should not be prosecuted for appearing in plays that have been previously licensed by the appropriate censor (*RETD* 1. 361).

The Lord Chamberlain in January 1704 blamed the acting companies for failing to provide the Master of the Revels with copies of new materials until they were ready to be staged; he urged the Master of the Revels to be more diligent in preventing any profanity or scurrility from being performed (*RETD* 1. 377). Almost immediately after that, on 17–20 January 1704, Queen Anne issued her proclamation against vice and immorality in the theatre. Among the edicts it contained were that no woman should be permitted to wear a vizard mask in the theatre, no person 'of what quality so-ever' should be permitted to go behind the scenes of the stage nor go on the stage, no person should be admitted without paying, and that it was the duty of the theatre managers and the actors to ensure that 'nothing be Acted in either of the Theatres contrary to Religion or Good Manners upon Pain of our High Displeasure, and of being silenced from further Acting'.[71]

---

[71] See Jackson, 'The Stage and the Authorities', 59.

Perhaps the most famous legal literary spectacle during this period was not an actual stage play, but a series of public events involving preaching, the circulation of quickly printed pamphlets, a public trial, and an outpouring of public demonstrations across the countryside. Dr Henry Sacheverell (bap. 1674–1724) was first impeached and then brought before the House of Lords for the sermon he preached before the Lord Mayor of London in St Paul's Church on 5 November 1709 and subsequently published under the title of *The Perils of False Brethren*. The original sermon, which took nearly one and a half hours to deliver, was a fiery denunciation of the 'sectarist and schismatics of whatsoever wild, romantic or enthusiastic notions so as to make the House of God not only a den of thieves but a receptacle of Legions of Devils'.[72]

Sacheverell had been known for his outspoken attacks on dissenters during his time at Oxford, but it was this London audience and the subsequent printing and sale of an estimated 100,000 copies of the sermon that drew the alarmed gaze of the government.[73] Describing the 1689 Toleration Act as having had the effect of 'indulg[ing] and cherish[ing] such monsters and vipers in our bosom' (p. 25), Sacheverell charged that it was re-creating the religious and political environment that had caused the Civil War and the death of Charles I. The 'false brethren' referred to in the title were members of the government, including the Lord Treasurer, Godolphin, who was attacked by Sacheverell under the nickname 'Volpone', the rascally con artist of Ben Jonson's satiric comedy. The charges brought against Sacheverell included that he asserted there had been no active resistance in the 1688 Revolution, that he maintained that the Act of Toleration was 'unwarrantable', that he asserted that, under the reign of Anne, the Church of England was in 'great peril and adversity', and that, in her government, 'there are men of characters and stations in Church and State who are False Brethren and do themselves weaken, undermine and betray and do encourage and put it in the power' of enemies of the constitution.[74]

As historians have noted, Sacheverell's trial drew so much public attention that there was a 'paper war' of pamphlets both excoriating and defending him, some 500 items being preserved from that period.[75] The bookseller John Dunton (see *MV* 5.IV), for example, weighed in with *The Bull-Baiting: Or Sach—ll Dress'd up in Fire-Works. Lately brought over from the Bear-Garden in Southwark; and Expos'd for the Diversion of the Citizens of London* (1709). Dunton describes it on the title page as his observations on 'a Scandalous Sermon *Bellow'd* out at St Pauls';[76] after working through Sacheverell's sermon as it was printed, Dunton concludes, 'I can tell the Dr what I believe, would tend more to the Strength and Credit of the Church, than the Tything of Mint

---

[72] Sacheverell, *The Perils of False Brethren*, 13.

[73] See Downie, *Robert Harley*, 115–17, and W. A. Speck, 'Sacheverell, Henry (*bap.* 1674, *d.* 1724)', *ODNB*.   [74] See Holmes, *The Trial of Dr Sacheverell*, 280–2.

[75] See Downie, *Robert Harley*, 177, n. 53, and Madan, *A Critical Bibliography*.

[76] Dunton, *The Bull-Baiting*, title page.

and Annise: And 'tis CHARITY, MODERATION, and (which is more available still, to make Religion amiable) *more exemplary Lives of the Clergy of all sorts'* (p. 11). The anonymous pamphlet *The Mischief of Prejudice; or, some Impartial Thoughts about Dr Sacheverell's Sermon* (1710) more moderately takes the form of a dialogue between Citizen and Countryman, where Citizen patiently has to correct Countryman for believing that Sacheverell is a victim of being a good churchman and that the term 'Moderation' is a highly charged term of opprobrium. Other titles described it as a *Pulpit-War: Or, Dr S—ll, the High Church Trumpet, and Mr H—ly, the Low-Church Drum, Engaged. By the way of* DIALOGUE *between the Fiery Dragon, and Aspiring Grasshopper* (1710), offering its reader a verse exchange between Sacheverell and his public rival Benjamin Hoadly (1676–1761), the bishop of Winchester, with Sacheverell coming out with the last word.

The trial evolved into an elaborate piece of political theatre. There was so much interest in the trial that space in Westminster Hall had to be adapted in order to accommodate both the Houses of Parliament and nearly 1,000 spectators, requiring the efforts of Sir Christopher Wren and an army of workmen to have it ready for the opening day on 27 February 1710. Indeed, demand for seats was so high that, on the 23rd, the House announced that seven tickets could be issued to those appearing at the trial, 'on personal application', but commentators noted disparagingly the practice of 'all the ladies... making advance to the lords to get tickets from them to see and be seen at the trial'.[77] As the trial progressed, there were night-time riots in London, and dissenting chapels were destroyed as the crowds grew increasingly aggressive in their support of Sacheverell. Although the Lords found Sacheverell guilty in March, his sentence was comparatively light given the history of punishments handed down; he suffered no imprisonment or fine, but simply was barred from preaching for three years. High Church clergy and their Tory sympathizers viewed the trial and this lenient verdict as a triumph; bonfires appeared in celebration in Westminster, and in Oxford there was a procession in his honour, while in Exeter outside the cathedral the works of Sacheverell's arch rival, the Low Church and Whig-supported Bishop Benjamin Hoadly, were publicly burned.

On a much less dramatic scale during this same time, the dramatist, prose fiction writer, and political journalist Delarivier Manley (c.1670–1724) likewise found her writing catching the eye of hostile Whig readers in 1709 (see CV 5.III). In October of that year, nine days after the publication of Manley's *Secret memoirs and manners of several persons of quality of both sexes, from the new Atalantis, an island in the Mediterranean*, a secretary of state's warrant was issued for the arrest of Manley, the printers John Woodward and John Barber (the latter of whom was the printer of the Tory periodical the *Examiner*, which Manley and Jonathan Swift would edit) (see CV 5.III), and the bookseller John

---

[77] Quoted in Holmes, *The Trial of Dr Sacheverell*, 120.

Morphew for seditious libel. Manley remained in the gaol until 5 November and was eventually tried on 13 February 1710. The only surviving account of her trial appears in her highly fictionalized memoirs *The Adventures of Rivella*, where she records in her defence that she was amazed that they had charged 'a woman to her trial for writing a few amorous trifles' (see *CV* 5.IV).[78]

Her defence was that indeed this was simply a translation of a piece of fiction, and that all of the characters and events were inventions. She was acquitted, as one can imagine none of her targets in this sexually salacious *roman à clef* wished particularly to stand forward and identify themselves. Almost immediately, however, 'keys' or guides were published permitting readers to identify the characters in *New Atalantis* as leading Whig politicians and their wives. She had particularly targeted John Churchill, Duke of Marlborough, and his wife, Sarah, confidante of Queen Anne, suggesting that the paths to power went through the bedrooms of influential people. This racy satire is credited by some historians, along with the atmosphere created by Sacheverell's sermon and trial, in helping the Tories to bring down the Whig ministry.[79] The government and the church may have desired to reform the public at large, but, in 1700–14, readers and playgoers still found ways of obtaining news of the latest scandal or seeing dramas that pushed the boundaries of social propriety and set the tone of popular debate and entertainment.

III. Kit-Cats and Scriblerians: Clubs, Wits, the *Tatler*, the *Spectator*, and *The Memoirs of Martin Scriblerus*

While coffee houses and public meeting places still served as the informal homes of booksellers and writers (see *CV* 2.II), the turn of the century also saw the creation of specific clubs with select membership and public identities deeply engaged in both literary and political pursuits. Of these, the writings of Kit-Cats and the Scriblerians have retained their prominence through generations of readers, and their members created several of what have been viewed by subsequent decades of criticism as the signature literary works of the period.

The precise origins and date of the founding of the Kit-Cat Club remain unclear, but by the first decade of the eighteenth century the London group whose members included politicians, prominent physicians, artists, writers, publishers, and patrons was more than a dining and drinking club for London gentlemen. A powerful network based on friendship and mutual interests, the Whig Party Club may originally have been a private association among the supporters of William III, but it was brought together in a public way in the 1690s by the publisher Jacob Tonson (see *CV* 3.III), Dryden's long-time printer

---

[78] Manley, *The Adventures of Rivella*, 110–11. See Ros Ballaster, 'Manley, Delarivier (*c*.1670–1724)', *ODNB*.   [79] See Downie, *Robert Harley*, 115–16.

and collaborator. Tonson even created a room in his house at Barn Elms in Surrey in 1703 for its meetings and to house the celebrated 'Kit-Cat Portraits' done by the court painter Sir Godfrey Kneller. In earlier decades, Dryden had held court at Will's Coffee House, where aspiring young writers, including William Congreve and John Vanbrugh, gathered to meet other writers and to gain a foothold in the world of commercial literature, but, unlike the Kit-Cats, this group was not strongly associated with any single political party. The Kit-Cats, although often at odds with each other on an individual level, promoted a generalized political, cultural poetic with the aim of celebrating the English national character.

The prolific satirist Ned Ward, the author of *The London Spy*, writing in 1709 in *The Secret History of Clubs*, stated that the Club got its name from its original meeting place, a London tavern owned by Christopher Catling, the Cat and Fiddle in Gray's Inn Lane, and the mutton pies, or 'cats' that he made and sold there. Ward, who was not an admirer of Tonson or the Club, places it within his survey of apocryphal social groups including 'The Farting Club', 'The Club of Ugly Faces', and 'Bawd's Initiating Club', as well as other real ones such as 'The Beef-Steak Club', founded by the actor Richard Estcourt around 1705, and the anti-Charles I 'Calves-Head Club', which allegedly met every 30 January to celebrate the regicide.[80] Ward depicts Tonson under the name of 'Bocai', as 'an Amphibeous Mortal, Chief Merchant to the Muses' and a literary pirate; the original members he characterizes as 'a parcel of Poetical young Springs, who had just Wean'd themselves of their Mother University'[81]—members such as Congreve, Matthew Prior, and Addison, who, Ward, sneered, seemed unable to control their desire to burst into verse on royal occasions, such as the death of Queen Mary (see CV 4.V). Sir Richard Blackmore, in a poem published in 1709, had a more flattering portrait of the origins of the Club and its members. Writing in a mock-heroic style, Blackmore declares:

> Kit-Cat Wits sprung first from Kit-Cat's Pyes.
> BOCAI the mighty Founder of the State
> Led by his Wisdom, or his happy Fate,
> Chose proper Pillars to support its Weight,

and 'All the first Members for their Place were fit, | Tho' not of Title, Men of Sense and Wit'.[82]

Blackmore's poem goes on to describe how the rising fame of the Kit-Cats angered the 'Blockhead Race | Which the long Robe, Camp, Gown and Court disgrace' (p. 8). Continuing Dryden's characterization of bad poets and hack writers who 'never deviate into sense' in his mock epic *McFlecknoe* (see CV 4.V) and foreshadowing Pope's creation of the Queen of Dullness in *The Dunciad*, Blackmore portrays the Blockheads as rebelling against Tonson's

---

[80] Orihel, ' "Treacherous Memories" '.   [81] Ward, *The Secret History of Clubs*, 360, 361.
[82] Blackmore, *The Rise and Progress of the Kit Cat Club*, 5.

'Throne, by Sense and Wit upheld', and calling on the Hiberean 'God of Dulness', whose temple 'With rude Magnificence high in the Air | Thick Walls of Mud the Pond'rous Roof did bear' (p. 10). This

> Idol is compos'd of massy Lead,
> And Wreaths of Poppy Flowers adorn his Head.
> Lolling and yawning in his Chair of State,
> And dropping down his Head the drowsy Figure sate. (p. 11)

The Club, whatever its original purpose, gained powerful patrons, both literary and political, as well as powerful enemies. Charles Sackville (1643–1706), Earl of Dorset (see *MV* 3.III), was an early member; as the tensions between Whig and Tory escalated in Parliament in 1710 as the health of Queen Anne continued to decline, raising challenges to the Hanoverian succession, the most powerful members of the Whig party, the so-call Junta under William III (see *CV* 5.III), were also Club members, including Thomas Wharton, 1st marquess of Wharton, John Somers, Baron Somers, Charles Spencer, 3rd Earl of Sunderland, and Charles Montagu, Earl of Halifax. Although historians are hesitant to assign any specific political policy to the Club itself, given that it kept no minute record book of its meetings, in general its members were staunch supporters of the Hanoverian succession during the reign of Queen Anne and vigorously opposed to the peace negotiations proposed by the Tory government headed by Robert Harley, the Earl of Oxford, in 1711 during the War of the Spanish Succession (1701–14), all matters of grave concern that occasioned an outpouring of political pamphleteering by both Whig and Tory.

In their publications, members of the Kit-Cat Club shared a general belief in the power of cultural politics, and that art, whether literary, architectural, or dramatic, should help to inspire a new nationalism and secure support for building a prosperous and secure society based on Whig principles favouring the growth of commerce and religious toleration. In 1704, the Kit-Cats came together through subscription to finance the construction of a new theatre, the Queen's Theatre, Haymarket, designed by fellow member and dramatist John Vanbrugh (see *CV* 5.II). Vanbrugh, who had recently completed building Tonson's house at Barn Elms and was working on Castle Howard, wished to increase London venues for the Queen's favourite musical entertainments, and it was specifically designed to stage opera. Its site, a former stable yard, drew derision from the Tory writers—Daniel Defoe noted sardonically, 'Apollo spoke the word | And straight arose a Playhouse from a turd'—while fellow Kit-Cat Dr Samuel Garth applauded the triumphant transformation in terms that mirrored the Whigs hopes for the country: 'Your own magnificence you here survey, | Majestic columns stand where dunghills lay, | And cars triumphal rise from carts of Hay.'[83]

---

[83] Defoe, *Review of the Affairs of France*; Garth, 'Prologue Spoken at the Opening of the Queen's Theatre', in Garth, *The Poetical Works of Sir Samuel Garth*, 131. See Field, *The Kit-Cat Club*, ch. 9.

Vanbrugh and Congreve were made the theatre's artistic directors. The theatre would seat 900; it was lavishly decorated, with baroque gilded arches, and featured concentric balconies supported by columns, and its ceiling was painted to display 'Queen Anne's Patronage of the Arts', surrounded by the adoring Muses. The Queen was invited for a private performance prior to the theatre's official opening; shortly afterwards, she created a new licence for a new company 'reposing especial trust and confidence in Our Trusty and Well-beloved' Congreve and Vanbrugh to make every effort to reform 'the Abuses and Immorality of the Stage'.[84] As critics and historians have noted, this was particularly ironic, as Jeremy Collier in his 1690s attack on the immorality of the stage had singled out both Vanbrugh and Congreve as particularly egregious offenders (see *MV* 4.IV).

The Club was also strongly identified with refined literary culture as opposed to Grub Street commercialism and popular vulgar entertainments (see *MV* 5.IV). In the case of Addison and Steele, their political appointments and allegiances and the themes of their poetry and dramas were inextricably linked. Addison and Steele had formed a close friendship while schoolboys at Charterhouse in the 1680s. Addison, who had become a fellow of Magdalen College, Oxford, in 1698, had been well regarded as a poet of both English and Latin verses in the 1690s (see *CV* 4.V); in 1704, he published *The Campaign*, a long poem celebrating Marlborough's victory at Blenheim, and in 1708 was elected MP for Lostwithiel and given the post of secretary to Lord Wharton, newly appointed lord lieutenant of Ireland. Steele had also been publishing commendatory verse during this period as well as having his play *The Tender Husband* (1705) produced, supposedly amended by Addison (see *CV* 5.II). Significantly for his future literary output, in 1707, Steele was appointed editor of the *London Gazette*, the official news publication (see *CV* 5.III), by fellow Kit-Cat member Arthur Maynwaring (1668–1712); Maynwaring was at that time the Duchess of Marlborough's private secretary and was an influential patron for William Congreve as well as the actress Anne Oldfield. Steele began the *Tatler* in April of 1709, making good use of what he had learned about periodical publications while in charge of the *London Gazette*.[85]

Addison, too, wrote for the stage, producing the opera *Rosamond* (1707), dedicated to Sarah Churchill, Duchess of Marlborough. Addison, whose derision of Italian opera will be discussed later, chose for his theme the popular story of 'The Fair Rosamund', loosely based on Thomas Deloney's ballad on the life and death of Rosamund Clifford (before 1140?–1175/6). Clifford had been the mistress of Henry II, the founder of the Plantagenet dynasty; according to legend, he had created a pastoral bower for her at Woodstock, accessible only through a complex maze. Music for Addison's opera was provided by Thomas Clayton, who had been successful with his earlier Italian opera,

---

[84] Quoted in Field, *The Kit-Cat Club*, 138.
[85] Calhoun Winton, 'Steele, Sir Richard (*bap.* 1672, d.1729)', *ODNB*.

Arsinoe; as critics have noted, this new English opera was a failure, although Addison's lyrics were applauded (see *CV* 5.II).

In terms of promoting a Whig cultural poetics, however, it was a coherent and cohesive statement. Masques and operas, as has been noted, have frequently been read as political in nature, and certainly the Master of the Revels kept a keen eye on potentially disruptive content (see *MV* 5.II); in Addison's opera, however, it is the politics of praise rather than subversion.[86] Painted on the stage set was the image of how Blenheim Palace, the nation's gift to Marlborough for his military victories built on the ruins of Woodstock Palace, would appear after Vanbrugh had completed it; Addison's lyrics highlight the ways in which future glories arise from past ruined ones, further suggesting the links between past and present greatness. The prologue by Kit-Cat bon vivant and mentor to the young Alexander Pope, William Walsh (bap. 1662–1708), directly references Marlborough as Mars, god of war, and Henry II, but declares that 'Vertue now these statelier Mansions grace'. Critics have pointed to the repeated use of the terms 'British' and 'Britain' in the piece, which would perhaps have been particularly striking for the original audience, given that the Act of Union (see *CV* 5.I) between England and Scotland received royal approval two days after the opera's performance, and two months later in May 1707 the Act came into force.[87]

In the opera, Henry II is given a vision of what Rosamund's pastoral bower will become. 'Look up and see | What, after long revolving Years, | Thy Bow'r shall be!' and the stage direction explains '*Scene changes to the Plan of Blenhelm Castle*': 'Behold the glorious Pile ascending!'[88] Perhaps even more significant than the vision of a splendid national monument to an English hero arising from this historic ruin is Addison's decision to have a happy rather than a tragic ending. In his version, Rosamund is not poisoned by a jealous Queen Eleanor; instead Henry chooses conjugal happiness over his lust. As critics have noted, the event itself was a triumph of the construction of English national heritage.

In 1710, however, the victorious commander in chief of the British army in that conflict and Kit-Cat member, John Churchill, 1st Duke of Marlborough (1650–1722), found his power and influence with Queen Anne lessening as the estrangement grew between her and his wife, Sarah, Duchess of Marlborough. Sarah Churchill had long enjoyed a position of power and prestige in the court, from the 1670s when she had danced in the court masque *Calisto* with the then awkward young Princess (see *MV* 3.I) to her elevation in the Queen's court in 1702 to positions as groom of the stole and keeper of the Privy Purse. She was a passionate supporter of Whig policies. She became a target of satire herself, and many rejoiced when the Queen dismissed her from the court (see *MV* 5.V;

---

[86] On the difficulty of construing allegory, application, and subversion in opera of the period as a genre characteristic, see Hume, 'The Politics of Opera'.

[87] See Hammond, 'Joseph Addison's Opera *Rosamond*'.   [88] Addison, *Rosamund*, 28.

CV 5.IV). Her husband's fortunes fell at the same time as hers: following accusations that Marlborough had privately profited from the war, inflamed in part by Jonathan Swift's attack on him in his *Conduct of the Allies* (1711), the Queen dismissed her most successful general. Briefly, the Whigs found themselves excluded from the inner circle of political power, with Robert Harley, Earl of Oxford, now calling the game, and the satirists of both parties waging a paper propaganda war (see CV 5.III).

'The Song of the Kit-Cat Club' (1711), printed in the satiric pamphlet collection *The state bell-mans collection of verses, for the year 1711*, has them declaring 'We may for *Interest Loyalty* pretend | But a true *Whig* can be no *Prince's Friend*, | *Power* is his Aim, and *Wealth* his chiefest End'.[89] Jonathan Swift, writing for the Tory party in 1712, contributed *A Letter of Thanks from my Lord W[harton] to the Lord Bp of S. Asaph, in the Name of the Kit-Cat-Club*: in 1712 William Fleetwood, Bishop of Asaph, published four of his sermons preached before Queen Anne, and in its preface he was critical of the choices made by the Lord High Treasurer, Robert Harley, 1st Earl of Oxford, Swift's patron. It so incensed the Tory House of Commons that it was ordered to be burned on 12 May 1712, but the *Spectator* had also printed the preface in its no. 384. Fleetwood's own response to the event was to dismiss the burning in a letter to Bishop Burnet on 17 June 1712 as 'a piece of revenge taken by a wicked party, that found themselves sorely stung'.[90] Adopting the persona of Wharton, Swift, in the mock epistle, addresses Fleetwood from the perspective of the Club.

It was with no little Satisfaction I undertook the pleasing Task, assigned me by the Gentlemen of the *Kit-Cat-Club*, of addressing your Lordship with Thanks for your late Service so seasonably done to our Sinking Cause, in reprinting those most excellent Discourses, which you had formerly preached with so great Applause, though they were never heard of by us, till they were recommended to our Perusal by *The Spectator*,

it opens silkily.[91] 'The World will perhaps be surprized, that Gentlemen of our Complexion, who have so long been piously employed in overturning the Foundations of Religion and Government, should now stoop to the puny Amusement of reading and commending Sermons', Swift continues, thus labelling the Kit-Cat members as a group of atheists.

The public face of the Kit-Cat Club, however, and the one immortalized by subsequent generations viewing the party, was that of genteel toleration, cultivated sensibilities, and a vision of the English as nation apart, as staged by dramatists, celebrated in the pages of the *Tatler* and the *Spectator*, and represented in Kneller's forty-eight informal portraits of the members done between the late 1690s and 1720. In particular, Addison's stoic tragedy, *Cato* (1713), with a prologue by Alexander Pope and an epilogue by fellow Kit-Cat Dr

---

[89] *The state bell-mans collection*, 15.   [90] Quoted in Swift, *Works*, ed. Scott, 4. 180.
[91] Swift, *Letter of Thanks*, 5.

Samuel Garth (see CV 5.II), struck a chord of sympathy among audiences whether Whig or Tory.

Unlike *Rosamund*, *Cato* was extremely successful throughout the eighteenth century. Cato, who nobly resists the tyranny represented by Julius Caesar, reflects on themes of the liberty of the individual in the face of arbitrary government oppression. Pope's prologue emphasizes that, unlike earlier generation's pathetic she-tragedies (see MV 4.IV), this tragedy is designed to appeal to reason and to patriotism:

> Here tears shall flow from a more gen'rous cause,
> Such tears as patriots shed for dying laws.
> He bids your breasts with ancient ardour rise,
> And calls forth Roman drops from British eyes:
>
> .   .   .   .   .
>
> No common object to your sight displays,
> But what with pleasure Heav'n itself surveys,
> A brave man struggling in the storms of fate,
> And greatly falling with a falling state.[92]

Its topics concerning the nature of patriotism when confronted by tyranny resonated with audiences not only in England but also in New England, where it was very popular as well.

The most enduring and celebrated collaboration arising from the Kit-Cats was the creation of a series of periodical papers devoted not to news events but to essays on contemporary issues. The *Tatler* (1709–11) and the *Spectator* (1711–14) (see Figure 6), the first begun by Steele and the second by Addison, with multiple contributors during their runs, were briefly continued in Steele's the *Guardian* (12 March–1 October 1713), with contributions from Addison, Thomas Tickell, Ambrose Philips, and Alexander Pope.[93] These were not the first periodicals that had enjoyed a wide popular readership but they carried the form in a different direction and, rather than proving to be ephemeral publications, were collected, consolidated, bound in volumes, and reprinted throughout the eighteenth and nineteenth centuries, valued both for their content as well as for their literary style (see CV 5.III for discussion of their physical format and distribution). As subsequent generations of readers have noted, sociability, friendship, and the promotion of rational ethical behaviour are the heart of the schemes proposed in these volumes, and the elegantly written pieces involved numerous techniques to keep readers intrigued as well as instructed.

The *Tatler* first appeared on 12 April 1709, when Steele, having lost his position at court in 1708 after the death of Prince George, had turned again to journalism. The paper was issued three times a week on Tuesdays, Thursdays,

---

[92] Addison, *Cato*, 'Prologue'.
[93] Bond (ed.), *Spectator*; Aitken (ed.), *Tatler*; quotations from the *Spectator* and the *Tatler* are cited from these editions. See also Stephens (ed.), *Guardian*; *The Spectator Project* <http://www2.scc.rutgers.edu/spectator/project.html> (accessed 28 April 2017).

and Saturdays to match the schedule of the London post (see CV 5.III) and each issue was dated, frequently as coming from a particular coffee house, and written by 'Isaac Bickerstaff', a persona Steele took from Jonathan Swift's character predicting the death of the astrologer John Partridge in his 1708 series of satires on the same (see CV 5.IV). 'All accounts of gallantry, pleasure, and entertainment, shall be under the article of White's Chocolate-house', Bickerstaff assures his readers, whom he declares will be both male and female, 'poetry, under that of Will's Coffee-house; learning, under the title of Grecian; foreign and domestic news, you will have from St James's Coffee-house; and what else I shall on any other subject offer, shall be dated from my own apartment' (no. 1, 12 April 1709) (see MV 3.I). Steele thus was committed from the beginning to offering a diverse collection of topics in his paper, ranging from literary criticism and politics to contemporary fashionable life. In the dedication of the collected papers to Arthur Maynwaring published in an octavo format in 1710 under the title *The Lucubrations of Isaac Bickerstaff Esq; Revised and corrected by the author*, Steele explains that 'The general Purpose of this Paper, is to expose the false arts of Life, to pull off the Disguises of Cunning, Vanity, and Affectation, and recommend a general Simplicity in our Dress, our Discourse, and our Behaviour'.[94]

The theatre is an important topic in the early *Tatler*, and the essays show the shifting tastes of the time. In no. 3, 14 April 1709, a review of a performance of Wycherley's *The Country Wife* (see MV 3.I) is offered, and, while the acting is applauded, the general moral tone is not: 'the character of Horner, and the design of it, is a good representation of the age in which that comedy was written; at which time love and wenching were the business of life, and the gallant manner of pursuing women was the best recommendation at Court'. In the following issue, no. 4, 18 April, a successful opera is targeted for critique: *Pyrrhus and Demetrius* by Adriano Morselli was performed to 'great applause', which Bickerstaff feels is a pity, since 'the stage being an entertainment of the reason and all our faculties, this way of being pleased with the suspense of them for three hours together, and being given up to the shallow satisfaction of the eyes and ears only, seems to arise rather from the degeneracy of our understanding, than an improvement of our diversions', he states emphatically (see CV 5.II). This opera being primarily in Italian, the contents of it were thus incomprehensible to most of the English audience, a topic to which Addison would return in numerous *Spectator* issues, including nos 1, 5, and 13 (see Figure 5).

In addition to literary criticism, Steele and his contributors did not hesitate to address contemporary issues ranging from the stupidity of duels of honour (no. 25), the lottery (nos 124, 203), and the corruption of popular taste by crude entertainments (nos 12, 99), to absurdities in women's exaggerated fashions (Addison, no. 116). Steele goes after the figures of the rake and the coquette, stock characters in many of the entertainments created in the 1670s

---

[94] Steele, *Lucubrations*, p. v.

and 1680s, in nos 27 and 107. The rake is 'the most agreeable of bad characters', Bickerstaff announces; 'his faults proceed not from choice or inclination,
but from strong passions and appetites, which are in youth too violent for the
curb of reason, good sense, good manners, and good nature: all which he must
have by nature and education, before he can be allowed to be, or have been of
this order' (9 June 1709). He concludes that, 'As a rake among men is the man
who lives in the constant abuse of his reason, so a coquette among women is
one who lives in continual misapplication of her beauty'. In a later issue Steele
focuses on this female version of passions ungoverned by reason (no. 107,
15 December 1709). The essay opens when a despondent young man visits
Bickerstaff to ask how to handle his unhappiness in love: 'the Woman my Soul
doats on', who, having initially encouraged him, now has given her heart to
another. Bickerstaff regretfully informs him that the woman in question is a
coquette, which he defines as being 'a chast Jilt', and admits that 'about the
Thirtieth Year of my Age, I received a Wound that has still left a Scar in my
Mind, never to be quite worn out by Time or Philosophy'.

Steele developed the character of Bickerstaff to become an engaging,
although eccentric, and ageing figure, tended by his faithful servant Pacolet,
sitting amid his books of astronomy and reflecting on the changing ways of the
world. In particular, Bickerstaff reflects on how the concept of 'gentleman' has
changed over generations. For Bickerstaff, a 'gentleman, or man of conversation', displays 'the height of good breeding is shown rather in never giving
offence, than in doing obliging things' and the most necessary qualification is
'good judgment' of the company he is in (no. 21). In contemporary society, he
laments in nos 24 and 26, written by Addison, even a 'Pretty Fellow' can pass
for a gentleman: the very pretty fellow 'practices a jaunty Way of Behaviour',
highlighting his own wit and activities, and heedless of giving offence.
Bickerstaff's half-sister, Jenny Distaff, was created by Steele in no. 10 to narrate
the female perspective on such issues, taking on the role of a female editor and
'authoring' six of the issues at her brother's 'invitation'. 'My brother Isaac
having a sudden occasion to go out of town', she opens in no. 10, 1 May 1709,
'ordered me to take upon me the despatch of the next advices from home, with
liberty to speak it my own way; not doubting the allowances which would be
given to a writer of my sex'. Jenny Distaff contributes her views not only on
'the Empire of Beauty' in no. 10 but also on marriage and on male manners.
Her success with readers is suggested by the appearance of the *Female Tatler*
on 8 July 1709, featuring one Mrs Crackenthorpe.[95]

The successor to the *Spectator* was the *Guardian*, published daily and running between 12 March and 1 October 1713, which featured several of the contributors to early collaborative works. Tonson would publish a collected volume in 1714. In the first essay, the character of the first-person narrator was
explained: 'I should not have assumed the Title of Guardian, had I not maturely

---

[95] Italia, *The Rise of Literary Journalism*, 43–8.

considered, that the Qualities necessary for doing the Duties of that Character, proceed from the Integrity of the Mind, more than the Excellence of the Understanding.'[96] Readers should demand of a Guardian that he be 'Faithful, to be Honest, to be Just', as well as 'a Pleasant, Ingenious, and Agreeable' gentleman. 'The main Purpose of the Work', he declares, 'shall be to protect the Modest, the Industrious, to celebrate the Wise, the Valliant, to encourage the Good, the Pious, to confront the Impudent, the Idle, to contemn the Vain, the Cowardly, and to disappoint the Wicked and Profane' (p. 3). The essays are designed to further 'the Advancement of the Conversation of Gentlemen, the Improvement of Ladies, the Wealth of Trader, and the Encouragement of Artificers', and essays relating to 'those who excel in Mechanicks, shall be considered with particular Application'. The goal, he states, is 'to make the World see the Affinity between all Works which are beneficial to Mankind is much nearer, than the illiberal Arrogance of Scholars, will, at all times allow' (pp. 3–4). Finally, he concludes, the goal of the paper is 'no less, than to make the Pulpit, the Bar, and the Stage, all act in Concert in the care of Piety, Justice and Virtues' (pp. 4–5).

Writing to his friend John Caryll in June 1713, Alexander Pope agreed that the *Guardian* was a weak replacement for the *Spectator*, but defended the contributions by Steele, saying 'those he writes himself are equal to any he has wrote', but noting that Addison, like Pope, was only contributing once a month.[97] Of the 176 essays, Steele wrote 82, and others were contributed by Addison, Pope, Thomas Tickell, George Berkeley, Eustace Budgell, and Ambrose Philips. Instead of a gentleman's club, the narrative thread was woven around the members of the Lizard family, 'what passes at the Tea Table of my Lady Lizard' and 'the Members of this Family, their Cares, Passion, Interest and Diversion shall be represented from time to time, and News from the Tea Table of so accomplished a Woman' (p. 8). In general, the topics of the paper focused on matters of literary style and taste, from deriding fulsome dedications and bombastic stage practices, to Pope's observations on 'recipes' for epic (no. 78), the humane treatment of animals (no. 61), and gardens (no. 173).

Issue no. 62 has been attributed to George Berkeley (1685–1753), who would become the Church of Ireland bishop of Cloyne. He had been recruited by fellow Irishman Steele when Berkeley was visiting London in 1713. In no. 62, the narrator returns to Westminster School and reflects on his childhood. He ponders on the pleasures of 'the grateful Employment of admiring and raising themselves to an Imitation of polite Stile, beautiful Images, and Noble Sentiments of Ancient Authors', which will be eroded once they leave the school, replaced by 'Law-*Latin*, the Lucubration's of our Paltry News-mongers, and that swarm of vile Pamphlets which corrupt our Taste and Infest the Publick' (pp. 262–3). Schools and universities, he concludes, are 'Nurseries of Men for the Service of the Church and State', and to refine the taste to enjoy 'those Entertainments

---

[96] *The Guardian* (1714), 2.   [97] Pope, *Correspondence*, 1. 176–7.

which afford the highest Transport, without the Grossness or Remorse that attend vulgar Enjoyments' (p. 264).

During his London visit, Berkeley wrote several of the essays to combat 'free-thinking', published *The Ladies Library* with Jacob Tonson, a three-volume collection of readings on the family, social conventions, and religion, and joined the literary circle of Pope and Dr John Arbuthnot, the Scriblerians.[98] Unlike the Kit-Cat Club, the Scriblerians, although sharing numerous connections between members, were not based around a physical meeting space, but instead formed in 1714 around a group of writers who enjoyed writing collaboratively, notably Swift, Pope, and Thomas Parnell. They, in turn, brought in friends and patrons, including the poet and dramatist John Gay, the Queen's physician and prolific Tory satirist John Arbuthnot, and Henry St John, 1st Viscount Bolingbroke, with occasional visits from Swift's patron, Robert Harley, 1st Earl of Oxford. Their collaborative persona was one Martin Scriblerus. Pope in retrospect recalled the formation of the club as being to satirize pedantry:

The design of the *Memoirs of Scriblerus* was to have ridiculed all the false tastes in learning, under the character of a man of capacity enough that had dipped in every art and science, but injudiciously in each. It was begun by a club of some of the greatest wits of the age: Lord Bolingbroke, the Bishop of Rochester, Mr Pope, Congreve, Arbuthnot, Swift, and others. Gay often held the pen, and Addison liked it very well and was not disinclined to come into it.[99]

There had been an earlier scheme for producing a periodical, *The Works of the Unlearned*, which Pope mentions in a letter of 21 October 1713, which may have been the seed for this scheme.[100] At this point in his life, Pope had successfully published not only his *Pastorals* (1709), but also *An Essay on Criticism* (1711), *Messiah, A Sacred Eclogue* (1712), and the first version of his mock epic, the *Rape of the Lock* (1712), as well as his collaborations with Addison and Steele (see MV 5.V). By late 1713, Pope and Swift were distancing themselves from the Whig writers, and the Scriblerians as a loose group were more closely associated with the Tory party. Pope's *Windsor-Forest* (1714), which had undergone a long gestation as part of Pope's socially circulated manuscript verse, appeared revised in 1714, apparently at the urging of its dedicatee, Lord Lansdowne, a strong Tory spokesman; the historical poem is in part a celebration of the peace to be brought about by the Treaty of Utrecht, one of the principal causes that the Tory party laboured to attain.

The Scriblerians as a group met only a few times in March and April 1714 before Swift returned to Ireland, Pope and Parnell left London for Binfield and Bath, where Pope concentrated his attentions on his translation of the *Iliad*, and Gay in August was given an appointment in the embassy at Hanover. When

[98] Stephens (ed.), *Guardian*, 27–8; M. A. Stewart, 'Berkeley, George (1685–1753)', *ODNB*.
[99] Spence, *Observations, Anecdotes, and Characters*, 1. 56.
[100] Pope, *Correspondence*, 1. 195.

Arbuthnot late in 1713 proposed completing the scheme, the others were less enthusiastic. Swift believed that Arbuthnot himself was the best suited to carry out that task: 'every day [you] give better hints than all of us together could do in a twelvemonth; And to say the Truth, Pope who first thought of the Hint has no Genius at all to it, in my Mind. Gay is too young; Parnel has some Ideas of it but is idle', Swift concludes, 'I could putt together, and lard, and strike out well enough, but all that relates to the Sciences must be from you'.[101] Arbuthnot, then the Queen's physician, had in 1712 published his five-part John Bull satires as well as Proposals *for printing a very curious discourse…a treatise of the art of political lying* and he may have provided the place for the Scriblerians' meetings in the house he had gained from his appointment as physician of Chelsea Hospital. He appears, however, to have been disinclined to tackle Martin Scriblerus on his own.

In the end, the group became physically dispersed but nevertheless maintained contact through correspondence and occasional meetings. Parnell returned to Ireland in 1714 and had one more reunion with his London friends in 1718, but died on his return journey home. Swift, who wrote to Pope on 20 September 1723 of his desire 'to establish a Friendship among all Men of Genius', would not see his London friends after 1727. Arbuthnot, Gay, and Pope did continue to collaborate, producing the comedy *Three Hours after Marriage* in 1717, but *Memoirs of the Extraordinary Life, Works, and Discoveries of Martinus Scriblerus* was not published until 1741 as part of Pope's *Works in Prose*.

IV. Booksellers and the Book Trade: John Dunton, Edmund Curll, Grub Street, and the Rise of Bernard Lintot

> Do you know that Grub Street is dead and gone last week? No more ghosts or murders now for love or money. I plied it pretty close the last fortnight and published at least seven penny papers of my own, besides some of other people's; but now every single half sheet pays a half penny to the queen. The Observator is fallen; the Medlays we jumbled together with the Flying Post, the Examiner is deadly sick; the Spectator keeps up and doubles its price; I know not how long it will hold.
>
> Jonathan Swift, *Journal to Stella*, 2. 553–4, 1 August 1712

In his letter to Esther Johnson, 'Stella', Swift was highlighting the damage done to the periodical publication trade with the imposition of the Stamp Tax (see *MV* 5.II). Grub Street as the home to entrepreneurial booksellers and

---

[101] Swift, *Correspondence*, 2. 46.

writers for hire, however, was far from dead. The careers of two prominent figures in the Grub Street trade, John Dunton and Edmund Curll, and the rise to
prominence of the literary publisher Bernard Lintot offer some insights into the
changing conditions of the trade for both the publishers as well as the writers
during the decade in which copyright law was being shaped. While the height of
John Dunton's (1659–1732) career as a bookseller peaked in the 1690s, Dunton's
1705 autobiography *The Life and Errors of John Dunton, Late Citizen of
London* offers an unparalleled glimpse into the lives and labours of men and
women in the book trade, publishers, authors, and consumers. The London
publishing career of Edmund Curll (d. 1747) took a different route from
Dunton's. He was never a member of the Stationers' Guild, although he
was invited to become one in 1710, operating instead as a member of the
Cordwainer's Company.[102] With the lapse of the Licensing Act in 1695 (see *MV*
4.II), printers were no longer compelled by law to be a member, and historians
have argued that, during the period between 1695 and the Statute of Anne in
1710, literary 'piracy' or the publication of texts without the author's consent
or selling of the rights became a literary cultural phenomenon and Edmund
Curll was the most notorious and apparently shameless practitioner.[103] Bernard
Lintot (1675–1736), who also began his career as a literary publisher in the late
1690s, in contrast, focused his business on securing the rights to plays performed
at the Theatre Royal, and soon became the rival of the venerable Jacob Tonson
in publishing the leading literary figures of the early part of the century.

Dunton was the son of a long line of Anglican ministers, but as he recorded
in his memoir he had no inclination to follow in their footsteps, having as
he said 'a strange Kind of Aversion' to study (Dunton, *Life and Errors*, 9).
He was sent to London when he was 15 and apprenticed to the well-regarded
Presbyterian bookseller Thomas Parkhurst. Made free of the Stationers'
Company in late 1681, the young Dunton began a career during which, he
records, he produced over 600 titles, although many of these have never been
subsequently traced.[104] While most of his books were devotional materials and
sermons, he also produced inexpensive chapbooks, some political treatises,
and some miscellanies. His innovation in the 1690s was the development of
popular periodical formats, which encouraged readers to send their poetry,
observations on topics, and requests for advice to him for publication in an
interactive exchange; this was particularly successful with women readers, for
whom he also published *The Ladies Dictionary* (1694). Among these periodicals
were the *Athenian Gazette*, which became the *Athenian Mercury* (see *CV* 4.II;
CV 5.III); subsequently the *Athenian Mercury* was edited and published as
a four-volume collection between 1703 and 1710 under the title *The Athenian
Oracle*, suggesting the popularity of the contents. Having fallen on hard times

---

[102] Rogers, 'The Uses of the Miscellany', 91.
[103] Johns, *The Nature of the Book*, 168 and ch. 7; see also Johns, *Piracy*.
[104] Parks, *John Dunton*, 43.

and in ill-health, Dunton penned his memoirs and turned to pamphleteering and hack writing himself until his death in 1732.

Curll's career is perhaps best known to subsequent generations because of the writers he managed to antagonize, including Jonathan Swift, Alexander Pope, John Gay, and Matthew Prior. Initially in his career, like Dunton, Curll combined forces with other small London publishers and collaborated to corner the market on topical pamphlets and broadsides. They were not averse to creating news as well as publishing it. Curll, Benjamin Bragge, and John Baker jointly wrote and produced several pamphlets about the sensational witchcraft trial of Jane Wenham in 1712—Bragge wrote three declaring her innocence and Baker published three announcing her guilt, all in association with Curll.[105] Also like Dunton, Curll was keenly attuned to readers' tastes and purchasing patterns, and many of his publications were inexpensively priced at 1s. or 2s. As with Dunton's list, many of the titles Curll produced so rapidly and inexpensively to meet popular demand have not survived.

While Dunton was experimenting with formats to attract genteel female readers, Curll became notorious for publishing books and pamphlets that shocked and offended many men. One of his first publications was a volume combining Dunton's *The Athenian Spy* with a work of pornography, *The Way of a Man with a Maid* (1706). He became embroiled in a pamphlet war concerning cures for syphilis: in *The Charitable Surgeon* (1708) published by Curll, the unknown author asserted that the best cures could be purchased at Curll's shop. He also dismissed those made by a rival, John Spinke, who defended himself in a series of pamphlets, *Quackery Unmask'd . . . A Scourge for a Conceal'd Quack* (1711), which were in turn answered by Curll in the newspaper the *Post Boy*. Curll's use of newspaper advertisements suggests his appreciation that publicity of any sort, good or bad, could increase sales. He used advertisements extensively throughout his career, to announce new titles and also to spark interest through creating controversy. He also used advertisements to solicit information and anecdotes after the death of a well-known person to create quickly printed short biographies, frequently reissuing them including new materials, or at least the title pages suggesting that they did. Joseph Addison writing in 1716 in *The Free-Holder* described this as a general practice but seems to target Curll in particular as among the species of the '*Grub-Street* Biographer, who watch for the Death of a great Man, like so many Undertakers, on purpose to make a Penny out of him . . . exposing the private Concerns of Families and sacrificing the Secretes of the Dead to the Curiosity of the Living'.[106]

Like Dunton, Curll's early business thrived. In 1710, he opened a shop on Fleet Street at the sign of the Dial and Bible; not long after, in 1712, he was able to open another shop in Tunbridge Wells. During this same period, Curll began publishing works by Jonathan Swift without his permission, including

---

[105] Raymond N. MacKenzie, 'Curll, Edmund (d. 1747)', *ODNB*.
[106] Addison, *Free-Holder*, 207.

Meditations upon a Broomstick, and creating 'keys' to *A Tale of a Tub* (1710) (see CV 5.IV), which revealed the identity of Swift as the author on its title page. As scholars have noted, this custom of naming previously anonymous publications was characteristic of Curll's practices and obviously contributed to the anger many writers directed towards him in later years, perhaps most notoriously Alexander Pope after the unauthorized publication of *Court Poems* in 1716.[107]

He also published collections of miscellaneous pieces and assigned them authors, often without the permission of the writers. Swift wrote to Stella upon the unauthorized appearance of Curll's *Miscellanies by Dr Jonathan Swift* (1711) that 'that villain Curll has scraped up some trash, and calls it Dr Swift's miscellanies, with the name at large'.[108] Curll dared to challenge Jacob Tonson's rights to the works of Matthew Prior; when Prior published an advertisement objecting to Curll's announcement of a second volume of his works in 1716, Curll not only proceeded to print *A Second Collection of Poems on Various Occasions*, but also published his own announcement saying that Prior's was spurious.

By 1718, Curll's reputation was such that his name could be used as an epithet. 'There is indeed but one bookseller eminent among us for this abomination, and from him the crime takes the just denomination of Curlicism', the anonymous author of the article in *Mist's Journal*, 5 April 1718, declared: 'the fellow is a contemptible wretch a thousand ways: he is odious in his person, scandalous in his fame: he is marked by Nature, for he has a bawdy countenance, and a debauched mien; his tongue is an echo of all the beastly language his shop is filled with, and filthiness drivels in the very tone of his voice'. Dunton, on his part, reflecting on what governed his own practice as a bookseller, declared that 'I would never go upon any design that interferes with another man's Project; but the contrary is grown so common and so notorious at this day, that the *whole Trade* has almost ruined its reputation and its honesty at once. This is but a *learned way* of robbery at best' (Dunton, *Life and Errors*, 88).

Both men also employed a host of writers for hire, the so-called hacks of Grub Street. The actual Grub Street (ironically now renamed Milton Street) was in a poor section of London in the parish of St Giles-without-Cripplegate. It became so closely associated with journalists and writers for hire that the *OED* now has one definition for 'grub' as meaning 'a person of mean abilities, a literary hack'. Such writers apparently gained the label of 'hack' writers because, like the hackney carriages available to be flagged down on the streets, their services were for hire, and they would take you wherever you would like to go; popular slang also applied this term to prostitutes. A prolific contributor to this Grub Street literature, Edward 'Ned' Ward (1667–1731), in *A Trip to Jamaica* (1698) described the life of a Grub Street writer as being 'much like

---

[107] Karian, *Jonathan Swift*, 65–6; Straus, *The Unspeakable Curll*; Baines and Rogers, *Edmund Curll*, ch. 4.
[108] Swift, *Journal to Stella*, 1. 269.

that of a Strumpet', explaining that, 'if the Reason by requir'd, Why we betake our selves to so Scandalous a Profession as Whoring or Pamphleteering, the same exusive [*sic*] Answer will serve us both, viz. That the unhappy circumstances of a Narrow Fortune, hath forc'd us to do that for our Subsistence, which we are much asham'd of'.[109] Ward, a prolific publisher who saw most of his writings through the press himself, continued offering his observations on London and the times until his death in 1731.[110]

The overwhelming number of associations with the terms 'grub street' and 'hack' were negative. Jonathan Swift in *A Tale of a Tub* (1704) mocked the '*Grub-Street* Brotherhood' for producing endless editions of miscellanies and popular ephemeral publications under the guise of poetry such as '*Westminster Drolleries, Delightful Tales, Compleat Jesters*, and the like'.[111] Alexander Pope would provide the most famous literary rendition of this class of writer in *The Dunciad*, first published in 1728 and enjoying two further expansions. In it he creates a mock epic with its target not only 'dull' or bad writers, but also in particular mercenary ones, willing to write on any topic or from any point of view for a price. John Dunton, having himself been reduced to writing for hire, described in a 1706 pamphlet *The Living Elegy* one of his detractors as, 'a Poetical Insect—A meer Grub-Street Poet—The worst sort of Hackney—a Murderer of Paper—(Nothing he writes Sells)—The Common Scribler of the the Town, that writes and drinks, as he can St[ea]l, or borrow, [or] Coyn Wit'.[112] As Pat Rogers has described the prevalent antipathy by writers such as Pope and Swift to this subculture, grub street hacks 'were manufacturing to order, a product—literature—which in the past had largely been the preserve of the learned, the leisured, and the secure'.[113]

In his *Life and Errors*, however, Dunton is kinder to the writers he employed on 'projects' and 'designs' he devised for them. After his invaluable listing of the London booksellers and printers with whom he dealt—for example, 'Mrs Tacy Sowle…both a *Printer* as well as a *Bookseller*, and the Daughter of one; and understands her Trade very well, being a good *Compositor herself*. Her love and piety to her aged Mother is eminently remarkable' (Dunton, *Life and Errors*, 300)—and the book auctioneers and 'the honest (Mercurial) Women' who sold his periodicals, he describes the other writers he employed and published. Some, like Richard Steele and Daniel Defoe, were important figures, but others were clearly educated young men who found themselves in London in search of a living. Dunton characterizes the versatile Charles Gildon as being 'well acquainted with the Languages, and writes with a peculiar Briskness, which the common Hacks can't boast of', while a 'Mr Philips' is a 'Gentleman of good Learning, and well born. He'll write you a Design off in a very little Time, if the Gout (or Claret) don't stop him' (Dunton, *Life and Errors*, 241).

---

[109] Ward, *A Trip*, 'To the Reader'. [110] See Troyer, *Ned Ward*, app. A.
[111] Swift, *A Tale of a Tub*, 42. [112] Dunton, *The Living Elegy*, 47.
[113] Rogers, *Hacks and Dunces*, 280.

One Mr Bradshaw Dunton describes as 'the best accomplish'd Hackney-Author I have met with; his Genius was quite above the common size... You cou'd propose to him no Design, within the Compass of Learning, but he knew to go through with it' (Dunton, *Life and Errors*, 241–2). In contrast, 'Mr Ames' was 'originally a coat-seller; but had always some yammerings upon him after Learning and the Muses' and is compared unfavourably to Mr Ridpath (see *CV* 5.III), 'a considerable Scholar... but by some unfortunate Accident or other, the Fate of an Author came upon him' (Dunton, *Life and Errors*, 239). The prolific Tom Brown (see *MV* 5.V; *CV* 5.IV) was also considered by Dunton to be a good scholar and a wit, but unfortunately 'the Urgency of his Circumstances won't allow him Time enough to lay out his Talents' and that ''tis extream Pity that a Man of *so fine Parts*, and so well accomplish'd every other way, should spend his time upon a *few romantic Letters*, that seem purely designed to debauch the Age, and overthrow the foundations of Religion and Virtue' (Dunton, *Life and Errors*, 238).

As Dunton's lists reveal, it was not only men who inhabited Grub Street and created its literary world. Part of what Pat Rogers described as the subculture of Grub Street involved families as well as single men and women in the book trade. Writers such as Susanna Centlivre, prior to her successes on stage, was a denizen, as were Delarivier Manley, Eliza Haywood, and Elizabeth Thomas, the latter two of whom Pope would skewer in *The Dunciad*.[114] As critics have observed, the expanding commercial opportunities for writers and booksellers meant increasing opportunities for women not only as writers and the familiar figure of the female hawker or Mercury woman (see *CV* 1.III) but also as publishers and artisans producing books and pamphlets.[115] Dunton was in general supportive of these women in the business, who were typically widows or daughters of printers, but, when Sarah Malthus, who printed several books for him, appeared to be implicated in Dunton's bankruptcy, he had no hesitation in labelling her 'the Famous Publisher of Grub-Street News', who 'Copies her Religion and Honesty from Hackney Authors'.[116]

A woman printer who had Dunton's respect was the formidable Elinor [Eleanor] James (1644/5–1719), who was involved in the print trade for over forty years, publishing more than ninety of her own pamphlets and broadsides between 1681 and 1716.[117] In her broadside *Mrs James's Advice to All Printers*, she reflected on the changes she had seen in the publishing trade over the course of her long career in it, and suggests some of the tensions arising during a period of transition from the model of the lived-in printing shop contained within the house and a hierarchical family structure, to the 'insubordination' of her recent apprentices, who seek employment elsewhere with other printers if they are dissatisfied with their working conditions, printers who had not had

[114] Ingrassia, *Authorship, Commerce, and Gender*.
[115] McDowell, *The Women of Grub Street*, ch. 1.   [116] Dunton, *The Whipping Post*, 33.
[117] Paula McDowell, 'James, Elinor (1644/5–1719)', *ODNB*.

the 'charge and trouble of bringing them up, which is too frequently practiced among you to the ruin of the trade in general'.[118]

Grub Street—its writers, publishers, printers, hawkers, and vendors—would continue to hold its own identity well into the nineteenth century. Its productions in the first decades of the 1700s were reflections of what readers wanted but they also display efforts by entrepreneurial literary promoters experimenting with new genres and new ways to attract readers. Although many of the titles written and produced by the writers and publishers of this group have vanished, through Dunton's memoir and Curll's long and notorious career traces remain of their efforts in marketing texts and making the most of an expanding consumer print culture.

In contrast to Dunton and Curll, Bernard Lintot was able to pay his authors relatively well. His accounts, for example, show payments of £30 to Farquhar for his comedy *The Beaux's Stratagem* and £50 15s. for Nicholas Rowe's 1714 *The Tragedy of Jane Shore*.[119] What would seal Lintot's reputation as the leading publisher of literary works in the first part of the eighteenth century was his early association with the young Alexander Pope and his circle of friends (see MV 5.V). In his poem *Verses to be Prefix'd before Bernard Lintot's Miscellaneous Poems and Translation by Several Hands* (1712), Pope places him in the history of printing in association with the master printer of the Renaissance, quipping, 'Others with *Aldus* would besot us; | I, for my part, admire *Lintottus*'. By combining his efforts with those of Tonson, with whom he had thirteen publication agreements, and aggressively advertising his books and authors in his *The Monthly Catalogue* (1714–16), Lintot secured the literary reputations of his authors, and kept them in the readers' view through frequent reprints, which were continued by his son Henry well into the 1750s.

V. 'The Great Business of Poetry': Poets, Pastoral, and Politics

> To BRITAIN'S QUEEN the Nations turn their Eyes,
> On Her resolves the Western World relies,
> Confiding still, amidst its dire Alarms,
> In ANNA's councils, and in CHURCHILL's arms:
> Thrice happy Britain, from the kingdoms rent,
> To fit the guardian of the continent!
>
> Joseph Addison, *The Campaign, A Poem, To His Grace The Duke Of Marlborough* (1704)

---

[118] Quoted in McDowell, *The Women of Grub Street*, 50, n. 26.
[119] See Nichols, *Literary Anecdotes*, for Lintot's account records.

Now awful beauty puts on all its arms;
The Fair each moment rises in her charms,
Repairs her smiles, awakens every grace,
And calls forth all the wonders of her face.

Alexander Pope, *The Rape of the Lock* (1714)

The poetry of the first decade and a half of the 1700s was ambitious—
ambitious in its public claims of speaking for the nation and in its quiet experimentation. Poets of the period engaged closely with ongoing debates over the
grounds for establishing literary merit, with the continuing rivalry between
'ancient and modern' (see CV 4.III), and with contemporary domestic and
foreign events. The poetry of the period was also pragmatic—the events and
persons celebrated in verse could secure patrons; political attacks or even
satires on matrimony could say in rhyme what otherwise might have proved
problematic in prose. Readers in the first decades enjoyed poetry of all sorts,
judging from the prolific publication of verse in a variety of formats ranging
from broadsides to 700-page miscellany volumes, and writing poetry could bring
both men and women social, cultural capital and, with changing publication
practices, possibly even an actual profit.

Many poets both social and professional continued to be printed initially
in periodical publications, including the *Spectator* and the *Guardian*, as well as
in miscellanies collecting verse and translations by several people. Editors of
periodicals actively encouraged their readers to contribute verses (see CV 5.III).
Poems celebrating national events, such as Joseph Addison's *The Campaign*,
published by Jacob Tonson (see MV 5.III) on the occasion of the Duke of
Marlborough's decisive military victory over the French at the Battle of Blenheim
(1704), were typically published initially as pamphlets before being collected in
miscellanies. These miscellanies often had no particular organizing theme or
principle and frequently ran to 300 or more pages of verse.

The series of miscellanies begun by John Dryden and Tonson in 1684 (see
MV 4.I) continued after Dryden's death, with reissues of the earlier volumes
such as *Sylvae* in 1702 and the appearance of new collections. These miscellanies
were often 500–600 pages long: Tonson's *Poetical Miscellanies: The Sixth Part*
(1709), which will be discussed later, offered 670 pages of original verses
and translations, some by new poets, such as Alexander Pope and Jonathan
Swift, and others by established ones, including Nicholas Rowe and William
Wycherley. Several of the other miscellanies published during this period kept
earlier poets alive for new readers, typically advertising in their titles that,
while the names would be familiar, the contents were new and 'never before
printed': one such compilation volume was the 1707 collection issued by
Benjamin Bragge, *The Miscellaneous works of the Right Honourable the late
Earls of Rochester and Roscommon*. Likewise John Baker published a substantial
octavo, *A Collection of Divine Hymns and Poems on Several Occasions: by the
E. of Roscommon, Mr Dryden, Mr Dennis, Mr Norris, Mrs Kath. Phillips,*

Philomela, and others. Most of them never before Printed (1709). This volume brought together several generations of poets, including Elizabeth Singer, to be discussed later, as well as several poems by unnamed 'young ladies' and some simply described as 'by an unknown hand'.

Collections of verse by single, highly regarded earlier poets also appeared during the period. James Watson, an Edinburgh printer, published *A Collection of all the Poems written by William Drummond, Of Hawthornden* (1711). Tonson's young rival for the literary trade, the publisher Bernard Lintot (1675–1736) (see *MV* 5.IV), in addition to publishing play texts, also produced a miscellany of Shakespeare's poems, *A Collection of Poems, in two volumes; being all the miscellanies of Mr William Shakespeare, which were publish'd by himself in the year 1609* (1709), in two volumes, the first containing the narrative poems, the second the first quarto version of the sonnets. In his advertisement to the reader, Lintot states that he acquired *The Passionate Pilgrim*, the 'Remains' of Shakespeare 'in a little stitch'd Book, printed at London for W. Jaggard, in the Year 1599. It is generally agreed', Lintot observed, that Shakespeare died 'about the Year 1616 so that it appears plainly they were published by himself, being printed 17 years before his Death' (recent Shakespeare scholarship, however, disagrees). Edmund Curll, not to be outdone, employed Charles Gildon (see *MV* 5.IV) to edit another volume of Shakespeare's sonnets, which was published in 1710, mimicking in its format and appearance Nicholas Rowe's six-volume edition of Shakespeare's plays, published also in 1709 by Tonson.[120] This last collection proved to have the most impact on the ways in which subsequent generations read and imagined Shakespeare: as critics have noted, Rowe, himself a popular playwright, was primarily interested in making Shakespeare understandable to contemporary readers, and he thus introduced helpful apparatus, including character lists, stage directions, scene divisions, and descriptions of settings, which became standard features of later editions.[121]

The composition of some miscellanies was based on location rather than subject matter, showcasing literary life outside London. Lintot published the *Oxford and Cambridge Miscellany Poems* (1708), a 400-plus-page compilation that mingled contributions from young scholars and dons with those of distinguished graduates such as Dryden and Otway. The popular spa town of Tunbridge Wells apparently also inspired poets: *The Tunbridge-Miscellany: consisting of Poems, &c. Written at Tunbridge-Wells this summer. By several hands* (1712) was published by Curll, who had opened a bookshop there, which was followed by yearly collections featuring local verse written in 1713 and 1714. The 1714 miscellany expanded its content to include a prose description of Bath by 'Nestor Ironside, esq' borrowed from the *Spectator* (see *MV* 5.III) and contains such original poetic gems as 'The Snoring Husband' and 'Upon Two Ladies in a Riding Habit', revealed in a note to be 'Mrs L—y, and Mrs G—y':

---

[120] See Burrow, 'Life and Work', 18.
[121] See Milhous and Hume, *The Publication of Plays*, 235–36.

> Now in Revenge, behold the Brightest Fair,
> Who conquer most, the Manly Habit wear,
> And try to hide beneath the Male Attire,
> Those Charms, for which a thousand Youths expire.[122]

Several notable individual collections included posthumous editions of the poems of John Wilmot, Earl of Rochester, *Poems on Several Occasions. By the R. H. the E. of R* (1701), Sir Charles Sedley, *Miscellaneous Works* (1702), John Dryden, *Poems on Various Occasions; and Translations from Several Authors* (1701), and the Quaker Mary Mollineux, *Fruits of Retirement; or, Miscellaneous Poems, Moral and Divine* (1702), as well as the works of Thomas Brown (4 vols, 1709) and the two-volume edition of the works of the Duke of Buckingham (1707). This is not to suggest that individual contemporary poets eschewed the publication of their own collected verse. In the first four years of the decade alone, there were a significant number of single volumes by poets in mid-career. These included those by the minister John Pomfret, *Miscellany Poems on Several Occasions* (1702), which would achieve eleven editions by 1748, by Sarah Fyge Egerton, who had refuted Robert Gould's misogynist satire as a teenager (see MV 4.V), and who published after her marriage *Poems on Several Occasions Together with a Pastoral* (1703), by Mary, Lady Chudleigh (bap. 1656–1710), *The Ladies Defence* (1701) and *Poems on Several Occasions* (1703), who, although living in Devon, initially had had her poems carried from Exeter to Jacob Tonson in London by John Dryden, and the ageing William Wycherley, *Miscellany Poems* (1704), which the young Alexander Pope helped to prepare for print.

Several poets who published single pieces initially later compiled collections of their works. John Pomfret (1667–1702), who had written an elegy on the death of Queen Mary in the 1690s, published *The Choice: a Poem* (1700) celebrating a life of comfortable culture in the countryside with Horace, Virgil, Juvenal, and Ovid (see MV 5.I). In 1702, *Miscellany Poems on Several Occasions. By the Author of the Choice* appeared, reprinting *The Choice* along with a Pindaric on death and one upon 'The Divine Attributes' on the themes of unity and Eternity. Likewise, Edmund Arwaker (*c.*1660–1730), the chaplain to the Duke of Ormond, who had offered commendatory verses on royal occasions in the 1680s, published in 1708 *Truth in Fiction: Or, Morality in Masquerade. A Collection of Two hundred twenty-five Select Fables of Aesop, and other Authors*, highlighting the continuing popularity of the verse fable. The physician Bernard Mandeville (bap. 1670–1733) likewise published *Some Fables after the Easie and Familiar Method of Monsieur de la Fontaine* (1703), which he enlarged under the title *Aesop Dress'd* (1704); this was followed by *The Grumbling Hive* (1705), a long verse fable that in turn would be incorporated into his prose exploration of the worldly benefits of human passions, *The Fable of the Bees, or, Private Vices, Publick Benefits* (1714).

---

[122] *The Tunbridge-Miscellany*, 5.

The book-length publications by Mollineux, Fyge, Singer, and Chudleigh display a diverse pattern of how poets envisioned their writings and how such writings came to print. The poems of Mary Mollineux, who lived and died in Liverpool, were published posthumously in 1702 by the Quaker printer Tace Sowle, although her cousin Frances Owen, who introduces the works, explains that they were enjoyed by family and fellow Quakers during her life. Mollineux wrote to 'Convince and Prevail upon the Mind, to affect and raise the Soul upon Wings of Divine Contemplation',[123] and the poems were published to comfort and encourage the reader, especially younger readers. Many of her poems are simply titled 'Contemplation' or 'Meditation', and there are numerous verse letters to friends and relatives, employing a variety of verse forms.

Fyge herself published her volume of verse in 1703, very much against the wishes of her clergyman husband. Fyge, who had gained some public recognition while still quite young for her verse rebuttal of Robert Gould's misogynistic satire (see *MV* 4.V), had some experience with London publishing. She dedicated the volume to Charles, Lord Halifax; she apologizes in it for her 'unskillful Muse', explaining that many of the poems had been written when she was less than 17, and 'long they lay in a neglected Silence' prior to 'an unlucky Accident forc'd them to the Press'.[124] Nevertheless, the volume comes with several poems of commendation to usher in the verses, one by the rising dramatist Susanna Centlivre (see *MV* 5.I; *CV* 5.II), suggesting that, even when not residing there, she was engaging with a London literary group. The prefatory poems praise the skills of 'Clarinda' for her mastery of verse forms ranging from panegyric to satire, highlighting the public nature of Fyge's poetry.

Mary Chudleigh and Elizabeth Singer Rowe would each publish several volumes of their collected writings during their lifetimes. Chudleigh spent much of her life in Devon and enjoyed a social literary circle there; John Dryden, visiting nearby Ugbrook Park while working on his translation of Virgil, had hoped to use one of her commendatory poems on it in his 1697 edition, but it arrived too late to be included. Dryden also showed her verses to William Walsh and William Wycherley in London, who voiced their approval. Chudleigh, after her name became known through her publications, enjoyed an extensive correspondence with Mary Astell, Elizabeth Thomas, and John Norris (see *MV* 5.I; *CV* 4.V).[125] She first appeared in print with her dialogue verse response to a wedding sermon that had been dedicated to her by a local cleric advocating grovelling wifely submission. Her retort, *The Ladies Defence* (1701), features a witty female commentator, Melissa, who takes on the arguments made by stock characters such as the boorish country squire and the misogynist cleric. It had circulated in manuscript form among her female friends prior to their urging her to print it. In 1703, her *Poems on Several Occasions* was printed by

---

[123] Mollineux, *Fruits of Retirement*, 'To the Reader'.
[124] Fyge, *Poems*, 'Dedication'.   [125] See Ezell, 'Introduction'.

Lintot, with a second edition in 1709; in her preface she describes her verses as 'a Picture of my Mind, my Sentiments all laid open to their View', and the volume contained occasional verse as well as a frequently recopied satire 'To the Ladies' beginning 'Wife and Servant are the same, | But only differ in the Name'.[126] Chudleigh's final volume, *Essays upon Several Subjects in Prose and Verse* (1710), was more sombre in tone, many of the prose and verse essays dealing with loss of children and enduring illness and pain.

Elizabeth Singer Rowe (1674–1737) was raised in Frome, Somerset, where she was educated in French, Italian, and perhaps Latin by the son of the Thomas Thynne, Viscount Weymouth, of Longleat. She published her verse poems under the sobriquet of Philomela by sending them in 1691, supposedly unbeknown to her parents, to Dunton's periodical the *Athenian Mercury*; between 1693 and 1696, she frequently published there (see CV 4.V), resulting in 1696 in her *Poems on Several Occasions: Written by Philomela*. Through her family and literary connections, she met Matthew Prior when he visited Longleat in 1703, whose romantic proposals she rejected, but she apparently used his help to place her translation of Tasso in the *Poetical Miscellanies: The Fifth Part* (1704) issued by Tonson. That year, too, she appeared prominently in *Divine hymns and poems on several occasions...by Philomela, and several other ingenious persons* (1704), which was revised in 1709, appearing as *A Collection of Divine Hymns and Poems* (1709). She married in 1709 a fellow poet at Bath, Thomas Rowe (1687–1715); in the later part of her life, she continued to publish her verses and, after his death, to memorialize his life and works. Her final literary efforts were in prose, when she created a sequence of short fictions, often mingling verse, *Friendship in Death: in Twenty Letters from the Dead to the Living* (1728).[127]

She saw herself as an explicitly Christian poet. In the dedication to Sir Richard Blackmore of the 1704 volume, she applauded his moral vision as a poet, declaring that 'the best Poetry, and Manly Sense, are very consistent; and that Wit never appears so illustrious, as when she borrows her Themes from Virtue and Religion'.[128] In the preface, which is not signed, it is declared that good poetry should inflame the passions, but only the appropriate ones: 'Now the great Business of Poetry as ev'ry one knows is to paint agreeable Pictures on the Imagination, to actuate the Spirits, and give the Passions a Noble Pitch', it states, and 'all its daring Metaphors, surprising turns, melting Accents, lofty Flights, and lively Descriptions, serve or this End'. Poetry is inherently sensual, and 'while we Read we feel a strange Warmth boyling within, the Blood dances through the Veins, Joy lightens in the Countenance, and we are insensibly led into a pleasing captivity' ('Preface'). This same sense of poetry as a religious vocation is at the heart of Rowe's poem 'The Vision' published in Tonson's

---

[126] Margaret J. M. Ezell, 'Chudleigh [née Lee], Mary, Lady Chudleigh (*bap.* 1656–1710)', *ODNB*.
[127] See Backscheider, *Elizabeth Singer Rowe*. [128] *Divine hymns*, 'Dedication'.

Poetical Miscellanies: The Fifth Part (1704), where the young poet, having debated what should be the subject matter of her verses—

> I take my lyre and try each tuneful string,
> Now war, now love, and beauty's force would sing;
> To heavenly subjects now, in serious lays,
> I strive my faint, unskillful voice to raise[129]

—falls asleep and is visited by an angel, who directs her to take God as her subject.[130]

One admirer of Rowe's poetry was the independent minister Isaac Watts (1674–1748). He had been educated at the dissenting academy in London and had first published his verse as *Horae Lyricae* (1706), 'poems chiefly of the Lyric kind', celebrating among other topics 'Vertue, Loyalty, and Friendship'. He would expand and reprint it in 1709. With both Greek and Latin epigrams on the title page, Watts's printer clearly signalled to the reader that the contents of the volume would not only be lyrics, but also works by a Christian poet at home with the classics. In his lengthy preface, Watts describes his desire to reclaim pagan and secular poetry for heaven. 'Almost in vain have the Throne and the Pulpit cried, *Reformation*, while the Stage and Licentious Poems have waged open War with the Pious Design of Church and State', Watts declares: 'the Press has spread the Poyson far, and scatter'd wide the Mortal Infection; Unthinking Youth have been allured to Sin beyond the Vicious Propensities of Nature, plung'd early into Diseases and Death, and sunk down to Damnation in Multitudes'.[131] While clearly manifesting his own familiarity with classical poets and multiple languages, English religious verse, Watts suggests, has 'no need of these Tinsel Trappings; the Glories of our Religion in a plain Narration and a simple Dress have something brighter and bolder in them, something more surprising and Divine, than all the Adventures of Gods and Heroes' (sig. A2ᵛ). Christian belief should inspire poets more profoundly, and poetry, in particular song, should be part of ministry, Watts asserts,

for touching the Springs of Passion will fall infinitely on the side of the Christian Poet; our Wonder and our Love, our Pity, Delight, and Sorrow, with the long train of Hopes and Fears, must needs be under the Command of an Harmonious Pen, whose every Line makes a part of the Reader's Faith, and is the very Life or Death of his Soul. (sig. A4ʳ)

From his preface and the inscriptions of many of his verses to teachers and friends, it is clear that Watts began composing poems while still a student; he states firmly that 'Poetry is not the Business of my Life' and that his sacred songs 'were never written with a design to appear before the Judges of Wit, but only to assist the Meditations and Worship of Vulgar Christians'. If the

---

[129] *Poetical Miscellanies. The Fifth Part*, 375.
[130] See Backscheider, *Eighteenth-Century Women Poets*, 113–23; Kennedy, *Poetic Sisters*, ch. 3.
[131] Watts, *Horae Lyricae*, sig. A2ᵛ.

volume has a good reception, 'these are but a small part of two hundred Hymns of the same kind which are ready for Public Use'. In the preface, he warns that he will experiment with the lyric following the models of Horace and Casimire (see *MV* 1.III; *CV* 1.V), as well as blank verse to achieve 'its peculiar Elegance and Ornament', while reverting in his Pindarics to the shorter lines favoured by the classical writers rather than 'Excessive Lengths to which some Modern Writers have stretched their Sentences'. He also makes conscious reference to the necessity of his sacred songs being able to be sung sensibly, even by those of the 'plainest capacities'.

Following the success of his first publication, Watts soon followed it with the promised *Hymns and Spiritual Songs* (1707, enlarged 1709). In the preface to the second edition, Watts laments the sad state of psalmody in worship services. 'I have been long convinc'd, that one great Occasion of this Evil arises from the Matter and Words to which we confine all our Songs',[132] he observes:

Some of 'em are almost opposite to the Spirit of the Gospel: Many of them foreign to the State of the New-Testament, and Widely different from the present Circumstances of Christians. Hence it comes to pass, that when spiritual Affections are excited within us, and our Souls are raised a little above this Earth in the beginning of a Psalm, we are check'd on a sudden in our Ascent towards heaven by some Expressions that are more suited to the Days of *Carnal Ordinances*, and fit only to be sung in the *Worldly Sanctuary*. (p. iv)

Watts's revision of the traditional metrical psalm emphasized the Christian application and likewise often employs a personal, individual voice.

In addition to using Scriptures as the source of Christian song, Watts desired his hymns be 'suited to the general State of the Gospel, and the most common Affairs of Christians' (p. vii). Watts's version of Psalm 114 was published in the *Spectator*, no. 461, on 19 August 1712, accompanied by a letter explaining his delight in translating it (see *MV* 5.III):

the 114th Psalm appears to me an admirable Ode, and I began to turn it into our Language. As I was describing the Journey of Israel from Egypt, and added the Divine Presence amongst them, I perceived a Beauty in the Psalm which was entirely new to me, and which I was going to lose; and that is, that the Poet utterly conceals the Presence of God in the Beginning of it.

His hymn 'Heavenly Joy on Earth' begins

> Come, we that love the Lord,
> And let our Joys be known;
> Join in a Song with sweet accord,
> And thus surround the Throne,

and declares that

---

[132] Watts, *Hymns*, p. iv.

> The Sorrows of the Mind
> Be banish from the Place!
> Religion never was design'd
> To make our Pleasures less.[133]

He did not shy away from contemporary issues or situations, offering hymns praising John Locke (see CV 4.IV), mourning the death of King William III, and, in 1714, one of his most famous hymns, lamenting the death of Queen Anne:

> Our God, our help in ages past,
> Our hope for years to come,
> Our shelter from the stormy blast,
> And our eternal home.[134]

These first two volumes contained several psalms, which Watts would eventually collect and expand into a volume published in *The Psalms of David Imitated in the Language of the New Testament* (1719), preceded by *Divine Songs Attempted in Easy Language, for the Use of Children* (1715). Watts's hymns, which celebrate a joyful community of worshippers as well as depict the pains of hell being visited upon those who persecute the church, became so popular over the course of the century that they were sung not only in congregational churches, but also in Presbyterian and Baptist ones, and they were highly influential on the development of the next several generations of British and American hymn-writers.[135]

In the American colonies, reading and writing religious poetry was among the principal pastimes of literate New Englanders, and the overall market for printed poetry was third only to sermons and almanacs.[136] Some were designed for specific audiences: the *Massachusetts Psalter* (1707), printed in Boston and done by Experience Mayhew, had both Pawkunnakut and English-language versions of the psalms.[137] Many of the published poets were Harvard-educated ministers:[138] Nicholas Noyes (1647–1717), the presiding magistrate in the notorious Salem witch hunt, was described by the bookseller John Dunton (see MV 5.IV) on his tour of New England as being 'all that's delightful in Conversation' (Dunton, *Life and Errors*, 176). Noyes was also a prolific occasional poet, sharing verses with other sympathetic New England Puritans; writing in 1706, he praised in verse Cotton Mather's efforts to educate African slaves (*The Negro Christianized An essay to excite and assist the good work, the instruction of Negro-servants in Christianity*), and he contributed

---

[133] Watts, *Hymns*, 155.   [134] See Parker, 'The Hymn as a Literary Form'.
[135] See Knott, *Discourses of Martyrdom*, 'Epilogue: The Hymns of Isaac Watts'; Escott, *Isaac Watts*.
[136] See Silverman, *Colonial American Poetry*; Hugh Amory, 'A Note on Statistics', Graph 5a, 'Leading Genres, by Place, 1640–1790', in Amory and Hall (eds), *History of the Book in America*, I. 511.
[137] See Szasz, *Indian Education*, 119.   [138] Shields, *Civil Tongues*, ch. 7.

commendatory verses printed in Mather's ecclesiastical history of New England, *Magnalia* (1702).

Reflecting on the melancholy need for elegies as being part of a minister's life, Noyes in his verses on Joseph Green observed that

> By over-praising of the Dead
> Nor they, nor we are Bettered.
> Poetick Raptures Scandalize,
> And pass with most for learned Lies,

and 'Such high Flights seem Design'd to raise | The *Poets*, not the *Person*'s praise'.[139] Another elegist, Benjamin Colman (1673–1747), who was also born in Boston and educated at Harvard, became acquainted with Elizabeth Singer Rowe when visiting England in 1695, sending her verses describing her in her rural setting as

> Such Eden's streams, and banks, and tow'ring groves;
> Such Eve herself, and such her muse and loves.
> Only there wants an Adam on the green,
> Or else all Paradise might here be seen.

On returning to Boston, he became the pastor of the Brattle Street Society; as part of his funeral sermon for the fiery minister Samuel Willard, Colman included an elegy, 'On Elijah's Translation', honouring his fellow clergyman in Virgilian epic style:

> I SING the man, by heaven's peculiar grace,
> The prince of prophets, of the chosen race,
> Rais'd and accomplish'd for degenerate times,
> To stem the ebb with faith and zeal sublime.

After his death, his son-in-law the Revd Ebenezer Turell wrote his biography, containing much of Coleman's verse, as well as that by his daughter Jane.[140]

The first fourteen years of 1700 also saw several notable national events that drew forth panegyrics, odes, and occasional verse to mark the occasions. The victories by the British army led by Churchill, in particular the Battle of Blenheim in 1704, were the occasion of much celebratory writing by poets, including Matthew Prior, Joseph Addison, Daniel Defoe, and John Philips. Matthew Prior, then serving as a commissioner of the Board of Trade and Plantations, wrote a mocking verse letter to the French poet Nicolas Boileau commiserating with him as the historiographer to the French king and having to write verses in praise of the defeated:

> What Turn wilt thou employ, what Colours lay
> On the Event of that Superior Day,

---

[139] 'An Elegy ... Joseph Green', 45; Hammond, *The American Puritan Elegy*, ch. 4.
[140] See Turell, *Life ... Benjamin Colman*, 36.

> In which One English Subject's prosperous Hand
> (So JOVE did will, so ANNA did command;)
> Broke the proud Column of thy Master's Praise,
> Which Sixty Winters had conspired to raise?[141]

Addison had no such problems as he focused in *The Campaign*, which appeared late in 1704 as well, on the figure of the victorious Duke of Marlborough as he marched across Europe:

> Our God-like Leader, e'er the Stream he past,
> The mighty Scheme of all his Labours cast,
> Forming the Wond'rous Year within his Thought;
> His Bosom glow'd with Battels yet unfought.[142]

John Philips (1676–1709) was the Oxford author of the very popular comic poem *Splendid Shilling*, which Addison in the *Tatler*, no. 249, would describe as 'the finest Burlesque Poem in the *British* Language'. It was written in imitation of Miltonic blank verse and published without his consent in 1701 as part of a miscellany; it appears to have drawn favourable attention to the young poet, as Philips, who had had no other verses published, was tapped in 1705 to create a Tory equivalent to Addison's panegyric. The result, *Blenheim, a Poem Inscrib'd to the Right Honourable Robert Harley* (1705), also written in blank verse, places Marlborough's victory in the context of classical epic battles. Thomas Tickell in his poem *Oxford* (1706), to be discussed later in this section, admired it and the poet:

> Unfetter'd in great Milton's strain he writes,
> Like Milton's angels, whilst his hero fights;
> Pursues the bard, whilst he with honour can,
> Equal the poet, and excels the man.

Daniel Defoe penned several poems celebrating the success of the English troops, which were published not only in London, but also in Edinburgh and Scotland. Dedicated to Queen Anne, *A Hymn to Victory by the Author of The True-born English-man* (1704) celebrates not only the victorious general, but also the character of the English queen:

> Your steady Councils, and discerning Sight,
> Lets loose his Glorious Sword, and shews it where to fight.
> The daring Hearts that in your Cause appear,
> They fight the Battel, but 'tis you make War:
> Their Courage may exalt the English Name,
> But 'tis the Sceptre helps the Sword to Fame.

Defoe's poetic output as well as his prose writings during this period were prolific and devoted to topical politics: in 1705 and 1706 alone, Defoe published

---

[141] Prior, *A Letter to Monsieur Boileau Depreaux*, 1.   [142] Addison, *The Campaign*, 4.

The Double Welcome. A Poem to the Duke of Marlbro as well as the long satire *Jure Divino*, another enlarged collection of his writings, *A True Collection of the Writings of the Author of The True-Born Englishman*, and two poems celebrating the Union with Scotland, *Caledonia* and *The Vision* (see CV 5.I).

Critics have pointed to the unusual amount of labour Defoe put into the composition and publication of *Jure Divino*.[143] Defoe's success with the 1701 verses of *The True-Born Englishman* (see MV 5.I, 5.II) led him to associate that poem with many of his subsequent publications, giving him an ongoing persona as the poet who spoke for the everyday English reader addressing national and foreign events and public figures. In *Jure Divino*, Defoe stakes his claim to serious literary attention: the folio volume, sold by subscription at fifteen shillings, features an author portrait showing him in an oval frame wearing a fashionable wig, with the inscription below from Juvenal's *Satire* 1, line 74, *Laudatur et Alget* '[Honesty] is praised and starves'. Done in heroic couplets in 12 books running over 8,000 lines, *Jure Divino* was, according to Defoe in his preface, written while he was imprisoned in 1703 (see MV 5.II), and it is a statement of his political philosophy, an attack on passive obedience and on the theory of the divine right of monarchs. '*Satyr*, the Grand Inquiry now begin, | Describe the Mortal, and describe the Sin', Defoe commands.

> The horrid contradicting Flight explode,
> And paint the Man that *thinks himself a God:*
> To the Exacter Test th' Ænigma bring,
> The *Kingly Slave*, and the more *Slavish King.*[144]

Like his shorter satires, it was quickly pirated but, unlike *The True-Born Englishman*, not reprinted.

Such was the interest in political poetry during this period that miscellanies were published offering the general reader the chance to purchase verses that typically had enjoyed popularity circulating in manuscript form previously as well as broadsides and other short ephemera. Volumes with titles such as *State-Poems; continued from the time of O. Cromwel. to the year 1697. Written by the greatest wits of the age* (1703) brought together earlier satires by Buckingham, Rochester, Marvell, Milton, Waller, and Dryden and combined them with university poems and contemporary verse, offering 'the best *Secret History*, of our Reigns, as being writ by such Great Persons as were near the Helm, knew the Transactions, and were above being brib'd to flatter, or afraid to speak truth', the anonymous compiler concludes.[145] Likewise, no information on the publisher or printer is given in these collections. By 1705, the contents of a pirated version of the series had ballooned to over 600 pages. Its title displays the complexity as well as the popularity of the format: *A New Collection of Poems Relating to State Affairs, from Oliver Cromwel to this*

---

[143] Backscheider, 'The Verse Essay'; Hunter, 'Defoe and Poetic Tradition'.
[144] Defoe, *Jure Divino*, p. vi.   [145] *State-Poems*, sig. A2ᵛ.

present Time: by the Greatest Wits of the Age. Its compilers boast in the preface that it contains all that was in the earlier compilations and more, but is priced at a mere six shillings as opposed to eighteen for the set of the three earlier volumes. A 1707 *Poems on Affairs of State, from 1620 to this present Year 1707* also included copperplate engravings satirizing the French king and the Elector of Bavaria.

When one surveys the many other poets publishing under their names and circulating their works during these years, one finds the beginnings of literary careers that would come to dominate critical discourse about the period, but also a host of others who have mostly dropped out of modern anthologies, or have been studied, not for their poetry, but for their prose, or their politics. Nineteenth- and twentieth-century readers often found the poetry of the first decades of 1700 impenetrable, in part because of the topicality of its best-known satires, but also because of its seeming fascination with creating and observing rules for writing: the nineteenth-century critic Matthew Arnold dismissed Dryden and Pope, saying that they are not 'classics of our poetry, they are classics of our prose'.[146] One more recent critic asserted that 'the Augustan period of literature in England remains today our most unread and, perhaps, unknowable body of texts'.[147]

This opaque view of the period's poetry has to some extent been shaped by Alexander Pope's later depiction of many of its poets in *The Dunciad* (1728–9, 1743)—what one recent critic has called the 'genius-and-dunce worldview'.[148] Among the writers listed and lampooned in book II of the *Dunciad* are several of the most prolific and popular poets writing in the first decade and a half of the century, including Ambrose Philips, Daniel Defoe, John Tutchin, the critic John Dennis, Charles Gildon, Thomas Tickell, and Sir Richard Blackmore. It should be noted that several of them were, in the early stages of Pope's successful literary career, his serious rivals. The period between 1709 and 1713 saw a heightening of tension between poets associated with different political parties; Addison's servant Daniel Button opened a coffee house in Rose Street not far from Tonson's offices, and it became the meeting place for Whig poets, what Pope would later call Addison's 'Little Senate', including such writers as Tickell, Dennis, Ambrose Philips, and Addison's cousin Eustace Budgell.[149] Swift, Prior, Gay, and Pope originally moved in the Whig Kit-Cat literary circles, but found themselves shifting over to the Tories and their great patrons; these poets still congregated at Will's and, along with John Arbuthnot and Swift's protégé Thomas Parnell, would found the Scriblerus Club (see *MV* 5.III).

Sir Richard Blackmore had his own poetic axes to wield on the reputations of other poets. He had published in 1705 *Eliza*, another epic poem in ten books,

---

[146] Arnold, *The Complete Prose Works*, 9. 179–81.
[147] Parker, *The Triumph of Augustan Poetics*, 7. An earlier critical defence of Augustan verse is Doody, *The Daring Muse*.
[148] Hunter, 'Missing Years', 435.   [149] Williams, *Poetry*, ch. 4.

dealing with Spanish conspiracies against Queen Elizabeth, and thus inviting a comparison with Queen Anne's position in the Wars of the Spanish Succession; according to the eighteenth-century critic Samuel Johnson, it 'dropped, as it seems, dead-born from the press'.[150] In *Advice to the poets. A poem. Occasion'd by the wonderful Success of Her Majesty's Arms, under the Conduct of the Duke of Marlborough, in Flanders* (1706), Blackmore struck back at his contemporary rivals and critics, mocking the efforts by some to celebrate the victories. 'Now high *Augusta*, now *Britania* rung | With Lyric Numbers, and Heroic Song', he begins sardonically,

> Adulterer Bards rehears'd their noble Thoughts
> And Infant Poets lisp'd their tender Notes
>
> .　　.　　.　　.　　.
>
> They all their Stores of Wit and Language drain'd;
> They rais'd their Voices, and their Sinews strain'd.[151]

'Ye mercenary Wits, who Rime for Bread', he admonishes, 'Ye unfledg'd Muses, this high Subject Dread'. Philips is ruthlessly dismissed:

> No more let *Milton's* Imitator dare
> Torture our Language, to torment our Ear
>
> .　　.　　.　　.　　.
>
> Let him no more his horrid Muse employ
> In uncouth Strains, pure *English* to destroy. (p. 10)

Congreve, Prior, and Walsh are, in Blackmore's opinion, the only poets worthy to be called such. In 1708, he would go after Tonson and the poets he published in *The Kit-Cats: a poem* (see MV 5.III).

During this period of intense literary and political rivalry, the adolescent Alexander Pope came to London from Binfield in Windsor Forest. His family had left London in 1700 to avoid and to attempt to mitigate the harsh penal laws against Catholics. Now back in London, the young Pope not only learned French and Italian, his reason for travelling there, but was able to cultivate friendship with and to be encouraged by established men of letters, including the actor Thomas Betterton, whom Pope apparently had known from his childhood from Betterton's farm near Reading, and William Congreve; George Granville, Baron Lansdowne (1666–1735), to whom Pope would address *Windsor Forest*, whose own volume of verse *Poems on Several Occasions* (1712) went through multiple editions; William Walsh, with whom Pope stayed in his country home in Abberley, Worcestershire, in the summer of 1707 and who read and commented on the young man's verses; and William Wycherley, whose poems Pope would help edit, rounded out an impressive circle of established poets and critics. It was through this circle of respected literary figures that Jacob Tonson first heard about Pope's pastorals and in 1706 wrote to the young poet asking to

---

[150] Johnson, *Prefaces*, 3. 81.　　　[151] Blackmore, *Advice to the poets*, 5.

publish them.[152] Pope, however, continued to seek advice and to circulate his manuscripts among these discriminating readers, as well as his friend and mentor Sir William Trumbull, recalling later that Walsh had told him that 'there was only one way left of excelling: for though we had several great poets, we never had any one great poet that was correct; and he desired me to make that my study and aim'.[153]

Shortly before Pope's twenty-first birthday, he made his first appearance in print in Tonson's *Poetical Miscellanies. The Sixth Part* (1709), publishing his translation of *The Episode of Sarpedon* from Homer and *January and May; Or, The Merchant's Tale. From Chaucer*. Other poets in the miscellany included Nicholas Rowe, Samuel Garth, and William Wycherley, and rising talents including Thomas Tickell, Elizabeth Singer Rowe, Anne Finch, Countess of Winchilsea, and Jonathan Swift. This over 700-page volume is bookended by two sets of pastorals: Ambrose Philips (bap. 1674–1749) had six pastorals at the start, and at its end were four by Pope. There were also two commendatory poems to Pope in the middle, one by Wycherley, 'To my Friend, Mr Pope, on his Pastorals' ('Young, yet Judicious; in your Verse are found | At strengthening Nature, Sense improv'd by Sound'[154]), and one by an unnamed admirer:

> The *Sylvan* Song your first Essay you chuse,
> The hardest, the least known, most moving Muse:
> But soon on Wings, above your Native Plains,
> You mount aloft in *Homer's* Godlike Strains;
> While you Divine *Sarpedon's* Fate deplore. (p. 260)

Swift's two poems were his translation of Ovid's 'Baucis and Philemon' and the occasional piece 'To Mrs Biddy Floyd'. Like Pope, Swift had circulated his verses in manuscript prior to their appearance in print: among his early readers was Joseph Addison, who in 1708 who helped him to revise 'Baucis and Philemon'. Both poems appear in several manuscript verse miscellanies prior to their publication in 1709 and both would be pirated and printed by Edmund Curll (see *MV* 5.IV; *CV* 5.IV).[155] 'To Mrs Biddy Floyd' is a compliment to a celebrated London beauty in the form of a 'recipe' by which the gods Cupid, Jove, and Venus create a lovely, modest young woman. It exists in eight manuscript collections under various titles including 'Cupid's Contrivance', 'On a Celebrated Beauty', and 'Upon Mrs Lloyd of Chester', the last of which was accompanied by 'The Reverse: or Mrs Cudd', describing the recipe for the creation of the female opposite, the character of a vain, coquettish slattern. While subsequent generations have focused critical attention on Swift's political writings and prose satires (see *CV* 4.II), it is clear that during his second stay in London, 1707–9, he was seriously cultivating his talents and reputation as a

---

[152] See Mack, *Alexander Pope*, ch. 5.
[153] See Sherburn, *The Early Career*; Ezell, *Social Authorship*, ch. 3.
[154] *Poetical Miscellanies. The Sixth Part*, 253.   [155] See Karian, *Jonathan Swift*, ch. 2.

poet; the *Tatler* would publish his modern London georgics, 'A Description of the Morning' (no. 9, April 1709) and 'A Description of a City Shower' (1710). Like Pope, he was initially embraced by the Whig literary circle before becoming disenchanted and becoming the editor of the Tory periodical the *Examiner* (see CV 5.III).

Many miscellanies during this period could boast of a contribution from the popular and celebrated Matthew Prior—the 1709 *Poetical Miscellanies. The Sixth Part* even offered an occasional poem 'Written in the blank Leaf of a Lady's *Prior*'. Prior himself brought out the collection in 1709 with Tonson. In his preface he notes that, 'the greatest Part of what I have Writ having already been Published, either singly or else in some of the Miscellanies, it would be too late for me to make any Excuse for appearing in Print', he observes wryly, 'but a Collection of Poems has lately appeared under my Name, tho' without my Knowledge' containing misattributions and poor copy. In self-defence of his reputation as a poet, although he declares that he was 'only a Poet by Accident', he organized his volume into the topics of 'Publick Panegyrics, Amorous Odes, Serious Reflections, or Idle Tales'. He also thanks Elizabeth Singer Rowe, who had given him permission to publish one of her pastorals, 'Love and Friendship', to go with his verses in response to it.

Another contributor to the 1709 volume, Anne Finch, Countess of Winchilsea (1661–1720), had previously published her long poem *The Spleen* anonymously, and it is with that poem she is identified in the volume. She had served as a maid of honour in the court of Mary of Modena at the same time as Anne Killigrew (see MV 4.I) but declared that she so dreaded being known as a 'Versifying Maid of Honour' that she either did not write while there or tightly controlled the readership of her early verses. Upon the flight of James II, she and her husband, as Jacobite sympathizers, retired to Kent (see CV 4.I), where Finch wrote, her husband corrected, and she compiled several manuscript copies of her collected verses.[156] In 1701, *The Spleen*, in the form of a Pindaric ode, was published in Gildon's *New Miscellany of Original Poems*; it explores melancholy and was her most popular poem in the eighteenth century. 'What art thou, Spleen, which ev'ry thing dost ape?' she opens wearily, and goes on to describe the many and varied ways in which the human mind can torment the human body.[157] It explores not only the mental aspect but also the bodily and the social. 'I feel my Verse decay, and my crampt Numbers fall. | Through thy black Jaundices I all Objects see, | As dark and terrible as thee', she writes of herself, then moves on to describe the effect of melancholy on those who live with the sufferer: 'Patron thou art of every gross abuse, | The sullen Husband's feign'd excuse', and

---

[156] 'Miscellany poems with two plays by Ardelia [manuscript], [*c*.1685–1702]', FSL MS N.b.3; Wellesley College, MA, 'Anne Finch MS, Poems'.
[157] Gildon, *New Miscellany*, 60.

By thee Religion all we know
That should enlighten here below,
Is veil'd in darkness, and perplext,
With anxious Doubts, with endless Scruples vext. (pp. 67–8)

On the return of the Finches to London in 1708, more of Anne's verses began to be printed. Delarivier Manley published two in *The New Atalantis* (see CV 5.IV), and three of her pastorals appeared in the 1709 *Poetical Miscellanies*. In 1712, her husband, Heneage Finch, became the 5th Earl of Winchilsea, and in the following year, her own volume *Miscellany Poems* appeared, first in an edition 'by a Lady' and then in another edition with her name on the title page. Her arrival in London corresponded with that of Pope and Swift; her volume was published by Swift's friend John Barber, also a Jacobite sympathizer, and the volume contained eighty-six poems and her play *Aristomenes*.

Finch offered pastorals celebrating the joys of retreat from the 'world', the most famous and approved by later generations, 'A Nocturnal Reverie'. This was praised by William Wordsworth in the process of condemning the poetry of Pope in his supplemental essay to *Preface to the Lyrical Ballads* (1815):

In such a *Night*, when every louder Wind
Is to its distant Cavern safe confin'd;
And only gentle *Zephyr* fans his Wings,
And lonely *Philomel*, still waking, sings,[158]

she opens, and describes the transformation of the rural landscape by the night, 'Their shortliv'd Jubilee the Creatures keep, | Which but endures, whilst Tyrant-Man do's sleep' (p. 292). Another pastoral, 'The Petition for an absolute Retreat', asks not only for rural solitude free of crowds, noise, gossip, statecraft, and strife, but also for

A Partner suited to my Mind,
Solitary, pleas'd and kind,
Slighting, by my humble Side,
Fame and Splendor, Wealth and Pride. (pp. 39–40)

Several poems are addressed to her husband, such as 'A Letter to Daphnis', which declares:

This to the crown and blessing of my life,
The much loved husband of a happy wife;
To him whose constant passion found the art
To win a stubborn and ungrateful heart,
And to the world by tenderest proof discovers
They err, who say that husbands can't be lovers. (p. 19)

---

[158] Finch, *The Poems of Anne, Countess of Winchilsea*, ed. Reynolds, 292.

As with the earlier verses of Katherine Philips (see *MV* 2.VI), still other of Finch's poems likewise celebrate women's friendships, such as her 'Friendship between Ephelia and Ardelia'.

Other of Finch's poems, however, take a different view of marriage and of women as they are regarded by society at large. One of the poems not printed in 1713 but opening one of her manuscript volumes, 'The Introduction', states:

> Did I, my lines intend for public view,
> How many censures, would their faults pursue,
>
> .   .   .   .   .
>
> True judges might condemn their want of wit,
> And all might say, they're by a woman writ.
>
> Alas! a woman that attempts the pen,
> Such an intruder on the rights of men,
> Such a presumptuous creature, is esteemed,
> The fault can by no virtue be redeemed. (p. 50)

In other unpublished poems, Finch displays her knowledge of earlier female poets, in particular Philips and Aphra Behn; in 'The Circuit of Apollo', described by critics as part of a seventeenth-century genre of a competition among poets, Finch depicts the god of poetry descending on a spot in rural Kent to judge who is the best poet, only to find all the competitors were women.[159] Finch sees the poetic genealogy of women who write as stemming from the matchless Orinda, but in this poem seems to prefer the passions of Astraea. Her published fables indeed show a distinct satiric edge, and one can easily see how both Pope and Swift became her literary friends at some point during this period. They perhaps all met after the publication of the 1709 *Miscellanies* through mutual friends, such as the painter Charles Jervas [Jarvis], but, as Finch's biographer points out, by 1713 Pope was enjoying dining with her and they were exchanging verses.[160]

Ambrose Philips had been publishing his verses since he was a student at Cambridge, with a poem on the death of Queen Mary in 1695 printed in *Lacrymae Cantabrigienses*. After that time, he had had numerous other occupations, beginning as a fellow at St John's, then a commissioned captain-lieutenant in 1705 fighting in Spain, being captured and escaping in 1707, and finally in 1709 arriving in Denmark as the secretary to the British envoy there. From that post, he would become the tutor to the son of the Lord Chancellor, Simon Harcourt. Addison was an admirer of Philips's pastorals as early at 1707 and through the *Guardian* had promoted Philips's successful tragedy based on Racine's *Andromaque*, *The Distressed Mother* (1712) (see *CV* 5.III,

---

[159] Hinnant, *The Poetry of Anne Finch*, 13, and McGovern, *Anne Finch*, 126.
[160] McGovern, *Anne Finch*, 102–4.

5.IV). Eventually Philips secured a position as tutor to the grandchildren of George I in 1714.

As mentioned in the commendatory verse to Pope, pastoral, like the Pindaric ode, was an ambitious genre choice for a young writer, but one that could establish one's credentials to be taken seriously as a poet. The youthful Elizabeth Singer Rowe, discussed earlier, had made her reputation as 'the Pindaric Lady', using the heightened dramatic possibilities of that genre, but the title of her 1704 volume highlighted that she also created pastorals. In the 1709 *Poetical Miscellanies. The Sixth Part*, Pope's and Philips's pastorals both have their own title page, setting them apart from the other mass of verse.

Pope's pastorals, as critics have observed, are quite different from Philips's: Pope's pastorals are organized around the four seasons; his model is Virgil, and the poems demonstrate his ability to master both elaborate poetic conventions as well as flowing and melodic lines, highlighting pastoral's artifice and his skills.[161]

> Oh! How I long with you to pass my Days,
> Invoke the Muses, and resound your Praise;
> Your Praise the Birds shall chant in ev'ry Grove,
> And Winds shall waft it to the Pow'rs above.
> But wou'd you sing, and rival *Orpheus* Strain,
> The wondering Forests soon shou'd dance again,
> The moving Mountains hear the pow'rful Call,
> And headlong Streams hang list'ning in their Fall![162]

Philips, in contrast, in his preface, accentuates 'a little Country Dwelling, advantageously situated amidst a beautiful Variety of Fields, Woods, and Rivers' (p. 17), claiming not only Virgil and Theocritus for his models but also Edmund Spenser. Philips's third pastoral, 'Albino', foregrounds the contemporary English setting, invoking Spenser,

> when amid the rural Throng
> He carol'd sweet, and graz'd along the Flood
> Of gentle *Thames*, made ev'ry sounding Wood
> With good *Eliza's* Name to ring around,

as his model, 'I my slender Musick raise, | And teach the vocal Vallies ANNA's Praise' (p. 17). The two shepherds mourning the loss of their comrade Albino, 'The Pride of Britain, and the darling Joy | Of all the Plains and ev'ry Shepherd Boy', decide to honour him each harvest: 'Old *Moulin* there shall harp, young *Mico* sing, | And *Cuddy* dance the Round amidst the Ring, | And *Hobbinol* his antick Gambols play' (p. 23).

---

[161] For a negative assessment of Pope's pastoral style, see the early biographer of Pope, Stephen, *Alexander Pope*, ch. 2; for more positive appreciations, see Spacks, *Reading Eighteenth-Century Poetry*, ch. 4.

[162] 'Summer', in *Poetical Miscellanies. The Sixth Part*, 736.

Four years after its appearance, this passage by Philips was quoted in the *Guardian* (no. 30, 15 April 1713) (see MV 5.III), as an example of what types of changes may be made to classical conventions of pastoral to render it more delightful, modern, and English. The author of the essay, Thomas Tickell (1685–1740), commends both Spenser and Philips, declaring, 'both have copied and improved the Beauties of the Ancients…as far as our Language would allow them, they have formed a Pastoral Stile according to the Doric of Theocritus, in which I dare not say they have excelled Virgil'. Tickell's early poem *Oxford* (1706) had been a topographical poetic description of the delights of Oxford and its countryside; Tickell had enjoyed numerous literary friend-ships there, including with the Professor of Poetry, Joseph Trapp, John Philips, and Samuel Cobb, who would publish his own volumes of verse, *Poems on Several Occasions* (1707) and *The Female Reign* (1709).[163]

In an earlier *Guardian* essay, one of a series of five—nos 22, 23, 28, 30, 32— Tickell had described pastoral as verse that

not only amuses the Fancy the most delightfully, but is likewise more indebted to it than any other sort whatsoever. It transports us into a kind of Fairy Land, where our Ears are soothed with the Melody of Birds, bleating Flocks, and purling Streams; our Eyes enchanted with flowery Meadows and springing Greens; we are laid under cool Shades, and entertained with all the Sweets and Freshness of Nature. It is a Dream, 'tis a Vision, which we wish may be real, and we believe that it is true. (*Guardian*, no. 22, 6 April 1713)

Tickell did not ignore Pope's pastorals, praising them in passing, but this was the final straw in response to the volume that clearly favoured Philips's contri-butions over those of Pope. In the *Tatler* shortly after the appearance of the 1709 volume, Steele had highlighted Philips's contributions without mention-ing Pope's at all, and in a *Spectator* number Addison added his praises of Philips with what certainly seems like a swipe at the younger poet. It begins well enough, with a sentence praising the 1712 *Miscellaneous Poems and Translations. By Several Hands* published by Lintot and edited by Pope, con-taining the first version of the *Rape of the Lock*, to be discussed later in this section: 'I am always highly delighted with the discovery of any rising Genius among my Countrymen. For this reason I have read over, with great pleasure, the late Miscellany published by Mr *Pope*, in which there are many excellent Compositions of that ingenious Gentleman.' He then devotes a paragraph to praising Philips:

I would recommend to their Consideration the Pastorals of Mr *Philips*. One would have thought it impossible for this Kind of Poetry to have subsisted without Fawns and Satyrs, Wood Nymphs, and Water Nymphs, with all the Tribe of rural Deities. But we see he has given a new Life, and a more natural Beauty to this way of Writing by substituting in the place of these Antiquated Fables, the superstitious Mythology which prevails among the Shepherds of our own Country. (*Spectator*, no. 523, 30 October 1712)

---

[163] Tickell, *Thomas Tickell*, ch. 2.

Pope met both Addison and Steele in 1711, about the time he also became acquainted with John Gay (1685–1732). At that time, Pope quickly became an active member of their literary circle (see *MV* 5.III), composing the prologue for Addison's opera *Rosamund* and contributing numbers to the *Guardian* (see *CV* 5.III), including a satirical piece on pastoral, no. 40, 27 April 1713, written in response to the series begun by Tickell. According to his biographers, Pope sent it anonymously to Steele, who apparently failed to recognize the irony in the hyperbolic praise of Philips's *'beautiful Rusticity'*. Indeed, the author claims to have found an even better example of natural rustic dialogue than Philips's in a supposedly ancient ballad written in the dialect of Somerset: 'Is this the Love that once to me you zed, | When from tha Wake thou brought'st me Ginger-bread?'[164]

John Gay would continue this spirited debate over the nature and naturalness of pastoral, publishing his own artful parody of it, *The Shepherd's Week* (1714). He had first appeared in print in May 1708 with a parody of John Philips's Miltonic georgic *Cyder*, called simply *Wine: A Poem*:

> Had the *Oxonian* Bard thy Praise rehears'd,
> His Muse had yet retain'd her wonted height;
> *Aerial* now in *Ariconian* Bogs
> She lies Inglorious floundering like her Theme.[165]

Gay had come to London from Devon to be apprenticed to a draper, but, once there, his former schoolmate, the dramatist Aaron Hill (1685–1750) (see *CV* 5.III), who at that time edited the periodical the *British Apollo*, became his literary mentor.[166] Gay perhaps became Hill's secretary but also began contributing pieces, including his farewell to the magazine, *The Present State of Wit* (1711), in the form of a letter to a friend in the country: complimenting Steele and Addison for the widespread moral and critical influence of the *Tatler* and the *Spectator* on shaping the taste and manners of its readers, the postscript snipes ungraciously at his former employer noting, 'I find I have quite forgot the *British Apollo*', since it has moved its quarters from the Town, 'where I am informed however it still recommends itself by deciding wagers at cards, and giving good advice to shopkeepers and their apprentices'.[167]

Moving from Hill's mentorship, Gay cultivated his acquaintance with Pope, addressing to him in 1713 *Rural Sports Inscribed to Mr Pope*, published by Tonson. By this time, Gay had been hired as the secretary to the ageing widow of the Duke of Monmouth (see *MV* 4.I). The original occasion of the poem was to celebrate the Peace of Utrecht; Gay declares to Pope that, although he is mired in London, where 'Each Rival Machiavel with Envy burns, | And Honesty forsakes them All by turns', he will retreat into Pope's vision of the countryside:

---

[164] *Guardian*, no. 40, 27 April 1713, p. 239.   [165] Gay, *Wine*, 6.
[166] See Brewster, *Aaron Hill*, ch. 1.   [167] Gay, *Present State*, 23.

> My Muse shall rove through flow'ry Meads and Plains,
> And Rural Sports adorn these homely Strains,
> And the same Road ambitiously pursue,
> Frequented by the *Mantuan* Swain, and You.[168]

In this georgic modelled on Virgil, Gay highlights country pleasures and sports such as hunting, fishing, and shooting rather than seasonal labour on the farm: 'But each revolving Sport the Year employ, | And fortifie the Mind with healthful Joy' (p. 21).

Gay's characteristic parodic mockery returned in force in *The Shepherd's Week* (1714). Throughout the 'Proeme' that precedes it, he uses an exaggerated pseudo-Elizabethan diction to ridicule Philips's notion of Spenserian pastoral and to support indirectly Pope's representation of true pastoral style as found in his *Guardian*, no. 40, essay: modestly the speaker declares, 'Great Marvell hath it been, (and that not unworthily) to diverse worthy Wits, that in this our Island of Britain…no Poet (though other ways of notable Cunning in Roundelays) hath hit on the right simple Eclogue after the true ancient guise of Theocritus, before this mine Attempt'.[169] Gay's rural characters have parodic Spenserian names: Lobbin Clout, Cloddipole, Bumkinet, Grubbinol, and Blowzelinda. The events in their lives are comic rather than tragic. They sleep under hedges, not in arbours, and their rural life is filled with actual unromantic labour: Marian the lovelorn milkmaid declares, 'My Sheep were silly, but more silly I', and recounts the unkindness of Colin Clout, but, when Goody Dobbin brings her cow to be bred, 'With Apron blue to dry her Tears she sought, | Then saw the Cow well serv'd, and took a Groat' (p. 18, 'Second Pastoral'). *The Shepherd's Week* is also notable for its illustrations by Louis Du Guernier. They show scenes of everyday rural village life, much as do Gay's poems, with the church in the background while social festivities such as dancing around the maypole or gathering at a gravesite are in the foreground.

Pope's own attempt at a serious georgic was published shortly after Gay's *Rural Sports* in 1713, and, like it, the occasion for its publication was the Peace of Utrecht, which brought an end to the Wars of the Spanish Succession. *Windsor Forest* had been in the process of composition long before the event leading to its publication, and had been read in manuscript by many of Pope's friends, including John Caryll.[170] Pope was persuaded to publish it by a request of George Granville, Lord Lansdowne, to whom he dedicated the printed version. Pope was one of many poets who published on the peace and its treaty, literary historians having recovered some seventy-four of them, including ones by Tickell, the dramatist Elkanah Settle, Thomas Parnell, and Bevil Higgons.[171] Pope's poem has received much more critical attention than any of the others, in part for its sheer literary merit, but also in connection with its denunciation—

---

[168] Gay, *Rural Sports*, 2. [169] Gay, *Shepherd's Week*, sig. A3ʳ.
[170] Ezell, *Social Authorship*, 67. [171] Foxon, *English Verse*, 2. 296.

or lack of it—of Britain's expansion into the North Atlantic slave trade as one of the provisions of the treaty.[172] The 'Asiento Clause' was highlighted in Queen Anne's speech to Parliament, where she announced that among the favourable terms secured for England was that English merchants would now for a thirty-year period be able to compete with the French and to provide 'one hundred and forty four thousand Negroes, *Piezas de India*, of both Sexes, and of all Ages, at the Rate of Four thousand and eight hundred Negroes, *Piezas de India*, in each of the said Thirty years'.[173]

As critics have pointed out, none of the other poems praising Queen Anne for the peace displays the slightest qualms about the slavery provision. Thomas Newcomb in *Pacata Britannia* (1713) plays with the conceit of the Amazonian warrior queen who nevertheless grieves the loss of her nation's sons, 'Till Albion own, as you her Fate pursue, | She bled with Glory to be wept by you'.[174] Parnell (1679–1718), one of the Scriblerians who was mentored by Swift (see *MV* 5.III), produced a poem intended for print, *On Queen Anne's Peace, Anno 1713*, which, however, was initially circulated in manuscript form. It also depicts Queen Anne as Europe's guardian, who now contemplates England at peace:

> Presenting peaceful images of good
> On Fancy's airy stage; returning Trade,
> A sunk Exchequer fill'd, an Army paid,
> The fields with men, the men with plenty bless'd,
> The towns with riches, and the world with rest.

Swift's patron Henry St John, Lord Bolingbroke, comes in for a large share of the praise. Parnell concludes, 'Great Britain arm'd, triumphant and ador'd, | Its State enlarg'd, its Peace restor'd again, Are Blessings all adorning Anna's Reign'.[175]

William Diaper (1685–1717), who had gained attention for his whimsical volume *Nereides: or, Sea-Eclogues* (1712), quickly followed it with a georgic set in English fairyland, *Dryades; Or, The Nymphs Prophecy* (dated 1713) published by Lintot. Swift had also introduced Diaper to Bolingbroke, and *Dryades* reflects this political patronage:

> If Bolingbroke, and Oxford with a Smile
> Reward the Song, nor scorn the meaner Style;
> Each bleeding Tree shall tell the Shepherd's Flame,
> And in its Wounds preserve the growing Name.[176]

Diaper also seems to be targeting the Whigs in general and Marlborough in particular, who was eventually to be brought down by charges that he profited from the war:

---

[172] See Brown (*Alexander Pope*, 40), who feels that Pope's verses tacitly accept and celebrate the conditions under which slavery was sanctioned for British economic ends, and Erskine-Hill ('Pope and Slavery'), who emphatically rejected such a reading.
[173] *The Assiento*, 3.   [174] Newcomb, *Pacata Britannia*, 9.
[175] See Griffin, *Swift and Pope*, ch. 1.   [176] Diaper, *Dryades*, 16.

> By foreign Wars intestine Factions thrive,
> The Dam destroy'd, the Imps not long survive
>
> .   .   .   .   .
>
> Designing Men the publick Welfare hate,
> Who cannot rise but on a ruin'd State. (pp. 18–19)

Fortunately, 'What specious colour'd Fraud, or secret Snare | Can *St. John*'s Prudence scape, or *Oxford*'s Care?' (p. 19).

Thomas Tickell offered *A poem, To His Excellency The Lord Privy-Seal, on the prospect of peace* published by Tonson, which went through multiple editions in 1713, and was praised by Addison in the *Guardian* essay in which he dismissed Pope's miscellany. Tickell, writing before the treaty was signed, imagines the celebrations that will ensue with the return of the English warriors to a welcoming country and observes:

> Her guiltless Glory just Britannia draws
> From pure Religion, and impartial Laws,
> To Europe's Wounds a Mother's Aid she bring,
> And holds in equal Scales the Rival Kings.[177]

Tickell focuses on Marlborough and his victories as they are immortalized in Blenheim Castle, and his trading of the business of war for the pleasures of the hunt.

Pope's poem celebrating peace likewise enjoyed multiple editions. *Windsor-Forest. To the Right Honourable George Lord Lansdown*, published by Bernard Lintot, does not immediately address the war or the peace, but instead moves slowly through time and history, placing Windsor Forest in multiple frames, from the poets who have preceded him, the Edenic past, and the Augustan golden future.

> The Groves of *Eden*, vanish'd now so long,
> Live in Description, and look green in Song:
> *These*, were my Breast inspir'd with equal Flame,
> Like them in Beauty, should be like in Fame.
> Here Hills and Vales, the Woodland and the Plain,
> Here Earth and Water seem to strive again,
> Not *Chaos*-like together crush'd and bruis'd,
> But as the World, harmoniously confus'd:
> Where Order in Variety we see,
> And where, tho' all things differ, all agree.[178]

Pope's guides through the landscape include those pastoral poets of the previous generation:

> Let by the Sound I roam from Shade to Shade,
> By God-like Poets Venerable made:

---

[177] Tickell, *To His Excellency*, 7.   [178] Pope, *Windsor-Forest*, 1.

> Here his first Lays Majestick *Denham* sung;
> There the last Numbers flow'd from *Cowley*'s Tongue. (p. 12)

Critics have observed the ways in which Pope's poem in many ways competes with Tickell's while maintaining its own Tory-inflected vision of who should be celebrated; Pope even wrote to his friend Caryll that he had some concerns that some of his lines might seem too similar to Tickell's, which had enjoyed three editions by this time.[179]

Pope's poem looks forward to a time of peace, but also to a time in which 'Earth's distant Ends our Glory shall behold, | And the new World launch forth to seek the Old':

> Oh stretch thy Reign, fair *Peace*! from Shore to Shore,
> Till Conquest cease, and Slav'ry be no more:
> Till the freed Indians in their Native Groves
> Reap their own Fruits, and woo their Sable Loves. (p. 17)

All agents of chaos and disorder such as faction, rebellion, and persecution will be banished, and Pope concludes by bowing out:

> Here cease thy Flight, nor with unhallow'd Lays
> Touch the fair Fame of *Albion*'s Golden Days.
> The Thoughts of Gods let *Granville*'s Verse recite,
> And bring the Scenes of opening Fate to Light. (p. 18)

Granville (1666–1735), who was influenced by Waller and by Dryden especially in his early staged plays—including *The British Enchanters* (1706) and his conversion of Shakespeare's *Merchant of Venice* into a comedy staged by Thomas Betterton, *The Jew of Venice* (1711)—published his *Poems Upon Several Occasions* in 1712. When *The British Enchanters* was revived in 1707, as his biographer has noted, Queen Anne is depicted as Oriana, bringing peace to the world;[180] in the version printed in *Poems Upon Several Occasions*, the concluding stage direction is 'Here a SCENE represents the Queen, and all the Triumphs of her Majesty's Reign' followed by a lengthy poem celebrating Queen Anne as the 'Guardian of Mankind'.[181] It was Granville who brought Pope and his poetry to Bolingbroke's attention prior to anything of Pope's being printed. Most of the contents of Granville's volume had not been previously published; Tonson states in the advertisement to the reader that the collection was published with the author's consent, and therefore the works are correct copies. Granville's poems range from topical poems on the marriage of James, then Duke of York, to Mary of Modena, to James as king and Mary as queen, a series of songs and occasional verse to 'Myra', as well as poems sent to him 'by a Lady' and his verses in response. He wrote verses to Dryden,

[179] Richardson, *Slavery and Augustan Literature*, chs 3, 4.
[180] Eveline Cruickshank, 'Granville, George, Baron Landsdowne and Jacobite duke of Albemarle (1666–1735)', *ODNB*.   [181] Granville, *Poems*, 266.

Waller, and Wycherley on writing poetry as well as the longer 'An Essay upon Unnatural Flights in Poetry':

> Poets are Limners of another kind,
> To copy out Idæas in the Mind,
> Words are the Paint by which their Thoughts are shown,
> And Nature is their Object to be drawn. (p. 172)

Such advice to poets, of course, also informs Pope's *Essay on Criticism*, which had appeared in print anonymously in May 1711 and doubtless was read in its earlier forms by Granville as well as William Walsh. It would quickly be reissued with Pope as its author and by 1719 had enjoyed six editions. It contains several of Pope's most quoted (often out of context or misquoted) lines: '*Fools* rush in where *Angels* fear to tread', 'A *little Learning* is a dang'rous thing', 'To Err is *Humane*, to Forgive, *Divine*'. Readers of the Earl of Roscommon's *Ars Poetica* (1680) and his *Essay on Translated Verse* (1684) (see MV 3.III; CV 4.III) would have been quite familiar with Pope's use of the long verse essay to discuss classical models and standards. In addition to giving pithy rules for evaluating and valuing verse that testify to his reading of Quintilian, Longinus, and Horace, Pope displays as well his familiarity with recent French critics (see CV 4.III) and his consciousness of taking his own place in the long history of criticism.[182]

> But where's the Man, who Counsel *can* bestow,
> Still *pleas'd* to teach, and not *proud* to *know*?
> Unbiass'd, or by *Favour* or by *Spite*;
> Not *dully* prepossest, nor *blindly* right;
> Tho' Learn'd, *well-bred*; and tho' well-bred, *sincere*;
> *Modestly bold*, and *Humanly severe*?
> Who to a *Friend* his *Faults* can freely show,
> And gladly praise the *Merit* of a *Foe*?
> Blest with a *Taste* exact, yet unconfin'd;
> A *Knowledge* both of *Books* and *Humankind*;
> Gen'rous *Converse*; a *Soul* exempt from *Pride*;
> And *Love* to *Praise*, with *Reason* on his Side?[183]

The ancients possessed such critics, Pope asserts, but in more recent history:

> But *we*, brave *Britons, Foreign Laws* despis'd,
> And kept *unconquer'd* and *unciviliz'd*,
> Fierce for the *Liberties of Wit*, and bold,
> We *still* defy'd the *Romans* as of old. (p. 35)

Only a few, such as Roscommon and Walsh, 'the Muse's Judge and Friend, | Who justly knew to blame or to commend', have upheld the standards of criticism to ensure that poetry continues to do the public, social work it should.

---

[182] See Smallwood, *Reconstructing Criticism*, ch. 9.   [183] Pope, *Essay on Criticism*, 31–2.

This provoked the poet–critic John Dennis to publish *Reflections Critical and Satyrical Upon a Late Rhapsody, Call'd An Essay Upon Criticism* (1711), also with Pope's publisher Bernard Lintot. Stating in the preface that he felt personally attacked by the poem, Dennis dissects it with a scalpel to demonstrate that Pope was 'a Slave to Authority and Opinion' paying 'servile Deference' to the ancients (see CV 4.III).[184] Dennis had hoped to publish by subscription a vastly expanded version of his *The Grounds of Criticism in Poetry* (1704), which would include appropriate rules for every genre and biographies of poets who demonstrated them, but it had so few subscribers he had been unable to create the full volume. Perhaps this added the venom to his attack on Pope, whom he infamously described as 'a hunch-back'd Toad', and a 'young, squab, short Gentleman, with the forementioned Qualifications, an eternal Writer of Amorous Pastoral Madrigals' (pp. 26, 29). 'Instead of setting his Picture to show', Dennis concludes, 'I have taken a keener Revenge, and expos' d his Intellectual, as duly considering that let the Person of a Gentleman of his Parts be never so contemptible; his inward Man is ten times more ridiculous', and he offers the sneering comparison which would be picked up by other satirists targeting Pope, 'it being impossible that his outward Form, tho' it should be that of downright Monkey, should differ so much from human Shape, as his immaterial unthinking part does from human Understanding' (p. 29).

Pope, however, was at that time engaged in other significant publications. His 1712 collection *Miscellaneous Poems and Translations*, published by Lintot, contained verses by himself, Thomas Betterton, and Dryden, as well as miscellaneous verse by 'other hands'. The opening piece is by Pope, his translation of the first book of Statius; in the preface to it he states that he 'hopes he need not Apologize for his Choice... which was made almost in his Childhood. But finding the Version better, upon Review, than he expected from those Years, he was easily prevail'd upon to give it some Correction', on the grounds that little of Statius had been previously translated. The concluding piece of the volume, however, does not bear Pope's name: *The Rape of the Lock. An Heroi-Comical Poem*, in two cantos.

Pope was familiar with the convention of mock-epics, including Dryden's satire on Thomas Shadwell and bad poets *Mac Flecknoe* (1682) and Garth's *The Dispensary* (1699) (see CV 4.V). The topic for his came from the request of his friend John Caryll to soothe the ruffled feathers of two prominent Catholic families over an incident when Robert Lord Petre cut a love lock from Arabella Fermor's tresses without her consent, and to 'laugh them together again'.[185]

> What dire Offence from Am'rous Causes springs,
> What mighty Quarrels rise from Trivial Things,
> I sing—This Verse to C—l, Muse! Is due;
> This ev'n Belinda may vouchsafe to view:

---

[184] Dennis, *Reflections*, 'Preface'.　　[185] Spence, *Observations, Anecdotes, and Characters*, 104.

> Slight is the Subject, but not so the Praise,
> If She inspire, and He approve my Lays.[186]

The essential elements, which would be developed in the four-canto version published under his name in 1714, are already established in the earlier one. The confusion of intrinsic, interior moral values and expensive, external commodities, the emptying of emblems of cultural signifiers and the substitution of glittering forms, and the war between the sexes are all on display: 'On her white Breast a sparkling *Cross* she wore, | Which *Jews* might kiss, and Infidels adore' (p. 356).[187] The use of zeugma heightens the sense that, in this fashionable world at court, priorities and values are curiously muddled:

> Here *Britain*'s Statesmen oft the Fall foredoom
> Of Foreign Tyrants, and of Nymphs at home;
> Here Thou, great *Anna*! Whom three Realms obey,
> Dost sometimes Counsel take—and sometimes *Tea*. (p. 359)

The expanded 1714 version was also published by Lintot, but this time with illustrations by Du Guernier and Pope's name on the title page. In the epistle addressed to Arabella Fermor, Pope explains that the poem initially was designed to be read by only a few 'Ladies, who have good Sense and Good Humour enough, to laugh not only at their Sex's little unguarded Follies, but at their Own', but that an imperfect copy 'having been offer'd to a Bookseller, You had the Good-Nature for my Sake to consent to the Publication of one more correct', even though he had finished only part of his design. He explains the 'machinery', a term 'invented by the Criticks, to signify that Part which the Deities, Angels, or Dæmons, are made to act in a Poem'.[188] In this mock epic, Pope has chosen 'a very new and odd Foundation, the *Rosicrucian* Doctrine of Spirits' ('Epistle').

The introduction of the Sylphs, ethereal creatures devoted to the preservation of young ladies' chastity, adds another layer of complexity to the issues raised in the earlier version of the poem. 'Know farther yet; Whoever fair and chaste | Rejects Mankind, is by some Sylph embrac'd', Pope announces, concluding the stanza with the observation:

> What guards the Purity of melting Maids,
>
> . . . . . .
>
> 'Tis but their Sylph, the wise Celestials know,
> Tho' Honour is the Word with Men below. (p. 5)

When Ariel, the chief sylph, informs Belinda's other attending spirits that 'black Omens threat the brightest Fair', it is clear that myriad dangers surround young women:

> Whether the Nymph shall break *Diana's* Law,
> Or some frail *China* Jar receive a Flaw,

---

[186] *Miscellaneous Poems and Translations*, 354.
[187] See also Benedict, 'Death and the Object'.   [188] Pope, *Rape of the Lock*.

> Or stain her Honour, or her new Brocade,
> Forget her Pray'rs, or miss a Masquerade,
> Or lose her Heart, or Necklace, at a Ball. (p. 16)

The society at Hampton Court that the young Belinda and her stalker, the Baron, inhabit is likewise a dangerous place: 'Hither the Heroes and the Nymphs resort, | To taste awhile the Pleasure of a Court', which appears to consist of 'various Talk'.

> One speaks the Glory of the *British Queen*,
> And one describes a charming *Indian Screen*;
> A third interprets Motions, Looks, and Eyes;
> At ev'ry Word a Reputation dies. (p. 20)

The court is a marriage market for fashionable young people, where one's reputation, it emerges, is actually more important than one's virtue or lack thereof. On the Baron's successful snipping of the lock, Belinda's friend Thalestris laments, 'Gods! Shall the Ravisher display your Hair, | While the Fops envy, and the Ladies stare!' She concludes thoughtfully what the outcome will be: 'Already hear the horrid things they say, | Already see you a degraded Toast, | And all your Honour in a Whisper lost!' 'How shall I, then', she muses, 'your helpless Fame defend? | 'Twill then be Infamy to seem your Friend!' (p. 36).

The young men of this society appear primarily interested in conquest and display, defined by objects they possess and exhibit. The Baron, seeking assistance of the gods to secure the lock of Belinda's hair, builds an altar made of French romances and offers as sacrifices 'all the Trophies of his former Loves', including a garter and half a pair of Gloves:

> Resolv'd to win, he meditates the way,
> By Force to ravish, or by Fraud betray;
> For when Success a Lover's Toil attends,
> Few ask, if Fraud or Force attain'd his Ends. (p. 12)

Bested by Belinda at court in a game of cards, the Baron is subsequently armed by one of the other court beauties, Clarissa, who gives him her scissors. On severing the lock, and while Belinda drinks her coffee, he declares:

> Let Wreaths of Triumph now my Temples twine,
> (The Victor cry'd) the glorious Prize is mine!
>
> . . . .
>
> While Nymphs take Treats, or Assignations give,
> So long my Honour, Name, and Praise shall live! (p. 28)

The 1714 version of the poem sold 3,000 copies in four days.[189] There are many features of Pope's treatment of the mock-heroic present in the multiple versions of *The Rape of the Lock*, which he revised again in 1717, which he

---

[189] See Nichol, 'Preface', in Nichol (ed.), *Anniversary Essays*, p. xx, for the publication history of the multiple 1714 editions.

would exploit in his later lengthy poem *The Dunciad* (1729, 1743).[190] There are epic battles and contests, catalogues of weapons and objects, journeys to the underworld, and supernatural intervention into the lives of mortals. Readers familiar with *Paradise Lost* would also have been aware that Pope was not merely concerned with classical epics and their machinery; the resonance between the two may well have been enhanced by the eighteen numbers of the *Spectator* by Addison, which had been devoted to the analysis of Milton's epic in 1711–12 (see *MV* 5.III).

While in the process of revising *The Rape of the Lock*, Pope had also been working on a proposal for a subscription publication, a translation of Homer's epic the *Iliad*, modelled after Dryden's successful single folio volume translation of Virgil (see *MV* 3.VI; *CV* 4.V). Pope imagined his as a series of six volumes done in a large quarto, each containing four books of the epic and including notes. It would, according to Pope's proposal, be printed on 'the finest Paper, and [with] a Letter new Cast on purpose, with Ornaments and initial Letters engraven on Copper'.[191] Also, unlike Dryden's enterprise, which required a single payment upfront, the *Iliad* could be paid for in five instalments over a five-year period. Even more striking were the terms that Pope as the translator secured from Lintot: in the contract he signed on 23 March 1714, not only did Pope control the quality of the paper and appearance of the text, but he was also to receive in payment 200 guineas per volume, in addition to 750 copies for distribution to his subscribers. Lintot retained copyright and could, after a month of the quarto's appearance, later publish it in whatever size and format he wished, but not on the same quality paper or with the engravings, making Pope, as his biographer observed, his own publisher for the subscription volumes and transforming Lintot into his agent.[192] The six volumes were completed in 1720, and his translation of the *Odyssey*, done with William Broome and Elijah Fenton, who had also been contributors to the 1712 *Miscellaneous Poems and Translations*, was finished by 1726. All told, Pope's payments for the *Iliad* and the *Odyssey* have recently been estimated to be around £10,000; as Pope himself would comment later, 'But (thanks to *Homer*) since I live and thrive, | Indebted to no Prince or Peer alive',[193] although, as recent commentators have described, Pope benefited greatly from the friendship and patronage of Burlington, Lansdowne, Bolingbroke, and Halifax, each of whom happily subscribed for multiple sets of the volumes.[194]

Pope would have need of his friends as well as patrons during this period. In May 1714, after Pope had signed his contract for the translation with Lintot,

---

[190] Rawson, 'Heroic Notes'.
[191] Pope, *Rape of the Lock*, 'Books printed for Bernard Lintott'.
[192] Mack, *Alexander Pope*, 267. See also Foxon, *Pope*, ch. 2.
[193] Pope, *The second epistle of the second book of Horace*, 6.
[194] See Griffin, *Literary Patronage in England*, ch. 6.

Thomas Tickell signed one for the same task with Jacob Tonson. Over time Pope became suspicious that Addison himself was behind his protégé's new venture, and perhaps even assisting in Tickell's translation. He recounted to Spence later in his life that, when dining one evening with Addison, Addison had warned him that Tickell intended to publish his version of Homer, but only book 1, which he had translated while at university.[195] As the publication of Pope's first volume approached in the spring of 1715, a series of pamphlets attacking both the project and Pope personally appeared. 'Sir Iliad Doggrel' offered Pope sarcastic advice in *Homerides: Or a Letter to Mr Pope. Occasion'd by his Intended Translation of Homer*. Pope's increasing physical deformity of the spine is highlighted on the title page with an epigram in Greek from Homer describing Thersites, 'his humped shoulders stopping over his chest'. In this charged and competitive environment, Tickell published his first volume two days after Pope did his in June 1715: Lintot wrote to Pope that Tickell's version 'is already condemn'd here and the malice & juggle at Buttons is the conversation of those who have spare moments from Politicks'.[196] Poetry, even the classical legacy, and its readers kept the contemporary political edge sharpened.

The death of Queen Anne on 1 August 1714, oddly, did not bring forth the outpouring of public verse by the most prominent poets of the day such as Prior, Congreve, Swift, or Pope, as had been the case with the mourning for the passing of Charles II (see *MV* 4.I).[197] The poems by Joseph Harris and John Dennis welcome King George even as they lament the passing of the Queen. Nevertheless, some were moved to immortalize the last of the Stuarts both as a queen and as a woman. An anonymous late fellow of New College, Oxford, imagined her comforting her people with her dying words in *Elegy on the Death of Her Most Gracious Majesty Queen Anne*. An unknown 'Lady of Quality' offered a dramatic dialogue poem between Constantia, Clemena, and Pacia, three ladies of the court. With the passing of the Queen, all previous order and decorum becomes confusion and disbelief:

> Fill'd with confused Cries the Palace seems;
> Haste, let us see. Oh my foreboding Dreams!
> Preserve us, Fate! Look yonder, *Pacia*, where
> The Regent's Nymphs run with distracted Air.[198]

The lawyer and hopeful dramatist Lewis Theobald (bap. 1688–1744), who had penned *A Pindaric Ode on the Union of Scotland and England* (1707) and the tragedy *Persian Princess, or, The Royal Villain* (1708), and who would end up in Pope's *Dunciad*, offered *The Mausoleum, a Poem: Sacred to the Memory of*

---

[195] Spence, *Observations, Anecdotes, and Characters*, 162–4.
[196] Quoted in Mack, *Alexander Pope*, 278.   [197] See Winn, *Queen Anne*, chapter 11.
[198] *A Poem Sacred to the Immortal Memory*, 5.

her Late Majesty Queen Anne (1714). Summarizing her life as a compound of virtues, Theobald declares:

> Where *Love* with *Pow'r* in sweet Confusion met,
> And *Majesty* with *Mercy* blended sat.
> An Union so compleat in Her was seen;
> She *Reign'd* a *Mother,* and She *Liv'd* a *Queen*![199]

---

[199] Theobald, *The Mausoleum*, 3.

Appendix: Table of Contents of *The Oxford English Literary History* *Volume 5: 1645–1714: The Later Seventeenth Century* (Companion Volume)

Bibliography

Pre-1750 Sources

(Unless otherwise stated, the place of publication for pre-1750 works is London.)

The Academy of Complements (1650).

The Academy of Pleasure (1656).

An account of the burning of the articles of the Union at Dumfries (Edinburgh, 1706).

An Account of the ceremonial at the coronation of Their Most Excellent Majesties, King James II and Queen Mary, at Westminster the 23 of April 1685 (1685).

An Account of the Societies for the Reformation of Manners in England and Ireland (1700).

An account of what passed at the execution of the late Duke of Monmouth (1685).

Addison, Joseph, *The Campaign, A Poem, To His Grace The Duke Of Marlborough* (1704).

Addison, Joseph, *Cato* (1713).

Addison, Joseph, *The Drummer; or, The Haunted House* (1716).

Addison, Joseph, *The Free-Holder* (1716).

Addison, Joseph, *Rosamond* (1707).

The address of John Dryden, laureat to His Highness, the Prince of Orange (1689).

Advice to the Maidens of London to forsake their fantastical top-knots (1691).

Advice to a parson, or, The true art of preaching, in opposition to modern practice written by a person of honour to Dr S—, his late chaplin (1691).

Allestree, Charles, *A sermon preach'd at Oxford…upon the 26th of July 1685* (1685).

Allestree, Richard, *The Gentleman's Calling. Written by the Author of the Whole Duty of Man* (1675).

Ames, Richard, *The Folly of Love. A New Satyr Against Woman together with The Bachelors Lettany* (1691, 1700).

Ames, Richard, *Sylvia's Complaint* (1692).

Ames, Richard, *Sylvia's Revenge* (1688).

An Answer to the Mantuan, or, False character lately wrote against womankind (1679).

The Apprentices Faithful Monitor (1700).

Arbuthnot, John, *A sermon preach'd to the people at the Mercat Cross of Edinburgh on the subject of the union* (1706).

'Ariadne', *She Ventures, and He Wins* (1696).

The arraignment and tryall with a declaration of the Ranters (1650).

The Assiento, or, Contract for allowing the Subjects of Great Britain the Liberty of Importing negroes into the Spanish America (1713).

Astell, Mary, *A Discourse Concerning the Love of God* (1696).

Astell, Mary, *Letters Concerning the Love of God* (1694).

Astell, Mary, *A Serious Proposal to the Ladies For the Advancement of their true and greatest Interest* (1694).

Astell, Mary, *Some Reflections Upon Marriage, Occasion'd by the Duke and Duchess of Mazarine's case* (1700, 1730).

Atkyns, Richard, *The Original and Growth of Printing* (1664).

Avery, Elizabeth, *Scripture Prophecies Opened* (1647).

Baker, Daniel, *This is a short relation of some of the cruel sufferings (for the truths sake) of Katharine Evans & Sarah Chevers in the inquisition of the isle of Malta* (1662).

Banks, John, *Virtue Betray'd or, Anna Bullen* (1682).

Barker, Jane, *Poetical recreations consisting of original poems, songs, odes, &c. with several new translations: in two parts | part I, occasionally written by Mrs Jane Barker, part II, by several gentlemen of the universities, and others* (1688).

Baron, Robert, *An Apologie for Paris. For rejecting of Juno and Pallas, and presenting of Ate's golden ball to Venus* (1649).

Baron, Robert, *Erotopaignion, or, The Cyprian Academy* (1647–8).

Baron, Robert, *Mirza* (1655).

Baron, Robert, *Pocula Castalia* (1650).

Barrow, Isaac, *The duty and reward of bounty to the poor in a sermon preached at the spittal upon Wednesday in Easter week, Anno Dom. MDCLXXI* (1671).

Baudier, Michel, *The History of the Court of the King of China* (1682).

Baxter, Richard, *Mr Baxters rules & directions for family duties* (1681).

Baxter, Richard, *The Poor Man's Family Book . . . In plain familiar Conferences between a Teacher and a Learner* (1674).

Baxter, Richard, *Reliquaiae Baxterianae: Or, Mr Richard Baxter's Narrative of the Most Memorable Passages of His Life and Times*, ed. Matthew Sylvester (1696).

Baxter, Richard, *The Saints Everlasting Rest* (1650).

Beaumont, Francis, and Fletcher, John, *Comedies and Tragedies* (1647).

Beckman, Martin, *A description of the royal fireworks . . . the happy birth of the most illustrious Prince of Wales* (1688).

Behn, Aphra, *Abdelazer, or, The Moor's Revenge* (1677).

Behn, Aphra, *Agnes de Castro; Or, The Force of Generous Love* (1688).

Behn, Aphra, *The Amorous Prince; Or, The Curious Husband* (1671).

Behn, Aphra, *The Emperor of the Moon. A Farce* (1687).

Behn, Aphra, *The Fair Jilt; Or, The History of Prince Tarquin* (1688).

Behn, Aphra, *The History of the Nun; Or, The Fair Vow-Breaker* (1689).

Behn, Aphra, *The Luckey Chance* (1687).

Behn, Aphra, *Lycidus, or, The lover in fashion* (1688).

Behn, Aphra, *The Miscellany, Being a Collection of Poems by Several Hands* (1685).

Behn, Aphra, *Oroonoko, or, The Royal Slave* (1688).

Behn, Aphra, *A Pastoral Pindarick. On the Marriage of the Right Honourable the Earle of Dorset* (1685).

Behn, Aphra, *A pindarick poem on the happy coronation of His Most Sacred Majesty James II and his illustrious consort Queen Mary* (1685).

Behn, Aphra, *A pindarick on the death of our late sovereign* (1685).

Behn, Aphra, *A Poem on her Sacred Majesty Catherine Queen Dowager* (1685).

Behn, Aphra, *Romulus And Hersilia; Or, The Sabine War* (1682).

Behn, Aphra, *The Rover Parts 1 & 2* (1677, 1681).

Beraldus, Prince of Savoy, A Novel. In Two Parts (1675).

Betterton, Thomas, *The History of the English Stage from the Restoration to the Present Time* (London, 1741).

Birkhead, Henry, 'The Female Rebellion', Bodl. Tanner 466; UG Hunter 635.

Blackborrow, Sarah, *Herein is Held Forth the Gift and Good-Will of God* (1659).

Blackmore, Richard, *Advice to the poets. A poem. Occasion'd by the wonderful Success of Her Majesty's Arms, under the Conduct of the Duke of Marlborough, in Flanders* (1706).

Blackmore, Richard, *Prince Arthur: an Heroick Poem in Ten Books* (1695).

Blackmore, Richard, *The Rise and Progress of the Kit Cat Club* (1709).

Blackmore, Richard, *A Satyr Against Wit* (1700).

Blith, Walter, *The English Improver Improved* (1653).

Blount, Charles, *A Just Vindication of Learning* (1679).

Blount, Charles, *Reasons humbly offered for the liberty of unlicens'd printing to which is subjoin'd the just and true character of Edmund Bohum, the licenser of the press* (1693).

Blount, Thomas, *The Academy of Eloquence* (1654).

Blount, Thomas, *Boscobel, or, The history of His Sacred Majesties most miraculous preservation after the battle of Worcester, 3 Sept. 1651* (1660).

Blount, Thomas, *Glossographia: or a Dictionary, Interpreting all such Hard Words* (1656).

Boate, Gerard, *Irelands naturall history* (1652).

Book of Common Prayer (1662).

Bowles, Edward, *Newes from Brussels* (1659).

Boyer, Abel, *Letters of wit, politicks and morality* (1701).

Boyle, Francis, *Discourses and Essays, Useful for the Vain Modish Ladies and their Gallants* (1696).

Boyle, Robert, *An Account of a Statical Hygroscope and its Uses, A Fragment about the Natural and Preternatural State of Bodies, and A Sceptical Dialogue about the Positive or Privative Nature of Cold* (1676).

Boyle, Robert, *The Excellency of Theology Compar'd with Nature Philosophy (as both are Objects of Men's Study) Discours'd of in a Letter to a Friend* (1675).

Boyle, Robert, *New experiments physico-mechanicall, touching the spring of the air, and its effects* (1660).

Boyle, Robert, *Of the high veneration man's intellect owes to God, peculiarly for his wisedom and power by a Fellow of the Royal Society* (1685).

Boyle, Roger, *Parthenissa* (1651–5).

Bradstreet, Anne, *The tenth muse* (1650).

Bremond, Sebastian, *The Happy Slave* (1677, 1685).

Bremond, Sebastian, *Hattige* (1680).

Bremond, Sebatian. *Homais, Queen of Tunis* (1681).

A brief description of the excellent vertues of that sober and wholesome drink, called coffee (1674).

A Brief and True Narration Of the Late Wars Risen In New-England (1675).

Brinsley, John, *A Looking Glasse for Good Women* (1645).

Brome, Alexander, *The Poems of Horace* (1661).

Brome, Henry, *Bibliotheca Digbeiana* (1680).

Brome, Richard, *Five New Playes* (1653).

Brown, Tom, *Amusements serious and comical, calculated for the meridian of London* (1700).

Brown, Tom, *Commendatory Verses, on the Author of the Two Arthurs, and the Satyr against Wit* (1700).

Brown, Thomas, *Letters from the Dead to the Living* (1702).

Browne, Thomas, *Pseudodoxia epidemica, or, Enquiries into very many received tenents and commonly presumed truths* (1646).

Browne, Thomas, *Religio Medici* (1642, 1659, 1682).

Bullokar, John, *An English Expositour, or Compleat Dictionary* (1674).

Bunyan, John, *A Book for Boys and Girls: Or Country Rhymes for Children* (1686).

Bunyan, John, *Christian Behavior* (1663).

Bunyan, John, *Come and welcome to Jesus Christ* (1686).

Bunyan, John, *A Discourse Upon the Pharisee and the Publicane* (1685).

Bunyan, John, *A Few Sighes from Hell* (1658).

Bunyan, John, *Grace Abounding to the Chief of Sinners* (1666).

Bunyan, John, *The Holy War* (1682).

Bunyan, John, *I will Pray with the Spirit* (1662).

Bunyan, John, *The Life and Death of Mr Badman* (1680).

Bunyan, John, *The Pilgrim's Progress from This World to That which is to come Delivered under the Similitude of a Dream* (1678).

Bunyan, John, *Prison-Meditations, Directed to the Heart of Suffering Saints and Reigning Sinners by John Bunyan In Prison* (1665).

Bunyan, John, *Profitable meditations fitted to mans different condition* (1661).

Bunyan, John, *Sighs from Hell: Or, The Groans of a Damned Soul* (1675).

Bunyan, John, *Some Gospel-Truths Opened* (1656).

Burnet, Gilbert, *Enquiry into the measures of submission to the supream authority, and...the grounds on which is may be lawful or necessary for subjects to defend their religion, lives, and liberties* (1688).

Burnet, Gilbert, *Pastoral Letter to the Clergy of his Diocese Concerning the Oaths of Allegiance and Supremacy to King William and Queen Mary* (1689).

Burnet, Gilbert, *Reflections upon a pamphlet entituled, Some discourses upon Dr Burnet and Dr Tillotson* (1696).

Burrough, Edward, *To the Whole English Army* (1659).

Burthogge, Richard, *Prudential reasons for repealing the penal laws against all recusants and for a general toleration* (1687).

Burton, Henry, *The grand impostor unmasked, or, A detection of the notorious hypocrisie and desperate impiety of the late Archbishop, so styled, of Canterbury* (1645).

Burton, John, *The History of Eriander* (1661).

Butler, Samuel, *Hudibras. The First Part. Written in the time of the late Wars* (1662).

C., H., *An epitomy of history. Wherein is shewn how severall princes and nations, came to their particular countries and dominions* (1661).

Care, Henry, *The Female Secretary* (1671).

Carey, Henry (trans.), *The history of the wars of Italy* (1663).

Carleton, Rowland, *Diana, Dutchess of Mantua, or, The persecuted lover a romance* (1679, 1681).

Cartwright, William, *Comedies, tragi-comedies, with other poems* (1651).

Cavendish, Margaret, Duchess of Newcastle, *The Description of a New World, called the Blazing-World* (1668).

Cavendish, Margaret, Duchess of Newcastle, *The Life of the Thrice Noble, High, and Puissant Prince William Cavendish* (1667).

Cavendish, Margaret, Duchess of Newcastle, *Nature's Pictures drawn by fancies pencil to the life* (1656).

Cavendish, Margaret, Duchess of Newcastle, *Observations upon Experimental Philosophy to which is added The Description of a New Blazing World* (1666).

Cavendish, Margaret, Duchess of Newcastle, *Poems and Fancies* (1653).

Cavendish, Margaret, Duchess of Newcastle, *Poems and Phancies* (1664).

Cavendish, Margaret, Duchess of Newcastle, *CCXI Sociable Letters* (1664).

Cellier, Elizabeth, *Malice Defeated: Or a Brief Relation of the Accusation and Deliverance of Elizabeth Cellier* (1679).

Cellier, Elizabeth, *The Tryal of Elizabeth Cellier, the Popish Midwife* (1680).

Centlivre, Susanna, *The Gamester* (1705).

Centlivre, Susanna, *Love at a Venture* (1706).

Centlivre, Susanna, *The Perjur'd Husband, Or, the Adventures of Venice A Tragedy* (1700).

Centlivre, Susanna, *The Platonick Lady* (1707).

Centlivre, Susanna, *The Wonder: a woman keeps a secret* (1714).

The Challenge sent by a young lady to Sir Thomas &c., or, The Female War (1697).

Chamberlayne, William, *Pharonnida* (1659).

The Character of a Coffeehouse, with the Symptomes of a Town-Wit (1673).

The Character of the Rump (1660).

Charles I, *Eikon Basilike; The Pourtrature of His Sacred Majestie in His Solitudes and Sufferings* (1649).

Charles I, *The Kings Cabinet Opened: or, Certain Packets of Secret Letters & Papers* (1645).

Charles I, *His Majesties Prayers which He Used in Time of his Sufferings* (1649).

Charles II, *An Act for Safety and Preservation of His Majesties Person and Government against Treasonable and Seditious practices and attempts* (1661).

Charles II, *King Charles II. his declaration to all his loving subjects of the kingdom of England. Dated from his Court at Breda in Holland, the 4/14 of April 1660* (1660).

Charles II, *A proclamation for calling in and suppressing of two books written by John Milton* (1660).

Charles II, *A proclamation for the suppression of coffee-houses* (1675).

Chidley, Katherine, *Good Counsell, to the Petitioners for Presbyterian Government* (1645).

Chidley, Katherine, *A New Yeares-Gift, or a Brief Exhortation to Mr Thomas Edwards* (1645).

Child, Josiah, *A Treatise Wherein is Demonstrated ...that the East-India Trade is the Most National of All Trades* (1681).

Chillingworth, William, *The Apostolicall Institution of Episcopacy* (1644).

Church, Benjamin, *Entertaining Passages relating to Philip's War* (1716).

Cibber, Colley, *An apology for the life of Mr Colley Cibber, comedian, and late patentee of the Theatre-Royal. With an historical view of the stage during his own Time* (1740).

Cibber, Colley, *The Careless Husband* (1704).

Cibber, Colley, *The Double Gallant* (1707).

Cibber, Colley, *The Lady's Last Stake, or, The Wife's Resentment* (1704).

Cibber, Colley, *Love's Last Shift* (1696).

Cibber, Colley, *She Wou'd and She Would Not: or, The Kind Imposter* (1702).

Clarke, Samuel, *Lives of Sundry Eminent Persons* (1683).

Cleveland, John, *The Character of a London-Diurnall* (1645).

Clifford, Martin, *Notes upon Mr Dryden's poems in Four Letters by M. Clifford…to which are annexed some Reflections upon the Hind and the panther, by another hand* (1687).

Cobb, Samuel, *Poetae Britannici: A Poem, Satyrical and Panegyrical* (1700).

The Coffee-Houses Vindicated (1675).

Cokayne, Aston, *Small poems of divers sorts* (1658).

College, Stephen, *A Ra-Ree Show* (1681).

College, Stephen, *A true copy of the dying words of Mr Stephen Colledge* (1681).

Collier, Jeremy, *A Short View of the Immorality and Profaneness of the English Stage, together with the Sense of Antiquity upon this Argument* (1698).

Collins, An, *Divine Songs and Meditacions* (1653).

A Common-Councell holden the first day of May 1660 (1660).

The Commonwealth Mercury (1658).

A Comparison Between the Two Stages, With an Examen of The Generous Conqueror and some Critical Remarks on the Funeral (1702).

The Compleat Courtier: or, Cupid's Academy (1683).

Congreve, William, *Amendments of Mr Collier's False and Imperfect Citations* (1698).

Congreve, William, *Incognita; Or, Love and Duty Reconciled* (1692).

Congreve, William, *The Judgment of Paris* (1701).

Congreve, William, *The Old Bachelor* (1693).

Congreve, William, *The Way of the World* (1700).

Cooper, Andrew, *Stratologia or The history of the English civil warrs in English verse* (1660).

Cooper, Joseph, *The art of cookery refin'd* (1654).

Cooper, William, *Catalogus variorum & insignium librorum* (1680).

Coppe, Abiezer, *A Fiery Flying Roll* (1650).

Coppe, Abiezer, *Some Sweet Sips of Some Spiritual Wine* (1649).

Coppin, Richard, *Truths Testimony* (1649).

Cotton, Charles, *The Compleat Gamester* (1674).

Cotton, Charles, *The Fair One of Tunis: or The Generous Mistress* (1674).

Cotton, Priscilla, and Cole, Mary, *The Priests and People of England we Discharge our Consciences and Give them warning* (1655).

Cowley, Abraham, *A Proposition for the Advancement of Experimental Philosophy* (1661).

Cowley, Abraham, *The Mistress; or, Several Copies of Love Verses* (1647).

Cowley, Abraham, *Poems* (1656).

Cowley, Abraham, 'To The Royal Society' (1667).

Cowley, Abraham, *Verses, Written upon several Occasions* (1663).

Cowley, Abraham, *The Works of Mr Abraham Cowley* (1668).

Cox, Nathaniel, and Kirkman, Francis, *An exact catalogue of all the comedies, tragedies, tragi-comedies, opera's [sic], masks, pastorals and interludes that were ever yet printed and published till this present year 1680* (1680).

Craftie Cromwell: Or, Oliver ordering our New State. A Tragi-comedie (1648).

Crane, Richard, *A Short But a Strict Account Taken of Babylons Merchants, Who are now Forcing the Sale of their Old, Rusty, Cankered Ware, upon the People of these Nations* (1660).

Crashaw, Richard, *Steps to the Temple: Sacred Poems, with other Delights of the Muses* (1646).

Cressy, Serenus, *Fanaticism fanatically imputed to the Catholick church by Doctour Stillingfleet and the imputation refuted and retorted by S.C. a Catholick* (Douay?, 1672).

Cressy, Serenus, *The Church History of Brittany* (1668).

Critical remarks on Mr Rowe's last play, call'd, Ulysses. A Tragedy (1706).

Crowne, John, *Calisto, or, The Chaste Nimph* (1675).

Curll, Edmund, *The Complete Key to the Tale of a Tub; With some Accounts of the Authors, The Occasion and Design of Writing it, and Mr Wotton's Remarks Examin'd* (1710).

Cynthia with the tragical account of the unfortunate lovers of Almerin and Desdemona (1687).

Dampier, William, *A New Voyage Round the World* (1697).

Dampier, William, *Voyages and Descriptions* (1699).

Darby, Charles, *The Union a poem humbly dedicated to the Queen* (1707).

Dauncy, John, *The history of the thrice illustrious Princess Henrietta Maria de Bourbon, Queen of England* (1660).

Davenant, William, *Gondibert* (1650).

Davenant, William, *A proposition for advancement of moralitie, by a new way of entertainment of the people* (1654).

Davies, John, *The civil warres of Great Britain and Ireland containing an exact history of their occasion, originall, progress, and happy end by an impartiall pen* (1661).

Davies, John, *The voyages and travels of the ambassadors sent by Frederick, Duke of Holstein, to the Great Duke of Muscovy and the King of Persia begun in the year M.DC.XXXIII. and finish'd in M.DC.XXXIX* (1669).

Dawson, Thomas, *A Book of Cookery* (1650).

Deacon, John, *The Grand Impostor Examined, or, The life, tryal, and examination of James Nayler, the seduced and seducing Quaker with the manner of his riding into Bristol* (1656).

A Declaration from the Harmless and Innocent People of God, Called Quakers, against All Sedition, Plotters, and Fighters in the World (1660).

A Declaration from the Harmless and Innocent People of God, Called Quakers (1660).

Defoe, Daniel, *The Consolidator; or Memoirs of Sundry Transactions from the World in the Moon* (1705).

Defoe, Daniel, *An Essay on the Regulation of the Press* (1704).

Defoe, Daniel, *A History of the Union of Great Britain* (Edinburgh, 1709).

Defoe, Daniel, *Jure Divino* (1706).

Defoe, Daniel, *The Pacificator* (1700).

Defoe, Daniel, *The Poor Man's Plea*, 3rd edn (1700).

Defoe, Daniel, *The Review* (1704–13).

Defoe, Daniel, *The Review of the Affairs of France* (1705).

Defoe, Daniel, *Shortest Way with the Dissenters* (1702).

Defoe, Daniel, *The True-Born Englishman* (1700).

Defoe, Daniel, *A True Relation of the Apparition of One Mrs Veal* (1705).

Defoe, Daniel, *The Vision, a poem* (Edinburgh, 1707).

DeLaune, Thomas, *A Narrative Of The Sufferings Of Thomas DeLaune* (1684).

DeLaune, Thomas, *Plea For The Nonconformists* (1683, 1706).

Delightful and Ingenious Novells (1686).

The Delinquent's Passport (1658).

Denham, John, *A panegyrick on His Excellency the Lord General George Monck* (1659).

Dennis, John, *Essay on the Opera's after the Italian Manner* (1706).

Dennis, John, *The Impartial Critick, or, Some observations upon a book, entituled, A short view of tragedy, written by Mr Rymer* (1693).

Dennis, John, *Iphigenia* (1700).

Dennis, John, *Letters upon several occasions written by and between Mr Dryden, Mr Wycherly, Mr ——, Mr Congreve, and Mr Dennis, published by Mr Dennis with a new translation of select letters of Monsieur Voiture* (1696).

Dennis, John, *The musical entertainments in the tragedy of Rinaldo and Armida all compos'd by Mr John Eccles and writ by Mr Dennis* (1699).

Dennis, John, *Reflections Critical and Satyrical Upon a Late Rhapsody, Call'd An Essay Upon Criticism* (1711).

Dennis, John, *Rinaldo and Armida* (1689).

Dennis, John, *The Usefulness of the Stage* (1698).

Diaper, William, *Dryades; Or, The Nymphs Prophecy* (1713).

Dillion, Wentworth, 4th Earl of Roscommon, *Essay on Translated Verse* (1684).

Discommendatory Verses, on those which are Truly Commendatory, on the Author of the Two Arthurs, and the Satyr against Wit (1700).

The Distressed Gentlewoman (1691).

Divine hymns and poems on several occasions...by Philomela, and several other ingenious persons (1704).

Don Samuel Crispe: Or, The Pleasant History of the Knight of Fond Love (1660).

Dorrington, Theophilus, *The Excellent Woman described by her true characters and their opposites* (1692).

Drake, James, *The Antient and Modern Stages Survey'd* (1699).

Drake, Judith, *An Essay in Defence of the Female Sex* (1696).

Dryden, John, *Absalom and Achitophel* (1681).

Dryden, John, *Albion and Albanius* (1685).

Dryden, John, *All for Love; or, The World Well Lost* (1677).

Dryden, John, *Annus mirabilis: The Year of Wonders, 1666* (1666).

Dryden, John, *Aureng-Zebe* (1675).

Dryden, John, *Britannia rediviva, a poem on the birth of the prince* (1688).

Dryden, John, *The Conquest of Granada by the Spaniards in two parts* (1672).

Dryden, John, *Don Sebastian* (1690).

Dryden, John, *Examen poeticum* (1693).

Dryden, John, *An Evening's Love, Or The Mock-Astrologer* (1671).

Dryden, John, *The Hind and the Panther* (1687).

Dryden, John, *The Kind Keeper, or Mr Limberham* (1678).

Dryden, John, *The Loyal Brother* (1682).

Dryden, John, *Marriage à la Mode* (1673).

Dryden, John, *Miscellany Poems* (1684).

Dryden, John, *Notes and Observations on The Empress of Morocco* (1674).

Dryden, John, *Ovid's Epistles* (1680).

Dryden, John, *A Poem on the Death of His late Highness, Oliver, Lord Protector of England, Scotland, and Ireland* (1659).

Dryden, John, *The satires of Decimus Junius Juvenalis translated into English…to which is prefix'd a discourse concerning the original and progress of satire* (1693).

Dryden, John, *The State of Innocence, and Fall of Man* (1674).

Dryden, John, *Sylvæ: Or The Second Part of Poetical Miscellanies* (1685).

Dryden, John, *Troilus and Cressida* (1679).

Dryden, John, *The Works of Virgil* (1697).

Dryden, John, and Howard, Sir Robert, *The Indian Queen* (1665).

Dudley, Lord North, *A Forest Promiscuous of Various Seasons Productions* (1659).

Dudley, Lord North, *A Forest of Varieties* (1645).

Duffett, Thomas, *Beauties Triumphant* (1676).

Duffett, Thomas, *The Mock-Tempest, or, the Enchanted Castle* (1675).

The Duke of Norfolk's Case with reasons for passing his bill (1700).

Dunton, John, *The Bull-Baiting: Or Sach—ll Dress'd up in Fire-Works* (1709).

Dunton, John, *The Life and Errors of John Dunton, Late Citizen of London* (1705)

Dunton, John, *The Living Elegy* (1706).

Dunton, John, *The Whipping Post: or, A Satyr upon Every Body* (1706).

D'Urfey, Thomas, *The Banditti, or, A ladies distress* (1686).

D'Urfey, Thomas, *A Commonwealth of Women* (1686).

D'Urfey, Thomas, *The Famous History of the Rise and Fall of Massaniello* (1700).

D'Urfey, Thomas, *The Virtuous Wife, or, Good Luck at Last* (1680).

The Dutch Damnified (c.1664).

Eachard, John, *Mr Hobbs's state of nature considered* (1672).

Edwards, John, *A Discourse Concerning the Authority, Stile, and Perfection of the Books of the Old and New-Testament* (1693).

Edwards, Thomas, *Gangraena: Or a Catalogue and Discovery of Many of the Errours, Heresies, Blasphemies and Pernicious Practices of the Sectaries of This Time* (1646).

Edwards, Thomas, *Reasons against the independant government of particular congregations* (1641).

Eikon Alethine (1649).

Elborough, Robert, *London's calamity by fire bewailed and improved in a sermon preached at St James Dukes-Place wherein the judgements of God are asserted* (1666).

An Elegy on the Death of his Sacred Majesty King Charles the II of Blessed Memory (1685).

An Elegy on James Scot, late Duke of Monmouth (1685).

Eliana. A New Romance: formed by an English Hand (1661).

'Eliza', *Eliza's babes, or, The virgins-offering being divine poems and meditations written by a lady* (1652).

Englands Deliverance, Or, God's Gracious Mercy at the time of Misery (1688).

England's Joy (1660).

'Ephelia', *Female Poems On several Occasions* (1679).

Evagoras (1677).

Evans, Arise, *A Rule from Heaven* (1659).

Evans, Arise, *To The Most High and Mighty Prince, Charles the II…an Epistle* (London, 1660).

Evelyn, John, *An Apology for the Royal Party: Written in a Letter to a Person of the Late Councel of State* (1659).

Evelyn, John, *Sculptura, or, The history, and art of chalcography and engraving in copper* (1662).

Evelyn, Mary, *Mundus Muliebris: or, The Ladies Dressing-Room Unlock'd, ... Together with the fop-dictionary, compiled for the use of the fair sex* (1691).

An exact narrative of the tryal and condemnation of John Twyn (1664).

The Examination, Confession, Trial and Execution of Joan Williford, Joan Cariden and Jane Holt (1645).

The Examiner (1712).

Familiar and courtly letters, written by Monsieur Voiture (1700).

Fane, Francis, *The Sacrifice* (1686).

Farquhar, George, *The Beaux's Stratagem* (1707)

Farquhar, George, *The Constant Couple, or, A Trip to the Jubilee* (1699).

Farquhar, George, *Discourse upon Comedy* as part of *Love and Business* (1702).

Farquhar, George, *The Recruiting Officer* (1706).

Fell, Margaret, *The examination and tryall of Margaret Fell and George Fox* (1664).

Fell, Margaret, *A Paper concerning such as are made Ministers by the will of man* (1659).

Fell, Margaret, *Womens speaking justified, proved and allowed* (1666).

Female Excellence, or, Woman display'd in several satyrick poems by a person of quality (1679).

The Female Wits (1696).

Ferguson, Robert, *A Representation of the Threatening Dangers Impending over Protestants in Great Britain* (1687).

First Article of Act of Union (1707).

Fisher, Samuel, *Christianismus redivivus* (1655).

A Flaming Whip for Lechery: Or, the Whoremasters Speculum (1700).

Flatman, Thomas, *Poems and Songs* (1674).

Flemming, Robert, *Theokratia, or the Divine Government of Nations Considered and Approved* (1700).

Ford, Thomas, *Logos autopistos, or, Scriptures Self-Evidence* (1667).

Forster, Mary, *These Several Papers was Sent to Parliament* (1659).

Fox, George, *A collection of many select and Christian epistles, letters and testimonies written on sundry occasions* (1698).

Fox, George, *Concerning sons and daughters, and prophetesses speaking and prophecying, in the law and the gospel and concerning womens learning in silence and also concerning womens not speaking in the church* (1661).

Fox, George, *Fifty-nine Particulars laid down for the Regulating things, and the taking away of Oppressing Laws, and Oppressors, and to ease the Oppressed* (1659).

Fuller, Thomas, *Feare of Losing the Old Light* (1646).

Fuller, Thomas, *Good Thoughts in Bad Times* (1645).

Fuller, Thomas, *The history of the worthies of England* (1662).

Fyge, Sarah, *Female Advocate* (1686, 1687).

Fyge, Sarah, *Poems on Several Occasions together with a Pastoral* (1703).

Gay, John, *The Present State of Wit* (1711).

Gay, John, *Rural Sports Inscribed to Mr Pope* (1713).

Gay, John, *The Shepherd's Week* (1714).

The Generous Rivals, or, Love Triumphant. A Novel (1711).

Gibbs, James, *A Consolatory Poem Humbly Addressed to her Royal Highness* (1700).

Gildon, Charles, *Letters and Essays, on Several Subjects ... to John Dryden, Esq., Geo. Granvill, Esq., Walter Moile, Esq., Mr Congreve, and Mr Denis, and other ingenious men of th' age by several gentlemen and ladies* (1694).

Gildon, Charles, *Miscellaneous Essays and Letters* (1694).

Gildon, Charles, *New Miscellany of Original Poems* (1701).

Gildon, Charles, *The Post-Boy Rob'd of his Mail, Or, The Pacquet broke* (1692).

The golden island, or, The Darian song in commendation of all concerned in that noble enterprize of the valiant Scots (Edinburgh, 1699).

Gould, Robert, *Love Given O're* (1683, 1685).

Gould, Robert, *Poems, chiefly consisting of satyrs and satyrical epistles* (1689).

Gould, Robert, *Satyr against Man* (1689).

Granville, George, Baron Lansdowne, *Poems Upon Several Occasions* (1713).

Green, Thomas, *A lamentation taken up for London that late flourishing city* (1665).

Grew, Neheniah, *Musaeum regalis societatis, or, A catalogue and description of the natural and artificial rarities belonging to the Royal Society and preserved at Gresham College* (1681, 1686).

The Guardian(1714).

Hamilton, John, Lord Belhaven, *The Lord Beilhaven's [sic] speech in Parliament . . . on the subject-matter of an union betwixt the two kingdoms of Scotland and England* (Edinburgh, 1706).

Hammond, William, *Poems by W.H.* (1655).

Hardy, Nathaniel, *Lamentation, mourning, and woe sighed forth in a sermon preached . . . after the dismal fire in the city of London* (1666).

Harrington, James, *The Censure of the Rota upon Mr. Miltons Book* (1660).

Harrison, Joseph, *The Lamentable Cry of Oppression* (1679).

Hartlib, Samuel, *Considerations Tending to the Happy Accomplishment of Englands Reformation* (1647).

Hartlib, Samuel, *An essay for the advancement of husbandry-learning, or, Proposition for the errecting [sic] collegde of husbandry* (1651).

Harvey, Gideon, *A discourse of the plague containing the nature, causes, signs and presages of the pestilence in general, together with the state of the present contagion* (1665).

Head, Richard, *The English Rogue Described* (1665).

Head, Richard, *Jackson's Recantation* (1674).

Head, Richard, *The Miss Display'd, With all Her Wheedling Arts And Circumventions . . . By the Author of the First Part of the English Rogue* (1675).

Head, Richard, *Nugae Venales* (1674).

Head, Richard, *O-Brazile Or The Inchanted Island Being A perfect Relation of the late Discovery . . . Of An Island On the North of Ireland* (1675).

Head, Richard, *The Western Wonder: Or O Brazeel, An Inchanted Island discovered* (1674).

A Help to a National Reformation (1700).

Herrick, Robert, *Hesperides or, The works both humane & divine of Robert Herrick, Esq.* (1648).

Heylyn, Peter, *Cyprianus anglicus, or, The history of the life and death of the Most Reverend and renowned prelate William, by divine providence Lord Archbishop of Canterbury* (1670).

Heylyn, Peter, *Ecclesia restaurata, or, The history of the reformation of the Church of England* (1660–1).

Heyrick, Thomas, *The new Atlantis a poem, in three books: with some reflections upon The hind and the panther* (1687).

Hickes, George, *Some discourses upon Dr Burnet and Dr Tillotson* (1695).

The history of Caledonia, or, The Scots Colony in Darien...by a Gentleman lately arriv'd (1699).

The History of Nicerotis (1685).

Hobbes, Thomas, *Leviathan or The Matter, Forme and Power of a Common Wealth Ecclesiasticall and Civil* (1651).

Hodges, Nathaniel, *Vindiciae medicinae & medicorum* (1666).

Holland, Samuel, *Romancio-Mastix: Or a Romance on Romances* (1660).

Hooke, Robert, *Micrographia, or, Some physiological descriptions of minute bodies made by magnifying glasses* (1665).

Howard, Edward, *Poems and Essays with A Paraphrase on Cicero's Laelius* (1674).

Howard, Mary, Duchess of Norfolk, *A Vindication of her Grace, Mary Dutchess of Norfolk* (1693).

Howell, James, *Epistolae Ho-Elianae* (1647).

Howell, William, *An institution of general history from the beginning of the world to the monarchy of Constantine the Great* (1661).

Hubbard, William, *A Narrative of the Troubles with the Indians in New-England* (1677).

Hubberthorne, Richard, *The horn of the he-goat broken* (1656).

Hubberthorne, Richard, *The immediate call to the ministry of the Gospel* (1654).

Hutchinson, Lucy, *De Rerum natura* (1675).

Ingelo, Nathaniel, *Bentivolio and Urania* (1660).

James II, *An Account of what His Majesty said at His First Coming to Council* (1685).

James II, *By the King a Proclamation...12 Feb 1687* (1687).

James II, *The Several declarations together with the several depositions made in council on Monday the 22d of October 1688 concerning the birth of the Prince of Wales* (1688).

Janeway, James, *Saints Incouragement* (1674).

Janeway, James, *A Token For Children* (1672–3).

Jatropoton (1700).

Jessey, Henry, *The Lord's Loud call to England* (1660).

Jevon, Thomas, *The Devil of a Wife* (1686).

Johns, William, *The Traitor To Himself, Or Mans Heart his greatest Enemy* (1678).

Jordan, Thomas, *Bacchus Festival* (1660).

The Justice of Peace His Calling. A Moral Essay (1684).

Killigrew, Anne, *Poems by Mrs Anne Killigrew* (1686).

King, William, *Some Remarks on the 'Tale of a Tub'* (1704).

Kirkman, Francis, *The Counterfeit Lady Unveiled. Being a full Account of the Birth, Life, most remarkable Actions, and untimely Death of Mary Carleton, Known by the Name of the German Princess* (1673).

Kirkman, Francis, *The English rogue continued, in the life of Meriton Latroon, and other extravagants comprehending the most eminent cheats of most trades and professions* (1671).

Kirkman, Francis, *The famous and delectable history of Don Bellianis of Greece, or, The honour of chivalry* (1671).

Kirkman, Francis, *A True, perfect, and exact Catalogue of all the Comedies, Tragedies, Tragi-Comedies, Pastorals, Masques, and Interludes* (1661).

Kirkman, Francis, *The Unlucky Citizen* (1673).

Langbaine, Gerard, *An account of the English dramatick poets, or, Some observations and remarks on the lives and writings of all those that have publish'd either comedies, tragedies, tragi-comedies, pastorals, masques, interludes, farces or opera's in the English tongue* (1691).

The last words of Coll. Richard Rumbold, Mad. Alicia Lisle, Alderman Henry Cornish, and Mr Richard Nelthrop (1685).

The Late Duke of Monmouth's Lamentation (1685).

Lawes, Henry, *Ayres and Dialogues* (1653–8).

Lead, Jane, *A Fountain of Gardens* (1697, 1700).

Lead, Jane, *Heavenly Cloud now Breaking* (1681).

Lead, Jane, *The Messenger of an Universal Peace, or, A Third Message to the Philadelphian Society* (1698).

Lee, Nathaniel, *Caesar Borgia* (1679).

Lee, Nathaniel, *Lucius Junius Brutus, father of his country* (1681).

Lee, Nathaniel, *The Massacre of Paris* (1690).

Lee, Nathaniel, *Oedipus* (1678).

Lee, Nathaniel, *Sophonisba* (1675).

Leslie, Charles, *Querela temporum, or, The danger of the Church of England* (1694).

L'Estrange, Roger, *Considerations and Proposals in order to the regulation of the press* (1663).

L'Estrange, Roger, *Fables of Aesop and Other Eminent Mythologists* (1692, 1699).

L'Estrange, Roger, *Five Love Letters from a Nun to a Cavalier* (1678).

L'Estrange, Roger, *Interest Mistaken, or, The Holy Cheat* (1661).

L'Estrange, Roger, *L'Estrange his Apology: with a Short View of some Late and Remarkable Transactions* (1660).

L'Estrange, Roger, *No Blinde Guides, In answer To a seditious Pamphlet of* J. MILTON'S (1660).

A letter sent into France to the Lord Duke Buckingham His Grace of a great miracle wrought by a piece of handkerchefe, dipped in His Majesties bloud (1649).

A Letter to Mr Congreve on his Pretended Amendments etc. of Mr Collier's Short View of the Immorality and Prophaneness of the English Stage (1698).

A Letter to Ferguson (1684).

Letters of Love and Gallantry and Several other Subjects, All Written by Ladies, 2 vols (1693–4).

The Levellers Levell'd (1647).

The Life of Donna Rosina, A Novel (1700).

Lilburne, John, *England's Birth-right Justified* (1645).

Locke, John, *Essay Concerning Human Understanding* (1690).

Locke, John, *Essay Concerning Toleration* (1667).

Locke, John, *A letter concerning toleration humbly submitted* (1689).

Locke, John, *The reasonableness of Christianity as delivered in the Scriptures* (1695).

Locke, Matthew, *Psyche* (1675).

London Undone; or, A Reflection upon the Late disasterous fire.

Lougher, John, *Sermons on Several Subjects* (1685).

Love without Measure: Or, the Young Man's Delight, and the Maiden's Joy (1693–5?).

Lovelace, Richard, *Lucasta, epodes, odes, sonnets, songs* (1649).

Lovelace, Richard, *Lucasta. Posthume Poems of Richard Lovelace* (1659).

The loyal subjects exultation, for the coronation of King Charls the Second (1661).

Mackenzie, George, *Aretina; or, The Serious Romance...Part first* (1660).

Major, Elizabeth, *Honey on the rod, or, A comfortable contemplation for one in affliction; with sundry poems on several subjects* (1656).

Makin, Bathsua, *An Essay to Revive the Antient Education of Gentlewomen* (1675).

Manley, Delarivier, *The Adventures of Rivella* (1715).

Manley, Delarivier, *The New Atalantis*, 2 vols (1708, 1710).

Manley, Delarivier, *The Royal Mischief* (1696).

Manley, John, *De rebus belgicis, or, The Annals and history of the Low-Countrey-warrs* (1665).

Mantuan English'd, and paraphras'd: or, The character of a bad woman (c.1679).

Markham, Gervase, *The English house-wife* (1615).

Marnettè, Mounsieur, *The perfect cook* (1656).

Marsh, Henry, *A new survey of the Turkish empire and government* (1663).

Marvell, Andrew, *An Account of the Growth Of Popery, And Arbitrary GOVERNMENT* (1677).

Marvell, Andrew, *Miscellaneous Poems by Andrew Marvell, Esq* (1681).

Marvell, Andrew, *The Rehearsal Transpros'd* (1672).

Masham, Damaris, *A Discourse concerning the Love of God* (1696).

Masson, David, *The Life of John Milton*, 7 vols (1859–94).

Mather, Increase, *A brief history of the war with the Indians in New-England* (1677).

Mayne, Jasper, *To His Royall Highnesse, The Duke of Yorke On our late Sea-fight* (1665).

Mercurius Candidus (1647).

Mercurius Elencticus (1647–9).

Mercurius Matrimonialis: or, Chapmen for the ladies lately offered to sale by way of auction Procured by one of their own sex (1691).

Mercurius Politicus (1650–60).

The Midwife of Poplar's Sorrowful Confession and Lamentation in Newgate (1693).

Millington, Edward, *A choice catalogue of the library of John Parsons* (1682).

Milton, John, *Areopagetica* (1644).

Milton, John, *Colasterion: A Reply to a Nameless Answer Against the Doctrine and Discipline of Divorce* (1645).

Milton, John, *Considerations touching the likeliest means to remove hirelings out of the church, wherein is also discoursed of tithes, church-fees, church revenues, and whether any maintenance of ministers can be settled by law* (1659).

Milton, John, *Eikonoklastes in answer to a book intitl'd Eikon basilike* (1649).

Milton, John, *The history of Britain* (1670).

Milton, John, *Paradise Lost* (1667, 1674).

Milton, John, *Paradise Regained and Samson Agonistes* (1671).

Milton, John, *Poems of Mr John Milton, both English and Latin, compos'd at several times* (1646).

Milton, John, *Poems, &c. Upon Several Occasions...With a small Tractate of Education to Mr Hartlib* (1673).

Milton, John, *The Readie & Easie Way to Establish a Free Commonwealth* (1660; 2nd edn, 1660).

Milton, John, *The tenure of kings and magistrates proving that it is lawfull, and hath been held so through all ages, for any who have the power, to call to account a tyrant, or wicked king* (1649).

Milton, John, *Tetrachordon: expositions upon the foure chief places in scripture, which treat of mariage, or nullities in mariage* (1645).

Milton, John, *A treatise of civil power in ecclesiastical causes, shewing that it is not lawfull for any power on earth to compell in matters of religion* (1659).

Mirabilis annus, or the year of prodigies and wonders (1661).

Mirabilis annus secundus or the second year of prodigies (1662).

Mirabilis annus secondus: or, the second part of the second years prodigies (1662).

A miracle of miracles: wrought by the blood of King Charles the First (1649).

Miscellaneous Poems and Translations. By Several Hands (1712).

The Mischief of Prejudice; or, some Impartial Thoughts about Dr Sacherverell's Sermon (1710).

Mollineux, Mary, *Fruits of Retirement, or Miscellaneous Poems* (1702).

Monmouth, James Scott, Duke of, *The Declaration of James, Duke of Monmouth ... for delivering the kingdom from the usurpation and tyranny of James, Duke of York* (1685).

Monmouth Degraded Or James Scot, the Little King in Lyme (1685).

Monmouth Routed, and Taken Prisoner. With his Pimp the Lord Gray (1685).

Montagu, Charles, and Prior, Matthew, *The Hind and the Panther Transvers'd to the Story of the Country Mouse and the City Mouse* (1687).

Monteage, Stephen, *Debitor and Creditor Made Easie: or, A Short Instruction for the attaining the Right Use of Accounts* (1675).

A Morning's Discourse of a Bottomless Tubb (1712).

The Most Strange and Wonderful Apparitions of Blood and Signs and Wonders from Heaven with a True Relations of a Monster Born in Ratcliffe Highway (1645).

Motteux, Peter (trans.), *The History of the most Ingengious Knight Don-Quixote de la Mancha* (1700).

Motteux, Peter, *The Island Princess* (1699).

Mountfort, William, *Doctor Faustus, with the Humours of Harlequin and Scaramouche* (1697).

Murrell, John, *Murrells two books of cookerie and carving* (1650).

The Murthers Lamentation (1694).

Nedham, Marchamont, *Crafty Cromwell Or, Oliver ordering our New State. A Tragi-comedy* (1648).

Nedham, Marchamont, *The Levellers Level'd* (1647).

Nedham, Marchamont, *Mercurius Pragmaticus* (1647–9).

Nedham, Marchamont, *Mistris Parliament Brought to Bed of a Monstrous Childe of Reformation* (1648).

Neville, Henry, *The Isle of Pines Or, A Late Discovery of a fourth Island in Terra Australis, Incognita* (1668).

A New Meeting of Ghosts at Tyburn (1661).

Newcomb, Thomas, *Pacata Britannia* (1713).

News from Parnassus (1681).

News from the Sessions at the Old-Bayly (1674–5).

Newton, Isaac, *Philosophiae naturalis principia mathematica* (1686).

The Nine Muses, Or Poems Written by Nine Severall Ladies Upon the Death of the late Famous John Dryden, Esq (1700).

Norris, John, *Letters concerning the love of God* (1695).

Nye, Stephen, *An accurate examination of the principal texts usually alledged for the divinity of our Saviour* (1692).

Oates, Titus, *Sound advice to Roman Catholics* (1689).

Ogilby, John, *The Entertainment of His Most Excellent Majestie Charles II* (1662).

Okeley, William, *Ebenezer; or, A Small Monument of Great Mercy, Appearing in the Miraculous Deliverance of William Okeley* (1675, repr. 1676, 1684).

Oldenburg, Henry (ed.), *Philosophical Transactions* (1665).

Oldmixon, John, *A Complete History of Addresses, from their First Original under Oliver Cromwell to this Present Year 1710*, 2nd edn (1710).

Oldys, Alexander, *The Fair Extravagant, or, the humorous bride. An English novel* (1682).

Oldys, Alexander, *The female gallant, or, The wife's the cuckhold a novel* (1692).

Otway, Thomas, *The Orphan* (1680).

Otway, Thomas, *Venice Preserve'd, or A Plot Discovered* (1682).

Otway, Thomas, *Windsor Castle, in a Monument To our late Sovereign K. Charles II* (1685).

Ozell, John, *La Gitanilla: the little gypsie. A novel. Written by Miguel de Cervantes Saavedra* (1709).

P., R., *Londons Lamentations* (1666).

Pagett, Ephraim, *Heresiography, or, A Description of the Heretickes and Secretaries of these Latter Times* (1645).

The Papist Prayers for Father Peters (1688).

Parker, Samuel, Bishop, *History of his own Time* (1727).

Parnell, Thomas, *On Queen Anne's Peace, Anno 1713* (1713).

A Passionate Satyr on a Devilish Great He-Whore who lives yonder at Rome (1675).

Patrick, Simon, *A Friendly Debate betwixt two neighbours* (1668).

Patrick, Simon, *The Heart's Ease, or A Remedy Against Trouble* (1660).

Patrick, Simon, *The Parable of the Pilgrim* (1664).

Peaps, William, *Love in It's Extasie: Or the Large Prerogative* (1649).

Penn, William, *The great case of liberty of conscience once more briefly debated & defended* (1670).

Penn, William, *No Cross, No Crown* (1669).

Penn, William, *The Reasonableness, of toleration, and The Unreasonableness of Penal laws And Tests* (1687).

Penn, William, *Reasons Why The Oaths Should not be made A Part of the Test To Protestant Dissenters* (1683).

Penn, William, *Truth Exalted* (1668).

Perfect Occurrences of Parliament (1644–6).

A Phanatique league and covenant, Solemnly enter'd into the Assectors of the good old cause (1659).

Phelps, Thomas, *A True Account of the Captivity of Thomas Phelps at Machaness in Barbary* (1685).

Philips, Katherine, *Letters from Orinda to Poliarchus* (1705).

Philips, Katherine, *Poems by the incomparable Mrs K.P.* (1664).

Philips, Katherine, *Poems by the most deservedly admired Mrs Katherine Philips, the matchless Orinda* (1667).

Phillips, Edward, *Theatrum Poetarum, Or, A Compleat Collection of the Poets, Especially The most Eminent, of all Ages* (1675).

Phillips, John, *The Tears of the Indians* (1656).

A Pindarick-poem upon His Most Sacred Majestie's late gracious indulgence, in granting a toleration, and liberty of conscience in matters of religion (1687).

Pix, Mary, *The Beau Defeated, or, The Lucky Younger Brother* (1700).

Pix, Mary, *The inhumane cardinal, or, Innocence betray'd a novel* (1696).

A poem occasioned by His Majesties most gracious resolution declar'd in His Most Honourable Privy Council, March 18, 1686/7. For liberty of conscience (1687).

A Poem Sacred to the Immortal Memory of her Most Excellent Majesty, Anne, Late Queen of Great-Britain (1715).

Poems On Affairs of State: From The Time of Oliver Cromwell, to the Abdication of K. James the Second (1697).

Poetical Miscellanies: The Fifth Part (1704).

Poetical Miscellanies. The Sixth Part (1709).

Poisson, Raymond, *The Gallant Ladies or the Mutual Confidence* (1685).

Polwhele, Elizabeth, *The Faithful Virgins, or The Lawyer Cheated* (1671).

Pomfret, John, *The Choice* (1699).

Pomfret, John, *Reason* (1700).

Pope, Alexander, *Essay on Criticism* (1711).

Pope, Alexander, *The Rape of the Lock* (1714).

Pope, Alexander, *The second epistle of the second book of Horace* (1737).

Pope, Alexander, *Verses to be Prefix'd before Bernard Lintot's Miscellaneous Poems and Translation by Several Hands* (1712).

Pope, Alexander, *Windsor-Forest. To the Right Honourable George Lord Lansdown* (1713).

The Pope burnt to ashes (1676).

Popery Routed: Or, Father Peter's Farewel to London City (1689).

Powell, Thomas, *Humane Industry* (1661).

Powell, Vavasor, *The Bird in the Cage Chirping* (1662).

Powell, Vavasor, *Tsofer bepah or The bird in the cage* (1661).

Power, Henry, *Experimental Philosophy* (1663).

The Practical Part of Love. Extracted out of the Extravagant and Lascivious Life of a Fair but Subtle Female (1660).

Prior, Matthew, *A Letter to Monsieur Boileau Depreaux; Occasion'd by the victory at Blenheim* (1704).

The Princess Cloria, or, The royal Romance (1653, 1661).

Proceedings of the Old Bailey, 17th January 1677 (1677).

A Proposal for a National Reformation of Manners (1694).

Proposals for Selling the Swimming Girdles (1700).

Prynne, William, *Foure Serious Questions of Grand Importance* (1644).

Prynne, William, *Histrio-mastix* (1633).

Prynne, William, *The Sovereigne Power of Parliaments* (1643).

Prynne, William, *Twelve Considerable Serious Questions* (1644).

Prynne, William, *A Vindication of Four Serious Questions* and *Truth Triumphing over Falshood* (1645).

Quarles, Francis, *Emblems* (1635).

Quarles, Francis, *The Profest Royalist: His Quarrell with the Times* (Oxford, 1645).

The Queens closet opened. Incomparable secrets in physick, chirurgery, preserving, candying, and cookery (1655).

Radcliffe, Alexander, *The Ramble* (1682).

Ravenscroft, Edward, *Mamamouchi: Or, The Citizen Turn'd Gentleman* (1675).

Reasons Humbly offered to be considered before the Act for Printing be renewed (1693).

Reasons Humbly Offered, why the Importation of Foreign-wrought...other Stuffs made of Wool, should be prohibited (1700).

Reasons Humbly Offered...for laying a further Duty on all Forreign Paper (1700).

Reasons Humbly Offered for the Liberty of Unlicens'd Printing (1693).

The revoltex [*sic*]. *A trage-comedy acted between the Hind and panther, and Religio laici, &c.* (1687).

Renwick, James, *The Testimony of some persecuted Presbyterian ministers of the Gospel* (1688).

Rich, Robert, and Tomlinson, William, *A true narrative of the examination, tryall and sufferings of James Nayler* (1657).

Richardson, Samuel, *The necessity of toleration in matters of religion* (1647).

Rigby, Joseph, *The Drunkards' Prospective, or Burninge Glasse* (1655).

Richardson, Elizabeth, Baroness Cramond, *A Ladies Legacie to her Daughters* ([1625] 1645).

Robinson, Henry, *The Falsehood of Mr William Pryn's Truth Triumphing* (1645).

Rogers, John, *Ohel, or Beth-shemesh...published for the Benefit of all Gathered Churches, More Especially in England, Ireland, and Scotland* (1653).

Rowe, Elizabeth Singer, *Poems on Several Occasions: Written by Philomela* (1696).

Rowe, John, *Tragi-Comaedia. being a brief relation of the strange, and Wonderfull hand of God discovered at witny* (1653).

Rowe, Nicholas, *The Ambitious Step-Mother* (1701).

Rowlandson, Mary, *The soveraignty and goodness of God, together with the faithfulness of his promises displayed*, 2nd edn (Cambridge, 1682).

Russel, Robert, *The Wedding Garment: or, The honourable state of matrimony* (1692).

Rycaut, Paul, *The History of the Turkish Empire from the year 1623 to the year 1677* (1677).

Rymer, Thomas, *The Tragedies of the Last Age Consider'd* (1678).

S., R., *The foundation of preaching asserted* (1687).

Sacheverell, Henry, *The Perils of False Brethren* (1709).

Sad and Dreadful news from Dukes-place near Aldgate: Or, a True Account of a Barbarous and Unnatural Self-Murther Committed by Dorcas Pinkney (1686).

Saltmarsh, John, *An end of one controversie* (1646).

Saltmarsh, John, *The Fountaine of free grace* (1645).

Saltmarsh, John, *Free-grace: or, the flowings of Christ's blood freely to sinners* (1645).

Saltmarsh, John, *Sparkles of glory, or Some beams of the morning-star* (1647).

Sancroft, William, *The proceedings and trial in the case of the most Reverend Father in God, William, Lord Archbishop of Canterbury*, ed. Thomas Basset and Thomas Fox (1689).

Sandys, George, *Sandys travels containing an history of the original and present state of the Turkish Empire, their laws, government, policy, military force, courts of justice, and commerce, the Mahometan religion and ceremonies, a description of Constantinople, the Grand Signior's seraglio, and his manner of living* (1615).

A Satyr Against Coffee (1675).

Scotland's Grievances Relating to Darien (1700).

Scudéry, Madeleine de, *Artamenes* (1653).

Sedley, Charles, *Bellamira, or The Mistress* (1687).

Settle, Elkanah, *A Defence of Dramatick Poetry* (1698).

Settle, Elkanah, *Notes and Observations on The Empress of Morocco Revised* (1674).

Shadwell, Thomas, *Bury-Fair* (1689).

Shadwell, Thomas, *A congratulatory poem on His Highness the Prince of Orange his coming into England written by T.S., a true lover of his country* (1689).

Shadwell, Thomas, *The Libertine* (1676).

Shadwell, Thomas, *Ode on the anniversary of the King's birth* (1690).

Shadwell, Thomas, *Ode to the King on his return from Ireland* (1690).

Shadwell, Thomas, *The Squire of Alsatia* (1688).

Shaw, Samuel, *Minerva's Triumph* (1683).

Sheffield, John, *The Works of John Sheffield, Earl of Mulgrave, Marquis of Nomanby, and Duke of Buckingham*, 2nd edn, 2 vols (1729).

Shepard, Thomas, *New Englands Lamentation for Old Englands present Errours* (1645).

Shepherd, Samuel, *Merlinus Anonymous* (1659).

Sheppard, Samuel, *Loves of Amandus and Sephronia* (1650).

Shirley, James, *Poems* (1646).

The Shutting Up Infected Houses As it is practised in England (1665).

Smith, Francis. *A satyr upon injustice, or, Scroggs upon Scroggs* (1680).

Smith, William, *Ingratitude Reveng'd, or, A Poem Upon The Happy Victory Of His Majesties Naval Forces Against The Dutch* (1665).

The Solemn Mock Procession of the Pope, Cardinalls, Jesuits, Fryers, &c (1679).

South, Robert, *Sermons preached upon several occasions* (1679).

South, Robert, *Twelve Sermons* (1724).

Southerne, Thomas, *The Fatal Marriage, or, The Innocent Adultery* (1694).

Southerne, Thomas, *The Loyal Brother* (1682).

Southerne, Thomas, *Oroonoko* (1695).

Spenser, Edmund, *The Faerie Queene* (1590).

Sprat, Thomas, *History of the Royal Society of London for the Improving of Natural Knowledge* (1667).

Stanley, Thomas, *Poems and Translations* (1647, 1651).

Stanley, Thomas, *Poems by Thomas Stanley* (1651).

The state bell-mans collection of verses, for the year 1711 (1711).

State-Poems; continued from the time of O. Cromwel. to the year 1697 (1703).

Steele, Richard, *The Englishman: Being the Sequel of the Guardian* (1714).

Steele, Richard, *The Lover* (1714).

Steele, Richard, *The Lucubrations of Isaac Bickerstaff Esq* (1710).

Steele, Richard, *The Lying Lover* (1717).

Steele, Richard, *Mr Steele's Apology for Himself and His Writings, Occasioned by His Expulsion From the House of Commons* (1714).

Steele, Richard, *The Tatler* (1709–11).

Steele, Richard, *The Tender Husband* (1705).

Stephens, Anthony, *Miscellany Poems and Translations by Oxford Hands* (1685).

Stevenson, Matthew, *Florus Britannicus* (1662).

Stillingfleet, Edward, *Irenicum, a weapon-salve for the churches wounds* (1662).

Stillingfleet, Edward, *Origines sacrae, or, A rational account of the grounds of Christian faith* (1662).

Stillingfleet, Edward, *A rational account of the grounds of Protestant religion* (1665).

Stillingfleet, Edward, *A sermon preached before the honourable House of Commons at St Margarets Westminster, Octob. 10, 1666* (1666).

Stillingfleet, Edward, *The Unreasonableness of a New Separation* (1689).

A Strange and Wonderful Example of God's Judgements (1645).

Strong, James, *Joanereidos: Or Feminine Valour* (1645).

Stubbe, Henry, *A censure upon certaine passages contained in the history of the Royal Society as being destructive to the established religion and Church of England* (1670).

Stubbe, Henry, *Legends no histories, or, A specimen of some animadversions upon The history of the Royal Society* (1670).

Suckling, John, *Fragmenta aurea. A collection of all the incomparable peeces written by Sir John Suckling, and printed by a friend to perpetuate his memory* (1646).

Suckling, John, *The Last Remains* (1659).

A supplement (to the paper called, Reasons humbly offered to be considered before the Act for Printing be continued, &c.) (1693).

The Sweet-Singers of Israel, Or, The Family of Love (1678).

Swift, Jonathan, *A Full and True Account of the Battel Fought last Friday, Between the Antient and the Modern books in St James's library* (1704).

Swift, Jonathan, *A Letter of Thanks from my Lord W[harton] to the Lord Bp of S. Asaph, in the Name of the Kit-Cat-Club* (1712).

Swift, Jonathan, *A Tale of a Tub* (1704).

Tate, Nahum, *Cuckold's Heaven, or An Alderman No Conjuror* (1685).

Tate, Nahum, *Poems by Several Hands* (1685).

Tate, Nahum, *The Sicilian Usurper* (1681).

Tatham, John, *The Rump, Or, the Mirrour of the late Times* (1660).

Taubman, Matthew, *London's Great Jubilee* (1689).

Taubman, Matthew, *London's Triumph* (1685).

Taubman, Matthew, *London's Yearly Jubilee* (1686).

Tavernier, Jean-Baptista, *The six voyages of John Baptista Tavernier, Baron of Aubonne, through Turky, into Persia and the East-Indies* (1677, 1680).

Taylor, Jeremy, *Discourse on the Nature, Offices, and Measures of Friendship...in answer to a letter from the most ingenious and virtuous M.K.P.* (1657).

Taylor, Jeremy, *Holy living in which are described the means and instruments of obtaining every virtue* (1656).

Taylor, John, *The Causes of the diseases and distempers of this kingdom* (1645).

Taylor, John, *Full and True Account of the Notorious Wicked Life of that Grand Impostor John Taylor; one of the sweet-singers of Israel* (1677).

Temple, William, *Miscellanea. In four essays...the second part* (1690).

Theobald, Lewis, *The Mausoleum, a Poem: Sacred to the Memory of her Late Majesty Queen Anne* (1714).

Thomson, John Henderson, *A Cloud of Witnesses for the Royal Prerogatives of Jesus Christ* (1714).

Thrænodium Britannicum: A Funeral Poem to the Memory of William Duke of Glocester (1700).

Tickell, Thomas, *Oxford* (1706).

Tickell, Thomas, *A poem, To His Excellency The Lord Privy-Seal, on the prospect of peace* (1713).

Tillotson, John, *Fifteen sermons on several subjects* (1702).

Tillotson, John. *The Wisdom of being Religious* (1664).

Tobias' Observation (1687).

Torshell, Samuel, *The Womans Glorie* (1645).

Trapnel, Anna, *Anna Trapnel's Report and Plea* (1654).

Trapnel, Anna, *The Cry of a Stone, or, a relation of something spoken in Whitehall* (1654).

Trotter, Catherine, *Agnes de Castro* (1696).

Trotter, Catherine, *The Fatal Friendship* (1698).

A True Account of the Behavior, Confession, and Execution of William Charley and Ann Scot (1685).

A True and Exact Relation of the Severall...Late Witches...at Chelmesford (1645).

A True narrative of a wonderful accident which occur'd upon the execution of a Christian slave at Aleppo in Turky (1676).

The Tunbridge-Miscellany: consisting of Poems, &c. Written at Tunbridge-Wells this summer. By several hands (1712).

Turell, Ebenezer, *The Life and Character of the Reverend Benjamin Colman, D.D.* (Boston, 1749).

Tutchin, John, *The Foreigners. A Poem* (1700).

Twysden, Roger, *The Commoners Liberty, or, The English-Mans Birth-Right* (1648).

Upon the Present Plague at London and His Maiesties Leaving the City (1665).

Van Heldoren, J. G., *An English and Nether-dutch Dictionary* (1674).

Vanbrugh, John, *The Pilgrim* (1700).

Vanbrugh, John, *The Provok'd Wife* (1697).

Vanbrugh, John, *The Relapse, or, Virtue in Danger* (1696).

The Vanity of Female Pride a true relation of a sow that Pig'd seven monstrous pigs (1691).

Vaughan, Henry, *Olor Iscanus* (1651).

Vaughan, Henry, *Poems with the Tenth Satire of Juvenal Englished* (1646).

Vaughan, Henry, *Silex Scintillans* (1650, 1655).

Vertue rewarded, or, The Irish princess a new novel (1693).

Villiers, George, Duke of Buckingham, *The Rehearsal* (1671).

Vincent, Thomas, *God's terrible voice in the city* (1667).

A voice to the city, or, A loud cry from heaven to London setting before her sins, her sicknesse, her remedies (1665).

Waller, Edmund, *Divine Poems* (1685).

Waller, Edmund, *Instructions to a Painter for the drawing of the posture & progress of His Ma[jes]ties forces at sea* (1666).

Waller, Edmund, *Poems &c* (1645).

Waller, Edmund, *Upon the late storme, and of the death of His Highnesse ensuing the same* (1658).

Ward, Edward, *Female Policy Detected* (1695).

Ward, Edward, *The London Spy compleat, in eighteen-parts*, 2 vols (1703).

Ward, Edward, *The rambling rakes, or, London Libertines* (1700).

Ward, Edward, *The Secret History of Clubs* (1709).

Ward, Edward, *Step to Stir-Bitch-Fair with remarks upon the University of Cambridge* (1700).

Ward, Edward, *A Trip to Jamaica* (1698).

Watson, Richard, *The Panegyrike and the Storme* (1659).

Watts, Isaac, *Horae Lyricae* (1706).

Watts, Isaac, *Hymns and Spiritual Songs* (1707, 1709).

Weamys, Anna, *A Continuation of Sir Philip Sydney's Arcadia* (1651).

Wesley, Samuel, *Maggots: Or Poems on Several Subjects* (1685).

Wharton, Anne, 'Love's Martyr; or Witt above Crowns. A Tragedy', BL Add. MS 28,693.

White, Dorothy, *A Warning to all the Inhabitants of the Earth* (1659).

Whitfield, William, *The Idolaters Ruine and Englands Triumph; Or The Meditations of a Maimed Souldier* (1645).

Wigglesworth, Michael, *The Day of Doom* (1662).

Wild, Robert, *Iter boreale*, (1660).

Wilkins, John, *Ecclesiastes, or, A discourse concerning the gift of preaching as it fals [sic] under the rules of art* (1646, 1690).

William III, *A proclamation, for preventing and punishing immorality and prophaneness* (1699).

Wilmot, John, Earl of Rochester, *A Satyr Against Mankind* (1675).

Wilmot, John, Earl of Rochester, *Valentinian* (1685).

Wither, George, *Collection of Emblemes* (1635).

Wither, George, *A proclamation in the name of the King of kings* (1662).

Wither, George, *Speculum Speculativum, or, A Considering Glass* (1661).

Wither, George, *Vox Pacifica: A Voice Tending to the Pacification of God's wrath* (1645).

Wolley, Hannah, *A Supplement to the Queenlike closet* (1674).

à Wood, Anthony, *Athenae Oxonienses* (1691).

The Women's Petition against Coffee (1674).

Wotton, William, *A defense of the reflections upon ancient and modern learning* (1705).

Wotton, William, *Reflections upon Ancient and Modern Learning* (1694).

Wright, James, *Historia histrionica, an historical account of the English stage* (1699).

Wycherley, William, *The Country Wife* (1675).

Wycherley, William, *The Plain-Dealer* (1676).

Yalden, Thomas, *The Temple of Fame* (1700).

Post-1750 Sources

Achinstein, Sharon, *Milton and the Revolutionary Reader* (Princeton University Press, 1994).

Adams, J. Q. (ed.). *The Dramatic Records of Sir Henry Herbert* (Yale University Press, 1917).

Aercke, Kristiaan P., 'Congreve's *Incognita*: Romance, Novel, Drama?' *Eighteenth-Century Fiction*, 2 (1990), 293–308.

Aitken, George A. (ed.), *The Tatler*, 4 vols (Duckworth & Co., 1899).

Altaba-Artal, Dolors, *Aphra Behn's Feminism: Wit and Satire* (Susquehanna University Press, 1999).

Amory, Hugh, and Hall, David D. (eds), *History of the Book in America*, vol. 1, *The Colonial Book in the Atlantic* (Cambridge University Press, 2000).

Amussen, Susan, *Caribbean Exchanges: Slavery and the Transformation of English Society, 1640–1700* (University of North Carolina Press, 2007).

Andrea, Bernadette, *Women and Islam in Early Modern English Literature* (Cambridge University Press, 2007).

Andreadis, Harriette, *Sappho in Early Modern England: Female Same-Sex Literary Erotics, 1550–1714* (University of Chicago Press, 2001).

Apetrei, Sarah L., 'The "Sweet Singers" of Israel: Prophecy, Antinomianism and Worship in Restoration England', *Reformation and Renaissance Review*, 10 (2009), 1–23.

Apetrei, Sarah L., *Women, Feminism and Religion in Early Enlightenment England* (Cambridge University Press, 2010).

Aravamudan, Srinivas, *Tropicopolitans: Colonialism and Agency, 1688–1804* (Duke University Press, 1999).

Armitage, David, 'The Scottish Vision of Empire: Intellectual Origins of the Darien Venture', in John Robertson (ed.), *A Union for Empire: Political Thought and the British Union of 1707* (Cambridge University Press, 2006), 97–121.

Arnold, Matthew, *The Complete Prose Works of Matthew Arnold* (University of Michigan Press, 1975).

Astbury, Raymond, 'The Renewal of the Licensing Act in 1693 and its Lapse in 1695', *Library*, 5th ser., 33 (1978), 296–322.

Aubrey, John, *Aubrey's Brief Lives*, ed. Oliver Lawson Dick, 3rd edn (Secker & Warburg, 1958).

Aubrey, John, *Brief Lives with An Apparatus for the Lives of our English Mathematical Writers*, ed. Kate Bennett, 2 vols (Oxford University Press, 2015).

Auchter, Dorothy, *Dictionary of Literary and Dramatic Censorship in Tudor and Stuart England* (Greenwood Press, 2001).

Avery, Emmett L., 'Dancing and Pantomime on the English Stage, 1700–1737', *Studies in Philology*, 31 (1934), 417–52.

Avery, Emmett L., and Scouten, Arthur H., *The London Stage, 1660–1700: A Critical Introduction* (Southern Illinois University Press, 1968).

Backscheider, Paula R., 'Cross-Purposes: Defoe's *History of the Union*', *Clio*, 11 (1982), 165–85.

Backscheider, Paula R., *Daniel Defoe: His Life* (Johns Hopkins University Press, 1989).

Backscheider, Paula R., *Eighteenth-Century Women Poets and Their Poetry: Inventing Agency, Inventing Genre* (Johns Hopkins University Press, 2005).

Backscheider, Paula R., *Elizabeth Singer Rowe and the Development of the English Novel* (Johns Hopkins University Press, 2013).

Backscheider, Paula R., *Spectacular Politics: Theatrical Power and Mass Culture in Early Modern England* (Johns Hopkins University Press, 1993).

Backscheider, Paula R., 'The Verse Essay, John Locke, and Defoe's *Jure Divino*', *ELH* 55 (1988), 99–124.

Bahlman, Dudley W. R., *The Moral Revolution of 1688* (Yale University Press, 2007).

Baines, Paul, and Rogers, Pat, *Edmund Curll, Bookseller* (Oxford University Press, 2007).

Baldwin, Olive, and Wilson, Thelma, 'The Harmonious Unfortunate: New Light on Catherine Tofts', *Cambridge Opera Journal*, 22 (2010), 217–34.

Baldwin, Olive, and Wilson, Thelma, 'The Singers of *The Judgment of Paris*', in Kathryn Lowerre (ed.), *The Lively Arts of the London Stage, 1675–1725* (Ashgate, 2014), 11–26.

Ballaster, Ros, *Fabulous Orients: Fictions of the East in England, 1662–1785* (Oxford University Press, 2005).

Ballaster, Ros, *Seductive Forms: Women's Amatory Fiction from 1684 to 1740* (Oxford University Press, 1992).

Barash, Carol, *English Women's Poetry, 1649–1714: Politics, Community, and Linguistic Authority* (Oxford University Press, 2000).

Barber, Hugh, *The Quakers in Puritan England* (Yale University Press, 1964).

Barnard, John, McKenzie, D. F., and Bell, Maureen (eds) *The Cambridge History of the Book in Britain*, 4. *1557–1695* (Cambridge University Press, 2002).

Barnes, Geraldine, 'Curiosity, Wonder, and William Dampier's Painted Prince', *Journal for Early Modern Cultural Studies*, 6 (2006), 31–50.

Bartolomeo, Joseph F., *A New Species of Criticism: Eighteenth-Century Discourse on the Novel* (University of Delaware Press, 1994).

Bassnett, Madeline, 'Recipe Books and the Politics of Food in Early Modern English Women's Writings', Ph.D. dissertation, Dalhousie University, 2008.

Bateson, F. W., '*The Double Gallant* of Colley Cibber', *RES* 1 (1925), 343–6.

Battigelli, Anna, *Margaret Cavendish and the Exiles of the Mind* (University Press of Kentucky, 1998).

Bauman, Richard, '*Let Your Words Be Few*': *Symbolism of Speaking and Silence among Seventeenth-Century Quakers* (Cambridge University Press, 1983).

Bawcutt, N. W. (ed.), *The Control and Censorship of Caroline Drama: The Records of Sir Henry Herbert, Master of the Revels, 1623–1673* (Clarendon Press, 1996).

Beal, Peter, *In Praise of Scribes: Manuscripts and their Makers in Seventeenth-Century England* (Clarendon Press, 1998).

Beal, Peter, *Index of English Literary Manuscripts* (University of Michigan Press, 1980–93).

Beaumont, Agnes, *The Narrative of the Persecutions of Agnes Beaumont*, ed. Vera J. Camden (Colleagues Press, 1992).

Beesemyer, Irene, 'Sir George Mackenzie's *Aretina* of 1660: A Scot's Assault on Restoration Politics', *Scottish Studies Review*, 4 (2003), 41–68.

Behn, Aphra, *The Works of Aphra Behn*, ed. Janet Todd, 7 vols (Pickering and Chatto, 1992–6).

Bell, Maureen, 'A Dictionary of Women in the London Book Trade, 1540–1730', MA thesis, Loughborough University, 1983.

Bell, Maureen, 'Elizabeth Calvert and the "Confederates"', *Publishing History*, 32 (1992), 5–49.

Bell, Maureen, 'Offensive Behavior in the English Book Trade, 1641–1700', in Robin Myers, Michael Harris, and Giles Mandelbrote (eds), *Against the Law: Crime, Sharp Practice and the Control of Print* (Oak Knoll Press, 2004), 61–80.

Bell, Walter George, *The Great Plague in London in 1665* (John Lane, The Bodley Head, 1924).

Benedict, Barbara M., 'Death and the Object: The Abuse of Things in The Rape of the Lock', in Don Nichol (ed.), *Anniversary Essays on Alexander Pope's 'The Rape of the Lock'* (University of Toronto, 2015), 131–49.

Bennett, Jim, Cooper, Michael, Hunter, Michael, and Jardine, Lisa, *London's Leonardo: The Life and Work of Robert Hooke* (Oxford University Press, 2003).

Berman, Ronald, 'The Values of Shadwell's *Squire of Alsatia*', *ELH* 39 (1972), 375–86.

Betz, Siegmund A. E., 'The Operatic Criticism of the "Tatler" and "Spectator"', *Musical Quarterly*, 31 (1945), 318–30.

Birch, Thomas, *The History of the Royal Society of London*, 4 vols. (1756–7).

Bjornson, Richard, 'The Picaresque Novel in France, England, and Germany', *Comparative Literature*, 29 (1977), 124–47.

Black, Jeremy, *The English Press in the Eighteenth Century* (Croom Helm, 1987).

Blagden, Cyprian, 'Notes on the Ballad Market in the Second Half of the Seventeenth Century', *Studies in Bibliography*, 6 (1954), 161–80.

Boas, F. S., *An Introduction to Eighteenth-Century Drama, 1700–1780* (Greenwood Press, 1953).

Bond, D. F. (ed.), *The Spectator*, 5 vols (Oxford University Press, 1965).

Booy, David, 'General Introduction', in Booy (ed.), *Personal Disclosures: An Anthology of Self-writings from the Seventeenth Century* (Ashgate Publishing, 2002), 1–19.

Borland, Francis, *The History of the Scotch Settlement at Darien* (Glasgow, 1779).

Bossy, John, *The English Catholic Community, 1570–1850* (Darton, Longman and Todd, 1975).

Boswell, Eleanore, *The Restoration Court Stage (1660–1702)* (Harvard University Press, 1932).

Bottrall, Margaret, *Every Man a Phoenix: Studies in Seventeenth-Century Autobiography* (John Murray, 1958).

Bowie, Karin, 'Public Opinion, Popular Politics and the Union of 1707', *Scottish Historical Review*, 82 (2003), 226–60.

Bowie, Karin, *Scottish Public Opinion and the Anglo-Scottish Union 1699–1707* (The Royal Historical Society/Boydell Press, 2007).

Bowyer, John Wilson, *The Celebrated Mrs Centlivre* (Duke University Press, 1952).

Boyle, Robert, *The works of the Honourable Robert Boyle. In six volumes. To which is prefixed The life of the Author*, vol. 1 (1772).

Bradbury, Jill Marie, 'New Science and the "New Species of Writing": Eighteenth-Century Prose Genres', *Eighteenth-Century Life*, 27 (2003), 28–51.

Braddick, Michael, *God's Fury, England's Fire: A New History of the English Civil Wars* (Penguin, 2009).

Bratton, Jacky, 'Reading the Intertheatrical, or, the Mysterious Disappearance of Susanna Centlivre', in Maggie B. Gale and Viv Gardner (eds), *Women, Theatre and Performance: New Histories, New Historiographies* (Manchester University Press, 2000), 7–24.

Brewster, Dorothy, *Aaron Hill: Poet, Dramatist, Projector* (Columbia University Press, 1913).

Brotton, Jerry, *The Sale of the Late King's Goods: Charles I and his Art Collection* (Palgrave Macmillan, 2006).

Brown, B. C. (ed.), *The Letters and Diplomatic Instructions of Queen Anne* (1935; repr. Funk & Wagnalls, 1968).

Brown, Cedric C., 'Recusant Community and Jesuit Missions in Parliament Days: Bodleian ms. Eng. Poet. B. 5', *Yearbook of English Studies*, 33 (2003), 290–315.

Brown, John, *John Bunyan: His Life, Times, and Works* (1885), rev. edn, ed. Frank M. Harrison (Hulbert Publishing Company, 1928).

Brown, Laura, *Alexander Pope* (Oxford University Press, 1985).

Brown, Laura, 'The Romance of Empire: *Oroonoko* and the Trade in Slaves', in Felicity Nussbaum and Laura Brown (eds), *The New Eighteenth Century: Theory, Politics, English Literature* (Methuen, 1987), 41–61.

Bruce, Thomas, *Memoirs of Thomas, earl of Ailesbury*, ed. W. E. Buckley, 2 vols, Roxburghe Club, 122 (1890).

Budge, Frances Ann, *Annals of Early Friends: A Series of Biographical Sketches* (Henry Longstreth, 1880).

Bunyan, John, *A Relation of My Imprisonment*, in John Bunyan, *Grace Abounding to the Chief of Sinners and the Pilgrim's Progress*, ed. Roger Sharrock (Oxford University Press, 1966).

Burnaby, William, *The Dramatic Works of William Burnaby*, ed. F. E. Budd (Scholartis Press, 1931).

Burnet, Gilbert. *A History of My Own Time*, ed. M. J. Routh, 6 vols (Oxford University Press, 1823).

Burnet, Gilbert. *A Supplement to Burnet's History of My Own Times: Derived from his Original Memoirs*, ed. H. C. Foxcroft (Clarendown Press, 1902).

Burrow, Colin, *Epic Romance: Homer to Milton* (Oxford University Press, 1993).

Burrow, Colin, 'Life and Work in Shakespeare's Poems', in Stephen Orgel and Sean Keilen (eds), *Shakespeare's Poems* (Taylor & Francis, 1999), 1–37.

Burrows, Donald, *Handel*, 3rd edn (Oxford University Press, 2001).

Burton, Thomas, *Diary of Thomas Burton*, ed. J. T. Rutt, 4 vols (H. Colburn, 1828).

Bush-Bailey, Gilli, *Treading the Bawds: Actresses and Playwrights on the Late-Stuart Stage* (Manchester University Press, 2006), 114–20.

Bywaters, David, 'Venice, its Senate, and its Plot in Otway's *Venice Preserv'd*', *Modern Philology*, 80 (1983), 256–63.

Canfield, J. Douglas, and Payne, Deborah (eds), *Cultural Readings of Restoration and Eighteenth-Century English Theatre* (University of Georgia Press, 1995).

Capp, Bernard, 'Popular Literature', in B. Reay (ed.), *Popular Culture in Seventeenth-Century England* (Routledge, 1985), 198–243.

Carslaw, W. H., *The Life and Times of James Renwick* (Alexander Gardner, 1900), 89.

Catalogue of the Collection of Autograph Letters and Historical Documents Formed...by Alfred Morrison (1897).

Cavendish, Margaret, Duchess of Newcastle, *Sociable Letters*, ed. James Fitzmaurice (Broadview Press, 1997).

Cavendish, William Duke of Newcastle, *Ideology and Politics on the Eve of Restoration: Newcastle's Advice to Charles II, transcribed and introduced by T. P. Slaughter* (American Philosophical Society, 1984).

Chalmers, Hero, 'Dismantling the Myth of "Mad Madge": The Cultural Context of Margaret Cavendish's Authorial Self-Presentation', *Women's Writing*, 4 (1997), 323–40.

Chalmers, Hero, *Royalist Women Writers, 1650–1689* (Clarendon Press, 2004).

Chernaik, Warren, *Sexual Freedom in Restoration Literature* (Cambridge University Press, 1995).

Cibber, Colley, *An Apology for the Life of Colley Cibber*, ed. B. R. S. Fone (University of Michigan Press, 1968).

Clare, Janet, *Drama of the English Republic, 1649–60* (Manchester University Press, 2002).

Clarendon, Edward Hyde, Earl of, *The History of the Rebellion and Civil Wars in England*, ed. W. D. Macray, 6 vols (Clarendon Press, 1958).

Clarendon, Edward Hyde, Earl of, *The life of Edward, earl of Clarendon. Being a continuation of the history of the great rebellion from the restoration to his banishment in 1667*, 3 vols (Clarendon Press, 1827).

Clarke, Bob, *From Grub Street to Fleet Street: An Illustrated History of English Newspapers to 1899* (Ashgate Publishing, 2004).

Clarke, Elizabeth, 'Diaries', in Michael Hattaway (ed.), *A Companion to Renaissance Literature and Culture* (Blackwell, 2000), 609–14.

Clarke, Sandra, 'Shakespeare in the Restoration', *Literature Compass*, 2 (2005), 1–13.

Clifford, John G., *Eyam Plague, 1665–1666* (rev. edn, J. Clifford, 2003).

Coffey, John, 'Puritanism and Liberty Revisited', *History Journal*, 41 (1998), 961–85.

Collé-Bak, Nathalie, 'The Pilgrim's Progresses of Bunyan's Publishers and Illustrators, or the Role of Illustrations in the Lie of a Text/Book', *Book Practices and Textual Itineraries*, 1 (Éditions Universitaires de Lorraine, 2011), 157–82.

A Collection of Letters, Never before printed: Written…to the Late Aaron Hill, Esqu. (1751).

Colley, Linda, *Captives* (Pantheon Books, 2002).

A Complete Collection of State Trials and Proceedings for High Treason and other Crimes and Misdemeanors, compiled by Thomas Jones Howell, 21 vols (printed by T. C. Hansard, for Longman, Hurst, Rees, Orme, and Brown, 1816).

Congreve, William, *Letters and Documents*, ed. John C. Hodges (Harcourt, Brace & World, 1964).

Connelly, Roland, *The Women of the Catholic Resistance in England, 1540–1680* (The Pentland Press, 1997).

Considine, John, *Academy Dictionaries 1600–1800* (Cambridge University Press, 2014).

Cooke, A. L., and Stroup, Thomas B., 'The Political Implications in Lee's "Constantine the Great"', *Journal of English and Germanic Philology*, 49 (1950), 506–15.

Cooper, Tim, *Fear and Polemic in Seventeenth-Century England: Richard Baxter and Antinomianism* (Ashgate Publishing, 2001).

Copeland, Nancy, *Staging Gender in Behn and Centlivre: Women's Comedy and the Theatre* (Ashgate Publishing, 2004).

Corbett, Margery, and Lightbown, R. W., *The Comely Frontispiece: The Emblematic Title-Page in England, 1550–1660* (Routledge & Kegan Paul, 1979).

Cordner, Michael, 'Marriage Comedy after the 1688 Revolution: Southerne to Vanbrugh', *Modern Language Review*, 85 (1990), 273–89.

Corman, Brian, 'Congreve, Fielding, and the Rise of Some Novels', in Shirley S. Kenny (ed.), *British Theatre and the Other Arts, 1660–1800* (Folger Shakespeare Library; London and Toronto: Associated University Presses, 1984), 257–70.

Corns, Thomas N. (ed.), *A Companion to Milton* (Oxford University Press, 2001).

Corns, Thomas N. (ed.), *The Royal Image: Representations of Charles I* (Cambridge University Press, 1999).

Corns, Thomas N., *Uncloistered Virtue: English Political Literature, 1640–1660* (Clarendon Press, 1992).

Corp, Edward, *A Court in Exile: The Stuarts in France, 1689–1718* (Cambridge University Press, 2004).

The Correspondence of Bishop Brian Duppa and Sir Justinian Isham, 1650–1660, ed. G. Isham, Northamptonshire Record Society, 17 (1951).

Cowley, Abraham, *The Civil War*, ed. Allan Pritchard (University of Toronto Press, 1973).

Crawford, Katherine, *European Sexualities, 1400–1800* (Cambridge University Press, 2007).

Crist, Timothy, 'The Expiration of the Printing Act in 1679', *Publishing History*, 5 (1979), 49–77.

Crist, Timothy, 'Government Control of the Press after the Expiration of the Printing Act in 1679', *Publishing History*, 5 (1979), 49–77.

Croissant, De Witt C., 'Studies in the Work of Colley Cibber', *Bulletin of the University of Kansas Humanistic Studies*, 1 (1912), 6–8.

Crump, Galbraith M., 'Thomas Stanley's Manuscript of his Poems and Translations', *Transactions of the Cambridge Bibliographical Society*, 2 (1958), 359–65.

Cuder-Dominguez, Pillar, *Stuart Women Playwrights, 1613–1713* (Ashgate Publishing, 2013).

Curtis, T. C., and Speck, W. A., 'The Societies for the Reformation of Manners: A Case Study in the Theory and Practice of Moral Reform', *Literature and History*, 3 (1976), 45–64.

Da Costa, Palmira Fontes. *The Singular and the Making of Knowledge at the Royal Society of London in the Eighteenth Century* (Cambridge Scholars Press, 2009).

Damrosch, Leo, *Jonathan Swift* (Yale University Press, 2013).

Daston, Lorraine J., and Park, Katharine, *Wonders and the Order of Nature, 1150–1750* (Zone Books, 2001).

Davies, Adrian, *The Quakers in English Society, 1655–1725* (Clarendon Press, 2000).

Davies, G. (ed.), *Papers of Devotions of James II, Being a Reproduction of the MS in the Handwriting of James the Second* (Roxburgh Club, 1925).

Davies, Michael, *Graceful Reading: Theology and Narrative in the Works of John Bunyan* (Oxford University Press, 2002).

Davies, Michael, ' "Stout and Valiant Champions for God": The Radical Reformation of Romance in *The Pilgrim's Progress*', in N. H. Keeble (ed.), *John Bunyan: Reading Dissenting Writing* (Peter Lang, 2002), 103–32.

Davis, Lennard, *Factual Fictions: The Origins of the English Novel* (Columbia University Press, 1983).

Davis, Paul, *Translation and the Poet's Life: The Ethics of Translating in English Culture, 1646–1726* (Oxford University Press, 2008).

Day, Robert Adams, *Told in Letters: Epistolary Fiction before Richardson* (University of Michigan Press, 1966).

Day, W. G. (ed.), *The Pepys Ballads*, 5 vols (D. S. Brewer, 1991).

Deazley, Ronan, *On the Origin of the Right to Copy: Charting the Movement of Copyright Law* (Hart Publishing, 2004).

Defoe, Daniel, *An Essay on the Regulation of the Press (1704)*, repr. with introduction by John Robert Moore, Luttrell Society Reprints no. 7 (Basil Blackwell, 1947).

Dennis, John, *Reflections Critical and Satyrical, upon a Late Rhapsody, Call'd, An Essay on Criticism*, in *Works*, ed. E. N. Hooker, 2 vols (Johns Hopkins University Press, 1939–43).

Dennison, James T., *The Market Day of the Soul: The Puritan Doctrine of the Sabbath in England, 1532–1700* (University Press of America, 1983).

Di Meo, Michele, and Pennell, Sarah (eds), *Reading and Writing Recipe Books* (Manchester University Press, 2012).

Dobie, Madeleine, 'Translation in the Contact Zone: Antoine Galland's *Mille et une nuits: contes arabes*', in Saree Makdisi and Felicity Nussbaum (eds), *The Arabian Nights in Historical Context: Between East and West* (Oxford University Press, 2008), 25–50.

Dobranski, Stephen B., *Milton, Authorship, and the Book Trade* (Cambridge University Press, 1999).

Dodds, John Wendell, *Thomas Southerne, Dramatist* (Yale University Press, 1933).

Dodds, Lara, *The Literary Invention of Margaret Cavendish* (Duquesne University Press, 2013).

Dolan, Frances E., 'Gender and the "Lost" Spaces of Catholicism', *Journal of Interdisciplinary History*, 32 (2002), 641–65.

Dolan, Frances E., *Whores of Babylon: Catholicism, Gender and Seventeenth-Century Print Culture* (Cornell University Press, 1999).

Domínguez-García, Beatriz, 'Female Relationships in Mary Pix's *The Beau Defeated*', *Sederi*, 8 (1997), 135–40.

Doody, Margaret Anne, *The Daring Muse: August Poetry Reconsidered* (Cambridge University Press, 1985).

Doran, J., *'Their majesties' servants': Annals of the English Stage*, 2 vols (John C. Nimmo, 1864).

Dowd, Michelle M., and Eckerle, Julie A. (eds), *Genre and Women's Life Writing in Early Modern England* (Ashgate Publishing, 2007).

Downes, John, *Roscius Anglicanus, or, An historical review of the stage* (1708), ed. Judith Milhous and Robert D. Hume (London: The Society for Theatre Research, 1987).

Downie, J. A., *Robert Harley and the Press: Propaganda and Public Opinion in the Age of Swift and Defoe* (Cambridge University Press, 2008).

Downie, J. A., 'What if Delarivier Manley Did Not Write *The Secret History of Queen Zarah?*' *Library*, 5 (2004), 247–64.

D'Oyley, Elizabeth, *James, Duke of Monmouth* (Geoffrey Bles, 1938).

Dragstra, Henk, 'The Last Farewell to the World: Semi-Oral Autobiography in Seventeenth-Century Broadside Ballads', in Henk Dragstra, Sheila Ottway, and Helen Wilcox (eds), *Betraying Ourselves: Forms of Self-Representation in Early Modern English Texts* (St. Martin's Press, 2000), 166–82.

Dryden, John, *The Letters of John Dryden with Letters Addressed to Him*, ed. Charles E. Ward (Duke University Press, 1942).

D'Urfey, Thomas, *The Songs of Thomas D'Urfey*, ed. Cyrus Lawrence Day (Harvard University Press, 1933).

Eckerle, Julie A., *Romancing the Self in Early Modern Englishwomen's Life Writing* (Routledge, 2013).

Edmond, Mary, *Rare Sir William Davenant: Poet Laureate, Playwright, Civil War General, Restoration Theatre Manager* (St. Martin's Press, 1987).

Ehrenpreis, Irwin, *Mr Swift and his Contemporaries* (Methuen & Co., 1967).

'An Elegy upon the Much Lamented Death of the Reverend Mr Joseph Green', in *The Historical Collections of the Topsfield Historical Society*, 12 (1907), 37–47.

Elias, Richard, 'Political Satire in *Sodom*', *SEL* 18 (1978), 423–38.

Elliott, Robert C., 'Swift's *Tale of a Tub*: An Essay in Problems of Structure', *PMLA* 566 (1951), 441–55.

Endelman, Todd M., *The Jews of Britain, 1656 to 2000* (University of California Press, 2002).

Erickson, Amy Louise, *Women and Property in Early Modern England* (Routledge, 1993).

Erskine-Hill, Howard, 'Pope and Slavery', in Howard Erskine-Hill (ed.), *Alexander Pope: World & Word* (British Academy, 1998), 27–54.

Escott, Henry, *Isaac Watts: Hymnographer* (Independent Press, 1962).

Estill, Laura, *Dramatic Extracts in Seventeenth-Century English Manuscripts: Watching, Reading, Changing Plays* (University of Delaware Press, 2015).

Evans, Charles, *Friends in the Seventeenth Century* (The Friends' Bookshop, 1875).

Evelyn, John, *The Diary of John Evelyn*, ed. E. S. De Beer, 6 vols (Oxford University Press, 1955; repr. 2000).

Ezell, Margaret J. M., 'Elizabethan Isham's Books of Remembrance and Forgetting', *Modern Philology*, 109 (2011), 71–84.

Ezell, Margaret J. M., 'The *Gentleman's Journal* and the Commercialization of Restoration Coterie Literary Practices', *Modern Philology*, 89 (1992), 323–40.

Ezell, Margaret J. M., 'Introduction', in *The Poems and Prose of Mary, Lady Chudleigh*, ed. Margaret J. M. Ezell (Oxford University Press, 1993).

Ezell, Margaret J. M., 'Late Seventeenth-Century Women Writers and the Penny Post: Early Social Media Forms and Access to Celebrity', in Patricia J. Pender and Rosalind

Smith (eds), *Material Cultures of Early Modern Women's Writing* (Palgrave Macmillan, 2014), 140–57.

Ezell, Margaret J. M., 'Never Boring, Or Imagine my Surprise: Interregnum Women and the Culture of Reading Practices', in Rivka Swenson and Elise Pugh (eds), *The Eighteenth-Century British Imagination: Contiguities and Extensions: Essays in Honor of Patricia Meyer Spacks* (University of Delaware Press, 2008), 155–69.

Ezell, Margaret J. M., 'Performance Texts: Arise Evans, Grace Carrie, and the Interplay of Oral and Handwritten Traditions during the "Print Revolution"', *ELH*, 76 (2009), 49–73.

Ezell, Margaret J. M., 'Seventeenth-Century Female Author Portraits, Or the Company she Keeps', *ZAA*, 60 (2012), 31–45.

Ezell, Margaret J. M., *Social Authorship and the Advent of Print* (Johns Hopkins University Press, 1999).

Ezell, Margaret J. M., 'The Times Displayed: Late Seventeenth-Century English Commemorative Broadsheets and Media Hybridity', in Sandro Jung and Stephen Colcough (eds), *Yearbook of English Studies*, 45 (2015), 12–24.

Ezell, Margaret J. M., *Writing Women's Literary History* (Johns Hopkins University Press, 1996).

Feather, John, 'The English Book Trade and the Law 1695–1776', *Publishing History*, 12 (1982), 51–76.

Feather, John, *A History of British Publishing* (Routledge, 2003).

Ferguson, Moira, 'Oroonoko: Birth of a Paradigm', in Moira Ferguson, *Subject to Others: British Women Writers and Colonial Slavery, 1670–1834* (Routledge, 1992), 27–49.

Field, Ophelia, *The Kit-Cat Club: Friends Who Imagined a Nation* (HarperCollins, 2008).

Finch, Anne, *The Poems of Anne, Countess of Winchilsea*, ed. Myra Reynolds (University of Chicago Press, 1903).

Fisk, Deborah Payne, 'The Restoration Actress', in Susan J. Owen (ed.), *A Companion to Restoration Drama* (Blackwell, 2001), 79–91.

Fitzgerald, Percy Hetherington, *A New History of the English Stage*, 2 vols (Tinsley Brothers, 1882).

Fitzmaurice, James, 'Front Matter and the Physical Make-up of *Natures Pictures*', *Women's Studies*, 4 (1997), 353–67.

Fitzmaurice, James, 'Introduction', in Margaret Cavendish, *Sociable Letters* (Broadview Press, 1997).

Fitzmaurice, James, 'Margaret Cavendish in Antwerp: The Actual and the Imaginary', *In-between: Essays and Studies in Literary Criticism*, 9 (2000): 29–39.

Forker, Charles R., 'Robert Baron's Use of Webster, Shakespeare, and other Elizabethans', *Anglia*, 83 (1965), 178–98.

Foss, Michael, *The Age of Patronage: The Arts in England, 1660–1750* (Cornell University Press, 1971).

Fox, Adam, *Oral and Literate Culture in England, 1500–1700* (Oxford University Press, 2000).

Fox, George, *The Journal of George Fox*, ed. John L. Nickalls (Cambridge University Press, 1952).

Foxon, David, *English Verse, 1701–1750*, 2 vols (Cambridge University Press, 1975).

Foxon, David, *Libertine Literature in England, 1660–1745* (University Books, 1965).

Foxon, David, *Pope and the Early Eighteenth-Century Book Trade*, rev. and ed. James McLaverty (Oxford University Press, 1991).

Frank, Marcie, *Gender, Theatre, and the Origins of Criticism from Dryden to Manley* (Cambridge University Press, 2003).

Fraser, Antonia, *Royal Charles: Charles II and the Restoration* (Dell, 1980).

Freehafer, John, 'The Formation of the London Patent Companies in 1660', *Theatre Notebook*, 20 (1965), 6–30.

Freke, Elizabeth, *The Remembrances of Elizabeth Freke 1671–1714*, ed. Raymond A. Anselment (Cambridge University Press for the Royal Historical Society, 2001).

Friedman, Jerome, *Blasphemy, Immorality, and Anarchy: The Ranters and the English Revolution* (Ohio University Press, 1987).

Friedman, Jerome, *The Battle of the Frogs and Fairford's Flies: Miracles and the Pulp Press during the English Revolution* (St. Martin's Press, 1993).

Fry, Michael, *The Union: England, Scotland and the Treaty of 1707* (Birlinn, 2006).

Fryer, Peter, *Staying Power: The History of Black People in Britain* (Pluto Press, 1984).

Furbank, P. N., and Owens, W. R., *The Canonisation of Daniel Defoe* (Yale University Press, 1988).

Furbank, P. N., and Owens, W. R., *A Critical Bibliography of Daniel Defoe* (Pickering & Chatto, 1998).

Furbank, P. N., and Owens, W. R., *A Political Biography of Daniel Defoe* (Pickering & Chatto, 2006).

Gallagher, Catherine, *Nobody's Story: The Vanishing Acts of Women Writers in the Marketplace, 1670–1820* (University of California Press, 1995).

Garcia, Beatriz Dominguez, 'Female Relationships in Mary Pix's *The Beau Defeated*', *Sederi*, 8 (1997), 135–40.

Garth, Samuel, *The Poetical Works of Sir Samuel Garth* (1773).

Geduld, Harry M., *Prince of Publishers: A Study of the Work and Career of Jacob Tonson* (Indiana University Press, 1969).

Gelber, Michael Werth, *The Just and the Lively: The Literary Criticism of John Dryden* (Manchester University Press, 1999).

Gibson, William, *The Church of England, 1688–1832: Unity and Accord* (Routledge, 2001).

Gill, Catie, *Women in the Seventeenth-Century Quaker Community: A Literary Study of Political Identities, 1650–1700* (Ashgate Publishing, 2005).

Gillespie, Stuart, *English Translation and Classical Reception: Towards a New Literary History* (John Wiley & Sons, 2011).

Globe, Alexander, *Peter Stent London Printseller* (University of British Columbia Press, 1985).

Goldberg, Jonathan, *Sodometries: Renaissance Texts, Modern Sexualities* (Stanford University Press, 1992).

Goldie, Mark, 'The Revolution of 1689 and the Structure of Political Argument', *Bulletin of Research in the Humanities*, 83 (1980), 473–564.

Gollapudi, Aparna, *Moral Reform in Comedy and Culture, 1696–1747* (Ashgate Publishing, 2011).

Gollapudi, Aparna, 'Why Did Steele's *The Lying Lover* Fail? Or, The Dangers of Sentimentalism in the Comic Reform Scene', *Comparative Drama*, 45 (2011), 185–211.

Gould, Philip, 'Reinventing Benjamin Church: Virtue, Citizenship and the History of King Philip's War in Early National America', *Journal of the Early Republic*, 16 (1996), 645–57.

Graham, Elspeth, 'Intersubjectivity, Intertextuality, and Form in the Self-Writings of Margaret Cavendish', in Michelle M. Dowd and Julie A. Eckerle (eds), *Genre and Women's Life Writing in Early Modern England* (Ashgate Publishing, 2007), 131–50.

Greaves, Richard L., *Glimpses of Glory: John Bunyan and English Dissent* (University of Stanford Press, 2002).

Green, I. M., 'The Persecution of "Scandalous" and "Malignant" Parish Clergy during the English Civil War', *English Historical Review*, 94 (1979), 507–31.

Green, Ian, *Print and Protestantism in Early Modern England* (Oxford University Press, 2000).

Greene, Jody, *The Trouble with Ownership: Literary Property and Authorial Liability in England, 1660–1730* (University of Pennsylvania Press, 2005).

Greer, Germaine, et al., eds, *Kissing the Rod: An Anthology of Seventeenth-Century Women's Verse* (Farrar, Straus & Giroux, 1989).

Gregg, Pauline, *King Charles I* (University of California Press, 1984).

Griffin, Dustin, *Literary Patronage in England, 1650–1800* (Cambridge University Press, 1996).

Griffin, Dustin, *Swift and Pope: Satirists in Dialogue* (Cambridge University Press, 2010).

Griffin, Robert J., 'Anonymity and Authorship', *New Literary History*, 30 (1999), 877–95.

Griffin, Robert J., 'Introduction', in Robert Griffin (ed.), *The Faces of Anonymity: Anonymous and Pseudonymous Publication from the Sixteenth to the Twentieth Century* (Palgrave Macmillan, 2003), 1–18.

Griffiths, Antony, *Prints and Printmaking: An Introduction to the History and Techniques* (University of California Press, 1996).

Grobe, Edwin P., 'Sebastien Bremond: His Life and his Works', Ph.D. dissertation, Indiana University, 1954.

Grundy, Isobel, 'Introduction', in *Lady Mary Wortley Montagu: Romance Writings*, ed. Isobel Grundy (Clarendon Press, 1996).

Guibbory, Achsah, *Christian Identity: Jews and Israel in Seventeenth-Century England* (Oxford University Press, 2010).

Hackett, Helen, 'Women and Catholic Manuscript Networks in Seventeenth-Century England: New Research on Constance Aston Fowler's Miscellany of Sacred and Secular Verse', *Renaissance Quarterly*, 65 (2012), 1094–124.

Hageman, Elizabeth H., 'Treacherous Accidents and the Abominable Printing of Katherine Philips's 1664 Poems', in W. Speed Hill (ed.), *New Ways of Looking at Old Texts* (ACMRS, 2008), 85–95.

Hageman, Elizabeth H., and Sununu, Andrea, ' "More copies of it abroad than I could have imagin'd": Further Manuscript Texts of Katherine Philips, "the matchless Orinda" ', *English Manuscript Studies*, 5 (1995), 127–69.

Haile, Martin, *Queen Mary of Modena: Her Life and Letters* (1905; facs. edn. Kessinger Publishing, 2007).

Halkett, Anne, *The Memoirs of Anne, Lady Halkett and Ann, Lady Fanshawe*, ed. John Loftis (Clarendon Press, 1979).

Hammond, Brean S., 'Joseph Addison's Opera *Rosamond*: Britishness in the Early Eighteenth Century', *ELH* 73 (2006), 601–29.

Hammond, Brean S., *Professional Imaginative Writing in England, 1670–1740* (Clarendon Press, 1997).

Hammond, Jeffrey A., *The American Puritan Elegy: A Literary and Cultural Study* (Cambridge University Press, 2000).

Hammond, Paul, *The Making of Restoration Poetry* (D. S. Brewer, 2006).

Harbage, Alfred, *Annals of English Drama, 975–1700*, revised by S. Schoenbaum (Routledge, 1964).

Hardacre, P. H., 'The Royalists in Exile during the Puritan Revolution, 1642–1660', *Huntington Library Quarterly*, 16 (1953), 353–70.

Harris, Brice, 'Captain Robert Julian, Secretary to the Muses', *ELH* 4 (1943), 294–309.

Harris, Brice, *Charles Sackville sixth Earl of Dorset: Patron and Poet of the Restoration* (University of Illinois Press, 1940).

Harris, Michael, *London Newspapers in the Age of Walpole* (Fairleigh Dickinson University Press, 1987).

Harris, Tim, *London Crowds in the Reign of Charles II: Propaganda and Politics from the Restoration until the Exclusion Crisis* (Cambridge University Press, 1987).

Harris, Tim, *Restoration: Charles II and his Kingdoms, 1660–1685* (Penguin, 2006).

Harris, Tim, *Revolution: The Great Crisis of the British Monarchy, 1685–1720* (Penguin, 2007).

Harth, Philip, 'Political Interpretations of *Venice Preserv'd*', *Modern Philology*, 85 (1988), 345–62.

Hartnoll, Phyllis (ed.), *The Oxford Companion to the Theatre* (Oxford University Press, 1983).

Hayton, David, 'Moral Reform and Country Politics in the Late Seventeenth-Century House of Commons', *Past & Present*, 128 (1990), 48–91.

Hearne, Thomas, *Remarks and Collections of Thos Hearne*, ed. C. E. Doble et al., 11 vols (Oxford Historical Society, 1885–1921).

Henriques, H. S. Q., *The Jews and English Law* (Bibliophile Press, 1908).

Herman, Ruth, *The Business of a Woman: The Political Writings of Delarivier Manley* (Associated University Press, 2003).

Herman, Ruth, 'Enigmatic Gender in Delarivier Manley's *New Atalantis*', in Chris Mounsey (ed.), *Presenting Gender: Changing Sex in Early Modern Culture* (Bucknell University Press, 2001), 202–24.

Herman, Ruth, 'Similarities between Delarivier Manley's *Secret History of Queen Zarah* and the English Translation of *Hattige*', *Notes & Queries*, 47 (2000), 193–6.

Highfill, P. H., Burnim, K. A., and Langhans, E. A., *A Biographical Dictionary of Actors, Actresses, Musicians, Dancers, Managers, and other Stage Personnel in London, 1660–1800*, 16 vols (Southern Illinois University Press, 1973–93).

Hill, Christopher, 'Bunyan's Contemporary Reputation', in Anne Laurence, W. R. Owens, and Stuart Sim (eds), *John Bunyan and His England, 1628–1688* (1990; repr. Bloomsbury Academic, 2003), 1–16.

Hill, Christopher, *Change and Continuity in 17th-Century England* (Yale University Press, 1974).

Hill, Christopher, *The World Turned Upside Down: Radical Ideas during the English Revolution* (1972; Penguin Books, 1984 edn).

Hind, A. M., *Engraving in England in the Sixteenth and Seventeenth Centuries*, ed. Margery Corbett and Michael Norton, 3 vols (Cambridge University Press, 1964).

Hinds, Hilary, *God's Englishwomen: Seventeenth-Century Radical Sectarian Writing and Feminist Criticism* (Manchester University Press, 1996).

Hinnant, Charles, *The Poetry of Anne Finch: An Essay in Interpretation* (University of Delaware Press, 1994).

Hirst, Derek, 'Reading the Royal Romance: Or, Intimacy in a King's Cabinet', *Seventeenth Century*, 18 (2003), 211–29.

Hobby, Elaine, *Virtue of Necessity: English Women's Writing, 1649–1688* (Virago Press, 1988).

Hoffman, Arthur W., 'Dryden's Virgil: Some Special Aspects of the First Folio Edition', *The Courier*, 19 (1984), 61–80.

Hofmeyr, Isabel, *The Portable Bunyan: A Transnational History of The Pilgrim's Progress* (Princeton University Press, 2004).

Holland, Peter, *The Ornament of Action: Text and Performance in Restoration Comedy* (Cambridge University Press, 1979).

Holmes, Geoffrey, *The Trial of Dr Sacheverell* (Methuen, 1973).

Hook, Lucyle, 'Introduction', in anon., *The Female Wits*, Augustan Reprint Society (William Andrews Clark Library, 1967).

Hopkins, David, *Conversing with Antiquity: English Poets and the Classics, from Shakespeare to Pope* (Oxford University Press, 2010).

Hopkins, David, 'Milton and the Classics', in Paul Hammond and Blair Worden (eds), *John Milton: Life, Writing, Reputation* (Oxford University Press for The British Academy, 2010), 23–41.

Hopkirk, Mary, *Queen Over the Water: Mary Beatrice of Modena, Queen of James II* (John Murray, 1953).

Hotson, Leslie, *The Commonwealth and Restoration Stage* (Harvard University Press, 1928).

Howard, W. Scott (ed.), *An Collins and the Historical Imagination* (Ashgate Publishing, 2014).

Howe, Elizabeth, *The First English Actresses* (Cambridge University Press, 1992), 82–90.

Howe, Sarah, 'The Authority of Presence: The Development of the English Author Portrait, 1500–1640', *Papers of the Bibliographical Society of America*, 102/4 (2008), 456–99.

Hughes, Ann, *Gangraena and the Struggle for the English Revolution* (Oxford University Press, 2004).

Hughes, Derek, *English Drama 1660–1700* (Clarendon Press, 1996).

Hull, Suzanne W., *Chaste, Silent & Obedient: English Books for Women, 1475–1640* (Huntington Library, 1982).

Hulse, Lynn, ' "The King's Entertainment" by the Duke of Newcastle', *Viator*, 26 (1995), 355–405.

Hume, Robert D., *The Development of English Drama in the Late Seventeenth Century* (Clarendon Press, 1990).

Hume, Robert D., 'Elizabeth Barry's First Roles and the Cast of "The Man of Mode"', *Theatre History Studies*, 5 (1985), 16–19.

Hume, Robert D. (ed.), *The London Theatre World, 1660–1800* (Southern Illinois University Press, 1980).

Hume, Robert D., 'Opera in London, 1695–1706', in Shirley Strum Kenny (ed.), *British Theatre and the Other Arts, 1660–1800* (Folger Shakespeare Library, 1984), 67–91.

Hume, Robert D., 'The Politics of Opera in Late Seventeenth-Century London', *Cambridge Opera Journal*, 10 (1998), 15–43.

Hume, Robert D., *The Rakish Stage* (Southern Illinois University Press, 1983).

Hunt, Arnold, *The Art of Hearing: English Preachers and their Audiences, 1590–1640* (Cambridge University Press, 2010).

Hunter, J. Paul, *Before Novels: The Cultural Contexts of Eighteenth-Century Fiction* (New York: W. W. Norton, 1990).

Hunter, J. Paul, 'Defoe and Poetic Tradition', in John Richetti (ed.), *The Cambridge Companion to Daniel Defoe* (Cambridge University Press, 2009), 216–36.

Hunter, J. Paul, 'Missing Years: On Casualties in English Literary History, Prior to Pope', *Common Knowledge*, 14 (2008), 434–44.

Hunter, J. Paul, 'Who Wrote What? The Question of Attribution', *Eighteenth-Century Fiction*, 8 (1996), 519–22.

Hunter, Lynette, 'Books for Daily Life: Household, Husbandry, Behaviour', in John Barnard, D. F. McKenzie, and Maureen Bell (eds), *The Cambridge History of the Book*, iv. *1557–1695* (Cambridge University Press, 2002), 514–32.

Hunter, Michael, *The Royal Society and its Fellows, 1660–1700: The Morphology of an Early Scientific Institution*, 2nd edn (British Society for the History of Science, 1994).

Huntington, William Reed, *A Short History of the Book of Common Prayer* (T. Whitaker, 1893).

Hutchinson, Lucy, *Memoirs of the Life of Colonel Hutchinson*, ed. N. H. Keeble (London: Dent, 1995).

Hutchinson, Lucy, *The Works of Lucy Hutchinson*, vol. 1, *Translation of Lucretius*, Reid Barbour and David Norbrook (eds) (Oxford University Press, 2012).

Hutton, Ronald, *Charles II: King of England, Scotland, and Ireland* (Oxford University Press, 1989).

Hutton, Ronald, *The Restoration: A Political and Religious History of England and Wales, 1658–1667* (Clarendon Press, 1985).

Ingle, H. Larry, *First among Friends: George Fox and the Creation of Quakerism* (Oxford University Press, 1994).

Ingrassia, Catherine, *Authorship, Commerce, and Gender in Early Eighteenth-Century England* (Cambridge University Press, 1998).

Italia, Iona, *The Rise of Literary Journalism in the Eighteenth Century: Anxious Employment* (Routledge, 2005).

Jack, Ian, *Augustan Satire: Intention and Idiom in English Poetry 1660–1750* (Oxford University Press, 1952).

Jackson, Alfred, 'The Stage and the Authorities, 1700–1714 (As Revealed in the Newspapers)', *RES* 14 (1938), 53–62.

Jackson, Clare, 'Union Historiographies', in T. M. Devine and Jenny Wormald (eds), *The Oxford Handbook of Modern Scottish History* (Oxford University Press, 2012), 338–54.

Jacob, James R., and Raylor, Timothy, 'Opera and Obedience: Thomas Hobbes and *A Proposition for Advancement of Moralitie* by Sir William Davenant', *Seventeenth Century*, 6 (1991), 205–50.

Jajdelska, Elspeth, *Silent Reading and the Birth of the Narrator* (University of Toronto Press, 2007).

James II, *The Life of James the Second, King of England*, ed. James Stanier Clarke, 2 vols (1816).

James II, *The Memoirs of James II*, ed. A. Lytton Sells (Indiana University Press, 1962).

James II, *Papers of Devotions of James II*, ed. G. Davies (Roxburghe Club, 1925).

Jenkins, Harold, *Edward Benlowes: Biography of a Minor Poet* (Harvard University Press, 1952).

Johns, Adrian, *The Nature of the Book: Print and Knowledge in the Making* (University of Chicago Press, 2000).

Johns, Adrian, *Piracy: The Intellectual Property Wars from Gutenberg to Gates* (University of Chicago Press, 2010).

Johnson, James William, 'Did Lord Rochester Write *Sodom?*', *Publications of the Bibliographical Society*, 81 (1987), 119–53.

Johnson, Samuel, 'The Life of Dryden', in G. B. Hill (ed.), *Lives of the English Poets*, 3 vols (Clarendon Press, 1905; repr. 1967).

Johnson, Samuel, *Prefaces, biographical and critical, to the works of the English poets*, 5 vols (1781).

Josselin, Ralph, *The Diary of the Rev. Ralph Josselin 1616–1683*, ed. E. Hockliffe, Camden 3rd ser., vol. XV (Camden Society, 1908).

Journal of the House of Lords, vol. 13, *1675–1681* (1767–1830), BHO <http://www. british-history.ac.uk/lords-jrnl/vol13> (accessed 20 April 2017).

Justice, George, *The Manufacturers of Literature: Writing and the Literary Marketplace in Eighteenth-Century England* (University of Delaware Press, 2002).

Kachur, B. A., *Etherege and Wycherley* (Palgrave Macmillan, 2004).

Karian, Stephen, *Jonathan Swift in Print and Manuscript* (Cambridge University Press, 2010).

Kaul, Suvir, 'Reading Literary Symptoms: Colonial Pathologies and the *Oroonoko* Fictions of Behn, Southerne, and Hawksworth', *The South Pacific in the Eighteenth Century: Narratives and Myths*, ed. Jonathan Lamb, *Eighteenth-Century Life*, 18 (1994), 80–96.

Keeble, N. H., *The Literary Culture of Nonconformity in Later Seventeenth-Century England* (Leicester University Press, 1987).

Kennedy, Deborah, *Poetic Sisters: Early Eighteenth-Century Women Poets* (Rowman & Littlefield, 2013).

Kenyon, John, *The Popish Plot* (Phoenix Press, 1972).

Kewes, Pauline, *Authorship and Appropriation: Writing for the Stage in England, 1660–1710* (Clarendon Press, 1998).

Killigrew, Anne, *'My Rare Wit Killing Sin': Poems of a Restoration Courtier*, ed. Margaret J.M. Ezell (ITER & CRRS, 2013).

Killigrew, Anne, *Poems by Mrs. Anne Killigrew*, intro. Richard Morton (Scholars' Facsimiles & Reprints, 1967).

Kilroy, Gerard, *Edmund Campion: Memory and Transcription* (Ashgate Publishing, 2005).

Kincade, Katheleen, 'The Twenty Years' War: The Defoe Bibliography Controversy', in Kevin Lee Cope and Robert C. Leitz (eds), *Textual Studies and the Enlarged Eighteenth Century: Precision as Profusion* (Lexington Books, 2012), 133–68.

The King Against Taylor (aka Rex v. Taylor) in Pleas of the Crown, comp. Sir John Tremaine, ed. John Rice, trans. Thomas Vickers (Buffalo, 2003).

King, John N., *Milton and Religious Controversy: Satire and Polemic in Paradise Lost* (Cambridge University Press, 2000).

King, Kathryn R., 'Cowley among the Women: Or, Poetry in the Contact Zone', in Jeanne Wood (ed.), *Women and Literary History: "For there She Was"* (University of Delaware Press, 2003).

King, Kathryn R., *Jane Barker, Exile: A Literary Career, 1675–1725* (Oxford University Press, 2000).

King, Peter, *The Life and Letters of John Locke: With Extracts from his Journals and Common-Place Books* (H. G. Bohn, 1858).

King, William, 'Useful Transactions for May–June 1709; Preface to Part III', in *The Original Works of William King* (1776).

Kitchin, George, *Sir Roger L'Estrange: A Contribution to the History of the Press in the Seventeenth Century* (K. Paul, Trench, Trübner and Co., 1913).

Klempe, P. J., ' "I Have been bred upon the Theatre of death, and have learned the part": The Execution Ritual during the English Revolution', *Seventeenth Century*, 26 (2011), 323–45.

Knoppers, Laura, 'Opening the Queen's Closet: Henrietta Maria, Elizabeth Cromwell, and the Politics of Cookery', *Renaissance Quarterly*, 60 (2007), 464–99.

Knott, John Ray, *Discourses of Martyrdom in English Literature, 1563–1694* (Cambridge University Press, 1993).

Korshin, Paul J., 'Types of Eighteenth-Century Literary Patronage', *Eighteenth-Century Studies*, 7 (1974), 453–73.

Lacey, Andrew, *The Cult of King Charles the Martyr* (Boydell and Brewer, 2003).

Lamb, Julian, *Rules of Use: Language and Instruction in Early Modern England* (Bloomsbury, 2014).

Lamb, Julian, 'Wittgenstein and Early English Dictionaries', in Philippa Kelly and L. E. Semler (eds), *Word and Self Estranged in English Texts, 1550–1660* (Ashgate, 2010), 15–32.

Langhans, Edward, 'The Post-1660 Theatres as Performance Spaces', in Susan J. Owen (ed.), *A Companion to Restoration Drama* (Blackwell, 2001), 3–18.

Langhans, Edward A., 'The Theatres', in Robert D. Hume (ed.), *The London Theatre World, 1660–1800* (Southern Illinois University Press, 1980), 35–65.

Lanser, Susan S., *The Sexuality of History: Modernity and the Sapphic, 1565–1830* (University of Chicago Press, 2014).

Lawler, John, 'Introduction', in *Book Auctions in England in the Seventeenth Century (1676–1700)* (Elliot Stock, 1898).

Lecky, William Edward Hartpole, *A History of England in the Eighteenth-Century*, 7 vols (Longmans, Green, and Co. 1904).

Lehmann, Gilly, *The British Housewife: Cookery Books, Cooking and Society in Eighteenth-Century Britain* (Prospect Books, 2003).

Lepore, Jill, *The Name of War: King Philip's War and the Origins of American Identity* (Alfred Knopf, 1998).

Lewalski, Barbara K., *The Life of John Milton*, rev. edn (Blackwell, 2003).

Lewcock, Dawn, *Sir William Davenant, the Court Masque, and the English Seventeenth-Century Scenic Stage, c.1605–c.1700* (Cambria Press, 2008).

Lewis, Jayne Elizabeth, *The English Fable: Aesop and Literary Culture, 1651–1740* (Cambridge University Press, 1996).

Lindenbaum, Peter, 'Milton's Contract', in Martha Woodmansee and Peter Jaszi (eds), *The Construction of Authorship: Textual Appropriation in Law and Literature* (Duke University Press, 1994), 175–90.

Lindgren, Lowell, 'Handel's London—Italian Musicians and Librettists', in Donald Burrows (ed.), *The Cambridge Companion to Handel* (Cambridge University Press, 1997), 78–91.

Linker, Laura, *Dangerous Women, Libertine Epicures, and the Rise of Sensibility, 1670–1730* (Ashgate Publishing, 2011).

Locke, John, *The Correspondence of John Locke*, ed. E. S. de Beer, 8 vols (Clarendon Press, 1976–89).

Loewenstein, David, 'The Radical Religious Politics of *Paradise Lost*', in Thomas Corns (ed.), *A Companion to Milton* (Blackwell, 2003), 348–62.

The London Jilt, ed. Charles H. Hinnant (Broadview Press, 2007).

Longfellow, Erica, '*Eliza's Babes*: Poetry "Proceeding from Divinity" in Seventeenth-Century England', *Gender and History*, 14 (2002), 242–65.

Loscocco, Paula, 'Inventing the English Sappho: Katherine Philips's Donnean Poetry', *Journal of English and Germanic Poetry*, 102 (2003), 59–87.

Loughlin, Marie H., ' "Touching the ground of Truth": An Collins and Sectarian Spiritual Autobiography', in W. Scott Howard (ed.), *An Collins and the Historical Imagination* (Ashgate Publishing, 2014), 137–54.

Love, Harold, 'But Did Rochester Really Write *Sodom?*', *Papers of the Bibliographical Society of America*, 87 (1993), 319–36.

Love, Harold, *English Clandestine Satire, 1660–1702* (Oxford University Press, 2004).

Love, Harold, *Scribal Publication in Seventeenth-Century England* (Clarendon Press, 1993).

Loveman, Kate, *Reading Fictions, 1660–1740: Deception in English Literary and Political Culture* (Ashgate Publishing, 2008).

Loveman, Kate, *Samuel Pepys and his Books: Reading, Newsgathering, and Sociability, 1660–1703* (Oxford University Press, 2015).

Loveridge, Mark, *A History of Augustan Fable* (Cambridge University Press, 1998).

Lowerre, Kathryn, 'Dramatick Opera and Theatrical Reform: Dennis's *Rinaldo and Armida* and Motteux's *The Island Princess*', *Theatre Notebook*, 59 (2005), 23–40.

Lowerre, Kathryn, *Music and Musicians on the London Stage, 1695–1705* (Ashgate Publishing, 2009).

Luckett, Richard, 'The Fabric of Dryden's Verse', *Publications of the British Academy*, 67 (1981), 289–305.

Ludlow, Edward, *A Voyce from the Watch Tower: Part Five, 1660–1662*, ed. A. B. Worden, Camden Society, 4th ser., 21 (1978).

Luttrell, Narcissus, *A brief historical relation of state affairs, from September 1678 to April 1714*, 6 vols (Oxford University Press, 1857); 2 vols (repr. Cambridge University Press, 2011).

Luttrell, Narcissus, *The Parliamentary Diary of Narcissus Luttrell* (Clarendon Press, 1972).

Luxon, Thomas H., *Literal Figures: Puritan Allegory and the Reformation Crisis in Representation* (University of Chicago Press, 1995).

Lynch, Kathleen M., *Jacob Tonson, Kit-Cat Publisher* (University of Tennessee Press, 1970).

Lynch, Kathleen, *Protestant Autobiography in the Seventeenth-Century Anglophone World* (Oxford University Press, 2012).

Macaree, David, 'The Flyting of Daniel Defoe and Lord Belhaven', *Studies in Scottish Literature*, 13 (1978), 72–80.

McCullough, Peter, *Sermons at Court: Politics and Religion in Elizabethan and Jacobean Preaching* (Cambridge University Press, 2011).

McDowell, Nicholas, *The English Radical Imagination: Culture, Religion, and Revolution, 1630–1660* (Clarendon Press, 2003).

McDowell, Nicholas, *Poetry and Allegiance in the English Civil Wars: Marvell and the Cause of Wit* (Oxford University Press, 2008).

McDowell, Nicholas, 'A Ranter Reconsidered: Abiezer Coppe and Civil War Stereotypes', *Seventeenth Century*, 12 (1997), 173–205.

McDowell, Nicholas, and Smith, Nigel (eds), *The Oxford Handbook of Milton* (Oxford University Press, 2009).

McDowell, Paula, *The Women of Grub Street: Press, Politics, and Gender in the London Literary Marketplace, 1678–1730* (Clarendon Press, 1998).

Macfarlane, Alan, *The Family Life of Ralph Josselin* (W. W. Norton, 1977).

McGovern, Barbara, *Anne Finch and her Poetry: A Critical Biography* (University of Georgia Press, 1992).

Mack, Maynard, *Alexander Pope: A Life* (W. W. Norton, 1985).

Mack, Phyllis, *Visionary Women: Ecstatic Prophecy in Seventeenth-Century England* (University of California Press, 1992).

Mackenzie, Donald, 'Rhetoric versus Apocalypse in *The Holy War*', *Bunyan Studies*, 2 (1990), 33–45.

McKenzie, Donald Francis, and Bell, Maureen (eds), *A Chronology and Calendar of Documents Relating to the London Book Trade, 1641–1700*, 3 vols (Oxford University Press, 2005).

McKeon, Michael, *The Origins of the English Novel, 1600–1740* (Johns Hopkins University Press, 1987).

McKeon, Michael, *The Secret History of Domesticity: Public, Private, and the Division of Knowledge* (Johns Hopkins University Press, 2009).

McKim, Anne, 'War of Words: Daniel Defoe and the 1707 Union', *Journal of Irish Scottish Studies*, 1 (2008), 29–44.

MacLeod, Catherine, and Alexander, Julia Marciari, *Painted Ladies: Women at the Court of Charles II* (National Portrait Gallery, 2001).

McManus, Clare, 'Women and English Renaissance Drama: Making and Unmaking "The All-Male Stage"', *Literature Compass*, 4 (2007), 784–96.

McShane, Angela, '"*Ne Sutor ultra Crepidam*": Political Cobblers and Broadside Ballads in Late Seventeenth-Century England', in Patricia Fumerton and Anita Guerrini (eds), *Ballads and Broadsides in Britain, 1500–1800* (Ashgate Publishing, 2010), 207–28.

McVeagh, John, *Thomas Durfey and Restoration Drama: The Work of a Forgotten Writer* (Ashgate Publishing, 2000).

Madan, F. F., *A Critical Bibliography of Dr Henry Sacheverell* (University of Kansas Press, 1978).

Magro, Maria, 'Spiritual Autobiography and Radical Sectarian Women's Discourse: Anna Trapnel and the Bad Girls of the English Revolution', *Journal of Medieval and Early Modern Studies*, 34 (2004), 405–37.

Maguire, Nancy, *Regicide and Restoration: English Tragicomedy, 1660–1671* (Cambridge University Press, 1992).

Major, Philip, '"A Credible Omen of a More Glorious Event": Sir Charles Cotterell's *Cassandra*', *RES* 60 (2009), 406–30.

Major, Philip (ed.), *Thomas Killigrew and the Seventeenth-Century English Stage* (Ashgate Publishing, 2013).

Major, Philip, '"Twixt Hope and Fear": John Berkenhead, Henry Lawes, and Banishment from London during the English Revolution', *RES* 59 (2007), 270–80.

Major, Philip, *Writings of Exile in the English Revolution and Restoration* (Ashgate Publishing, 2013).

Mambretti, Catherine Cole, 'Orinda on the Restoration Stage', *Comparative Literature*, 37 (1985), 233–52.

Mandelbrote, Giles, 'Richard Bentley's Copies: The Ownership of Copyrights in the Late 17th Century', in A. Hunt, G. Mandelbrote, and A. Shell (eds), *The Book and its Customers, 1450–1900* (Oak Knoll Press, 1997), 55–94.

Mandell, Daniel R., *King Philip's War: Colonial Expansion, Native Resistance, and the End of Indian Sovereignty* (Johns Hopkins University Press, 2010).

Mann, Alastair J., *The Scottish Book Trade, 1500–1720: Print Commerce and Print Control in Early Modern Scotland* (Tuckwell, 2000).

Mann, Alastair J., '"Some Property is Theft": Copyright Law and Illegal Activity in Early Modern Scotland', in Robin Myers, Michael Harris, and Giles Mandelbrote (eds), *Against the Law: Crime, Sharp Practice and the Control of Print* (Oak Knoll Press, 2004), 31–60.

Markley, Robert, *The Far East and the English Imagination, 1600–1730* (Cambridge University Press, 2006).

Marshall, Alan, *The Strange Death of Edmund Godfrey: Plots and Politics in Restoration London* (The History Press, 2013).

Marshall, Ashley, *The Practice of Satire in England, 1658–1770* (Johns Hopkins University Press, 2013).

Martindale, Charles, *John Milton and the Transformation of Classical Epic* (Rowman & Littlefield, 1986).

Marvell, Andrew, *The Poems of Andrew Marvell*, ed. Nigel Smith. rev. ed. (Routledge, 2007).

Massarella, Derek, *A World Elsewhere: Europe's Encounter with Japan in the Sixteenth and Seventeenth Centuries* (Yale University Press, 1990).

Masson, David, *The Life of John Milton*, 7 vols (Macmillan, 1859–94).

Matar, Nabil I., *Turks, Moors and Englishmen in the Age of Discovery* (Columbia University Press, 1999).

Maul, Jeremy, 'Robert Baron's *Cyprian Academy* (1647)', *Notes and Queries*, 33 (1986), 393–4.

Mendelson, Sara, 'Stuart Women's Diaries', in Mary Prior (ed.), *Women in English Society, 1500–1800* (Methuen, 1985), 181–210.

Milhous, Judith, 'The Multi-Media Spectacular on the Restoration Stage', in Shirley Strum Kenny (ed.), *British Theatre and the Other Arts, 1660–1800* (Folger Shakespeare Library, 1984), 441–66.

Milhous, Judith, *Thomas Betterton and the Management of Lincoln's Inn Fields 1695–1708* (Southern Illinois University Press, 1979).

Milhous, Judith, and Hume, Robert D., 'New Light on English Acting Companies in 1646, 1648, and 1660', *RES*, NS 32 (1991), 487–509.

Milhous, Judith, and Hume, Robert D., 'Opera Salaries in Eighteenth-Century London', *Journal of the American Musicological Society*, 46 (1993), 26–83.

Milhous, Judith, and Hume, Robert D., *The Publication of Plays in London 1660–1800: Playwrights, Publishers and the Market* (British Library, 2015).

Milhous, Judith H., and Hume, Robert D. (eds), *A Register of Theatrical Documents, 1660–1737*, 2 vols (Southern Illinois University Press, 1991).

Milhous, Judith, and Hume, Robert D. (eds), *The Vice Chamberlain Coke's Theatrical Papers 1705–1715* (Southern Illinois University Press, 1982).

Miller, C. William, 'A Source Note on Boyle's *The Generall*', *Modern Language Quarterly*, 8 (1947), 146–59.

Miller, John, *Popery and Politics* (Cambridge University Press, 1973).

Milton, John, *Paradise Lost: Book III and IV*, ed. Arthur Wilson Verity (Cambridge University Press, 1911).

Mish, Charles C., *English Prose Fiction, 1600–1700: A Chronological Checklist* (Bibliographical Society of the University of Virginia, 1967).

Molekamp, Femke, *Women & The Bible in Early Modern England: Religious Reading and Writing* (Oxford University Press, 2013).

Montagu, Lady Mary Wortley. *Lady Mary Wortley Montagu: Romance Writings*, ed. Isobel Grundy (Oxford: Clarendon Press, 1996).

Moore, Rosemary Anne, *The Light in their Consciences: Early Quakers in Britain, 1646–1666* (Pennsylvania State University Press, 2000).

Moote, L. Lloyd, and Moote, Dorothy C., *The Great Plague: The Story of London's Most Deadly Year* (Johns Hopkins University Press, 2006).

Moretti, Franco, *Graphs, Maps, Trees: Abstract Models for Literary History* (Verso, 2005).

Morgan, Charlotte E., *The Rise of the Novel of Manners: A Study of English Prose Fiction Between 1600 and 1740* (Columbia University Press, 1911).

Morgan, Fidelis, *The Female Wits: Women Playwrights of the Restoration* (Virago, 1981).

Morley, Henry, *Memoirs of Bartholomew Fair* (1880).

Morse, H. B., *The Chronicles of the East India Company Trading to China, 1635–1834*, 5 vols (Oxford University Press, 1926).

Mortimer, Sarah, *Reason and Religion in the English Revolution: The Challenge of Socinianism* (Cambridge University Press, 2010).

Motteux, Peter, *The Island Princess: British Library Add. MS 15318, a Semi-Opera*, ed. Curtis Alexander Price and Robert D. Hume (University of Michigan Press, 1985).

Mudge, Denver Bradford K., *The Whore's Story: Women, Pornography, and the British Novel, 1684–1830* (Oxford University Press, 2000).

Mulvilhill, Maureen E., 'Introduction', to *Ephelia* in *The Early Modern Englishwoman: A Facsimile Library of Essential Works: Printed Writings 1641–1700*, ser. ii, pt two, vol. 8 (Routledge, 2003).

Murphy, Andrew, *Shakespeare in Print: A History and Chronology of Shakespeare Publishing* (Cambridge University Press, 2003).

Murray, Nicholas, *World Enough and Time: The Life of Andrew Marvell* (St Martin's Press, 2000).

Myers, Robin, Harris, Michael, and Mandelbrote, Giles (eds), *Against the Law: Crime, Sharp Practice and the Control of Print* (Oak Knoll Press, 2004).

Narveson, Kate, *Bible Readers and Lay Writers in Early Modern England: Gender and Self-Definition in an Emergent Writing Culture* (Ashgate Publishing, 2012).

Nate, R., 'Rhetoric in the Early Royal Society', in T. O. Sloane and P. Oesterreich (eds), *Rhetorica Movet: Studies in the History of Modern Rhetoric in Honour of Heinrich F. Plett* (Brill, 1999), 215–31.

Nethercot, Arthur H., 'The Reputation of Abraham Cowley 1660–1800', *PMLA* 38 (1923), 588–641.

Nevitt, Marcus, 'Thomas Killigrew's *Thomaso* as Two-Part Comedy', in Philip Major (ed.), *Thomas Killigrew and the Seventeenth-Century Stage* (Ashgate Publishing, 2013), 113–32.

Newton, Isaac, *The Correspondence of Isaac Newton*, ed. H. W. Turnbull, 7 vols (1959; repr. Cambridge University Press, 2008).

Nichol, Don (ed.), *Anniversary Essays on Alexander Pope's 'The Rape of the Lock'* (University of Toronto, 2015).

Nichols, John, *Literary Anecdotes of the Eighteenth Century*, 9 vols (1812–16; facs. repr. AMS Press, 1966).

Nicoll, A., *History of Restoration Drama 1660–1700* (Cambridge University Press, 1928).

Niemeyer, Carl, 'The Earl of Roscommon's Academy', *Modern Language Notes*, 49 (1934), 434–7.

Norbrook, David, *Writing the English Republic: Poetry, Rhetoric and Politics 1627–1660* (Cambridge University Press, 1999).

North, Roger, *The Life of the Honourable Sir Dudley North…and of the Honourable and Reverend Dr John North* (1754).

North, Roger, *Roger North on Music Being a Selection of his Essays written during the years c.1695–1728*, ed. John Wilson (Novello, 1959).

Novak, Maximillian E., *Daniel Defoe: Master of Fictions* (Oxford University Press, 2001).

Novak, Maximillian E., 'Who Wrote What? The Question of Attribution 2: Whither the Defoe Canon?' *Eighteenth-Century Fiction*, 9 (1996), 89–100.

Nussbaum, Felicity, *On the Brink of All We Hate: English Satires on Women, 1660–1750* (University of Kentucky Press, 1984).

O'Brien, John, 'The Character of Credit: Defoe's "Lady Credit", The Fortunate Mistress, and the Resources of Inconsistency in Early Eighteenth-Century Britain', *ELH* 63 (1996), 603–31.

Orihel, Michelle, ' "Treacherous Memories" of Regicide: The Calves-Head Club in the Age of Anne', *Historian*, 73 (2011), 435–62.

Orr, Bridget, *The Empire on the English Stage, 1660–1714* (Cambridge University Press, 2001).

Orr, Leah, 'Attribution Problems in the Fiction of Aphra Behn', *Modern Language Review*, 108 (2013), 30–51.

Orr, Leah, 'Genre Labels on the Title Pages of English Fiction, 1660–1800', *Philological Quarterly*, 90 (2011), 67–95.

Osborn, James M., 'Thomas Stanley's "Lost" Register of Friends', *Yale University Library Gazette* (1958), 1–26.

Owen, Susan J., 'Tragedy II: Thomas Otway's *Venice Preserv'd*', in Susan J. Owen, *Perspectives on Restoration Drama* (Manchester University Press, 2002), 121–46.

Parker, Blanford, *The Triumph of Augustan Poetics: English Literary Culture from Butler to Johnson* (Cambridge University Press, 1998).

Parker, Kenneth L., *The English Sabbath: A Study of Doctrine and Discipline from the Reformation to the Civil War* (Cambridge University Press, 1988).

Parker, M. Pauline, 'The Hymn as a Literary Form', *Eighteenth-Century Studies*, 8 (1975), 392–419.

Parks, Stephen, *John Dunton and the English Book Trade: A Study of his Career with a Checklist of his Publications* (Garland, 1976).

Parsons, A. E., 'A Forgotten Poet: William Chamberlayne and *Pharonnida*', *Modern Language Review*, 45 (1950), 296–311.

Patterson, Annabel, *Censorship and Interpretation: The Conditions of Writing and Reading in Early Modern England* (University of Wisconsin Press, 1984).

Patterson, Annabel, 'The Country Gentleman: Howard, Marvell, and Dryden in the Theatre of Politics', *SEL* 25 (1985), 491–509.

Payne, Deborah C., ' "And Poets shall by Patron-Princes Live": Aphra Behn and Patronage', in Mary Ann Schofield (ed.), *Curtain Calls: British and American Women and the Theatre, 1660–1820* (Ohio University Press, 1999), 105–19.

Payne, Deborah C., 'Theatrical Spectatorship in Pepys's Diary', *RES* 66 (2015), 87–105.

Peacey, Jason T., 'Order and Disorder in Europe: Parliamentary Agents and Royalist Thugs 1649–1650', *Historical Journal*, 40 (1997), 953–76.

Pearl, Jason H., *Utopian Geographies and the Early English Novel* (University of Virginia Press, 2014).

Pepys, Samuel, *The Diary of Samuel Pepys*, ed. R. Latham and W. Matthews, 11 vols (University of California Press, 1970–83; repr. 1995; repr. 2000).

Pepys, Samuel, *The Pepys Ballads*, ed. W. G. Day, 5 vols (D. S. Brewer, 1991).

Perry, Ruth, *The Celebrated Mary Astell: An Early English Feminist* (University of Chicago Press, 1986).

Perry, Ruth, 'Writing the History of English Feminism', *Tulsa Studies in Women's Literature*, 2 (1983), 101–6.

Peters, Kate, *Print Culture and the Early Quakers* (Cambridge University Press, 2005).

Pettegree, Andrew, *The Invention of News: How the World Came to Know about Itself* (Yale University Press, 2014).

Philips, Katherine, *The Collected Works of Katherine Philips, 'The Matchless Orinda'*, vol. 2: *The Letters*, ed. Patrick Thomas (Stump Cross Books, 1990).

Pierce, Kathryn, 'The Coronation Music of Charles II', unpublished thesis, Master of Music, Bowling Green State University, 2007.

Pincus, Steve, *1688: The First Modern Revolution* (Yale University Press, 2009).

Pittock, Joan H., *Henry Birkhead, Founder of the Oxford Chair of Poetry (1617–1697): Poetry and the Redemption of History* (Edwin Mellen Press, 1999).

Plank, Steven, 'Introduction', in *John Eccles: Rinaldo and Armida* (Recent Researches in the Music of the Baroque Era) (A–R Editions, 2011).

Plomer, H. R., 'Secret Printing during the Civil War', *Library*, NS 5 (1941), 374–403.

Poems on Affairs of State, Augustan Satirical Verse, 1660–1714, ed. George de F. Lord, 7 vols (Yale University Press, 1963–75).

Pollak, Ellen, *Incest and the English Novel, 1684–1814* (Johns Hopkins University Press, 2003).

Pollock, John, *The Popish Plot: A Study in the History of the Reign of Charles II* (Duckworth, 1903).

Pope, Alexander, *The Correspondence of Alexander Pope*, ed. George Sherburn, 5 vols (Clarendon Press, 1956).

Porter, Roy, *Rewriting the Self: Histories from the Renaissance to the Present* (Routledge, 1997).

Porter, Stephen, *The Plagues of London* (The History Press, 2008).

Potter, Lois, 'Pirates and "Turning Turk" in Renaissance Drama', in Jean-Pierre Maquerlot and Michèle Willems (eds), *Travel and Drama in Shakespeare's Time* (Cambridge University Press, 1996), 124–60.

Potter, Lois, 'The Plays and the Playwrights: 1642–60', in Philip Edwards et al. (eds), *The Revels History of the Drama in English*, vol. IV, *1613–1660* (Methuen, 1981), 294–8.

Potter, Lois, 'The Royal Martyr in the Restoration: National Grief and National Sin', in Thomas Corns (ed.), *The Royal Image: Representations of Charles I* (Cambridge University Press, 1999), 240–87.

Potter, Lois, *Secret Rites and Secret Writing: Royalist Literature, 1641–1660* (Cambridge University Press, 1989).

Prebble, John, *The Darien Disaster* (Holt, Rinehart & Winston, 1968).

Price, Curtis A., 'The Critical Decade for English Musical Drama, 1700–1710', *Harvard Library Bulletin*, 26 (1978), 38–76.

Price, Curtis A., *Henry Purcell and the London Stage* (Cambridge University Press, 1984).

Price, Curtis A., *Music in the Restoration Theatre* (UMI Research Press, 1979).

Pulsipher, Jenny Hale, *Subjects unto the Same King: Indians, English, and the Contest for Authority in Colonial England* (University of Pennsylvania Press, 2005).

Quintana, Richard, *The Mind and Art of Jonathan Swift* (Oxford University Press, 1936).

Randall, Dale B. J., *Winter Fruit: English Drama, 1642–1660* (University Press of Kentucky, 1995).

Raven, James, *Bookscape: Geographies of Printing and Publishing in London before 1800*, Panizzi Lectures (British Library, 2014).

Raven, James, 'Booksellers in Court: Approaches to the Legal History of Copyright in England before 1842', *Law Library Journal*, 104 (2012), 115–34.

Raven, James, *The Business of Books: Booksellers and the English Book Trade* (Yale University Press, 2007).

Rawson, Claude J. (ed.), *The Character of Swift's Satire: A Revised Focus* (University of Delaware Press, 1983).

Rawson, Claude, 'Heroic Notes: Pope's Epic Idiom Revisited', in Howard Erskine-Hill (ed.), *Alexander Pope: World & Word* (British Academy, 1998), 69–110.

Rawson, Claude, *Swift's Angers* (Cambridge University Press, 2014).

Raymond, Joad, *The Invention of the Newspaper: English Newsbooks, 1641–1649* (Clarendon Press, 1996).

Raymond, Joad, *Making the News: An Anthology of the Newsbooks of Revolutionary England, 1641–1660* (St. Martin's Press, 1993).

Raymond, Joad, *Pamphlets and Pamphleteering in Early Modern Britain* (Cambridge University Press, 2006).

Reed, John Curtis, *Humphrey Moseley, Publisher*, Oxford Bibliographical Society Proceedings & Papers, vol. 2, pt 2 (Oxford, 1929).

Rees, Emma L. E., *Margaret Cavendish: Gender, Genre, Exile* (Manchester University Press, 2003).

Revard, Stella P., 'Cowley's *Pindarique Odes* and the Politics of the Inter-Regnum', *Criticism*, 35 (1993), 391–418.

Revard, Stella P., 'Thomas Stanley and "A Register of Friends"', in Claude J. Summers and Ted-Larry Pebworth (eds), *Literary Circles and Cultural Communities in Renaissance England* (University of Missouri Press, 2000), 148–72.

Rich, Julia A., 'Heroic Tragedy in Southerne's *Oroonoko* (1695): An Approach to a Split-Plot Tragicomedy', *Philological Quarterly*, 62 (1983), 187–200.

Richards, Penny, 'A Life in Writing: Elizabeth Cellier and Print Culture', *Women's Writing*, 7 (2000), 411–25.

Richards, Thomas, *Religious Developments in Wales (1654–1662)* (The National Eisteddfod Association, 1923).

Richardson, John, *Slavery and Augustan Literature: Swift, Pope, and Gay* (Routledge, 2004).

Richetti, John, *The Life of Daniel Defoe: A Critical Biography* (John Wiley & Sons, 2008).

Richetti, John J., *Popular Fiction before Richardson* (Clarendon Press, 1969).

Roach, Joseph R., *It* (University of Michigan Press, 2007).

Roberts, David, *Thomas Betterton: The Greatest Actor of the Restoration Stage* (Cambridge University Press, 2010).

Robertson, Randy, *Censorship and Conflict in Seventeenth-Century: The Subtle Art of Division* (Pennsylvania State University Press, 2009).

Robinson, David M., *Closeted Writing and Lesbian and Gay Literature* (Ashgate Publishing, 2006).

Robinson, Herbert Spencer, *English Shakespearian Criticism in the Eighteenth Century*, 2nd edn (Godrian Press, 1968).

Rogers, Pat, 'The Dunce Answers Back: John Oldmixon on Swift and Defoe', *Texas Studies in Literature and Language*, 14 (1972), 33–44.

Rogers, Pat, *Hacks and Dunces: Pope, Swift and Grub Street* (Barnes and Noble, 1972).

Rogers, Pat, 'The Uses of the Miscellany: Swift, Curll and Piracy', in Paddy Bullard and James McLaverty (eds), *Jonathan Swift and the Eighteenth-Century Book* (Cambridge University Press, 2013), 87–100.

Rollins, Hyder E., *Analytical Index to the Ballad-Entries (1557–1709) in the Registers of the Company of Stationers of London* (University of North Carolina Press, 1924).

Rollins, Hyder E., 'A Contribution to the History of the English Commonwealth Drama', *Studies in Philology*, 18 (1921), 267–333.

Rose, Craig, *England in the 1690s: Revolution, Religion, and War* (Blackwell, 1999).

Rose, Mark, *Authors and Owners: The Invention of Copyright* (Harvard University Press, 1993).

Rosenfeld, Sybil, 'The Players in Norwich, 1669–1709', *RES* 12 (1936), 129–38.

Rosenfeld, Sybil, 'The Restoration Stage in Newspapers and Journal, 1660–1700', *Modern Language Review*, 30 (1935), 445–59.

Rosenfeld, Sybil, 'Some Notes on the Players in Oxford 1661–1713', *RES* 19 (1943), 366–75.

Rosenfeld, Sybil, *Strolling Players and Drama in the Provinces: 1660–1765* (Cambridge University Press, 1939).

Ross, Sarah Gwyneth, *The Birth of Feminism: Woman as Intellect in Renaissance Italy and England* (Harvard University Press, 2009).

Roth, Cecil, *The French Connection: A History of the Jews in England* (Clarendon Press, 1941).

Rousseau, G. S., 'The Pursuit of Homosexuality in the Eighteenth Century: Utterly Confused Category and/or Rich Repository?', *Eighteenth-Century Life*, 9 (1985), 132–68.

Rowlands, Guy, 'An Army in Exile: Louis XIV and the Irish Forces of James II in France, 1691–1698', *Royal Stuart Papers*, 60 (London: Royal Stuart Society, 2001).

Runge, Laura, *Gender and Language in British Literary Criticism, 1660–1790* (Cambridge University Press, 1997).

Runyon, Daniel Virgil, *John Bunyan's Master Story: The Holy War as Battle Allegory in Religious and Biblical Contexts* (Edwin Mellen Press, 2007).

Salzman, Paul, 'Alterations to *The English Rogue*', *The Library*, 6th ser., 4 (1982), 49–56.

Salzman, Paul, *English Prose Fiction, 1558–1700: A Critical History* (Oxford University Press, 1985).

Sandys, John Edwin, *A History of Classical Scholarship: From the Revival of Learning to the End of the Eighteenth Century in Italy, France, England and the Netherlands (1903–1908)* (facs. repr., Cambridge University Press, 2011).

Sarasohn, Lisa T., *The Natural Philosophy of Margaret Cavendish: Reason and Fancy during the Scientific Revolution* (Johns Hopkins University Press, 2010).

Sargent, Carole Fungaroli, 'How a Pie Fight Satirizes Whig–Tory Conflict in Delarivier Manley's *The New Atalantis*', *Eighteenth-Century Studies*, 44 (2011), 515–33.

Schonhorn, Manuel (ed.), *Accounts of the Apparition of Mrs Veal*, Augustan Reprint Society, no. 115 (William Andrews Clark memorial Library, 1965).

Schultz, Eric B., and Tougias, Michael J., *King Philip's War: The History and Legacy of America's Forgotten Conflict* (W. W. Norton, 2000).

Schwoerer, Lois G., *The Ingenious Mr. Henry Care, Restoration Publicist* (Johns Hopkins University Press, 2001).

Schwoerer, Lois G., *The Revolution of 1688–89: Changing Perspectives* (Cambridge University Press, 2004).

Scodel, Joshua, 'The Cowleyan Pindaric Ode and Sublime Diversions', in Alan Houston and Steve Pincus (eds), *A Nation Transformed: England after the Restoration* (Cambridge University Press, 2001), 201–10.

Scott, Mary Augusta, 'Elizabethan Translations from the Italian: The Titles of Such Works Now First Collected and Arranged with Annotations', *PMLA* 11 (1897), 377–484.

Scott-Bauman, Elizabeth, *Forms of Engagement: Women, Poetry and Culture, 1640–1680* (Oxford University Press, 2013).

Scouten, Arthur H., and Hume, Robert D., ' "Restoration Comedy" and its Audiences, 1660–1776', *Yearbook of English Studies*, 10 (1980), 45–69.

Seidel, Kevin, '*Pilgrim's Progress* and the Book', *ELH* 77 (2010), 509–34.

Sewell, William, *The History of the Rise, Increase, and Progress of the Christian People Called Quakers*, 2 vols (1881).

Shapin, Steven, and Schaffer, Simon, *Leviathan and the Air-Pump: Hobbes, Boyle, and the Experimental Life* (Princeton University Press, 2011).

Shaw, Jane, 'Religious Love', in Ros Ballaster (ed.), *The History of British Women's Writing, 1690–1750* (Palgrave Macmillan, 2010), 189–200.

Shawcross, John, *John Milton: The Self and the World* (University Press of Kentucky, 1993).

Shell, Alison, 'Divine Muses, Catholic Poets and Pilgrims to St Winifred's Well: Literary Communities in Francis Chetwinde's "New Hellicon" (1642)' in Roger D. Sell and Anthony W. Johnson (eds), *Writing and Religion in England, 1558–1689: Studies in Community-Making and Cultural Memory* (Ashgate Publishing, 2009), 273–88.

Shepard, Leslie, *The Broadside Ballad: The Development of the Street Ballad from Traditional Song to Popular Newspaper* (Legacy Books, 1978).

Shepherd, John Robert, *Statecraft and Political Economy on the Taiwan Frontier, 1600–1800* (Stanford University Press, 1993).

Sherburn, George, *The Early Career of Alexander Pope* (Clarendon Press, 1934).

Sherman, Sandra, *Finance and Fictionality in the Early Eighteenth Century: Accounting for Defoe* (Cambridge University Press, 2005).

Shields, David S., *Civil Tongues and Polite Letters in British America* (University of North Carolina Press, 1997).

Siebert, Frederick, *Freedom of the Press in England, 1476–1776* (University of Illinois Press, 1965).

Silverman, Kenneth, *Colonial American Poetry* (Hafner Publishing, 1968).

Skerpan-Wheeler, Elizabeth, 'Authorship and Authority: John Milton, William Marshall, and the Two Frontispieces of *Poems 1645*', *Milton Quarterly*, 33 (1999), 105–14.

Skouen, Tina, 'Science versus Rhetoric? Sprat's *History of the Royal Society* Reconsidered', *Rhetorica*, 29 (2011), 23–52.

Slagle, Judith B., 'Thomas Shadwell's Censored Comedy, *The Lancashire-Witches*: An Attack on Religious Ritual or Divine Right?' *Restoration and Eighteenth Century Theatre Research*, NS 7 (1992), 54–63.

Smallwood, Philip, *Reconstructing Criticism: Pope's Essay on Criticism and the Logic of Definition* (Associated University Presses, 2003).

Smith, Bruce R., 'Afterword: Ballad Futures', in Patricia Fumerton and Anita Guerrini (eds), *Ballads and Broadsides in Britain, 1500–1800* (Ashgate Publishing, 2010), 317–23.

Smith, Geoffrey, *The Cavaliers in Exile, 1640–1660* (Palgrave Macmillan, 2003).

Smith, Geoffrey, ' "A Gentleman of Great Esteem with the King": The Restoration Roles and Reputations of Thomas Killigrew', in Philip Major (ed.), *Thomas Killigrew and the Seventeenth-Century English Stage* (Ashgate Publishing, 2013), 151–74.

Smith, Helen, *'Grossly Material Things': Women and Book Production in Early Modern England* (Oxford University Press, 2012).

Smith, Nigel, *Andrew Marvell: The Chameleon* (Yale University Press, 2010).

Smith, Nigel, *Literature and Revolution in England, 1640–1660* (Yale University Press, 1994).

Smith, Nigel, 'Paradise Lost from Civil War to Restoration', in *The Cambridge Companion to Writings of the English Revolution*, ed. N. H. Keeble (Cambridge University Press, 2001), 251–67.

Smyth, Adam, 'Almanacs, Annotators, and Life Writing in Early Modern England', *ELR*, 38 (2008), 200–44.

Smyth, Adam, *Autobiography in Early Modern England* (Cambridge University Press, 2010).

Smyth, Adam, 'Printed Miscellanies in England, 1640–1682: "store-houses of wit" ', *Criticism*, 42 (2000), 151–84.

Smyth, Adam, *'Profit and Delight': Printed Miscellanies in England, 1640–1682* (Wayne State University Press, 2004).

Snider, Alvin, '*The Curious Impertinent* on the Restoration Stage', *Seventeenth Century*, 21 (2006), 315–34.

Sommerville, C. John, *The News Revolution: Cultural Dynamic of Daily Information* (Oxford University Press, 1996).

Sowerby, Robin, *The Augustan Art of Poetry: Augustan Translation of the Classics* (Oxford University Press, 2006).

Spacks, Patricia Meyer, *Reading Eighteenth-Century Poetry* (Wiley-Blackwell, 2009).

Speck, William, 'Politics and the Press', in Michael Harris and Alan Lee (eds), *The Press in English Society from the Seventeenth to Nineteenth Centuries* (Associated University Press, 1986), 47–63.

Spence, Joseph, *Letters from the Grand Tour*, ed. Slava Klima (McGill-Queen's University Press, 1975).

Spence, Joseph, *Observations, Anecdotes, and Characters, of Books and Men*, ed. J. M. Osborn, 2 vols (Clarendon Press, 1966).

Sprague, Arthur Colby, *Beaumont and Fletcher on the Restoration Stage* (Blom, 1965).

Spufford, Margaret, 'First Steps in Literacy: The Reading and Writing Experiences of the Humblest Seventeenth-Century Spiritual Autobiographers', *Social History*, 4 (1979), 407–35.

Spufford, Margaret, *Small Books and Pleasant Histories: Popular Fiction and its Readership in Seventeenth-Century England* (University of Georgia Press, 1982).

Spurr, John, *English Puritanism, 1603–1689* (Macmillan, 1998).

Starnes, De Witt T., and Noyes, Gertrude E., *The English Dictionary from Cawdry to Johnson 1604–1755* (John Benjamins Publishing, 1991).

Starr, George, 'Why Defoe Probably Did Not Write *The Apparition of Mrs Veal*', *Eighteenth-Century Fiction*, 15 (2003), 421–50.

Statutes of the Realm, vol. 6, 1685–94, ed. John Raithby (Great Britain Record Commission, 1819).

Steele, Robert, *Tudor and Stuart Proclamations, 1485–1714*, 2 vols (Oxford University Press, 1910).

Stephen, Leslie, *Alexander Pope* (1880; repr. Cambridge University Press, 2011).

Stephens, John Calhoun (ed.), *The Guardian* (University Press of Kentucky, 1982).

Stiebel, Arlene, 'Subversive Sexuality: Masking the Erotic in Poems by Katherine Philips and Aphra Behn', in Claude J. Summers and Ted-Larry Pebworth (eds), *Renaissance Discourses of Desire* (University of Missouri Press, 1993), 223–36.

Straus, Ralph, *The Unspeakable Curll* (Chapman and Hall, 1927).

Swift, Jonathan, *The Correspondence of Jonathan Swift*, ed. Harold Williams, 5 vols (Clarendon Press, 1963).

Swift, Jonathan, *Journal to Stella*, ed. Harold Williams, 2 vols (Clarendon Press, 1948).

Swift, Jonathan, *The Works of Jonathan Swift*, ed. Sir Walter Scott (Archibald Constable and Company, 1824).

Syfret, R. H., 'The Origins of the Royal Society', *Notes and Records*, 5 (1948), 75–137.

Szasz, Margaret Connell, *Indian Education in the American Colonies, 1607–1783* (University of Nebraska Press, 2007).

Szechi, Daniel, *1715: The Great Jacobite Rebellion* (Yale University Press, 2006).

Szechi, Daniel, 'Scottish Jacobitism in its International Context', in T. M. Devine and Jenny Wormald (eds), *The Oxford Handbook of Modern Scottish History* (Oxford University Press, 2012), 355–69.

Teague, Frances, *Bathsua Makin, Woman of Learning* (Bucknell University Press, 1998).

Teague, Frances, and Ezell, Margaret J. M. (eds), *Bathsua Makin and Mary More with a Reply to More by Robert Whitehall: Education English Daughters: Late Seventeenth-Century Debates*, associate editor Jessica Walker (ITER and ACMRS, 2016).

Temple, Kathryn, 'Manley's "Feigned Scene": The Fictions of Law at Westminster Hall', *Eighteenth-Century Fiction*, 22 (2010), 573–98.

Teonge, Henry, *The Diary of Henry Teonge, Chaplain on Board his Majesty's ships Assistance, Bristol, and Royal Oak, Anno 1675 to 1679* (Charles Knight, 1825).

Thirsk, Joan, *Food in Early Modern England: Phases, Fads, Fashions, 1500–1760* (Hambledon Continuum, 2007).

Thomas, David, Carleton, David, and Etienne Anne, 'Theatre Censorship under Royal Prerogative', in *Theatre Censorship: From Walpole to Wilson* (Oxford University Press, 2007), 6–23.

Thomas, Keith, 'Women and the Civil War Sects', in Trevor Aston (ed.), *Crisis in Europe, 1560–1660* (Doubleday, 1967), 332–57.

Thompson, Roger, 'The London Jilt', *Harvard Library Bulletin*, 23 (1975), 289–94.

Thompson, Roger, 'Two Early Editions of Restoration Erotica', *Library*, 32 (1977), 45–8.

Thompson, Roger, *Unfit for Modest Ears: A Study of Pornographic, Obscene and Bawdy Works Written or Published in England in the Second Half of the Seventeenth Century* (Macmillan, 1979).

Tickell, Richard Eustace, *Thomas Tickell and the Eighteenth-Century Poets (1685–1740)* (Constable & Co, 1931).

Todd, Janet, *The Critical Fortunes of Aphra Behn* (Camden House, 1998).

Todd, Janet, *The Secret Life of Aphra Behn* (Rutgers University Press, 1997).

Todd, Janet, *The Sign of Angelica: Women, Writing and Fiction, 1600–1800* (Columbia University Press, 1989).

Tomlinson, Sophie, ' "She that Plays the King": Henrietta Maria and the Threat of the Actress in Caroline Culture', in Gordon McMullan and Jonathan Hope (eds), *The Politics of Tragicomedy: Shakespeare and After* (Routledge, 1991), 189–207.

Toulalan, Sarah, *Imagining Sex: Pornography and Bodies in Seventeenth-Century England* (Oxford University Press, 2007).

Traub, Valerie, *The Renaissance of Lesbianism in Early Modern England* (Cambridge University Press, 2002).

Treadwell, Michael, 'The Stationers and the Printing Acts at the End of the Seventeenth Century', in John Barnard, D. F. McKenzie, and Maureen Bell (eds), *The Cambridge History of the Book in Britain*, iv. *1557–1695* (Cambridge University Press, 2002), 755–76.

Trolander, Paul, *Literary Sociability in Early Modern England: The Epistolary Record* (Rowman & Littlefield, 2014).

Trolander, Paul, and Tenger, Zeynep, *Sociable Criticism in England, 1625–1725* (University of Delaware Press, 2007).

Troyer, Howard William, *Ned Ward of Grub Street: A Study of Sub-Literary London in the Eighteenth Century* (Harvard University Press, 1946).

Trumbach, Randolf, 'The Birth of the Queen: Sodomy and the Emergence of Gender Equality in Modern Culture, 1660–1750', in Robert Shoemaker and Mary Vincent (eds), *Gender and History in Western Europe* (Arnold, 1998), 160–73.

Tsai, Shih-Shan Henry, *Maritime Taiwan: Historical Encounters with the East and West* (M. E. Sharpe, 2008).

Turner, James G., 'Bunyan's Sense of Place', in Vincent Newey (ed.), *The Pilgrim's Progress: Critical and Historical Views* (Liverpool University Press, 1980), 91–110.

Turner, James G., *Libertines and Radicals in Early Modern London: Sexuality, Politics and Literary Culture, 1630–1685* (Cambridge University Press, 2002).

Uglow, Jenny, *A Gambling Man: Charles II and the Restoration* (Faber, 2009).

Ustick, W. Lee, 'The Courtier and the Bookseller: Some Vagaries of Seventeenth-Century Publishing', *RES* 5 (1929), 146–8.

Van Der Zee, Henri, and Van Der Zee, Barbara, *William and Mary* (Alfred A. Knopf, 1973).

Vaughan, Virginia Mason, *Performing Blackness on English Stages, 1500–1800* (Cambridge University Press, 2005).

Vickers, Brian, 'The Royal Society and English Prose Style: A Reassessment', in B. Vickers and N. Struever (eds), *Rhetoric and the Pursuit of Truth: Language Change in the Seventeenth and Eighteenth Centuries* (William Andrews Clark Memorial Library, 1986), 3–76.

Vieth, David, *Attribution of Restoration Poetry* (Yale University Press, 1963).

Visconsi, Elliott, *Lines of Equity: Literature and the Origins of Law in Later Stuart England* (Cornell University Press, 2008).

von Maltzahn, Nicholas, 'The First Reception of *Paradise Lost* (1667)', *RES* 47 (1996), 479–99.

von Maltzahn, Nicholas, 'Laureate, Republican, Calvinist: An Early Response to Milton and *Paradise Lost*', *Milton Studies*, 29 (1993), 181–98.

von Maltzahn, Nicholas, *Milton's History of Britain: Republican Historiography in the English Revolution* (Clarendon Press, 1991).

Vries, Marleen de, 'Literature of the Enlightenment, 1700–1800', in Theo Hermans (ed.), *A Literary History of the Low Countries* (Camden House, 2009), 293–368.

Walker, Claire, 'Prayer, Patronage, and Political Conspiracy: English Nuns and the Restoration', *Historical Journal*, 43 (2000), 1–23.

Walker, J., 'Censorship of the Press during the Reign of Charles II', *History*, NS 35 (1950), 219–38.

Walker, Patrick, *Six Saints of the Covenant*, ed. D. Hay Fleming (Hodder & Stoughton, 1901).

Wall, Cynthia, *The Literary and Cultural Spaces of Restoration London* (Cambridge University Press, 2006).

Walsh, Marcus, 'Swift's *Tale of a Tub* and the Mock Book', in Paddy Bullard and James McLaverty (eds), *Jonathan Swift and the Eighteenth-Century Book* (Cambridge University Press, 2013), 101–18.

Walsh, Marcus, 'Text, "Text", and Swift's "A Tale of a Tub"', *Modern Language Review*, 85 (1990), 290–303.

Walsham, Alexander, *Catholic Reformation in Protestant Britain* (Ashgate Publishing, 2014).

Walters, Lisa, *Margaret Cavendish: Gender, Science and Politics* (Cambridge University Press, 2014).

Walton, James, 'On the Attribution of "Mrs Veal"', *Notes & Queries*, 54 (2007), 60–2.

Warner, William B., *Licensing Entertainment: The Elevation of Novel Reading in Britain, 1684–1750* (University of California Press, 1998).

Watkins, John, *Representing Elizabeth in Stuart England: Literature, History, Sovereignty* (Cambridge University Press, 2002).

Watson, George, 'Dryden and the Jacobites', *Times Literary Supplement*, 16 March 1973.

Watt, Ian, *The Rise of the Novel: Studies in Defoe, Richardson, and Fielding* (University of California Press, 1957; repr. 2001).

Watt, Teresa, *Cheap Print and Popular Piety, 1550–1640* (Cambridge University Press, 1991).

Weamys, Anna, *A Continuation of Sir Philip Sidney's Arcadia*, ed. Patrick Colborn Cullen (Oxford University Press, 1994).

Webster, Charles, 'Introduction', in *Samuel Hartlib and the Advancement of Learning* (Cambridge University Press, 1970).

Webster, Jeremy, *Performing Libertinism in Charles II's Court: Politics, Drama, Sexuality* (Palgrave Macmillan, 2005).

Weil, Rachel, *Political Passions: Gender, the Family and Political Argument in England, 1680–1714* (Manchester University Press, 2000).

Weiser, Brian, *Charles II and the Politics of Access* (Boydell Press, 2003).

Welch, Anthony, *The Renaissance Epic and the Oral Past* (Yale University Press, 2012).

Weldon, John, *The Judgment of Paris*, ed. David W. Music (A-R Editions, 1999).

West, Philip, *Henry Vaughan's Silex Scintillans: Scripture Uses* (Oxford University Press, 2001).

Westfall, Richard S., *Never at Rest: A Biography of Isaac Newton* (Cambridge University Press, 1983).

Whatley, C., *The Scots and the Union* (Edinburgh University Press, 2006).

Whitaker, Katie, *Mad Madge: The Extraordinary Life of Margaret Cavendish, Duchess of Newcastle* (Basic Books, 2002).

White, Arthur F., *John Crowne: His Life and Dramatic Works* (Western Reserve University Press, 1922).

White, Arthur F., 'The Office of Revels and Dramatic Censorship during the Restoration Period', *Western Reserve University Bulletin*, 34 (1931), 5–45.

Williams, Abigail, *Poetry and the Creation of a Whig Literary Culture, 1681–1714* (Oxford University Press, 2005).

Williams, J. A., 'English Catholicism under Charles II: The Legal Position', *Recusant History*, 7 (1963), 123–43.

Williams, Sheila, 'The Pope-Burning Processions of 1679, 1680, and 1681', *Journal of the Warburg and Courtauld Institutes*, 21 (1958), 104–16.

Willie, Rachel, *Staging the Revolution: Drama, Reinvention and history, 1647–72* (Manchester University Press, 2015).

Wilmot, John, Earl of Rochester, *Earl of Rochester: The Critical Heritage*, ed. David Farley-Hills (Routledge, 1972).

Wilmot, John, Earl of Rochester, *The Works of John Wilmot, Earl of Rochester*, ed. Harold Love (Oxford University Press, 1999).

Wilson, Brett D., *A Race of Female Patriots: Women and Public Spirit on the British Stage, 1688–1745* (Bucknell University Press, 2011).

Wilson, John Harold, *Court Satires of the Restoration* (Ohio State University Press, 1976).

Wilson, John Harold, *The Influence of Beaumont and Fletcher on Restoration Drama* (Ohio State University Press, 1928).

Wilson, John Harold, 'Theatre Notes from the *Newdigate Newsletters*', *Theatre Notebook*, 15 (Spring 1961), 79–84.

Winn, James Anderson, *John Dryden and his World* (Yale University Press, 1989).

Winn, James Anderson, *Queen Anne: Patroness of Arts* (Oxford University Press, 2014).

Wiseman, Susan, *Drama and Politics in the English Civil War* (Cambridge University Press, 1998).

Wolfe, Heather, 'The Scribal Hands and Dating of *Lady Falkland: Her life*', *English Manuscript Studies*, 9 (2000), 187–217.

Woolley, David, 'The Textual History of *A Tale of a Tub*', *Swift Studies*, 21 (2006), 7–26.

Worden, Blair, *Literature and Politics in Cromwellian England: John Milton, Andrew Marvell, Marchamont Nedham* (Oxford University Press, 2007).

Worden, Blair, 'Milton's Republicanism and the Tyranny of Heaven' in Gisela Bock, Quentin Skinner, and Maurizio Viroli (eds), *Machiavelli and Republicanism* (Cambridge University Press, 1990), 225–45.

Worden, Blair, 'Milton, *Samson Agonistes* and the Restoration', in Gerald MacLean (ed.), *Culture and Society in the Stuart Restoration* (Cambridge University Press, 1995), 111–36.

Worden, Blair, *The English Civil Wars, 1640–1660* (Phoenix, 2010).

Worden, Blair, ' "Wit in a roundhead": The Dilemma of Marchamont Nedham', in S. D. Amussen and M. A. Kishlansky (eds), *Political Culture and Cultural Politics in Early Modern England: Essays Presented to David Underdown* (Manchester University Press, 1995), 301–37.

Wright, Gillian, *Producing Women's Poetry, 1600–1730: Text and Paratext, Manuscript and Print* (Cambridge University Press, 2013).

Wright, L. B., 'The Reading of Plays during the Puritan Revolution', *Huntington Library Bulletin*, 6 (1934), 73–108.

Würzbach, Natascha, *The Rise of the English Street Ballad, 1550–1650*, trans. Gayna Walls (Cambridge University Press, 1990).

Yadav, Alok, 'Fractured Meanings: "Hudibras" and the Historicity of the Literary Text', *ELH* 62 (1995), 529–49.

Zinck, Arlette, 'From Apocalypse to Prophecy: The Didactic Strategies of *The Holy War*', in N. H. Keeble (ed.), *John Bunyan: Reading Dissenting Writing* (Peter Lang, 2002), 183–98.

Zook, Melinda S., *Radical Whigs and Conspiratorial Politics in Late Stuart England* (Pennsylvania State University Press, 1999).

Index

Figures are indicated by an italic *f* following the page number.